ALSO BY MARIE ARANA

Bolívar: American Liberator

Lima Nights

Cellophane

The Writing Life: Writers on How They Think and Work

American Chica: Two Worlds, One Childhood

Three Crucibles
in the
Latin American Story

SILVER, SWORD, AND STONE

MARIE ARANA

Simon & Schuster
New York   London   Toronto   Sydney   New Delhi

Simon & Schuster
1230 Avenue of the Americas
New York, NY 10020

First Simon & Schuster hardcover edition August 2019

SIMON & SCHUSTER and colophon are registered trademarks of Simon & Schuster, Inc.

For information about special discounts for bulk purchases, please contact Simon & Schuster Special Sales at 1-866-506-1949 or business@simonandschuster.com.

The Simon & Schuster Speakers Bureau can bring authors to your live event. For more information or to book an event, contact the Simon & Schuster Speakers Bureau at 1-866-248-3049 or visit our website at www.simonspeakers.com.

Interior design by Carly Loman

Manufactured in the United States of America

10   9   8   7   6   5   4   3   2

Library of Congress Cataloging-in-Publication Data

Names: Arana, Marie (Writer), author.
Title: Silver, sword, and stone: three crucibles in the Latin American story / Marie Arana.
Description: New York: Simon & Schuster, 2019.
Identifiers: LCCN 2018057093|ISBN 9781501104244 (hardback) | ISBN 1501104241 (hardback)
Subjects: LCSH: Gonzales, Leonor. | Buergos, Carlos. | Albró, Xavier, 1934—|Latin America—Biography. |Latin American—History.|BISAC: HISTORY/Latin America/ General. | SOCIAL SCIENCE/Developing Countries.
Classification: LCC F1407 .A685 2019 | DDC 920.08—dc23 LC record available at https://lccn.loc.gov/2018057093

ISBN 978-1-5011-0424-4
ISBN 978-1-5011-0502-9 (ebook)

In memory of
María Isabel Arana Cisneros,
"Y sabe lo todo,"
godmother, inquisitor, and dazzling mentor

CONTENTS

LATIN AMERICA TODAY

Ciudad Juárez
Sonora Desert
Sierra Madre
MEXICO
Gulf of Mexico
Havana
Yucatán
CUBA
DOMINICAN REPUBLIC
PUERTO RICO
Veracruz
Mexico City
— *Lacandón*
Chiapas •
BELIZE
HAITI
Santo Domingo
HONDURAS
Caribbean Sea
Atlantic Ocean
GUATEMALA
EL SALVADOR
NICARAGUA
Caracas
COSTA RICA
PANAMA
Medellín •
VENEZUELA
★ Bogotá
COLOMBIA
EQUATOR
Quito
ECUADOR
Amazon River
PERU
Pacific Ocean
Lima ★
Cuzco •
BRAZIL
La Paz •
Andes Mountains
BOLIVIA
PARAGUAY
São Paulo •
• Rio de Janeiro
CHILE
URUGUAY
Santiago ★
Buenos Aires ★
ARGENTINA
Rio de la Plata
Atlantic Ocean

0 Miles   1000   2000
0 Kilometers   2000

Tierra del Fuego

Cape Horn

© 2019 Jeffrey L. Ward

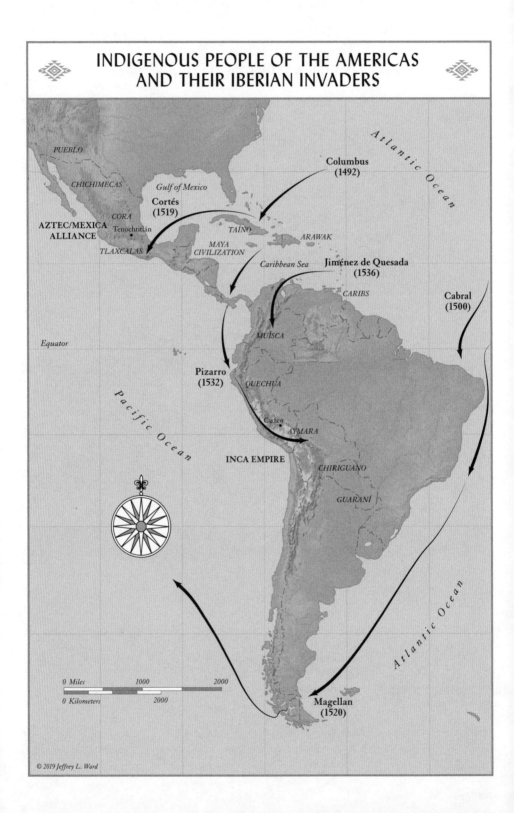

INDIGENOUS PEOPLE OF THE AMERICAS AND THEIR IBERIAN INVADERS

PUEBLO

CHICHIMECAS

Gulf of Mexico

Columbus
(1492)

Atlantic Ocean

Cortés
(1519)

CORA

AZTEC/MEXICA
ALLIANCE   Tenochtitlán

TAÍNO

ARAWAK

TLAXCALAS

MAYA
CIVILIZATION

Caribbean Sea

Jiménez de Quesada
(1536)

CARIBS

Cabral
(1500)

Equator

MUISCA

Pacific Ocean

Pizarro
(1532)

QUECHUA

Cuzco

AYMARA

INCA EMPIRE

CHIRIGUANO

GUARANÍ

0 Miles   1000   2000

0 Kilometers   2000

Magellan
(1520)

Atlantic Ocean

© 2019 Jeffrey L. Ward

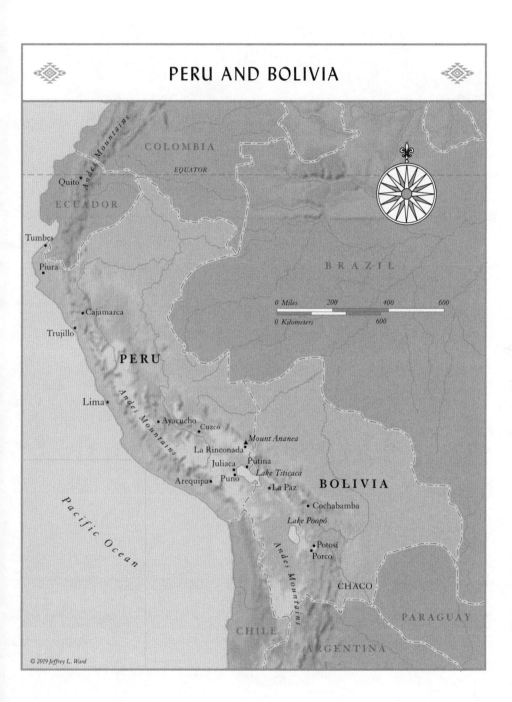

PERU AND BOLIVIA

COLOMBIA

EQUATOR

Quito★

ECUADOR

Andes Mountains

Tumbes

Piura

BRAZIL

0 Miles   200   400   600

0 Kilometers   600

Cajamarca

Trujillo

PERU

Lima★

Andes Mountains

Ayacucho

Cuzco

Mount Ananea

La Rinconada

Juliaca   Putina

Arequipa   Puno   Lake Titicaca

★La Paz   BOLIVIA

Cochabamba

Lake Poopó

Potosí

Porco

Pacific Ocean

Andes Mountains

CHACO

CHILE

PARAGUAY

ARGENTINA

© 2019 Jeffrey L. Ward

SILVER, SWORD, AND STONE

CHAPTER I

STILL SEEKING EL DORADO

———————————— ❖ ————————————

Peru is a beggar sitting on a bench of gold.

—Old Peruvian adage

In the stinging cold just before dawn, Leonor Gonzáles leaves her stone hut on a glacial mountain peak in the Peruvian Andes to trudge up a path and scour rock spills for flecks of gold. Like generations before her, she has teetered under heavy bags of stone, pounded it with a crude hammer, ground it to gravel with her feet, crushed it to a fine sand. On rare, lucky days, she teases out infinitesimally small motes of gold by swirling the grit in a mercury solution. She is only forty-seven, but her teeth are gone. Her face is cooked by a relentless sun, parched by the freezing winds. Her hands are the color of cured meat, the fingers humped and gnarled. She is partially blind. But every day as the sun peeks over the icy promontory of Mount Ananea, she joins the women of La Rinconada, the highest human habitation in the world, to scale the steep escarpment that leads toward the mines, scavenging for all that shines, stuffing stones into the backbreaking rucksack she will lug down-mountain at dusk.

It might be a scene from biblical times, but it is not. Leonor Gonzáles climbed that ridge yesterday during the *pallaqueo*, the hunt for gold her forebears have undertaken since time immemorial, and she will climb it again tomorrow, doing what she has done since she first accompanied her mother to work at the age of four. Never mind that a Canadian mining company less than thirty miles away is performing the same task more efficiently with hulking, twenty-first-century machinery; or that just beyond Lake Titicaca—the cradle of Inca civilization—Australian, Chinese, and United States corporate giants are investing millions for state-of-the-art equipment to join the Latin American mining bonanza. The business of digging deep into the earth's entrails to wrest glittering treasures has long, abiding roots on this continent and, in many ways, defines the people we Latin Americans have become.

Leonor Gonzáles is the embodiment of "silver, sword, and stone," the triad of this book's title—three obsessions that have held Latin Americans fast for the past millennium. "Silver" is the lust for precious metals; the infatuation that rules Leonor's life as it has ruled generations before her: a frantic hunt for a prize she cannot use, a substance that is wanted in cities she will never see. The passion for gold and silver is an obsession that burned brightly before Columbus's time, consumed Spain in its relentless conquest of America, drove a cruel system of slavery and colonial exploitation, sparked a bloody revolution, addled the region's stability for centuries, and morphed into Latin America's best hope for the future. Just as Inca and Aztec rulers made silver and gold symbols of their glory, just as sixteenth-century Spain grew rich and powerful as the preeminent purveyor of precious metals, mining remains at the heart of the Latin American promise today. That obsession lives on—the glistening troves extracted and sent away by the boatloads—even though the quarries are finite. Even though the frenzy must end.

Leonor is no less a product of "silver" than she is of the "sword," Latin America's abiding culture of the strongman that accompanies it: the region's proclivity, as Gabriel García Márquez, José Martí, Mario Vargas Llosa, and others have pointed out, to solve problems by unilateral and alarming displays of power. By brutality. By a reliance on muscle, coercion, and an overweening love for dictators and the military: *la mano dura*, the iron fist. Violence was certainly the easy expedient in the day of the war-loving Moche in AD 800, but it grew more so under the Aztec and Inca Empires, was perfected and institutionalized by Spain under the cruel tutelage of Cortés and Pizarro, and became ingrained during the hellish wars of Latin American independence in the nineteenth century. State terrorism, dictatorships, endless revolutions, Argentina's Dirty War, Peru's Shining Path, Colombia's FARC, Mexico's crime cartels, and twenty-first-century drug wars are its legacies. The sword remains as much a Latin American instrument of authority and power as it ever was five hundred years ago when the Dominican friar Bartolomé de Las Casas lamented that the Spanish colonies were "choak'd up with Indian Blood and Gore."

No, Leonor Gonzáles is no stranger to oppression and violence. Her ancestors, people of the altiplano, were conquered and forced into labor by the Incas and then reconquered and enslaved by Spanish conquistadors. For centuries, her people were relocated by force at the whims of the *mitmaq*—the compulsory labor system that the Inca Empire, and then Spain, demanded of the vanquished. Or they were taken away in the Church's "reductions": massive resettlements of indigenous populations in the ongoing enterprise to save their souls. In the nineteenth century, Leonor's people were herded at sword's point to fight and be sacrificed on opposing sides of the revolution. In the twentieth century, they were driven higher and higher into the snowy reaches of the Andes to escape the wanton massacres of the Shining Path. But even in that airless aerie, eighteen thousand feet above sea level, the sword has continued to be master. Today in the wild, lawless mining town of La Rinconada, where murder and rape are rampant—where human sacrifices are offered to mountain demons and no government police chief dares go—Leonor is as vulnerable to brute force as her forebears were five hundred years ago.

Every day when she rises, Leonor touches a small, gray stone that she keeps on a ledge by her cot, near a faded photograph of her dead husband, Juan Sixto Ochochoque. Every night, before she crawls under a blanket with her children and grandchildren, she touches it again. "His soul rests inside," she told me when I visited her in her frigid one-room hut, no larger than ten feet squared, where she lives on the lip of a mountain glacier with two sons, two daughters, and two grandchildren. She and Juan, the ruddy-faced miner in the photo, were never actually married; no one in Leonor's acquaintance has ever taken the Church's vows. To her, Juan is her husband and the father of her children; and, from the day a mine-shaft collapsed, and his lungs filled with the deadly fumes that killed him, that round, gray stone at the head of her bed has come to represent him even as it represents the whole of Leonor's spiritual life. Like many indigenous people—from the Rio Grande to the Tierra del Fuego—Leonor accepts Catholic teachings only as they reflect the gods of her ancestors. Virgin Mary is another face for Pachamama, Earth Mother, the ground beneath our feet, from which all bounty springs.

God is another word for Apu, the spirit that dwells in mountains, whose energy comes from the sun and lives on in stones. Satan is Supay, a demanding rascal-god who rules death, the underworld, the dark entrails of ground below ground, and needs to be appeased.

Leonor's stone stands for the third obsession that has held Latin America in its grip for the past thousand years: the region's fervent adherence to religious institutions, whether they be temples, churches, elaborate cathedrals, or piles of sacred rock. The first order of business when pre-Columbian powers conquered one another a thousand years ago was to pound the others' gods to rubble. With the arrival of the conquistadors in the Americas, the triumphant monuments of stone erected by the Aztecs and the Incas to honor their gods were often reduced to mere pedestals for mighty cathedrals. The significance was not lost on the conquered. Rock was piled on rock, palaces were built on top of palaces, a church straddled every important indigenous temple or *huaca*, and religion became a powerful, concrete reminder of who had won the day. Even as time wore on—even as Catholicism became the single most powerful institution in Latin America, even as some of its adherents began to be wooed away by Pentecostalism—Latin Americans have remained a resolutely religious population. They cross themselves when they pass a church. They build shrines in their homes. They carry images of saints in their wallets, talk to their coca leaves, hang crosses from rearview mirrors, fill their pockets with sacred stones.

Leonor is not alone in her thrall to silver, sword, and stone. The majority of Latin Americans are bound to her by no more than a few degrees of separation. Extracting ore in Mexico, Peru, Chile, Brazil, and Colombia has resumed the primacy it had four hundred years ago, and the business of mining has gone a long way to redefine progress, boost economies, lift people out of poverty, and touch every aspect of the social fabric. Precious minerals pass from rural to urban handlers, from brown hands to white, from poor to rich. The gold that is dug from the rock beneath Leonor's hut fuels an elaborate economy: the seedy beer hall a few steps from her door, the flocks of child prostitutes down-mountain in Putina, the bankers in Lima, geologists in Canada, socialites in Paris, investors in China. It is an industry whose profits ultimately go overseas to Toronto, Denver, London, Shanghai, much as gold once crossed the

Atlantic Ocean in Spanish galleons and made its way to Madrid, Amsterdam, and Peking. The general flow of revenue has not changed. It lingers briefly—enough for a beer at the cantina or a fly-bitten shank of goat to hang from the roof beam—and then it goes out. Away. Over there.

The "sword," too, has weathered history, from the keenly honed slate blades that Chimú warriors used to disembowel their enemies, to the crude kitchen knives deployed by Zeta gangsters in the Mexican city of Juárez. A culture of violence persists in Latin America, lurking in shadows, waiting to erupt, threatening the region's fitful progress toward peace and prosperity. The sword has been the ever-ready instrument in this precinct of stark inequalities: as useful in Augusto Pinochet's 1970s Chile, among a largely white, literate population, as in today's blood-soaked streets of Honduras among the illiterate poor. The ten most dangerous cities in the world are all in Latin American countries. Little wonder that the United States has seen a flood of desperate immigrants fleeing Mexico, Guatemala, Honduras, El Salvador. Fear is the engine that drives Latin Americans north.

As for "stone's" purchase on the spirit, there is no question that organized religion has played—and continues to play—a crucial role in these Americas. From the days of the Inca, when the great rulers Pachacutec Inca Yupanqui and Tupac Inca Yupanqui "turned the world" and expanded the empire by conquering vast swaths of South America and forcing the vanquished masses to worship the sun, faith has been a weapon of coercion as well as an instrument for social cohesion. The Aztecs shared the Incas' appetite for conquest as well as a keen appreciation for the uses of religion. But they had a starkly different approach to conversion: they often adopted the deities of the newly conquered with the understanding that someone else's god might have much in common with one's own. Stroll through any Mesoamerican or Andean village, and you will find lively expressions of those ancient beliefs in contemporary art and ritual traditions.

Today, although various Amerindian, African, Asian, and European faiths are practiced in Latin America, the region remains firmly stamped with the one Spain imposed on it more than five hundred years ago. It is adamantly Catholic. A full 40 percent of all the world's Catholics reside here, and, as a result, a strong bond unites the believers, from Montevideo, Uruguay, to Monterrey, Mexico. Indeed Simón Bolívar, who liberated six South American republics, imagined the Spanish-speaking, Catholic nations of those Americas as a potentially powerful unified force in the greater world. The Spanish Crown may have worked mightily to keep its colonies from communicating, trading, or establishing human concord, but it joined them forever when it led them to the feet of Jesus. In the end, Bolívar was never able to fashion a strong Pan-American union from the diverse, restless population of Spanish-speaking Christians that he liberated. But the Church today remains, as it was in Bolívar's time, the most trusted institution in all of Latin America.

This is a book about three components of Latin American society that have shaped it for a thousand years. It does not pretend to be a definitive, comprehensive history. Rather, it is meant to cast light on the legacy of the Latin American people and on three elements of our past that may suggest something about our future. Certainly there are other obsessions we share that make for a brighter portrait of the region: our infatuation with art, for instance; our enthusiasm for music, our culinary passions, our love of rhetoric. The Spanish language that flows from the pens of Latin Americans has produced one of the most strikingly original literatures of our time. There are also few regional traits that shine more brightly than our fidelity to family or our propensity for human warmth. But none of these, in my view, has moved populations, marked the landscape, and written history as forcefully as Latin America's fixations on mining, or its romance with brute force, or religion.

These obsessions are not tidy strands that can be addressed as independent narratives. Their histories over the course of the past one thousand years have clashed, overlapped, become intricately intertwined, just as gold, faith, and fear are tightly woven skeins in the life of Leonor Gonzáles. But Latin America's inclinations to religion and violence, along with its stubborn adherence to an ancient form of extractive commerce that doesn't necessarily lead to lasting development, have fascinated me for years. I believe the history of these inclinations can tell us much about who we Latin Americans are. And we are, as a historian once said, "a continent made to undermine conventional truths," a region unto ourselves, unlike any other, where theories or doctrines fashioned elsewhere seldom have purchase. I also believe that, for all the years I have spent following the ways and warps of this skeined history, it cannot possibly tell the whole story.

How do you explain a hemisphere and its people? It's an impossible task, really, made more complicated by five hundred years of skewed historical record. All the same, I am convinced that there is a commonality—a concrete character, if you will—that emerges from the Spanish American experience. I am also convinced that this character is a direct product of the momentous confrontation between two worlds. We are defined by a grudging tolerance born of this experience. There is no northern equivalent.

In Latin America, we may not always know exactly what breed we represent, but we do know that we are more bound to this "New World" than we are to the "Old." After centuries of unrestrained mixing, we are more brown than white, more black or Indian than some might think. But, since raw political power has been held stubbornly by every anxious generation of "whites" since First Contact, a true reckoning of our identity has always been a tenuous proposition. Call it what you will, but the enduring presence of indigenous history in Latin America—quite unlike its counterpart in the North—suggests there is a very different explanation here. I offer mine in all humility in hopes of relaying something of the perspective it has given me.

Although my father's family has had roots in Peru for almost five hundred years, my grandmother Rosa Cisneros y Cisneros de Arana was a great enthusiast of all things Spanish. She often spoke to me of Spain's custom of sending sons into different walks of life as a way of building the pillars of a robust society. One son, as the logic went, would be a man of the world (a lawyer, politician, or businessman); the second, a military man; the third, a priest. The first would ensure prosperity by having a hand in the nation's power and wealth; the second would maintain the peace by serving his country as a soldier; the third would throw open the gates to heaven by teaching us the way to God. I never saw reference to this custom made in history books, although I heard of it again and again as I traveled the countries of Latin America. In time, I saw that a banker, a general, and a bishop were indeed pillars of our shared society; they were precisely what kept the oligarchy, genders, and races in the rigid caste system that Spain had created in the first place. That triumvirate of sovereignty—of princes, soldiers, and high priests—had held for the Incas, Muíscas, Mayans, and Aztecs as well. In many cases, a supreme ruler was expected to be all three. Call it what you will, but the formula of triangulated control has worked for centuries in the Americas of the South. It allowed ancient cultures to expand and conquer. It allowed colonizers a firm lock on the pockets, fists, and souls of the colonized. For all Latin America's gifts to the world—for all the storied civilizations of our past—the region continues to be ruled by what has always held sway here. By silver, sword, and stone.

PART ONE

SILVER

Once upon a time, my little dove, there was a dazzling city, floating on a blue lake, radiating such brilliance that, seen from afar, it seemed to be made of silver. They called it Tenochtitlán.

—Myths, Fables, and Legends of Ancient Mexico

CHAPTER 2

VEINS OF A MOUNTAIN GOD

＊◈＊

Descend to the mineral depths and find, in those grim metal veins, mankind's struggle on earth.

—Pablo Neruda, "Canto General"

POTOSÍ, BOLIVIA

The long drab, arid plateau between Porco and Potosí on the Bolivian altiplano is surely one of the most desolate landscapes on earth. What the ancient Incas described as a region of sparkling lakes and leaping fish—a grassland alive with alpaca, vicuña, chinchilla—has become a barrens that beggars the imagination. The brush is scarce. The earth is turned. To the northwest, Lake Poopó, second only to Lake Titicaca in size, has disappeared entirely; today it is an endless expanse of crazed sediment, a cemetery of aquatic life. What you see, as you cross the valley of Tarapaya and approach Porco or Potosí, the ancient medullas of Inca and Spanish dominion, is what you might see in any mined territory in this part of the world—a lunar scape, pitted with murky ponds that reek of ruin. The waterfowl are gone; few birds flap overhead save the occasional vulture. There is a rank odor about, the stench of dynamite and anatomical decay. Even the shearing winds and freezing rain cannot mask the smell.

Along the road to Cerro Rico, the fabled "rich mountain," there are heaps of stone. An occasional figure slips past, weaving through the rubble. These are itinerant miners, springing from that bare and boundless plain like mythical soldiers, toting their worldly possessions on their backs. Eventually you come upon the famed red promontory and the city that sprawls at its feet. This is Potosí, once one of the largest urban centers of the Western Hemisphere: a metropolis, during its heyday in the 1600s, as populous and vibrant as Paris or London or Tokyo. A mighty cathedral clings to its heart. For as far as the paved streets will lead, you see rickety mansions with intricate Moorish balconies—lumbering phantoms of a splendid past. Thirty-six churches in varying states of dilapidation punctuate the decline. The storied city of silver is no longer. Gone are the stately palm trees, the silks from Canton, the Neapolitan shoes, the London hats, the perfumes from Araby. No one in Paris finery leans from the balconies anymore. A lonely dog howls from a rooftop. It is hard to believe that this was the seat of modern globalization as we know it—the sixteenth-century economic marvel that drove European commerce and prefigured the industrial age.

But that is precisely what Potosí once was. In the one hundred years between 1600 and 1700, Potosí single-handedly supplied more than one hundred million kilos of the silver that made the Peruvian Viceroyalty one of the most vibrant financial enterprises in the world. Lima grew rich because of Potosí. Metal mined by Indian hands poured into European capitals, giving that region the bullion it desperately needed, stimulating the economy and allowing capitalism to stamp out feudalism and become the prevailing wave of the future. Spain used that infusion of wealth to enrich its aristocrats, wage war against England, curb the spread of Protestantism, and ensure the dominion of the Hapsburg Empire. But the money did not stay in Spain. As England marched into the industrial age, boosted by the solvency that Latin American mines provided, and as Europe forged ahead, expanding its commercial reach, Spain stagnated—resolutely agricultural, doggedly tied to the past—and its colonies' hard-won silver slipped through its fingers. Wealth moved on to build lavish fortunes elsewhere. The stain of that failure is still visible in this legendary boom town. Potosí.

At the edge of it, climbing in chaotic angles up Cerro Rico's jutting rock, are a scattering of tin houses. Here and there, huts of stone. A string of humanity moves in and out of the holes that scar the face of the mountain. Along the precipitously winding paths, flocks of women in wide woolen skirts hurry with food and rude implements; children shoulder bags of rock. There isn't much to carve away from Cerro Rico now. Legend has it that the many thousands of tons of silver extracted from this colossus would have built a gleaming bridge from here to Madrid. But the red leviathan seems deflated now; a tired heap that bears little resemblance to the soaring peak of sixteenth-century engravings. Riddled with tunnels, it is a fragile grid on the verge of collapse, a labyrinth of perils. The hopeful remain, but the bonanza has moved on.

It wasn't like this when Huayna Capac, the Lord Inca, traveled between Potosí and Porco five hundred years ago, before the civil wars, before the plagues, and before the fateful conquest of his empire. Porco had long been one of the main sources of precious metals for the Incas. Since the thirteenth century, when the empire is said to have originated, the Inca lords traded no metals, nor did they use them as currency; they valued the glittering substances as sacred symbols of their gods, essential elements in the ritual worship of sun, moon, and stars. Gold, with its resplendent yellow, was a reflection of the heavenly body that ruled by day, the father of all earthly life. Silver represented the white deities who lit the night sky and commanded the seas. Copper was the swift current of lightning, a force to be revered. These metals were mined under strict supervision of the Lord Inca's administrators in Cuzco. In Porco, the oversight was meticulous, as slaves scrabbled for silver with deer antlers and carried it away in animal skins. Reserved for the exclusive use of the nobility, these metals were hammered into strikingly original ornaments: ceremonial breastplates, gilded raiments, ritual altar pieces, decorative sculptures, funerary baubles, household decor. There was no incentive to steal or hoard them, nor search out their source, since they had only one use and only one consumer. They were mined as the emperor's ceremony demanded. Nothing more.

That all changed with the reign of Huayna Capac, the eleventh Inca sovereign, who loved gold and silver with an abandon his royal forebears did not share. It wasn't enough to have the sacred sun temple, Coricancha, arrayed in gold, or his chambers' walls lined with silver, or his ceremonial raiments bespangled with both. This Lord Inca wanted to eat and drink from them, demanded that his chairs and litters be made of glittering metals, commissioned statues of himself and his ancestors made from hammered gold. His overweening love for these hard-won metals meant that the empire had to step up production, and it brought on a covetousness and oppression never in evidence before.

Huayna Capac was at the height of his power when he visited his mines in Porco in the early 1500s. Handsome, well built, a warrior king who had expanded his realm to far corners of his universe, he decided to take a grand tour to review those conquests, expel invaders, and stamp out the rebel factions. It was beyond his capacity to appreciate that dominion, but just then, at that pivotal moment in history, he presided over the greatest empire on earth. Bigger than China's Ming dynasty, more vast than Ivan the Great's Russia, larger than the Byzantine, Songhai, Aztec, or Ottoman Empires, the Inca Empire was more sprawling than any European state of its time. Huayna Capac ruled over lands that stretched for more than 2,500 miles, or roughly the distance between Stockholm and Riyadh. The Tahuantinsuyo, as he called it, was a territory as long as North America is wide, the most formidable domain this civilization would ever hold, and it had taken more than three centuries and eleven generations to build it. Huayna Capac had begun his reign just after Columbus's fateful landing in Santo Domingo, and he would die just before Francisco Pizarro rode across his lands to plant an alien flag on the sacred Temple of the Sun. But now—right now, in the glow of Huayna Capac's preeminence—he was mounting an expedition to beat back a Guaraní invasion in the South and reassure his people that they had his protection against the wild, marauding tribes of the known world.

As the emperor and his armies crossed the valley of Tarapaya, he decided to stop in Porco and visit the silver mines. It was just after the turn of the sixteenth century, and although he didn't know it, the winds of change and an epic plague had already been loosed on the peoples of that hemisphere. Hernán Cortés would soon capture the powerful emperor Montezuma and cripple the Aztecs at the Battle of Tenochtitlán. Pedro de Alvarado would sweep into Mayan territory and kill its ruler, Tecún Uman. Silver and gold had already left indigenous hands and crossed the Atlantic in what would become a brisk traffic to Seville, and a virulent strain of smallpox had traveled the seas in the opposite direction. But in the sublime isolation that Huayna Capac inhabited as he surveyed his empire, aloft on his litter of gold, the journey to Porco was a perfunctory visit.

As his retinue continued across the valley, the Lord Inca noticed an imposing peak on the southern horizon. It commanded that stretch of the Andean cordillera—the imposing mountain range that runs like a spine from Venezuela to Argentina—not only because of its height but also because of its rust-red hue. Pointing to it, he opined that surely it contained rich lodes of some precious metal. Legend has it that he ordered his miners to investigate, and, as they did, a mighty roar of displeasure arose from the belly of the mountain. Terrified, the miners withdrew. Earthquake, thunder, whatever the reason, the Inca potentates never did insist on exploring the mountain. Some say it was because the promontory was considered sacred, holding within it a great spirit—an *apu*, a mountain god; others, because there was no particular urgency, as long as the royal court had what it needed. It was not until a decade after the conquest, when a lowly miner for the Spanish Crown stopped to warm himself on a winter's night, that everything changed. He saw a trickle of molten silver gather at the base of his fire, evidence of the bounty within. Soon after that, his Spanish overlord expropriated the discovery and made Potosí known round the world.

MOUNT ANANEA
Peru, 1829–2009

> *On the fourth day, the All Powerful beautified the world with the sun, moon, and stars. Once these were in the firmament, the sun gave birth to gold and the mines, and the moon saw about the silver.*
> —Bartolomé Arzans de Orsúa y Vela, 1715

In 1829, three hundred years after Huayna Capac made his grand sweep of the altiplano and pointed prophetically to the red mountain of Potosí, a young Irish geologist, Joseph Barclay Pentland, dashed off a letter to the celebrated explorer Alexander von Humboldt and, in it, pointed to the wealth of precious metals that might be found just north of that territory. Potosí's glories were past, finished, its treasures sacked, its investors in ruins. But there were hard rock deposits of gold on higher ground four hundred miles away, Pentland assured Humboldt, especially in the Cordillera de Carabaya, on the forbidding slopes of the hoary behemoths that circled the highest navigable body of water in the world: Lake Titicaca.

The diplomat geologist—as interested in metal as in foreign affairs—had just returned to Lima, Peru, after a grueling two-thousand-mile mule ride through the rugged highlands of Bolivia. The wars of independence had just ended, Spain had been thoroughly routed from American shores, and Britain's foreign secretary, George Canning, who had been watching the revolution with keen interest, was eager to assess Latin American mining and see what was in it for England. The great liberator Simón Bolívar, fresh from freeing Peru and founding Bolivia—and an avid fan of the British to boot—had welcomed Pentland to the task. Being an energetic social climber of the first order, Pentland now wrote about Latin American possibilities to Humboldt, Charles Darwin, and other great scientists of the day. As Huayna Capac had pointed presciently to Potosí three centuries before, Pentland now pointed emphatically to the promontories of the Carabaya cordillera, where future fortunes would be made.

The Carabaya mountain chain, which straddles Peru and Bolivia due north of Lake Titicaca and cradles Mount Ananea, was certainly not virgin ground to fortune hunters. Over the centuries, the glacial grind and lacerating winds had eroded the rock, hacked off enormous boulders, and coaxed forth the treasures that lurked within. According to Inca lore, gold nuggets as large as a human skull had rolled from cracks in the stone. One trophy was said to be as large as a horse's head. El Inca Garcilaso de la Vega, Huayna Capac's great-nephew, had written that the mountain contained gold beyond our imagining. He had good reason to think so: his lordly grand-uncle had sent a contingent to mine there. But the terrain had proved impossible: the peaks too vertiginous, the cold too punishing. Before long, the Incas stopped their operations in Ananea. The Spanish, too, eventually abandoned their mines, but for different reasons. The shafts, which bored deeper into the glacial rock than any Inca pit, had collapsed under ice and snow.

Ironically enough, Pentland's projection, like the mines themselves, remained frozen in time as Bolívar's newly liberated republics fell, one by one, into political and economic chaos. The gold and silver lodes that had been exploited to such advantage in Incan and colonial days were

now left to the caprices of a string of despots and their temperamental regimes. It wasn't until the Latin American mining industry experienced
a vibrant renaissance at the turn of the twenty-first century that Bolivian
geologists revived Pentland's work and credited the Irishman for his meticulous analysis of the rich arteries that coursed through the geologically
exuberant Carabaya. He had described, almost two centuries before, the
Potosís that were yet to come.

In 2004, even as Pentland's name was being resurrected on the Bolivian
side of the cordillera by functionaries wanting to attract foreign investors, Leonor Gonzáles's husband, Juan Ochochoque, was alive and laboring in the pitch-black mines of Mount Ananea, in the very region
that Pentland had indicated would be the golden way of the future.
After his meager breakfast of pig's ear broth cooked over an improvised
ethyl burner, Juan would head out with a pickax over his shoulder. Although he was a man of the twenty-first century, he was also a miner in
the centuries-old lottery of *cachorreo*, a system in which a laborer works
thirty days for no pay before he is allowed to keep whatever rock he can
lug out on his back. Daylight would reveal whether or not it contained
gold. Sometimes Juan's haul was enough for a few days of water and
food; sometimes it yielded nothing at all.

Juan's days began in the freezing penumbra of dawn and ended long
after nightfall. Joining the files of shadowy figures snaking up the muddy
paths, he entered the mine to be swallowed into a deeper darkness. Night
was a permanent state—tunnels, his natural habitat—and, like any noc-
turnal creature, Juan learned to navigate the stygian labyrinth of Ananea
and suffer its fetid damp. There were few rules in the makeshift, informal enterprises dedicated to hewing that icy rock, but those that existed
were firm: no female was allowed to enter that underworld—no one
could risk the bad luck a woman might bring. Miners had to trust one
another, share what little they had, and make offerings to the god of all
miners, the lord of dark places, Supay. Chewing coca leaf to brace themselves against an airless gloom, hunched by cramped channels of stone,
speaking to no one so as to conserve the scant oxygen, they trudged past
husks of spent dynamite, pools of chemical waste, the leering, horned
effigies of Supay, the litter of past sacrifices, until they were a thousand

feet into the mountain's heart. For Juan, it was, in every way but one, the repetition of an ancient practice.

With this essential difference: no miner in the service of the Inca would have dared penetrate a mountain so deeply. Perhaps because each was seen as harboring its own god, perhaps because the Incas had strong constraints against forcing slaves to suffer ill health—perhaps because so little gold or silver was needed for such exclusive purposes—mining in the time of the Incas was largely superficial, scraping a mountain's surface, or scooping out a cave, rather than plunging a three-hundred-meter hole into its flank. Shaft mining, after all, would have represented a flagrant violation of the most physical manifestation of a god, or *apu*, which was the mountain itself. Perhaps that is why the lion's share of gold that the indigenous extracted was from rivers, sifted carefully from coursing silt. Indeed, the Huallaga River, which starts high in the Andes and flows majestically through the Amazon jungle, is said to have been so laden with gold that it made mining elementary for the Incas. But any explanation we might offer for a reticence to bore deep into Pachamama, the sacred earth, would be conjecture. We have no real explanation for this.

In truth, "real" explanations for the continent's indigenous past are rare. Reconstructing pre-Columbian history or culture is a tenuous business. But there are facts we can deduce. The Incas and Aztecs did not see time as we see it: for them, it consisted of different cycles, other dimensions. Its organization was largely binary—rain versus drought; day versus night; harvest versus hunger—and time raveled in a way that reflected a profoundly held belief in the eternal repetition of order and chaos. The Aztec world view, too, was deeply binary: there was earth below, sky above; fire and water; darkness and light. But for all the seeming simplicity of this cosmology, much about these ancient societies was fluid, complex, built on a sense that while the physical world might be clear and evident, human affairs were not.

To be an ordinary mortal in the Inca realm was to inhabit a transitory existence: work was interchangeable, rotational, highly disruptive. As in later totalitarian systems under Joseph Stalin or Mao Tse-tung, whole populations were often uprooted and mobilized, families divided, all for the convenience of the state and its economic necessities. Rebel tribes would be relocated to areas where they could be watched by loyal subjects. Peons knew to expect a life of constant upheaval. A man in the labor force, the *mitmaq*, might scavenge for gold in a nearby mine, or harvest maize in a far field, or be sent to bear arms in war. A lifetime of travail in one line of work—a single industry—was almost unheard of. A laborer in this ever-revolving system might be required to fish for three months, be free to spend another three dancing and drinking, and then be called to resume labors elsewhere. We know from chronicles— or from evidence in tombs—how great rulers lived and died, but history has left scant record of the commoners.

Complicating our ability to fully appreciate the past, the Incas and Aztecs had no writing. Although the Mayans perfected a complex system of glyphs we can now decode, the Incas and Aztecs preserved the past in oral histories handed down through generations or, in the case of the Incas, through knotted string *quipus* historians are only now beginning to understand. Moreover, much of what we know about these ancient cultures is tainted by European bias—filtered through Spanish chroniclers, priests, or mestizos striving to please their colonial masters. The mark of the conqueror is all too clear in the extant "record." In it, we read that the New World indigenous are heathen, unenlightened barbarians, a disposable race, hardly human; even though we now know that in many ways they were more evolved than Europeans. The Inca moral code, for instance—*ama suwa, ama llulla, ama qhella* (do not steal, lie, or be slothful)—was deeply ingrained in the Andean people. Eventually, when the colonial system locked into place, the accepted, popular gloss was that Indians were beasts of burden, whatever their rank in the preconquest universe, and their just reward was to serve the higher order of Spain. As a result, historians must navigate a quagmire of opinion and prejudice to understand even the most basic contours of indigenous life.

So what, if anything, can we conclude about these cultures' interest in gold and silver? There is plenty of physical evidence that the Incas held a reverence for precious metals. Gold had been part of their belief system from the very beginning, since the day that Manco Capac and Mama Ocllo, the founding patriarch and matriarch, along with their brothers and sisters, allegedly left the hollows that surround Lake Titicaca to seek the sacred land on which to found their empire of the Sun. The Sun God, as legend had it, had armed them with a gold rod that would sink deep into the earth when it recognized Qosqo—Cuzco—the earth's umbilical, the center from which their dominion would radiate to far corners of the world. That larger world was Tahuantinsuyu, and their charge was to penetrate it, enlighten it, and bring more hands and souls to the labors and glories of worshiping the Sun.

As the Inca Empire expanded, following a logic that is altogether different from any known model of conquest, precious metals became the symbols of its mandate, if never its currency or goal. The Incas fanned out from the holy medulla of Cuzco gradually, methodically, growing ever more powerful as they subjected others to their faith and will. Tribes were subsumed with promises of a more comfortable life, a grander community, a better god. The more rebellious were conquered in brutal wars. Once subdued, the *curacas*, or tribal leaders, were sent with their families for reeducation in Cuzco. When they returned to their tribes, prepared to rule in fealty to the Incas, a favorite son or brother would be detained indefinitely in the capital as a way of ensuring loyalty.

Each Inca emperor advanced the cause, bringing more worshippers to the Sun, creating a mighty webwork that grew along *ceques*: lines that reached like rays from Coricancha—the Temple of the Sun, the empire's vital heart—to borderlands of conquest. Mobilizing a massive army of forced laborers, the Incas split rock, raised fortresses, and built storehouses and holy sanctuaries, as well as the magnificent Royal Road, the Capac Ñan, a road system traversing every possible landform and stretching twenty thousand miles from Argentina to Colombia—a span nearly four times as long as China's Great Wall, and the equivalent of traveling from Lima to Tokyo and back two times. To glorify that expansion, they combed gold from rivers, carved silver from mountains, hacked copper from open pits, and sent it all back to ever more powerful lords in Cuzco. The walls of Coricancha, the "golden realm" of the Incas, were tiled in gold. Silver hung from its ceilings. Elaborate gardens made entirely of intricately wrought metals were fashioned for the emperor's delectation. Indeed, every utensil in his house was made of precious metal. Gold was the "sweat of the sun"; silver, the "tears of the moon." As such, these substances were cherished gifts from the heavens, signaling the essential connection between the earthly and the divine. The European intruders who came to these lands scavenging for riches never did understand this fundamental difference: to the Inca, gold was light's refuge in a never-ending battle against the dark, a manifestation of the holy, a bridge between man and his creator. Only the anointed ruler, who himself descended from gods, could own such sacred stuff.

So revered were these metals and so personal their ties to the Lord Inca—who was, after all, primogenitor, Christ, and king—that when he died, no inheritance was possible. His mansion would be shuttered with all his gleaming possessions inside, exactly as he had left them. The belief was that he would hold court in the afterlife and come again to reinhabit those rooms someday. His bowels were meticulously removed and buried in a temple with his gold and jewels. His fingernail and hair clippings, painstakingly accumulated over the course of his lifetime, were stored away to be deposited in sacred places. His mummified remains, perfectly embalmed to resemble him at the peak of his powers, were placed on a throne in Coricancha, along with the mummies of all the other dead Lord Incas, to await the moment of return. He would continue to rule, as vigorously as when he was alive, through family representatives—or *panaca*—who would consult his corpse, control the narrative of his reign, and impart his ongoing will. So it was that all the gold, silver, and precious artifacts that an Inca took with him to eternity were seen more as tribute than principal. They were more illusory than real, more connected to the gods than to mortals, more a testament to collective memory than currency to be coveted in the here and now.

But halfway through the 1400s, with the spread of empire by two dynamic Inca rulers, Pachacutec and Tupac Inca Yupanqui, gold and silver began to be regarded as a mark of earthly glory.

Pachacutec decreed that only the royal family could wear these precious metals, while Tupac Inca Yupanqui returned from conquests with trains of llamas weighed down by silver. Huayna Capac, who delighted in symbols of power and grandeur more than either his father or grandfather, honored the birth of a son by commissioning a chain of gold that reached from one end of Cuzco's marketplace to the other. An army of men was required to carry it.

These metals were not forged in the same way as gold or silver were forged in Europe—by pouring liquid metal into molds. The American Indians didn't value metal for its solidity but for its malleability and resilience. They fashioned masterpieces by hammering the metal into sheets, pounding it with mallets until they were left with a tough and brilliant foil. Working the sheets around sturdy molds, they would then solder the parts to form a magnificent, glittering whole.

With time, the Incas became renowned for these symbols of power, and, because of ongoing conquests, news of their love for them spread through the continent. They became known as the people who wore glitter: the white kings. The shining. The warriors of sun and moon. This is not to say that they were the first civilization on the continent to develop precious metals or that they had a monopoly on production. Indeed, the art of metallurgy had been flourishing in the Americas for thousands of years. The Chavín culture, which dominated Peru's coastline for much of the millennium before Christ, had excelled in metalwork. Like the Incas, they had pounded gold into intricate jewelry and headdresses, sewed it into garments, valued it as a badge of nobility, proof of a higher order, a more aristocratic bloodline. The "Lady of Cao," a Mochica priestess who ruled the Peruvian coast in AD 300, was buried with a splendid array of jewelry, as well as elaborate crowns, nose rings, and scepters.

The Andean cultures that followed—the Moche and the Chimú—were equal masters, especially of silver. Eventually metalwork was taken up by the powerful Muísca people, a highly sophisticated confederation that inhabited the Colombian highlands and, in the fifteenth century, began producing exquisite gold for its chieftains. Indeed, it was around a particular Muísca prince, or *zipa*, that the legend of El Dorado took hold: the young eminence was said to be so wealthy, so accustomed to an abundance of shimmering metals, so winsome and athletic, that he would dust himself with a thick layer of gold powder before plunging into Lake Guatavita for his daily swim.

So it was that the art of metalwork spread along the cordillera and prospered in Andean isolation, the strict property of royalty in cultures that dominated those mountains for more than three thousand years. But at some point during the eleventh century—even as Norman invaders swept into England and Vikings slunk home, even as Spain suffered the grip of the Arab conquest—an invasion of a very different kind was taking place in the Americas. Trade from the Andes gradually began to creep up the continent and across the Caribbean, and the art of metalworking began to pique the interest of peoples elsewhere in the hemisphere. Call it gossip, cupidity, curiosity, trade route serendipity, but it was then—almost five hundred years before the arrival of the conquistadors—that a wider interest in precious metals began in earnest, spreading that mastery through Panama and the Caribbean to the great civilizations of the North.

TENOCHTITLÁN
Mexico, 1510–1519

> *There was no sin then. No disease. No aching in the bones. There was no gold fever.*
>
> —Chilám Balám, c. 1650–1750

Intercontinental trade, which began to proliferate along the coasts—especially in precious shells and feathers—brought metallurgy to Mesoamerica. By the turn of the first millennium AD, the Mayans, whose extraordinarily advanced culture was thriving in what is now Guatemala and Mexico, began to mine silver, gold, and copper for the same purpose as the Andeans: as a mark of nobility; as a way to distinguish class. Just as the Egyptian Queen Hatshepsut draped herself in gold frippery and dusted her face with silver, the Mayan potentates used shiny metals to signal their growing power. It did not occur to the Mayans, or to any of the early Andean cultures, for that matter—as it had to the Egyptians, Romans, and Germans—to forge something as utilitarian as arms and tools from iron ore. Not until the rule of Huayna Capac had the Incas begun to use bronze in crowbars, knives, and axe heads. And not until the Aztecs began fashioning copper spears in the fifteenth century was metal used for killing. Stone was the preferred bludgeon, obsidian the favored impaler, and though iron was plentiful in the landscape that surrounded these first nations, they did not mine it or imagine it as weapons until conquistadors disembarked on their shores. Much as the load-bearing wheel was unknown in the Western hemisphere until

European contact, metal would not enter the American imagination as cudgel or currency until the conquest imposed it in radical and transformative ways.

In truth, Spain's startling encounter with the people of the "Indies" brought it face-to-face with an original world, entirely distinct from any that Europe had ever imagined. Certainly it was a world beyond the conquistadors' capacity to understand—one they hardly paused to consider, having crossed seas not to learn about civilizations but to enrich themselves, reap honors, and evangelize the natives by force, if need be. In turn, the hemisphere into which they had sailed was hardly prepared for such bewildering aliens. For millennia, the so-called New World had felt comfortably old to its inhabitants—a "great island, afloat in a primordial sea." Isolated from the rest of the world and left to its own devices, it was a land teeming with residents. They were descendants of the people of Beringia, who had once inhabited a remote strip of grassland between Siberia and Alaska that, nineteen thousand years before, had been overrun by the Bering Sea. Migrating south, as waters rose and separated them from Asia and Europe, these newly indigenous Americans were flung far and wide by necessity and a pioneer spirit. They adapted to terrain, became a profusion of cultures, conducted wars as well as commerce, and developed strong tribal identities and a vigorous appetite for conquest.

By the 1400s, when Europe was no more than a modestly populated area roughly the size of Brazil, indigenous Americans occupied every habitable area of their hemisphere, from the Arctic tundra to the Caribbean islands, and from the Andean peaks to the deepest redoubts of the Lacandón Jungle. It was, to put it plainly, a world brimming with people. By 1492, historians say, there were one hundred million of them— one-fifth of the human race—and they had become distinct cultures and tribes. The Mayans had abandoned the great cities of Tikal and Chichén Itzá to fan out into the countryside. The Aztec capital, Tenochtitlán, was a bustling home to a quarter million residents—quadruple the population of London at the time. But beyond the city limits, the Aztecs governed twenty-five million more, double the density of the population of India or China. The Inca capital, Cuzco, too, was a humming metropolis. At the height of Incan power, Cuzco held two hundred thousand citizens, with as many as thirty-seven million more under its control—more than the Arab caliphate that had once held Spain, the Middle East, and northern Africa in its clutches. Though a vast and surpassingly difficult geography separated them, the great civilizations that were destined to defend the hemisphere against the Spanish invader shared striking commonalities. This was so evident by the 1500s that conquistadors were able to repeat strategies of conquest by assuming that the Aztecs and Incas were virtually identical in important ways: they were highly hierarchical, with a single emperor, perceived simultaneously as god, king, high priest, and supreme warrior. Both considered themselves People of the Sun. Both the Incas and the Aztecs had subjugated others over great expanses of land, and so had acquired many enemies. Thrones did not pass automatically from father to eldest son, which made the process vulnerable to intrigue and manipulation. Both cultures practiced human sacrifice and incest, and therefore were handily labeled by Christians as abominators. Both employed sophisticated techniques of engineering, agriculture, timekeeping, and astronomy, and so a vast knowledge base was immediately available to their conquerors. Both worshipped the sun and moon and glorified them in art. Perhaps most significant of all to the plundering Spaniards, both had reached zeniths in the production of gold, silver, and copper and had erected vast and efficient slave systems that could support—even increase—the output.

Indeed, the Aztec ruler Montezuma, like the Inca Huayna Capac, favored gold and silver adornments above all others. Whereas rulers of more ancient times in Central America had preferred emeralds, amethysts, jade, turquoise, and precious stones, Montezuma arrayed himself in ear spools and lip plugs of gold, as well as nose rings and silver necklaces. Gold—"the excrement of the gods," as the Aztecs called it—was available only in limited supply in Mesoamerica, harvested largely from the rivers of Oaxaca and seen as the exclusive preserve of the royal family. But when the Aztecs launched conquering incursions in the early 1400s, they annexed neighboring territories that were rich in silver, establishing mines that the Spanish would adopt, expand, and make world famous: Taxco, Zacatecas, Guanajuato, and the prodigal veins of Sierra Madre— some of which are still in operation today. "What can be grander than a barbarian lord," Hernán Cortés crowed to the Spanish king about Montezuma, "wearing phony baubles . . . alongside gold and silver ornaments that no goldsmith in the world could rival."

That meeting between Cortés and Montezuma in 1519 was, as far as we know, the first in which a Spaniard beheld an American sovereign in all his magnificent glory. Cortés had seen no one remotely like this Indian in Hispaniola or Cuba, where he had spent fifteen years serving the Spanish Crown. Born into a family of impoverished nobility and all too eager for the metal that would restore his status, Cortés reckoned correctly that the eminence before him was a man of formidable power. Those baubles would bring him glory.

Montezuma II was the *huey tlatoani*, the supreme leader of the Mexica Triple Alliance, an agglomeration of tribes that included three city-states: the Aztec metropolis of Tenochtitlán, as well as the neighboring cities of Texcoco and Tlacopan. The language he spoke—the elegant, mellifluous tongue of Nahuatl, still spoken in areas of Guatemala and Mexico today—was part of a vast family of languages spoken by the Comanche, Shoshone, and Hopi peoples. His empire, expanded vigorously by eight generations of Aztec leaders before him, was a territory roughly the size of Britain. As the *huey tlatoani*, or "reigning speaker," of this scrappy, pugnacious federation, he held unrivaled power in Mesoamerica. But he hadn't been born into that role. Montezuma II had been elected democratically in 1502 by a small cabal of elders. Chosen from among the princes of Tenochtitlán's royal families, he seemed an appealing candidate. He was deliberate, serious, with a pronounced gift for oratory. He was also, by all apparent evidence, an unpretentious young man. When the old men sent for Montezuma to tell him of their decision, legend has it that they found him sweeping the temple floors.

All that was to change. Charismatic, dignified, tall, the emperor Montezuma had impeccable personal habits and demanded as much from those around him. He bathed twice a day, favored lavish clothes and jewelry, was finicky about food, and discreet about sexual affairs. His long, triangular face, punctuated by an assiduously groomed goatee and a piercing gaze, gave him the appearance of an alert fox. Infinitely charming when he chose to be, he had an army of concubines who fussed over him and answered his every whim. It was said he took special potions to boost his virility and, at one point, had impregnated as many as 150 of his concubines at the same time. It was also said he was strong, nimble, and an excellent archer, attributes that—at least at first—earned him the wide-eyed admiration of his warriors.

If the ruling elders thought the mild-mannered man sweeping the temple floors would be a tractable and easily controlled puppet, they were soon proven wrong. Once the initiation rituals were done—his nose pierced; his limbs pricked and bled as custom demanded—Montezuma turned to the business of making his predecessors' vast dominion into an empire all his own. History books, especially those written by early European chroniclers, describe Montezuma II as a weak and anxious ruler, a coward in the face of peril. Nothing could be further from the truth. He was cunning, ambitious; a consummate strategist. As years passed, he grew increasingly ruthless in human affairs, fierce in command, and surpassingly cruel in war. He would become—as the Nahuatl name Montezuma actually means—a raging, unforgiving force.

He had good reason for wanting to bring change to the Mexicas: it was clear something drastic needed to be done. The Triple Alliance had grown so quickly, become so unruly, that it was threatening to come apart at the seams. Tribes conquered in brutal wars had begun to chafe under their Aztec masters. A general truculence had swept over the land, and, as a result, an angry spirit of rebellion lingered in the outlying territories like a low-grade fever. The populace, battered by ongoing fears of violence, was in a constant state of agitation. To keep them under control, Tenochtitlán's military now commandeered every aspect of society, turning a former theocracy of priests and Sun worshipers into a virtual paramilitary state. Soldiers were deployed at the slightest provocation, and a coterie of powerful generals had emerged to edge out the nobility on important state decisions. Soon the military was involved in commerce as well, serving as guard for a burgeoning class of powerful merchants that traded in all manner of goods from the shores of the Caribbean to the banks of the Rio Grande. The central plaza of Tenochtitlán had become nothing so much as a magnificent, well-policed bazaar for rich, freewheeling entrepreneurs, and a lively trade of gold and silver—once the province of kings and princes—was now a buoyant market at large.

Here was a profound cultural shift. Precious metals under the Aztecs had become a commodity like any other. Just as shells, feathers, and tools were fungible currencies in the vibrant marketplace of the day, so too were the "excrement" and "tears" of the gods. The manufacture of gold and silver was now so widespread among the Mexicas that citizens at the periphery of empire paid tributes to the state in bracelets and necklaces; even ingots and precious stones. A wealthy protobourgeoisie had materialized to accommodate it. To some, this economic exuberance might have signaled a welcome progress, but, to Montezuma, it was one more indication that things had gone badly awry. Too many liberties had been taken. The economy no longer answered to the state, and, for this progressively ungovernable bedlam, the military was to blame. Authority needed to be put back into the hands of the nobility. His government would clamp down.

Montezuma's first move was to reverse modifications that his predecessor, the warrior-emperor Ahuitzotl, had made to the very fabric of Mexica society by favoring a man's merit over his caste. Montezuma spared no time in dressing down the plebeian soldiers who had risen through the army's ranks to exercise what he perceived as exaggerated power. Never mind that they had spilled their blood to win him an empire. They were commoners, undesirables, and would be treated as such. He ordered them to wear simple cotton tunics and shave their heads. In a time when style and vestment defined one's status in the ruling hierarchy, this was a humiliating blow. Among those fighting forces, after all, were officers who had suppressed rebellions and maintained authority in time of perpetual war. To Montezuma's armies, this draconian response seemed misplaced, excessive. Resentment began to simmer among the rank and file.

The corrections did not stop there. Intent on consolidating the royal house's power, Montezuma II now declared that a nobleman's bastard children—whose status in Aztec society had never been questioned—would no longer enjoy hereditary rights. Not surprisingly, a wave of abortions followed. Montezuma's 150 expectant concubines made haste to terminate their pregnancies, convinced that their issue would have no place in the Aztec future. That purge, which began quietly enough in palace boudoirs, turned into a very public bloodbath when the emperor sent his guards to slay all the tutors and handmaids of the imperial nursery. He wanted it made clear that the purification and reeducation of the bloodline was to be complete.

Montezuma then moved to reduce the power of the wealthy merchants, the majority of whom were living splendidly in the neighboring metropolis of Tlatelolco. Once he had extracted a healthy tribute from them, he introduced a new economic model. Henceforward, the empire's financial center would be in the imperial palace, hefty taxes would be the order of the day, and, with manufacture under unilateral control, the merchants of Tlatelolco would be reduced to mere distributors. The state's most desirable commodities—including gold, silver, and copper—would be held under strict supervision of the state.

In these ways did Montezuma II achieve his goal to centralize power, although the fury he reaped as a result would ultimately be his undoing. No famine, no plague, no war—and Montezuma's rule was eventually visited by all three—would be as ruinous as the loathing he now invited from his subjects. He was as hated within his realm as without. Enemies made auguries about the *tlatoani*'s imminent destruction and the return of an angry, vengeful god. Evil omens began to be reported: a tongue of fire had pierced the night sky and brought down a rain of sparks. A thunderbolt had ripped through the volcano god's temple. A comet with a long, sinister tail had streaked overhead at sunrise. The lake waters surrounding Tenochtitlán had foamed up in a rolling boil. An army of men hunched over galloping deer had been glimpsed in a clouded mirror. The evidence for impending doom was so overwhelming that rebellious tribes took heart and began to look for alliances with anyone willing to wage war against the tyrant of Tenochtitlán. And yet no one could doubt that the man had done what he had set out to do: he had secured unconditional power for the Aztec nobility. He had preserved the purity of his race. Sisters in royal families would now continue to wed their brothers, as was the custom; cousins would propagate with cousins; and the sacred blood of ancestors would be passed on in a perfectly preserved chain. No one, not even the most celebrated warrior, could penetrate that closed circle. As for the gold and silver that Montezuma so favored, it was now corralled within the perimeters of his imperial walls.

If Hernán Cortés thought Montezuma's glittering gewgaws were worthy of the Spanish king's attention, he had a point: the *tlatoani*'s treasures were marvels of surpassing beauty. They had so dazzled Cortés that he saw little else. More than the breathtaking sight of the luminous capital on the lake—more than the impulse to take that shining citadel by force—it was the gold and silver that gleamed from Montezuma's throat that piqued Cortés's ambition. Nothing else mattered much after that: not the culture that the Mexica represented, or the history that had gone before, or the architectural splendors of a differently imagined universe. It was the "barbarian lord's baubles" that launched the cruel history that was to follow.

QUITO
Ecuador, 1520

> *With the Pacific to the west and the Amazon to the east, the Incas were confident that they had absorbed almost all civilisation.*
> —John Hemming, *The Conquest of the Incas*

Even as Montezuma fretted about racial purity, three thousand miles away, the Lord Inca Huayna Capac, too, began to worry about the integrity of his royal line. He came to the conclusion that it was high time he married one of his sisters and produced a solid heir to the throne. The Lord Inca had hundreds of concubines by whom he had left a sizable progeny, but like his counterpart in the land of the Mexicas, he descended from a long line of rulers who believed that marrying within the royal family would ensure purity of bloodline and a legitimate successor. The marriage he finally consummated with his sister produced Huascar, a spoiled, capricious boy whose privileged place in the royal household evoked nothing so much as an inflated sense of entitlement. To mark his arrival, Huayna Capac called for a lavish festival and a chain of pure gold, thick as a man's forearm and long enough to span the main plaza of Cuzco. On the appointed day, a legion of noblemen from all corners of the Tahuantinsuyu paraded the seven-hundred-foot cable through the streets, dancing joyously, holding the gold aloft so that it gleamed in the sun. The name Huascar itself means "chain" in Quechua, the language of the Incas, and, true to the moniker, the boy remained firmly fettered to Cuzco, unwilling to stray far from his father's palaces. Born of high blood, raised with every assurance that he was the chosen one, Huascar did not inherit his father's expansive spirit or his curiosity about the work of empire and the lands and mines from which his fortune sprang. Arriving at manhood at a remove from his more adventurous, illegitimate brothers and from the wayfaring Huayna Capac himself, Huascar gained a reputation as something of a wastrel. Cruel, cowardly, and vain, he developed the habit of demanding sexual favors from other noblemen's wives. Although he could not possibly have foreseen it, his character, like that of Montezuma's, would play a central role in the loss of empire.

Maintaining the royal bloodline was not the only preoccupation these two great civilizations shared. Montezuma was fully engaged in battling rebellions in far reaches of empire when Huayna Capac began to be pestered by similar troubles. Faraway conquests by dead ancestors now plagued the living. Huayna Capac's father, Tupac Inca Yupanqui, one of the most aggressive expanders of the Tahuantinsuyu, had built roads, bridges, and crossed the desolate Atacama Desert many decades before to push his empire's frontiers to the remote shores of what is now Chile. In the process, he had found metal making in full swing among the conquered tribes of the South. Triumphant in those forays and addicted to adventure, Tupac Inca had gone on to conquer lands in the North, and, in Quito, he was delighted to find that there, too, there were mineral rewards in the newly won ground. Pressing on to the Galapagos Islands, he came away with a surprisingly bountiful booty of dark-skinned slaves, gold curios, brass chairs, and the hide and jawbone of a beast he had never encountered before in the flesh: a horse. His victorious armies came home to Cuzco weighed down with gold, silver, emeralds, spondylus, turquoise, and—most precious of all—jade. Tupac Inca happily installed all of it in his palaces and temples, thrilling the royal family, securing his place in legend, and inspiring his son Huayna Capac to greater glories.

Not everyone was elated by Tupac Inca's exploits. The conquered became increasingly resentful about their enslavement to distant despots and gods. Whereas Tupac Inca had spent a lifetime expanding his rule, his son now found himself faced with the task of simply holding on to what had been won. The troubles began in the South, in highlands that surrounded Lake Titicaca, precisely where the empire's most productive silver and copper mines were located—precisely where mining would focus for the next five hundred years. A skilled warrior and passionate defender of his father's demesne, Huayna Capac now sent forth his powerful armies to quell a number of bloody insurgencies. He decided to follow these with a goodwill expedition. He was completing a "pacification" tour of the borderlands in Chile, assuring himself that the royal mines were out of harm's way, when he learned that the conquered peoples of the North, too, were rising up against him. Near Tumbes and Quito, where rivers glittered with gold, his governors had been found with their throats slit. Leaving Huascar to govern in Cuzco, Huayna Capac called for his younger sons Atahualpa and Ninan Cuyochi to prepare for a military campaign that would wind north through the towering cordillera, cross the eyebrow of the jungle, and make its way along the magnificent Royal Road, the Capac Ñan, to root out the malcontents.

Not least on Huayna Capac's mind as he crossed his vast empire with a retinue of thousands, stopping at sumptuous rest houses along the way, were his mineral riches. Enamored of his father's glittering spoils and fired by a material avarice unmatched by his predecessors, Huayna Capac was determined to keep a merciless lock on the Tahuantinsuyu. He assembled a vast army of hundreds of thousands as he traveled overland, pressing the locals into service. Eventually he prosecuted a harsh war against the people of Quito, but the fighting was so fierce and the Quiteños so stubborn that at the end of it, his royal troops were left starving and in rags. When, at last, the Inca received a mighty wave of reinforcements from Cuzco, he was able to repel the colossal force that had united against him: the naked, wild men of the Quillacingas tribe, the obdurate freedom fighters of Pasto and Cayambe, and the cannibals of Caranqui who had been stalking those gold-rich highlands for years, ripping out the hearts of many an Inca warrior who dared cross into it.

Unnerved, the Lord Inca's opponents scattered into the hills. It was a hard-fought war, lasting many years, and slaughter on both sides was so common that the lakes ran red with the blood of the fallen. All the same, Huayna Capac was determined to keep his grip on that geologic wonderland—crazed with emeralds and shot through with the lambent essence of sun and moon—and so urged his warriors to unimaginable brutality. Forbidding the capture of prisoners, he ordered his armies to decapitate tens of thousands of enemy soldiers and cast their headless corpses into the waters. Today a lake in the Ibarra region of Ecuador is still known in Quechua as Yahuarcocha: "pool of blood."

By the time Quito was "pacified"—a horrifying, grisly process that took more than a decade to accomplish—there was hardly a Quiteño male left over the age of twelve. "You are all children now," Huayna Capac proclaimed as he declared peace and went off to rest in the palace his father had built in nearby Tumipampa. The Inca dedicated himself to building magnificent lodgings for himself in numerous locations to secure his domination. He oversaw the mass conversion of Quiteños to sun worship, to the language of Quechua, to the labors that Cuzco required. Aided in this brutal business of subjugation by his son Atahualpa—born of a Quito princess—and his eldest son, Ninan Cuyochi, the Lord Inca settled into the fertile, scenic valleys of the region, transferring his court from Cuzco to Tumipampa and governing the empire from afar. So it was that even as he succeeded in securing the frontiers, Huayna Capac ended up fracturing the carefully forged firmament of Tahuantinsuyu, creating a new capital in Quito, a rift in its armies, doubts about the succession, and leaving capricious, unstable Huascar to manage Cuzco, the umbilical of an increasingly volatile world.

It was during this time, in the late 1520s, as he enjoyed the bucolic comforts of Tumipampa, that the Inca potentate began to hear strange reports about sightings his spies had made along the coast, near Tumbes. Messengers—*chasquis*—who ran long distances to deliver news to the Inca, reported that they had seen bearded men with fair skin and ferocious countenances approach the shore in large wooden houses. Huayna Capac asked the *chasquis* what part of the world these strangers had come from, but the messengers could say only that they appeared to travel the seas in those houses, and that they came ashore during the day and slept adrift at night. They were bold, loud, foul smelling, and could move like the wind on water. They could make a terrible thunder issue from their vessels, along with wild bursts of fire and puffs of dark smoke. They could split a tree from a great distance. They could kill with invisible arrows. Communicating with little more than mime and hand signals, the bearded ones had asked about the lord of the land. What was his name? Where did he live?

Hearing this, Huayna Capac was stunned, not a little frightened. He asked the *chasquis* to repeat the stories again and again, marveling at the strangeness of their testimony, fearful of what it might mean. Some years earlier, an oracle had predicted that the Twelfth Inca would be the last. He hadn't given the augury much credence at the time, but here it was now—as ominous as thunder, as real as sundered trees—and all of it coming so soon after his glorious defense of the Tahuantinsuyu. He was, after all, the Twelfth Son of the Sun.

Some chronicles paint Huayna Capac as audacious in his contact with those foreigners. One Spanish friar recounted that two of his countrymen wandering ashore were captured by chasquis and brought to the Lord Inca, whereupon he granted them an audience and heard them out. Interpreting their gestures, he deduced their interest in his jewelry. He was taken aback by the pettiness of that fixation and angered by rumors that such ragtag vagabonds posed any danger to his rule. As the friar told it, Huayna Capac had the intruders hacked to pieces, cooked, and served up to his court for dinner. In yet another historic, highly graphic account of the conquest, the Andean chronicler Felipe Guaman Poma de Ayala depicts a conversation between Huayna Capac and the sailor Pedro de Candía: "Is this the gold you people eat?" the Inca ruler asks the hungry Spaniard in perfect astonishment, offering a plate of gold nuggets. "*Kay quritachu mikhunki?*"

Fearless or fearful, if Huayna Capac was tormented by the possibility of an alien invasion, that darkening cloud on the Pacific littoral vanished as quickly as it had appeared. The wooden houses sailed off to the north, taking their bizarre, bearded masters with them, and, as weeks went by, other perils took their place. A plague of epic proportions, such as never had befallen the inhabitants of those lands, is said to have torn along the coast, felling hundreds at first, then thousands, and hundreds of thousands. It was a horrible, nameless sickness, manifesting in red, inflamed sores that morphed into suppurating pustules, eating at human flesh, spreading indiscriminately from village to village and from shoreline to mountain. In time, as Huayna Capac's armies marched along the

Capac Ñan, carrying the disease with them, the pestilence coiled over the cordillera, aided by random vectors—cloth, food, sandflies—until it consumed Cuzco and wiped out countless members of the royal family as well as their servants. Eventually Huayna Capac, who lingered in his beloved gardens in Huancavilca, not far from Quito, became infected with the disease and, feeling all too mortal, called his *orejones*—his noblemen—to his bedside to talk about the future of the empire.

Perhaps he had forgotten, in his fevered state, that he had designated Huascar for the throne long before, when he had consorted with his sister for the specific purpose of breeding the Thirteenth Inca. Perhaps, being away from Cuzco for so many years, he had forged stronger bonds with his sons Atahualpa and Ninan Cuyochi, the princes who had been warring loyally by his side. All the same, Huayna Capac was suddenly and quite impulsively convinced that his throne should go to the eldest of these, Ninan Cuyochi. He was lucid enough, however, to seek assurances that he was making the right choice. To decide the question, his high priests hastily conducted a ritual of the *kalpa*, in which they read the inflated lungs of a slaughtered llama. What they beheld in that ballooned mass was unequivocal: Ninan Cuyochi was the wrong choice. When the priests undertook another *kalpa* to determine the suitability of Huascar, he, too, was deemed unfit for the task.

Even as these rituals were taking place, Huayna Capac's servants observed a marked decline in their old master. The plague was not only cankering his flesh, it had taken a firm hold on his mind. The Lord Inca was hallucinating, seeing tiny apparitions who spoke to him, claimed to have come for him, and were calling him away. Quickly, his servants sent two teams of *chasquis* to the oracle at the Temple of Pachacamac to ask what should be done to save him. The shamans in that faraway shrine to the creator consulted with the god of the underworld, Supay, who answered that the Inca should be taken from his bed immediately and put out in the full light of the great Sun.

The Lord Inca was being carried out to absorb the healing powers of the all powerful Sun, when the *orejones* decided that they would ignore the unfavorable *kalpas*, solve the question of succession at once, and give the crown to Ninan Cuyochi, who was lodging close by. When they found the young prince in his chambers, however, they were horrified to see that he was laid out, ravaged by the disfiguring disease, lifeless. Hastening to inform Huayna Capac that there was no choice now but to give the throne to Huascar, the *orejones* arrived too late once again. Moments after the old Inca had been carried into the harsh light of day, he breathed his last.

So it was that the empire reeled from one catastrophe to another, from a series of wars that had purposefully butchered thousands to a plague that mindlessly devoured the rest. Now, adding to the chaos, came a struggle for succession between two bitterly contending factions: Huascar's Cuzco, and Quito under Huayna Capac's surviving warrior son, Atahualpa. Some historians say that the Lord Inca had every intention of installing two successors—that he deliberately set out to divide his kingdom north and south, understanding that it had grown unwieldy. Others say that these were decisions made at the spur of the moment, possibly under psychotic delusions, and that Huayna Capac was not the discerning, visionary leader that his father or grandfather had been.

Whatever the case, there is no question that the death of the Twelfth Inca marked a distinct end to an era. The empire was split, the seeds of discord sown. It was almost as if Tahuantinsuyu itself felt the air whistling out of the grand, inflated bubble it had become. The Lord Inca's heart was gouged from his breast and buried in Quito, and his embalmed body was carried to Cuzco with great pomp, the flustered *orejones* insisting he was still alive. It isn't known exactly when the people understood that their leader was dead. Only the closest and most loyal members of the elite knew, and they guarded that secret as long as they could, waiting for a clear leader to emerge. When the cortege finally arrived in Cuzco after many months of travel, his mummy was taken from its ornate litter and placed alongside those of his ancestors in the glittering halls of Coricancha, Temple of the Sun. Four thousand family members, concubines, and servants were sacrificed in solemn rituals to ensure that Huayna Capac had all the vassals he needed to serve him in the next world. The Twelfth Inca came to be as adored in death as he had been in life, celebrated in lavish ceremonies alongside his idol Guaraquinga—a giant, solid gold statue that he had commissioned during the pinnacle of his rule. They scarcely knew it at the time, but the people of Tahuantinsuyu were mourning their last true emperor. Grief stricken, thronging the capital's great plaza, they surged into the colossal Temple of the Sun to offer their prayers and lamentations.

CUZCO
Peru, 2010

> *There it was. The face of the sun, wrought from a slab of pure gold.*
> —El Inca Garcilaso de la Vega, 1605

Almost five centuries later, Juan Ochochoque, Leonor Gonzáles's ailing husband, too, made his tortured way from the gold mines of La Rinconada to the Temple of the Sun to offer prayers and lamentations. Suffering from acute mercury and cyanide poisoning after the collapse of his mine shaft, his legs were swollen, his breathing labored, his skin ulcerated, his mind unstable. He traveled with his youngest daughter on a bone-rattling bus trip from the foot of Mount Ananea to the walls of the once mighty Coricancha, now stripped of all precious metals and dwarfed by the great church that squats on top.

His mission was simple, and no different from what an ancestor might have undertaken in the 1500s at any of the sacred *huacas.* Juan went to solicit a blessing, reverse an ill wind. By then, he was desperate to save his life along with the lives of his wife and seven children, and he seemed to be out of options. There were few choices for a sick, indigent man perched on a glacial rock eighteen thousand feet up in a man-made wasteland. He had crouched in the mine shafts too long, bargained with the demon Supay too often. He had surrendered body and soul to the icy mountain range the canny Irish geologist Joseph Pentland had pointed to almost two hundred years before. The only thing Juan could see that might rescue him now was to take himself to the umbilical of the world: to Cuzco and its Temple of the Sun, where a high priest might lay hands on him and heal his suppurating wounds. Bartering all his savings—the flecks and chips of residual metal that miners call "seeds"—he bought two fares for a trip that would consist of four bus rides in one direction and four buses back, on seven hundred miles of rugged road.

Juan left Mount Ananea before daybreak on a frigid Friday morn-

ing in December 2008 and reached Cuzco with his ten-year-old daughter Senna just as the sun slipped over the white peaks of Vilcabamba,
shrouding the city in darkness. With one hand on a cane and the other
on Senna's shoulder, he hobbled down Avenida El Sol to the Church of
Santo Domingo, where the glorious Temple of the Sun had once stood.
They reached the main entrance just as the last visitor was saying good
night and the doors were swinging shut. Pleading with the priest at the
threshold, Juan explained why he had come, but he was told that there
would be no laying on of hands until Monday. For all of Juan's supplica-
tions, the answer was unwavering. Finally, the holy man simply stopped
speaking and quietly closed the door.

Juan could not have known it, but twenty feet below those immense
doors were the stones that had once held the fabled, coruscating rooms
through which Huayna Capac had once strode, honoring the ancient
gods and reveling in the power of his empire. The Lord Inca had returned to those golden halls with his veins plump with embalming fluid,
his afflicted skin masked by the tanning process. A few years later, his
mummy was ferreted out of Cuzco, along with his giant idol, as word of
the advancing "bearded ones" spread through the capital like waves of a
brand-new plague.

Juan sat on the steps of the Church of Santo Domingo, weighing his
options. He had no more money. He had bartered his last "seeds" on bus
fare. Slowly, and with Senna's help, he rose and hobbled back to the bus
station. Within a week, he was dead.

As strange as it might seem, a slight but strong link binds the fate
of Juan Ochochoque to that of Huayna Capac. That link is made of
metal. Juan's demise was a result of the ravages of a lifelong search for
gold—a substance he would never own or use. Huayna Capac's was
the result of a disease brought upon him by conquerors who were after
nothing so much as his sacred ore. Emperor and pauper, united by race
and language—divided by caste, ambition, and five hundred years of
history—both ended their time on earth as casualties of fortune; victims
of an alien lust. That legacy of distant desires and a native's inability to
truly comprehend them would only intensify in the tumultuous centuries to come.

CHAPTER 3

METAL HUNGER

<hr/>

Inca: "Is this the gold you people eat?"
Spaniard: "We eat this gold."

—Felipe Guaman Poma de Ayala, 1615

THE AWAKENING

In 1492, when Spain launched its flimsy bid for global power and sent Columbus to claim lands beyond the Pillars of Hercules—the edge of the known world—the indigenous empires that dominated the Americas were entering a fragile and volatile era. But they hardly knew it. Huayna Capac was young, ambitious, carefree, and had just taken the reins from his illustrious father. Montezuma II had yet to begin his rule and impose a stern corrective on the Triple Alliance. The two feisty Muísca rulers who would consolidate a gold-rich federation near Bogotá—and then die defending it—were hardly born. Spain, too, was poised on the verge of a radical transformation, a total reversal of its hobbled, inchoate past; but it hardly knew this as well.

Queen Isabella I and King Ferdinand V, Spain's sovereigns at the time, had inherited a war-weary nation, a rude conglomeration of two kingdoms, cobbled together hastily as a result of their elopement twenty-three years before. Somehow, by dint of an iron will, deft politics, and a fierce commitment to Christianize the peninsula, they managed to consolidate Iberia's fragmented loyalties against the last vestiges of Arab occupation. In 1492, after decades of grisly warfare, they won Granada and drove the Moors from the peninsula once and for all.

None of this had been easy. The fair-skinned, red-haired Isabella, whose father had died when she was three and whose mother had been mentally unstable ever since, had endured a string of betrothals imposed on her by her older half brother, King Henry IV of Castile. Henry was known throughout Spain as El Impotente, an appellation that alluded as much to his lack of sexual prowess as his meager abilities to lead. His frankly libidinous second wife was known to have had numerous lovers among the rakes of Castile's royal court and eventually produced a child, Juana la Beltraneja, whose shaky hereditary claims would bedevil Isabella's path to the throne.

When Isabella was a girl of six, living with her unhinged mother in the gloomy castle to which King Henry had virtually exiled them, she had become betrothed to her second cousin Ferdinand, the five-year-old son of the king of Aragon. But within a few years, her wastrel brother king, who had frittered away Castile's wealth and plunged the kingdom into ruinous debt, began to look around frantically for an alliance with a more prosperous, powerful entity, and saw Isabella's hand as a possible medium. Henry ignored his father's previous agreement with Aragon and casually offered Isabella to a series of moneyed noblemen in distant royal houses. By the time the girl was ten, he had wrenched her from her mother's side, brought her to his court, and begun to cultivate her for just such a marriage. Some years later, when rebellion threatened to end his disastrous reign, he reneged on all agreements and—out of sheer desperation—promised her to one of the richest men in his court, Pedro Girón Acuña Pacheco, who owned a spectacular castle in Valladolid and had agreed to pay the royal treasury a vast sum of money. Young Isabella, a devout Catholic, prayed to be spared this degrading union; those prayers were answered when Don Pedro suddenly became ill and died on his way to consummate their wedding. Isabella was fifteen years old. Soon after, in 1469, she took advantage of that slender rupture of fate to elope with the heir presumptive to whom she had been engaged in the first place, young Ferdinand of Aragon.

When Isabella and Ferdinand mounted their thrones as king and queen of the united houses of Castile and Aragon, their newly wrought merger was in virtual ruin. The royal coffers were almost empty. Gold, which had been the fiduciary standard of Europe since the 1300s, was in alarmingly short supply. The production of silver, which was the coin of the realm and had been mined in Andalusia since 3000 BC, had all but trickled to a stop. Everywhere the new queen and king looked, there were debts to repay, battles to engage. Over the years, the Christian kingdoms of Iberia had gradually pushed back the Moors, who had swept in from northern Africa in the eighth century and occupied the peninsula for seven hundred years. Despite the bloody crusades of the Reconquista and the hundreds of battles that had consumed generations of Iberians, when Isabella and Ferdinand were handed the scepter, the Umayyad Caliphate still occupied the kingdom of Granada, a massive swath of land straddling southern Iberia. Between 1482 and 1491, King Ferdinand directed all his attention to an unremitting war with the Moors, a ferocious military campaign that won back Granada inch by inch and finally expelled the caliphate at long last on January 2, 1492.

Arabs had not been Iberia's only masters. A long history of conquest had predated the Moors. The peninsula had been colonized by Phoenicians, Greeks, Carthaginians, Romans, Visigoths. Every invasion had had its dose of political ambition, but overwhelmingly the aim of occupiers and conquerors had been to raid the region's silver or gold—those glistening substances that coursed through Iberian waters, crazed the rock of Spain's mining meccas, Río Tinto and Las Médulas, and had become the preferred hard currency of the Continent. At the close of the fourteenth century, seven-eighths of all gold imported by the Republic of Genoa, one of the largest purveyors of the metal, came from Iberia, and five-sixths of that, from Seville. Enslaved and humiliated for centuries, forced to mine their terrain for the enrichment of faraway potentates, the Iberians yearned for leaders who could turn history on its ear and end a millennium of exploitation. Queen Isabella and King Ferdinand were those leaders. By 1475, they had become keen participants in regional European trade. By January 1492, they had defeated the Moors, demanded the forced conversion of Jews, established Spain by spirit if not by politics, and begun the furious enterprise of driving foreigners from the peninsula.

Spain emerged from centuries of foreign domination with a crusading spirit, a passionate commitment to forge an exclusively Christian nation. It also emerged with all the rage and truculence necessary to achieve it. Diving into the business of expelling Arab potentates and Jewish moneylenders, Isabella and Ferdinand called for a brutal and fanatical purge that employed torture, set "infidels" against one another, raided homes and businesses alike, and filled the royal coffers with desperately needed funds. The Inquisition, as practiced by the Catholic Church in the twelfth century, had focused on heresy and depravity within the ranks of the faithful; now, in the fifteenth, it took a distinctly ethnic turn: it began persecuting Muslims and Jews. Especially harsh against conversos—converts to Catholicism—who all too often were suspected of secretly maintaining ties to their old religions, the Inquisition began setting converted Jews (Marranos) against Jews, and converted Muslims (Moriscos) against Muslims. The Emirate of Granada, with whom Castile and Aragon had sparred for years, was now progressively rent by civil divisions, and Ferdinand took advantage of that internal chaos to attack those contested lands.

By the time Granada surrendered to King Ferdinand on January 2, 1492, a hundred thousand Moors were dead; two hundred thousand more had emigrated; and, of the two hundred thousand that remained, most were subject to stern laws of conversion. The Jews, too, were given the choice to convert or leave, and by the time the Spanish Inquisition began in earnest—ushered in by a papal bull—more than half the Jewish population of Castile and Aragon had been forcibly expelled, and several thousand summarily executed. Open atrocities—burnings at the stake, autos-da-fé, the widespread confiscation of valuable possessions—all these took place in city squares, with royalty present and an almost festive air. Europeans visiting Spain at the time were appalled by the public acceptance of these executions. Less visible, perhaps, were the hurried efforts to hide one's ancestral line, or prove a conversion, or integrate as fully as possible: the ancestors of Saint Teresa of Ávila, the famed Carmelite mystic, were Jews, as may have been those of the great master of Spanish letters Miguel de Cervantes. As irony would have it, the first inquisitor-general of Castile and Aragon, a Dominican priest named Tomás de Torquemada, had been born into a Jewish family and, fired by zeal that only radical conversion can bring, went on to prosecute chilling cruelties against his own people.

It was a nervous age, the anxiety such that it spurred Spain, as all Europe, toward a feral self-protection. For financial security. For gold.

That hunger hardened into outright greed by the end of the fifteenth century, when it became clear that the production of this metal would not be enough, by any measure, to satisfy the gargantuan demands of the European economy. There were wars to prosecute, empires to build. Even Pope Pius II, a remarkably forthright pontiff who had written openly about his carnal appetites and the son he had sired, lamented the Church's lack of funds: "The problem of money predominates," he wrote, "and without it, as they commonly say, nothing can be done aright." The new monarchs of Spain felt that accursed greed for gold—*auri sacra fames*—keenly when their arch rival, King Afonso V of Portugal, sent fortune hunters to scour Africa for gold in the 1470s and established a vigorous trade at San Jorge de Mina, in what is now Ghana.

Queen Isabella, too, had sent her navies to trawl the west coast of Africa for riches, and, in 1478, as thirty-five of her caravels returned from the Gulf of Guinea weighed down with bullion, Portuguese ships intercepted them and seized all their cargo. The Battle of Guinea followed, a bitterly fought contest for the Atlantic waterways and the lucrative slave trade that accompanied them. Spain emerged victorious, at least on land: King Afonso surrendered to its "Catholic Monarchs," giving Isabella the right to retain her dominion and consolidate an empire with Ferdinand. But Portugal was the clear winner at sea. Afonso was given unfettered access to a number of Atlantic strongholds and the wealth they represented: the mines at Guinea; the strategically located ports on the Azores, Madeira, and Cape Verde islands; control over large tracts of northern Africa; and more than 1,500 pounds of gold. All that the treaty left to Spain, as far as maritime possibility, was the Canary Islands, a cluster of parched, impoverished islands off the Barbary Coast. In other words, Spain's navies had but one option if they wanted to expand their queen's rule: they would need to brave a sea rife with pirates, make a fleet course south to the Canaries and then swing west, ever west, beyond the Pillars of Hercules. It was certainly a logistical challenge. But the wider implication of the treaty was obvious: the world beyond Europe's shores was for the taking. Conquerors had only to raid lands, colonize the darker races, and divide the map—brutally, if need be—into spheres of influence.

If Spain had dreams of expansion, Portugal continued to thwart them. Even as Isabella and Ferdinand battled the Moors, struggling to unify the peninsula under their command, Afonso's successor, King João, busily established a vigorous trade along Africa's Gold Coast, explored the Congo, and launched the Atlantic slave trade, a monopoly Portugal would hold for more than a hundred years. Lisbon had become a center of exploration, a polestar for mapmakers. It was there that many starry-eyed sailors of that boisterous age came to launch their fortunes. Among them were two brothers from Genoa, sons of a humble weaver, who had abandoned their father's stuffy little workshop for a life on the high seas. Bartholomew Columbus, the younger of the two, became a skilled mariner and maker of sea charts; Christopher, on the other hand, preferred wild, seafaring forays along the coast of Africa with Portuguese slave traders. When the famous Portuguese explorer Bartolomeu Dias rounded the Cape of Good Hope in 1488 and returned to Lisbon with promises of gold, Christopher Columbus was there to hear him. Columbus had been immersed in the work of plotting out trade routes, analyzing maps, poring over astronomical charts, pondering cosmographical theories, worrying his copy of *Imago Mundi* until it was frayed, stained, overrun by notes in his trademark jittery hand.

By then, Columbus's petition to Portugal's King Joao for three caravels had been roundly rejected. Columbus was convinced that a trade route to India—the same route that Bartolomeu Dias had been seeking to the East—could be found by sailing west, and so he had written to Paolo Toscanelli, a famous astronomer in Florence, to inquire his opinion. Columbus was especially interested in the route west of the Canary Islands, bypassing Portuguese territory altogether. The Florentine scholar did not hesitate. He referred Columbus to a letter and a map he had sent many years before to a Lisbon priest, who, in turn, had shared it with King Afonso. Sail due west from Lisbon, the letter said, and in time you will find yourself in the city of Kwang Chow. Before you reach it, you will come upon the land of Cipango (Japan). The map placed the hulking island of Cipango squarely in the far reaches of the Atlantic, exactly where the Americas would be found. "This island is rich in gold, pearls, and gems," the astronomer added provocatively, echoing the fervor of the age. "Its temples and palaces are roofed with solid gold."

CRUCERO
Peru, 1988

Gold and slaves. The first corrupts all it touches. The second is corrupt in itself.

—Simón Bolívar, 1815

Five centuries later, Leonor Gonzáles's future husband, Juan Ochochoque, too, was feeling the allure of gold, the urge to leave an old world behind, climb the dirt trails to higher ground, chase metal fortunes. For all his thirty-three years, he didn't have much to show for his life's work: two teenage daughters, a woman who had shamed him with another man, a score of unsettled debts. He had abandoned the work he had inherited from his father, tending a fragile herd of alpaca against the glacial cold, shearing and selling the wool, butchering the older ones for meat. He had left behind the arduous work of digging trenches as a lowly conscript in the Peruvian army. The Maoist guerrilla forces of the Sendero Luminoso, or Shining Path, were cutting a murderous path through the Peruvian highlands, burning government property, hanging dogs from lampposts, assassinating village leaders, and displacing hundreds of thousands. The army was no longer building much; it was struggling to fight back. Campesinos, country people like him with no combat training, were fleeing to safety in the big cities or higher still, into the punishing altitudes of the Andes.

Even as his woman took off for Puno with the other man, Juan told his teenage daughters that he would come for them when his fortunes improved. One frigid morning, he bought a pickax with the little money he had, left the little village of Crucero, and trudged up-mountain for four days through the rough volcanic rock that flanks the Rio Carabaya. On the fifth day, he arrived in Ananea, a humming little marketplace, where a soupmonger offered him a bowl of broth and a place to sleep in return for scrubbing down his stall and scouring out the pots. On the next day, Juan reached La Rinconada—a cluster of glistening tin roofs against a wide expanse of snow. Just under the blinding white, he could barely make out the black holes. There, tapping into the veins of the mountain known as Sleeping Beauty, hundreds of laborers worked the icy mines that had been founded by Incas, abandoned by Spaniards, and reinvigorated by those fleeing the terrorist peril. He promised one of the friendlier men a portion of his wages for a spot on the dirt floor of his hut.

So it was that Juan Ochochoque became a peon in the mines of La Rinconada. He was not allowed to mine at first, relegated to the business of sweeping out the shaft, hauling out stones. But eventually he was admitted to the circle of *barreteros*, prospectors who set out with an iron rod from time to time to determine where a likely vein might be. Juan never mastered the rod, but with his affable nature and forthright manner, he rose to warrant the trust necessary to enter a mine with men whose very lives depended on one another. Mining *cachorreo*, the age-old colonial system in which a man split rock for thirty days for no pay until—on the thirty-first—he was allowed to carry out one backload for himself, he saved enough to become self-sufficient. It was at about that time that he came upon the discovery that would change his life forever.

Her name was Leonor Gonzáles, a young woman with two small daughters. She was small, spirited, with bright eyes and glossy black braids. She bustled here and there, climbing up the cliffs with the *pallaqueras*— the rock spill scavengers—when she could. Either that or sell this and that on the roadside. A bite of food. A bit of knitting. There seemed to be no men in her life, save her old, wizened father and a wastrel uncle. They said that the man who had given her children had gone off to the mines one morning and never come back. The demons within had claimed him.

THE TATTERED DREAMER
Spain, 1492

> *As centuries unfold, the Ocean, loosening its bonds, will reveal an enormous land, a new world . . . and Thule will no longer be the outer rim of the Universe.*
>
> —Seneca (a Spaniard), AD first century

As 1482 slipped into 1483 and Portuguese trade on the coast of Africa flourished, Columbus cut a strange, outlandish figure, hurrying through

Lisbon in a frayed coat, with his prematurely white hair askew and Toscanelli's map firmly in hand. But if he was little interested in personal riches, he was well aware that money was an asset without which nothing would get "done aright." Gold was what expanding kingdoms fed on; silver was the spark that fired global exploration. He sailed out of Lisbon secretly in 1484, penniless, widowed, with a young son to feed and staggering debts to honor, but he left with formidable assets of his own: a passionate conviction and the verbal capacity to communicate it. Making his way from the port at Palos to Seville and then Córdoba, he paid countless visits to the royal household, prattling on to anyone willing to listen about pavilions roofed in gold and the great khans of Cipango. When at last he was able to convince Queen Isabella to sponsor an expedition beyond the latitudes of the Unknown—beyond the *nec plus ultra* of antiquity—he had learned that more than continuing the Holy Crusade, perhaps even more than the prospect of converting heathen souls to Jesus, riches were what his king and queen were after. Ferdinand and Isabella had grown weary of dealing with intermediaries; they needed to find a direct route to the treasure troves of the Indies. The financial pressures were ever more onerous. The time to act was now.

On April 17, 1492, Isabella, the redheaded queen with the cool green gaze, finally persuaded her husband that they should reach beyond the confines of their known world and make a bid for distant conquests. They signed the Capitulations of Santa Fe, a document that invested Columbus, for all perpetuity, with the titles of "Admiral of the Ocean Seas" and "Viceroy of the Indies," which included all islands and continents he would discover. There was everything to gain, little to lose. They had invested no troops, no management oversight, few funds. "Columbus's enterprise," an enthusiastic investor gushed, "will add many carats to the stature and renown of Your magnificent Highnesses!"

Columbus undertook the enterprise knowing that carats were precisely what he had to secure. "Gold is a wonderful thing!" he wrote from the shores of the New World, suggesting that his sailors were virtually sweeping it from the sand. "From gold springs all treasure! With gold one can achieve anything on this earth, even pass through the very gates of Heaven!" From his very first landing on a small island in the Bahamas, Columbus was as interested in that dazzling substance as he was in the new race of man before him. He wrote to Ferdinand and Isabella of the friendly youths who swarmed down to greet his ships: "a handsome people: with hair not curly, but straight and thick, like the mane of a horse." They were naked, guileless, seemingly "poor in everything." But soon, he was adding, "I was alert to the task of ascertaining whether or not they had gold, and I could see that some of them had bits of it hanging from their noses. Signaling with their hands, they told me that, going south and steering round the island, I would find a king who had vast stores of the stuff." The gold was so plentiful in that other land, he was told, that people drank from goblets of gold. There are no fewer than one hundred allusions to gold and silver in Columbus's reports to his king and queen during the three months between October 12, 1492, and January 12, 1493. In truth, he was finding precious little of it, but in his accounts, gold is omnipresent, seductive, glittering just out of reach. The indigenous Americans, quick to see what was on the admiral's mind, goaded him: a little farther, just behind that island—there, toward the horizon—he would find men with more riches and women more beautiful to behold. But there was something else, something apart from the gold that piqued Columbus's interest: a sense that he might do whatever he wanted with these people. "They have no experience with arms," he wrote his king and queen, "and they are suitable to take orders and be made to work, sow, and do anything else that may be needed, and build towns and be taught to wear clothes and adopt our customs."

When Columbus sailed west, he had been a medieval man from a medieval world, surrounded by medieval notions about Cyclops, pygmies, Amazons, dog-faced natives, antipodeans who walk on their heads and think with their feet—about dark-skinned, giant-eared races who inhabit the lands where gold and precious gems grow. When he set foot on American soil, however, he did more than enter a new world: he stepped into a new age, and that step would have lasting consequences. The Age of Discovery (1450 to 1550) would clarify much about this world; it would also ignite cultural confrontations and fusions quite unlike any that had gone before. Cutting a path through that entirely original universe, Columbus could only work with what he knew. He had landed, as far as he understood from Toscanelli's map, on an island somewhere off the coast of India. Having studied Marco Polo's travel journals, he expected to find those islands replete with spice fields and gold mines there for the taking. If he could catch the right wind, he would come upon the hulking island of Cipango and eventually the mainland of Cathay, where Kublai Khan's palaces shone in the distance, gems were traded for pepper, and gold was as plentiful as brick.

This was the vision Columbus held in his head, and the one he shared with his king and queen even as he navigated far seas and wrote to them about sights no European had ever witnessed. Much later, during his fourth voyage, when he already had outposts in Santo Domingo, Cuba, and Panama, and was shipping gold and slaves to Seville, he remained convinced he was on the verge of finding Japan, stumbling into a grand bonanza. As he skimmed the coast of what is now Honduras, Nicaragua, and Costa Rica, marveling at the gold his sailors raked from the riverbeds and the pearls they swept up "like chaff," he wrote to Ferdinand and Isabella that he was nearing the River Ganges. A scant year before, he had written to Pope Alexander: "I have secured one thousand four hundred islands as well as three hundred thirty three leagues of the continent of Asia for my lords, the King and Queen. Here there are mines of all manner of metal, but especially gold and copper. There is brazilwood, sandalwood, aloes. . . . This island is Tarsus, Scythia, Ophir, Ophaz and Cipango. We call it Hispaniola."

It was not immediately apparent that Columbus's New World had been born of a geographical error. The Old World, flabbergasted by the revelations, struggled to understand. As news of his discoveries spread through Europe—as he returned in April 1493, making a deliberate point to land first in Portugal, which had declined to sponsor him, and then sail triumphantly to the Spanish port of Palos—Europeans flocked to witness the "New World wonders." Columbus took his exotic caravan overland, making his way in a breathtaking procession from Seville to Barcelona, where King Ferdinand and Queen Isabella awaited. His sailors paraded past an exuberant public, holding aloft their colorful, fantastical trophies—pineapple, chili, corn, squash, avocado, guava, papaya—and the people marveled. Jewel-bright macaws, monstrous and lumbering iguanas—animals never seen before in Europe—were ferried past in crates. Six handsome Indians in loincloths led the parade, sporting turquoise, gold masks, and bangles. There were baskets filled with gold mirrors, silver hoops, belts wrought from riotously colored feathers, barrels of gold nuggets. It was a grand show—a *pars pro toto*—to persuade Spain that Columbus's error had actually been a resounding success; that he would now fulfill all the financial expectations of his king and queen. Perhaps, if the show was persuasive enough, it would buy him the time to reach the real India and find true wealth. He needn't have worried. When all was said and done, the Catholic monarchs fell to their knees and thanked God for the bounty.

The year 1492 had turned out to be a boom year for Ferdinand and Isabella. Truly, the heavens had smiled on them. They had done the Church's bidding, purged their fledgling empire of Muslims and Jews. They had defended themselves against a belligerent neighbor. They had consolidated Spain. And now they were opening a new frontier in the Indies, where boundless riches awaited. Pope Alexander, Aragonese by birth and a friend of King Ferdinand's, was one of the first to receive a gift of gold from Columbus. With it came Isabella's plea to help protect Spain's claims to the newly discovered lands. She implored the pope to support them against Portugal's King João, who, having learned of Columbus's discoveries firsthand, immediately dispatched a hostile letter, claiming all territories—by virtue of earlier treaties—for the Portuguese Crown. In Rome, the pontiff grandly spread out a map of the hemisphere and drew a straight line from pole to pole, assigning everything west of it to Ferdinand and Isabella; everything east, to King Joao. The Americas, except for the hump that is now Brazil, would be Spanish. Africa would be Portuguese.

An arduous voyage through tempest and hazard had finally brought Columbus the glory he craved. No longer the threadbare dreamer of Lisbon, he was a hero to his royals, an inspiration to all Europe. In May, as his six Indian chattel were baptized with great fanfare in Barcelona, Columbus was granted the title of captain general of the Indies. Eventually he was given his own coat of arms, more ships and munitions, equipment to facilitate metal mining, and the confidence that, through the Capitulations of Santa Fe, his binding agreement with the king and queen, he would claim a percentage of all discoveries. And so dreams of gold and silver proliferated throughout the Old World. Sailors, swordsmen, gentlemen, miners, peasants—some employed by the Crown, others escaping dubious pasts—thronged to the Spanish port of Cádiz to enlist in the admiral's glittering enterprise. Isabella's well-known love for jewelry, amplified now by these prospects, took on new meaning when Ferdinand hectored the outbound crews: "Get gold! Humanly, if possible. But attain it, whatever the cost."

The cost would be high. Columbus's next three voyages were fraught with peril and brought modest rewards. In 1495, in desperation, he issued an infamous edict, ordering all male Arawak Indians in Hispaniola over the age of thirteen to produce large hawk's bells of gold every three months; if they did not, their hands would be hacked off. And yet everywhere he ventured—whether he was marauding villages, establishing strongholds, or scouring the coasts for any glint of treasure—there was little of the stuff Ferdinand had called for. Frustrated, Columbus turned to other opportunities. He began to engage spiritedly in the slave trade, a commerce he knew well from his exploits in Africa. By his second voyage, he had captured 1,500 Taíno men, women, and children, and herded the 550 best specimens to the slave markets of Seville. By the end of that trade, as many as five million souls would be trapped and sent elsewhere. "Slaves are the primary source of income for the admiral," the Dominican friar Bartolomé de Las Casas later complained, fanning the flames of Columbus's ruin.

Blamed for appalling cruelties—the burning and destruction of entire villages, the abduction of slaves, the staggering losses in population—Columbus was taken prisoner by the King's administrator, shackled, and shipped back to Spain. The reasons given were countless, among them the simple fact that he had promised so much and delivered so little. His accusers, streaming back to *tierra madre* from Hispaniola, were legion, and although the very Catholic Isabella was not inclined to believe them, the more pragmatic Ferdinand lent them an ear. Hadn't Columbus's dreams been a drain on the Crown's treasury? they asked. Didn't his meager booty refute all the extravagant pictures he had painted—the glorious, glittering mountains of metal that promised to rival King Solomon's ancient mines? Worst of all, hadn't a great fraud been perpetrated on Spain? Hadn't the prim, Catholic, teetotaling queen been led to think that she was spreading the faith, when, in fact, her reign was disseminating nothing so much as greed, death, and destruction? The implication was clear: Columbus had either deceived his king and queen with gross exaggerations, or he had wronged them by wicked malfeasance. It was the first time—to be followed by uncountable others—that Europe would be accused of abusing its colonial powers. And indeed, when the Crown's emissary arrived in Hispaniola to investigate Columbus's crimes, he was greeted by the sight of seven corpses swinging from the gallows—luckless Spaniards who had run afoul of *El Capitán*'s orders.

When a disgraced Columbus arrived in Seville in 1500, the royals were aghast to learn that the great man was in chains. He was freed immediately, his reputation swiftly reinstated. He would continue to be admired for his bold explorations, his expansion of Spain's influence in the world, his evangelical service to the Church, his maritime genius. But unfulfilled promises of gold would dog him. And questions about the lengths to which a conquering power should go would throw Europe into a lengthy and heated debate: Were the indigenous humans, after all? Could they be herded and bound like beasts of burden? The titles of "Admiral of the Ocean Seas" and "Viceroy of the Indies," which had been revoked when Seville's enforcers had put Columbus under arrest, were never restored. The world would continue to think of him as a man of formidable deeds and riches, but in truth he was deeply in debt, his finances in disarray, his income nonexistent. By 1506, the year he died, Columbus had been reduced to living out of a common boardinghouse in Valladolid, fighting stubbornly to claim what he believed to be lawfully his: one-tenth of all royal profits in the New World, a percentage of future trade, and one-third of the profits due him as Admiral of the Ocean Seas. In all, his wage would have amounted to more than half the income from the Indies, far more than "the royal fifth" the Crown demanded for itself.

Columbus would never find the fame and fortune he sought. He had seen more parrots than gold, more naked Indians than richly bejeweled headsmen. In all his travels through lands he had mistaken for Ophir, Ophaz, and Cipango, he had never seen a city. There had been little more than makeshift villages to plunder. He would die a bitterly disappointed man. He had lost his riches, his reputation, his eyesight. Ferdinand and Isabella would fear he had also lost his mind. For the rest of their lives, his sons, Diego and Fernando, would struggle in vain to claim what the king and queen had promised him in the first place. Ships would come and go from the New World, making thousands of crossings with more dreamers and schemers aboard—all of them with impossible visions dancing in their heads. It would take two bold excursions and three more decades for a new generation of scrappy adventurers to transform America into Spain's shining prize.

THE BARBARIAN'S BAUBLES

Fateful omens in the sky. One like a spark of fire, one like a flame of fire, one like a false dawn: as if it were bleeding, as if it were piercing the sky.
—Nahua witness, 1517

Even as Columbus was limping from ship to shore in Jamaica—casting about for gold, crippled by gout, fending off mutineers—a young notary from Spain's Extremadura joined the westward passage and scudded across the seas to Hispaniola. He was Hernán Cortés, barely eighteen, slightly older than Columbus's youngest son, and a distant relative of another adventurer, Francisco Pizarro, who would ply those same waters a few years later. It was 1504. Ten thousand pesos of gold had been harvested from Hispaniola; a ruthless, new governor had been installed in Columbus's place; and Queen Isabella, who had never quite recovered from the sudden, unexplained death of her only son, the crown prince, had taken ill and begun to withdraw from government affairs.

It didn't take long for Cortés to grasp how haphazard and unproductive earlier expeditions had been—how flagrant the mismanagement, how tragic the devastation. His generation of conquistadors, that of Pizarro, Vasco Nuñez de Balboa, and Hernando de Soto, would take the conquest to new heights and to more remote reaches of the hemisphere, but Cortés was perhaps first to recognize that to achieve long-term success and to best exploit the potential wealth of these new lands, Spain would need to put down roots and establish a permanent presence.

He had a point. Spain had not approached the conquest of the Indies in any systematic way. There had never been a true, declared commitment to discovery: no armies and navies employed to the task, no grand

investment in the enterprise. Even as King Ferdinand took Spain's soldiers into wars in Europe, hoping to expand his power in the Old World,
Isabella was essentially approving New World expeditions that were undertaken by civilians, funded by independent investors, and joined by
ambitious young hidalgos from the poorest outposts of the peninsula.
The understanding was simple enough: the Crown would give a fortune
seeker its blessing, expect one-fifth of all mineral profits from his venture, and he would be expected to shoulder the lion's share of the costs,
either with his own money or with additional funds from underwriters.
Some, like Columbus, had experience in the gold or slave trade in Africa. More often, the conquistadors were jobless, rootless, wild—raised
by generations of men who had taken violence to new heights in wars
against the Muslims of Granada. They were, in short, children of cru-
saders, and they held God's banner high as they set out to conquer infidels and scour the Indies for treasures.

The governor of Hispaniola in 1504, Nicolás de Ovando, was a pugnacious former commander in the Moorish wars who had been sent by
Queen Isabella with express instructions to liberate Columbus's Taíno
slaves and treat them as well as any Spanish subjects. But once declared
free, the Taíno refused to mine, and Ovando swiftly reinstated Columbus's harsh measures. The Crown looked the other way. "Forasmuch
as my Lord King and Myself have ordered that the Indians living on
the island of Hispaniola be considered free and not subject to slavery,"
Isabella instructed Ovando from her sickbed, "I order you, Our Governor . . . to compel the Indians to cooperate with the Christian settlers on
said island, to work on their buildings, and to mine and collect gold and
other metals." In other words, killing and genocide were un-Christian,
un-Spanish, and intolerable, but "compelling" the Indians to mine was
a necessary sin.

Cruel in nature and a former commander in Ferdinand's brutal war
against the Moors, Ovando proceeded to inflict a series of gruesome massacres on the Taíno as he applied himself to exploiting the mines at all
costs. By then, Isabella was dead, Ferdinand was engaged in one Machiavellian scheme after another, and the conquistadors were learning that
they could feign obedience to the Crown and do exactly as they pleased.

Spain was very far away. All a conquistador needed to do was shout the king's *requerimiento* in Spanish from a far hill, command uncomprehending natives to surrender to Spain and Jesus, and, with a notary present to record things, he could then wage war, round up slaves, and force them to work the mines. Within three years, even as young Cortés romanced the island's women, acquired an appetite for derring-do, and kept books for the governor, Ovando extracted a quarter million more pesos of gold from Hispaniola. He did so by virtually sacrificing the Taíno people. Indians who refused to labor in the mines were killed outright. This single-minded obsession with mining meant that Indians did not plant or harvest; eventually famine, disease, and suicide reduced that robust community of a half million to a feeble sixty thousand. Forty years after Columbus's landing, the Taíno would be virtually decimated and the gold of Hispaniola gone.

When Cortés landed in Santo Domingo, he was received warmly in the house of Governor Ovando, whom he had met in Spain. Told he would be given a sizable tract of land to settle, the youth was taken aback. "I came to get gold!" he sputtered in amazement, "not plow soil like a peasant!" The governor assured him that husbandry was the best way to build funds for his exploits. Accordingly, Cortés was given a generous plot in that perpetually verdant land and a *repartimiento* of Indians to work it. For several years, he oversaw their labors in his fields and worked as a notary in a nearby settlement, breaking the monotony with love affairs that often landed him in trouble. From time to time, he joined efforts to suppress the violent insurrections that bedeviled the conquistadors on that unhappy island, and so learned much about indigenous warfare and the brutal tactics necessary to foil it.

He was dashing, handsome, physically agile, irrepressibly genial, and a lively conversationalist, so he swiftly became a favorite among his fellow Spaniards. He also acquitted himself admirably in skirmishes against rebellious Indians, which won him a place in the expedition that set out to conquer Cuba in 1511. The *adelantado* in charge, Diego Velazquez de Cuéllar, was quick to see the natural leader in Cortés and rewarded him generously for his valor. He was granted an even more enviable tract of land in Cuba and a larger contingency of indigenous slaves to tend it. By the age of twenty-eight, Cortés was a relatively wealthy young man.

His work as a notary had predisposed him to be an able manager of his Cuban estate, and, given his rare talent for recognizing opportunity and persuading others to his side, he was soon making his name as one of the most successful importers of sheep and cattle to the Indies. He was, in other words, a rancher—albeit a restless one—whose most pressing concern, until his marriage to the governor's sister-in-law, was his consuming passion for the ladies. There was, in all this, little evidence of the lust for gold he had expressed so early upon his arrival. But all that would change when Vasco Núñez de Balboa, a petulant, debt-ridden hog farmer from Cortés's home province, discovered a way to the Pacific in 1513, and slave hunters, returning to Cuba after hair-raising raids on Indian villages, told of unimagined riches in a land they called Castilla de Oro. The Gold Castle. Panama.

Vasco Núñez de Balboa, as charismatic an adventurer as any, had escaped his creditors in Hispaniola and sailed to Castilla de Oro as a stowaway, tucked into a ship's barrel along with his dog. When he was discovered, the captain threatened to strand him on the nearest island, but Balboa won him over with wit and acuity. Within a few years, he had reconnoitered the area with a contingent of men, subdued a number of recalcitrant tribes, and founded Santa María, the first permanent settlement on the American mainland. It was there that Balboa's men began to hear that there were wealthier tribes elsewhere, and an impulse to mutiny began to rise among those who wanted to pursue those chimeras. The men had already appropriated what little precious metals and stones the local tribes possessed. Squabbles over gold reached such a fever that one day, as Spaniards were weighing a chieftain's gifts and arguing over the distribution, the Indian, appalled at the crass cupidity, knocked over the scales and shouted, "If you're so ravenous for this that you abandon your homes to wreak havoc in distant lands, I'll show you a province where you can gorge yourselves on gold and satisfy your desires!" He pointed firmly south.

Balboa's gold ambitions were so extreme that eventually they took him across the isthmus to the other side. At noon on September 25, 1513, accompanied by Indian guides, he stood on an Urrucallala mountain peak and thought he detected a seductive shimmer on the far horizon.

Days later, with sword in hand and the banner of Virgin Mary on high, he waded into a vast ocean, claiming it and all the lands it touched for the Spanish Crown. He named it Mar del Sur—South Sea, because he had been on a southern course to reach it—and so it was that a new coast of the Americas opened to European exploration. The Pacific Ocean. The sea that lapped the Asian shores Spain had been looking for all along.

The coming years brought a flurry of discoveries as ships set sail from Cuba and Hispaniola and conquistadors streamed back and forth with slaves, gold, pearls, and all they had seized, traded, or stolen outright. Although Balboa had established himself as governor of the South Sea and begun to explore the Pacific, the very body of water that Columbus had been searching for all along, he would not live much longer. Resentment quickened among his fellow conquistadors, and in early 1517 his father-in-law, Pedrarias Dávila—known as the "Wrath of God"— accused him of high treason. One of Balboa's men, the shrewd and opportunistic Francisco Pizarro, was assigned to take him prisoner and drag him to the dungeons of Acla in irons as an example to any Spaniard who would defy his master and take fortune into his own hands in the Americas. The hapless discoverer of the Pacific was judged, sentenced, and put to death in the public square. After one swing of the axe, the executioner hoisted Balboa's severed head, thrust it on a pole, and left it to the mercy of flies.

The dreamers were not deterred. When an expedition returned from Panama a few months later with rumors of a gold-rich civilization in the North, more Spaniards yearned to take fortune into their own hands. Hernán Cortés, fed up with domestic ventures, longed to return to the golden dreams of his youth. He let Cuba's governor—his father-in-law, Diego Velázquez—know that he wanted to lead a gold-hunting expedition, and when Velázquez took him up on it, Cortés accepted the commission immediately. But even as Cortés busily prepared for an expedition, Velázquez, whose greed was boundless, began to worry that the young man was in it for himself. Indeed, Cortés had liquidated all his businesses, mortgaged all he owned, recruited five hundred of Velázquez's men, and outfitted a fleet of eleven ships with scant help from anyone else. Suspecting that the governor was about to withdraw his commission, Cortés rushed to set sail. "Fortune favors the daring!" he later wrote to the only man he would now obey: the newly crowned boy sovereign of Spain, King Carlos I, grandson of Ferdinand and Isabella. Daring would turn out to be Cortés's stock in trade.

Even as Cortés's ships skimmed away from Santiago de Cuba one gusty November night in 1518, the morbidly obese Governor Velázquez paced the shore, panting, roaring with rage, charging his brash young captain with mutiny. The governor had yet to receive permission from Spain to conquer new soil, and Cortés was well aware of it. The young man's precipitous departure under a starless sky could mean only one thing: he would wrest glory for himself.

With all the cunning and charm he could muster, Cortés worked to win Velázquez's troops to his side. As they headed for the promised bounty, he played on their greed for gold, convinced them that the governor was intent on cheating them out of it, and argued that their allegiance, in any case, should not be to Velázquez but to the Spanish king. Although a number of soldiers would remain loyal to the governor throughout the expedition, most did not argue. They were, after all, eager recruits, recent fugitives from penury and adolescence, fleeing a drab, desolate Spain with only one goal in mind: to get rich or die trying. They understood little about these latitudes and what it would take to lay claim to their precious store, but they knew they would need to be resolute. The Old World had to prevail over the New.

They hardly knew where the "gold-rich" ground might be, whether it was arable or sand, what human life inhabited it. For all the insistence that they were on a mission to save souls, precious few cared about the spiritual welfare of the indigenous. What they did care about was crystal clear: there were fortunes to be made, slaves to be pressed into service, treasures to ferry home. If Spain demanded that priests and notaries accompany them, they would comply, but it was seizure and booty that mattered most, not missionary work or the letter of the law. As one of them described it, they were sure of but one thing: "God would see to it that the lands we found were teeming with gold, pearls, or silver." The rest would be up to them. They would fight those lands into submission if need be, take and divide the spoils. Even the pope had decreed they had every right to do this. And they would make very sure that the king got his royal fifth.

BELLA DURMIENTE
Mount Ananea, 1965

> *There she is, the mountain we call Sleeping Beauty, in my town of
> tears.*
>
> —Resident, La Rinconada, 2013

In 1965, when Leonor Gonzáles was little more than two, her father,
whose ancestors had been miners on the Bolivian side of the Carabaya
mountains, left those lands for Sleeping Beauty, *la Bella Durmiente*, the
legendary mountain where it was said gold was good and government,
minimal. Like generations before him, her father was trying to make a
living for his woman and children, but he had watched his own father
fail in the mines of Untuca, where the business of gold had ground to a
standstill; and his grandfather, too, had not done well in the ancient Inca
quarries at Gavilán de Oro. Born in that unforgiving cordillera, where
failure had hardened failure, Leonor had watched her father set out with
his pickax before dawn, heading into the dark even as he gulped down
his soup. Pig soup, that fortifying elixir she had learned to conjure from
the animal's ear and serve one man after another in generations of the
hunt for El Dorado.

Times hadn't changed much. Gold was still the object. The irony was
that the precious dust was there often enough; certainly enough to en-
courage the clamor. The potential win for any of them was but a fraction
of the overall discovery, but her people had done this before: endured a
bitter reward after the removal of "the royal fifth," after the contractors'
thirty-to-one, after the ceaseless drain to a world elsewhere. There remained, in that hard calculus, overseers to obey. A punishing quota to
satisfy. The physical toll of survival. One day, as she tended to her two
small children in the freezing confines of her grandfather's one-room
hut where her little family lived, she watched her man don his coat and
cap and go off into the black of night, never to be seen again. They told
her he had been swallowed whole by the mine's god, the unpredictable,
insatiable El Tío. They told her he had drunk too much at one of the
brothels and met his match in a fatal brawl. Some said he had staggered

out of the mine in a daze, onto the freezing altiplano, and been carried off by two hard-eyed vultures.

He was gone.

NORTH FROM YUCATÁN
Mexico, 1519

> *"That's it?" said the captain. "This is all you are offering as welcome?"*
> *"It is all we have, my lord."*
> —Hernán Cortés and Montezuma's messenger, 1519.

Landing in Cozumel, Cortés's army moved quickly to the north, rounded the peninsula of Yucatán, swarmed overland, and engaged the natives in bloody battle. Although it was one Spaniard for every three hundred Indians—thousands of brightly painted faces racing at them over the savannah—Cortés's men handily routed them, falling upon them with all the force of their cavalry. The Indians were stunned by the sight of a bizarre enemy galloping toward them, pounding the earth with metal hooves. Horses had never been seen before in the Americas, and their effect was calamitous for the Indians. For the first terrifying moments of the invasion, they believed they were witnessing the approach of a terrifying beast: a sword-wielding leviathan with two heads and four legs. Alarmed by the wheeling animals, the slavering mastiffs alongside, the deafening cannon balls overhead, the Indians beat a hasty retreat and surrendered the next morning. Forty chieftains, clad in richly woven mantles, waving incense and bearing gifts of gold, food, and slaves, begged Cortés to cease the slaughter. They had lost eight hundred men to the steel swords and guns. Cortés had lost two.

It was immediately apparent to Cortés that any gold these natives might produce was flimsy, all too scarce, and probably filched from else-where, but he was intrigued by their description of the Mexica, a fiercely ambitious empire in the North that was said to have much of it. The Mexica were roundly hated for their rapaciousness and brutality; a war-rior culture that combed the land for captives to offer up in human sacri-fices, ripping fresh hearts from the living to satisfy hungry gods. Clearly, this was the powerful civilization that Spaniards had heard about all along. But Cortés had not lost time in his exploits in the Yucatán. He had gained allies and would continue to do so, accumulating collaborators as he advanced.

Before continuing toward the setting sun, where the Mexica were rumored to be, Cortés dashed all possible hope of desertion by scuttling his ships and making conquest his men's sole avenue to survival. Every Spaniard, including every deckhand on the ships' crews, was now committed to the journey inland. No one would stay behind. He incorporated two "tongues"—interpreters he had recruited along the way—who proved essential to the effort. One was a shipwrecked Spanish priest named Gerónimo de Aguilar, who had escaped cannibals, wandered the Yucatán for years, and become fluent in the language. The other was a winsome Aztec slave, La Malinche, who had been captured by Mayans and so was proficient in both languages. Offered to Cortés as war booty, La Malinche would quickly learn Spanish and become his personal translator, lover, and slave. She would wield remarkable authority, trusted as she was by conquistadors and revered by the conquered tribes. The principal negotiator in the exchange between Cortés and the Aztec emperor, she would be Cortés's avatar, strategic advisor, and mother of his first child: in other words, a slave with extraordinary power. Without her, any human interaction between Spaniards and Mexicans—and perhaps the very conquest itself—would have been impossible.

By the time Cortés came upon the great capital of Tenochtitlán, where the emperor Montezuma II resided, he had learned a thing or two about the challenges he would face in the land of the Mexicas. Unlike Columbus, he had seen cities here that matched Granada in size and architecture, rivaled the Republic of Venice in reach and governance. He had seen bustling marketplaces, where gold and silver were traded briskly. Everywhere he looked, he would later remark, he saw order, intelligence, courtesy, and a land graced with beautiful valleys. Mexico was a thriving territory—carefully cultivated, profitably harvested, bristling with people. But it had not escaped Cortés that, in outlying areas especially, their emperor, Montezuma, was roundly despised. He quickly understood that if he were to ally with these malcontents in borderlands of empire, he might gain military advantage, but he would also run a perilous course of provocation. He could see, too, that the Mexica alliance was a vast machinery of commerce and war, a fact made ever more vivid as he pressed overland—through cities, over brush, skirting volcanoes—and witnessed its power firsthand. From caciques, the tribal leaders who spoke candidly to La Malinche, Cortés learned of Montezuma's traits and eccentricities: his devotion to the war god, his grisly sacrifices, his cupidity, his love of luxury, his caprices. From Montezuma's ambassadors, who brought Cortés bribes to keep him from entering the city—gigantic discs of gold and silver, exquisitely woven fabrics, finely worked jade—he was now sure that he was approaching a formidable but anxious and mercurial emperor. From Montezuma's nephew, who ventured out to greet him when it was clear that the Spaniards would not be averted easily, Cortés witnessed a pomp and splendor the likes of which he had never seen. But he could not have anticipated the sight before him as he and his troops crossed the towering Sierra Madre, stood on high ground, and beheld the Mexican capital in the distance for the first time.

It was early morning when Cortés's army and its tribal cohort arrived at the causeway that separated the lakes and led into the great city of Tenochtitlán. Spread out before them, like a shimmering string of beads, were urban clusters that virtually sprang from the water; others that sprouted from dry land. And then there was the vast island city of Tenochtitlán itself, suspended on a blue lake, radiating such brilliance that, seen from afar, it seemed to be made of silver. The Spaniards were as dazzled as they were fearful of what might become of them in so grand a metropolis. Cortés's men compared the sight to the moment in the legendary tale of *Amadís of Gaul*, the most popular chivalric romance of the day, when the hero and his companions first lay eyes on Constantinople—it had been the tale that inspired them to join the conquest in the first place. Was this city before them not the realization of a dream? Elaborate temples rose from the lake like great stone lilies. As they approached, they could see how spacious and well built they were—how beautiful the stonework, the carved cedar, the sweet-scented trees, the rose gardens, the canoes that skimmed gracefully along the canals. As one soldier later wrote, "I do not know how to describe it, seeing things that had never been heard of or seen before, not even dreamed about. . . . I stood looking at it all and thought that never in the world would there be other discoveries such as these."

If Cortés harbored any apprehensions about the potential of this strange New World to deliver the wealth he and his king craved, those doubts would be dispelled now. Earlier conquests had been relatively modest: Columbus and his crews had subjugated villages of naked tribespeople easily, taken what they wanted by cunning or brute force. Spain's firm grip on Hispaniola, Cuba, and the coast of Panama had brought a modicum of hard-won gold, pearls, a new slave trade, and a growing plantation economy, but the vast metropolis Cortés was entering now was something else—something with infinitely more luster and promise.

Rattled by his visitors' brazenness, Montezuma made it clear that he wanted no Spaniards in his capital and delegated his nephew to bribe Cortés with an additional three thousand pesos of gold, along with a plea that Cortés turn back for any number of desperately concocted reasons: because food in the city was scarce, because Montezuma was indisposed, because the roads were perilously rough. The emperor had determined from spies and ambassadors that what the bearded men wanted was silver, gold, precious stones, and he had offered Cortés annual tributes of these in as great quantities as his king required. But these offers and gifts only sharpened Cortés's appetite. His army pressed on with greater resolve and with all the attendant support of the Aztecs' most rabid enemies. Cortés had it on good authority that Montezuma had contemplated capturing and killing twenty Spaniards to prevent them from coming any nearer. Or allowing them all to enter Tenochtitlán and then killing every last one. But at every turn, Cortés's unfailing charm—and his assurances to Montezuma's emissaries that he wanted only to see the great capital and relay a message from King Carlos—paved his way into the heart of the Aztec polestar.

Montezuma finally relented and agreed to admit the impertinent, mercenary courier from the faraway kingdom. If Cortés had an advantage, it was this: he was being given a courtesy on the assumption that he was an ambassador, not an aggressor. A king or chieftain in these lands would have had the prerogative to attack; a diplomat would not. Some chroniclers—including Cortés himself—have claimed that Montezuma

believed that the fair-haired Spaniard arriving on his shores was the in-
carnation of the legendary god-king Quetzalcoatl, who had sailed off
to the east many years before, vowing to return and rule again. It may
be convenient to think that Mexicans lived in fear of an angry god's triumphant return. It was certainly convenient for Cortés to pose as one. It
may also be useful to project a certain insecurity—and illegitimacy—on
the part of a great civilization so easily conquered. But these are Western
projections on the Amerindian mind, not likely true. Once he was persuaded that the brash captain approaching his inner sanctum was a mere
functionary delivering greetings from a king, Montezuma warily threw
open the doors.

The meeting with Montezuma on November 8, 1519, confirmed
every hope Cortés nurtured about wresting glory and a sizable fortune
for the Crown. The Mexican emperor received his guest cordially at the
causeway to the capital: he arrived on a litter under a magnificent can-
opy of emerald-green feathers, encrusted with gold and silver and hung
with pearls and jade. As a coterie of caciques helped him from his perch,
Cortés could see that the soles of the emperor's sandals were of pure gold;
the straps, adorned with glittering gems. Montezuma approached in
full regalia, as lords busily swept the earth and rolled out a rug beneath
him, anticipating his every step. Cortés was astonished by "the barbarian
king's baubles"—thrilled by the validation of his quest to find them. He
swung off his horse to offer the great man his hand. Startled by that surprising gesture, Montezuma did not take it, and so the Spaniard reached
for something else instead. He produced a necklace of stained glass beads
scented with musk and draped it around his host's neck. Cortés then
moved to embrace the man, but was restrained by Montezuma's vigilant
entourage. To touch the great Aztec lord, much less to gaze on him so
openly, was considered a great affront.

It's worth noting here that to the fastidious, hygiene-conscious Aztecs, the Spanish conquistadors were a foul, slovenly lot. Sixteenth-
century Europeans were largely indifferent to personal cleanliness and
unaccustomed—even averse—to bathing. Indeed, whenever Aztec
emissaries visited with the Spaniards, they insisted on fumigating them
with incense before an exchange. All the same, Montezuma welcomed
the rude Spaniard warmly. He lodged him splendidly in his father's pal-

ace, awarded him a highly coveted necklace of gold, and regaled him for days with sumptuous dinners.

Cortés's crudely outthrust hand was a harbinger of more indignities to come. As he later informed King Carlos, the conquistador had already decided that "it would benefit" the king to hold Montezuma hostage, seize his power, and claim the empire for Spanish rule. Six days after ingratiating himself to the emperor, Cortés got word that two Spaniards had been killed by Indians in a distant city. He took advantage of that news to blame his host, put Montezuma in irons, and take him prisoner in his own apartment. Montezuma's royal court, paralyzed by this unexpected turn of events, could do nothing lest the invaders kill their sovereign and inspire their enemies to war.

Even as Cortés plotted the most efficient way to fully hijack the empire and avail himself of its riches, he continued to dupe Montezuma with trumped-up accusations. He explained to his prisoner, with courteous apologies, that he was simply meting out justice, reconnoitering the area, and serving his god and king. He insisted that he be shown the mines from which Montezuma obtained his exquisite gold. Alarmed by the indignity, fooled by Cortés's charm, the Mexican obliged all too willingly. He called for his servants to accompany four detachments of Spaniards to the provinces—to Cosalá, Tamazulapa, Malinaltepec, and Tenimes—where gold was being panned from the rivers. A full report on the empire's gold operations was the result, with postscripts on the land that lay between: Mexico's fields were bursting with maize, beans, cacao, chicken farms. The land not only promised Spain metal fortunes, it was a bread basket, too.

We cannot presume to know what Montezuma was thinking, but the actions speak for themselves: he agreed to whatever his amiable captor wanted. Lodged in the comforts of his own father's palace, issuing directives as if he were still in full charge, he demanded that Cortés's every desire be satisfied: Artists produced maps of navigable rivers. Chieftains of conquered tribes sent gold on the backs of slaves. Whole cities were commanded to defer to the Spaniards as they built fortresses and amassed booty. Within the course of five months, Cortés had collected and melted down a veritable mountain of artifacts, jewelry, gold bars, and silver sheets amounting to almost a million pesos. One-fifth of that plunder, which today would have been worth more than $20 million, was eventually sent to King Carlos in a single shipment. Cortés kept an equivalent fifth for himself, and the rest was divided up among his troops, according to rank and service. For all the claims that Spain's conquest of the Indies was a mission to enlighten the world and spread God's word to the infidels, little mention of that sacred ministry was made in the initial report to the Crown. Like Columbus's first letter to Ferdinand and Isabella, Cortés's letter to King Carlos made clear the objective. Spain's radiant lodestar in the New World was hard gold.

GOLD LUST

They come armed with lightning . . . and they belch fire.

—Montezuma's messengers

We can only imagine the Aztec emperor's puzzlement at Cortés's metal obsessions. Montezuma was partial to gold—he liked to wear it—but it was little more than an ornament, really, and certainly not the most precious. The small jade stones, *chalchihuites*, which he had lavished on Cortés before his arrival and now offered in greater number, were far more valuable to him. One small stone, Montezuma assured Cortés, was worth two large loads of gold. The emperor could not have known that precious metals were the prize that had driven centuries of European history. It was gold—and before that, silver—that had emerged in the 1300s as the preferred specie of Europe's monied classes after the massive human losses during the Black Death, and then five hundred years later in the Great Famine. The near constant warfare that followed that dark era in Europe had produced a rash of demands for ransoms. Gold was needed throughout the fourteenth century, if only as a means to rescue kings and free their armies. Eventually gold became the fungible commodity that drove the economy from Constantinople to Calais. But no one had more of it than the merchants of Venice, who had amassed vast stores of gold and silver in a brisk market of slaves and lumber, making their city the most prosperous in Europe.

By 1500, however, the amount of gold in Europe had dwindled to a few meager tons. According to one historian, "the total amount of gold in Europe in all forms—coins, hoards, and every manner of adornment and decoration—could have been fashioned into a cube only two meters in each dimension." Indeed, in the century before Columbus's discovery, the bullion reserves in Europe had shrunk by half. Little wonder that Spanish and Portuguese navigators were eager to find the legendary golden empires of the Orient. Now, holding a great emperor hostage, Cortés stood a chance to grant his own king—the newly proclaimed ruler of the Holy Roman Empire—the "greater Kingdoms and Dominions Your Royal heart so desires."

Montezuma's apparent goodwill and cooperation did not sit well with Cortés's allies in the outlying provinces of Mexico. Rebellions flared as tribes that had signed on with Cortés defected altogether and refused to pay tribute to either side. But the greatest threat to Cortés came when another fleet of Spanish ships carrying nine hundred men and led by Captain Pánfilo de Narváez arrived at Veracruz, the seaport Cortés had founded and where he had sunk all his ships. Narváez had been sent by none other than Diego Velázquez, governor of Cuba, who, in his own relentless quest for gold, had declared all-out war on his mutinous captain. Even as some of Cortés's men were scouting out Montezuma's gold mines near Veracruz, they stumbled upon the new arrivals, informed them about Cortés's triumphs and newly won treasures, and—seduced by promises of greater rewards and a safe passage home—defected to Velázquez's side.

Montezuma had been told of the fleet's arrival, but he did not say a word about it to Cortés. Even in captivity, he had managed to stay informed. Indeed, through his spies, Montezuma secretly began sending gifts of gold and food to Narváez's crews, hoping that this internecine breach among Spaniards might serve to foil his captor and save the empire. But in a fateful moment of confusion, Montezuma let slip the news to Cortés, and Cortés, suddenly grasping his perilous position, prepared frantically for the struggle that was sure to follow. He offered his men more gold for their loyalty. By now, gold and jewels had become firm badges of power among conquistadors. The higher the station, the more ornamentation they would flaunt. They pinned the hard-won metal to their chests, draped heavy gold chains—*fanfarrones*—around their necks, looped them ostentatiously around their shoulders. Cortés understood that the only way to maintain his troops' allegiance was to assure them that they stood to win more. Wasting no time, he left the command of Tenochtitlán to his deputy, led a squadron against the new Spanish incursion, and succeeded in capturing Captain Narváez and buying his men's loyalty with ever more metal promises.

All the same, things were not going well back in the Mexican capital. The retinue of Spaniards left behind began to fear that the locals would soon overpower them. One night, as crowds gathered in the sacred Patio of the Gods for dancing and ritual festivities, Cortés's deputy Pedro de Alvarado panicked and, sensing a revolt, ordered a massacre. The Spanish forces, such as they were, rode out onto the square with their guns and swords, butchering hundreds mercilessly. The city was stunned, momentarily numb, but, in time, fought back with avenging fury. So it was that Cortés returned to a Tenochtitlán reeling with violence. Desperate to improvise a response, he sent the captive Montezuma out to calm the angry hordes. The emperor did as he was told and implored protesters to stop, but the rebel chieftains called out that he was no longer their sovereign—the power now belonged to his younger brother, Cuauhtémoc. Montezuma could barely absorb that humiliation before a hail of stones rained down on him, striking him senseless to the ground. Those last bitter blows at the hands of his own people proved too much for the emperor to bear. He refused all efforts to bind his wounds. Even as rioters pummeled the palace walls with blazing torches—even as Cortés, ironically, was forced to defend the emperor's ground—Montezuma expired. The battle that raged into the night was all-consuming, feral. Streets and canals ran with blood and buildings were devoured by flames as Aztec loyalists, intent on routing the conquistadors once and for all, came at Cortés's stronghold in waves. There was no choice now for the Spaniards but to flee the capital en masse. But how could they leave behind their accumulated plunder—the whole point of the invasion?

The conflagration that followed would have monumental consequences, but most striking in that swiftly unfurling history were the many hundreds of thousands of gold pesos that Cortés stood to lose in the flight from Tenochtitlán. Gold had been foremost in his mind, as it had been in the minds of Velázquez, Narváez, and the soldiers who served them. It had been the aim, purse, bank—mover of armies. It had been uppermost, too, in the collective mind of the powers that drove them: the king, the pope, and the newly conceived Council of the Indies, founded precisely to manage all the riches Spain stood to gain in the New World. Mexicans quickly learned to play Spaniards for that weakness, set them against one another over it, and, through the many months they had spent in the company of those bearded strangers, they could only marvel at the intensity of that lust.

Shouting to his men, Cortés called for an immediate evacuation of the capital, and his besieged soldiers gathered their wits for a desperate exodus. With the assistance of their newfound collaborators, the Tlaxcalans, they attempted to make off with as much booty as they could carry. As one soldier described it:

Cortés ordered his . . . servants to bring out all the gold and jewels and silver, and loaned them many Tlaxcalan Indians for the purpose, and they placed all of it in the Hall. Cortés told the King's officers . . . to take charge of the gold belonging to His Majesty, and he gave them seven wounded and lame horses and one mare, and many friendly Tlaxcalans, more than eighty in number, and they loaded them with parcels of it, as much as they could carry, for it had been melted down into very broad ingots, and much gold still remained in the Hall piled up in heaps. Then Cortés called his secretary and the King's Notaries and said: "Bear witness for I can do no more with this gold. We have here in this apartment and Hall over seven hundred thousand pesos of gold, and, as you have seen, it cannot be weighed nor placed in safety. I now give it up to any of the soldiers who care to take it, otherwise it will be lost among those dogs of Mexicans."

The soldiers made a run for the looted treasures, eagerly seizing the jade along with the solid gold bars, knowing full well that in this faraway land, the natives valued stone more than metal. They took what they could, tucking it wildly into their belts, shoving it under their armor. Narváez's troops, newly arrived and electrified to see so much wealth piled in one place, loaded themselves with it. In the frenzy, they tried to lug away more in hastily improvised boxes. Rushing from the city, scrambling across the causeway bridges, the Spaniards were set upon by the Aztecs, and some were sent tumbling into the lake. Looking back, a Spaniard caught a glimpse of the dead horses, wounded Indians, and boxes laden with gold, bobbing briefly on the surface, only to sink out of sight.

For all the material losses Cortés suffered in that hasty retreat, he soon found that he had accumulated an abundance of soldiers and ammunition. With four thousand Tlaxcalans as reinforcement, Cortés handily drove back the Aztecs who chased him into the countryside. Along the way, he was able to recruit other disgruntled tribes—the Cholulas, the Tepeacas, and warriors from neighboring territories—who were anxious to settle scores with their Mexican overlords. Over the next months, as Spanish ships arrived from Cuba and Jamaica, and as the cohort proceeded to capture and enslave whole villages, Cortés soon had a formidable population under his control. It wasn't long before he was planning to recover the capital.

First, however, he wanted the gold back. Gathering his troops at their first encampment, Cortés could see full well that they had carried off a good portion of the precious store. Even in those makeshift circumstances, ingots were being traded, gambled, fought over viciously among the ranks. Cortés issued a proclamation ordering his soldiers to produce all the treasures they had grabbed or pay a heavy penalty. He would take it by force if he had to, he told them, and when he had it all counted, he would allow them to keep one-third of what they had managed to haul away. "This order of Cortés's," one Spaniard groused, "seemed very wrong indeed." After all, in the panic of their flight from the Mexican capital, he had urged them to have at it, pilfer whatever they could, and they had done so with every assurance that it was theirs now. A royal scribe had been present to make it law.

But there were other, more urgent troubles. A rabid war was afoot, and all the furies would be unleashed as Cortés and his armies, honed now by privation and combat, systematically worked their way back to Tenochtitlán, leveling the empire as they went. By the time Cortés forced a surrender from Emperor Cuauhtémoc in August 1521, many a Spaniard would have his beating heart ripped from his chest, and thousands of Indian corpses would lie strewn on the roads that led to that shining city on the lake. But Cortés would emerge from that abattoir a heroic figure, exalted in Europe, highly decorated by his king—an exemplar for every conquistador who followed.

It was precisely during these years that Spain's King Carlos I, the Holy Roman emperor, whose ambitions had spiraled vigorously after Cortés's spectacular conquest of Mexico, decided to change his coat of arms so that the two rampant black eagles that characterized his insignia now paraded grandly through the Pillars of Hercules. He added the heraldic motto, "Plus Ultra," or "Ever Beyond," for not only had his Holy Roman Empire sailed well past "non plus ultra," the perilous brink of medieval lore, "beyond" had become its dominion, cash cow, and playground. This ambition, coupled with the superstition of the age—that God would pardon any means, however cruel, to bring converts to the Church of Rome—was the fertile loam in which the subjugation of America flourished. The conquistadors' aim was metal riches, but their agency was Christian conversion. As the great sixteenth-century writer Lope de Vega put it, "Under faith's banners, they went searching for silver and gold." The lure was irresistible; the alibi, unimpeachable. The animating war cry "Santiago! Y cierra, España!" ("Saint James! And charge, Spain!"), shouted at the start of every assault or skirmish, conjured, at least in their minds, the grand, noble crusades of yore. It pledged rapine to a higher cause; to the glory of God. It mitigated the greed.

And why not? In a time when Pope Julius II was riding into battle in full armor and paying for holy wars by selling "indulgences"—paper certificates that promised anyone rich enough to buy them a welcome relief from purgatory—it was clear that the Church had come to the realization that it needed the bullion and would use any means to raise it. There was a Basilica of Saint Peter's to build, after all; a Protestant Reformation to stamp out. In time, King Carlos's close ties to Rome would prove mutually profitable for Church and Spain alike. As the king's navies appropriated the wealth of the Indies and established plantations, mines, and a thriving colonial economy, Spain and Catholicism grew hand in hand in power and dominion. Only Napoleon I and Adolf Hitler at the heights of rule have commanded a larger area of Europe. But

Spain's dominion would go on to radiate to far corners of the east and west—from the Americas to the Philippines, an empire on which the sun never set, as the Holy Roman emperor liked to put it—so that King Carlos's authority would eventually surpass Alexander the Great's and Julius Caesar's. But that ongoing initiative would take not only gold, it would also take silver. It would take a Peru.

CHAPTER 4

TRAIL OF THE WHITE KING

❖

Atahualpa had said there was a small mountain they lit with fire,
and when that fire died out, there was melted silver in it.

—Pedro Pizarro, 1571

You might suppose that Spain's conquest of the grand sweep of territory from Argentina to Colorado was a sprawling enterprise undertaken by hundreds of principals from radically different backgrounds. But it was not so. The conquistadors who succeeded Columbus and locked much of the Americas under Spanish rule were a tight circle of like-minded individuals, many of them from harsh boyhoods in the Extremadura, some even related by blood, and most schooled in indistinguishable realities. Vasco Núñez de Balboa, who discovered the Pacific; Hernán Cortés, who conquered the Aztecs; Pedro de Alvarado, who conquered Cuba, aided Cortés in Mexico, and then went on to subjugate much of Central America; Francisco Pizarro, who conquered the Incas; Pedro de Valdivia, who founded what is now Chile; Francisco de Orellana, who explored the Amazon and founded what is now Ecuador; and Hernando de Soto, who explored Indian territory from Florida to Arkansas— all hailed from within fifty miles of one another in the impoverished, drought-ridden, impossibly torrid highlands of western Spain. The links can be surprising: Balboa claimed the same dusty little birthplace as De Soto. Pizarro was born an easy day's ride from Cortés's childhood home. Indeed, Pizarro, Cortés, and Orellana were all distant cousins and served in the same expeditions. Nicolás de Ovando, the governor who brought Pizarro and Cortés to the New World, was also related to both. Balboa was son-in-law to his commanding officer, Cortés was brother-in-law to his. But perhaps the greatest bond among these men was that they were sons of war: their fathers, uncles, cousins had battled the Italians, the French, the Moors, and they had all inherited a strong loyalist and fighting spirit. Conquering the Americas was truly an enterprise of brothers.

As the great historian of Latin American conquest John Hemming once wrote:

> The men who went on these ventures were not mercenaries: they received no pay from the expedition's leader. They were adventurers who took passage to the Americas in the hope of making their fortunes. In the early days of conquests, any reward for these desperadoes had to come from the Indians themselves. They were predators hoping for easy plunder. Their food and personal service came from the Indians they hoped to rob. . . . The Spanish adventurers were like packs of hounds, roaming the interior to pick up a scent of gold. They sailed across the Atlantic full of bravado and ambition and then filled the tiny coastal settlements, hoping to grow rich as parasites on the native population.

It stands to reason, then, that these men—far from home, tied by blood, fueled by personal ambition—were well aware of one another's successes and failures. Pizarro had studied Cortés's strategies of conquest meticulously. He had pored over every move and countermove his young cousin had employed to bring the Mexican Empire to its knees. By 1522, when he first heard about Cortés's remarkable exploits, Pizarro had been a stolid, reliable soldier of fortune with extensive lands, one of the wealthiest residents of Panama. He had worked his way into Governor Pedrarias Dávila's confidence by conquering the Pearl Islands. He had proven his loyalty by arresting his own leader, Balboa, and bringing him to a harsh justice. He had raided villages, capturing Indians for the lucrative slave trade. But Pizarro was nearing fifty and still answering to others, waiting for destiny's doors to fling open and offer a greater prize. That opportunity arose in 1523, when Pascual de Andagoya, a Basque colleague, returned to Panama from an exploratory trip down the San Juan River in what is now Colombia. Andagoya's reports were transfixing. He told of great wealth just beyond reach—just south of the most southerly point he had reached—and he described how he had "discovered, conquered, and pacified Pirú." The Pirú Andagoya had found was a pugnacious chieftain who ruled the wilds of Chochama and had attacked him in vicious battle. Once vanquished, Pirú had become useful to Andagoya, schooling him in the region and informing him about the powerful "White King" of the south, whose colossal empire, he said, was bursting with metal riches. But for all Andagoya's successes—his foothold on the continent, his self-appointed rule over the green valleys of Cali and Popayán—he had returned to Panama wasted by battle and illness, too frail to return to the realm of Pirú.

Here was the opening Pizarro had longed for. Electrified by rumors about Pirú—the name now for all land south of Panama—and its powerful, rich White King, Pizarro angled to buy Andagoya's ships and conduct a more purposeful exploration of the region. But he was working against time. King Carlos had already contracted explorer Ferdinand Magellan to find a sea route to the coveted spice islands of Asia, and, by 1520, Magellan's fleet had skirted Brazil and reached a great river that coiled south from the Andes. They called it Río de la Plata, the river of silver. Magellan, too, had heard of the legendary emperor: the Guaraní Indians had told of a sovereign whose throne, garment, and emblem were made of a shimmering metal, and whose very essence was forged from silver. But for all the Portuguese forays into that river, the White King was nowhere to be found.

All the same, in 1535 Pedro de Mendoza, who had already made a fortune in the mutinous sack of Rome, sailed to the southern tip of the American continent, looking for the White King's gold. What he found instead was syphilis and starvation, and his men ended up in the swamps of Buenos Aires, eating the soles of their boots. Yet no one was deterred. Soldiers of fortune continued to be enchanted by the siren song of silver, Pizarro not least among them. Like many of his cohort, he claimed he was serving Catholic Spain, bringing Christianity to benighted Indians—the politically correct pablum of the time—but he was an avid participant in the race for worldly riches, as captivated by the myth of the White King as any of his predecessors, and he knew full well that whoever got there first stood to win them for himself.

Pizarro had come far, in human terms as well as on the seas. Born the illegitimate son of a lesser nobleman and a servant girl, deprived of an education that typically accompanied higher birth, he had spent his boyhood tending swine. Illiterate, he would remain so for his entire life, but he grew tall, well made, confident—traits inherited from his father— and soon he was dreaming of life beyond the mire and moil of pigpens. By sixteen, Pizarro had escaped to Seville, where losers became sailors and the Guadalquivir River flowed seductively to the sea. Within a year, he decided to follow his father's military example and sign on to fight in King Ferdinand's armies, although the news of Columbus's adventures had begun to fire his imagination. Lit by the fever of the day, Pizarro later joined Governor Nicolás Ovando's fleet and sailed for Hispaniola in 1502. Within five years, half of his shipmates were dead and the entire native population of Hispaniola decimated by war and disease, but somehow Pizarro managed to survive. In fact, he was thriving, excelling at hunting gold and slaves—the grueling business of conquest. He was in his element.

Participating eagerly in feverish raids on the Indians of Hispaniola's interior, Pizarro handily proved his martial prowess. He was bold, tenacious, surpassingly skilled at breaking rebellious natives and forcing them to work the mines. A trusted, personal guard to Governor Ovando, he was eventually moved along in the same capacity to Governor Pedrarias Dávila in Panama. Pizarro may not have been as lettered or learned or clever as his comrades Cortés and Balboa, but he was a loyal warrior, valiant in battle, and surprisingly resourceful under duress. A man of few words and impressive carriage, he was seen as a natural leader. In Panama, he added another advantage. His *encomienda*, or plantation— flush with grain and a thriving cattle business—became decidedly profitable. He was awash in money.

Eventually Pizarro merged his plantation with those of two other men he trusted: Diego Almagro, an illiterate soldier, who, like him, had been born illegitimate and shunned, but had gone on to make his mark as a fighter and spirited slaver; and Hernando de Luque, a clergyman possibly of Sephardic origin, who was rich, talented in finance, and a confidant of Governor Pedrarias's. Together the three formed a company that combined properties and businesses, shared costs, and divided all profits. One for all, all for one. They formalized their pact according to old medieval tradition: by attending mass in Panama's modest church, sharing a communion host three ways, and vowing undying loyalty to one another. They resolved to buy ships, outfit a crew of more than one hundred men, and undertake the exploration of Pirú. Pizarro would be captain and commander of the expedition; Almagro, in charge of assembling all arms and provisions; and Luque, manager of their funds. It didn't take long to convince Pedrarias to authorize the voyage: the governor was not asked to contribute a penny to the enterprise but was promised a representative portion of all treasures found.

The first voyage was a rout. The two ships commissioned—a shabby brigantine pompously named *Santiago* (after the patron saint of Spain), and its creaky companion, a small caravel—were in perilous condition, unfit for the task. They slid out to sea on November 14, 1524, bearing 110 Spaniards, a few Indians, four horses, a dog of war, and no wind in their sails. Lagging to shore at the Pearl Islands, Pizarro waited for north gales to sweep them south, but he was forced to idle for three more weeks, his supplies dwindling. When the crew did manage to push off, fickle winds nudged them along as far as the mangrove swamps where Andagoya had begun his exploration inland. But in the interim, they had endured a wasting hunger, plagues of mosquitos, and debilitating tropical rains. By February, they had yet to see one Indian. Pizarro set off inland, but he was soon put off by the inhospitable mountains and an impassable tangle of trees. He returned to sea and navigated farther south, where they found an abandoned camp, a few trinkets of gold, and the ghoulish remains of a cannibal feast.

After six months of unimaginable starvation, Pizarro's crew counted fifty scrawny men—half the original complement—and, for all the fine words Pizarro could summon about the gold and silver that lay ahead, it was clear the expedition was in grave peril. The worm-eaten ships had begun to take on water; they would not carry them much farther. The Spaniards ventured inland, in desperation, to raid Indian villages for food, but this was dangerous work with meager results, and, ultimately, suicidal. The Indians, naturally, defended their turf. Naked, flesh eating, painted for war and armed with poison arrows, they tracked the intruders as they moved overland or down the coast, engaging them in hostilities. Pizarro was wounded critically in one foray. Almagro, in a separate attack, lost an eye. Eventually Pizarro and Almagro understood that, for all the humiliation of admitting defeat, they had no choice but to return to Panama, repair their ships, and start all over again.

In 1526, even as the great Inca Huayna Capac moved across his vast empire with a retinue of thousands—and even as the Holy Roman emperor King Carlos I consolidated his power as the ruler of the Catholic world, inviting a flurry of wars and provoking the Protestant Reformation— Pizarro launched a second voyage to Pirú. It was almost as shabby as the first and had not been easy to mount, but, at the very end, after enormous sacrifices, it offered a glint of promise.

By then, Governor Pedrarias had lost all faith in the enterprise. His own grandiose plans for the conquest of Nicaragua had run aground, and he had no time for Pizarro's folly. Exploratory ventures such as Pizarro's represented a potentially calamitous drain on a newly established settlement. All of Panama counted only four hundred Spaniards and a limited quantity of food and supplies. For Pizarro to make off with a quarter of the Spanish population, not to mention precious stores of maize, horses, and ammunition—all in the midst of an occupying effort, all in the name of treasures he might never find—was a formidable risk for any governor. Pizarro found himself cobbling together a fleet as best he could, defending it on all sides, and encountering more hazards than he thought possible.

From the moment it set sail in January 1526, the expedition seemed doomed to failure. Pedrarias's parting act had been to promote Almagro to second captain, dealing a stinging insult to Pizarro's authority and sorely wounding his vanity. Nothing would be quite right between Pizarro and Almagro after that. The voyage was arduous, and months would go by as they engaged indigenous Americans in one skirmish after another, moving ever south, raiding villages along the coast for food, scouring their huts for any trace of precious metals. The natives seemed to have expected them this time, and they defended their camps fiercely. But there were alligators, too, and strange fevers, and an inescapable hunger that honed Spanish desperation as they lumbered in heavy armor through the impossible green. Near the San Juan River, where Andagoya had proclaimed himself governor five years before,

Pizarro managed to invade and crush an entire hamlet, making off with gold that was worth fifteen thousand ducats and a herd of captives for the slave markets in Panama. There were reasons to move on.

Soon, however, his men were too wretched to do so. Every week, three or four were expiring of disease or starvation. Pizarro decided to send his own ship south to search for gold and silver, and Almagro's ship north to secure reinforcements from Panama. He would remain on the desolate island of Gallo, marooned with his little band of raggedy men. Fighting off snakes, foraging among roots, suffering thunderbolts that split the night skies, they remained on that island for another hellish seven months. A few of the more desperate men had managed to slip a note to Governor Diego de los Ríos in the shipment that had gone off with Almagro. Pleading to be released from Pizarro's ruthless charge, they wrote: "Ah, mister Governor! See this for what it is! There, with you, goes the trapper [Almagro]; here, with us, sits the butcher [Pizarro]." When the governor received it, he ordered a full-scale inquiry of Pizarro's mission.

But as months slipped by, the ship Pizarro had sent south under captain Bartolomé Ruiz returned with some startling news. Five hundred miles away, just off the coast of what is now Ecuador, Ruiz had chanced upon a fleet of merchants' rafts so immense and sophisticated as to suggest a far greater civilization than he had ever encountered in the New World. The captain had no way to know this, but the natives on those rafts were subjects of the Lord Inca Huayna Capac, who, at that moment, was 150 miles inland, in the bucolic comforts of his palace in Tumipampa. What Ruiz did know for certain—and had concrete proof of in hand—was that these were a people who made and traded metal.

"They were carrying many pieces of silver and gold for adorning the body . . . crowns and diadems, belts and bracelets, armor for the legs and breastplates . . . mirrors decorated with silver, and cups and other drinking vessels. They carried many wool and cotton mantles, shirts and tunics. . . . They had some small weights to weigh gold, resembling Roman workmanship."

The Indians seemed refined, worldly, more friendly than any he had met before. And they were also ferrying emeralds, ceramics, and luxuriously soft textiles the likes of which he had never seen in Spain. Knowing he needed validation of this discovery, Ruiz and his men seized the ship and captured three of the natives to train as translators for Pizarro—the rest jumped overboard and swam desperately for shore.

Ironically enough, as Pizarro listened raptly to Ruiz's account—a thrilling affirmation of what he had believed all along—very different news was heading his way from the North. Panama's governor De los Ríos, deeply alarmed by the desperate message from the crew, had dispatched a detail, commandeered by Captain Juan Tafur, to round up Pizarro's men and force them to return. Whether the governor had been moved by the malcontents or by other disgruntled members of Almagro's crew, he was adamant that those seeking rescue should be brought back to Panama. But if as many as twenty wanted to persevere under Pizarro, he would approve an expeditionary ship. When Captain Tafur's detachment arrived at the island of Gallo, none of the men wanted to carry on Pizarro's mission. They were in tatters, unshod, emaciated, and they wept for joy to see Tafur's ships approach—virtual prisoners freed from bondage. Pizarro strode out to greet Tafur only to be handed the governor's orders along with the news that his entire crew had elected to return. He was devastated but kept his emotions in check. He had always been an austere man, taciturn, more given to rudeness than urbanity. Calmly, soberly, he drew his sword from its sheath, walked toward his crew, and made a horizontal gash in the sand. "On that side," he said, gesturing toward the waiting ship, "is Panama, where you will be poor. On this side is Peru, where you will be rich. Let the good Spaniard choose his course."

A long silence descended over his men. Eventually Ruiz, who had witnessed with his own eyes the promise of Huayna Capac's empire, crossed slowly to Pizarro's side. One by one, twelve more followed. With such scant numbers, Tafur insisted that the expedition be terminated there and then, as the governor had decreed, but Pizarro knew that to return to Panama now would be to lose face as well as foothold. After Cortés's victories, the appetite for conquest was at a frenzied high, and any conquistador who got wind of the White King's riches would surely rush to claim them. Pizarro decided that Ruiz would return with the others, reunite with Almagro, find another ship, and rejoin the expedition as soon as he could manage. Pizarro would stay where he was. It was a strikingly defiant choice, given that he and the remaining twelve would wait seven more punishing months before they would see relief. Unable to convince Pizarro otherwise, an irked Tafur transported Pizarro and his die-hards to an uninhabited island safe from potential attack, dumped their allotment of maize on the sand to rot, and sailed away.

Governor de los Ríos was furious to learn that Pizarro had countermanded his orders and stayed in the field with so few men. At first, he refused to send a ship with reinforcements. But Almagro, who was still in Panama trying to amass arms and provisions to bolster the expedition, pleaded passionately that it would be barbaric for the governor to condemn Spaniards to a sure death. A ship was finally granted, with the stipulation that Pizarro had six months to make his way back to Panama. Pizarro and his men rejoiced to see it approach, having been castaways for more than a year in those remote waters. They had suffered crippling bouts of dysentery, malaria, heat stroke, and malnutrition, but sheer force of will and an abundance of fresh fish had ensured their survival. With them on that wild little patch of green, and seldom noted by history, was a band of slaves: African blacks as well as the young indigenous merchants Ruiz had abducted on his southern foray. The natives on that island would be invaluable: they had learned enough Spanish to serve as translators. They would prove crucial to the conquest of legendary Pirú.

Pizarro's tenacity was eventually rewarded. Sailing south with enough supplies, but no weapons of war, they crossed into the Gulf of Guayaquil and saw their first Incan city, Tumbes. These were the lands that had been conquered by Tupac Inca a generation before and defended ferociously by Huayna Capac since. Like the merchants Ruiz had encountered earlier, the people of Tumbes received the Spaniards cordially. They flocked to the shore, intensely curious about their ships, their beards, their peculiar, baffling behavior. It was clear to the Spaniards who had sailed this coast before that the intervening year had brought significant changes. A sense of instability was afoot; a civil war was being fought. Surveying the coast from his ship, Pizarro sent two men ashore to scout the city and see if there was any material wealth to be found. Both men returned with separate but arresting reports: there was a fortress, said the first, filled with breathtaking metal treasures and fortified by six walls. The second told him that when the natives had asked about his arquebus, a weapon the likes of which they had never seen, he'd demonstrated its use by splitting a thick beam of wood with a single shot. The Indians had been astounded by the gun's power, falling to the ground in abject terror when the lead ball roared to its mark.

Here was the intelligence Pizarro needed. He and his men were literally on the verge of a great civilization, "the product of centuries of development in complete isolation from the rest of mankind," as one observer put it. Here, too, were the glittering metals Ruiz had seen: the silver and gold so coveted by the Spanish Crown. And yet, for all the sophistication of this new culture, the sound of a single gunshot had brought the people of Pirú to their knees.

History raveled quickly after that. Pizarro's six-month franchise would soon be over, and he needed to return to Panama in great haste. He knew all too well that, like Cortés, he had defied his governor and could no longer rely on his support. Sailing back, filled with conviction, he made plans to take his project directly to Seville. Within months of arrival, he boarded another ship for Hispaniola and, from there, sped on to Spain to seek the higher blessings of the Crown. He arrived in Seville in the summer of 1528, accompanied by a throng of Indians and llamas, bearing treasures he had accumulated along the coast. As illiterate as he was, Pizarro was eloquent, persuasive—a natural dream weaver—and he succeeded in holding the court spellbound with tales of his brave adventures and the glittering prizes that lay in store.

King Carlos was won over by the stern conquistador and said so to his court. A year later, the queen, acting for her husband, made Pizarro a nobleman by granting him a marquisate and favoring him with the famed Capitulación de Toledo. In it, he was made governor for life of that distant territory, with power to explore, conquer, and forcibly settle more than six hundred miles of shoreline, from what is now the northernmost border of Ecuador to the southern reaches of Peru. Almagro and Luque were granted substantially less—Almagro was made the commandant of the town of Tumbes; Luque, its bishop—slights that would fester to fatal proportions in time. But fundamental to the Capitulación were its stipulations about the gold: whatever precious metals were found in faraway Peru would not be subject to the Crown's royal fifth, as was customary, but taxed by a mere 10 percent. The incentive to seek gold in that land, then, would be far greater than anywhere else in the Indies. The lure of even more gains would come to define the spirit of the conquest of the Incas, and the future of the Americas for generations to come.

PIZARRO'S LAST SHOT

Castrate the Sun! That's what those strangers came to do.

—Chilám Balám

Pizarro's decision to appeal directly to the throne was joined by a singular stroke of good fortune: Hernán Cortés happened to be in Toledo at the same time. Cortés, with his natural charisma and engaging swagger, had deeply impressed the king and queen, who listened to his colorful accounts with enormous gusto. A decade into his governorship, the conquistador of Mexico had not been having an easy time of it in the New World, beset as he was by accusations of greed, cruelty, and rank abuse of power. But here, in the salons of Toledo, he mingled easily and charmed the ladies of the court with gifts of Mexican treasures. By then, a formidable river of silver had begun to flow from Mexico's mines to the king's coffers, inspiring a general forbearance of Cortés's alleged transgressions. It also inspired the envy of France, which openly encouraged French privateers on the high seas to raid it. Cortés was not shy to flaunt his spoils of conquest and, prostrating himself before Carlos for theatrical effect, dedicated the vast expanse of Mexico and all its material wealth to the young monarch. The gesture wasn't lost on the king: Mexico represented more territory than all Europe under his rule, from the Canary Islands to the River Danube. Awarded many honors, a hero at the very zenith of his fame, Cortés had set the stage for any conquistador poised to vanquish a great civilization. It was only natural that he and Pizarro would meet in Toledo's gilded halls.

Cortés's mother was a Pizarro, surely disposing the two distant cousins to an amicable encounter. Moreover, they had both served in the expedition led by Nicolás de Ovando. They saw each other at least once in Toledo, if not a number of times. Cortés, like any other Spaniard deployed to the Indies, had heard about the fabled kingdom of Pirú. He wanted to hear more about Pizarro's adventures directly. The meetings between them went well, despite their stark differences: Pizarro was taciturn, unlettered, uncomfortable in his skin; Cortés was magnetic, sunny, a practiced and graceful writer. All the same, Cortés inspired the older man with his confidence and counsel. There was much to learn from the conquest of the Aztecs: the details of his strategy, the collaboration with enemies, the initial overtures to Montezuma, the sudden capture, the extortion of gold and silver, the cleverly constructed illusion that the people's emperor still ruled. It stands to reason, then, that Pizarro's conquest would resemble Cortés's victory to the letter. What is more difficult to fathom is why two great civilizations separated by so much distance and history succumbed to the same strategies in the same way.

In truth, for all the seeming similarities, the Mexicas and Incas were as different from each other as Egypt is from Rome. Despite Montezuma's efforts to tamp down freedoms, his empire had evolved into a largely urban, highly entrepreneurial society. Mesoamerica was a buzzing network of competing enclaves and markets, with a monetary system based on copper and cacao. Huayna Capac's empire, on the other hand, was rural, nestled in a mountain aerie, highly centralized, and its currency—if you could say it had one—was slave labor. The Mexica confederation traded freely, bought and sold metals, and allowed for a certain social mobility. The Inca's Empire of the Sun, however, arrogated all metal and power to its ruling class—its literal and figurative umbilical in Cuzco—and maintained a firm hand on all goods.

Pizarro's great luck was that, for at least one brief moment in time, Cortés's strategy was actually viable in the lands where Pizarro had been granted unfettered power. For an unprecedented window of a dozen years, from 1518 to 1530, Spain had a distinct advantage. Inca and Aztec rulers were beset by a common dilemma: their territories had grown unwieldy, rebellious, torn asunder by too many loyalties. This social disorder was joined by a silent weapon the conquistadors didn't even know they had. Smallpox, the scourge a Spaniard carried with him in his person, had coiled down that virgin hemisphere like a swift snake, spreading from tribe to tribe, decimating the Indian population. It had been a deadly, agile incursion, preceding the first footfall of a Spanish boot on those southern sands.

There were, all the same, enormous challenges. Pizarro may have seen Tumbes from a distance, even held Incan treasures in his hand, but he had no real understanding of the people who inhabited the continent, aside from the vivid picture Cortés had re-created for him about a place a continent and a half away. Pizarro didn't know the name of the capital, Cuzco, or the fact that it sat one thousand miles inland, cradled by a range of majestic mountains. He didn't know that the civilization didn't have an array of deities—as Aztecs did—but one supreme being; that its emperor was worshipped as a direct descendant of the Sun. Nor did he know the name Huayna Capac, the Lord Inca who had presided over that realm—a vast territory three thousand miles long and several hundred miles wide, which reached from the southernmost part of Colombia to the heart of Chile, and from the Amazon jungle to the sea. But by the time Pizarro sailed for those lands at the end of 1531—this time with four more Pizarros, an army of two hundred men, warhorses, battle dogs, and a full complement of ammunition—the Incas were indeed in disarray, just as the Aztecs had been when Cortés had encountered them.

Huayna Capac was dead, victim of a savage plague that had annihilated god-king and slave alike. His sons Atahualpa and Huascar, who ruled in the North and the South, respectively, were locked in a bitter war for the ascendancy. The conquered tribes of the Incas—reduced, traduced, and exploited—had come to see this royal breach as an opportunity to rebel. So it was that a providential instability was rocking Peru when Pizarro stepped out on its desolate coast, saw mutilated corpses swinging from trees, and marched to Cajamarca for his fateful first meeting with the Lord Inca.

Gleaming from the written record of that initial contact is the ardently sought metal: the gold the Spaniards hoped to see dangling from ears, the silver curios for which they sacked houses, the pounded copper bits that had been so abundant in Mexico. They marauded their way through the countryside, doing what they knew best—enslaving locals, plundering villages for food and treasures, enlisting the loyalty of malcontents. When Atahualpa sent one of his nobles to investigate rumors of an approaching horde, the emissary returned to report "that there were about one hundred ninety, including ninety on horseback more or less; that they were lazy robbers . . . bearded thieves who had come from the sea, and that they came riding large llamas like those of [the fearsome tribespeople,] the Collao." They were unruly, insubordinate, filthy. Atahualpa had more problems to worry about than a rowdy band of barbarians. They were pests, little more. "He took them for nothing," it was reported. Even so, he was curious to see them. He allowed them to advance.

Atahualpa was not in Cajamarca when the Spaniards finally arrived on Friday, November 15, 1532. He had repaired to his pleasure house several miles away to rest, fast, and take the thermal waters before resuming his bloody war against Huascar. Pizarro ordered his brother Hernando Pizarro and Captain Hernando de Soto to ride out to the rest house with twenty-four horsemen and announce themselves to the sovereign. Through a translator, they were to ask him where the Spaniards could lodge and when Pizarro could expect to meet him.

They found Atahualpa sitting on a lavish stool in the middle of a courtyard, surrounded by a formidable assembly of guards and servants. Fearing for their lives, the Spaniards never dismounted. The emperor seemed utterly indifferent to the unkempt riders and their high-spirited, snorting horses. In a voice filled with disdain, he scolded them for pillaging the countryside and ransacking his storehouses. But his tone changed considerably when Hernando Pizarro offered to turn Spanish energies to fighting Huascar; soon Atahualpa was calling for his servants to serve the Spaniards a ceremonial drink. Fermented *chicha*, the favored strong drink of the Inca, arrived in elaborate golden chalices and was handed up to the two horsemen. Perhaps from the sheer elation of seeing such clear evidence of the Inca's wealth, perhaps out of fear that the drink might be poisoned, the Spaniards turned the cups in their hands and spilled the *chicha* on the ground. Atahualpa was taken aback, offended, but young Pizarro and de Soto managed to allay the awkwardness. They went back to Cajamarca with three vital pieces of news: First, an enormous army attended the emperor, and it was flush with victory, in full battle order. Second, the delicately wrought golden goblets they had been proferred suggested great wealth and remarkable metallurgical sophistication. The news that exhilarated Francisco Pizarro most, however, was the third: Atahualpa had reassured them he would return to Cajamarca the next day. The Lord Inca had set his own trap.

Atahualpa was so confident that the Spaniards posed no threat that he accepted the visitors' assurances at face value. He didn't bother to arm his soldiers. Indeed, in numbers alone, the Incan army had an overwhelming advantage. The Spaniards, huddled in their quarters on the plaza as the inky night blanketed Cajamarca, trembled at the prospect of the imminent encounter. They peered out from their high perch and saw row after tidy row of shining, white tents in the valley, the campfires beside them twinkling "like a brilliantly star-studded sky." The advance party estimated Atahualpa's army at approximately 40,000, but they had said that to mitigate the alarm. It was clear that Pizarro's 170 men were looking at no fewer than 80,000. And, in their countryside escapades, they had seen evidence of the brutality of which those warriors were capable. "I myself witnessed," recalled Pizarro's cousin Pedro, "many Spaniards who, totally unaware, pissed themselves from pure terror that night."

When Atahualpa marched toward them the next day, the Spaniards were all too alert to the spectacle unfolding before them in that valley. There were roughly eight thousand Peruvians in his immediate retinue, parading in perfect formation, with gold and silver headdresses glinting in the late-afternoon sun. They sang as they marched, their voices reverberating through the hollows. As dusk began to throw long shadows over the landscape, they entered the city square, a vast, empty space of about fifty acres, embraced by long, squat buildings. Atahualpa was aloft on a colossal litter fitted with silver handles and carried by eighty richly dressed lords. His seat was surrounded by shimmering gold plates and riotously colored parrot feathers. Circling his head was the Lord Inca's traditional crown: a band with a red tassel at the brow and a cockscomb of pounded gold trembling above it. A heavy necklace of emeralds gleamed from his ample chest. He was a handsome man of about thirty, burly in stature, solemn in demeanor, with unnaturally bloodshot eyes.

Atahualpa was surprised not to find the Spaniards waiting for him in the plaza. He thought perhaps his mighty army had scared them off. In truth, they were battle ready in their armor and chain mail, hunched over their horses, hiding inside the massive buildings and lurking within the narrow alleyways. The most strapping among them, expert artilleryman Pedro de Candía, stood guard behind the imposing dais at the deepest part of the square. Puzzled, Atahualpa halted his advancing litter and called out, "Where are they?"

The first to emerge was Friar Vicente de Valverde, who hurried out toward the emperor with one of the young translators. Holding a crucifix aloft in one hand and a breviary in the other, the priest invited Atahualpa to come forward from his litter and dine with Governor Pizarro, but the emperor did not take the lure. He told the priest that he would not budge until the Spaniards had repaid him for everything they had stolen or consumed in their rampage through his kingdom. Valverde then launched into a recitation of the *requerimiento*, the mandatory cry of conquest that declared King Carlos their new ruler, Jesus Christ their savior, and warned that any effort to resist would be met with harsh measures. The translator dutifully rendered the words in Quechua. Flustered, Atahualpa stopped him midsentence and barked that his people needed no new rulers or gods. He asked what the priest was holding. Valverde came forward and handed him the holy book. The Inca turned it over in his hands but did not succeed in opening it. Ignorant of the strict etiquette demanded in the presence of a sun king, the priest reached out to assist him, and, furious, Atahualpa thwacked him on the arm. When the emperor did manage to flick open the volume, he glanced briefly at its pages, then flung it angrily to the ground. Terrified, the boy translator scurried to pick it up and hand it to the friar.

Valverde was outraged. He gathered the folds of his robe and hurried back to Pizarro. "Did you not see what just happened?" he seethed. "Go at those enemy dogs! March out! I absolve you!" That was all the provocation Pizarro needed. Just as Atahualpa stood on his litter and called to his guards to make ready to withdraw, the conquistador signaled to his artilleryman to fire the cannons into the square. The Spaniards spilled out of the buildings on horse and on foot, shouting the ancient battle cry against infidels: "Santiago!" The Peruvians, unarmed and defenseless against this onslaught, were mowed down by blades and guns where they stood, readily massacred. Pizarro's overriding goal was to take Atahualpa alive, as Cortés had taken Montezuma. He tried to pull the emperor from his seat, hacking off hands and arms as the noblemen struggled to maintain their grip on the litter. Even so, the Indians labored to carry their king, holding him up with their bleeding stumps. "Their efforts were of little avail," one chronicler reported. "Every one of them was slaughtered." Eventually, as the chaos and carnage mounted, Atahualpa was toppled to the ground and Pizarro was able to frog-march him into one of the buildings.

Panic stricken, the Peruvians tried to flee the square, but the gate was too small to allow so many thousands through at once. The conquistadors made easy victims of the rest. Those who weren't trampled were beheaded or shot. Those who broke free were chased and lanced out in the fields. As Titu Kusi Yupanki—Atahualpa's nephew—described it:

> They pulled him from his litter by force, turned it upside down, seized his insignia and headband, which among us is the crown, and took him prisoner. . . . That square was enclosed by walls and all the Indians were inside like llamas. There were a great many of them and they could not get out, nor did they have any weapons—they had not brought them because of the low opinion they held of the Spaniards; all they had were slings and ceremonial knives. . . . The Spaniards killed them all—with horses, with swords, with guns— just as one might slaughter llamas, for nobody could defend himself. From more than 10,000 men there did not escape 200. And when all were dead they took my uncle Atahualpa to a cell, where they kept him bound all night, with a chain around his neck.

In little more than two hours, which was all there remained of daylight, nearly the entire retinue was annihilated. During it all, no Indian had raised a weapon against a Spaniard. At the end of it, thousands lay dead in the square or out on the open plain, beyond Cajamarca's gates. The living were hobbled or missing arms, left to bleed to death where they fell. With the emperor held hostage, a terrible dread gripped the army in the valley, little more than a mile away. Many thousands of warriors were there—skilled and battle ready—but they were stunned, leaderless, unwilling to attack, lest their god-king be killed in retaliation.

Later, as Pizarro held Atahualpa captive in his own quarters, the Inca was asked why he had been so feckless, so trusting. He answered with a sad smile that he had anticipated a very different outcome. He had fully intended to seize the Spaniards' horses, which were the assets he most admired. He would have bred them, mastered them, used them against his enemies. He would have sacrificed a few Spaniards to the great god Sun and castrated all the rest, reducing them to menials in his household or eunuchs for his concubines. At least one historian has conjectured that the Lord Inca could not imagine otherwise. He was flush with victory, ruler of his world. Besides, why would the Spaniards, with so much to lose, risk all in a suicide mission? The odds had been so compellingly against them. Nor could Atahualpa have imagined that they would strike first, without warning or provocation, or even before a token meeting between him and Pizarro. All he had seen or heard of the Christians bespoke a rank disorganization. A lazy disposition. He hadn't imagined the guns and steel.

Pizarro's first order of business was to get the gold. With Atahualpa as virtual puppet, issuing orders at his command, Pizarro disbanded the army that waited in the valley, sent the soldiers home, and enslaved the rest, forcing a harsh new reality on the empire. "The Spaniards took all who were brave and noble and reduced us to servants, *yanakunas*," one Inca historian wrote. The complex social hierarchy of the Inca was toppled overnight, never to recover: Atahualpa's courtiers were forced to menial roles; the women, including the virgin order of *acllas*, were systematically assaulted, creating an ongoing culture of rampant sexual abuse. Having brought no women with them, the Spaniards appropriated them at will, conjugating with them freely and creating a new breed of human: the mestizo. Throughout, what was uppermost in the conquistadors' minds was the wealth they could take home. Pizarro's troops raided Atahualpa's rest house and military camp, making a clean sweep of all that was gold or silver. In a frenzy approaching delirium, Hernando de Soto seized "eighty thousand pesos of gold, seven thousand marks of silver, and fourteen emeralds. The gold and silver was in monstrous effigies, large and small dishes, pitchers, jugs, basins, and large drinking vessels. Atahualpa recognized these as his table service, and commented that the Indians who had fled the encampment had taken a great deal more."

Cajamarca was looted, its buildings scoured for anything that shone.

The dead were stripped of their headdresses and jewelry; the living, forced to render up more. Spanish squadrons rode out into the countryside, demanding all precious metals, burning villages as they went. Atahualpa, who craved his freedom as urgently as Pizarro craved treasure, soon saw that the glittering stuff interested his captors far more than service to King Carlos or the forced imposition of Christianity. He understood that he himself was no more than a disposable convenience toward this burning goal; it was only a matter of time before they killed him and moved on. In a desperate attempt to save his own life, he offered his famous ransom: one large room stacked to the ceiling with gold; two more filled with silver. Pizarro eagerly agreed.

Clearly, Atahualpa believed that all the metalwork of the kingdom would be meager recompense for his liberty. He also believed that Pizarro would honor the bargain—that he would take his booty and go home. The Inca ordered his people to systematically strip all temples and palaces of their treasures and bring them to Cajamarca under strict supervision. Llamas weighed down with the empire's gold and silver streamed into the plaza for months, as Spaniards marveled at their good fortune. Never before in Spain's thirty-five-year sack of the New World had such magnificent lucre been imagined, much less seen. All of Columbus's dreams and Cortés's plunder combined did not approach it. From the sacred Sun Temple of Cuzco's Coricancha alone, a ton and a half of gold was hacked from the walls and sent to navigate the treacherous Andean passes on the backs of slaves and beasts. Huascar, reckoning Atahualpa's enemies to be his friends, offered to send the Spaniards more, but Atahualpa, hearing about this from his spies, dispatched two generals and an army of forty thousand to stop him. Huascar was killed soon after, as he made his way to Pizarro in chains.

With a civil war afoot and Peru's difficult terrain to cross, it took far longer to fill the rooms than Atahualpa had hoped. For eight months, he endured a soul-crushing captivity, struggling to answer Pizarro's demands and ingratiate himself with promises. He had assured the governor that it would take no more than two months to deliver the ransom, which meant he would be free by mid-January 1533. But by May, the metal was still in transit. By June, the mounting spoils had yielded a formidable collection of art and ornamentation—seven tons of gold and thirteen of silver—a pile no Inca would have valued for its inherent worth, but any European monarch would have yearned to have at his disposal. By 1534, the conquistadors had wrung an estimated ten metric tons of twenty-two-carat gold and seventy tons of silver from the cities of Cajamarca and Cuzco. In today's market, that plunder would have been worth approximately a half billion dollars.

The gleaming prize was guarded jealously by Pizarro himself in that adjoining warehouse; no other Spaniard could lay claim to it. As months passed, he ordered local goldsmiths to start melting the silver into tidy ingots, just as Cortés had commanded the Mexicans to do a dozen years before. In June they began the melting and assaying of gold. Every day, the Indian metalworkers were forced to render thousands of master-pieces into a quarter ton of shippable bullion, destroying the painstaking artistry they had achieved in the first place. By the middle of July, it was finished. With the exception of a few objects that were put aside for King Carlos as evidence, not a single piece survived. The raw, refined metal bricks that emerged from the furnaces were engraved with the royal stamp, ensuring that 10 percent of the precious harvest had been separated for delivery to the Crown.

In the interim, the governor's brother Hernando Pizarro was sent to find the fount of the Incan riches—the gold and silver mines—as well as raid the ancient Temple of the Creator God at Pachacamac. As it turned out, Pachacamac offered little more than an infinitely dark cave, a ghoulish sacrificial slab, and a startled cluster of holy men, one of whom was dispatched to Cajamarca to answer to Atahualpa for having failed to protect him. But the mines were a different story. As narrow a role as they'd had in the world of the Incas, they were now the be-all and end-all of the world to come. By the time Hernando Pizarro returned to report his findings, the ransom had been collected, Atahualpa had been garroted and killed, Almagro had arrived from the Caribbean with more troops and new demands, but the way of the future was lit and clear. Spain's encounter with the Inca Empire would spur a flow of precious metals the likes of which the Old World had seldom seen. That influx from Peru and Mexico would go on to fuel the birth of global capitalism, establish the financial viability of Europe, pique the commercial appetites of Asia, and polarize the social dynamic of Latin America for centuries to come.

POTOSÍ
1545–1700

*Stone upon stone on a bedrock of rags? Coal upon coal, and in its depths,
tears? Fire in the gold, and in that gold, a trembling drop of red blood?*
—Pablo Neruda, "The Heights of Machu Picchu"

The conquest of America's great civilizations—the Inca, Maya, Mexica, and Muísca—had a profound effect on Spain and, in time, the entire world. Rugged soldiers of fortune became affluent landowners; an ever-larger wave of adventurers and royal overseers poured into the hemisphere to win more wealth for themselves and the Crown. By 1542, America had been divided into two viceroyalties that answered directly to the king: the Viceroyalty of New Spain (composed of the colonies in North and Central America, as well as Venezuela and the Philippines) and the Viceroyalty of Peru (which took up the entire continent, from Panama to Patagonia, except for Venezuela and Brazil, the latter of which was Portuguese). There was still much money to make, more laurels and privileges to collect: Diego Alvarado left Cortés in order to get richer with Pizarro. Hernando de Soto left Peru to find greater treasures in Florida. Francisco Pizarro became so prosperous, having assigned one-fifth of all the Peruvian plunder to himself, that eventually he was in a position to extend personal loans to the king. The vast holdings of Hernán Cortés, from the sands of the Sonora Desert to the jungles of Lacandón, made him the most prosperous mogul in Mexico. The greed was infectious, and with it came rampant exploitation. Wherever gold, silver, or copper could be found, native populations were compelled to dig more, yield more, in hellish conditions that would have been deemed intolerable by Indian rulers. Any early restraints on human abuse that conquistadors imposed gingerly in the name of Jesus were abandoned, and, as Indians were killed off in alarming numbers, a brisk traffic in African slaves began. Between 1500 and 1800, five times more blacks than whites entered the Americas—all of them as human chattel.

The conquistadors and slavers learned quickly that blacks were more suited to field work, to laboring in the sugar, indigo, cacao, and coffee plantations; barrel-chested Andeans had a distinct advantage mining at high altitudes, where oxygen was scarce and the cold winds, perpetual. So it was that the demands of faraway masters came to shape the social landscape. Much as the Incas had displaced entire populations to meet the military and engineering needs of the Tahuantinsuyu, Spain now imposed its metal and commercial ambitions on the hemisphere. The goal was to make the conquered peoples extract as much mineral wealth as they could. Native Americans were forced into reductions, separated from their families, herded and sent to labor wherever the colonists decreed. But, in a way, the slave, too, would have a firm hold on his master: by the middle of the sixteenth century, the Spanish economy was almost entirely dependent on Mexican and Peruvian ore and on the labor of American Indians. A spirited flow of New World bullion had bankrolled King Carlos's wars, created a buoyant trade from Panama to Peking, and transformed Spain into a money forge that would drive Europe into the modern age.

Latin American indigenous cultures, which had lived in splendid isolation for centuries, now became radical agents of change for regions they never knew existed. As the Indians quickly learned, they themselves were totally expendable; it was the earth on which they stood that had become the desirable commodity. For five centuries to come, its veins would be bled, its viscera extracted, refined, and sent elsewhere. At first, the conqueror's obsession was gold, the elusive chimera of El Dorado—a stubborn belief in the myth that a trove of it awaited them somewhere in the middle of the continent. But soon enough it became clear that the most prodigal asset in the Indies was its silver, and it lay deep underground. Nowhere was this more evident than in Potosí, where the craze for white ore became frantic.

Legend has it that Diego Huallpa, an indigenous miner traveling from the Spanish quarry at Porco on a bitter cold night in January 1545, built a fire on Potosí's rust red flank to warm himself. By morning, a puddle of molten silver had gathered around the fire's smoldering ashes. Thrilled by this fortuitous find, Huallpa managed to scratch out a considerable pile of ore over the course of the next few weeks, but he soon realized that he needed help to amass and transport his cache. A fellow laborer who assisted him on the assumption that he would share in the profits eventually squabbled with Huallpa over the size of his share and, to settle scores, revealed the serendipitous discovery to a Spanish overseer. The large-scale excavation of Potosí began shortly thereafter.

A mere dozen years after Pizarro stepped foot on Peruvian soil, the conquistadors had a fully developed system in place for extracting metals and forcing the indigenous population into the mines to do it. Gold had been scarce, but silver was plentiful. So much so, that failing to find iron, they were forced to shoe their horses with the precious white substance. One conquistador whose jaw was blown off during a battle with the Incas had his chin reconstructed entirely in the metal. In the Mexican silver mines of Zacatecas and Taxco, production was so great by the 1540s that Spain soon commanded the bullion market in Europe. But the miners of the Inca, unlike those of the Mexica, had centuries of experience with mining and amalgamation. As a result, a silver bonanza sprang up in Potosí.

Immigrants flocked to the Andean highlands from every corner of Europe, hoping to strike it rich or at least profit from the increasingly wealthy magnates who gathered on that dusty, rockbound terrain. Miners and overseers were soon joined by merchants and mayordomos, tailors and lace makers, cabinetmakers and glassblowers, singers and dancers, countesses and whores. By 1574, a steady influx of Indian captives and African slaves was generating the great majority of the world's silver, much of it gouged from the precipitous red flanks of Potosí's Cerro Rico, all of it melted down and transformed into Spanish *reales*. Mule trains and caravans of llamas scrolled across the altiplano, over the vaulting mountain peaks, making the five-week trek to the Pacific port of Callao. Creaky, rat-infested ships then ferried the precious cargo to the western coast of Panama, where the silver was either transported up the coast to Acapulco and Veracruz or across the jungle to the Caribbean coast. At Cartagena, it was loaded onto galleons and sent across the Atlantic to Seville, which, in a profligate burst of spending, hurried the hard-won bullion through banks in London or Amsterdam to merchants in Poland, Constantinople, and Russia.

As Latin American silver shot through the marketplaces of Europe, the settlements in Mexico and Peru mushroomed into great Spanish viceroyalties. To keep a strong grip on them, conquistadors stripped locals of all power, constructed churches atop their temples, palaces atop their places of government, and redirected their labor to the mines. Cortés's and Pizarro's conquests were soon producing 99 percent of all the silver in the hemisphere. In the course of the next two centuries, Potosí alone would ship forty thousand tons of the white ore to Europe. Latin America as a whole would fuel Europe's banks with 136,000 metric tons of silver, a full 80 percent of the world's output. The hauls were so large, so valuable—a single galleon might carry two million pesos—that massive convoys of more than sixty ships became necessary to protect them from pirates on the high seas. The danger was constant, the piracy lucrative, and a brisk commerce was soon created by English and Dutch privateers whose governments encouraged the rapine. Most infamous among pirates, perhaps, was the English adventurer Francis Drake, who sailed the Caribbean, trading African slaves for tobacco, sugar, and cotton, but turned his sights farther south as the frenzy for silver grew. He raided the mule trains as they crossed overland from Potosí. He attacked the port of Cartagena as cargo was loaded into the ships, making off with vast payloads of bullion. So coveted was silver in Europe that Queen Elizabeth I rewarded Drake's robberies with a knighthood.

It was this itinerant silver, product of Native American and, later, African hands, that became the vanguard of global capitalism and eventually swept northern Europe into the industrial age. But it may also have been the first major instance of racial exploitation for global profit. The dark races produced the currency; the whites reaped the returns. An intense theological debate soon arose in Europe about the legitimacy of the Spanish conquest, the treatment of native peoples, and the essential nature of the indigenous races. Were they human, after all? Or were they—as Europe had decided long before—like black Africans, insensate beasts of burden? But for all the moral intensity of the debate, it turned out to be all talk. The rank exploitation continued. Eventually Seville passed injunctions to mitigate the abuse, but conquistadors simply looked the other way and carried on with the cruelty, leading the very Italian Pope Paul IV to say in a fit of pique that Spaniards were "heretics, schismatics, accursed of God, the Offspring of Jews and Marranos, the very scum of the earth." It was a calumny the English and Dutch were only too happy to promulgate.

By 1570, as England grappled with questions of religious tolerance, and Queen Elizabeth turned a cautious eye to foreign commerce, Spain was already carrying on a highly profitable trade with China—all of it based on New World silver. As much as two million to three million pesos were making their way, legally and illegally, to Manila and Peking every six months from Acapulco. Three decades later, that figure multiplied six times. Striking a productive vein in Potosí could fuel an exuberant economic boom across the Pacific, and Asian cities began to flourish as a result, profiting from the traffic. One traveler reported that the international markets in Southeast Asia were so spirited that more than eighty languages were being spoken in the port of Malacca. Fleets that shipped silver to the Orient would sail back freighted with silks, porcelain, sandalwood, and ivory, so that the palatial houses of Mexican and Peruvian silver magnates were—quite absurdly for that era—bursting with Chinese and Japanese art. Even the wounded sailors, convalescing in ramshackle hospitals, were eating off Ming porcelain plates.

By 1600, Potosí held a population that rivaled London's and Tokyo's. It was more congested than the bustling port of Venice, easily the largest urban concentration in the Western Hemisphere. But the Imperial City, as King Carlos called it, was also known for its drunkenness, flamboyance, and wanton degeneracy. A mere eleven years after Diego Huallpa's campfire discovery, Potosí celebrated the coronation of King Carlos's successor—King Philip II—with a wild, decadent party that lasted twenty-eight days and cost eight million pesos. By the middle of the seventeenth century, when the Massachusetts Bay Colony was still a fledgling settlement struggling to maintain its tenuous hold on America, Potosí had produced such a vast abundance of silver that its name had entered the literary canon: Cervantes, in his immortal classic *Don Quixote*, coined the phrase "Vale un Potosí!" Rich as Potosí. There was nothing grander, more exuberant, more filled with promise than that ruddy brown hump of South American ground.

Greed followed on greed. To capitalize on his success and grow the profits, King Philip needed miners—legions of them. In 1569 he sent Viceroy Francisco de Toledo to install a more efficient system of forced labor in Peru. Toledo ended up using the system of reductions, which Spain had established in the Caribbean—to drive whole populations of the indigenous to places where hard labor was needed. The initial argument was that, in order to Christianize heathens, the Spaniards needed to disrupt local traditions, destroy the prevailing culture, and break down all tribal ties, but the reality was that reductions were a convenient way to herd the indigenous into work gangs and force them to pay tributes. In order to marshal the massive silver production that Spain now demanded, Toledo revived the ancient *mita* (*mitmaq*) system, which the Incas had used to coerce the conquered to work their fields, build their roads, and fight their wars.

Toledo's *mita* in Potosí became the largest, most crushing system of labor exploitation in the Spanish colonies. All indigenous males between eighteen and fifty years of age who inhabited the two-hundred-square-mile expanse from Peru to Argentina were wrenched from their homes, marched in chains across the altiplano, and made to toil in the mines of Potosí. Some fled this fate, but most hardly resisted, accustomed as they were to the massive migrations—and punishing taxes—the Incas had imposed for generations. For all the familiarity of these practices, however, mining had never been so ruthless under the Incas. It had been rotational; the mita had been intermittent; there was a certain lenience in play. All the same, just as the Indians came to understand the overweening avarice of their conquerors, the Spaniards were understanding a crucial acquiescence in the Indians. Throughout the Americas, with very few exceptions, it was merely a matter of killing the indigenous leaders, purging the nobility, and then extending the oppression that was already in place. Forcibly, swiftly, the conquistadors collapsed an intricate hierarchy into one powerless underclass. For the Spanish, the new social order represented a formidable victory; for the indigenous, a catastrophe. A genocide. As one Inca nobleman lamented to his captor:

> Your excellence, I am the captain of these people . . . and yet I have received many insults since Christians entered these lands. Before, we were lords, now we are slaves. Not only do Christians want us to serve you as we were once served—as gentlemen and officers—but

now we have been degraded to one humble class. You want all of us to bear your cargoes, be your bricklayers, build your houses, be your laborers, sow your fields. Think if it's truly just to do us this grievous wrong.

Eventually that same system would force natives to work the deadly mercury mines to harvest the quicksilver necessary for amalgamation. The indigenous were not only compelled to pound rock for twelve months in the dank crawl spaces of Potosí, they were dragooned for two more months to toil in the dread Santa Barbara mercury mines of Huancavelíca, more than one thousand miles away, in what is now Peru. Most became bound to those mines for life, as were their wives and descendants. Trapped in the frigid black of a mercury shaft, a miner was likely to lose his teeth, go blind, and suffer an early, excruciating death. As his corpse decomposed, puddles of mercury would be found in his grave. With women and children stirring mercury with their feet, entire populations risked eradication. It became clear that to be consigned to these places was to be sent to slaughter. Legions of Indians disappeared into the mountains, preferring starvation or death by freezing to the scourge of the mercury mines. Mothers broke their children's bones to render them unfit to mine. As strict as they were, the Incas had never subjected their peons to such terrors. A priest who visited Santa Barbara in the 1630s described the mines as "living images of death, black shades of eternal hell." Two centuries later, the conditions were hardly better. A British soldier passing through observed that to be made to mine was a virtual death sentence. Many a man of the cloth would claim that the overlords, too, inhabited a parallel inferno: the corruption, cupidity, venality, and drunkenness of Potosí's silver moguls had made affluence a hell of a different kind.

By 1700, the bubble had burst. Potosí went dry. The rich abandoned the withered teat of Cerro Rico for more promising lodes—a gold rush in Brazil, a silver boom in Mexico—and the city slumped into a pitiful shadow of itself. By 1825, when Simón Bolívar's armies finally liberated those lands, it was clear Potosí had been deep into free fall. Like the fabled empire of King Ozymandias, it slid into prolonged dilapidation, all the more poignant for the city's coat of arms, which crowed over that arid ruin: "I am rich Potosí. Envy of all kings." Potosí was but one in a long series of booms and busts that the region's mining would experience in centuries to come. Spain had been first to extract America's mineral riches and appropriate them for a global market, but other foreigners would follow, and precious metals would continue to slip through Latin America's fingers before heading for distant shores.

In the end, Spain was little transformed by the torrent of silver that coursed into its ports on its way elsewhere. Kings directed their fifths to finance their holy wars against a growing wave of European Protestantism. They used them to indulge sybaritic habits, enrich their friends, reward the nobility. The flow was out rather than in, as Latin America's hard-won silver paid for the court's every whim. Silver enabled the Hapsburgs to engage in wars that gripped Europe for the greater part of a century; it imported luxuries that only princes might use; it brought on an inflation so massive that it eventually bankrupted Spain. No industrial advances came of that silver windfall; no bridges, no roads, no factories; no true betterment of life for the ordinary Spaniard. As one seventeenth-century economist lamented at the height of the metal influx, "Out of its great wealth, the republic of Spain has extracted utter poverty." The "easy money" had been for the happy few.

Those who truly profited in the end were the English and Dutch, who broadcast an unremittingly negative view of Spain, rode the crest of Spanish America's economic stimulus, and went on to produce steam engines, textile mills, ironworks, shipbuilding yards, steel foundries, and powerful, international banks. In 1785 a newly independent United States of America signaled its economic ambitions by fixing its dollar firmly to the value of the Spanish peso. By the early 1800s, it, too, had joined the era of mechanization. But Spain remained stubbornly agricultural, never joining the industrial age it had labored so mightily to facilitate. In the end, its romance with New World silver actually may have promoted its irrevocable decline rather than consolidated its power. King Carlos I's grandiose motto, *"Plus Ultra"*—"Ever Beyond"—took on new meaning as the empire's riches spilled out and away, ultimately impoverishing the country for the foreseeable future, building fortunes in territories beyond Spain's control.

VETA MADRE, MOTHER LODE
1800–1824

> *One does not establish a dictatorship in order to safeguard a revolution;*
> *one makes a revolution in order to establish a dictatorship.*
> —George Orwell, *Nineteen Eighty-Four*

Latin America's conviction that it needed to break free from the monarchy that had shackled it for three hundred years didn't come until the 1800s, but the logic of liberation had been spelled out a half century before by French Enlightenment thinker Montesquieu. "The Indies and Spain may be two powers under the same ruler," he wrote in 1748, "but the Indies are the principal, while Spain is no more than an accessory. To bind a principal to an accessory is a pointless political exercise. The Indies will always be the more compelling power." It was becoming clear to all but the Spanish factotums: Latin American labor had been the animating spirit of the age—the dynamo, the genie—making faraway kings rich, transforming all Europe into an economic engine. The principal was the people, the muscle, the backs, the work. The Americas needed Spain no more.

No one appreciated this more keenly than the Creoles—*los criollos*: the white, American-born rich who managed the mines, ran the haciendas, and produced the wealth, yet had no real power or voice in their own government. For centuries, colonial rule had been kept strictly in the hands of Spain's emissaries, merchants, or midlevel functionaries with little to recommend them beyond the fact that they had been born on Spanish soil. Bright, educated Creoles with deep roots in the Americas had to submit to an ever-revolving door of these lesser masters. Only the Spanish-born were allowed to govern, trade, own stores, or sell goods. No American was permitted to sell for his own profit on the streets, much less plant grapes, establish vineyards, make spirits, grow tobacco or olive trees. Spain fiercely suppressed all American entrepreneurship. It brooked no competition and forced brutal regulations on American initiatives, for it was earning the equivalent of billions of dollars a year by obliging its colonies to buy even the most basic goods from Spain.

Creoles could see that very different histories were being made elsewhere. Their counterparts in North America had shed predatory masters, fought a revolution, and won. In Europe, French commoners had shucked the status quo and sent their king and queen to the guillotine. To the south, Brazil, which was now furnishing 80 percent of all gold circulating in Europe, had begun to chafe under its iron-fisted, Portuguese bosses. Yet Spanish America was singlehandedly—dutifully—continuing to fuel Madrid's wars and caprices with its colossal reserves of silver.

Indeed, by 1800, a veritable torrent of silver flowed from Veracruz to Havana to Cádiz. Never in the history of Spanish America had so much ore been extracted to secure Spain's survival. Having laid waste to Potosí, Madrid now latched onto Mexico as its prize, a fecund host to which the Crown became resolutely, parasitically affixed. The Veta Madre—as the mother lode at very heart of Central America was known—became Spain's new fiscal mammary. Even so, all the silver of Mexico would not be enough: in 1804, finding himself strapped for cash, the Spanish king, Ferdinand VII, imposed a punishing new tax, carried out largely by the Catholic Church and requiring Mexican mining magnates to hand over a steady stream of pesos to line the royal purse. These Creole tycoons, whose accumulated wealth rivaled that of the most moneyed classes in Europe, now provided the king with a dizzying 250 million silver pesos in the course of a few decades, for which they were compensated with titles of nobility. The Creoles surrendered their metal fortunes, coughed up personal savings, and in the bargain were dubbed counts, dukes, and marquises. But they still had no political power.

In the autumn of 1807, when Napoleon I invaded Spain and put its king under arrest, the Creoles and rebels of Latin America saw their window of opportunity. Galvanized by Spain's swift emasculation and paralysis—an unexpected bit of good fortune—they sparked a rolling war for independence that, for the better part of twenty years, convulsed the hemisphere from California to Cape Horn, the southernmost tip of South America. But even when the violence ceased, the liberation of more than a dozen republics did not usher in an era of peace and prosperity. Freedom did not convert the Americas into a vast economic force for its own profit. Quite the contrary. After the revolutions had expelled Spain, the victory cries had died down, and white Creoles managed to snatch liberty from the black and brown hands that had won it, a bloody-minded era followed. The wars of independence could not have been won without vast armies of black and Indian slaves, yet that went ignored. Revolutionary heroes were assassinated or driven to ruin. Generals took power, and fledgling governments began to spar about the new borders. Racial violence erupted and was tamped down, violently, by the very whites who had dominated before.

The great mines, as a result, fell to utter ruin. The prolific veins of the Veta Madre, which had yielded 342 million pesos in the course of the previous century, were now choked with debris, their shafts flooded and useless, their miners dispersed by war. The famed silver and gold harvests of the New World plummeted to a trickle. In the majestic cordillera of the Andes, the mines of Peru, Colombia, and Bolivia were either abandoned or demolished, first through war and then through intermittent waves of anarchy. Once financial engines of the world, Peru and Mexico now fell into postrevolutionary chaos. Mexico, rent by cycles of brutality and lawlessness, would survive thirty-eight governments in its first twenty-five years of freedom. Peru—the anxious heart of a gutted empire—proceeded to have twenty presidents in twenty years.

The principles of Enlightenment—freedom, democracy, reason—which had been battle cries for the Latin American liberators, were tossed to the wayside as rich whites scrambled to appropriate the wealth and power the Spaniards had left behind. Seizing all privileges, they held them fast, consigning Indians and blacks to virtual slavery. Just as the conquistadors had adopted the dictatorial ways of the Incas and the Aztecs, Creoles now borrowed Madrid's concept of absolute rule. The extraordinary sacrifices made by black and Indian revolutionary armies were forgotten, and the darker races were returned to the rung they had inhabited since the conquest: the very bottom.

As this difficult history settled, other prejudices stiffened. Latin America, having galvanized an economy that had connected Europe, the Middle East, and Asia, now began to be perceived as the troubled spawn of Spain; the unruly orphan of a failed power. It was a minor actor, no longer a "principal" in the wider world. What it needed in this unfolding phase was guidance, management, a new supervisor. London bankers rushed in with loans, making Mexico a bit player in Britain's vast economic empire. "*We* slip in between!" the British foreign minister crowed gleefully, "plant ourselves in Mexico . . . we link once more America to Europe." Thomas Jefferson's smug suggestion that the United States might want to snatch Latin America for itself "piece by piece" began to prove true as the growing giant turned a hungry eye to the south. The rest raveled quickly: by the close of the nineteenth century, Brazil's gold rush had come and gone; tin and copper gradually replaced silver and gold in the Andes. Bird dung—or nitrates—now served as the region's most promising mineral trade; a war would be fought over the dung islands that dotted the Pacific from Chile to Peru. Foreign opportunists flooded in to pick at the leavings. One British company impounded black slaves to work the pits of Minas Gerais, once the most coveted gold mines of Brazil. Other British corporations moved quickly to take over Mexico's prize silver deposits. Even as the United States massacred its own Indian population at the Battle of Wounded Knee in 1890, American enterprises were investing hundreds of millions of dollars in mines where Mexican Indians labored. A rabid racism froze in place throughout the hemisphere, and Latin America dug in for another century of pillage.

CHAPTER 5

BLIND AMBITION

In the long course of history many substances have been used as currency. . . . Only two, the precious metals gold and silver, have endured.

—Ludwig von Mises

Legend has it that Ai Apaec, the creator god of the Moche people—a fierce, powerful civilization that inhabited the rim of the Pacific during the first century—fell helplessly in love with Pachamama, the goddess who ruled the earth and all riches that lay below. He was a cunning god: part spider, part reptile, part jaguar. A fiend with long fangs and an insatiable lust for human sacrifice, Ai Apaec had a fondness for lopping off heads. Yet some say he was the fount of life itself. Snakes coiled from his ears, horns jutted from his head. Scorpions, lizards, and crabs were his preferred companions. A notched belt circled his waist. He was god of high places, and his elements were mountain and sky, but he was also drawn—as yin to yang, male to female—to the dark, secret passages of the earth.

They say that Ai Apaec prized mountains because it was on those promontories that Pachamama reached up to receive him. They also say that come winter, he would betray his moon wife to plunge deep into Pachamama's loins, boring his way through the loam and rock to spill his seed on the deepest part of her being. Eventually the spawn of that union would emerge in surprising ways: copious harvests, rich deposits of clay, streams teeming with gold. But the journey from mountain to the heart of Pachamama would not be easy: Ai Apaec would need to claw his way through black universes, vanquish monsters, and offer peace to strange gods, and brotherhood to his spirit creatures: the owl, the gull, the vulture.

As remarkable as it seems, given the relative isolation of ancient American cultures, versions of this story appear throughout the hemisphere at different points in time. The names and details may differ, but the deities are recognizable: creator gods who live in the skies but have a pronounced attraction to the underworld. At the site of the renowned archeological marvel Chavín de Huántar, for instance—a sacred sanctuary tucked into the Andes 250 miles from the Moche ruins on the Pacific coast—there is a statue of just such an idol, although the civilization that worshiped it preceded the Moche by a thousand years. The only way to reach Chavín de Huántar is to follow a labyrinth of pitch-black tunnels to the very heart of darkness. There, in the temple's airless penumbra, is a towering sculpture with a fearsome face, long fangs, and large, round eyes cast skyward. Its right hand is raised, the left one points down, signaling heaven and earth. The fingers have long, reptilian claws. Serpents spring from two protuberances on his head. He wears a low, notched belt.

More than 2,000 miles north, in the depths of the Yucatán jungle, a Mayan divinity bears a striking similarity to those Andean likenesses. His name is Kinich Ahau. The Mexican god has long fangs; a serpent springs from his head; his taloned hands are pointed in opposite directions: the right one up, left hand down. His large eyes squint at the sun. A macaw is his spirit brother. Often he is portrayed with insects circling his head. He is the fearsome jaguar god of the underworld, also known as the Night Sun. But he is also the dark star that lights the world—the blazing heavenly body that plummets to earth, descends to its entrails, and begins a subterranean journey that goes from west to east, to rise again on the other horizon.

For yet another American culture—the Aztec—the earth itself is Coatlicue, a goddess who combines attributes of Pachamama and the creator god. Her skirt is a mantle of writhing snakes. Her fingers and toes are clawed. Her neck is festooned with skulls, human hearts. Spiders, scorpions, centipedes are her companions. She is life and death in one; our birth mother with an insatiable lust for human sacrifice. Her teats sag with the effort of feeding the children she will ultimately devour.

There is a reason why Indians of Latin America are hesitant to gouge the earth beneath their feet. It is from her that all life flows; to her that all life will return. Ride a microbus down the winding roads of the Andean sierra toward a tunnel, and you may see a devout farmer dutifully get off, walk around the bluff, and meet the bus on the other side. The others on the bus will be patient about this reluctance to mindlessly penetrate ground—the roots of indigenous cultures run deep—they know he feels it would be a violation of the Earth Mother to do otherwise.

So it was for Juan Ochochoque and those who labored beside him in the gold mines that pock the frigid peak they call Sleeping Beauty. Their fickle home, La Rinconada, the highest human habitation in the world, is little more than a precarious cluster of tin and stone that girds the heights of Mount Ananea. And yet, for all the altitude, Juan and his cohort are creatures of a life lived below. Like Ai Apaec, lord of the mountains, these miners inhabit the skies but suckle the earth's dark heart.

Come the keen, menacing blue just before dawn, when Leonor set about making his breakfast, Juan would always feel a certain dread. Soon he would be plunging deep into the flank of that glacial mountain, hunching his way down its burrows to hack at the stubborn rock. He always brought a few leaves of coca and a bit of *chicha* to offer Pachamama against the offense. Now and then, he took part in the *wilancha*, a ritual sacrifice to the mother in which snow-white llamas are slaughtered at the mine's entrance, their beating hearts ripped from their chests, their gushing blood smeared on the verge of the jagged orifice where men, and only men, can pass into the darkness. At the main tunnel's deepest point, where the way parts to take miners to far arteries of Sleeping Beauty's loins, they will find the trickster god El Tío, "the Uncle," the idol whose face—as jolly as it is sinister—reminds them that luck is often the brother of hazard; that danger can bring opportunity. With El Tío's favor, the rock slide that someday will bury them, the glacier that will crush their bones, the explosion that will splatter them into eternity might be avoided today. All these catastrophes are certain to come eventually. But today—who knows?—they might find a hidden vein of gold. El Tío will decide.

El Tío is god of the mines, lord of the underworld. Horns jut from his head. A miner's light glares from his cap. His teeth are fangs. His arms are festooned with snakes. He inhabits a universe of subterranean creatures. He is Ai Apaec, night crawler, web maker, venomous creature. Comfortable in the Earth Mother's gut, he commands the flow. Since the early days of the conquest, priests have called him a demon—a devil who reigned over the mines—and, to accommodate Catholic overseers, miners gave him horns, a goat's head, a goatee. But he is not the face of evil. He is not the fallen angel of Christian lore. Like Kinich Ahau and Coatlicue, he is half light, half darkness. Half rising sun, half night pilgrim. He is what might rescue a miner or send him to oblivion. Part mother, part monster. He is a Pan-American god.

So it is that the collective memory of ancient divinities lives on through millennia, connecting the green of the Yucatán to the arid exuberance of the Andes. These echoes may not be recorded in history books, for history is ever told by the conqueror, but the evidence is there if we open our eyes.

Take the Spanish word *Tío*, for instance. Uncle. Early chronicles tell us that Indians had difficulty pronouncing *D*; it did not exist in their languages. So the Spanish word for God—*Dios*—was often rendered as *Tios*, and when terrifying semblances of El Tío emerged in the mine shafts, the Spaniards dismissed him—along with all the other underworld gods—as Lucifer. But the indigenous realm is not the Spanish realm; its gods are not the God of Scripture. It may be in places as mundane as mines that these differences are most apparent.

For Juan Ochochoque, El Tío was a useful idol. In a netherworld in which fate can mete out a miserable death or a shining nugget of gold, a man needs a trickster god. El Tío, who knows full well that all miners are violators living on borrowed time, might look favorably on a supplicant today. Juan always remembered to save a few extra coca leaves, bring a cigarette, and lay these tokens of faith at El Tío's feet.

BEGGARS ON A BENCH OF GOLD

"¡Oh, Perú de metal y de melancolía!"
—Federico García Lorca, "A Carmela, la Peruana"

Peru is booming these days. It is one of the fastest-growing economies in Latin America. At times in past decades, the country has boasted one of the highest growth rates in the world, rivaling the colossal engines of

China and India. It is one of the world's leading miners of silver, copper, and lead. It is Latin America's most exuberant fount of gold. It is an up-and-coming producer of natural gas. It harvests and sells more fish than any other country on the planet, save China.

But it is gold that has gripped Peru all over again—that age-old fever that fueled the conquest, stymied the Incas, and set a defining course for a hemisphere. More than five hundred years later, the rush is in full frenzy: a blind, overriding ambition not unlike the one that fueled the dreams of Pizarro. Minerals are the country's main export; mining, its principal source of foreign exchange. Rushing to accommodate the caprices of an alien hunger, Peru is once more defined by what it can dig out and ship away.

In 2009 Peru extracted a total of 182 tons of gold from its mountains and rain forests, the highest production of gold in all of South America. In 2016 it produced less. Every year has seen a drop in output, which is hardly surprising, since there is so little of this precious stuff in the world. "In all history," one source reports, "only 161,000 tons of gold have been mined, barely enough to fill two Olympic-size swimming pools." More than half of the world's supply has been extracted in the last fifty years. Little wonder that the price of gold has soared in past years; little wonder, too, that multinational companies have scrambled to wrest it from remote corners of the globe.

But multinational giants are not the only ones to join the hunt. Economists have calculated that illegal mining operations run by upstart bosses such as those who employ the likes of Juan Ochochoque have increased by more than five times in the last ten years. It is an expansion largely due to organized crime. Investigators report that more than a quarter of all gold mined in Peru is illegal. But the percentages are higher elsewhere: 33 percent of all gold mined in Bolivia, 75 percent of gold mined in Ecuador, 80 percent of gold mined in Colombia, and 90 percent of Venezuelan gold is produced illegally. Meanwhile, the production from legal mines, from which whole nations might profit, has fallen drastically during the same period. "Illegal mining is crowding out the legal," one Peruvian economist lamented. Improvised, primitive, toxic mines have claimed a firm place in the boom, although they wreak havoc on the environment. In Peru, illegal mining is now twice as profitable as trafficking cocaine.

The repercussions are punishing. No logger, no matter how destructive—or any other breed of tree-clearing agricultural entrepreneur, for that matter—has cut as ruinous a path through the nerve centers of biodiversity as an illegal miner does in this part of the world. Deforestation from mining in the Peruvian Amazon alone tripled from more than five thousand acres per year to more than fifteen thousand each year after the gold rush that followed the 2008 global financial crisis. The depredations have not abated. Massive swaths of rain forest are lost annually to mining, and that amount continues to exceed the damage done by other industries. Depending on whether you stand on the Brazilian side of the Amazon or the Peruvian side, that's equivalent to wiping out an area the size of Manhattan in five days, or the entire metropolitan area of Denver in a month. Except that the planet doesn't rely on Manhattan or Denver as much as it does on this humid stretch of earthly terrain. The Amazon rain forest is nothing less than the planet's lungs. Home to more than half of the species of the world's plants and animals, it cleans up our global emissions, flushes out carbon dioxide. Without it, we cannot breathe.

But illegal miners often go where the rest of us fear to tread, and the Amazon jungle is one of those places. The impossibly high flanks of the Andes are another. Juan's bosses staked their claim on the godforsaken peak of Mount Ananea. It is why La Rinconada's mines alone yield as much as ten tons of gold a year—worth up to $460 million on the open market. It is why the number of inhabitants on La Rinconada's icy, forbidding rock—less than ten thousand when Juan Ochochoque arrived twenty-five years ago—has multiplied so frantically ever since.

Today there are seventy thousand souls in that soaring aerie. More than half work the frozen tunnels of Mount Ananea, most are with families, and all are in the service of a buoyant global market. There is no legal oversight, no benevolent employer, no operational government, no water, no sewer system, no functioning police. Every year, more and more newcomers press into that lawless encampment, building huts on the near vertical cant of a dizzying promontory—harboring hope that this may be the day they strike a gleaming vein, cleave open a wall to find a fist-sized nugget. They think they'll stay only as long as it takes to find one. There are just enough stories of random fortune to keep the insanity alive.

Peruvians call the mines at La Rinconada "informal," a euphemism for illegal, a status without which Peru's economy would come to a screeching halt. For fifty years now, the Peruvian government has turned a blind eye to increasingly wretched conditions in this remote community, its agents unwilling to scale the heights, brave the cold, take control. Even the Catholic Church has given up sending priests. In the interim, what was once a region of crystalline lakes and leaping fish has become a Bosch-like world that challenges credulity. The scrub is gone. The earth is turned. What you see instead, as you approach that distant glacier, is a lunar landscape, pitted with rust-pink lakes that reek of cyanide. The waterfowl that were once abundant in this corridor of the Andes are gone; no birds flap overhead, no alpaca graze on the hillsides. There is no grass in sight. The odor is overwhelming; it is the rank stench of the end of things: of chemical burn, of rot, of human excrement. Even the permafrost, the whipping winds, the driving snow cannot shield the smell. As you ascend, all about you are vast heaps of garbage, a choking ruin, and sylphlike figures picking idly through it. Closer in are teetering huts of tin and stone, leaning out at 70-degree angles, narrow alleys oozing with raw sewage, a string of humanity streaming in and out of the black holes that scar the cliffs. Along the precipitously winding road, you see hundreds of women in wide skirts scrabble up a steep escarpment to scavenge rocks that spill from the mine shafts. The children who aren't toted in slings— the ones who are old enough to walk—shoulder their own bags of stone.

A miner lucky enough to find work once he reaches this mountain inferno labors in subzero temperatures, in the suffocating dark, wielding a primitive pick—much as his forebears did a half millennium ago. In the course of that work, he risks lung disease, toxic poisoning, asphyxiation, nerve damage. He exposes himself to glacial floods, collapsing shafts, wayward dynamite, chemical leaks. The altitude alone is punishing: at fifteen thousand feet, a human body can fall victim to pulmonary edema, blood clots, kidney failure; at eighteen thousand, injuries can be more severe. To counter them, miners chew wads of coca. Like slaves of the ancient mita, they carry pocketfuls of the leaf to curb their hunger, blunt exhaustion. If they live to work another day, they celebrate by drinking themselves into a stupor. The ore they extract—ground down, leached with mercury, purified in a blazing furnace—may make their bosses and their bosses' bosses very rich; but for the vast majority who toil in that high circle of hell, gold is as elusive as a glittering fool's paradise.

The system of *cachorreo*, used by contractors throughout the Andes, is akin to the mita that the Incas once used to shackle their conquered tribes, and then Spain used all over again to shackle the Incas. Today under *cachorreo*, a worker surrenders his identity card to his employer. He labors for thirty days without pay. On the thirty-first day, if he is lucky, he is allowed to mine the shaft for his personal profit. But he can take only as much as he can carry on his back. By the time a miner struggles out under his cargo of stones, grinds it, and coaxes the glittering dust free, he may find he has precious little for his efforts. Worse still, because he must sell his gold to the ramshackle, unregulated "Compro Oro!" ("I Buy Gold!") establishments in town, it will fetch the lowest price possible. On average, a miner in La Rinconada earns $170 a month—$5 for every day of grueling labor. On average, he has more than five mouths to feed. If he has a bad month, he will earn $30. If he does very, very well, he will earn $1,000. In most cases, workers simply go up the hill, spend their hard-won cash on liquor and whores, and count themselves lucky if they make it home without a brawl. Crime and AIDS are rampant in La Rinconada. If work doesn't kill a man, a knife or a virus will. Few miners here reach fifty.

It is hard to imagine, as we hover over the gleaming counters of jewelry stores in Paris or New York, or even Jakarta or Mumbai, that gold can take such a hallucinatory journey, that the process remains so medieval—that so little has progressed in five hundred years of human history. But if La Rinconada today is the Potosí of half a millennium ago, it is so only in the grinding misery of the mines. There are no socialites in La Rinconada; no visiting orchestras or opera singers; no Chinese Ming treasures; no tailors from London or *parfumeurs* from Paris; no imported delicacies; no lace-clad courtesans from Cádiz. There are only ramshackle dives and bordellos to which thousands of hoodwinked, prepubescent girls from Cuzco or Arequipa are abducted to service the addled young men who trawl La Rinconada's nights in search of oblivion. Six dollars for an ordinary hooker; twenty for a beauty. HIV and tuberculosis are common here. Violence is the rule of law. The only gold to be seen is in bucketfuls of urine that spill from high windows onto the ubiquitous mud as it coils its way to ponds where the children wade. Or in the tiny seed of gold that will buy a thirteen-year-old virgin. Drunks stagger through the neon-lit night. Toddlers slip and fall, giggling, into the sewage. Young girls with vacant eyes stare out from dingy doorways, hoping for an easy few tricks before morning. Down the way, a brawl will produce a corpse. No one will identify the killer. By dawn, it will have been offered to El Tío, fickle lord of the mines, modern-day avatar of Ai Apaec, the fanged god of all creation.

Families like Juan Ochochoque's, laboring for generations under the spell of gold's promise, live in abject poverty here, barely able to eke out an evening meal. The world boom has not translated to better lives for them. It is not too different in the gold mines of Cajamarca, Peru (one of the most productive mines in the world, owned by the American giant Newmont Mining Corporation); or in Puerto Maldonado, where anarchic pit mines have mutilated the jungle; or in Mexico, for that matter, where an average miner—the highest paid in Latin America—takes home $15 a day. In Cajamarca, which has poured nearly $1.5 billion of gold into the global market in a single year, three in four residents live in numbing poverty. Today one out of five Peruvian families live on less than $1 a day. In the outlying areas of Cuzco, where Australian and American companies are busily ferreting Peru's gold out into international markets, more than half the population earns less than $35 a month. The ordinary Latin American, in other words, may perch on some of the world's most valuable mineral wealth, but as an Italian traveler observed more than a century ago, that fool "is a beggar, sitting on a bench of gold."

A NEW KIND OF COLONIALISM
1900–Present

> *To live perpetually at the mercy of two colossuses, alienated between two forms of colonial servitude, never really to be free.*
> —Mario Vargas Llosa, 1996

No industry characterizes the Latin American story more vividly than mining. Since the time of the Incas, when Huayna Capac forced distant nations to surrender the "sweat of the Sun" to glorify his palaces—to the time Pizarro extorted a colossal ransom from Atahualpa before subjecting him to the *garrote vil*—to the fateful moment when the earth crashed down on Juan Ochochoque, collapsing his mine and effectively ending his life, the narrative has not altered. A thousand years later, it is the same. At the core of it is an alien hunger, a foreign craving, an outward suction. It is as if the conquest imposed by Inca, Aztec, or Spaniard had never left. The continent is still defined by external forces.

Mining may be the most vivid example, but it is not the only commerce that informs this gyre. Consider the rampant profiteering of the United Fruit Company, an American corporation that, for well over a century, controlled vast areas of land from the Caribbean to the Andes. United Fruit, championed in the 1950s by US Secretary of State John Foster Dulles and his CIA director brother, Allen, exploited the region's poverty via its cheap labor, bribed government officials, dominated transportation networks, and shipped rich, profitable harvests to North America and Europe. "El Pulpo," the locals called it. The octopus. It was ravenous, took much, and gave little. Like the colonial power that preceded it, United Fruit herded legions of workers at will, cleared forests, drained marshlands, blocked indigenous rights, suppressed labor rebellions, and bled all the profits to foreign pockets. Today that company calls itself Chiquita Brands International. Its fiercest competitor was another American outfit, Standard Fruit and Steamship, founded by Joseph Vaccaro, a Sicilian cane cutter from New Orleans whose modest investment in one ship grew into a mammoth business. Vaccaro was an all-American success story, a bootstrap wonder, but his fortunes came at a cost for Latin America. Eventually his ships were transporting coconuts, pineapples, and bananas from Honduras and other rural outposts in the Caribbean to cities around the world, making him a very rich man. But gains, like fruit, continued to be devoured abroad. That company is now Dole International.

Few newspapers reported it, but both companies, United and Standard—more alert to the rivalry between them than to the calamitous damage they were leaving behind—used brutal tactics in the countries in which they operated. Racing to put harvests on distant tables, they hired death squads, instigated coups, and caused murder and mayhem as they tamped down any semblance of protest. In 1928 the Colombian government took its cue from bosses of United Fruit and crushed a strike, massacring as many as two thousand peons, including women and children. The bloody events were recounted in Gabriel García Márquez's powerful 1967 novel *One Hundred Years of Solitude*. But American companies didn't always rely on locals to do their dirty work. In the first thirty-five years of the twentieth century, the US military invaded Latin America twenty-eight times, all in the name of "banana interests."

Other southern resources were in demand. Chief among them, perhaps, was sugar, which Christopher Columbus had brought to Cuba when he set sail to the New World for a second time. Columbus would die consumed by his gold obsession, but less than three centuries later, the tiny sprouts he transported whimsically from the Canary Islands grew into the most important agricultural product cultivated in South America. The gargantuan global market they engendered became one of the most epochal demographic forces in world history. It was because of sugar that millions of enslaved Africans were dragooned from their homelands and transported to the Americas. And it was because of sugar that the hemisphere's natives were relocated to climes they were constitutionally incapable of surviving. For two hundred years, Europeans made vast fortunes from Columbus's transplanted shoots, enriching kings as well as bankers, leaving a monstrous trail of atrocities in their wake. A German traveler in the sixteenth century noted that Queen Elizabeth I had pleasant enough eyes, but her teeth were disconcertingly black, a defect common enough in the English from an excessive fondness for sugar. The sweet crystal was wanted everywhere. "White gold," the Londoners called it. "Mother of slavery" was its name in latitudes farther south.

By the nineteenth century, more than six million tons of sugar were being produced in Latin America every year, most of it grown in Cuba or Brazil, most of it harvested in grueling conditions. Today almost two billion tons are generated annually, half of it from Latin American countries, half of which continues to enrich only the importers. As one chronicler put it more than two hundred years ago, "I do not know if sugar and coffee are essential to the happiness of Europe, but I know well that they have accounted for the unhappiness of two great regions of the world: America has been depopulated so as to have land on which to plant them; Africa has been depopulated so as to have people to cultivate them."

Looming large in the history of extraction is the story of oil: in 1912 the London-Amsterdam powerhouse Royal Dutch Shell drilled its first commercial oil well in Venezuela. The rewarding gush should not have been surprising. Here was the country with the largest hydrocarbon reserves in the Western Hemisphere—fifth in the world in proven inventory. Seven years later, Shell bought up vast oil reserves in Mexico. What wasn't taken by Shell in the Americas was taken soon after by Standard Oil, the brainchild of American magnate John D. Rockefeller. Oil shortages in the United States had made foreign incursions imperative, at least in Rockefeller's eyes. Standard Oil, later part of the ExxonMobil empire, helped itself to oil in Venezuela, Mexico, Brazil, Argentina—wherever there was oil to be found. But eventually Latin Americans began to demand it for themselves: President Lázaro Cárdenas of Mexico nationalized his country's oil wells in 1938, in response to the violent, xenophobic convulsions of the Mexican Revolution in the second decade of the twentieth century. Venezuela nationalized its fields in 1976, hoping to spur growth. Caving in to international demand several years later Venezuela nationalized them once again in 2007, under the revolutionary regime of President Hugo Chávez. Oil might have been the one commodity in all of Latin America that Latin American presidents were not willing to surrender entirely to foreign trade.

That wasn't always the case. Coffee, cacao, cotton, rubber—all these became fair game for any businessman audacious enough to rush Latin American shores. In the nineteenth and twentieth centuries, as the region hobbled its way out of a savage revolution and three hundred years of colonial rule, Latin America became a playground for hustlers, frauds, rapacious capitalists, and adventurers with questionable pasts, much as it had been in the days of the conquistadors. The Creoles—rich whites who had appropriated all the wealth and power left behind—encouraged them. Foreigners were welcomed eagerly, invited to do as they liked, as long as cash flowed to the Creoles' coffers. And flow, it did.

An agitated century ensued. In the early 1900s, a number of London banks invested in high-grade rubber from the Amazon, an operation earning the equivalent of $5 billion a year even as tens of thousands of rain forest Indians were slaughtered in the process. American middle-men muscled their way into the coffee business, lording over Central American livelihoods for generations. Wall Street bankers financed bands of assassins who marauded their way through Nicaragua, El Salvador, and Honduras, forcing loans and taking over businesses. Their agents reinstated old-time slavery, setting the region back hundreds of years. Unlike the Spanish conquest and colonization, however, there were no designated sages—no Council of the Indies—to pull on their respective beards and consider the human carnage. Instigating this free-for-all with something approaching glee, US President William Taft crowed, "The day is not far distant when three Stars and Stripes at three equidistant points will mark our territory: one at the North Pole, another at the Panama Canal, and the third at the South Pole. The whole hemisphere will be ours, in fact, as, by virtue of our superiority of race, it already is ours morally." He was only repeating what Thomas Jefferson had proposed one hundred years before.

As years wore on—as American businessmen took over land, ports, customshouses, treasuries, governments—and natives began to question those tactics and rebel, marines were sent in "to protect the lives and interests of US citizens." In most cases, a creeping Communism was given as the reason why: as the Machiavellian argument went, the United States was not going to stand by and allow foreign interventions—real or ideological—to threaten its God-given dominion. Didn't the Monroe Doctrine, the venerable old 1823 declaration, which stated that "any portion of this hemisphere" is part and parcel of the American ambit, make this clear enough? As President Franklin Delano Roosevelt is famously reputed to have proclaimed about Rafael Trujillo, the ruthless military strongman who ruled the Dominican Republic in one of the bloodiest eras of Latin American history, "I know he is an SOB, but at least he is *our* SOB." Indeed, the northern leviathan was willing to unleash considerable martial might to prove it was in charge. One highly decorated US Marine, a major general who had served in Latin America, reflected:

> I spent thirty-three years and four months in active service as a member of our country's most agile military force—the Marine Corps. I served in all commissioned ranks from a second lieutenant to major

general. And during that period, I spent most of my time being a high-class muscle man for Big Business, for Wall Street, and for the bankers. In short, I was a racketeer, a gangster for capitalism. . . . I helped make Mexico, especially Tampico, safe for American oil interests. I helped make Haiti and Cuba a decent place for the National City Bank to collect revenues. I helped in the raping of half a dozen Central American republics. . . . I helped purify Nicaragua for the international banking house of Brown Brothers. I brought light to the Dominican Republic for American sugar interests. I helped make Honduras "right" for American fruit companies. During those years, I had, as the boys in the back room would say, a swell racket. I was rewarded with honors, medals, promotion. Looking back on it, I feel that I could have given Al Capone a few hints. The best he could do was to operate his racket in three districts. I operated on three continents.

The British, for all their rapacity in colonial matters, were not as overtly political or military about interventions. As one historian explains: they didn't have to be. England kept a tight rein on the Latin American purse. British diplomats made sure that commercial treaties favored London banks. They pandered to the white oligarchy, encouraged the expansion of large haciendas, favored control by a handful of rich, powerful families, and perpetuated the ongoing grind of racial discrimination. London bankers carried out the bulk of Latin American trade in Europe; they became virtual treasurers to their governments. In the end, it was London's banking district that managed affairs, undermined the region's independence, cranked up national debts, and made countries entirely reliant on British speculators. If Latin American commodities were being sucked dry by American bosses, its fiscal assets were being siphoned away by English financiers.

The twenty-first century has brought changes. Credit that to a growing awareness among the Latin American upper class that the continent has never been truly its own; and among the lower classes that bosses have been too far away to allow them to address their grievances. As one shrewd nineteenth-century Chilean statesman put it, "For the Americans of the north, the only Americans are themselves." Such is the deeply held opinion in the other America, even though for almost two hundred years now, that opinion is held with a grudge bordering on adulation. *El Imperio*, they call the United States—The Empire—home of the legendary, villainous Darth Vader, ruler of a distant star. Where does the money go? *El Imperio*, they say with a nod and a shrug. Who foments the coups and the revolutions? *El Imperio*, of course. Who maintains the status quo? *El Imperio*, if that's what *El Imperio* wants. And so on.

If factories have been slow to come to this part of the world, it is because, after having been forbidden manufacture by Spain for three hundred years, newly independent republics found themselves beholden to foreign corporations that systematically discouraged development for a century and a half more. Gradually, over the course of the past eighty years, the Americas of the South have tried to cut their own path, nationalize businesses, switch axes of power, and make alliances with Asia, perfectly aware that businessmen in faraway places can be as emasculating as Spanish viceroys on the ground. Like Spain, with its punishing *repartimiento de mercancía*—the colonial system that forced Indians to buy goods they didn't need in exchange for metals Spain craved—foreign entities that wrest natural resources from Latin America expect to sell their own goods there in return. Indeed, today a staggering 40 percent of all US exports go to Latin America. It is a market that generates millions of North American jobs.

This can make for a fierce sense of entitlement. When the United States has done business in Latin America—Anaconda Copper in Chile, for instance, or the Drummond Company's coal operations in Colombia—it is because it expects exclusivity and complete control. For many years, American companies brooked no competition from locals nor any challenge to their jurisdiction. In 1973 Chile's threat to nationalize Anaconda Copper was sufficient rationale for President Richard Nixon and National Security Advisor Henry Kissinger to sanction the bombing of Chile's presidential palace, oust Salvador Allende, and pave the way for the installation of military strongman Augusto Pinochet. Forty years later, facing resistance by Colombian workers in American mining enterprises, President Barack Obama announced he would send "brigade commanders with hands-on counterinsurgency experience" to subdue dissenters. There have been many such examples of US military intervention in the Americas in the past half century, from Mexico to Paraguay.

But, along the way, by virtue of public outrage, El Imperio curbed its zeal. It had to. In 2012, the same year that President Obama threatened a US military corrective in Colombia, Latin American leaders at the Summit of the Americas in Cartagena united to challenge America's profile in the region. They called for Washington to lift its Cuban embargo, imposed back in 1958, arguing that it had been far too damaging to the hemisphere, and "to do more to combat drug use on its own turf" rather than send arms and "advisors" to fight drug lords in theirs—a strategy that has failed spectacularly. By then, Latin America was eagerly seeking to expand economic ties with China, India, the Middle East—regions that did business without demanding political tit for tat. Taking their own reins, they decided to determine their economic future for themselves. In 2015, while attending a conference with Cuba's president Raúl Castro in Panama City, President Obama responded by striking a very different note. He offered something of an apology, saying: "The days in which our agenda in this hemisphere presumed that the United States could meddle with impunity, those days are past."

All the same, in at least one respect, Latin America remains caught in an age-old wheelwork. Its romance with metal hunger continues, as if it can't quite let go of the fever that has held it fast since Columbus set foot on the Bahamas. Brazil, one of the largest producers of iron ore, for instance, ships most of its metal abroad. The lion's share goes to China, even though China is the world's number one producer of iron (leagues ahead of Brazil) and even though Brazil loses money in the bargain. The romance extends, too, to the old colonial practice of letting someone else wear the big hat and pocket the profits. Peru may be one of the world's top ten producers of gold, but the overwhelming majority of its mines are not owned by Peruvians. They are owned, managed, and operated by corporations in China, Canada, the United States, Brazil, England, Mexico, or Australia; and most of what Peruvian hands rout from the Andes or the Amazon is sent to glitter on another side of the globe. Indeed, Asia now consumes most of the gold that is gouged from the bowels of the planet. Metal imperialism—not terribly different from that practiced in the sixteenth century—still prevails in the copper mines of Chile, the coal mines of Colombia, the diamond fields of Brazil, the silver quarries of Mexico, even as profits are funneled away to London, Beijing, Zurich, Melbourne, Toronto, Johannesburg, or Butte, Montana. As President Danilo Medina of the Dominican Republic pointed out a few years ago: for every $100 of gold it rips from the Dominican countryside, Barrick Gold Corporation—whose owners reside in Canada—will receive $97 of the profits and the Dominican people, $3. For him at least, "That is simply unacceptable."

Perhaps the fact that almost half of Colombia is managed by multinational mining companies, or that Mexican mines are dominated by Canadians, is not so troubling if you believe in exuberant markets and the triumphs of global consumerism, but what the boom leaves behind in Latin America is devastating: rampant pollution, a wanton destruction of the rain forest, toxic rivers and lakes, rising morbidity and mortality levels, an epidemic of child labor, ongoing poverty, and a ravished landscape. Few places expose the dark side of the global economy more starkly than the illegal mines that are multiplying today in Latin America, but even the legal ones have proven ruinous. For every simple gold ring that goes out into the world, 250 tons of rock must move, a toxic pound of mercury will spill into the environment, and countless lives—biological and botanical—will struggle with the consequences. It doesn't take a social scientist or a chemist to walk through that wasteland and reckon the costs.

CAJAMARCA
2011

Gold is chemically inert. . . . its radiance is forever. In Cairo, a tooth bridge made of gold 4,500 years ago is good to go in your mouth today.
—Peter L. Bernstein, *The Power of Gold*

In 2006, as the post-9/11 economy rumbled into being, gold prices soared. The trend reflected a new global skittishness: hoarding was on the rise, and gold was the preferred investment. The irony is that every niche of the gargantuan gold industry that made substantive profits in that first bullish decade of 2000—from Tiffany's flagship store on Fifth Avenue to the mom-and-pop shops of Mumbai—owes global terrorism a debt of gratitude for its rising profits. After the sobering events of 9/11, when three hijacked airplanes plunged into the hearts of Wall Street and the Pentagon, and the dollar began to lose ground, gold began its meteoric upward spiral. Everyone seemed to want it, especially in the form of jewelry, and especially in countries whose populations were clawing their way toward the middle class: India and China accounted for the highest demand for gold, their surging numbers driving the prices ever skyward. One ounce of gold, which sold on the global market for $271 on September 11, 2001, sold for $1,920 a decade later, a whopping increase of 700 percent. That boom prompted an equivalent explosion in the population crowding into illegal mining grounds. From bangles to bullion, and from Bern to Beijing, precious metals were seen as the best insurance against a nervous age.

Ironically, the frenzy reached the valley where—480 years before—Pizarro had once held Atahualpa hostage for much the same reason. But for all the metal the conquistador demanded, and for all the gold and silver Atahualpa had hauled to him from the four corners of the Tahuantinsuyu, it turned out that the greatest reserve the Inca held was right underfoot. The valley of Cajamarca, that high, windswept stretch of land where so much colonial history had been written, was harboring some of the richest deposits of gold in the world. The largest gold operation in all South America—the US-owned Yanacocha mine—was busily turning rock to reach it.

That spring, villagers who inhabited the area around Yanacocha decided to block the roads and declare war on the company's toxic and predatory practices. The corporation that owned Yanacocha, Newmont Mining, had just announced a mammoth new project a few miles away, not far from the very fields where the Inca had seen freedom for the last time. They called it Conga, and it stood to be more colossal, more prolific than any gold mine Latin America had ever known. Denver executives estimated it would bring them a billion dollars a year in gold and a half billion in copper.

The residents of Cajamarca wanted none of it. A bloody stand-off between them and the mine's armed security forces followed. Five protesters were killed. But Conga began to be built anyway.

A few years later, in 2011, a humble subsistence farmer named Máxima Acuña de Chaupe refused to be evicted from her farm, a little patch of ground that lay inconveniently within the parameters of Conga's blueprints. One frigid morning, her property was overrun by armed police: she was beaten unconscious, her mud shack destroyed, her family injured. The assault was disavowed by Newmont and the Peruvian government, but it had been bold, brutal, unequivocally captured on a cellphone and was enough to radicalize the mine workers, who soon called a strike against the American giant. Their complaints were loud and clear: they had been laboring in wretched conditions. The people of Cajamarca were among the poorest citizens of Peru. Not only had Newmont appropriated the land of their ancestors, it had provoked the battery of a defenseless grandmother, ravaged the environment, and endangered their children with toxic substances that spilled into their rivers day and night.

Not long before, a German scientist had confirmed that the once-sparkling lakes of Cajamarca had been dangerously contaminated with cyanide; two million Peruvians inhabiting that lush, fertile valley were now at risk for chemical poisoning. But there was more than environmental despoliation at issue. There was the question of rank exploitation. Once the Peruvian gold was excavated, processed, and shipped abroad, Peru stood to retain only 15 percent of Newmont's gargantuan profits. Moreover, in a year in which Newmont carved three million ounces of gold from those heights (worth $3.7 billion), more than half the residents were living on $100 a month.

The protesters in Cajamarca were so outraged by the seeming injustice of this—and Peruvians around the country expressed such immediate sympathy—that troops in riot gear were called out to contain what officials in Lima feared was a larger threat to the Peruvian economy. On July 4, 2013, the leader of the protest, a Catholic priest, was taken by force from a bench in a public park, arrested, and roughed up before he was let go. President Ollanta Humala, who had won the presidency on a socialist vote, now said with unequivocal free-market conviction that Conga would continue, albeit with closer government oversight. Peru's mineral boom, in other words, was sacrosanct, not to be disrupted. Gold trumped water, money quashed justice, and world markets took precedence over the rural poor.

Remarkably, the opposite proved true. Máxima Acuña prevailed, at least for a little while. The diminutive Peruvian invited protesters onto her contested land, spoke out whenever asked, and refused to back down against the American Goliath. Eventually she attracted the attention of a number of international organizations that were all too happy to trumpet Newmont's human and environmental depredations: the Inter-American Commission on Human Rights, the Organization of American States, Amnesty International. Newmont was forced to halt all progress at Conga. Caught in suspended animation for five more years, the company finally decided in April 2016 to walk away from the project. The locals celebrated, Máxima Acuña was given a prestigious international prize, and a New York journalist dubbed her "the badass grandma" who had challenged big mining. But even as Newmont announced it would abandon Conga, its executives in Denver were busily working toward expanding their mines at Yanacocha, an alternate deliverance, promising sales of nearly $1 billion a year for at least five years. A few months later, a band of hit men broke into Máxima Acuña's home and gave her and her husband another thrashing.

LA RINCONADA
2002

We would not say Jesus, Mary, Joseph, nor make the sign of the cross, because the place belonged to Tío, the devil.

—Andean miner, 1972

Leonor Gonzáles could be Máxima Acuña's sister for the way the two speak, the Quechua inflections they share, their tiny statures, their essential fortitude, the fierce principles of family and hard work that characterize the indigenous women of the Andes. But there are differences. Leonor lives and works in a remote aerie, high up in the mountains, where only illegal miners go. Máxima lives just outside the historic city of Cajamarca, indigenous South America's losing ground, the very place where worlds once collided, where white won against brown and locals still answer to outsiders.

There are other, more observable differences in these women. Although they were born in the same year, Leonor looks to be twice Máxima's age: her skin is disfigured by a relentless sun, raw from the glacial winds. She is missing teeth. Her hands, unlike Máxima's, do not dance when she talks. They are gnarled, stiff—the hands of someone who scrabbles up cliffs, hunting through rock spills. They lie in her lap like broken relics. Her eyes, once a sparkling onyx, have turned milky gray. Leonor has spent her life as a *pallaquera*, a sifter of discarded stone; Máxima is a farmer. For all the beatings Máxima has suffered at the mercy of hired thugs, her eyes are bright, her movements graceful, her smile pleasing. Life itself, on the other hand, has left an all-too-visible scar on Leonor. Its ravages mar her face, just as mines pock the face of the towering peak they call Sleeping Beauty.

From the day she was born in a tin shack on the flank of that mountain, Leonor's life has never been free of troubles, but it was tolerable enough when her husband, Juan Ochochoque, was alive. At least they could shoulder the burdens of hardship together. Somehow, between the pittance Juan earned in the soul-crushing system of *cachorreo* and the rare moments when Leonor would crack open a stone to find a tiny miracle inside, they eked out enough soles to feed them and their four children. They were poor—bone poor, always poor—but, in the fortress of that small stone hut, they were whole. They sang.

All of that changed one snowy morning in 2002. Juan had been breaking rock in a far corridor of the mountain, tirelessly scouting its veins, when a colossal chunk of glacier broke off far above, crashed down the slope, and collapsed the shaft where he was working. His son Jhon, eleven years old, was in the mine at the time, helping to drag out the gravel. Juan never did describe the horror in all its detail to Leonor, but she could imagine it: The slam of ice. The rock on rock. The sudden black. And then the choking dust, the chemical stink, invading every millimeter of his lungs, stinging his eyes. The only thing Jhon remembers of that fateful moment is the sound of his father's squawks as the man tried, frantically, to find the boy—scrabbling toward him on his knees, pushing through the debris, calling for him with a voice he himself hardly recognized.

The two managed to claw their way out of the shattered hole. They thanked El Tío for the deliverance, but they were never the same after that. Juan could not walk, could not breathe. The chemical fumes had seared his lungs. It took three men to carry him down. They met Leonor running up the path the other way. She had heard the terrifying detonation, the rumble of rock shooting through the perforated mountain like some diabolical roulette. She had seen the thick cloud of dust hanging ominously over the mine's entrance, flicking its black tail into the frigid sky. Leonor looked about desperately for her son and—after a heart-stopping moment—found him trailing after his father, dazed, unaided, miraculously unharmed. But he had emerged from that calamity with a sickness the Indians call *susto*: a fear that forever grips the soul, a panic that will not go away.

As days wore on, the children could see that a shadow had fallen over their father. Juan was suffering a very manifest physical deterioration. He had always marched out before dawn, tramping through ice and mud to hammer away at the mine's recesses. Now his legs had ballooned to three times their size. He was off balance, confused, in agony. His arms grew weak. His joints ached, his hands shook; he could scarcely bend his knees. He couldn't shuffle more than a few yards, much less climb to the mine. Before long, he began to have seizures; and then came the constant, bone-rattling cough. He made his way through La Rinconada holding on to walls, gasping for air.

In the course of a fleeting moment, Juan Ochochoque had become a marginal citizen. He now joined the women, the children, the maimed, and the dispossessed—those relegated to distaff roles in a full-blooded macho society. He was too sick to do women's work: *quimbaleteo*, for instance, a practice that dates to the Incas, in which a person stands on a boulder and rocks back and forth, grinding the ore to a fine sand and coaxing the silver out with mercury. Or *pallaqueo*, Leonor's work, in which a woman scales the escarpments, scavenging whatever promising bits spill from the mines, and stuffing them into a rucksack. Nor could he do even the simplest work: the *chichiqueo*, which requires a woman or child to stoop over a standing pool of chemically tainted water for hours, picking through gravel for whatever shines. These were impossible tasks in his condition. But he had to do something: there were children to raise, six mouths to feed. Within weeks, he decided to cook for a living.

Hunched over an ethyl-alcohol burner on the bare earth of his hut, he produced pot after pot of soups and stews. At noon, he sent his family into the streets to sell them. At night, he drank whatever alcohol was left, hoping to dull the humiliation.

The labors of Juan's children, which until then had been sporadic and secondary, now became indispensable, primary. Although he encouraged them to attend the run-down little school where miners who knew how to read and write taught in their off-hours, they all went to work when they could. His eldest daughter, Mariluz, eleven years old, dedicated herself to her mother's work, the *pallaqueo.* Jhon lugged water from trucks that rumbled up-mountain from Lake Titicaca and sold it to pimps in the cantinas. Senna, five years old, dedicated herself to chopping ingredients for Juan's stews. When she turned seven and able to earn a wage, she went to work scouring out the squat holes in La Rinconada's public toilet.

But they all stayed on in La Rinconada. Like most families that had inhabited mining towns for generations, it was what they knew.

Less than two years later, their father was dead. His bloated body—shot through with chemical toxins—had reached crisis point as he exited a bus at the foot of Sleeping Beauty, trying desperately to find a cure. He had sought help wherever he could find it: he had visited witch doctors, made offerings to El Tío, consulted with social workers who drifted up now and then from Juliaca. He had even traveled to Cuzco with Senna—to the convent perched on top of the ancient sun temple—hoping a priest might lay on hands. But his body gave out suddenly as Leonor helped him across the road after a choppy ride down-mountain. Crumpling to a heap, he gasped for air, clutching at his throat as a deep guttural squawk rattled from the depths of his being. Leonor cannot recall much of what happened after that. Only her terror. Only his bulging eyes, the sudden red of his face, and then the color draining away entirely. Juan Ochochoque's long battle with La Rinconada's poisons was over.

In those last few months of life, Juan had left a powerful lesson for his children. It was he who had pointed out—as they puttered about, cooking, telling stories, singing, making the best of things—that they were not like him. They did not need to be like him. He, like most on Mount Ananea, was a benighted man, a throwback to another time: Illiterate. Unworldly. Doomed. They, on the other hand, had futures beyond the age-old cycle that had trapped him. Senna was good at words, good at rooting out the right ones, good at polishing them to a fine shine. Jhon could fix things, determine how they worked; he had a knack for solving problems. Mariluz might run a business someday, if she would just set her mind to it—have her own food stall on the square. Henrry, a mere baby, was destined for better things, too, although it was hard to say what. You will dig yourselves out of this cursed mountain, he told them. You are miners of a different kind.

If those who labor in illegal mines—the most dynamic and productive branch of South American mining today—do so in conditions their fore-bears endured five hundred years ago, it is probably because something fundamental hasn't changed. If multinational operations bring scant progress to the communities on which they depend, it is probably be-cause more is being taken than given. Then and now, there is a sameness at work, a dogged consistency, a stubborn mind-set in occupier and oc-cupied alike. For all the strides made in the economic progress of Latin America—the growth rates, the steady reduction of poverty, the gradual emergence of a middle class—the ruling brain often remains the same.

As the feisty Uruguayan writer Eduardo Galeano put it almost fifty years ago: some nations win, others lose. It may not be a zero-sum game, exactly, but Latin America has specialized in losing since Europeans, flush with a Renaissance sense of self, ventured across the seas and buried their teeth in the throats of the indigenous. In North America, where English colonists virtually eradicated the Indian and broke the African, whites looked around, saw themselves in the majority, and framed themselves as undisputed victors. Since time immemorial in Latin America, how-ever, Indians have looked around, seen themselves in the majority, and remain losers still. By now, they and their descendants have become past masters at losing. Riches surrendered by the ubiquitous Earth Mother—whether it be silver, sugar, oil, or human capital—have been gathered up by invaders, forged into profits, and swept away to a far metropolis.

Much has been made of the inherent failures of Latin America. It is, as global economists say, the most unequal continent in the world, a region whose economic potential was sapped first by the Spanish Crown and then sapped some more by whites who inherited that power.

During the nineteenth century, when ordinary North Americans, not just the rich or elite, surged to the fore as the most inventive citizens on the planet—creating patents, establishing public institutions, fomenting competition—Latin American elites adopted policies and institutions that enriched them but impoverished everyone else around them. Whereas, by 1914, there were almost thirty thousand banks operating in the United States, there were only forty-two in all of Mexico—and two controlled more than 60 percent of the nation's wealth. The same was true throughout Latin America. Competition was discouraged. Industrialization was prevented. Innovation was stifled. Even education for the masses of indigenous and poor went ignored. Why educate someone when what you want is a pair of hands, a strong back, and blind obedience? As a result, Latin American republics became extractive by nature: they concentrated all power in a tiny elite, placed few restraints on their staggering clout, and invited the rest of the world in to exploit the land and its people.

Little wonder that the mentality that ruled in the days of the conquistador simply continued, with the difference that there was now no uniformity in government. No systematic rule of law. Despots, dictators, rich hacienda owners, unscrupulous opportunists looking for enrichment—these were the kings in that unruly century from 1830 to 1930. To be white was to be master. To be brown was to be locked into a menial class. Latin America emerged from its wars of independence ravaged, and, although its revolutionary armies had been largely people of color, governments were improvised to keep those races in servitude and give whites the seats of power. Bigotry, institutionalized by the Spaniards, now hardened under their descendants, the fair-skinned criollos and the European immigrants who joined them, and a virulent racism became the region's tinderbox. Even as Simón Bolívar lay dying, the territories he had liberated became wild, ungovernable. He fretted in his deathbed that Latin America was no strong, united force against the world, after all, no bulwark against colonial predators. Those who had served his revolution had plowed the sea. And indeed, the chaos was endemic. Corruption became widespread, morality slipshod, ambitions tyrannical. Coups and bullies prevailed. The strongest, as always in these Americas, did as they pleased.

Throughout this volatile history, it was miners—of silver, gold, copper—who served as proverbial canaries in the coal shaft. Although precious metals yielded vast fortunes in Latin America—for Spaniards, for whom wealth was the paramount object of conquest, or for foreigners, who looked for full veins and cheap labor—silver and its like have always been more profitable to faraway powers than to those who live on the ground. The rule of the market is supposed to be simple: if you possess something others want, you stand to benefit handsomely. And yet, the lust for these glittering prizes has brought more despoliation than development, more drain than gain. "Mining is the hole through which the vitality of the country escapes," the Bolivian intellectual Sergio Almaraz Paz wrote fifty years ago. "In more than three centuries, it has left nothing, absolutely nothing . . . it is a passing prosperity that translates to an empty shell."

That is certainly as true for Leonor Gonzáles today in the wild, glacial reaches of La Rinconada as it is for Cajamarca's Máxima Acuña, trying to survive on the brink of one of the most profitable multinational mining companies in the world. For many who have relied on the silver hunt as livelihood, there is no question that it has been a gamble. It is a wager with El Tío, a question of survival. It is also rank speculation for the overseer, the investor, governments. As the Scottish economist Adam Smith wrote more than two hundred years ago in a comment that is still meaningful today: "Of all those expensive and uncertain projects which bring bankruptcy, there is none perhaps more perfectly ruinous than the search after new silver and gold mines. It is perhaps the most disadvantageous lottery in the world, or the one in which the gain of those who draw the prizes bears the least proportion to the loss of those who draw the blanks."

And yet it is the lottery on which Latin America's future still depends.

HISTORY'S GHOSTS

National wealth consists in the abundance . . . and national poverty in
the scarcity of Gold or Silver.

—Adam Smith, 1776

We know what the mining lottery says about opportunists who chase metal
dreams. What does it say about the people who, for centuries now, have been
subjected to those opportunists? Leonor Gonzáles has never quite been free
of her husband's improvident quest for gold, although her children now
live down-mountain, away from the blinding chemicals, the glacial cold,
the grinding hunger. Every Friday at dawn, nevertheless, she boards a ramshackle bus that takes her on a bone-rattling journey from Juliaca, where
the family now lives, to Putina, where she takes another bus up-mountain
over an ice-crazed road, past a pocked and desolate moonscape. Six hours
later she is in La Rinconada, inside the pile of stones Juan built for her and
their family. Squatting over a blue flame on the dirt floor, she stirs the stew
she will sell as miners stagger out of the darkness into the light.

Juan's quest to wring life from the veins of Mount Ananea still
lures Leonor because it was her father's quest, her grandfather's, her
great-grandfather's—a hunger that has raveled through her people's one
thousand years of fickle history without yielding much in return. She
certainly cannot make a living in the riotous city of Juliaca, where her
children struggle to advance, where skills are far higher than her own,
where work is impossible for an illiterate widow of the mines.

The irony is that, although globalization began with Spain's first
boatload of Montezuma's metal—the cargo that triggered world trade,
lifted faraway populations, and sparked the industrial age—for hundreds of years, the vast majority of Latin Americans like Leonor were
left behind to wallow in primitive conditions. Whereas open frontiers in
the United States of America or trade routes in Europe and the Far East
meant real opportunity for ordinary people prepared to risk the venture, in Latin America, land and open trade were available only to the
politically powerful: the Spanish-born rulers, the white oligarchs who
came after them, the landed gentry who held all the property to begin

with. *Plata*, or silver, the lodestone of the conquistadors, became *plata*, the universal Latin American word for wealth in general. That there has been as much progress as there has been in the last two decades—that more *plata* has funneled down and lifted so many out of poverty—is miraculous indeed. That countries such as Brazil, Mexico, Chile, Peru, and Colombia have been more vigilant of their patrimony, less willing to submit to foreign masters, is perhaps the "turning of the world," the fundamental revolution in thinking that the great Incas Pachacutec and Tupac Yupanqui wanted for their people.

But the past is a teacher. If there is a foundational cornerstone in these Americas, it is the impulse to extract and exploit—mandated by conquest, perfected by Spain, extended through history. Freedom, the rule of law, "the shining city on a hill": these guiding principles have come late to Latin America. We are a people shaped by coercion and submission. This is never more evident than in the mines; never more defining than when native Americans are sent to dig metal for a distant master. Call it metaphor, call it simplified history, but it is also fact: an extractive economy is the shackle that has bound Latin America since Columbus set boots on its shores. That extractive economy has been inimical to true prosperity in these lands. Money courses through, businesses expand, economists register the growth, but growth in this part of the world is a fragile business. Usually it has meant that the rich grow richer, the powerful more powerful. If there is human progress, it is ephemeral, and it usually comes because something has been forfeited in the bargain.

Argentina, Ecuador, Brazil, Peru, and Colombia have seen a growing middle class in the first stretch of this century, but the question is whether they can sustain the corresponding expectations. A single coup, a threat of civil unrest, a rampant wave of corruption, a fall in the price of commodities—all of these are common enough—is often all it takes to bring progress to a standstill. History is ever combustible in this cradle of cultural shock, this land of violent amalgamation. Unlike North America, where Indians were herded, reduced, exterminated, and their brutal history suppressed or forgotten, Latin America still lives with its colonial and postcolonial scars. A legacy of abuse, resentment, and distrust has wormed its way deep into the character of our people. "Silver" was the start. It continues to be a holy grail. And it is proving to be a hard master.

PART TWO

SWORD

The distant past never disappears completely, and all its wounds,
even the most ancient, still drip blood.

—Octavio Paz, *The Labyrinth of Solitude*

CHAPTER 6

BLOOD LUST

Question: When did Peru fuck up, exactly?

—Mario Vargas Llosa, 1969

Answer: The moment it was born. The insemination was all wrong, brutal, and it birthed a wounded nation, at war with its other half, the Indian.

—Jeremías Gamboa, 2017

Carlos Buergos is at large. Nobody knows where he is. Not his former wife. Not his friends. Not his correctional officer. Lorton Prison in Virginia, which held him for a while, no longer exists. The inmate information system that monitored him has lost track. He came barefoot to this country from Cuba in 1980 and, after a profligate ten years, was arrested, imprisoned, and then set free on a blue-sky summer morning in 2001 to make his way in freedom as best he could. The last he was heard from was in a plaintive call to his ex-wife: How could their six-year-old son have died while he was gone? Had the boy been ailing for long? Sick even in the womb? Was it a curse that he, as father, had brought on him? The woman simply hung up the phone.

He moved on. Back to Miami, Dade County, the ground he had kissed when he crawled off a ramshackle boat to deliverance.

Seared into the memory of every Marielito who arrived from Cuba in 1980 is a terrified exodus from one coast, a dazed arrival on another. Every once in a while, those memories rush back. The knock at the door. The stone-eyed police. The neighbors shrieking "Escoria! Gusano!" ("Scum! Worm!") and wielding rocks. The bumpy bus ride through the

Cuban countryside to the port of Mariel. The regiments of rifle-toting guards. The fierce-faced dogs. The biblical mass of humanity huddled beneath the hiss of a nearby electric plant. And then the heart-stopping sight of thousands of American boats bobbing in the water, waiting.

In the scant six months from April to September of that year, the Mariel boat lift brought 125,000 Cubans to the United States in one of the most remarkable waves of immigration in recent American history. It began when a driver seeking asylum rammed his van through the gates of the Peruvian embassy in Havana on April 1, 1980. A fight broke out. A guard was shot. When Fidel Castro pulled Cuban security forces out of the area, ten thousand Cubans flooded the embassy grounds, clamoring to leave. Furious, Castro opened the borders and announced that anyone who wanted to leave was welcome to go. American adventurers in Florida—largely Cuban Americans—took to their boats, descending on the northern coast of Cuba by the thousands, eager to save the oppressed.

The Freedom Flotilla, President Jimmy Carter called it, and it was an invitation as clear and open as the one carved in stone: "Give me your tired, your poor . . . the wretched refuse of your teeming shore." The new arrivals poured into Florida, jamming immigration facilities, straining police and welfare services, and giving Americans one more reason not to reelect their president.

The lives of the Marielitos converged fleetingly when they boarded those boats and traveled the open sea together. Some, like Carlos Buergos, arrived shirtless, shoeless, without so much as a scrap of paper bearing their name. Months later, they had all dispersed to hundreds of cities and towns throughout the United States, each taking a divergent path. A few worked their way up the American dream to become successful entrepreneurs. Others sought educations and became teachers, lawyers, doctors. The rest found work doing what they had always done: as musicians, menial laborers, construction workers, farmhands, kitchen help. Still others remained trapped by an angry past. Buergos's violent trajectory eventually led him to forfeit the very liberty he had won in coming to America—a paradox he was to contemplate in a prison cell for many years.

"America," the philosopher and writer George Santayana once wrote, "is the greatest of opportunities and the worst of influences." For many Latin Americans who enter the country as political or economic fugitives, life can be good and the work rewarding, but for just as many, it can be a bewildering maze. The context is so radically different, the opportunities exhilarating, the temptations irresistible, the potential failures, stark. Undertaking to become an immigrant can be a voyage every bit as stormy as the ninety miles from Mariel.

Although Castro implied that anyone who wanted to leave Cuba was either criminal or insane, most Marielitos were law-abiding citizens who passed themselves off as "antisocials" or "misfits" to qualify for the exodus. Of the 125,000 who came, according to the US Immigration and Naturalization Service, the great majority hailed from ordinary lives in Cuba and proceeded to ordinary lives in the United States. A small fraction of them—about 2,500—were convicts and mental cases thrown into the mix by Castro.

One of those was Carlos Buergos, eldest son of a stevedore, a wiry, blond, hazel-eyed descendant of Cubans and Eastern Europeans— a happy-go-lucky guy and convicted thief. He was hardly twenty-five when he clambered onto Florida soil, but he had already accumulated a history of misadventure.

His family was not the reason. His parents had raised nine children, a normal enough circle of siblings. But by the time America got him, he had fought in the hardscrabble war in Angola, crawled on his belly through a wilderness of corpses, been imprisoned in Havana for stealing and butchering horses, and then, on his release, been convicted again for attempting to escape Cuba. He was exactly the kind of Cuban that Castro did not want.

On May 9, 1980—one year into his twelve-year sentence for the attempted escape—Buergos's dungeon threw open its doors, and he was taken to the port of Mariel. There, with very little ado, his wildest dream came true: he was put on a cargo boat bound for Key West. Forty-eight hours later—sunburned, sun blind, and dehydrated—he was whisked through a processing center with thousands of other refugees and put on a bus to Fort Chaffee, a military base in Arkansas. Five months later, he was in Washington, DC, free to go out into the crisp October afternoon.

IN THE BEGINNING

*Man wasn't born to live without purpose like a jungle animal, with
no trace of humanity—in the interest of civilization, it is urgently
incumbent on us to put into chains or destroy barbarians who live like
savages in the wild.*

—Editorial, *El Mercurio*, Chile, 1859

On the face of it, Carlos Buergos's peccadilloes may have seemed petty by
the time he reached twenty-five. He was a rapscallion, certainly; a damaged war veteran, perhaps; a scofflaw with two criminal convictions:
horse theft compounded by highly contraband butchery, as well as a desperate attempt to escape his country. But to better understand Carlos's
journey requires a backward glance at the history—of the island, of the
region, of a wild strain of violence that has crazed the Latin American
story for more than five hundred years.

By the end of the fifteenth century, when the Spaniards arrived, the
island that would become Cuba had long been subject to violent interventions, as had many of the scattered islands of the Caribbean. The Caribs,
a warrior tribe that swept up from the heartland of South America and
launched northward from its shores, had become expert navigators and,
over the course of centuries, raided the docile island populations, enslaving females and castrating males. So it was that when Christopher Columbus stepped onto the Cuban shore on October 28, 1492, a history of
terror and colonization had already rattled through the region, leaving
the Arawak people—including the Taíno, and the Ciboney—hopeful
that the Spanish interlopers might actually be defenders against an age-
old scourge.

The Spaniards turned out to be anything but saviors to the Arawak.
Or to the Caribs, for that matter. By 1519—barely a generation after the
arrival of the conquistadors—the native population of Cuba had been
decimated: by displacement, by disease, but most drastically by the Spanish order to slaughter any Taíno who dared resist his new masters. The
conquering governor who would eventually feud with Hernán Cortés
over the conquest of Mexico, Diego Velázquez, had ordered his men to

force the Taíno to the mines. There was a perpetual shortage of labor, and the Spaniards wasted no time in raiding the surrounding islands for slaves and transporting whole populations to Cuba in bondage. The natives of Cuba, who by then were starving, having lost their ancient farmlands to Spanish cattle ranches, resisted at first. They refused to go quietly; refused to work. Many rose up in rebellion, killing their invaders in random ambushes or clear provocations.

To impose a corrective, the Spaniards swept into the village of Caonao and hacked off the inhabitants' arms, legs, and breasts, leaving three thousand men, women, and children to die. "I saw here cruelty on a scale no living being has ever seen or expects to see," wrote the friar Bartolomé de las Casas. But for all the friar's remorse, the killing did not stop. The head tribesman of the Taíno was assured by his captors that, if he converted to Christianity before he was burned at the stake, he would go to heaven. He spat out his answer: if Catholics were all going to heaven, he would vastly prefer hell, so that he would never be forced to witness such cruelty again.

The Caribs, who were roundly feared in the New World, did not fare much better. When Columbus returned on his second voyage in 1493 and found all the Spaniards he had left behind gone, dead—killed in a wave of xenophobia—he decided to take an even more aggressive tack. He found it useful to call any tribespeople he encountered "Caribs" so that his men could enslave entire populations with impunity. The Caribs reputedly practiced cannibalism—although whether they killed to eat or ate the already-dead is up for debate, and the whole claim may have been a rumor promulgated largely by the Spaniards—but it proved to be a handy distinction. As far as the Spanish Church was concerned, there were three Indians who warranted capture and enslavement: cannibals, idolaters, and sodomizers. The Caribs were said to be all three. Columbus's writings reveal that he was very aware of the profit and advantages that might accrue if he accused whole tribes of cannibalism or simply labeled them all as Caribs in order to dispose of them as he wished. In such ways did Columbus institutionalize the concept of good and bad Indians, and then assign labels freely to suit his purposes. In time, all who inhabited the coast of Venezuela as well as the Antilles—from Cuba to Curaçao—were accused of cannibalism and thus were candidates for hard labor in the mines. The indigenous peoples of Mexico, Ecuador, and Colombia were eventually labeled Caribs, too, leaving them open to whatever whims the conquistadors had in mind: slavery, rapine, even extermination.

When Columbus put a number of "Caribs" in chains and brought them to Spain after his second voyage, the chaplain of Queen Isabella's court dropped his books to rush down to the open market at Medina del Campo and see the New World monsters for himself. The holy man later wrote that, as he watched "the cannibals" being herded back onto the boats, he couldn't help but think that they "showed all the ferocity and bestiality of fierce African lions when they realize they've fallen into a trap. Anyone who lays eyes upon them will admit to a kind of horror in the gut, so atrocious and diabolical is the savagery that nature and cruelty have imprinted on their faces. I confess this as much for myself as for those who accompanied me *more than once* to look upon them there."

It was the effect Columbus had intended. The stage was now set for the rampant brutality that would follow in the Americas. It was no surprise then, ten years later in 1503, when the queen spelled it out in the event there was any doubt: "If such cannibals continue to resist and do not admit and receive my Captains or men on such voyages by my orders, nor hear them in order to be taught our Sacred Catholic Faith and be in my service and obedience, they may be captured and are to be taken to these my Kingdoms and Domain and to other parts and places and be sold."

As a result, thousands of indigenous tribespeople who were arbitrarily labeled Caribs were forced into slavery, or driven into jungle or mountain, or killed. Within twenty-five years, most of the Indians of Cuba were gone, their lands replaced by livestock. By 1520, the Indians of Hispaniola had been uprooted and shipped off to hard labor elsewhere. Within a half century, because indigenous populations in the New World had been so reduced by war, disease, and starvation, the conquistadors called for a broader definition of the criteria under which locals could be enslaved. Women and children became fair game. A village of tribespeople might be called Caribs for the convenience of the capture, or the kill. Sir Walter Raleigh, no lover of Spain or Portugal— joked that he himself was a Carib—a cannibal—fair game.

Eventually the Spanish Crown granted licenses to make war against the Caribs *a sangre y fuego*—that is, to lay waste to populations entirely. In Brazil, which Pedro Álvares Cabral had colonized in 1500, the Portuguese continued the ruthless practices that had been lucrative for them on the African coast, where they had been slaving since the 1460s. Mass killings, torture, brutality—learned to perfection in the Crusades, in the wars to expel the Moors, in the rape of Africa—became an easy expedient for conquest and settlement. And then acceptable governing tools. In the age-old campaign to expel the Muslims and Jews from Iberia, after all, the goal had always been "*limpieza de sangre*," or racial purity. That term, "cleanliness of blood," in all its airbrushed arrogance, brings to mind the muddy contemporary expression "ethnic cleansing," which, truth be told, means genocide.

Indeed, as the friar las Casas recorded, "Spaniards would brag about their panoply of cruelties, each trying to best the other on novel ways to spill blood." They excelled in torturing Indians for information, slaughtering a crowd to force an entire village into submission, practicing their swordsmanship by carving Tainos from chest to groin, spilling their entrails. "All this, and more, I saw, so foreign to human nature," las Casas wrote sadly. "I shudder to tell it." The bloodletting that followed in the Americas—as well as the atrocities imposed on ten million Africans who were abducted, enslaved, and shipped across the seas to replace the natives' dwindling numbers—did not abate for hundreds of years, until 1804, when the French colony of Saint Domingue rose up, slaughtered its white masters, and established the Republic of Haiti, at which point a collective shudder rippled up and down Latin America's spine, from the Rio Grande to Tierra del Fuego, and the downtrodden dared to think that they might try violence in return.

Spain had come to the Americas with a long history of racial bloodlust: the Muslims of Granada had slaughtered its Jews; Castile's Catholic king personally led a bloodbath against Semites; in time, more than a hundred thousand Jews were massacred in the 1391 pogroms; King Ferdinand's wars against the Arab infidels, which ended the very year that Isabella sent Columbus to do his will in the New World, had forged generations schooled in "holy wars" and their attendant brutalities. Portugal was no different. Accustomed to maritime adventures in which it was sport or good business to invade the lands of the darker races and subjugate incompatible universes, Iberia was convinced it was ready for whatever the New World would bring. Hadn't medieval lore held that the periphery of their known world harbored cannibals, dog-faced humans, and monsters of nature? Reality could hardly be worse. And yet the Iberians were not alone in their appetite for venturing beyond their territories and enslaving distant populations. As fate would have it, when Old World met New on the warm sands of the Caribbean, the native peoples of the Americas knew something about the business of rampant ambition. They, too, had seen their share of conquest and conflagration. They, too, had been erstwhile conquerors.

For all the contemporary revisionist scholarship that has portrayed Latin American Indians as docile, peaceable innocents in the face of Spanish and Portuguese ruthlessness, the archaeological evidence suggests otherwise. Indigenous America had its war hungry as well as its peaceful nations. From Cape Cod to Cape Horn, the pre-Columbian hemisphere teemed not only with large, diverse populations but also with bellicose tribes that reveled in vanquishing their neighbors and appropriating their wealth. The Taíno, portrayed by Columbus as the "good," peace-loving Indians of the Americas, indeed had been known for their wars and butchery. The Spaniards eventually decimated the Taíno in Cuba and Hispaniola, reducing them in the course of fifteen years—by disease, forced labor, and outright massacre—from one million souls to a pitiable sixty thousand. But it does history no service to claim that the Taíno were not proud fighters in their own precolonial sphere.

There is no argument about the pugnacity of the indigenous of Central America, however. The Tlaxcalans, skilled warriors who eventually collaborated with Hernán Cortés in overpowering Montezuma, had been engaged for the better part of a century in a state of perpetual war against the Aztecs. The Aztecs themselves were past masters at genocide, memorializing their truculence in vast, fearsome walls of severed heads. The skull towers at Tenochtitlán alone were said to number as many as 136,000 decapitated crania, embedded into the stone. One can only imagine the carnage in the killing fields of the Mexica, the horrific stench of death, the deranged cries of victory as one head after another was ripped from its trunk and borne high. Raising a hewed head by the hair was seen as controlling an enemy's vital force—the head itself was the governing member, to be sure, but, to the indigenous American, a man's mane contained his spiritual essence, his *vis vitae*. In 1487, a mere five years before the New World arrival of the conquistadors, Montezuma II's predecessor, Ahuitzotl, conducted a mass execution of his enemies, ordering his armies to capture and behead eighty thousand victims in order to end a punishing drought and famine, revivify the Empire of the Sun, and consecrate the holy site of his Templo Mayor. These were trophies offered to the Aztec gods, ensuring the orderly progress of seasons and the ongoing renewal of the cosmos.

One of those gods, Xipe Totec, ruler of war as well as earthly abundance, was known as "the Flayer," since he wore masks or capes of flayed human skin, carved from the faces and bodies of live captives. Tied intimately to the notion of the natural world, ritual flaying among the Aztecs was a form of paying tribute to the miracle of a dry seed, which molts its husk before germination; bloodletting was a form of feeding the earth with vital energy; ripping a beating heart from a chest was tantamount to seizing the very wonder of life itself.

The Mayans, no strangers to these practices, had their infamous killing alleys, where advancing armies would be duped by a wall behind a wall, trapped, and slaughtered in vast numbers. They, too, favored decapitation and torture, and not only in times of war. There was the ballgame celebrating the powers of darkness and light, for example; the Mayans called it *pitz*. Before the start of a game, a Mayan priest would bash in a female prisoner's skull, lop off her head with a razor-sharp obsidian blade, and drag her bleeding body across the grounds of the ball court to feed the Earth Mother before a vigorous match of *pitz*. For this and other customary ceremonies, the Mayans and Aztecs needed captives, conquered tribes, sacrificial fodder. In such ways was warfare in those Americas seen as part and parcel of the ritual of worship—a necessary practice to perpetuate the natural order of things.

Although time and vast distances separate the ancient peoples of the Caribbean and Central America on the one hand and those of South America on the other, there is surprising concord in their uses of violence. The Aztec god Xipe Totec, "the Flayer," and the Moche god Ai Apaec, "the Decapitator," seem cut from the same cloth, conjured by similar imaginations. They both represent darkness and light, death and birth, chaos and order, folded—paradoxically, perhaps, to our Western minds—into a single figure. Great good was attributed to their benevolence, and great atrocities were carried out in their names. The Inca and Moche civilizations of Peru, too, may have brought a semblance of order to their citizens and appealed to a mass respect for the law, but they were also cultures built on a war model, in which land-grabbing, forced slavery, and human sacrifice were the governing principles of the day.

Imagine then, when such cultures, tempered by centuries of war and ambition, were faced by invaders as hard-bitten as the Spaniards and the Portuguese. As fate would have it, up and down the Americas at the very end of the fifteenth century, the most powerful of those cultures—the Caribs, Taíno, Aztecs, and Incas—all found themselves in reset mode, reorganizing after punishing defeats and civil wars, or crippled by a deadly plague that seemed to waft through before the invasion itself, like a diabolical herald of the catastrophe to come.

As for the tribes that were unprepared for pitched battle—the isolated Arawaks of the Bahamas, for instance—there was nothing to be done but face the onslaught. Columbus had commented on their languid, gentle nature when he first saw them on the shore of his New World, but he had no qualms about enslaving hundreds and shipping them off to die at sea or be sold at the slave markets of southern Spain.

The Muíscas—the formidable, emerald-rich federation of tribes nestled in the Andean highlands called Bacatá (Bogotá)—fared no better. By the time the Spanish expedition that had begun in the Caribbean port of Santa Marta wended its way more than six hundred miles upriver through jungle and mountain to reach the Muíscas, the vertiginous voyage had taken a heavy toll on the invaders. From the 700 men who began that expedition on the coast, only 160 survived. But Gonzalo Jiménez de Quesada was so driven by the vision of El Dorado and his conviction that the lord cacique of Bogotá was none other than the gold-dusted prince of lore, that he persevered, arriving in that Andean aerie prepared to do whatever necessary to bring it to its knees. No sooner did he arrive with his slavering mastiffs and his steel-toting soldiers than he demanded that the lord chieftain present himself. When he didn't, Jiménez de Quesada issued the order to fight, slaughter the population if need be, ransom its chieftains for gold, seize their emerald mines, and found a city for Spain. He called it Santa Fe de Bogotá—the sainted faith of Bogotá—a cynical twist, given that the lord cacique of Bogotá was killed, his successor—Sagipá—tortured and sacrificed, and if any sainted faith was expressed in the process, it was the faith that Jiménez would soon be a very rich man. Indeed, by the time the victory was secured and the booty gathered, he would steal more than seven thousand emeralds in the rout.

BRED IN THE BONE

It's not my fault. It's just my nature.

—Aesop

Anthropologists have a name for a mind-set born of hundreds of years of history: they call it transgenerational epigenetic inheritance. It is an emerging science, with much still to discover and understand, but the implications about the ways a social environment can influence the biology of an entire generation or a race of people are broadly suggested and profound. Some studies have focused on the ways that stress, social pressure, and hardship have affected certain races over generations. Others conclude that the effects of violence committed against a single parent can be passed on to a fetus in concrete genetic ways. A holocaust or attempted genocide, for instance, can have an abiding effect on the unborn. As can domestic violence. As can war. What does this suggest about an entire people whose history is steeped in violence and whose present generations to this day live with the echoes of brutality and bloodshed?

Latin American historians summon the ancient Greek fabulist Aesop to explain how such histories are not easily lost. It is a simple but memorable story. As Aesop tells it, a scorpion and a frog met one day on the bank of a river, and the scorpion, unable to swim, asked the frog to carry him across on its back. The frog asked, "How do I know you won't sting me in the journey?" The scorpion answered, "Fool! If I sting you, we'll both drown!" Satisfied, the frog allowed the scorpion to mount his back, and the two set out across the water. But halfway to the other shore, the scorpion leapt out and stung the frog. The frog, sensing the poison course through him, gasped, "Why in the world did you do that?" The scorpion shrugged and said, "It's not my fault. It's just my nature."

For Aesop, this inexplicable, core impulse was nature as the Greeks truly meant it. *Physis.* In Latin, *natura.* An essential quality, an innate disposition so ingrained that it is coded in our physical, chemical, biological selves. Some creatures are programmed to sting. Others will be stung. Over time, that behavior is learned, digested, imprinted on the self as surely as an Icelander, in all likelihood, has blue eyes, and an African is born with dark brown.

In other words, an inclination to violence can be a tangible, traceable pattern. The story of Latin America as we know it began with a confrontation so cataclysmic that it had a swift and dire impact. It didn't happen in a vacuum. The protagonists involved had brought separate, highly articulated histories to the moment. As for the indigenous, the most powerful among them were deeply attuned to their land and their gods; they were ambitious, evangelical, militaristic, sanguinary, with a highly developed sense of their mission and dominion. The invading conquistadors from Spain and Portugal were similarly attuned to king and god; they were equally ambitious, evangelical, militaristic, sanguinary, and they had fought Semite "infidels" in bloody, righteous wars for centuries—killing, enslaving, or expelling a half million in one decade alone—sharply honing a sense that *they* were the chosen ones.

Some contemporary historians depict the moment of first contact as unequal from the start: ruthless violence on the part of the Spaniards; a corresponding awe, naiveté—even cowardice—on the part of the indigenous. The evidence tells us this is not so. The great, developed civilizations—the Mexica, Inca, and Muísca—were all too willing and able to fight. Their natures and histories disposed them to do so. The surprising, inopportune arrival of the Spanish, the crippling disease they brought with them, the reeling horses, terrifying mastiffs, the miraculous "thundersticks," the alien battle conventions, the disorienting lies and deceit—all these contributed to the defeat of the great indigenous nations. It was not because they didn't know how to make war, and certainly not because they trembled at the prospect.

At the heart of that centuries-long confrontation was a deeply ingrained conviction—long instilled in the Spanish as well as in their indigenous counterparts—that extreme violence was justified, that invaders were often victors, that a strong arm would be necessary to keep the new order in place. Although Spain's Council of the Indies enacted laws to prevent adventurers from excessive acts of cruelty, the men on the front lines of conquest paid little attention to them. These were men well accustomed to countermanding orders and rebelling against their superiors. Cortés, Balboa, Pizarro—they had all bucked the system at some juncture of their careers, disobeyed the rules, launched out on their own. Although they paid voluble lip service to the king and their Christian faith, they had brought wild, rebellious impulses with them. Balboa, after all, had ignored all orders and appointed himself supreme leader in Castilla de Oro. Cortés had followed his example in Veracruz. In Paraguay, one of the conquistadors had gone so far as to put Governor Álvar Núñez Cabeza de Vaca on a ship and send him back to Spain in irons. Pizarro had snubbed his immediate bosses in favor of conducting his own version of conquest. They fought with one another, fought with their superiors. Finding themselves in pagan territory, beyond the reach of the Church or Spanish courts of justice, most exercised a wanton barbarity, and even the seemingly most principled among them did not try to stem the abuses. Rapacity, gold fever, a desperate courage against overwhelming odds, a hyperinflated sense of superiority, a basic contempt for the Indian—call it what you will—these are the impulses that galvanized them, and the effects on the indigenous world were cataclysmic.

When European intellectuals began to raise moral arguments against the spiraling genocide, the enslavement of whole populations, the hard labor under penalty of death, and the unbridled exploitation—Spanish adventurers argued that all these should be permissible, because banishment (the usual punishment for prisoners of war) was impossible in these latitudes, as was imprisonment. Moreover, they insisted, the "Indians didn't suffer whippings in the same way the Spanish did, because they lacked the same sense of honor." Indeed, they argued, harsh, penal labor might even be salutary for the heathen. In the process of regular, systematized labor, an Indian might acquire a suitable trade. Perhaps even good manners.

As Spain realized the magnitude of its luck and locked down on its newly won territories, the colonial structure it imposed was punitive in the extreme. Absolute rule became the hallmark. It is almost as if the Spanish understood from the very start that the only way they could hold on to their shining prize was to install a strictly authoritarian, suffocating vice. From the outset, as Spain began to pour governors, treasurers, and artisans into its colonies—as silver and gold began their steady, exhilarating flow from Mexico and Peru—the royal court insisted that viceroys and captain generals report directly to the king, making him the supreme overseer of American interests. King Carlos soon had many reasons besides precious metals to protect his grip on the American bonanza. Spain now controlled the entire world supply of cocoa. It extracted copper, indigo, sugar, pearls, emeralds, cotton, wool, tomatoes, potatoes, and leather from the New World and rerouted all of it from storehouses in Cádiz to points around the globe.

To prevent its colonial populations from trading in these goods themselves, Spain carefully constructed a rigid system of domination. All foreign contact was forbidden. Movement between the colonies was closely monitored. Contraband was punishable by death. No foreigners could visit the colonies without permission from the king. Only the Spanish born could own businesses, and no American-born subjects, no matter how aristocratic, were permitted to plant their own grapes, own their own vineyards, grow tobacco, make spirits, or propagate olive trees. And no American—even if his parents were Spanish born—could vote or take part in government. The Tribunal of the Inquisition, which Ferdinand and Isabella had put in place years before to keep a firm hold on the empire, called for penalties of death or torture for any number of perceived transgressions: books or newspapers could not be published or sold without express permission of the Council of the Indies, and many a rebel intellectual would be imprisoned and tortured for that crime. Colonials were barred from owning printing presses. Indeed, when Simón Bolívar, liberator of six republics, undertook his wars of independence in the early nineteenth century, he made a point of hauling a printing press onto the battlefield as a direct provocation to the Spanish masters. Under the king's rule, the implementation of every colonial document, the approval of every venture, the mailing of every letter was a long, costly affair that required Cádiz's approval. And woe to any foreign vessel that crossed into New World waters: non-Spanish ships were assumed to be enemy craft and attacked.

Stringent government was nothing new to indigenous America. What was new was that it was being enforced by a conquering tribe thousands of miles away. All the same, the basic parameters of conquest seemed familiar: Laws would subject them to the whims of a distant overlord. Their language, their customs, their gods—even their places of residence—would change according to alien needs and desires. The most disorienting aspect of all of this was that the conquerors they had been fighting for generations—the lordly Incas, ruthless Aztecs, powerful Muíscas—were now among the conquered, too.

It was thought that the Inca ruler Pachacutec, among the most successful in extending the Empire of the Sun, had perfected the art of conquest. It was he, after all, who had established the highly successful method of conquer and divide. Once a tribe was defeated in war, Pachacutec would divide it into two, north and south. The upper half would be called *hanan*; the lower, *hurin*. He would then goad the districts into competing against each other. Sundered geographically and psychologically, a population would be too preoccupied about its brother enemy to care much about its conqueror, and too exhausted to mount a unified rebellion against the Incas. To perpetuate these radical divisions—and create a Montague versus Capulet level of animus—the Incas instigated outright violence between the districts, even battle. The scheme was downright Machiavellian, highly strategic, meant to achieve several goals at once: maintain supremacy, forge skilled warriors for the Incan armies, foment useful jealousies, ensure widespread subjugation, yet keep the overall peace. Ritual battles became deeply ingrained in the social structure of the Andean people. So profoundly rooted, in fact, that, like the scorpion's sting, they emerged as the default reaction. Ritual violence has persisted through the centuries in the highlands of Peru. It has persisted, in truth, throughout the Latin American cosmos.

There is a great deal of evidence for this. Just as the Spaniards kept good records of every ounce of silver they took from the New World, every slave they brought into it, every newborn Indian whose soul the Church could now claim, they kept track of the bloody, recurring confrontations among the indigenous as they persisted—largely unchecked—throughout the course of colonial rule. The ritual battles were held seasonally, on festival days. If villagers had hoes, they used hoes to bludgeon one another; if they had stones, they used stones. It was understood that it was a matter of pride: a man fought for his district—his corner of the region, his little gang—and there was nothing a colonial overseer could do or would do to curb it. Eventually the Spaniards saw that these were rivalries they could exploit, twist, use to control their subjects. It became convenient to point to atrocities wrought by one Indian against another; point at how savage and violent the indigenous population truly was. By the late 1700s, in staged battles between Cuzco's Hanan and Hurin factions, Spanish courts documented cases in which children were being killed in the crossfire. And yet no charges were pressed; everyone understood that this was just how things were.

Even now, in full flower of the twenty-first century, Bolivians of the altiplano hold an annual festival called the Tinku, an ancestral ceremony that has taken place for seven hundred years. In it, thousands of villagers gather on an open stretch of land to get drunk and fight with sticks or stones, often to the death. "If a person dies, it is better for the fields," one man observes, wryly alluding to the ancient practice of spilling sacrificial blood upon the earth to make the crops grow. No police will try to stop it. The authorities understand that this is a day when frustrations will be vented, a people's existential wrath unleashed, and an age-old tradition honored. "Tinku is violent, but peaceful," a humble miner offers. "It is like man and woman, above and below, light and shadow." When morning comes, the sun will rise over the carnage, and, for the living, life will go on. Rivals will shake hands and say, "Thank you, brother; we have tested each other." Men will return to their labors. Widows will bury their dead. And Pachamama—Earth Mother—will swallow her blood sacrifices.

REBELLION

What concerns us most about the Inca civilization is not what has died but what remains.

—José Carlos Mariátegui, 1928

The ancient Indians had always been punctilious about giving Pachamama—or Coatlicue or Bachué—her seasonal quota of blood offerings. Humans were killed to end a drought, stop an earthquake, counter an eclipse. Virgins were strangled and thrown into Lake Titicaca, the umbilical of the world, to ensure fertility and abundance. Prisoners of war were dragged into temples in Mexico or Peru, beheaded, flayed, gutted, and left to pool their blood on stone altars. But these were premeditated, religious acts of violence, prepared meticulously by high priests, supervised ceremoniously, and practiced diligently for a thousand years. In the scant forty years between Columbus's landing and Pizarro's conquest of Peru, however, the violence was raised to an altogether different level. The killing fields of the Americas fed Pachamama a veritable ocean of human blood.

Scholars claim that a mere twenty-one years after Columbus's landing in the Bahamas, the swarming, heavily populated island of Hispaniola was effectively deserted. Almost eight million Amerindians had been killed by violence, abuse, or disease. Many, unwilling to entrust their fate to the invaders, committed suicide or perished in their attempt to escape. Within a few generations following that first encounter in the Caribbean, the vast majority—as many as 95 percent—of Latin American native peoples had been exterminated. Far from deserving to be memorialized by splendid monuments and grand avenues (as they are) from Caracas to Montevideo, the conquistadors need to be seen as all the evidence reveals them: as looters, liars, murderers, enslavers, oppressors—perpetrators of a hecatomb so vast and so enduring that it is difficult at this distance to truly comprehend it.

But belligerence and ambition were not the only tools of war the Europeans brought with them. There was also the scourge of smallpox, the secret weapon that Spanish conquistadors didn't even know they had. An anthropologist claims that one lone slave, arriving gravely ill in Mexico in 1520, months after Cortés's landing, was all it took to infect an entire population. Seeing the effects of a devastating plague all around them in that unfamiliar land, Cortés and his men could not possibly have factored in the science. To them, the magnitude of the dying was sure confirmation that God was on their side. To Montezuma and the Mexicans, it was a demoralizing signal that their gods had abandoned them. Even though Cortés landed on those shores with little more than six hundred men and the bizarre conviction that he could take on a military state of any size, his ambition suddenly seemed viable. All he needed to do was employ the ruthless butchery he had learned from his hard-bitten cohort in the Caribbean. When he sensed one of his men was disloyal, he executed the offending soldier on the spot. When he suspected an Indian of spying, he chopped off his hands and sent him, stumps bleeding, to the enemy camp. He deployed a deceptive diplomacy, made a few advantageous alliances, brandished guns in the face of spears, steel as opposed to oak, and lost only two hundred men in the enterprise. To understand the impact of the ensuing onslaught, the numbers say it best: by 1618, less than one hundred years later, Mexico's buoyant, indigenous population of about twenty-five million had plunged to a feeble one and a half million. It had lost more than 90 percent of its people. One year later, the Atlantic slave trade of African blacks to Latin America began.

That general trajectory was essentially the same with the Incas, since Pizarro was able to follow Cortés's winning strategy to the letter. Pizarro landed on the Peruvian coast with only 168 men and proceeded through that war-torn, beleaguered land to take on an empire of millions. Smallpox had preceded him, passed along from one seafaring indigenous merchant to another, until it broke into a full-fledged epidemic that ripped through much of South America by 1526. Pizarro's arrival in 1531, on the tail of that viral visitation, could not have been more fortunate for Spain. Even as disease was consuming the Inca Empire, the sons of Huayna Capac were sending their armies against each other in a mad *hanan* and *hurin*—north-south—war their father had effectively conceived. Once Pizarro killed Atahualpa and Huascar, and two more Lord Incas were slain in a relentless effort to exterminate the ruling class, the empire appeared to be beheaded. But they hadn't gone gently: within six years of conquest, the Incas had mounted a number of major, well-planned, and bold rebellions against their would-be masters. The last hereditary Lord Inca, Tupac Amaru—born twelve years after the arrival of the Spaniards—held out in the mountains, fighting the Spanish forces until they finally hunted him down in 1572, brought him to Cuzco with a rope around his neck, and executed him in a public spectacle for all to see. It was, according to an observer, a terrifying sight for the fifteen thousand Indians who were forced to witness the decapitation. Seeing the nephew of Atahualpa and Huascar brought to his knees and murdered, after witnessing forty years of an effort to exterminate every trace of Inca rule, the crowd raised such a loud lament that it "deafened the skies, making the heavens reecho with a terrible wailing."

By then, Francisco de Toledo, the viceroy who had arrived to govern the valuable, sprawling colony of Peru, claimed to be appalled at the "imbruted Spaniards" of this savage New World. In time, however, he abandoned that indignation and sent what was left of the indigenous to the mines, establishing a full-fledged silver economy that had more drastic consequences than the swords of conquest. Ten years later, the vast majority of the hemisphere—the entire South American continent, all of Central America, and North America as far as California—belonged to the Spanish king. Fifty years later, more than half the population of that area had been lost to diseases brought by white men: smallpox, tetanus, typhus, leprosy, and yellow fever, as well as a number of pulmonary, intestinal, and venereal diseases. (In come cases, the contagion was purposeful, proliferated by distributing infected blankets or tainted baubles to unsuspecting tribes.) Forty percent more perished from wars, executions, starvation, and hard labor—even suicide, as tribes fled the onslaught and lost themselves to the inhospitable wilderness of mountain and jungle.

We will never know how many indigenous wandered the Western Hemisphere before Columbus, since by the time the Europeans got around to counting them, so many had been killed by germs or swords. Scholars do tell us that when the Viceroyalty of Mexico celebrated its hundredth anniversary in the 1620s, the humming human population Cortés encountered in his march to Tenochtitlán had been reduced to a mere 700,000. Scholars also estimate that before the conquest, the hemisphere's indigenous population may have ranged anywhere from 40 million to 140 million. A century later, fewer than 9 million were alive.

As downtrodden and subjugated as the New World became under the Spanish boot, a natural impulse to violence against the oppressor finally began to flare in insurgencies throughout the hemisphere. The slow burn of anger had always been there. But the indigenous had been disoriented, hesitant to respond, paralyzed by colonial overlords too powerful to dislodge—forces that had hijacked and shackled whole civilizations. All the same, three centuries after Columbus's landing, the animus began to surface more boldly, especially as Spain lost more and more footing in the world. Simmering resentments that the colored races—now a veritable rainbow of crossbreeds—harbored against "whites" began erupting in short, sharp explosions of collective rage.

One of the most resounding of these occurred in Santa Fe de Nuevo Mexico in 1680. The Pueblo Indians, who had been crippled by one Spanish expedition after another for more than 150 years, had not had much success with insurrections. They had tried to beat back the hostile invaders, reject their enforced religion, buck all efforts at mass enslavement, but had been overcome by relentless reprisals from the other side. In 1598, when the colonial governor of Mexico, Juan de Oñate, set out with an expedition to colonize the fertile Rio Grande valley, an area already occupied by forty thousand Pueblo Indians, the Puebloans fought back. But they were overcome by Spain's superior war machine. The victorious Governor Oñate, wanting to show the Pueblo Indians a lesson, ordered his men to amputate the right foot of every indigenous male over twenty-five. To cap that punishment, he forced the women into slavery and separated the children from their families so that they could be indoctrinated fully in the Catholic faith.

It took almost one hundred years, but the resulting anger was so overwhelming that it exploded in a fierce Pueblo uprising in 1680. The Indians swept into the Spanish plantations, killed four hundred of the whites, including women, children, and priests, and then drove two thousand more out of the valley, effectively purging their land of whites. There was a brutal calculus at work here: in order to rid themselves of Spanish rule and reclaim their identity after almost two centuries of relentless ethnocide, the indigenous had decided they would need to extinguish the very existence of their overlords. In other words, the whites needed to go or die. The Puebloans proceeded to destroy all the churches and Christian images, dissolve marriages effected under Spanish missionaries, and try to restore the world as they had known it before the Europeans arrived. It did not last long. In 1692, twelve years after the bloodbath, the Spaniards swept back in to reclaim their dominion over the Rio Grande.

The next large-scale uprising in the colonies took place in Quito in 1765. Unlike the convulsion in Mexico, which was largely about land and identity, this one was economically driven. For years, the citizens of that Andean colony—largely weavers—had suffered a punishing decline in their livelihoods. There were reasons: they had endured a plummeting population of Indians in the highlands where wool was produced, a glut of cheap textiles was pouring in from Europe, and a vertiginous economic spiral had taken hold. Desperate to survive, the Quiteños turned instead to producing contraband—*aguardiente*, for example, a sugar-cane liquor easy enough to make in anyone's hut—and they found work in a buoyant underground that butchered wild animals, tanned leather, hawked food, and bootlegged fermented *chicha*. To quash this, the viceroy of New Granada (who effectively oversaw Ecuador, Colombia, and Venezuela) arbitrarily assigned all control of the viceroyalties' private stills, and all the taxes their liquor sales might raise, to the Royal Treasury in Madrid. His peremptory crackdown threatened to bring a thriving, illegal market to a halt and create an even more dire economic crisis. The people of Quito wanted no part of it. They rose up, took to the streets in a violent revolt, and ultimately expelled the Spanish, setting up a coalition that managed to govern that city for a year before a highly armed viceregal army stormed in and retook the power, beginning an era of harsher rule.

Fifteen years later, the winds of dissent, which had bedeviled the Viceroyalty of Peru for decades, reached the Bolivian altiplano like a gale force. An Aymara native named Tomás Catari had been trying for years to persuade his Spanish overlords to curb abuses against the Indians of the mineral-rich area of La Paz, but he got no results save jail sentences and brutal floggings. Upon his release, secured only because his supporters took a Spanish governor hostage and threatened to kill him, Catari decided to mount a revolt against the whites. In September 1780, Indian rebel groups began raiding and looting haciendas and exterminating not only Spaniards but also anyone who did not pledge loyalty to their revolution.

Months later, as if a mortal pressure cooker were at work, a bloody race war broke out in Peru. The trouble began when a mestizo *curaca*, who would eventually call himself Tupac Amaru II and claim to be a descendant of the last ruling Inca, seized the Spanish *corregidor* Antonio de Arriaga after a long and vinous lunch. Holding the government official captive in his own house, Tupac Amaru ordered the governor to summon two hundred regional leaders—Spaniards and mestizos alike—to the plaza at Tungasuca. When they arrived, Tupac Amaru demanded that the governor's Indian slave execute his own master. Then he marched on Cuzco with six thousand Indians, killing every white man, woman, and child in his way. This was no act of impulse. It was a last-gasp effort to turn history on its ear. Like Tomás Catari, Tupac Amaru had tried diplomacy at first, with no success whatsoever. For years, he had implored Arriaga to abolish the cruelties of the Indian tribute and be more humane to his subjects overall. Indeed, as the *curaca* responsible for collecting those tributes, he had run afoul of his Spanish masters for failing to do so. But his entreaties had gone ignored. Frustrated, angry, Tupac Amaru gathered a vast army of many more thousands, armed them with stolen muskets and hoarded arms, and issued his last warning to the Creoles, the American-born whites who had long expressed solidarity in their rage against the ruling Spaniards: "I have decided to shake off the unbearable weight and rid this bad government of its leaders. . . . If you elect to support me, you will suffer no ill consequences, not in your lives or on your plantations, but if you reject this warning, you will face ruin and reap the fury of my legions, which will reduce your cities to ashes. . . . I have seventy thousand men at my command."

The bloodshed lasted for two years, ripping through Spanish enclaves as mercilessly as the invaders had ripped into Indian villages centuries before. Tupac Amaru had said very clearly that in order to restore the old order he might need "to put an end to all Europeans." Moreover, in a fit of exultant hyperbole, Tupac Amaru claimed that he had received a royal order from Madrid to kill every *puka kunka* (literally, every red neck) who inhabited the Viceroyalty of Peru. His followers believed him. And it was precisely what they began to do. Euphoric, crazed by the rampant bloodletting, the victorious rebels danced, drunk, on the corpses of whites. There were reports that they fed on white flesh; that they ripped out hearts and painted their faces with the gore. Some, it was said, even indulged in the ancient practice of drinking from skulls. One leader demanded that the heads of all white eminences be severed and brought to him so that he could personally pierce their eyes. The news of these atrocities shocked the Creoles, who had encouraged revolt and wanted nothing more than to be rid of their colonial bosses. Now they could only recoil in horror. This was hardly the uprising against the king that they had hoped for. It was a race war. And it was as rabid against whites as their conquistador forebears had ever been against brown.

In the end, the royalist armies swept in and crushed the Andean rebels, costing the Indians some hundred thousand lives. Tupac Amaru II was captured and brought to Cuzco's plaza, just as his namesake Tupac Amaru had been brought to the same open square two centuries before. When the Spanish inspector general asked him for the names of his accomplices, he replied, "I only know of two, and they are you and I: you as oppressor of my lands, and I because I am striving to rescue it from your tyranny." Infuriated by the insolence of that reply, the Spaniard ordered his men to cut out the Indian's tongue and draw and quarter him on the spot. The directives were specific and registered officially to the letter:

> His hands and feet will be bound by strong cords to the girths of four horses, which will be galloped to four corners of the Tahuantinsuyu, ripping his body apart. The torso will then be taken to the promontory called Cerro Picchu, from whence he had the temerity to invade, intimidate, and lay siege to this city, and there it will be burned to ashes in a public bonfire. . . . Tupac Amaru's head will be sent to Tinta so that it can hang from the gallows for three days, after which it will be thrust on a stake at the main entrance to the city. One of his arms will be sent to Tungasuca, where he was a *cacique*, to be

displayed in the same way, and the other to the capital province of Carabaya. His legs will be dispatched, respectively, to Livitica and Santa Rosas in the provinces of Chumbivilcas and Lampa.

The inspector general's minions went about their grim business. They carved out his tongue with one whack of the sword. But the four horses to which they tied Tupac Amaru's wrists and ankles would not comply. Each time they hoisted the Inca up like a spider sprawled on a web, his hands and feet slipped through the straps, and he fell to the ground. The soldiers slit his throat instead; hacked off his head, hands, and feet; and sent them off to be displayed on pikes, as ordered, at various crossroads of six cities. The same was done to his wife, Micaela. The tortures and executions were repeated throughout the day until all members of his family were dispatched. When he saw his mother's tongue carved from her head, Tupac Amaru's youngest child issued a piercing shriek. Legend has it that the sound of that cry was so heartbreaking, so indelible, that it signaled the end of Spanish dominion in America.

Word of Tupac Amaru II's grisly fate electrified the colonies, inflaming and terrifying any and all who would contemplate a similar rebellion. For blacks, for whom slavery's inhumanities were untenable, the urge only grew. They had little to lose. But for white Creoles, who were, after all, part of the ruling class—if only by virtue of their skin—dreams of insurgency now spurred the fear that revenge would come not only from Spain but also from a massive colored population. Those fears were magnified in New Granada months later, when an army of twenty thousand marched against the far more powerful Viceroyalty in Bogotá to protest high taxes. One of the leaders, José Antonio Galán, an illiterate mestizo swept by the fever of the moment, proclaimed the black slaves free and exhorted them to turn their machetes against their masters. When they began to do just that, Galán was condemned to be hanged until dead, drawn and quartered, and beheaded, with his limbs sent to every district in which he had lived. To ensure that such a vile subject would never be born again, his house was dusted with salt, the grains tamped deep into the surrounding earth. It was a warning that revolt would be met with brute force—a prophylactic against all malcontents.

THE MACHETE, THREE HUNDRED YEARS LATER
Cuba, 1955–1970

The men who knew how to use a machete to cut cane demonstrated one day that they also knew how to use a machete to kill.

—Fidel Castro, 1962

Carlos Buergos, footloose and free until he found himself in a Cuban jail, and then—less than a dozen years after—in an American penitentiary, had been born at the cusp of revolution. It was August 1955. Cuba had been free of Spain's yoke for less than sixty years, but once again people were fretting about independence. The powerful whites, the predatory foreigners, the tyrannical government and corrupt oligarchs had become for them a yoke of a different kind.

Two years before, Fidel Castro had led a group of 150 rebels against one of the largest military garrisons in Cuba. The mission had been simple: to capture a massive repository of arms to bolster his revolution. For Castro and his rebels, the regime of Fulgencio Batista represented the epitome of a despotic, debauched, and essentially colonial rule. The banks, national resources—indeed, the entire economy under Batista, including the lion's share of industry—was now controlled by American companies. The Platt Amendment, passed by the US Congress in 1901, a few years after Cuba won its independence from Spain, had prohibited any foreign power aside from the United States from colonizing or entering into treaties with Cuba. It spelled out very clearly that America could intervene in Cuban affairs whenever it desired and could establish military bases wherever it felt necessary. Passed into Cuban law shortly thereafter, it remained in place for decades, making the island a virtual colony of the United States. In 1940, when Batista was elected president, the Platt Amendment was struck from the Cuban constitution to conform with Franklin Roosevelt's "Good Neighbor Policy" of 1933, but the spirit remained, Washington's dominion over the island lived on, and Batista continued to fortify ties with American businesses, lining his own pockets in the process.

Batista was, according to Castro, a *monstrum horrendum*, an illegal president who, after his first elected term, luxuriated for eight years between New York's famed Waldorf Astoria Hotel and Florida's Daytona Beach, manipulating Havana from afar and collaborating with the American Mafia. In 1952 he retook power in a military-backed coup and installed a puppet government dependent entirely on American commercial interests. By the late 1950s, Batista and his coterie had handed over more than 60 percent of all sugar production and profits to companies in the United States. Nearly half of all arable land was owned by American businesses. It was high time, according to Castro, for Batista, his criminal cronies, and US kleptocrats to be cast from Cuba altogether.

For all the grassroots support he was able to rally, Castro's fledgling rebellion against the Moncada Barracks ended badly, and Castro ended up in prison. But in May 1955, just as Carlos was reaching fetal maturity, ready to launch himself into a nervous world, Fidel and his brother Raúl Castro were freed on amnesty. Public opinion had soured on Batista's brazen 1952 power grab—a few distinguished Americans had begun to grumble about Cuban corruption, police brutality, and a reckless indifference to the poor—and Batista needed all the positive publicity he could muster. Someone suggested that amnesty for all political prisoners might be a timely palliative.

Jettisoned from Cuba's shores by Batista's rash publicity stunt, Castro and his rebels now repaired to the jungles of Mexico, where they met the Marxist Argentine doctor Che Guevara and began planning their next assault on Havana. It was precisely as Castro and Che hunched over crude maps of the Cuban archipelago, honing their strategy, learning what they needed to know from hardened veterans of the Spanish Civil War, that Carlos entered this mortal world and saw light for the first time. Castro and Che's combined curriculum was straightforward: they would use guerrilla warfare—the David versus Goliath principle of rebellion—pitting a tiny, nimble, and fearless force against a far larger, more cumbersome one. Just as Carlos blinked his eyes open for the first time, Castro issued his famous proclamation of war: "I believe the hour has come to claim rights, not request them—to seize rather than to beg."

Before Carlos's fifth birthday, Cuba had been turned inside out. Comandante Castro had landed on the jagged shore of southern Cuba with a tiny contingent of eighty-two rebels who—bedraggled, hungry, sea tossed, and sunburned—made their way through cane fields, fainting, stumbling, until they reached the inland region of Alegría de Pío. From there, they sped to take cover in the Sierra Madre mountains, before Batista turned his army against them. A furious guerrilla war followed, lasted two years, and gradually attracted a formidable army of Cubans to the rebel side. On New Year's Day 1959, frightened by their sharp reversal of fortune and fearing the worst, Batista and his deputies fled Havana, thousands of Cubans flooded the docks to hie to other shores, and, within a week, the *comandante* and his *barbudos*—the bearded ones— swept from their strongholds in the Sierra Madre to the panicked streets of the capital. The victory was instantaneous, the euphoria contagious. Carlos's father, who had worked for years as a stevedore, hauling sugar on and off ships and drinking himself into a rum stupor, was eventually sent to cut sugar cane in the emerald fields of Matanzas and prove his loyalty to the revolution.

By the time Carlos was ten, there wasn't enough to eat. There had been numerous reforms that had made life somewhat better for the poor—better access to education and medical care, improved hygiene— but there were seven hungry people under his father's roof, and a cane cutter's wage had not put enough food on the table. Worse, Cuban sugar production, which since the early 1900s had been the greatest in the world, now slipped to a far rung in the global commodities market. No amount of newly minted *revolucionarios* sent out to work the fields could match the burgeoning sugar boom in Brazil, India, and Europe. As Cubans liked to say, *sin azúcar no hay país*—without sugar, we have no country. And that was precisely what US politicians had in mind: to starve Cuba out of its fling with Socialism and incite the people to revert to their former ways. A massive trade embargo, put in place by the administration of President Dwight Eisenhower, expanded under his successor, John F. Kennedy, and adopted by their allies, was now squeezing the Cuban economy to the breaking point. After initial, unrequited overtures to the United States in 1960, Castro eventually turned to the Soviet Union to help feed the people. Carlos's father, too, turned to desperate measures: he began taking his eldest boy to bars to sing for a few centavos, or for a plate of bananas. The boy's anxieties, a product of his skittish time, played out in risky behavior: Carlos began to steal. Small thefts at first. Fruit from a neighbor's tree. Trinkets from a schoolmate. By the time he was thirteen and his voice had dropped, he was pilfering bottles of rum when the bartender wasn't looking, slipping them under his jacket, selling them in the barrio. He snitched from women's purses, grabbed whatever he could, and sold it clandestinely for the little pocket change it would bring him.

Carlos got beaten—often furiously—by schoolmates, storekeepers, neighbors, for these transgressions, but he learned to pick himself up, wipe blood from his face, laugh. He didn't have much respect for authority; he didn't have much respect for anything, really, apart from his immediate needs at hand. He wasn't in the minority in this. There were plenty of disillusioned young men around who felt as he did. Soon he fell in with a gang of fledgling delinquents, sulking on street corners, scheming against the machine.

Whenever his father was sober, he would try to correct Carlos's impulse to misbehave. But lectures left little impression on the boy. In 1970, when Carlos turned fifteen and Castro commanded all Cubans to head for the fields to double the sugar output to ten million tons and recover Cuba's historic place in the market, Carlos's father decided this was his opportunity to instill some discipline in the boy. He handed Carlos a machete and forced him to join in the punishing business of hacking at cane. It was there in those fragrant fields, redolent of sweetness, where African slaves had toiled for hundreds of years, that Carlos witnessed something that would change him forever. An argument between two men escalated into a brawl so murderous that one finally swung his machete and brought it down with a brutal stroke on his opponent's face. The halo of blood, the victim's electrifying howl, the dead silence afterward as the attacker glanced around, eyes wild—these were details, all too human, in a tableau he would never forget.

CHAPTER 7

REVOLUTIONS THAT SHAPED LATIN AMERICA'S PSYCHE

❖

They say grand projects need to be built with calm! Aren't three hundred years of calm enough?

—Simón Bolívar, 1811

MADRID
1807

Latin America had endured three hundred years of Spain's repressive rule when an unexpected window of opportunity flung open and forever altered history. That miracle arrived in the form of a scandal engulfing the royal house in Madrid. In the fall of 1807, King Carlos IV, a shallow man with a nervous temperament, sent a frantic letter to Napoleon Bonaparte of France, begging for help. He had just learned that his son, the crown prince Ferdinand, was plotting to dethrone him and possibly poison his mother. In truth, King Carlos had become the laughingstock of his country. His prime minister, Manuel de Godoy, had been cuckolding him for years. His wife, Queen María Luisa, whose sexual appetites and predatory habits were legendary, had taken a string of young, handsome bodyguards as lovers. A vain, flighty woman, she had frolicked her way from one paramour to another, persuading her witless husband to reward them with high stations, wreaking havoc with one misguided appointment after another. Indeed, it was her old inamorato Prime Minister Godoy who had declared a disastrous war on England, draining the empire's coffers and initiating Spain's headlong spiral to bankruptcy. All this was too much for young Prince Ferdinand, who had begun to despair at the royal house's preposterous state of affairs. He, too, dashed off a letter to Napoleon, inviting the emperor to choose a French bride for him, bless the wedding, and so unite the empires.

Napoleon saw his chance. Taking rank advantage of the family squabble, he persuaded the Spaniards that not only would he defend King Carlos's rule, he would conquer Portugal and make Iberia whole for him. The Treaty of Fontainebleau was signed in October of that year. Desperate to remain king, Carlos gave his blessing to Napoleon to march twenty-five thousand troops through Spanish territory to Lisbon. But come November, Napoleon sent quadruple that number, securing a firm foothold in Spain and overwhelming Lisbon in a bloodless coup. Queen Charlotte and the royal Braganza family had fled Portugal just in time, along with ten thousand loyal subjects, and resettled in Brazil, from which they would rule the Portuguese empire for the next eight years. Four months later, Napoleon's generals slipped into Spain's closely guarded fortresses and took control of the whole peninsula. Spain was paralyzed, under occupation. Its colonial administration, all financial interests, the iron reign of the Council of the Indies, suddenly ground to a complete halt.

But the colonies didn't know it. Even as ordinary Spaniards were showing their grit and astonishing the French by mounting a fierce guerrilla war, Spanish America lived on in languid, blissful ignorance. Though Napoleon's generals were sacking the *madre patria*'s cities, garroting its leaders, and raping its women, life in the colonies went on in its customary, backwater mode. Given Britain's implacable war against Napoleon and its yearlong blockade of Europe's shores, all communication with Latin America had virtually been gagged. To make matters worse, President Thomas Jefferson's misguided Embargo Act of 1807, which effectively throttled all overseas trade and crippled the hemisphere's markets, had compounded the regional isolation.

In Caracas, news that Spain had been savagely overrun by the French was not known until a full seven months later, in July 1808, when two old, dog-eared issues of the *London Times* arrived in the captain general's office, sent on by a dusty functionary in Trinidad. The journals seemed ordinary enough: four-page broadsheets with financial notices. But wedged in between the shipping news and the real estate offerings was the stunning revelation that Spain's king had been deposed and that

Napoleon now ruled the country. Andrés Bello, then secretary to the captain general of Venezuela, translated the notices for his boss, who simply dismissed them as English invention. The truth was confirmed days later when two ships, a French brigantine and an English frigate, arrived in Venezuela's port of La Guaira at precisely the same time and with versions of the same story. The French delegation hurried over the mountain that shields Caracas from the sea, presented itself in resplendent uniforms, and announced that Spain had capitulated—all its colonies, including the patch on which he now stood, now belonged to Napoleon. Not long after that, the English captain came huffing over the hump to proclaim the opposite: the French were flagrant liars, he said. Spain had yet to yield. Indeed, according to him, a junta in Seville had formed to represent the embattled nation, and Britain had pledged it unconditional support.

It was stupefying news to the Venezuelans. Were they to believe that Britain, which had fought Spain bitterly for centuries—whose pirates, among them Sir Francis Drake, had raided Spanish galleons and made off with the king's silver—was suddenly Spain's best friend? It was a pivotal moment for frustrated, embittered Creoles who had been denied power for three hundred years. Much as Napoleon had sensed opportunity in the king's sordid family spat, Caracas's homegrown and beleaguered aristocrats now saw opportunity in their king's sudden and total impotence. They decided to seize the reins, shape destiny, and wrest independence at last.

There were obstacles, and more than a few. Many rich, white colonials with strong family ties to Spain were adamantly against violent revolution. They wanted more rights, a bit more say in government, and certainly more control over their financial affairs. But they had no stomach for the bloody upheavals the French and Haitians had undertaken to win their independence. The Creoles also knew they were but a small coterie in a vast population. They could not count on the colonies' blacks, mulattos, and indigenous to rise alongside them against Spain. Indeed, the Creoles had been lording over the darker races, using and abusing them for hundreds of years. Naturally, slaves and menial laborers, who far outnumbered the whites, regarded all landowners with deep suspicion. They feared that, without Spain's flimsy laws, the whites would grow ever more brutal. With Spain, at the very least, one could point to a written code that censured maltreatment of the indigenous, even if that code consistently went ignored. With white Creoles, who knew what might happen?

A year went by as Spain's colonial governors fretted about their futures and Creoles debated one another to arrive at a revolution they could all agree on. The first declaration of independence, *"el primer grito"* ("first shout"), came a year later in 1809 in the halls of the Royal Audience of Quito. On August 10, in the dark just before dawn, a cabal of Creole revolutionaries barged into the royal palace and presented the sitting governor with an official order announcing that, according to the will of the people, his duties were over. The power was now theirs. It was a fleeting independence, lasting a mere seventy-three days and not, by any means, resounding with any bold assertions about the inherent rights of men. Indeed, the rebels were all too willing to express loyalty to Ferdinand VII, the king's feisty, ambitious son. But it was a tiny island of declared liberty in the course of centuries of imposed rule, and it showed, perhaps for the first time, that whites were as serious about breaking colonialism's shackles as the indigenous, who had endured far worse for hundreds of years. Eventually the viceroyal forces that surrounded Quito laid siege to the city and pounded it into submission, and by October 25, the revolutionaries were rotting in the dungeon, awaiting the hangman. Within a few months, in a grisly fanfare of public executions, they were all dead. Anyone who dared express sympathy, citizens were told, would be charged with high treason and killed. It was a teaching moment for the Spanish, a chastening one for Quiteños, but the lessons would soon be lost in the great wave of revolutions that followed.

BOLÍVAR'S WARS

He rode, fighting all the way, more miles than Ulysses ever sailed. Let the Homers take note of it!

—Thomas Carlyle, 1843

A far stronger revolt eventually bubbled up in Caracas, where the stakes were higher for the colonizer, if only because Venezuela ("little Venice") was a richer, more renowned colony. Leading the insurgency were two young brothers—scions of an aristocratic Creole family—who organized clandestine meetings in one of their family homes outside Caracas and lent their considerable wealth to the enterprise. They were Simón Bolívar and his older brother, Juan Vicente. Simón Bolívar, who was twenty-seven at the time, had accumulated life experiences well beyond his years. He had lost his father at three, his mother before he was nine, and—being an unruly, rebellious orphan who preferred the company of slaves—ended up being raised by stern, disapproving uncles, who sent him off to Madrid to acquire a modicum of discipline and sophistication. What he acquired instead was the conviction that Spain, the *madre patria*, was an incompetent master. Hosted by an aristocratic family friend who offered him a place to stay and an extensive library, Bolívar came of age as a frequent guest of the royal court in Madrid. There he was given a rare glimpse into the scandalous concupiscence that mired the royal family, but he also traveled to France and England, amassing a formidable knowledge of the literature and culture of the Enlightenment.

At nineteen, he married a lovely Spaniard with family connections in Venezuela, but was widowed months later when his young bride died shortly after he brought her to Caracas. For years, he wandered Europe, heartbroken and rudderless, squandering his days as a rake and voluptuary, drowning his sorrows in drink or the dance halls, and devouring the works of Voltaire, Montesquieu, and Thomas Paine. In Paris, he met the celebrated explorer and scientist Alexander von Humboldt, who had nothing but scorn for Spain's cruel colonial subjugation of the Americas. In London, he was mentored by Francisco de Miranda, who not only had fought in the American Revolution and later become friendly with George Washington and Alexander Hamilton, but who'd also gone on to command a French rebel army in the bloody uprising against King Louis XVI. As Bolívar immersed himself in the fervor of this liberal, antimonarchical cohort, he became increasingly radicalized. When he returned to Caracas, it was because he had sworn to dedicate himself to liberating his native land.

Bolívar wanted no part in a "soft" revolution. He was unwilling to wrest power as the Quito rebels had, while continuing to pledge loyalty to Ferdinand VII, now sovereign of the shaky, besieged edifice that was Spain. He had little patience for those who waved banners of liberty while swearing allegiance to a king. Unlike many of his fellow Creoles—unlike his own departed father, who had flirted with rebellion decades before—Bolívar understood that a revolution would never be won in the polite halls of government. It would need to engage the people. It might need to employ extreme violence.

Over the years, traveling through Napoleon's France and the Duke of Wellington's England, meeting fellow revolutionaries from numerous colonies in Latin America, his convictions about independence had grown rock hard and absolute. He knew Ferdinand VII all too well—an insufferable little whiner with whom he had sparred as a boy—a man for whom he had no respect whatsoever. And if Bolívar despised the prince, he loathed the queen, whose lechery was notorious and whose weaknesses he knew intimately through one of her many lovers, his boyhood friend Manuel Mallo. The strongest contempt, however, he reserved for Carlos IV, whose dithering inadequacies had enslaved an empire. Bolívar had spent too much time nursing his animus to let go of it now. His hatred for Spain had grown to such proportion that it dwarfed "the sea that separates us from her."

On April 19, 1810, revolutionaries stormed the palace in Caracas and let the governor know that the Venezuelan people wanted him gone. The governor protested, but when he stepped out onto his balcony, he saw a mass of humanity gathered in the main plaza, shouting him down. Within two days, he and his deputies were on a ship bound for Philadelphia. To Bolívar's chagrin, the new government called itself the Supreme Junta of Caracas Dedicated to Preserving the Rights of King Ferdinand VII. But its most pressing declarations expressed his dearest wishes: the colony would now engage in free trade; the Indians would no longer pay tribute or be enslaved for their inability to pay it; the slave market would be a thing of the past.

That year, like dominos tumbling in a row, the colonies of Buenos Aires, Bogotá, Quito, and Mexico declared their sovereignty, established juntas, and dispatched Spain's governors to the open seas. But the royalists' retribution would be fleet and brutal. Although Spain was impotent at first to defend its hold on its colonies, a vast army of royalist forces throughout the region mustered immediately to beat back and squelch

the epidemic of insurrections. Even as the bloodied head of Mexico's ferocious rebel priest Miguel Hidalgo swung from a rooftop in Guanajuato so that the world could see how Spain would deal with America's
revolutionaries, the hemisphere broke out in a hydra-headed war that
consumed the better part of fourteen years, leveled whole cities, brutalized the population, and fed Mother Earth with the blood of hundreds of
thousands. To bolster the Spanish army's numbers in that faraway land,
the king's generals mobilized blacks and Indians to fight on their side
and welcomed whole bands of hard-bitten roughriders who wanted no
truck with the white Creoles' bid for power.

The overseas royalist forces that converged on the fledgling rebellions held their own, spitting out Bolívar and his like, executing revolutionaries when they could, driving them into internal or external exile.
But there was nothing quite like the swift, draconian punishment the
madre patria loosed on its children when the French were finally crushed
at Waterloo and King Ferdinand turned all his lights on reconquering
the Americas. After the Napoleonic Wars, Spain emerged fiercer, more
terrible, more sharpened by combat than the revolutionaries could have
imagined. *La reconquista* fell like a heavy sword on the Indies, replete
with all the cruelty and truculence the conquistadors had brought to the
task in the first place.

Eventually the white Creoles realized they would have to look beyond their race for help in fighting Spain's ravenous war machine. In
Venezuela and Colombia, Bolívar understood that he would need to recruit the masses and unite the races: in order to populate his troops, he
sought soldiers among the indigenous, blacks, slaves, roughriders, the
infirm, the doddering, the impossibly young. Anyone capable of carrying a stick was hauled to the barracks and conscripted. Sailing back
to the South American mainland from exile in Haiti, he determined to
construct a new, unforgiving, wholly desperate revolution. He was well
aware that white aristocrats like him, who had sparked revolution for
economic and political profit, were simply not numerous enough to finish the job. Every bit of advice his mentor, the black president of Haiti,
Alexandre Pétion, had given him cemented another brick in his conviction. He would free the slaves, as Pétion had insisted he do. He would incorporate a democratic fighting force, employ unconventional guerrilla

tactics, feature the gambit of shock and awe. If necessary, he would go to violent extremes, as Haiti had done when its blacks butchered whites in the name of freedom. Whatever the costs, he would liberate his people from Spain.

In 1813, riding the muggy Río Magdalena from Cartagena to Cúcuta and then crossing the snowcapped cordillera to Venezuela, he engaged anyone who would join his last-ditch quest. At first, the only willing recruits came from society's dregs: slum dwellers, runaway slaves, out-of-work peasants, ex-convicts, near-naked tribesmen. They were un-trained, undisciplined, weaponless, shoeless, with little more than a pair of tattered trousers, a flea-ridden blanket, a frayed hat. In time, he cre-ated a fierce and formidable army, expert in resilience and surprise. As he went from success to success, battling his way back to Caracas, the city of his birth, he proclaimed a policy of "War to the Death" against all Spaniards, setting the revolution on a zero-sum course. He also sacri-ficed many a soldier in the enterprise.

But Bolívar had also opened the hearts and minds of Latin Americans to what they might become. He had been inspired by the Enlightenment, Thomas Paine's electrifying *Rights of Man*, the fundamental principle that no human being should be owned or subjugated by another. It was Bolívar, after all, who, with a higher moral instinct than Washington or Jefferson, saw the absurdity of embarking on a war for liberty without first emancipating his own slaves. Bolívar's war of independence took twice as long as the American Revolution, from 1810 to 1824, and, in the course of its staggering violence, he was beaten back, exiled twice—but he always returned, more fierce after the failures. "The art of victory is learned in defeat," he liked to say. Indeed, with every rout by a highly trained, vastly more equipped Spanish army, his improvised corps be-came stronger.

In time, improvisation became his most valuable weapon. Bolívar's charismatic appeal—his insistence on riding with his soldiers, sleep-ing alongside them on the ground, inspiring them to unimaginable heroism—became widely known as he swept from battle to battle, mus-tering recruits. Eventually he brought a formidable army to the task. They were black, Indian, mulatto slaves, merchants of the seas, pirates of the Caribbean, wild cowboys of the plains, invalids in hospitals, boy soldiers as young as eleven. Having declared an end to slavery a full half century before Abraham Lincoln's Emancipation Proclamation, Bolívar aimed to enlist a slave's rage. The vast underclass of urban and rural laborers didn't respond immediately, but eventually, moved by his eloquent exhortations about the rights of man, they flocked to join the army of liberation. They came to his ranks with no discipline, often bearing little more than a hoe or stick. Others came from across the sea—unemployed British veterans of the Napoleonic Wars in elaborate uniforms—paid to liberate America. Or they came from wealthy, white, disgruntled Creole families that had never known the merest sacrifice. But they had this much in common: they were all inspired by the Liberator's rhetoric and vision and, like him, were willing to apply a rabid violence to purging the land of "goths." They would be unstoppable.

By the end of that fierce and chastening war, Bolívar would single-handedly conceive, organize, and lead the liberation of six nations: Venezuela, Colombia, Ecuador, Peru, Bolivia, and Panama—a landmass the size of modern Europe. The liberation that José de San Martín executed so brilliantly at the same time in Argentina, Chile, and the capital of Peru had to be finished, little by little, by Bolívar's march through the inhospitable Andes. Working his way down the continent, he was ruthless about meeting brutality with brutality. By then, like-minded revolutions were ripping furiously through the Southern Cone—in Uruguay, under the valiant leadership of José Artigas, and in Paraguay, which pitted itself not only against the Spaniards but against the Argentines who wanted to annex it. The carnage would be staggering.

It didn't take long for the colonized to realize that the revolutions they had declared would be costly. By 1812, the Latin American people had seen much, absorbed the terrible calculus of victor and victim. But it would grow worse. In 1813 Bolívar's War to the Death captured and eliminated whole battalions of Spanish soldiers. One year later, José Tomás Boves—a barbarian of epic proportions, chieftain of a formidable horde of seven thousand roughriders—proclaimed his preference for Spain and massacred eighty thousand rebels. Unlike Boves, Bolívar was not inherently a violent man: killing sickened him. But, like his royalist foes, he well understood the uses of fear. The very kind of revolution that his aristocratic comrades wanted and thought they had started—

quick, easy, well argued, and civilized—was now ending in extremes of savagery. Bolívar admitted openly that all Spaniards he encountered on his first successful campaign "almost without exception were shot." That uncompromising policy had not sprung from a vacuum: a year before, King Ferdinand's commanding general had issued a royal order that called for the extermination of all rebels, without exception. It was akin to Tupac Amaru's desperate insurrection, mounted three decades before and met by Spain's chastening scourge. It was an all-or-nothing game. There would be no compromises. Only one side would survive. The result was a bloody conflict that reduced civilian populations in Latin America by a third. Whole cities were wiped off the map. The country-side was ravaged. The despoliation was complete. A Spanish official put it succinctly: "There are no more provinces left. Towns that had thousands of inhabitants are now reduced to a few hundred or even a few dozen. In some, there are only vestiges of human habitation. Roads and fields are strewn with unburied corpses; entire villages have been burnt; whole families are nothing but a memory."

The devastation reechoed throughout Latin America. It sped like a fulgent flame, provoking a population that had been assaulted and dominated for three hundred years. Hostility, suspicion, abominations became the norm. All of Spain's ire—learned in generations of war—had turned with a fresh fury against the Americas. And now all the accumulated rage of the colonized soared to meet it in kind. When the Spanish expeditionary force finally limped home in 1824, it was a fraction of the colossal fleet that had arrived a decade earlier.

THE KILLING THAT WOULD NOT STOP

They are children of the devil, not of the Moon and Sun, our deities, for they go from land to land killing, pillaging, plundering everything in sight.

—Inca Garcilaso de la Vega, 1605

The furor was such that it never truly receded. Even after winning independence from Spain in 1819, Venezuela went on in unabated frenzy to sacrifice a million more lives in skirmishes that lasted for seventy years, into the twentieth century. Mexico lost more than a half million in its bid for independence from Spain (1810 to 1821), only to carry on a brutal civil war against the Mayans that lasted thirty years more and claimed three hundred thousand more dead. One-quarter of its population perished in the course of those conflagrations. In the scant thirteen years between 1847 and 1861, almost half a million more Mexicans were lost to war, bringing the total carnage to a million and a half souls in the course of fifty years. The violence continued through the early twentieth century until it culminated in a second Mexican revolution, led by disgruntled peasants who realized with perfect clarity that their postrevolutionary masters would be more of the same: unfailingly white, dominated by foreign interests, and cruelly heedless of the colored masses. For all the liberty they had been promised, a century of independence had offered little but discord and conflict.

Between 1910 and 1920, the Mexican population was reduced in a fury of bloodletting. The evidence was there for all to see: corpses dangling from trees, civilians mowed down in the streets, mass graves in the desert. It had been an ongoing escalation of unimaginable cruelty; murder, executions, decapitations, torture, mutilations, and kidnappings were now the law of the land. No one was immune to the violence, even the apolitical—even immigrants who were uninvolved in the white-brown belligerence. To wit: the dawn of Mexico's century-long romance with the illicit drug trade began when landowners drove out or killed Chinese railroad laborers in order to seize the laborers' lucrative opium fields for themselves.

For all the uprisings and bloodshed, the violence never seemed to advance the colored masses. As Mexico entered the twentieth century, a full half of the peasant class—more than 80 percent of them indigenous—were still working on plantations of the rich or toiling for foreign bosses. Almost the entire population outside of Mexico City was landless and indigent. And restless. They still are. One hundred years after Pancho Villa and Emiliano Zapata stormed the capital to take over the presidential palace—two hundred years after Hidalgo ignited a bloody war for independence with his galvanizing shout from the plaza of Dolores, "el Grito de Dolores"—Mexico remains one of the ten most dangerous

places in the world. It shares that distinction with Honduras, Guatemala, Colombia, Venezuela, and Brazil.

Indeed, postrevolutionary carnage was seen in almost every newly liberated republic. But perhaps none reached the intensity of killing that
ravaged Paraguay in the nineteenth century. In that budding nation,
whose revolution had reduced it drastically from capacious province to
tiny landlocked state, José Gaspar Rodríguez de Francia, a virtual unknown, rose to absolute power. The enigmatic son of a Brazilian tobacco
planter and a locally born mother—three of whose siblings were certifiably deranged—Francia grew up with a marked grudge against the
established, moneyed classes. He seized the presidency soon after independence in 1811, proclaimed himself "El Supremo," Supreme and Perpetual Dictator of Paraguay, and immediately set about stripping the
colonial elite of their power. He was an irredeemable eccentric, to say the
least: a tall, gaunt, saturnine figure of a man who demanded that citizens
turn their backs or prostrate themselves when he passed, so as to pose no
threat to him. To answer his paranoid fantasies, windows in the houses
of Asunción clacked shut as he passed by. Citizens trembled with fear lest
they be singled out for one of his purges. He had never forgotten that the
parents of a Spanish girl with whom he had been infatuated as a young
man had rejected his overtures and accused him of being a mulatto: as
dictator, he forbade the Spaniards of Paraguay from marrying whites.

Francia was a strong-arm despot in the most dire sense. No sooner
had he taken power than he sealed borders, confiscated all foreign property, nationalized the Church's assets, cut all its ties to Buenos Aires and
Rome, and proceeded to purge the country of foreigners, educated officials, public intellectuals, even teachers. His goal was to achieve a fully
self-sufficient economy with no need of capital or ideas from the outside
world. As historian Thomas Carlyle, his contemporary, put it in the 1830s:

> Here, under our own nose, rises a new tyrant! Precisely when con-
> stitutional liberty was beginning to be understood a little, and we
> flattered ourselves that by due ballot-boxes, by due registration
> courts, and bursts of parliamentary eloquence, something like a real
> National Palaver would be got up in those countries,—arises this

tawny-visaged, lean, inexorable Dr. Francia; claps you an embargo on all that; says to constitutional liberty, in the most tyrannous manner, Hitherto, and no farther! . . . The ships lay high and dry, their pitchless seams all yawning on the clay banks of the Paraná; and no man could trade but by Francia's license. If any person entered Paraguay, and the Doctor did not like his papers, his talk, conduct, or even the cut of his face,—it might be the worse for such person! Nobody could leave Paraguay on any pretext whatever. It mattered not that you were man of science, astronomer, geologer, astrologer, wizard of the north. Dr. Francia had a gallows, had jailors, law-fiscals, officials; and executed persons, some of them in a very summary manner. Liberty of private judgment, unless it kept its mouth shut, was at an end in Paraguay. Paraguay lay under interdict, cut off for above twenty years from the rest of the world, by a new Dionysius.

Paraguay became an impermeable island, free from alien influence, a bastion of isolation—"the only Latin American country that foreign capital could not warp," as one historian put it. Ironically, for all the tyranny, by the end of Francia's rule, Paraguay had become one of the strongest economies in South America. The poverty and disease so rampant elsewhere were nonexistent within its closely guarded borders. Illiteracy had been eliminated. Francia's obstinacy and neuroses had succeeded in making Paraguay a bulwark of resistance against foreign encroachment—the region's most progressive country. Nestled at the very heart of the continent, facing trespass from every side, it was proving it could survive without its neighbors, without European or North American investment, without the privileges of free trade. In time, that inviolability rankled the foreign bankers and corporate moguls who had made profitable inroads in South America and engaged in vigorous commerce with Argentina and Brazil, just across Paraguay's frontiers. A considerable animus against Paraguay began to build in the peripheral universe of Brazil, Argentina, and Bolivia, and the British bankers who were financing those fledgling countries.

Francia died and was buried in 1840. His remains were later exhumed, defiled, absconded with, and ultimately discovered in a shabby box of dry noodles, his skull sent off to live on as a relic in the Museum of History. His reign was followed by confusion and turmoil, and three subsequent leaders were overthrown willy-nilly, in lightning succession. But by 1841, Francia's nephew Carlos Antonio López had stormed the presidential palace and taken the dictatorial perch. Short, stout, and deeply corrupt, "El Excelentísimo" proceeded to build an army of sixty-four thousand, by far the largest military force in South America. Enriching his own personal coffers, he ensured that when the presidency eventually passed to his son, Francisco Solano López, the López family was among the wealthiest, most powerful landowners in Paraguay. In time, the young, petulant Solano López turned on his own kin in a fit of paranoia. In a chilling move, fearing a secret plot against his rule, he ordered the execution of his own brothers. To satisfy lingering suspicions, he had his mother tortured and his sister shot.

But the real plot against Solano López turned out to be brewing well beyond the nation's borders. Argentina and Brazil had long had their eyes on Paraguay, yearning to carve up its territory and gain access to the Paraguay River, giving them access to fertile land and, farther north, the riches of the Amazon jungle. Toward this purpose, Brazil began encroaching on Paraguay's northeast farmlands. Argentina, in turn, goaded by British commercial interests, brazenly invaded Uruguay, which was just to Paraguay's south, and installed a puppet government there. Bolivia, which had long been an irritant, seemed poised to make a move of its own.

Paraguay was suddenly beset on all sides. A stubborn, arrogant man, López Solano now prepared to defend his borders against the belligerents. He ordered his formidable army to expel the poachers in the Northeast, prompting Brazil to storm across the frontier and engage the Paraguayans in a full-scale war. To retaliate, Solano López ordered an attack on the villages of Mato Grosso, which his huge army was only too happy to oblige, ransacking houses, burning farmland, and raping the women. His neighbors' riposte was fierce and immediate, almost as if it had been the desired goal all along: Brazil, Argentina, and the puppet government in Uruguay joined efforts, formed the infamous Triple Alliance, and mounted a punishing invasion of Paraguay. It was a genocidal war, even clearly articulated as such, and its goal was to eliminate the Paraguayan people entirely. The butchery was nothing short of savage. Even as the robust Paraguayan army was reduced to a ragged shadow—even while children as young as ten were sent out to fight with false beards glued to their faces—the killing continued. These struggling, fledgling American republics, like the mythological Saturn, were now devouring their own sons. Divvying up the spoils of the Paraguayan bloodbath, no one got richer than the British financiers—the Bank of London, Baring Brothers & Co., Rothschild & Co.—whose vaults had financed the incursion. Meanwhile, a nation of 900,000 had been brutally reduced to 221,000. Whole cities were empty of men; the overall male population plunged to 28,000. Paraguay became a ghost of itself—routed, emasculated—a land of women and girls. Striding away from the rubble and slaughter, the victors might have declared—as Huaya Capac had done almost four centuries before—"You are all children now."

The story was repeated, if less dramatically, in other fledgling Latin American countries. In centuries to come, dictators came in a multitude of varieties. But the trajectory was always the same, and "el dictador" became a necessary corrective in the public mind, a mythic creature homologous to the notion of the Latin American republic. Most began by touting the dicta of liberation, the voice of the people, the demands of revolution, the liberty at last from the depredations of colonialism. Eventually all headed toward the same end: the iron fist, the comforts of rigid rule, the routine familiarity of repression. As the Argentine writer Ernesto Sabato once said: "The most stubborn conservatism is that which is born of a triumphant revolution." And that is precisely what came of the Latin American wars for independence, not least in Paraguay. If it wasn't repression, dictatorship, and the heavy thumb, it was chaos and pandemonium.

Peru, the jittery seat of a lapsed empire, proceeded to have twenty presidents in the twenty years after Simón Bolívar liberated it. Bolívar himself had decided that the Latin American countries he had freed from colonial rule just weren't ready for democracy as his Enlightenment heroes had envisioned it. More than once, as he rode through the roiling hell of war, through the abattoirs of improvised military justice, Bolívar was forced to toss aside his ideals, make questionable decisions. The hard hand, he decided—*la mano dura*—was what was needed in the divided, infantilized continent Spain had wrought in the past three hundred years. His abandonment of democratic principles had started early: in Gran Colombia, Bolívar had arrogated all power to himself, attempting to avoid the fractiousness that had beset the early republic in Venezuela. Eventually Bolívar's rigorous dictatorial rule in Peru set the stage for the region's ongoing romance with dictators that would follow.

As Bolívar feared, chaos soon followed every liberated republic he left behind. Violence was met with a higher violence; corruption with a more firmly entrenched corruption. In Bolivia, just after the revolution, a debauched president, known for his sexual excesses, alcoholic rampages, and graft, fled the country but was hunted down by his brother-in-law and killed in the heart of Lima. In Ecuador, a roundly hated religious fundamentalist despot who had installed himself for a third presidential term was butchered on the cathedral steps in the full light of morning. In Quito, a dictator who tried to seize power too many times was thrown in prison and then murdered, his corpse dragged through the cobbled streets like a bouncing sack of refuse. Blood trickles down streets in Latin American literature for a reason. It is part of the region's legacy. It has been and continues to be so.

ISLAND FEVER
Cuba, 1870–1970

> *The people get the governments they deserve.*
>
> —Joseph de Maistre, 1811

Cubans, too, eventually felt the need to shuck their overlords, and when their dissatisfaction became fury in 1868, they fought for liberation for the next thirty years, losing half a million people—rebels and Spaniards—in the process. Once independence was won, and Spain was thrust from Cuba's shores, the island was quickly swept by another master: Mammon, a seemingly bottomless gluttony for riches. Prompted by postrevolutionary desperation and quickened by American ambition, seeds were laid for a half century of exploitation and corruption. Just as Mexico's dark-skinned races continued to be at the mercy of descendants of Spaniards, Cuba's brown remained hobbled by white, sacrificed to a full-fledged, booming capitalist economy. And just as silver had enslaved the hemisphere, a craving for sugar now shackled Cubans to Fulgencio Batista and his American minders. It was an inescapable reality throughout Latin America: the Spanish system had never been truly scuttled; its overlords had simply been replaced by home-grown tyrants and greedy foreigners. The downtrodden became filled with disillusionment; the wars of independence had been a rude trick. A sham.

When, in 1958, Fidel Castro and his revolutionary compadres rode that wave of discontent from the jungles of Mexico to the streets of Havana to purge Cuba of its capitalist masters, the sword fell once more on the Cuban people. By 1961, two thousand of them had been executed at the hands of Castro's revolutionary forces. By 1970, five thousand had been shot or hanged and dumped in mass graves. Twenty thousand more were rotting in dungeons as political prisoners. Half a million had fled the country and headed for asylum in Miami. If wars among the indigenous tribes in pre-Columbian Cuba had taken a grim toll five hundred years before, so had every "ism" that followed: colonialism, capitalism, communism. All had resorted to bloodshed: from outright butchery, to gangland revenge, to racial and political oppression, violence had remained the easy expedient.

The potential for unrest intensified in 1970 when Castro pledged to produce the Zafra de los Diez Millones, a whopping ten-million-ton harvest of sugar, breaking all records and doubling the production of the year before. In that single-minded pursuit, meant to prove that the new Cuba was a nimble, vibrant economy, Castro sent the entire population to the sugar fields to cut cane. By then, Fidel was the self-proclaimed dictator of Cuba: its prime minister of the Revolutionary Government, first secretary of the Communist Party, commander in chief of the Armed Forces, and president of agrarian reform. He governed as the old Spanish colonial Marquis of Havana once said one could easily govern Cuba: *con un violín, una baraja y un gallo fino*—with a fiddle, a deck of cards, and a fighting cock. His Zafra was not an idle goal; it became a dictum. Cubans who had been gainfully employed as doctors, professors, dockworkers, soldiers, farmers were abruptly directed to drop their professions and take up work as cane cutters. Castro's ten-million-ton campaign had come to stand, in his own words, for "far more than tons of sugar, far more than an economic victory. It is a test, a moral commit-ment. And precisely because it is a test and a moral commitment, we cannot fall short by even a single gram."

Every able-bodied man and woman was ordered to contribute to the challenge. Whole tracts of land were cleared for planting, trees felled, croplands abandoned, wildlife displaced. Ships sat in docks—unloaded—for months at a time, schools were shuttered, hospitals and prisons emptied. As one journalist described it:

> from every far corner of Cuba, men and women were summoned to battle for sugar production as if the country were at war. Beneath the soaring chimneys of giant American-built mills—now named after revolutionary heroes—laborers fed threshers around the clock, colossal turbines ground on incessantly, day and night. In the inky predawn, you could make out the shadows of enormous trucks as they lumbered through mud, delivering students, office workers, prisoners, soldiers. Hundreds of thousands filed silently along the roads, armed with machetes, tramping down paths redolent with a pungent sweetness. Their faces would soon show evidence of the *corte*—the harvest—as every whack of their machetes was answered by rigid stalks, whipping back like angry swords.

The face of Cuba soon exhibited more scars: foreign trade was virtu-ally paralyzed—a punishing hardship in an island country. Factories that produced raw materials were shut down, precious commodities were abandoned. Cuba's two-hundred-thousand-man army, by far the most aggressive military force in Latin America at the time, was called to slog in the cane fields, leaving a highly militarized, carefully managed country to the hazards of chance. Hundreds of hectares of banana trees went unharvested, left to rot and die. Animals perished without fodder. Cuba went hungry, transportation sputtered to a standstill, education halted. Castro's fixation had become an echo from the past: the Zafra was not unlike the conquistadors' rash, stubborn, ultimately catastrophic instinct to herd whole populations to the mines to satisfy Spain's lust for gold and silver. The effects had been backbreaking then, and they were backbreaking now. Famine swept over Cuba. Disease, corruption, and violence were not far behind. In the end, after all the sacrifices and the devastation, the Zafra fell considerably short of its mark. The goal of ten million was never met. And, in the process, the country was virtually gutted.

Castro was not deterred. Soon he was seeking increased assistance from the Soviet Union and looking for other ways to distinguish Cuba in the eyes of a larger world. Communist insurgencies had been bubbling up in a number of Third World countries: bands of guerrilla fighters, many of them Cuba inspired and Cuba supported, had been knocking about Guatemala, Venezuela, Colombia, Peru, Bolivia, and Uruguay since the 1960s; in the 1970s they were joined by Nicaragua, El Salvador, Brazil, and Argentina. But it was Africa that caught Castro's attention. A war on a far continent presented a distinct public relations opportunity for an ambitious country that had little currency to give but plenty of human muscle. This was the Cuba in which Carlos Buergos found himself when, out of work, barely emerging from adolescence, and on the verge of a free-wheeling profligacy, he was pressed into service to fight for the Communist cause in Angola. It was 1975, Carlos had just turned twenty, and despite his distinct lack of accomplishments, he was a young man in the prime of life: fit, robust, fearless, with just the right degree of impetuosity that might be useful in a guerrilla warrior. He shipped out to Angola, much as his thrill-seeking ancestors had shipped out from Spain hundreds of years before—hungry, expectant, cheeky, and thoroughly ignorant of the world he was stepping into.

TWISTED
Angola, 1975–1976

> *The chief says burn everything. By everything he means everything. Women, children, everything.*
>
> —General Ben Ben, Angola

Cuba's history with Angola had been slight, but its political sympathies were strong. A decade earlier, the African nation had sought independence in an all-out war against its colonial masters. This was a struggle Cuba could understand. For three centuries before that bid for freedom, Portugal had enjoyed a virtual monopoly on the West African slave trade, marauding the coast, capturing well over a million souls, and shipping them in shackles—and for considerable profit—to the New World. When human trafficking was finally banned in 1836, Lisbon was obliged to change its strategy. Now it urged its colonial avatars to continue to round up slaves, but instead of driving them onto ships, they forced them to toil on Angolan plantations. Within a century, Portugal was not only reaping the profits of a vigorous agricultural economy in Angola, it was also profiting from an unexpected bonus: a lively diamond trade. But the fate of this colony, like that of the Spanish colonies 150 years before, changed overnight when the *país mãe's*—the mother country's—government came to an abrupt end. An unexpected coup in 1974 brought political havoc to Portugal, overthrowing a Fascist dictatorship that had ruled it for four decades and marking the end of the Portuguese colonies in Africa. Angola, which had long fought a scrappy war against its colonizer, was suddenly fighting a bloody war against itself. Three separate factions began a ferocious battle for control of the newly independent nation: the leftist People's Movement for the Liberation of Angola (MPLA), supported wholeheartedly by the Soviet Union and Cuba; and the National Liberation Front of Angola (FNLA), along with the National Union for the Total Independence of Angola (UNITA), both of which were backed by apartheid South Africa, Israel, and the fervent anti-Communist realpolitik of the United States.

It was a rabid contest for the soul of a fledgling republic, until then one of the most developed, economically vibrant of African nations. Just as the Spanish Civil War had been prelude to the Second World War, the civil war in Angola now became a proving ground between two hostile superpowers—a grisly, brutal conflagration by proxy between Africans armed to the teeth by the Soviet Union and those fitted out by the United States. Cuba elected to fight shoulder to shoulder with the Communists, contributing whatever troops necessary to bring victory to the revolutionaries. It was a stubborn, perversely homicidal, seemingly never-ending bloodbath, and as a result, Cuba would pour half a million men into the country, hold out for seventeen years, and suffer thousands of casualties.

For Carlos, the call to serve had come without warning or explanation. The Cuban army began rounding up the unemployed, delinquents, punk rowdies like him—any able-bodied young men who might feed the maw of an ungovernable, distant war. At the time, Carlos was out of work, romancing a married woman, slumming with fellow ruffians in the Parque de la Libertad in sleepy Matanzas when, abruptly one balmy Friday morning, he was called to report to the military command. Suddenly there was a fist at the door, a brusque shout, and he was told to appear that afternoon, or the Cuban Revolutionary Armed Forces would come looking for him. It was December 1975. He had turned twenty a few months before.

The vast majority of youths who huddled that day in the dank, fusty army headquarters on General Betancourt Avenue were even younger. The presiding officer was pock-faced, gravel voiced, gruff. "You boys from Matanzas?" he growled, one eyebrow arched. Then he surprised them with a chilling snort, a sharp peal of laughter. "You're from Matanzas. And you're headed to matanzas. There will be plenty of matanzas where you're going. With your big, black, shiny AK-47s. Believe me, you'll get your fill of 'em." Massacres. The town of Matanzas ("killings") had been named for the slaughter of Spaniards on the shores of those crystal-blue waters nearly five hundred years before. The Cuban indigenous had not taken kindly to invaders. Carlos laughed nervously at the burly man's wordplay. He had no idea that the officer was deadly serious; that, as a recruit, he was poised to relive his boyhood trauma again and again, a hundred times over—the cane cutter with the blood halo, the machete suspended overhead—except that it would be seven thousand miles away and in more harrowing circumstances.

It was precisely in the last weeks of 1975 that the Soviet Union engaged in a massive airlift of Cuban soldiers and tens of thousands of Kalashnikov AK-47 assault rifles to the jungles of Angola. The Soviets would supply the hardware. The Cubans would supply the cannon fodder. Carlos would be surrounded by neophytes like himself—untrained farm boys and city wastrels, sent into a war they hardly understood. Thousands were gathered for *la previa*—boot camp—in military installations near San Antonio de los Baños, where they were taught to wield Soviet weapons and operate Soviet radios. One month later, Carlos and his cohort were informed they were going on a secret mission. Issued phony passports that ascribed phony occupations, they were loaded onto buses and taken in caravan to meet—to Carlos's bafflement and delight—Fidel and Raúl Castro. In the course of that indoctrination, they were told that their mission was to defend their black Communist brethren against imperialist white South Africans. They were hectored to fight fat-cat plutocrats, those shameless, blood-sucking American vampires who were raping Africa and supporting the corrupt government in Johannesburg. They were told to think of this war as akin to the great Communist revolution in which their forebears had risked and sacrificed their lives. Their contribution to the cause was, El Comandante assured them, an expression of "proletariat internationalism." More than that, the new recruits did not know. All the same, within a few weeks, there would be thirty thousand more of them. A decade later, it would be more than seventy thousand. Over the course of the war, almost 350,000. It was remarkable—if not unique in history—for a Third World country to undertake a military operation of that magnitude.

Carlos soon learned that the war they had joined was a brutal conflagration in which children as young as eleven were mustered to jungle skirmishes. Hard-bitten soldiers with human trophies flapping from their belts—ears, noses, fingers—were his comrades in arms. He found himself armed with an AK-47 bayonet, crawling on his belly through thick brush in night raids on villages. It was impossible, at times, to know who the enemy was. The white South African forces fighting the Communist insurgents used black Angolans to carry out the sorties. In the heat of battle, it was difficult to tell whether a man or boy creeping through the green with a knife in his teeth was friend or foe.

One moonless night, Carlos was deployed with a posse of young Angolans to penetrate a stubborn knot of American-funded and -equipped FNLA guerrillas who were holding out just beyond a mine-ridden field, south of his base of operations in Luanda. As they made their way toward the camp, they were spotted by a lone woman, walking through the high grass, carrying a jug on her head. The men dropped to the ground, and she began sprinting toward the enemy camp, putting their ambush in peril. One of the Angolans drew out a poison-tipped blowdart and swiftly shot it into the woman's spine, felling her like an animal. Shaken,

Carlos staggered ahead, clutching his AK-47 to his chest, swatting the insects that flitted about drinking his sweat, trying to block out what he had just seen. Suddenly, with no warning, and with a blood-curdling cry that seemed to rise from the belly of the earth, a wall of humanity sprang from the brush and rushed at them with machetes, shouting. Orange bursts exploded at his side, raising black smoke that stung his eyes and clouded the darkness. He could hear his comrades fall with loud thuds and cries, either by knife, or machete—he could not tell which. The gunshot seemed to be coming from his side. For a fleeting second, as he stumbled through the fumy night, he saw a man sprawled in the grass, his head cleaved open, pink spilling from his crown. Carlos moved on, startled, rubbing his eyes. In the chaos, he could not make out much more. The fighting seemed disembodied, deafening, and strangely elsewhere. Shooting and running, he made it to a cluster of trees and then, deeper still, into a forest, as the sounds of battle died off into an eerie silence.

He climbed into the branches of a tree, hoping to catch some sign of his squad, but there was none. Nothing to see save the flickering stars above. Nothing to hear but the loud chirp of crickets, the rustle of beetles, the croaking of frogs. He spent the rest of the night in that aerie, alert to the dark world around him. Come morning, saved by the natural compass of sunrise, he clambered down to head southwest, where he knew his camp to be. He hadn't been walking long when he was suddenly confronted by a mangy, yellow-eyed dog. It stiffened as he approached, bared its teeth, growled. He didn't dare shoot or provoke a bark, lest he would betray his position. He dropped to his haunches and scooted toward it slowly, quietly, leveling his bayonet at the blight-bitten fur. The dog snarled, spit a grayish froth, shifted this way and that, but eventually Carlos was able to get close enough to lunge at the cur with his blade. The steel slid through the thorax as if it were penetrating soft clay, exiting the other side. The dog hardly had time to issue a final whimper. It dropped in a heap where it stood.

Staggering ahead for hours, exhausted, Carlos finally spotted a fellow Cuban in a familiar green beret, guarding the perimeter of their camp. When he rejoined his unit, he learned that every last member of his squad, apart from him, had been hacked to death by machetes.

*   *   *

There would be long stretches with nothing to do but play ball in the dirt with Angolan children, a boom box nearby blaring Cuban rhumbas. There would be days spent trekking through the wild, scouting the landscape, dodging herculean spiders and spitting cobras. Enemy skirmishes would surprise, and violence would be met by cruder violence, upping the ante until Carlos understood that his best weapon was his raw animal instinct. Kill or be killed. Mistakes would be made with that calculus. And he made them. Fellow combatants would die at friendly hands. But, hewing to it, he always managed to live another day.

If Carlos had been a thief, a liar, and a petty swindler in Cuba, he had become a hardened killer in Angola. A soldier in Angola once asked, "What have they done to us? . . . sitting here in this landlocked place, imprisoned by rows of barbed wire in a land that doesn't belong to us, dying of malaria and bullets, fighting an invisible enemy, fighting the dark nights as thick and opaque as a mourning veil?" What they had done was forge yet another generation of Cubans well acquainted with the power of violence. Carlos vowed that if he ever made it out of Angola alive, he would try to reform, be more like his father. Hardworking, Responsible. He would put killing behind him. Maybe settle down, find a job, have a family. But in Castro's Cuba, he had never really had a job. He had never had an expertise. He had one now.

In time, his battalion was sent deeper into the interior to battle South African forces that were pressing toward Luanda. By then, Cubans were using flamethrowers to incinerate villages, low-flying planes to drop napalm on cattle ranches. Carlos was running through a field just south of Huambo one early morning in 1976, answering an order to charge, when he heard a sharp crack, and the world went black. A well-aimed bullet had ripped into his skull, grazed the edge of his brain, and exited the rear of his cranium. He would never know how much time passed between that headlong race across open meadow and his waking up in a medical bivouac somewhere in the African bush. When he finally regained consciousness, he felt a taut, heavy bandage gripping his head, a fetid cot beneath. His bones ached. His vision was blurred. It took awhile before he could make out the blue uniforms of the medics standing before him. They laughed as they recounted the trouble they'd had digging the lead slug from his head. "Made in USA," they told Carlos. It had left a hole in his skull and a deep, angry scar in his forehead.

They let him know that his condition was serious—serious enough that he would now be transported to the Americo Boavida Hospital in Luanda and processed for release along with a growing rank of Cuban amputees, bomb and knife casualties, burn victims: the gravely wounded, the mentally unstable. Within weeks, Carlos Buergos was spit back into civilian life in Havana. He had just turned twenty-one.

Cuba was not alone in putting its young in harm's way as Latin America moved on from its unfulfilled revolutions and entered the mid-twentieth century. By the 1970s, there was plenty of evidence that the brutality that had traumatized the region for five hundred years still persisted in one form or another, eroding the people's confidence that their countries might ever achieve the justice and equality that revolutions had promised. Just as Carlos was wending his way back to his father's rooms in Havana, conflagration tore like a fleet wind through all of the Americas. Other countries, inspired by Cuba, had been lured by Communism—their benighted poor imagining that Marxist dreams promised a sainted justice at last—but the United States had different ideas. Whatever political divisions were deviling America, whatever Democratic and Republican presidents took turns at its helm, the majority of its citizens could agree on at least one thing: Communism was the enemy, and it needed to be eradicated wherever it took root. If that meant sacrificing American lives, so be it.

Intent on maintaining its authority in the hemisphere—and fulfilling a doctrine put in place almost two centuries before—the United States government, under John F. Kennedy and Richard Nixon alike, pledged to support any force that would combat nascent Communism (or Socialism) and ensure Washington's preeminence in Latin America The perverse result was that, in protecting North American interests, violence became endemic in almost every country of Latin America. Guatemala, for one, soon found itself in a crucible of state-sponsored terrorism for that very reason. President Carlos Arana Osorio, a vindictive, corrupt former colonel boosted by hefty military support from the United States, imposed a state of siege, deploying death squads that would eventually arrest, torture, disappear, and execute nearly fifty thousand Guatemalans he considered political undesirables.

In Nicaragua, which at that time was the United States' major beef supplier, all-out insurgency was under way. Even as Carlos was trying to reenter civil life in Havana, martial law was declared in Nicaragua, and the entire Nicaraguan army—with Washington's help—began to lock down the country, razing whole villages as it went. Everywhere in these volatile countries, it seemed, as far as the United States was concerned, any whiff of Soviet or Cuban influence needed to be stamped out, supplanted with military control.

In Chile, which had just elected the openly Socialist president Salvador Allende, the disaffected right-wing generals chafed, itching to take back the reins. The president's first order of business had been to host his good friend Fidel Castro in a lavish and elaborate state visit during which Castro presented Allende with his own Kalashnikov rifle, newly engraved with Allende's name. "*A Salvador Allende, de su compañero de armas, Fidel Castro*," read the shining plaque on the butt end of the rifle: To Allende from his brother in arms. Nothing could have been more roiling to the right-wing Chilean generals than to have Castro bequeath the Cuban revolution's preeminent weapon to the Chilean president. Not long after, with the full blessings of the Central Intelligence Agency, President Nixon, and Secretary of State Henry Kissinger, the generals began planning a violent coup to take back the country. The deputy director of the CIA wrote in a secret memo: "It is firm and continuing policy that Allende be overthrown. . . . It is imperative that these actions be implemented clandestinely and securely so that the USG [US government] and American hand be well hidden." Nixon had already launched an economic war against Chile, trying to squeeze it into submission by choking off its vital supply line. "Make the economy scream!" Nixon instructed the CIA.

Shortly thereafter, in September 1973, the Chilean air force swept over the capital in a concerted air attack, strafed the presidential palace, and left President Allende dead by his own hand. The weapon he had used to kill himself was Castro's Kalashnikov. The coup had been surgical, chillingly effective, and it swept into power Augusto Pinochet, Allende's most trusted general. Never before in this highly democratic country had the military wielded such authority. Indeed, when a right-wing newspaper had suggested the army stage a coup to drive out the Socialists, Pinochet had feigned outrage and threatened to sue the editors, saying, "Such things are not done here." But such a thing had indeed been done, and Pinochet's power was absolute. Perceived enemies of the new state were soon rounded up and tortured or killed. The favored technique, so as not to waste bullets, was to force victims to lie on the ground while torturers drove trucks over them, crushing their heads. For the next seventeen years, Pinochet ruled with an iron hand, arresting 130,000 dissidents within the course of two years, exterminating thousands, and driving a quarter million Chileans into exile.

The governments of Argentina, Bolivia, Brazil, Uruguay, and Peru all fell like houses of cards in the same period between 1966 and 1973, overthrown in bloody military coups. What was at stake—what had always been at stake in Latin America—was the fundamental instability of a region defined five hundred years before by Spanish and Portuguese conquistadors: the essential exploitation at its core, the racial divisions, the extreme poverty and degradation of the vast majority, the entitlement and wealth of the very few, the corrosive culture of corruption.

In Mexico, the generation that grew up with Carlos erupted in protest in Mexico City in 1968, voicing a spirited objection to the vast sums of money being spent on the 1968 Summer Olympics, as opposed to addressing the very real necessities of the people. The government response was merciless, and the repression lasted for fourteen years. Three separate Mexican administrations from the late 1960s until 1982—in an ever-mounting spiral of violence—killed, tortured, or disappeared dissidents, political rebels, and anyone else they suspected might have had a hand in sowing discontent. They rounded up villagers, burned down houses, punished suspects with inhuman cruelty. Hundreds of students and political sympathizers were executed on the spot in what became known as "the Tlatelolco massacre," when soldiers and police fired into a plaza filled with ten thousand protesters. Almost a thousand were subsequently disappeared; two thousand more were tortured. The bad blood would bubble up many years later in surprising ways.

In Colombia, which had emerged from a decade of bitter civil war, the sixties and seventies were a jittery, high-wire crossing. *La Violencia,* which had dominated Colombia for much of the 1950s, had produced a staggering count of two hundred thousand dead in the murderous rage between the conservative rich and the liberal poor, and the wounds had hardly healed. Just as Carlos was bumbling through adolescence, laboring alongside his father in the sugar fields of Matanzas, a celebrated World War II lieutenant general, William P. Yarborough, father of the Green Berets, visited Colombia and laid out a "team effort" to train collaborators from every social class in tracking and rooting out Communists. If all went well, in Yarborough's estimation, those clandestine forces—peasants, workers, and professionals—would represent a formidable source of secret information; a counterinsurgency army they could call up at any time. Fidel Castro's success in Cuba and the danger it represented for American interests in the hemisphere worried the Washington pooh-bahs and the large corporations that stood to lose ground. The threat needed to be snuffed out. Harshly, if necessary.

It was, yet again, a time for violent reckoning. The proxy war between the United States and the Soviet Union in Angola was but a reecho of what was taking place in dozens of outposts south of the Rio Grande. One hundred fifty years after the most bitter wars of independence the world had known, fragile governments were toppling, reconstituting themselves, and toppling again. Washington, DC, intent on maintaining the hemispheric preeminence it had claimed emphatically with the Monroe Doctrine, was hard at work on "containment": stalling the Communist tide, preserving its hold on its interests. And yet, for all the very real chaos and suffering being felt in coups and revolts throughout the Americas, the US public was hardly aware of its government's role in the troubles—hardly cognizant of the turmoil it engendered. Latin America continued to be ignored by the greater American population. It was physically close, yet Europe seemed more simpatico, more approachable. Latin America was, to many of its northern neighbors, chaotic, enigmatic, and in need of a complete overhaul. That attitude was nothing new. When John Adams had been an ambassador to the Court of St. James's in 1786, he held that revolution in South America would be "agreeable to the United States" and that North Americans should do all they could to promote it. Once he became the second US president, however, he wanted little to do with "those People." Asked what he thought about lending a hand to South American independence, he had only this to say: "What could I think of revolutions and constitutions in South America? A People more ignorant, more bigoted, more superstitious, more implicitly credulous in the sanctity of royalty, more blindly devoted to their priests, in more awful terror of the Inquisition, than any people in Europe, even in Spain, Portugal, or the Austrian Netherlands, and infinitely more than in Rome itself."

Almost two centuries later, in 1973, the perception in Washington was no different. Nixon insisted that "if the poison of unrest and violent revolution" continued in Latin America, it would eventually spill up the hemisphere and "infect the United States." To him, the southern Americas were little more than a dangerously diseased appendage to be kept at bay. There was no risk that the United States doing as it willed in those latitudes would come back to haunt. "Latin America doesn't matter," he said. "People don't give a shit about the place." Henry Kissinger agreed. It was irrelevant. Less than trifling. "What happens in the south has no importance," the secretary of state asserted—a pronouncement he held to, except, of course, when the south got unruly and US assets were at risk. Infantilizing the region's people, dismissing them as irresponsible, he added that there was an essential weakness of character in "America's backyard." Half a millennium after Columbus unleashed a scourge on the New World, things hadn't changed much. Latin America was still a gold rush for conquistadors, a combat zone for predators, a wild frontier for the taking.

CHAPTER 8

THE RISE OF THE STRONGMAN AND THE DRAGONS ALONG THE WAY

Barbarians who resort to force and violence are incapable of cultivating anything. Hatred makes for a bad seed.

—José Martí, 1877

If Inca and Aztec emperors were ruthless and authoritarian—if Spanish conquistadors answered in kind—their descendants, the leaders of Latin America, would eventually follow example. The enlightened sought to forge democratic nations; others, beset by the challenges, resorted to extraordinary powers. Many found their keenest expression as strongmen. With Spain gone, the scramble for dominion became endemic; tin-pot generals and local warlords scrapped with one another for a parcel of land, a fiefdom to rule. Governing became far more difficult than anyone had imagined. Even the liberators—Antonio López de Santa Anna in Mexico, Juan Manuel de Rosas in Argentina, Bernardo O'Higgins in Chile, Bolívar in much of South America—forsook their liberal ideals to apply dictatorial powers, claiming that the chaos they had inherited could be tempered only by an iron hand. "I fought for liberty with all my heart," said Santa Anna, "but I soon saw my foolishness. Even one hundred years from now, the Mexican people will not be ready for liberty . . . despotism is the only viable government."

Bolívar was even more pessimistic. Plagued by squabbles in every republic he left behind, he was convinced that a bloody-minded era would follow. He lamented to a friend, "We have tried everything under the sun, and nothing has worked. Mexico has fallen. Guatemala is in ruins. There are new troubles in Chile. In Buenos Aires, they have killed a president. In Bolivia, three presidents took power in the course of two days, and two of them have been murdered." No one knew more than he how erratic his brethren could be and how imperfect the aftermath of liberation had been. Independence had been achieved—freedom, equality, and justice fought for—but, one after another, the new nations emerged with the same, entrenched system of castes and an even fiercer sense of white entitlement.

Surveying their fledgling Latin American republics, liberators quickly understood that the principles of Enlightenment, which had quickened revolution in the first place, would have to be abandoned, at least for the time being, in favor of the *mano dura*—the all-too-familiar hard hand. They themselves would apply it. There was too gaping a difference between poor and privileged, ignorant and educated, brown and white. There was too much opportunity for insurrections and race wars. In his "Letter from Jamaica," written during his exile in the Caribbean, Bolívar had brilliantly distilled Latin America's political reality. His people were neither Indians, nor mulattos, nor Spaniards, nor Europeans, he insisted, but an entirely new race. Monarchies had become abhorrent to them, and democracy—Philadelphia-style—could never function for a people so congenitally backward: a population that had been cowed and infantilized by three hundred years of persecution and slavery. "A democratic system, far from rescuing us, can only bring us ruin," he claimed. "We are a region plagued by vices learned from Spain, which, through history, has been a mistress of cruelty, ambition, meanness, and greed." In his view, neither kings nor constitutional congresses could tame these unwieldy Americas. But a firm authoritarian government might, especially if it were bolstered by a robust military. Overshadowed by a more immediate need for social order, social justice thereby took a back seat in Latin America, where it would lurk precariously for two hundred years.

So it was that even though the colonies were dead, the spirit of colonialism remained very much alive. Absolute power still beguiled. New republics became as oppressive, insular, and isolated as Spain had encouraged its colonies to be. Latin America's culture of violence, nurtured by wars of independence that had raged for fourteen years—a prolonged carnival of killing, unparalleled in the hemisphere—seemed to morph, almost overnight, into a culture of intimidation, with the landed gentry acquiring an ever sharper aptitude for cruelty, and a pumped-up military that never seemed to stand down.

In all this, order became an elusive prize. The hard-won wars that had reduced the Latin American populace by more than 25 percent simmered on in far corners of the hemisphere in a lingering belligerence: the patriot's cry became the political spat, the intrigue, the feuds, the assassinations, the border disputes, the heavy reliance on armed muscle. Every postcolonial Latin American country, except for Brazil, suffered this volatility, moving from lawlessness to rank despotism and crystallizing its class divisions along the way. One after another, they slid into civil wars. One after another, they institutionalized a devastating poverty. Coups and ruptures became ordinary, all-too-familiar consequences of a fundamental inability to cohere.

MEXICO
1860–1920

> *My grandfather, as he drank his coffee, spoke to me of Juárez and Porfirio . . . and the tablecloth smelled of gunpowder.*
> *My father, as he drank his brandy, spoke to me of Zapata and Villa . . . and the tablecloth smelled of gunpowder.*
>
> —Octavio Paz, "Mexican Song"

Within a few years of winning its independence, Mexico was swinging manically from one president to another. Santa Anna won and lost the presidency eleven times in the course of twenty years, each time burying and reburying—with full military honors and the archbishop's blessing—the amputated leg he had lost in war. He had been an unfortunate choice to lead a budding republic. Erratic, deeply corrupt, wildly autocratic, and all too reliant on brute force, Santa Anna arrogated public funds to his own pockets, sold off or lost vast tracts of land to the United States, and declared himself dictator-for-life, insisting his minions refer to him as "His Serene Highness." Eventually, once he was forced out of power and exiled, Mexico broke out in a bloody civil war between constituencies that remain at odds to this very day: the conservatives, who wanted power to remain with the Church, the military, and the old white elite; and the liberals, who wanted a more representative government that defended the rights of the lower class, the darker race. When the war was over, Mexico's first indigenous president, Benito Juárez, was given the task of picking up the pieces. The lawyer and former secretary of education had been exiled for his passionate objections to Santa Anna's corrupt government. He had been living in New Orleans and working in a cigar factory when he was called back to political activism.

As president, Juárez tried to establish some semblance of a democracy and cut back the vast, landed wealth of the Catholic clergy as well as the lingering power of the military. He moved to defend against the predatory advances of France, Spain, and Britain, which threatened to invade Mexico to reclaim its unpaid debts. But for all his egalitarian intentions and achievements, Juárez ultimately presided over a disastrously unruly decade. Springing to take advantage of the disorder, Napoleon III's troops invaded Mexico in 1861, ousted Juárez, and installed a teetering monarchy led by an Austrian prince, Maximilian I, and his wife, Princess Carlota. This, too, would founder before long.

Turmoil and civil unrest continued to addle the country until 1876, when Porfirio Díaz seized the helm and clamped down on Mexico for thirty-five consecutive years. Finally, under that strict *mano dura*, material progress began to be made. But for all his efforts to turn the tide and open the economy to a flood of foreign investment, Díaz was all too reliant on ruthless, crude force to address his every challenge. Corruption, repression, rapacious profiteering became Díaz's trademark, even resorting to the old Spanish practice of shaking down the masses when funds were short. Small farmers, struggling tradespeople, the poor—all paid a steep price in the process. Lands owned by the indigenous were considered uninhabited, open territory, and Díaz's government moved quickly to dispossess tens of thousands of Indians, handing over a land area the size of California to foreign speculators and investors. In this, Díaz was merely emulating his neighbors: the practice of selling off one's land and one's industries—the very infrastructure of a country—was endemic by now throughout Latin America. Whereas Spain had protected its interests relentlessly, siphoning off America's riches for its own prodigal purposes, dictators such as Díaz were all too willing to auction their countries to the highest bidder, and North American and European capitalists rushed in to buy. In the process, Díaz had all the chieftains of the Yaquis and the Mayans chained together and dumped in the Pacific Ocean. Half of the tribes' male populations were murdered or deported to the Yucatán. The priorities were made clear.

Eventually the Mexican people had enough of this. In 1910 they erupted in another defiant revolution, and this time it proved far more destructive than the one that had devoured the country a hundred years before. Tens of thousands of campesinos rushed to take action against their landlords, prosecuting a fierce race war that would ultimately topple Díaz's rule, install Francisco Madero as president, and then—just as precipitously—prompt a ruthless military coup backed by none other than the ambassador of the United States. One prominent Mexican historian reckons that no fewer than seven hundred thousand of his countrymen died in the violence. A quarter million more fled for their lives to the United States. Industrial production screeched to a halt as ranches, haciendas, and cities were demolished until Mexico resembled nothing so much as a ghostly postapocalyptic desert. As if this weren't enough blood to offer up to the gods of war, the enduring divide between powerful and powerless soon resulted in another wave of butchery: the pro-Catholic Cristero rebellion of the 1920s, which pitted Christian peasants against secular, anticlerical government forces, spread like a brushfire through the Mexican countryside and devoured seventy thousand more souls.

THE CONTEST FOR NICARAGUA
1847–1934

> *The war will come, my darling,*
> *And . . . the barbarian hordes*
> *trying to rob all we are and love.*
>
> —Gioconda Belli, "Canto de guerra"

Nicaragua, struggling to shed Mexico's influence, remove itself from its neighbors' vicissitudes, and gain its own foothold as an independent country, didn't survive much more than two decades before it was invaded by British forces in 1847. Clearly, it was seen as territory to be had, irrespective of whoever happened to inhabit it. Within three years, in a staggeringly brazen move, Britain and the United States signed a treaty granting unfettered access to an interoceanic trade route through Nicaragua. It was a unilateral decision enacted with an easy handshake between London and Washington and sealed without Nicaraguan consent.

The sting was lethal and immediate. A nascent nation, bullied by predators, had been stunned once more into slavish surrender. And, indeed, come 1856, it seemed as if that capitulation would be complete: a North American adventurer named William Walker tramped into Managua, handily duped the local politicians, assumed the presidency, and eventually sought annexation by the United States. His first order of business was to reinstate slavery. The logic was simple: Nicaragua's assets, especially as a workforce, were crucial to US ambitions. Nicaragua had productive gold mines as well as highly lucrative coffee plantations. There was money to be made; a highly industrialized, booming American economy to support. As blatant as the American intervention was, protests against it didn't do much good. For the next fifty years, US warships menaced the shores, and eventually, in 1910, a fully functioning puppet government answering to Washington was established.

Things went well for American interests in Nicaragua until ordinary Nicaraguans laboring in the mines and fields decided things weren't going very well for *them*. Until then, Nicaraguan violence had been low-grade, intermittent—random eruptions in an otherwise easily subjugated country. But by 1927, resentments exploded into a full-fledged guerrilla war. The next two decades were not unlike the bloodyminded conquest that had gripped that territory and decimated the population four hundred years before. Augusto Sandino, commander of the Army to Defend the National Sovereignty, launched a war, hoping to eject US forces and businessmen for good. But the US Marines, like the conquistadors who had preceded them, proved formidably stubborn. Not until 1934, seven years and five hundred spirited guerrilla skirmishes later, did the United States finally withdraw, leaving Sandino in power and its command to Nicaraguan military officer Anastasio Somoza García.

It was clearly understood, however, via a clear directive by the American ambassador, that Somoza was to have Sandino killed. Although to the rest of the world Sandino seemed to have achieved the picture-perfect revolution—a non-Soviet, non-Marxist uprising by a young, moderate population pitting itself against the embodiment of corrupt, dictatorial rule—the United States left no doubt that it would not tolerate Sandino's brand of nationalism. President Theodore Roosevelt's corollary to the Monroe Doctrine had put it plainly: the United States had every right to interfere in cases of flagrant and "chronic wrongdoing" in any Latin American country. And Sandino, as far as American interests were concerned, was a flagrant wrongdoer.

An unrepentant enemy and critic of the United States until the very end, Sandino was executed as he was exiting a gate of the presidential palace in Managua on February 21, 1934, alongside his brother and his top generals. Events raveled quickly after that: the country reverted to puppet status, a fiercely coercive regime was put in place, and Washington's choice, General Somoza, reigned unchallenged, ruthlessly imposing his sword as freely as any Spanish potentate had done before him. By the end of his reign, as many as fifty thousand Nicaraguans had been murdered and three hundred thousand more were either disappeared or rendered homeless by the government. Protected and funded by the United States, General Somoza—and eventually his sons—would rule Nicaragua with a hard hand for more than forty-three years.

THE DOMINICAN REPUBLIC
1900–1960

> *The fukú ain't just ancient history. . . . If you even thought a bad thing about Trujillo, fuá, a hurricane would sweep your family out to sea, fuá, a boulder would fall out of a clear sky and squash you, fuá, the shrimp you ate today was the cramp that killed you tomorrow.*
> —Junot Díaz, *The Brief Wondrous Life of Oscar Wao*

The harsh mill of souls was repeated again and again as Latin America stumbled from newly minted independence into the twentieth century. On the island of Hispaniola, the first permanent settlement Columbus established when he conquered, enslaved, and virtually exterminated the Taíno, violent rule had been the norm for more than four centuries. Buffeted by the aspirations of Spain, France, England, Holland, and the United States, the island had long been seen as a strategic target, a valuable port of trade. There was no stopping the savage disruptions on its shores: the constant flow of Spanish warlords; the fugitive slaves who raced down-mountain from time to time to kill and bedevil them; the invasion by nine thousand English soldiers ordered by Lord Protector Oliver Cromwell and led by Admiral William Penn; the brazen French buccaneers who constantly marauded the coast and preyed on sea traffic; the rich, powerful Dutch and Portuguese slave traders whose barbarism was all too well known in the ports; the rabid never-ending wars with Haiti. For twenty-two years, between 1822 and 1844, the part of the island now known as the Dominican Republic was occupied by Haiti in a brutal reign of counterrepression: Spanish was outlawed as a language, whites were forbidden to own land, all Church property was confiscated, and all relations with the Vatican were severed. Most landowners fled to other parts of the world.

The Dominicans entered the 1900s battered by a brutal and capricious history. They had seen thirty-eight governments flit past in the course of fifty years—an average of fifteen months for every rule. The new century brought little relief to that instability. Twelve administrations came and went from the presidential palace in sixteen years. The United States, seeing the potential havoc to its interests, moved quickly to occupy the capital and restore order. A series of American generals and puppets proceeded to rule the island for the next eight years. But although the United States officially packed up and exited Santo Domingo in 1924, the US Marines remained in neighboring Haiti for another decade. American influence would never quite leave the island.

In 1920 or so, Rafael Trujillo, a small-time Dominican criminal who joined the military and graduated to small-time police work, caught the eye of the US Marines who were occupying the island at the time. They offered him the opportunity to train for the municipal police force. Within five years, he was its commander in chief. The occupying Americans saw him as stabilizing figure in a potentially precarious era, and their support was unequivocal. Certainly he was on their side, a manipulatable pawn.

In 1930, running for the presidency, Trujillo threatened to torture and murder anyone who dared support the opposing candidate, and so, quite logically, he won the presidential palace in a landslide. In a dictatorship marked by decadence and corruption, he proceeded to arrogate all profits to himself and militate against any and all who opposed him. One after another, he eliminated enemies through outright force or intimidation. To keep them under his thumb, he placed the country under martial law, established a secret police, censored the press, killed dissidents. He also renamed the capital after himself—the ancient, historic Santo Domingo became Ciudad Trujillo—in the event anyone had doubts about who was in command.

In 1937, in a stunning show of racial absolutism, Trujillo ordered the massacre of more than twenty thousand Haitian immigrants who had crossed the island border to find work on the Dominican side. Although he had risen to power via American muscle—installed by US Marines and maintained for thirty-one years—he met his undoing via American pragmatism: the CIA, finally, out of pressure from Washington, began maneuvering to oust him from an increasingly embarrassing office. In 1961, after a failed attempt to assassinate his sworn enemy the president of Venezuela, Trujillo was gunned down by a gang of assassins, some of them identified as soldiers from his own army. In his wake, he left behind an untold number of human rights atrocities. He bequeathed the country one thing more: an abiding culture of fear.

COLOMBIA
1900–1948

> *It's the sound of things falling from on high, a fitful yet perpetual sound, a sound that never ends.*
> —Juan Gabriel Vásquez, *The Sound of Things Falling*

In those formative, postrevolutionary years, Colombia, favored since the conquistadors' days for its rich veins of gold, its emeralds, its fertile fields, provided yet another version of the volatile Latin American story. From the day Venezuelan liberator Bolívar declared its independence from Spain, the new republic went on to suffer rabid internecine wars between Bolívar's generals, one sputtering rebellion after another, a string of unstable governments. Even as the country entered the twentieth century, it erupted in the War of a Thousand Days, a bitter battle between liberals and conservatives over the price of coffee. The liberals represented the coffee growers, the laborers, and a laissez-faire economy; the conservatives, who had just snatched the presidency in a highly suspect election, were landed aristocrats out to get as much as they could from the booming coffee business. As many as 130,000 Colombians died in the carnage, farmlands were burned, banks fell to ruin. In the ensuing chaos, Panama, which had been part of Colombia since the wars of independence, now seceded boldly with the aid of the US government. For years, the United States, which had taken over the construction of the Panama Canal, had craved full control of the isthmus. In 1903, as US government reports describe it, President Theodore Roosevelt took full advantage of Colombia's disarray to achieve what he had long wanted. Having prodded Colombian revolutionaries to war in the first place, Roosevelt's administration now moved through the rubble to establish exclusive control, in perpetuity, over the Canal Zone.

Violence in Colombia became so commonplace during those years that ancient regional and tribal conflicts sprang from the mists of time to be fought anew by the descendants of rivals. Centuries of cultural, ethnic, and racial differences became fodder for new belligerence, and, in the process, bandits and drifters took to the streets to take rank advantage of the chaos. They stole, raped, ransacked the countryside, and plotted vendettas against ancient foes. A culture of bloodletting rushed from the past to plague the present. The scorpion, as in Aesop's tale, stuck to his nature and stung. So endemic was the murderousness that few were surprised when liberals celebrated their victory at the polls in 1930 with a series of massacres and assassinations and a spree of looting and burning, especially of churches, and especially in the state of Santander, where the fighting had been most fierce.

A mere generation later, in 1932, Colombia became embroiled in another war—this time in a border spat with Peru—over territory in the Amazon rain forest. The Peruvian president, sensing the Colombians were distracted by internal problems and lacked a strong military defense, decided to take back a sliver of land Peruvians had always considered theirs. A bitter struggle followed, and the respective military forces—tattered at best—went at each other viciously in the wilds of the Putumayo jungle. Not until the Peruvian president was shot dead by an assassin's bullet was a nervous truce reached. That awkward peace reigned in Colombia for a blessed few years, even as the conservative-liberal divide continued to vex the country. Now, nearing the mid-twentieth century, the nation's conservatives were chafing under twelve years of uninterrupted liberal rule. When a conservative president was finally elected in 1948, liberal fury broke loose and found its voice in a full-throated, eloquent orator. His name was Jorge Gaitán. Soon what little order there was began to ravel in perilous ways, and Colombia descended headlong into a violence hitherto unknown in postindependence America.

Gaitán was the highly charismatic leader of the Colombian Liberal Party, a former education minister who had staked his career on decrying violence and empowering the lower classes. He was staunchly anti-Communist, reserving his most bitter criticism for the primitive, homicidal tactics so prevalent among revolutionaries during those Cold War years. His speeches, vibrantly delivered and laced with vivid images of a world made of better angels, were captivating, inspiring. But when he was assassinated in cold blood on April 9, 1948, under mysterious circumstances, Gaitán's death changed the course of Colombian history and galvanized the Left in much of Latin America. News of his assassination was greeted by a spontaneous burst of outright barbarity.

It wasn't clear who had pounded three bullets into the head and neck of the beloved orator. Someone made the accusation and pointed at a young man—a hapless drifter—who happened to be present on the scene. The unfortunate youth was seized by the mob, lynched, pummeled to death, stripped naked, and dragged through the streets, marking the way with his blood. The Nobel Prize–winning novelist Gabriel García Márquez, who was witness to the deed, claimed that three well-dressed men had been involved: one who pointed at the sorry vagrant and blamed him for the crime, and two others who slipped away quietly in a shiny, new car.

But the killing didn't stop with the lynching. No more than ten minutes after the words "They've murdered Gaitán!" rang out in the streets, Bogotá was overrun with rioters. Within hours, they were surging through the capital, leaving hundreds of dead in their wake. El Bogotazo, as the uprising was subsequently named, would eventually crash through the rest of the country in waves of raw fury that pitted liberal and conservative armies against each other, lasted ten years, and left the fertile fields of Colombia strewn with more than three hundred thousand corpses. One man's death—blamed variously on the CIA, the Colombian Communist Party, the Soviet Union, Fidel Castro, random student revolutionaries, and the newly elected right-wing president, Mariano Ospina—had razed the capital's heart, sparked a homicidal civil war, forcibly displaced three million souls, and brought the country to financial ruin. At no time in memory, aside from the bullet that took the life of Austrian archduke Francis Ferdinand and sparked the First World War, had a slug of steel cost so much human life and suffering.

As fate would have it, none other than the young Fidel Castro was casting about Bogotá in 1948 when Gaitán was killed. Castro had gone to Colombia to protest, among other things, General Trujillo's reign of terror in the Dominican Republic, the Pan American Conference (precursor to the Organization of American States), and the United States' designs on the Panama Canal. At every opportunity during that trip—in student meetings, revolutionary cells, visits to politicians—Castro excoriated his declared enemies, the hidebound dictators that had proliferated throughout South America for the past one hundred years. According to him, Fascism, capitalism, imperialism, all aided and abetted by the colossus to the north, were cancers to be rooted out. Dictators were the ruin of Latin America, he insisted, and many of the most noxious had gathered right there in Bogotá for the Pan American Conference. "Trujillo was there!" he reflected later. "All of them were there." He had traveled to Colombia to rail against them, but he was also there to recruit Colombians to his revolutionary cause.

Castro had found considerable success in attracting Panamanian, Venezuelan, Dominican, and Argentine students to his mission—after all, a firm belief in the Marxist world view was taking root among the young in Latin America—and he suspected that Colombia, torn by years of political turmoil, would be fertile ground for a wider revolution. To assist him toward that goal, a group of Colombian university students inspired by his political passions and steeped in Gaitán's populist vision took it upon themselves to introduce Castro to Gaitán. The scruffy twenty-two-year-old Fidel must have seemed a starry-eyed neophyte to Gaitán, who by then was more than twice his age and a veteran of Colombia's hard-bitten realpolitik. All the same, when the two met, Gaitán was courteous to the callow revolutionary. In turn, Fidel gushed that the Colombian hero struck him as pleasantly "Indian" in manner, "intelligent, clever, friendly." He was thoroughly impressed with the man's brilliance and charm. Gaitán was polite, but demurred from promising Castro outright support, although he agreed to meet with the young man again. Castro was thrilled, confident that the meeting had gone well. All the same, he couldn't quite shake a strange premonition he had about the general mood of the country. "When I arrived in Colombia," he would say later, "it struck me as odd that every day there were newspaper notices about thirty deaths here, forty deaths there. It seemed there was a daily massacre in Colombia." Bogotá was a tinderbox, ready to explode.

Just before Castro was to meet with Gaitán again, Bogotá did just that. It erupted in a war that would last fifty years. Castro was on his way to Gaitán's office when the shout went up that the man had been murdered. Almost immediately, a biblical mass of protesters ran down the streets roaring with rage, destroying everything in sight. With so much fury about and the capital bursting into flames, Castro didn't hesitate. He grabbed an iron rod and, like everyone else, joined in the mayhem of destruction. "Bogotá! Another grand adventure!" he exclaimed much later, recalling the sheer thrill of it. This was anger, revenge, primitive justice. In the frenzy of it, he seized a government typewriter a fellow protester was trying to smash and flung it to the ground, shattering it completely. He sprinted to the plaza and wielded his cudgel like any other disillusioned Colombian in a fit of wrath. But this was no revolution as he had envisioned it. This was not what he was after. Killing, if and when his revolution came, he resolved, would have a purpose. A tactical edge, a strategic aim. Of that he was very certain.

WITNESS TO HISTORY
Havana, 1976–1980

> *Castro was in Angola because Angola was simply one more new and far more extravagant stage on which to fight the United States.*
> —Georgie Anne Geyer, *Guerrilla Prince*

Within thirty years, Fidel Castro's strategic aim was crystal clear. He had won his revolution, rid Cuba of imperialist powers, executed his enemies, and proved that one man could stand against a sea of foes. Shunned by the United States, welcomed into the Communist fold, and eager to engage a restless Latin America, he resolved that aiding the upstart Marxist revolution in Angola would almost certainly send the right message, achieve a wider purpose. He would prove that Cuba, despite its size and isolation, could have a profound influence in world affairs, stand for justice, make a mark in the global politic. Toward that end, he would join forces with the Soviets and engage in a proxy war against the United States.

Carlos Buergos did not know he had been witness to history when he returned from Angola in December 1976. He could not imagine that within a few months, forty-five thousand more Cubans like him would be deployed in Africa to carry on what his little battalion had modestly begun. In truth, he was hardly able to think at all as he stepped onto the tarmac with his head swaddled in a soiled bandage. His head throbbed, his bright-amber eyes were ringed by a deep purple, he had lost twenty pounds in the course of a few months. He was a shadow of the breezy, carefree youth he had been a year before when he flew across the Atlantic shoulder to shoulder with a plane full of boys. He had turned twenty-one in the interim—probably as he waited to be sent into the bush, somewhere on the periphery of Luanda. He wasn't sure. He realized that his birthday was long past only as he stared up at the clinic's lightbulb, after the bullet had been dug from his head.

He was flown to the military base outside Havana on Friday, December 3, the very day that Premier Castro, who had held undisputed power for seventeen years, assumed the presidency. He would occupy that position as Latin America's most lasting dictator for thirty-two more years. Carlos was unaware of the change. He was also unaware of Castro's recent threat, as the United States readied for bicentennial celebrations, that Cuba was fully prepared to be the most efficient terrorist machine, the most persistent thorn in the side of that neighboring leviathan. Oblivious to the global drama in which he had just taken part, the young veteran was herded from airfield to military quarters, lined up and counted along with the other wounded, and then discharged and spit out under the vast, blue sky. He hitched a ride with a sympathetic trucker and pitched his way through the streets of Havana until he reached his father's tiny apartment by nightfall.

It is unclear what happened after that. Carlos was patently unable to remember much. He drifted, made do. Recovering gradually, he tried to find work but had no luck. There were job shortages, housing shortages; the war in Africa seemed to be sucking all energy from the island. For all the fog of that first year, he remembered all too clearly the following one. There was less and less to eat on the table. He could see his father wasting away, cadaverous. His mother was frantic. Although Cuba was being praised around the world for its high literacy and low poverty rates, there was little to buy in the markets. More precisely, there was a distinct scarcity of meat.

The country's cattle, copious in the 1950s, feeding the millions, were no longer. The Communist Party was now forced to admit that it would need to criminalize the butchery of cows or risk a vast illegal market. The edict came from on high: anyone caught killing and butchering an animal would face at least ten years in prison. Cubans joked darkly that cows had become as sacred, as inviolable, as any Brahman in India. All the same, appetites were such that if a herd were hit by a train—if lightning struck a barn—Cubans would descend on the carcasses like vultures on carrion. Eventually the ban included horses. Butchering and selling one—even a dead one—might cost a man thirty years of his life, more at times than for cold-blooded murder. Yet for all the injunctions against the consumption of meat, an existential hunger prevailed, demand grew, and the black market spiraled. A spirited trade in horse meat became a viable career opportunity. Carlos, seeing his future in it, began to cast about for horse ranches where he might make a strike.

He found one in Camagüey, not far from the sugar field where he had watched a machete hack open a man's brow. He had seen far worse, risked far worse, in Angola. He did not hesitate. With a gang of like-minded friends, an improvised knot of small-time thugs—the flotsam of war—he set about plotting the crime. They would steal a truck. They would kill a horse in the dark before dawn. They would butcher it, stash it in tarps, and ferry it to a third location, where one of the men's brothers—a foreman in a food freezing factory—would store it until all suspicion was past. Eventually the authorities would find the vehicle abandoned in an empty lot. After that, in the fullness of time, Carlos and his little gang would sell the meat on the black market, where it would fetch enough to feed their families for several weeks. They would do this on Saturdays in the wee hours of morning while Cuba slept, giving them enough time to get the deed done, pack up the dismembered limbs, and flee to the outskirts of Havana before sunrise.

It went well. Surprisingly well. As it turned out, horse stables had far fewer guards than cow ranches. The first kill went unobserved, and was remarkably lucrative. Every part of the horse turned out to be profitable: the flesh, the bone, the hide, even the penis and tail were wanted for Santería voodoo rituals. There were several more kills after that. Soon, the little band fell into a pattern. There was the hunt for the perfect mark. The tracking of careless owners. The dedicated watch to observe workaday habits, dogs, the excitability of the horses. The heist of a suitable truck. The quick, lethal slit of the throat.

The foreman in the processing plant was all too accommodating; he argued for a larger cut of the profits. Carlos's hawker was skilled at keeping each sale secret, the buyer protected, the hand-off discreet. The little band was soon flush with money, carousing in bars, visiting houses of pleasure, their pockets jingling with coins. The world seemed an easy place. Until the day a police car appeared out of nowhere on the dirt road where they happened to be and flicked its headlights into high beam. It was November 1978. Carlos was arrested, convicted, and, without much ado, thrown into prison. By coincidence, days later, Fidel Castro, responding to President Jimmy Carter's pledge to drop all travel restrictions from Cuba, announced that the following year he would release three thousand "hard-core" criminals to the open waters facing Florida.

They would be political prisoners, Castro said: anti-Communists who had been behind bars since the 1960s.

Carlos didn't have to wait that long. In June 1979, only six months into his sentence and ten months from Castro's promised release, he was pulled from his cell, handed a paper bag with his old clothes, and told to go home. When he knocked on this father's door this time, however, it was made very clear to him that he was not welcome anymore. There were too many children under that roof, his father said—Carlos's younger brothers, like any ordinary human beings, had fathered babies—and Carlos was nothing but a bad influence. No help to them. No good.

Within three months, he was in jail again; this time for treason. He had tried to escape Cuba. In sheer desperation, he had patched together a raft made of old tires, bound it with hemp, and set out to sea with two other men. The military unit that captured him was not as gentle as the police had been the year before. They threw a lasso around him as if he were a wild animal and broke his arm in the struggle to pull him onto their craft. They roughed him up, brought him ashore, and thrust him into a dank dungeon in the fearsome Combinado del Este prison, just east of Havana and twenty-five miles from Mariel. His two companions weren't so lucky. They were shot dead as they leapt, terrified, into the watery expanse.

BODY COUNTS

Tierra del Fuego could prove suitable for cattle breeding; but the only drawback to this plan is that to all appearances it would be necessary to exterminate all the Fuegians.

—*London Daily News*, 1882

"Eat or be eaten, there's no getting around it," a character says in Mario Vargas Llosa's stark, brittle, and exquisitely brutal *La Ciudad y los Perros*. The novel, translated into English as *The Time of the Hero*, describes, among other things, how a Peruvian youth in a military academy who would rather write love letters than learn the ways of war will be expected to crawl on his belly, kill on command. One might say this is the goal of any warrior's education, except that in the Latin American context, the militarization of the young brings with it a good dose of extracurricular instruction: a boy, in the course of being a soldier, will learn the ways of corruption, the material benefits of military power; the handy peacetime uses of brute force. And, quite naturally, when this belligerence is loosed upon a population, the response—if people are brutalized enough—will be to respond in kind.

To most of the world, reading about extreme distemper in Latin America—as prone to exaggeration as that notion might be—might be to assume that the region is overwhelmingly, numbingly homicidal. Surely there is plenty of evidence for that: the hard-boiled, repressive dictators, the assassinations, the disappeared, the culture of corruption, the delinquency, the death squads, narcos, terrorists, gangland *pandilleros*; not to mention the barbed, electrified wire that sits atop our city walls. The images are constant in the media. Who can forget the past sixty years in the history of Mexico, Argentina, Honduras, Peru, Colombia, El Salvador? The mutilated bodies, the pot-clanging widows, the blank-eyed children? Right now, in any major city in the United States of America, or any number of urban neighborhoods of Europe, there are plenty of murder rates to compete, but the difference is that in those cities, violence always seems to surprise. It is largely a product of chance and misfortune. There is no surprise in the Latin American version. And, even if numbers fluctuate—if, for some reason, in any given year New Orleans can count more murders than Ciudad Juárez or San Salvador or Natal—the underlying calculus is undeniable.

Sometimes the murderousness can be chilling in its premeditated cruelty: in the late 1800s, in the southern swath of Chile and Argentina known as Tierra del Fuego, the Selk'nam people were declared "dangerous obstacles" to progress. Europeans had poured into the area, lured by a gold rush, and the indigenous who resisted the influx were deemed a nuisance. Despised, dismissed as less than human even in that advanced age, they were subjected to a campaign of vilification. Especially when the English recalled how repelled Charles Darwin had been by Fuegians when he visited Patagonia years before:

These poor wretches were stunted in their growth, their hideous faces bedaubed with white paint, their skins filthy and greasy, their hair entangled, their voices discordant and their gestures violent. Viewing such men, one can hardly make oneself believe that they are fellow-creatures, and inhabitants of the same world. It is a common subject of conjecture what pleasure in life some of the lower animals can enjoy: how much more reasonably the same question may be asked of these barbarians!

"There's so much to be done in Tierra del Fuego!" a London newspaper proceeded to editorialize breathlessly, but to accomplish it, one would need "to eliminate the Fuegians." And that is precisely what the coloniz-ers did. They paid Chilean and Argentine mercenaries to hunt and kill the Selk'nam. Armed thugs were compensated according to how many severed ears or testicles they could produce to prove the kills. More was offered if a pair of ears belonged to a pregnant woman and was accom-panied by a human fetus. Sheep were doused in strychnine in hopes that the Selk'nam would feed on them. A steady extermination took place, just as the London paper had called for it. The locals were engaged to carry it out. By the time the killing was over, thousands of Selk'nam were dead, and the few hundred who were left were herded onto reser-vations, where disease finished them off. Several years later, Argentina invited and admitted its largest European influx—almost two million immigrants of a whiter race.

As Tina Rosenberg's heartbreaking 1991 book *Children of Cain* puts it:

> Quantity is not the whole issue. Violence in Latin America is sig-nificant in part because so much of it is political: planned, delib-erate, carried out by organized groups of society against members of other groups. It is used to make a point. It is committed by the institution entrusted with the protection of its citizens. And it is justified by large numbers of people. It is different from the pur-poseless, random, individual violence of the United States. It is more evil.

And it is still there.

HIT MEN, GUERRILLAS, AND TORTURERS

A single person killed is a tragedy, but a million people killed are a statistic.

—Joseph Stalin, 1943

Sometime in June 1976—the precise moment is not known—the word *disappeared* took on new currency in Latin America. The verb suddenly morphed from passive to active: a death squad could disappear a person; that person was *el desaparecido*, the disappeared. The word came to vivid life on the Plaza de Mayo in Buenos Aires when hundreds of men and women began to congregate in slow, somber walks around the plaza's *La Estatua de Libertad*, carrying signs that bore witness to those who had suddenly disappeared in their families: the missing children, spouses, or grandchildren who had been dragged from their homes, tortured, summarily executed, or dropped into the big, blue sea, never to be seen again. It was a terrible coda to the civil war that had raged through Argentina after the death of President Juan Perón two years before.

The power vacuum in 1974 had been acute. Before expiring, Perón had installed his third wife, Isabel Perón, as vice president, and now, as Argentina's sovereign—as the first female in the world to hold the title of "president"—she had proved patently unprepared to fill the role. Isabel sorely lacked the grand, populist appeal of the former first lady—now dead for twenty-two years—Evita Perón.

Isabel had been a nightclub dancer in Panama City when Perón met her: a pretty, but distinctly shallow and unprepossessing woman with a fifth-grade education, whom he had married only because the Church had insisted on it when it learned he was cohabiting with a mistress. With Perón dead, all Isabel's shortcomings came into play, as well as her strange dependence on the police commissioner José López Rega, a former security guard in the presidential palace, who was fascinated, as she was, by occult divination and fortune-telling. She had promoted López to minister of social welfare but eventually relied on him as her de facto prime minister. Under his auspices, a secret death squad called the Triple A (Argentine Anti-Communist Alliance) was formed to liquidate increasingly pesky leftists. Within a year, he had killed 1,500 of them. The truculence was contagious. Right-wing paramilitary groups rushed out to battle Communist guerrillas in the streets, prompting a bloody conflict that seemed to have its own fiendish momentum. The leftist guerrillas, the Montoneros and others—largely university students and Catholic liberation theologists—answered with bombs or arson, kidnapping businessmen to fund their campaign and collecting some of the largest ransoms on record: $14 million for the abduction of an Exxon executive; $60 million for the Argentine grain moguls Jorge and Juan Born. By March 1976, a military coup had ousted Isabel Perón, established a government under General Jorge Rafael Videla called "The Trial"—eerily reminiscent of Franz Kafka's novel of the same name—and begun a reign of terror as murderous as any conquistador's rule.

Months later, the Guerra Sucia—the Dirty War—was in full throttle. Almost seven thousand more Argentines went missing within the course of a year. This was hardly a war; there had ceased to be combatants or any real give and take between foes. It was a campaign in which a muscular, armed military had brazenly undertaken to wipe out thousands of civilians, and it was fierce, unrelenting, and seemingly random. Hardly understood in its terrifying fullness at the time, a purge of inconvenient Argentines had begun. The goal was to rid the country of a wave of rebellious "Communist guerrillas" that had bedeviled the right-wing power structure for years. But it quickly became a genocide of leftists from any walk of life, including vague suspects, glancing associates, family members, and whomever the military didn't much like: journalists, social workers, labor leaders, teachers, priests, nuns, psychiatrists, poets. In other words, a massive population of Argentines who were averse to hard-line, *mano dura* rule.

When Argentina's steely military dictator, General Videla, who had overseen the hecatomb, was asked how the Argentine people should think about the thousands devoured by his maw of improvised justice, he answered archly that the question's logic was all wrong. The Argentine people had seen law work on their behalf. They deserved human rights, and those rights had been threatened in Argentina. In an argument that swelled to Orwellian proportion, he explained that the truly loyal, honest citizens had been faced with a metastasizing terrorist threat—

a Communist infiltration—and they needed to pay down that cancer in human blood. The victims, if there were victims, were nobodies. "Who is a disappeared person?" he asked rhetorically. "Anonymous. Nobody. He has no identity, is neither dead nor alive. Just disappeared." His answer was all too reminiscent of the answer given to the debate that had raged in Seville during the late fifteenth century: Were the victims of the conquest truly human? The answer five hundred years later was still a resounding no. Not if the presiding force decided otherwise. They were chaff—and by virtue of their resistance, totally expendable.

The mass extermination that took place during Argentina's Dirty War had been the brainchild of a sinister, secret campaign called Operation Condor, a concerted, multinational plan of repression hatched by right-wing dictators in the Southern Cone (Argentina, Bolivia, Brazil, Chile, Paraguay, and Uruguay; supported by Peru, Colombia, and Venezuela) and carried out by a vast network of secret police. The initial architects of the cooperation, security officials from those countries—many of whom had been trained at the US Army's School of the Americas during the 1960s and 1970s—gathered in Buenos Aires under the auspices of General Videla to collaborate on methods they might use against "subversives." The United States, a natural partner to anti-Communist initiatives in the region, was complicit, providing military and technical support to Operation Condor for more than two decades. Support began with Lyndon Johnson's administration in the late 1960s and continued through the end of Ronald Reagan's presidency in 1989, even though US government officials were fully aware of the extent of the atrocities. Indeed, in 1973, when Secretary of State Henry Kissinger received concrete evidence of the massacres, he stated that "however unpleasant" these circumstances might be, the overall situation was beneficial to the United States. "We want you to succeed," he told the Argentine foreign minister in no uncertain terms. "We do not want to harass you. I will do what I can."

In August 1976, when Kissinger was further informed that prominent subversives were not only game within Latin America but targeted abroad, he did not balk. Instead, on September 20 he instructed American ambassadors to stand down, not interfere with Operation Condor, and "take no further action" on deterring Latin American plots that might be under way. The very next day—September 21, 1976—a bomb under the car of former Chilean ambassador Orlando Letelier, a passionate critic of General Pinochet, exploded as he rode through Washington, DC's Sheridan Circle, hurling the car into the air and killing him as well as a young American aide. The Chilean secret police, under express orders by Pinochet, were the perpetrators. The claws of Operation Condor had reached into the very heart of the American capital.

Two years later, although wholesale murders were by now a daily occurrence in Argentina, the military regime hosted the soccer World Cup in Buenos Aires. Even as women were being impaled by cattle prods in their vaginas, even as men's anuses were being rammed by iron rods—even as prisoners were being flayed alive, or herded into concentration camps, or drugged and dropped from biplanes and helicopters into the Atlantic or the Paraná River—a grinning General Videla swanned through festivities with Secretary Kissinger, and the military ranks ran the games as efficiently as they did their torture machines. At the very apogee of the cruelty, with unidentified bodies washing ashore, with young girls being snatched screaming from buses, with a whole world watching, the 1978 World Cup closed with a victory for the home country. Argentina trounced the Netherlands by a score of 3–1. Thirty years later, when Argentina celebrated that victory, the memories were too painful. Nineteen of the twenty-two players didn't join in the revelry.

In the end, as many as thirty thousand Argentines were killed by their government in that tragic decade between 1973 and 1983. In Chile, we know that a quarter million were taken into custody and interrogated by the military; ten thousand more detained and tortured; in excess of three thousand killed. Within the same period, the Paraguayan armed forces disposed of two thousand corpses. Because of the covert nature of Operation Condor, its body count over the years and throughout its many affiliated countries may never be known, but scholars estimate that as many as sixty to eighty thousand may have been murdered, including thirty thousand "disappeared" or presumed executed, and four hundred thousand more who were jailed and tortured. It is a numbing calculus, so easy to dismiss for its sheer implausibility. But the reckoning was all too real. The human costs of Condor were higher than American losses in the Revolutionary War or the Vietnam War; higher than the number of casualties in all US engagements of the past half century, including wars in Iraq and Afghanistan. Perhaps as costly as American combat casualties in World War I. And yet the methodical killing continued long after Operation Condor closed its ledgers in Argentina. It swept through the continent like a malevolent plague.

EL SALVADOR, GUATEMALA
1960–1984

Let the history we lived be taught in the schools, so that it is never forgotten, so that our children may know.
—Commission for Historical Clarification, 1996

There was nothing uniform about the revolutionary contagion that ripped through Latin America in the 1960s and held it fast for the next four decades. Stark differences ruled its viral manifestations. After all, a white urbanite's impulse to rebel could hardly be the same as that of an indigenous banana laborer. Nevertheless, something galvanic was in the wind. The Cuban revolution had shown a generation of Latin Americans that a people could grab hold of its destiny and change it. As a result, Soviet agents were suddenly, gleefully everywhere in the region—in the capitals, in universities, in burgeoning Communist cells—sowing that message to a restless young. The logic was powerful and clear: the raw divisions of class or race, the gaping abyss between rich and poor, were no longer tenable. Whatever their color, revolutionaries across Latin America now insisted on a break with the old order, a more liberal society, a leveling of classes, a culmination of the Marxist dream. But there was no consensus on the Left as to how to achieve it. Where there *was* unity and cooperation, ironically, was on the opposing side, among the old guard, the rich families, the descendants of conquistadors, an established power base that was adamantly reactionary. The military crackdowns that followed from Montevideo to San Salvador had startling similarities: they all featured draconian generals, tanks in the streets, martial law, heavily armed security forces, undercover death squads. And they could all count on the United States to take their side.

Shortly after Castro's victory in Cuba, some of the countries buffering South America from Mexico—El Salvador, Guatemala, Honduras—a cluster known as Central America's "Northern Triangle," erupted in fiery insurgencies at about the same time. For decades, El Salvador had been a bomb waiting to detonate. The country's peasants had risen up in a massive revolt during the 1930s, but had reaped a deadly military retaliation called *la matanza*, "the slaughter." Thirty thousand of the most humble Salvadorans had been massacred and shoveled into mass graves. The army, ruled by the country's oligarchy—the "Fourteen Families"— and aided by the United States, dominated the jittery decades to come. But defiance was never far from the surface. It exploded once again in the course of the 1970s, when poverty rates in El Salvador were at 90 percent, wages plummeted by 70 percent, and the number of landless soared. Life expectancy among the poor had shrunk to thirty-seven years. Infant mortality and malnutrition were at all-time highs. As the wealthy turned a blind eye, left-wing guerrillas organized into a fighting force. When they were ready to challenge the right-wing military colossus, a deadly spiral of violence began.

For the full decade that followed, guerrillas proceeded to invade embassies, kill businessmen, and execute military commanders and police chiefs—targeting anyone who was perceived to be part of the machinery of oppression. They bombed factories, businesses, stores. They kidnapped the rich and held them ransom, scoring millions of dollars and netting a rogue popularity in the process. In 1979 they finally wrested power in a victorious coup over the old oligarchy. But it didn't last long. With the help of $4.5 billion from the United States, a fighting force called the Contras, and spirited support from Reagan's recently appointed and short-lived Secretary of State Alexander Haig, the old right-wing military slammed back with full force. A virulent civil war followed. For all the brutality perpetrated by guerrillas in the twelve years of that struggle—for all the arms and guns that poured in from Ethiopia and Vietnam to support the revolutionaries—the Salvadoran armed forces answered with a dwarfing detonation of fury. They unleashed death squads to eradicate any and all perpetrators, enlisted child soldiers, herded civilians into concentration camps. Mark Danner, reporting for *The New Yorker*, described the abattoir that the country had become:

Mutilated corpses littered the streets of El Salvador's cities. Sometimes the bodies were headless, or faceless, their features having been obliterated with a shotgun blast or an application of battery acid; sometimes limbs were missing, or hands or feet chopped off, or eyes gouged out; women's genitals were torn and bloody, bespeaking repeated rape; men's were often found severed and stuffed into their mouths. And cut into the flesh of a corpse's back or chest was likely to be the signature of one or another of the "death squads" that had done the work.

The Church protested, but the Salvadoran military answered by murdering nuns, declaring Jesuit priests enemies, and assassinating renowned human rights activist Archbishop Óscar Romero. When a quarter million faithful gathered before the cathedral in San Salvador to mourn the holy man's passing, military snipers on nearby rooftops shot into the crowd, killing forty-two and wounding two hundred. There seemed to be nothing the Salvadoran military could do that would prompt Washington to cease its financial support. In the carnival of killing that followed, untold numbers of Salvadorans were disappeared; one million were displaced; seventy-five thousand were murdered. The United Nations estimated that leftist rebels may have been responsible for approximately four thousand of those deaths. In contrast, more than seventy thousand murders were committed by right-wing military-controlled death squads.

Guatemala was no different. For years, it had been a virtual colony of American interests. The United Fruit Company, which owned vast tracts of lands in Guatemala, also controlled the railroads and the shipyards, as well as all modes of communication. But that unilateral control was suddenly threatened when citizens began to demand their rights. Beginning in 1960, one after another Guatemalan president fought that trend, sanctioning extrajudicial killings as protests against the prevailing regimes began to sweep the country. Like Cortés, who sent out armies to kill any Mayans who refused to work the mines, the military now relied on the sword to suppress defiance.

The troubles had started much earlier, in 1944, when Guatemalans decided to depose their corrupt dictator, hold a democratic election, and sweep Juan José Arévalo to power with a vigorous liberal platform of universal suffrage and a minimum wage. Arévalo was succeeded by President Jacobo Árbenz, who continued to defend the rights of the poor, nationalize the land, and parcel it out to the landless. Perceived by the United States as too Socialist for comfort in that volatile turf, Guatemala was soon targeted for a harsh correction. In 1954 the Central Intelligence Agency, supported by Secretary of State John Foster Dulles, masterminded a coup to topple Árbenz's government. They called its combatants "the army of Liberation," but Guatemalans were quickly disabused when activists were rounded up and thrown in jail, tortured, and executed. Any whiff of rebellion was labeled as Communist inspired or foreign born. Guatemala soon became a pilot program for American military and covert political intervention in the Caribbean—a training ground for any armed engagements that might emerge.

Castro's success changed all of that. With Cuba's sudden victory, Guatemalan hopes were spurred once again to dreams of self-determination. Rebellion, all too rashly stirred and all too swiftly quashed, became widespread as the 1960s unfolded in its full revolutionary glory. Nevertheless, circumstances changed when President Julio César Méndez of the Revolutionary Party was elected democratically, and the Guatemalan military, fearing an erosion of its power, stepped in to make demands: they would fight any rebel guerrillas on their own terms, they would brook no government interference, and they would answer to no judge. By 1966, mass disappearances had become common. Students, professors, political activists, outspoken civilians, foreign diplomats—all were potential targets. And with good reason, because the intellectual and informed community was precisely where revolution lay.

It was then that indiscriminate bombings of villages began. For the next fifteen years, Guatemala proceeded to ravage itself, urged on by US advisors who were fresh from the bedlam of the Vietnam War. Murder became high theater as death squads festooned corpses with propaganda and ghoulish warnings, or disseminated death lists, or marauded the streets unchallenged. With each presidency that followed, the violence seemed to mount exponentially: the constitution was suspended, a state of siege was declared, kidnappings and mass arrests became steady fare.

For all the brutality of the torture and disappearances that followed, however, the left-wing dissidents refused to be cowed. Only a massive earthquake in 1976 seemed to unify the population briefly, if only because a spirit of mutual survival prevailed. But soon enough the death squads were back in business: in one month alone, August 1977, they murdered sixty-one suspected revolutionary ringleaders. The rebel movement answered by doubling its numbers and moving to the desolate mountains of the western highlands. A taste of the genocide to come was felt in early 1980, when an indigenous delegation, appearing in the capital to denounce the murder of fellow villagers, was snubbed by Congress, its lawyer assassinated just outside the doors of the police headquarters. In order to bring attention to the burgeoning violence, protesters then occupied the Spanish embassy, but they were fatally foiled when the police hurled Molotov cocktails into the gated embassy grounds, burning alive almost everyone within. International opinion didn't seem to matter now. The military was hell-bent on taking power.

Passions were such that, in 1982, when General Efraín Ríos Montt hijacked the presidency in a violent coup, he lost all patience and identified the greater Guatemalan populace as the "internal enemy." He ordered entire rural villages destroyed, whole populations massacred. Eighteen thousand Guatemalans fell victim to state violence in the course of one year. Most were recalcitrant Mayan peasants in the West, who for centuries had bucked repression and to whom promises of justice had spoken most emphatically. Communities suspected as being rebellious were mowed down in wholesale executions, a large percentage of them women and children. The army by now was engaged in a full-scale war against dissent, striving to terrorize civilians into abandoning revolution. If it meant taking the lives of innocents, so be it. For the old guard, it meant preserving the world as they knew it; for the Americans who supported them, it meant keeping the world safe from the scourge of Communism. They ransacked village and town, indiscriminately raping females, young or old. Using techniques taught them by foreign advisors, they raided "safe houses" and snuffed out all life within. As an in-depth study of those years described it: "Methods of violence became ever more gruesome. . . . The army tended towards overkill, beheading their victims or burning them alive, and smashing the heads of children against rocks. The rape of women survivors, even when pregnant, became more common."

Just as atrocities appeared to be reaching a genocidal peak, just as the international image of President Ríos Montt's government couldn't possibly get worse, press coverage came to an abrupt halt and human right groups were suddenly nowhere to be seen, allowing the terror to escalate in a harrowing silence. Meanwhile, President Ronald Reagan's administration portrayed Ríos Montt's regime as a major improvement of human rights in Guatemala. He's "a man of great integrity," Reagan avowed, "totally dedicated to democracy." By the end of Guatemala's staggering losses, there were as many as two hundred thousand dead or disappeared. One in every thirty of its citizens had been sacrificed to the carnage.

NICARAGUA
1954–1984

In 1980 the statue of the Virgin of Cuapa began to ooze beads of sweat. The opposition press reported that it was suffering from materialism. A year later it reported that the Virgin had stopped sweating and had begun to cry.

—Dirk Kruijt, *"Revolución y contrarevolución"*

In Nicaragua, the echo of discontent resounded. And with good reason. A government funded by the United States and sapped by three generations of the Somoza family—a regime that had grown fat on coffee and banana profits—ruled the country with a greedy and stubborn hand. Most of Nicaragua's children under the age of five were undernourished, stunted. In parts of the countryside, illiteracy reached 90 percent. "I don't want educated people," Anastasio Somoza Debayle liked to say. "I want oxen." By the mid-1950s, by virtue of rampant corruption, the family had built an immense fortune for itself, virtually starving the country's peons, pocketing public funds, and socking it all away in its private empire of commercial and contraband operations. When an earthquake toppled Managua in 1972, killing 13,000 and displacing 750,000 more, Somoza and his family stole the disaster funds that poured in from abroad to reconstruct the country. Much as they stole the shiploads of cement and machinery. Even the beans and rice.

The outrage about these excesses was such that in 1978, at the crest of

Latin America's revolutionary wave, the Sandinistas—a rebel guerrilla force named after the assassinated liberal hero Augusto Sandino—set off a furious campaign of terror and kidnappings to bring world attention to the injustices. Protests had gotten them nowhere. Here and there, throughout the country, they began to launch bold sorties against Somoza's far more powerful National Guard. In retaliation, his air force unleashed a punishing, large-scale bombing of Nicaragua's cities. Suddenly the rebels were garnering international sympathy: Why was Somoza slaughtering his own people for making their will known—for demanding to be heard? Even President Jimmy Carter had to admit that enough was enough; President Somoza was intolerable and needed to be eased out of power. But "easing" was not part of a Latin American guerrilla's vocabulary. The momentum was such that, at noon on August 22, 1978, the Sandinista vanguard, *la frente*, stormed the National Palace, captured nearly two thousand people on the premises and held them for ransom. It was the start of a series of major, violent confrontations that would grip the country for the next decade. Eventually, a year later, in July 1979, the Nicaraguan rebel forces sent President Somoza and his mistress fleeing for their lives, and citizens swarmed Managua's central plaza to declare unequivocal victory for the rebels.

Within two and a half years—with Reagan in power in Washington, Managua in firm alliance with Moscow, and Nicaraguan arms flowing freely to rebels in El Salvador—the tenor of American involvement took a radical turn. In November 1981, the US president signed an order to slip covert funding to the "contras"—the counterrevolutionary force rallying to oust the Sandinistas. Meanwhile, in neighboring Honduras, American armed forces were hard at work training Central American soldiers to beat back Communists wherever they emerged—a progressively harder task in this increasingly volatile region. A few months later, in March 1982, a CIA operation blew up two bridges near the Honduran border and signaled the start of a new war. By the end of it, brother would fight brother, and fifty thousand Nicaraguans would lie dead in the coffee and banana fields. One by one, and for the next forty years, the Mesoamerican nations would cannibalize their own children much as the goddess Coatlicue gobbled her offspring or the great titan Saturn devoured his sons. Almost five hundred years later, that green, fertile funnel of ground—that strategic middle earth that coursed up from Panama, sparked Balboa's and Cortés's ambitions, and separated America north and south—was still under dispute. "You'd be surprised," said Ronald Reagan in a speech to the American people, reporting on his first official Central American trip. "They're all individual countries."

PORT OF EMBARKATION
May 1980

> *I have lived inside that monster, and I know its entrails; my sling is David's.*
>
> —José Martí, about the United States, 1895

Carlos Buergos, eldest son of nine—wiry, hazel-eyed descendant of Spaniards, happy-go-lucky convicted thief—was once more at the mercy of a political wind, although he didn't know it. He was hardly twenty-five when he was released from Cuba's Combinado del Este prison, ferried by a ramshackle government bus yet again—this time not to climb the skies to an uncertain future in Africa but to face the open sea. Of all the children who had emerged from his mother's womb, he was the kind of Cuban Castro did not want. Erratic, balky, perverse, with a big hole in his head and wont to criminal pursuits, Carlos was a disposable quantity.

On May 9, 1980, one year into his twelve-year sentence, Carlos's prison threw open its doors and he was taken to the port of Mariel. There, looking out on a flood of humanity and a sea bobbing with boats, he was confused. He had been presented with such mind-altering scenarios before: the blood spraying from the head of a dying cane cutter; or the army knocking on his door just as he was reveling in the arms of a married woman; or winning Africa to Communism until he was shipped home with a shattered skull; or bartering horse meat for drugs until he could ease the storm in his brain. This time he couldn't quite make out whatever he was meant to see. He had emerged from darkness to light, and the scene before him was dazzling. Stupefying. He could ascertain that there were people—men, women, children—scrambling to board a profusion of small boats, but he hadn't been told why, and his first impulse was to run.

CHAPTER 9

SLOW BURN

---························· ❖ ·····························---

Everybody in the Andes knows, when the devil comes to work his evil on earth, he sometimes takes the shape of a limping gringo stranger.

—Mario Vargas Llosa, *Death in the Andes*

Even as the United States was embroiled in the Watergate scandal, even as Britain was roughed up by the Angry Brigade, even as the Vietnam War roared into its last, tragic days, Latin America stumbled ahead, surrendering itself to increasingly violent upheavals, overshadowed by seemingly harsher headlines, hardly noticed by the wider world. By now, the revolutionary impulse that had cost millions of Latin American lives in the twentieth century had crept through the continent like a slow burn, fueled by resentments that had plagued it for more than five hundred years. Nevertheless, just as sixteenth-century Spain had grown rich on Latin American silver while the cruelest depredations were being imposed, the Colombian economy now grew handsomely in the twentieth century, piling a formidable body count alongside its profits. Indeed, between 1948 and 1953, even as Colombia erupted in an undeclared civil war called La Violencia, it continued to be the largest exporter of gold in the world.

The shattering riots of 1948 known as el Bogotazo, the repercussions of which had gone on to kill nearly a quarter of a million Colombians in the course of ten years, never really stopped. The violence carried on well beyond that, stacking corpses, creating a culture of violence that seemed to have a pulse of its own. By the time news of Central America's revolutionary fervor reached the mountain aerie of Bogotá in the early 1970s, Colombians already had a long history with Left-Right violence.

Hiding out in the hinterlands of Colombia, the country's rebels continued their stubborn resistance to the *mano dura*. With no security forces to protect them from a seemingly endless war, campesinos began to form armed bands, either to shield themselves from harm or, as criminals, to take advantage of the rampant disorder. Before long, there were more than twenty thousand armed commandos roaming the countryside, establishing their own "independent republics." In every sense, it seemed a throwback to the wild, lawless days of the revolution a century and a half before, when plainsmen and rural chieftains formed their own fiefdoms and fought scrappy, vainglorious wars. The military raids against those self-appointed rural vigilantes could be harsh and punishing—a killing field unto itself—and Communist insurgents offered to protect them, pledging to safeguard their rights. So it was that the infamous Revolutionary Armed Forces of Colombia (the FARC) was born, and a wider revolution was made. Throughout the 1970s, as the Marxist romance continued to kindle the Latin American imagination, the FARC expanded, recruiting more and more campesinos to its ranks. In the cities, disaffected university students joined forces and created the National Liberation Army (the ELN), a guerrilla movement that focused on random acts of terror meant to rattle the rich and topple their empires. At their height, the FARC and the ELN amassed a formidable infantry of twenty-three thousand, all dedicated to bombing, kidnapping, extortion, shootings, massacres—whatever it took to force the oligarchy to release its grip on the country.

The turmoil seemed enough to break any nation. Even so, it grew steadily worse. In the 1990s, when the cultivation of coca came to a sudden halt in neighboring Peru, the doors flung open for Colombia's powerful drug cartels to expand their businesses. The demand for cocaine was at an all-time high in the United States—more than ten million avid American users were making regular buys—and the cartels' opportunity to grow profits was irresistible. By 1995, the US cocaine market represented a record $165 billion, almost as much as the American agricultural and mining businesses combined. Coca fields began to spring up in the Colombian countryside as drug lords bought up land to fuel their operations, prompting an even more gigantic illegal market that ultimately financed the Left as well as the Right in that country. Billions of drug dollars flowed into Colombia, seducing and compromising the country's most vital public institutions, including its congress, police, and judicial system. With that staggering bonanza came a fiercer, more random level of violence, as narco-terrorists began to target government officials, journalists, politicians—anyone who got in the way. Two vast drug empires emerged—one in Cali, the other in Medellín—battling to dominate the booty.

Eventually, with cocaine bosses and FARC *comandantes* operating side by side in the interior, they forged strong alliances. Outlaw rules were now the only ones that mattered. Narcos, guerrillas, and right-wing paramilitary forces fought for control, creating a state of siege in which any citizen might be a mark. There were as many as three mass killings a month, seven kidnappings a day, eleven thousand child combatants in jungle and mountain. Gangland-style executions, beheadings, flayings, rapes, abductions, disappearances—unspeakable acts of barbarity—these were everyday occurrences now. There was hardly a Colombian alive whose family had not fallen victim to some form of violence. Indeed, three million were on the run; they were *los deplazados*—the displaced, wrenched from their homes, fleeing to protection in the cities. For all the proud history of the Colombian people, for all their storied culture, for all the natural riches of that emerald land, Colombia had become a criminal enterprise with thugs and butchers at the helm.

GONZALO THOUGHT

Everything but the power is an illusion.
                                    —Abimael "Gonzalo" Guzmán

The plague of violence spread quickly, almost as sinister and ruinous as the virulence that had ripped through and scarred the hemisphere a half millennium before in its conquest. Just as the furies of discontent in Argentina and Chile seemed to fly north to inflame Central America, Colombia's angry fate soon befell Peru, where rancor was ripe and racial grudges had been mounting for generations.

It all began in the Andean region of Ayacucho, one of Peru's poorest provinces—a sunny valley perched twelve thousand feet in the Andes, where Quechua people are known for their stubbornness, pride, and a staggering poverty. Here, of all places, Peruvians were presented with a sudden efflorescence of educational opportunity. In a concerted push to raise Peru's literacy rates, a series of governments in the 1960s and 1970s had decided to open schools and universities in the most remote, stick-poor areas of the country. One outcome was the stunning growth of Ayacucho's Huamanga University, which multiplied its student body fivefold in the course of six years. By 1977, it had grown by 33 percent, so that the university—faculty, students, and staff—now represented more than a quarter of the entire population of Ayacucho.

In a city of poor within a province of poor, where educational options were rare if not nil, this was an extraordinary development. Here was a thoroughly indigenous, highly ambitious, surprisingly egalitarian community of young Andean men and women poised to take full advantage of their unexpected good fortune. And here was a hyperpumped university, in turn, ready to take advantage of its sudden potential. Huamanga's classrooms were packed with a fresh-faced, impressionable accumulation of youths, fully vulnerable to indoctrination. Far from the insular, bigoted capital—far from "Lima La Blanca" and its privileged whites and gringo capitalists—students proceeded to parse and reparse, as undergraduates are wont to do, the history of their country's injustices. With a bold, charismatic professor named Abimael Guzmán stirring their passions, the students of Huamanga became the perfect breeding ground for the Sendero Luminoso, the Shining Path: one of the strongest—as well as the most violent, fanatical, sectarian, and frightening—guerrilla movements in Latin American history.

Guzmán, the illegitimate son of a reasonably well-off merchant in Arequipa, had been born in a small village outside the port city of Mollendo. He had been raised in modest circumstances in his mother's house until he was eight, at which point his mother, desperate to start a new life, abandoned the boy to his own fate. An uncle in Callao took custody of the waif, but it was hardly a kindness: he abused him, humiliated him, put him to work as a servant in his house. Although young Abimael hardly knew his father, he wrote to him now, explaining the cruelties to which he was being subjected, pleading to be rescued from his torments. Guzmán senior, an outsized personality who had fathered ten children by numerous women, was not particularly sympathetic, but the heartrending letter fell into the hands of his more charitable wife, who immediately took pity on the boy. The letter was proof of a good mind, she argued; the child deserved a better life. At the age of eleven, Abimael Guzmán was taken into his father's house in Mollendo and, under his stepmother's auspices, sent to a good school. He performed so well that he eventually aspired to study in nearby Arequipa, a hub of Peruvian intellectuals.

In the late 1950s, Guzmán became a law and philosophy student at the National University of Saint Augustine, a venerable Catholic institution in Arequipa, the most Peruvian of cities. Graduating with a strong academic record and a solid membership in the ever-expanding Communist Party in Latin America, he was recruited in 1962 to teach philosophy and politics at the University of Huamanga, high up in the Andes, in the sleepy mountain city of Ayacucho. Shy, portly, enigmatic, and puritanical, Guzmán may not have cut the figure of a charismatic revolutionary—and Ayacucho might not have been the obvious cradle for one—but he had concrete ambitions for Peru and the will to bring them to life.

It was there in that mountain redoubt that the rector of the university eventually heard out Guzmán's radical vision: having visited China on numerous fellowships, the young professor had come to admire what Mao Tse-tung had achieved with a massive, lumbering peasant society. Chairman Mao had proved that revolution did not have to begin in an urban center; the spark and fire could come from a rural movement. The rector was impressed: this was philosophy in action, ideology with muscle, and he encouraged his starry-eyed subaltern to proceed with his quest. Mao's achievements were Guzmán's ideal, his goal for a nation he felt had abandoned its Andean roots and been seduced by outside forces. He became convinced that the young, promising Quechua Indians under his tutelage—the progeny of generations of neglect—had the wherewithal to rise from centuries of abuse, honor their ancestors, and reclaim Peru for their children. What was needed was nothing short of a violent, catastrophic revolution: what the Incas called Pachacuti, turning the world on its ear. The new would have to level the old—the colonialism, the foreign imperialism, the wanton corruption, the cruelly imposed caste divisions—just as China had purged its past under Mao.

Taking the rector's encouragement as carte blanche, Guzmán began to think beyond mere theoretical goals and put his political convictions into play. With Huamanga University as his factory of transfiguration and Mao's principles as his bible, he taught his disciples to renounce history, turn society upside down, start the country anew.

By the mid 1970s, Guzmán's Communist Party of Peru, founded and nurtured at Huamanga University, had become a formidable guerrilla army of men and women willing to wage war against a government they claimed was ruled by avarice and manipulated by foreign interests. With a trusted cohort of commanding officers, Guzmán eventually left the university and established a paramilitary garrison, committed to training that army to violent insurrection. He ruled with all the absolutism of an iron-fisted dictator, calling himself Comrade Gonzalo, demanding that recruits sign a strict oath of loyalty not to the Shining Path but to him, and inculcating "Gonzalo Thought," which he claimed would cross national borders and spark world revolution. He was, according to a burgeoning brigade of fanatical followers, the Fourth Sword of Communism, after Karl Marx, Vladimir Lenin, and Mao.

The Shining Path could not have found a more fertile territory for its brand of terror. Peru, from 1968 to 1975, had been governed by Juan Velasco Alvarado, a moderate Socialist president intent on forging ties with Castro's Cuba and Allende's Chile. By the time the military staged a coup d'etat in 1975, Guzmán's Shining Path agents had taken every opportunity to penetrate that system, establish strategic posts within it, and learn the way it operated. The Path peppered the lower echelons of government with propaganda. It infiltrated the police and military, targeting neophytes with pamphlets and arming them with liberal supplies of dynamite pilfered from the region's mines. It encouraged soldiers in heavily armed garrisons to desert and take ammunition with them. By 1980, the Path was ready to activate its network. In May, on the eve of Peru's presidential election, it struck. Comrade Gonzalo's guerrillas stormed the election polls in the mountain town of Chuschi, burned the ballot boxes, and declared their larger ambition to overturn the Peruvian government and exterminate the ruling class.

The newly elected president, Fernando Belaúnde Terry, as well as everyone else in the bustling capital of Lima, dismissed the guerrillas as an

ungainly, unfocused agglomeration of lunatics. Ignoring them with pa-
trician disdain, Belaúnde buried their grievances, thinking they couldn't
possibly affect a wider purpose, and, in the interim, the Shining Path grew.
It moved through the countryside, killing the foremen of state-controlled
enterprises, earning the respect and loyalty of peasants who virtually had
been enslaved by the Lima network that Belaúnde represented. The dis-
sidence may have started in a small way, but soon enough the Path began
policing the aureole surrounding Ayacucho—and then the area that en-
compassed the entire Andean highlands—under the guise of protecting
the poor. Not long after, they left a gruesome calling card on the streets
of the capital: Lima awoke to find dead dogs hanging from lampposts,
suspended on banners that screamed "Deng Siao Ping, Son of a Bitch."

At first, the youths who populated the Path were green, unprepared,
ignorant of combat techniques or guerrilla warfare. But before long, as
success followed success, they became hardened warriors, their raids
more pointed, more strategic, their methods more savage. Eventually
the force represented a veritable army, cutting a wide swath through the
country, killing peasants who didn't agree with their campaign of terror or didn't join their forces. The reference to Deng Siao Ping had not
been idle: Deng, Mao's successor, had ended China's strict Marxist code,
opened its possibilities, and renewed its romance with foreign trade. The
crude signal of a dog's carcass became the Shining Path's way of letting
Peruvians know that a brutal extermination would follow if they succumbed to Deng's capitalist weaknesses. Dogs with slit throats began to
appear on the doorsteps of houses, strung up on factory gates, tossed over
the walls of military outposts. The signal was clear: as in Mao's China,
the establishment was immediately suspect; the powerful were a walking
dead. In a wild spree of bloodletting akin to Communist revolutionary
Pol Pot's horrific genocide in Cambodia, the Shining Path began torturing and executing anyone with the slightest connection to the state—
the police, the military, mayors, teachers—and any unfortunate civilians
who got in the way.

In time, the Path made lucrative alliances with drug traders who operated out of the jungle and remote areas of the sierra. The guerrillas
would provide security; the narcos would funnel them cash. So it was
that the Path needed no outside financiers. It was the first armed insur-

rection in Latin America that was virtually 100 percent free of foreign support, banking on drug money to train, arm, and run its day-to-day operations. Future terrorist organizations would learn from that example. By the late 1980s, the Shining Path controlled the vast majority of Peru's countryside in a grip of terror that swept from the northern border with Ecuador to the borders with Brazil and Bolivia.

This was no campaign of political persuasion. Guzmán's operatives used brute force to cow the population. If a female guerrilla flirted with a policeman and he responded to her advances, he might well be found with his throat slit and his weapon gone. If a band of guerrillas stopped a car on the open road, it was to crush skulls, gouge out eyes, and stuff dismembered penises into mouths. Children were sent off to blow up banks. Bomb squads leveled electric stations, plunging cities into darkness. Guerrillas attacked waterworks and rendered the neighborhoods dry. Mothers were made to murder their own children if they so much as whimpered and potentially betrayed an ambush. Farmers were forced to silence their dogs with their knives. If anyone objected, she or he would be killed outright. The idea was to move furtively, breed chaos, sow panic, weed out the power structure, bring the entire population under control. We will ford "a river of blood!" Guzmán exhorted his armies. We will hammer the countryside, clean out the pus, leave deserts behind.

To shatter the old order, guerrillas were trained to swoop into mountain villages and kill whoever was remotely associated with it. As one reporter put it, anyone suspected of ties with the state was a potential mark: "the local mayor; the health post's nurse; the peasant organizer managing farm cooperatives; the bank security guard; the European agronomist combating sheep fever; the peasant who owned too large a plot of potatoes; the student who went to the airport to pick up a political candidate arriving from Lima."

The Shining Path took its inspiration, in a larger sense, from Tupac Amaru II's full-tilt war against Spanish rule that had paralyzed the colony two hundred years before. That rebellion, which bloodied Peru from 1780 to 1783, eventually surpassed the death toll for the American Revolution, scattering a hundred thousand corpses through the Peruvian sierra. There is little doubt that Tupac Amaru and Abimael Guzmán shared a vision as well as a strategy: theirs would be a zero-sum war between oppressed and oppressor, brown versus white, mountain against city. But whereas Tupac Amaru's goal had been to kill Spanish *corregidores* and slaughter the whites, the Shining Path was slaughtering anyone who wouldn't join its ranks, including the very population to which it had promised justice: the indigenous.

"*La cuota*," Guzmán called it: killing innocents was part of the larger quota of blood that Peru would need to pay to rid itself of its capitalist poisons and usher in a more just age. If Shining Path guerrillas would die by the thousands in this bloodbath, then so be it; *la cuota* would demand a strict code of self-sacrifice, an unwritten willingness to die. The rebels would sow the wind and welcome the whirlwind. Indeed, the Shining Path quickly became the most radical expression of a desperate revolutionary body driven to extremes. *La guerra al muerte*—war to the death—was what Bolívar had called a very different revolution a century and a half before, but the message was almost identical. A purifying war. Against Spain, against the petrified hierarchy of Lima—a pitched revolution by an anarchist force that had nothing to lose. On the contrary, it had everything to gain. If the nation imploded, so much the better. As far as the Path was concerned, it was going to champion the trampled, the disdained—the very butt end of the country—and it would bite off the head of a power that had held them for five hundred years.

Unlike Tupac Amaru's army, Guzmán's insurgents managed to penetrate far corners of Peru and find their way into the very heart of the capital, wreaking havoc in rich neighborhoods and corridors of power, establishing offices in downtown Lima. But it didn't leave the poor alone. It cut through the shantytowns, killing the civic leaders, the priests, the social workers. The idea was to relay that there was only one way, and that way was the Path. The Peruvian Armed Forces added to the mayhem by fighting a rabid, unconditional war against the guerrillas, marauding the countryside and executing anyone who was remotely complicit—often killing at whim. Indeed, the military ended up being every bit as sadistic and genocidal as the revolutionaries, exterminating a large swath of the peasantry and rounding up equivalent numbers for torture and incarceration. Lima's prisons were so packed with suspects that when inmates rose up in one particular riot in 1986, 250 were slaughtered like sheep inside the penitentiary walls. When that

furious, blood-soaked decade was over, Guzmán's revolution had cost
Peru 70,000 souls. The displaced rural population, fearing for its life and
pouring into the capital for protection, built shacks wherever it could—
on sand and slope—creating rings of squalid shantytowns around the
center of Lima. A city of 800,000 became a city of 7 million. By 1990, one
out of every two Lima residents lived in a slum. Life was cheap, suffered
in dread. No one was surprised when a cholera epidemic erupted a year
later, sickened 322,000, and cut down a thousand more.

La cuota was being paid liberally on both sides now. In 1992, two days
after a bombing that blasted a quiet plaza and killed forty civilians in the
suburb of Miraflores, the Peruvian Armed Forces raided a university on
the outskirts of Lima on the presumption that all institutions of higher
education were hatcheries of trouble. Twenty-five students and teachers
were abducted, tortured, massacred, decapitated or torched, and dumped
in a ditch. Not one was a member of the Shining Path or any other terrorist group. But, by now, wanton violence seemed to be the only rule.

In 1995, three years after Guzmán was arrested in his hiding place
above a children's dance school in a quiet corner of the capital, the head
swung back to bite the tail: Lima took revenge on the mountain people.
Deciding to stem the growth of an unwanted, indigent population and
boost Peru's economic profile, President Alberto Fujimori ordered the
forced mass sterilization of indigenous women in the Peruvian sierra.
In a scourge of violence cloaked as a health measure and supported by
$36 million from the United States, more than 350,000 frightened Quec-
hua and Aymara women were herded into makeshift clinics without explanation, drugged without their consent, and subjected to surgery that
took knife to groin and severed any possibility of reproduction.

ADRIFT IN EL DORADO

America is the greatest of opportunities and the worst of influences.
—George Santayana

Carlos Buergos felt as if he were being born again as he approached the
ghostly landform he knew only as Cayo Hueso: bone reef, hard-nosed,

Key West. The sun was merciless, blinding, making it difficult to see the world into which he was being delivered. He had been in a dungeon long enough to favor the dark, and he strained now with both hands shielding his brow to make out the sliver of sand beyond the shimmering sea. As shouts rose, *"América! Bendito Dios!"* he, too, wanted to yawp with joy, although he could only manage a croak. Who would have imagined that butchering horses and breaking laws would bring him such good fortune? He was barefoot, shirtless, exactly as he had been when they opened the prison gates and shoved him onto a truck. His shoulders and arms were scorched. His lips were parched. His head pounded from his old wound. Someone punched him on the arm and pointed to shore. *"Fulas, papaya, y wisky, compay!"* Dollars, pussy, and whisky, my friend! He laughed. His appetites were more basic. He hadn't eaten for days.

He was but one of more than 125,000 desperate specimens of humanity—ragged, bedraggled, with little to identify them apart from their word. Even though efforts were made to discourage Americans from trying to rescue the masses that Castro called "human refuse" and "scum," President Jimmy Carter promised to welcome them "with open arms." Americans chartered motorboats, sailboats, shrimp boats, cargo ships, and rushed to Cuba's shores to save lives, sometimes using their accumulated savings to do so. US government flyers were tacked to walls of the receiving halls in the Florida Keys in advance of the Marieitos' arrival:

> To the Cuban refugees:
>   This great nation is offering you the opportunity of a new life, ample and full liberty, security and the guarantee of a peaceful, orderly life; we also offer you the chance for a rebirth and to be considered as a person. With all inalienable human rights before God and the people.

When the prison truck bearing Carlos and a few more convicts had arrived at Mariel, the hatch had swung open, releasing them to the port. Carlos had staggered toward the nearest cargo boat but was pushed back by a frenzied throng. Eventually he managed to board one, slipping behind what seemed like a large, agitated family. There were men in suits, dissidents in rags, malcontents, desperados, dreamers, homosexuals, the mentally handicapped, and the mentally ill—Cubans Castro no longer wanted. He glanced around but didn't see anyone he recognized. There were no army veterans, no thieves from Combinado del Este, no fellow convicts had made it aboard. Hours later, he was whisked through a processing center in Key West with thousands of others and put on a flight to Pennsylvania.

There they took him to Fort Indiantown Gap, a National Guard training center where tens of thousands of Marielitos were being held behind barbed wire as US government officials tried to decide what to do with them. Eventually he was shooed onto a bus headed for Fort Chaffee, a military base in Arkansas. Of the thousands of Cubans who went through that human thresher, fifty-five had criminal records, many of those as political prisoners. In the group arriving at Fort Chaffee's detention facility with Carlos, however, it seemed to him he was the only one. All the same, the people who inhabited the small town near the fort believed, as Cubans poured in, that Castro's word was true: here were criminals, reprobates, dangers to their community. Protests would follow, prison riots, and, in some cases, accusations of cruelty on the part of American jailers. And then suddenly, five months later, after a long bus trip, Carlos was in Washington, DC, free to wander the city streets.

At the Immigration and Naturalization Service in the heart of Washington, the staff did three things for Carlos: They found him a job as a busboy in American University's cafeteria at minimum wage, no tips. They gave him a monthly stipend of $150 until he was settled into the routine. And they rented a room for him in a crowded boardinghouse in a rough quarter of the Mount Pleasant neighborhood. No one asked whether he had been incarcerated before. No one told him he would be living in one of the most vibrant crack cocaine neighborhoods in the country, in the center of America's murder capital, in a city whose mayor himself, Marion Barry, was a flagrant cocaine user.

Disoriented, struggling with the English language, Carlos tried to better his circumstances. After a few months, he landed a second job washing dishes for Ridgewells, an upscale party caterer, to augment his meager salary. But life in this town turned out to be a perilous business. Coming home late one night from that second shift, he was robbed by three street toughs and shot in the stomach. For months, he nursed eight perforations in his intestine. Carlos underwent a colostomy, but he grew thinner, more gaunt and wasted, hardly able to eat.

He was well acquainted with shootings; had survived worse before. What he didn't know quite yet was that he didn't have to take the INS's counsel; there were faster ways to make money in America. Big money. He was learning from American junkies in his building that a spirited flow of crack cocaine was pouring into those streets. The city's leaders didn't seem to care. It was coming up from the Andes—grown in Peru, processed in Colombia, slipped north, and shipped through Mexico— all fueled and protected by terrorists. The Crips and the Bloods, the most truculent gangs in Los Angeles, were dealing directly with the Colombian cartels, funneling tidy bricks of the stuff by the truckload to Washington. The drug lord who facilitated it was working the very neighborhood where Carlos lived.

Recovering from his wounds, he started in on a carousel of short-lived jobs: waiting tables, bartending, hanging drywall for a construction company. But it was all with a difference now: he was determined to find out more about the drug world, the cash that flowed so easily around him. Everywhere he looked, it seemed, there were smooth talkers, sharp dressers, slick cars. This was not Havana, not Matanzas. Not Luanda or Mozambique. He began to be fascinated by it, drawn irresistibly to the nightly allure of the drug dealers, the discos, the high life, the fast women. He began snorting cocaine with friends, and before long, dealers were asking him to translate whoever was yammering in Spanish on the phone, or inviting him to accompany them to a Santería voodoo shop, a salsa club, a burrito place, a grocery store, to help them score deals. He would do this for a few grams, a quick high. He had never taken hard drugs before, and the rush seemed a revelation: the euphoria—that inexpressible feeling of immortality—the seductive flush of well-being. It was like nothing he had ever known, a balm for his pounding head, a distraction from his damaged gut. Soon he could think of little else.

Could it be so simple, after all, the good life in America? Sell some drugs, pack a weapon, make connections, rough up a few people. This wasn't so unfamiliar after all. He had been trained to wield a gun, brandish a knife. He wasn't averse to stealing, if necessary—none of this was new to him. He had cohabited with convicts, consorted with thugs, befriended killers. Was this, then, his most marketable skill in this land?

The slide into felony was gradual. Carlos met an older American woman at a mambo club: a fiftyish blonde with a good job, a daughter his age, and a nice enough apartment. Helen liked the way he danced, his funny English, his sense of humor, his nervous energy, his youth. She invited him to her bed and then, shortly thereafter, told him he could move in and make himself at home. It was a comfortable enough life, so much so that in time he began to skip work. Eventually, carousing with fellow junkies, he fell into misdemeanors, rowdy nights, drunk arrests. Official documents show that Carlos was apprehended by police in 1982 and 1983 for carrying a concealed weapon. "I was with a group of Cubans both times," he recalls, "and we were a little high in a 7-Eleven parking lot, maybe. We got rough. It got out of hand. The weapon was my drywall knife."

One day in 1984, he was offered several days' pay to deliver a suitcase of cocaine across town. Before long, he was taking packages here and there, over state lines, for anyone who asked. The capital had become prime crack country now—it was awash in drugs—and a new, charismatic nineteen-year-old kingpin, Rayful Edmond III, was running the show. On September 24, 1984, one of Edmond's henchmen sent Carlos off with several thick stacks of $100 bills to make a score in Springfield, Massachusetts, but as things unfolded, everything went wrong. When Carlos and his Mexican traveling companion checked into their motel room, the Mexican pulled a pistol, shot him in the back, and ran off with the money. Rushed to the emergency room, Carlos was hospitalized for weeks. The bullet is still lodged in his left hip.

Within months, he had a stiff cocaine habit. By 1987, crippled by pain and dismissed as a cokehead—a washout—he was doing errands for small-time dealers, keeping himself in gold chains and smart clothes, feeding a spiraling addiction. It was during this time that Carlos, now thirty-two, robbed a shop as well as a private house in Ocean City, Maryland, was caught, and served twelve months in jail.

In the interim, he met Clara, a young Venezuelan woman who was cleaning houses in Bethesda, Maryland. Responsible and hardworking, she tried to instill some order in his life, and, for a while, he was off drugs and working regularly as a drywall hanger. He had moved out of Helen's house and vowed to make a better life for himself. He and Clara married and had a baby boy in May of the following year.

In 1988 Carlos became a waiter at a tony Washington country club, commanding the best salary he had ever earned, but the job didn't last long. He quit in a huff when the headwaiter complained that he was slow and inattentive to the clientele. To take the place of one job, he found two: working room service at a Marriott hotel, and then heading out with his best friend to serve as a waiter in a Baltimore Holiday Inn. "I was getting right," he says, "trying hard." But when that friend died of cancer a few years later, Carlos stopped showing up at either job. Soon he was back on cocaine with a vengeance and into the netherworld of freaks and thugs who traded in it.

When a big-time drug dealer moved into his apartment building on Sixteenth Street, he began running cocaine again. This time for large drops, in spite of high risks. He was not himself. He was summoning nightmares from the African battlefields, feeling anger suffuse him in a murderous slow burn. Before long, his wife checked into a shelter for battered women, and then she moved into a separate apartment altogether, resolving to address the failing health of their three-year-old, who—like some children of addicts—had begun exhibiting signs of acute attention deficit disorder and emotional confusion.

On his own now, Carlos surrendered completely to his habit. He was pocketing no money, simply getting from one high to the next. Back on the streets, he was like a winter's leaf, buffeted by the winds of drugs and violence that had traveled north with him, riding a crest of terror he hadn't even known was there. By the time he landed in Lorton Prison for drug trafficking, he was a ghost of the young blond boy who had marched off to Angola twenty years before—a cadaverous, twitching, 130-pound wreck.

While Carlos was in prison, his four-year-old son died of heart failure, his wife drifted away. In 2001, Lorton penitentiary shut down to reopen as a community arts center. Correctional authorities were obliged to ship all inmates, including Carlos, elsewhere: to Georgia, South Carolina, Florida. In time, he was released into the American ambit, only to go on to do what he knew best: steal, kick in doors, threaten addicts for nonpayment, pistol-whip goons. He drifted from one town to another, looking for the next trick. And yet, wherever he went, he couldn't rid himself of certain memories: the sight of a machete landing on a man's brow; the sea of mutilated flesh on an African battlefield; the sudden black when a bullet hurled through his head; the flash of white as eight more drilled into his stomach; the sight of his wife, fleeing down the corridor with his son; the quick slam of lead invading his flank. It was just the way it was. It was just the way it had always been.

WAR WITHOUT END

The conquest has not yet ended, and neither has resistance to the conquest.

—Juan Adolfo Vásquez, 1982

It was certainly the way it had been in Cuba. Even after the revolution—even after the tumult of Castro's takeover and his subsequent political purges—it had continued to be a repressive country. Under the guise of reinventing it for the betterment of all, the Communists had created an Orwellian regime, a bully government, with punitive laws and a vast population of prisoners. Arbitrary arrests, torture, human rights violations were commonplace, as well as a culture of paranoia. All the same, from the 1960s to the end of the century, the Cuban model went on to inspire revolutions elsewhere in Latin America. This hadn't been difficult to do. Since memory served, the region had been a powder keg, a racial time bomb, waiting to combust. Despotism had become the norm, even in democratically elected regimes, and, with it, an inclination to hard-line absolutism, subjugation, cruelty. Violence became the continent's default, the modus operandi—simply the way the world worked.

History had made it so. The crucible that had created Latin America in the first place had joined two distinctly different and volatile people. Spain had emerged from a rabid war against Arab occupiers as well as a campaign to dominate the slave trade. The Spanish who sailed by the thousands to populate Latin America had been reliant on *hermandades*—vigilantes, rural police—to keep populations in check, often through brutal means. The indigenous empires they met in that distant land had been well acquainted with wars of conquest. Ritual human sacrifice. Violent repression was not an alien quantity here. Both sides knew the uses of crude savagery, and they relied on it, employed it, were undone by it. It was the natural course of things.

As history wore on, a pattern seemed to form. There were always juiced-up warriors with little to do, subjugated classes with little to lose. When the Portuguese king set out to populate Brazil, he sent unwanted, hardened criminals; Brazilian natives paid the price. When Spanish soldiers were dispatched to quell Latin American revolutions, they were fresh from a fierce guerrilla war against Napoleon's invading armies; in response, the rebels in the Spanish colonies mustered an equal violence. When France wanted to collect its debts from Mexico and claim the country in the bargain, it sent steely veterans from the Crimean War—a butchery followed. When, centuries later, foreign corporations in Latin America needed to install security forces, they employed cutthroat veterans of civil wars. Seasoned warriors were precisely what corporations wanted to safeguard their businesses: hard-bitten, unforgiving, and armed.

It was, as it had been for centuries, "*la época del perrero*," the era of the dogcatcher, in which reprisals were claimed and retaliations delivered—in which violations were alleged and retributions met. In Peru, one cannot help but see "a primitiveness, a ferocity" in the fundaments of society, wrote the Nobel Prize–winning novelist Mario Vargas Llosa, years after abandoning the political life. A Peru that, with so many past injustices and transgressions, could easily be reduced to vileness. But Peru is no different from its neighbors. It is just the way it has been in this calvary of culture shock. It is just the way it has been since time immemorial.

Vargas Llosa went on to spell out the Latin American malaise further in his Nobel lecture:

> The conquest of America was cruel, violent, as all conquests have been through time, and we must level a critical eye on its legacy, without forgetting that the perpetrator of those crimes and plunder were our own grandparents and great-grandparents. . . . When we gained our independence from Spain two hundred years ago, those who took power in the colonies, instead of redeeming the Indian

and atoning for ancient offenses, went on exploiting them with as much avarice and ferocity as the conquistadors and, in some countries, decimating or exterminating them completely. Let's be clear: for centuries, the emancipation of the indigenous has been entirely our responsibility, and we haven't succeeded in accomplishing it. It's an unresolved issue throughout Latin America. There is not one exception to this disgrace.

Here is the root of the violence, the reason why whites have monitored race so scrupulously—why priests recorded the cast of a newborn's skin so meticulously in ancient church annals and the powerful still guard it so jealously today. It is why, for so long, the colored have been ostracized, left out, undervalued in Latin America. Many a panegyric has been written about the grand, sweeping mestizoization of the region, and indeed race mixing was widespread from the beginning. There was no choice, as Spanish and Portuguese conquistadors conjugated freely with Indian and black women. All the same, *limpieza de sangre* has always been an old precept for those of Spanish ancestry: the notion of "purity of blood," of a gene pool that is free of indigenous, Jewish, Chinese, Arab, or black stock—even though "whites" with long histories in the Americas by now have acquired generous strains of each. The prejudice remains, although the reality has changed.

For a hundred years, *limpieza de sangre* was law in fifteenth-century Spain, and it required an official certificate, meant to exclude Jews and Arabs. Eventually the concept became more fluid, more corrupt: when Spain was in dire need of money in the early 1800s, it decided to sell *cédulas de Gracias al Sacar*, certificates that granted a light-skinned colored person in the colonies the same rights as every white: the right to be educated, to be hired into better jobs, to serve in the priesthood, to hold public office, to marry whites, to inherit wealth. In modern-day multiracial Latin America, the notion of *limpieza de sangre* has become even more fluid, although it remains a useful crutch for prejudice. Whiteness has a sliding scale. *"Es muy blanca la novia,"* a groom's proud parents will say—"The bride is very white"—glad that their future progeny will be whiter. It is why, as Bolívar lamented, and so many still insist, the revolution was never quite finished, and true equality, that shining goal of the Enlightenment, was never reached. Plumb the impetus for a crime, or for the deeper reasons for abiding anger, and the triumvirate of race, class, and poverty are almost always at the root of things in Latin America. It is why the culture of violence persists.

And it does persist. Of the fifty most violent cities in the world, forty-three are in Latin America. Of the twenty-five countries that boast the highest murder rates, nearly half are south of the Rio Grande. Today in Trujillo, Peru—Pizarro's proud city on the Pacific, my childhood home—for $100 or less, you can hire a *sicario* to shoot a creditor, dispatch an irritating neighbor, eliminate your wife's lover. It's as easy as going to Facebook or a digital marketplace called "Qué Barato!"—"How Cheap!"—to find exactly the right killer at the right price. You can do this in Cali, Colombia, too; indeed, no country at peace has registered Colombia's extreme levels of violence. In Buenos Aires, Argentina, it may cost you more—$10,000 is the going rate for a quick, efficient, premeditated murder this year—but it can be done. As one journalist has said, *sicarios* have done for murder in Latin America what the transistor did for the radio. The barbarity is protean, pervasive, and it permeates the very fabric of the region in other ways. In Maturín, Venezuela, today, for instance, a street criminal may lop off your hand if he takes a fancy to your watch; he may kill you outright for a good pair of shoes. It is the product of a numbing spiral of righteous violence that began in Latin America in the 1960s and went on to spur a frenzy in which rulers and rebels alike felt no moral or psychic constraints to their basest impulses.

In 2018, every day with stupefying regularity, more than a dozen Salvadorans were cut down in gang warfare. On a bad day, forty-five were flung onto trucks and hauled off to the morgue. At the time, El Salvador had the highest murder rate in the world—108 homicides per 100,000 people—more than one hundred times the rate of the United Kingdom, more than twenty times higher than in the United States, and more than ten times the global average. When, on January 17, 2017, an entire day went by without a single murder in that calamitous country, the news was reported as far away as Russia and New Zealand. Yet Salvadorans are not alone in this carnage. Latin America as a whole, a region that accounts for a mere 8 percent of the world's population, is responsible for 38 percent of the world's criminal killings. According to the magazine the *Economist*, the butcher's bill in this part of the Americas came to 140,000 murders in 2017, more than the casualties that have been perpetrated in all wars to date in the twenty-first century. Were we to count the maimed, the wounded, the raped, the tortured—those who may have survived the bloodbath—the numbers would be too staggering, too incomprehensible. And this in a world in which crime is generally on the decline and murder, rarer.

Where outright violence is less evident, political factions and criminal gangs have found other, more subtle ways to inflict cruelty: the foiled assassination attempts, the kidnappings and extortion, the arson, the stoking of public fear, the paranoia, the psychological tolls, the social wreckage, the starvation and displacement. In Venezuela in the twenty-first century, we have seen all these. Here, since 2014, when President Hugo Chávez's corpse was installed in a grand mausoleum, and his former bodyguard Nicolás Maduro took up the reins, street crime has been king, hunger and malnutrition rampant, corruption endemic, and it has launched a great wave of desperate Venezuelan refugees, taking off across Latin America, fleeing for their lives. We will never know the level of gore they are escaping: the Venezuelan government stopped reporting homicides in 2005.

Even in nations fortunate enough to have low crime rates, or drastically reduced incidences of assault—Costa Rica, for instance, or Panama—citizens end up reaping a profit from the mayhem all around them. The trade route for drugs making their way up the hemisphere courses through those more peaceful countries, after all, enriching them in the process and binding them to the overall misery. And whereas a country with a violent past may be far safer today—in Argentina, for example, or Ecuador, or Chile—history has shown that political climates in these volatile nations could flip, demagoguery could return, and the people would be sent barreling through the cycle again.

Latin America's inability to deal assertively with violence—the murders that go ignored, disappearances that are never prosecuted, assaults that remain unreported—is evidence of its acute judicial failures, and it is all too conspicuous in the corruption that is so widespread today. Fraud, bribery, extortion, which were flagrant and widespread during Spanish and Portuguese colonial rule, are still rampant today, so deeply a part of the culture that they have proved exceedingly difficult to curb, much less eradicate. Indeed, in most Latin American countries, even those claiming to be liberal democracies, bribes are such an accepted practice that business depends on them.

To wit, between 2004 and 2016, Brazil's gargantuan construction company Odebrecht was able to facilitate $3 billion of profit by buying off dozens of presidents and government officials with kickbacks totaling $800 million. The imposing statue of Christ that stands atop the brown hump of Chorrillos in the bay of Lima, Peru—an exact copy of the statue that spreads its arms over Rio de Janeiro—was a gesture of gratitude from Odebrecht's "corporate relations department" to President Alan García. Five out of the last six Peruvian presidents, including García, stand suspected of accepting bribes. Some have been reprimanded; two went to jail. Pedro Pablo Kuczinski was impeached due to clear evidence. García put a bullet through his brain. But most have gone unpunished. Government officials from Panama to Argentina have walked away with tens of millions of dollars at a time, many of them having insisted, ironically, that they made solid advances against corruption. Two recent Brazilian presidents have seen their demise over similar denunciations.

Odebrecht's sprawling scandal has laid bare the greed and venality of Latin America's political and business elite, but to ordinary citizens and the wider public, it has also hardened the belief that transparency and justice are distant goals in this part of the world. Corruption is simply a part of everyday life. According to the anticorruption activist organization Transparency International, one out of every three Latin Americans paid a bribe in the past year to police, doctors, or educators. It is precisely this arrogance, this sense of entitlement among those in authority, that feeds the fires of discontent among the vast, furious masses of the poor.

If history holds, the people's fury will be followed by rebellion, and rebellion will be followed by despotic rule. The people may even long for it; military dictatorships are decidedly efficient at quelling the chaos of revolution. Democracies may follow, but rank corruption—the plague that has held Latin America fast since conquistadors cheated the Crown and Spain cheated the New World in turn—will simply ramble ahead and ignite the fury all over again. Poverty, dependency, exploitation, revolution, graft, and then back to the iron hand. We have seen the cycle at work when liberators who promised a better future resorted to dictatorial rule, claiming it was for the good of the republic: General José Antonio Páez, a rough-riding hero of the revolution, made himself dictator in newly liberated nineteenth-century Venezuela; the great liberator Bolívar donned the dictator's mantle in Colombia and Peru; Mexican liberation brought two consummate despots, Agustín de Iturbide and General Santa Anna; Argentina's liberation brought the flagrant tyrant Juan Manuel de Rosas—and so on throughout the continent. We saw the cycle reborn in the regimes of Fulgencio Batista in Cuba, Anastasio Somoza in Nicaragua, Alfredo Stroessner in Paraguay, Rafael Trujillo in the Dominican Republic, Alberto Fujimori in Peru. As the Argentine writer Ernesto Sabato warned, revolutions can bring on the most hardheaded conservatism. That stubborn dictatorial streak reemerged in Castro's Cuba, Chávez's Venezuela, Perón's Argentina, all of them after vibrant, hope-filled, populist revolutions and after seemingly open, democratic elections. In every case, violence—or the threat of it—was a strongman's most potent weapon.

The impulse to violence was there at work in Chile, when General Pinochet's military cohort rained bombs on the palace of La Moneda in 1973 and annihilated Salvador Allende's presidency. It surfaced again a decade later in Guatemala when President Efraín Ríos Montt, claiming to save his people from terrorists, unleashed a campaign of extermination, costing the country hundreds of thousands of Mayan lives. This is not the pugnacity of random criminals in Europe or the United States; it is collective violence with a public and ritual character. We have seen it when the government of Peru exterminated 250 Shining Path inmates held in Lima's prisons, in what constitutes the deadliest massacre of political prisoners in modern Latin American history. We saw it in Argentina, when thousands of "political suspects" were herded off to concentration camps, and torture, murders, and disappearances became quotidian fare. We see it now in Brazil, with a right wing that wants to stem the tide of liberalism and corruption and bring back the old, conservative values—at whatever cost. We have seen it from Left and Right, in every possible stripe of the political spectrum, as terrorists and government officials resort to equivalent mayhem; as drug lords and soldiers dispatch mutilated corpses to one another as warning.

For all Latin America's propensity to breed dictators (or elected presidents who become dictators), violence is not always doled out by the *mano dura*. Nor are democratic governments necessarily a salve to the wanton truculence: Colombia, for instance, has not been ruled by a dictator for almost seventy years. No other country in the region (not even Chile, Uruguay, Costa Rica, or Venezuela before Chávez) has experimented more vigorously with democracy than Colombia. And yet the country has been racked by bloodshed and is one of the most homicidal nations in the world.

Mexico, too, despite strong democratic advances and constitutionally elected leaders, still suffers bitter cycles of violence, depending on the political winds and its crime-riddled economy. Democracy hasn't seemed to help this. Indeed, Venustiano Carranza, Mexico's first constitutional president, the politician who marked the beginning of the nation's hundred-year history as a democratic nation, was assassinated in 1920. A period of unrest followed, but since 1934, Mexicans have gone to the polls sedulously to elect their governments. And yet the country has been unable to rid itself of its violent propensities. These are primal catalysts, after all; bred in the bone, difficult to overcome.

Like many other Latin American countries, Mexico has been victim of its harsh past. A population that was approximately twenty million in the early 1500s was reduced to barely one million in the 1600s—decimated twice over by Europe's deadly diseases and Spain's brutal rule. Some call it genocide; others, a "demographic collapse." Three hundred years later, during Mexico's peasant revolution, one out of ten Mexicans died in a civil war unmatched in the hemisphere—one and a half million dead littered the fields, dangled from trees. Whereas that unimaginable catastrophe has made Mexicans wary of outright revolution, Mexico's rate of atrocities has continued with frightening regularity. We saw terror raise its head most emphatically in 2007 when President Felipe Calderón ordered the military to wage a decade-long *guerra al muerte* on drug lords, loosing a disastrous wave of bloodshed on his fellow countrymen, butchering the innocent along with the guilty and sending more than two hundred thousand to their graves.

A deeply ingrained impulse to brutality is bound to erupt most catastrophically in the slums, or *barriadas*, where hard resentments reign.

Democracy hasn't necessarily bought safety to the indigent: in the past half century, precisely during a time when democratic practices have spread and taken hold more firmly, the slums have exhibited an exponential growth in violent crime. This is largely because Latin American cities have experienced a rapid glut in their populations. Rural farmers, mountain folk—fugitives from terrorism, drug wars, and civil unrest in the 1960s and 1970s—began to flock to the urban hearts by the tens of thousands, seeking protection, joining the ranks of the desperately poor and unemployed. The clearest expression of class anger has been in gang violence, which cropped up in the squalid shantytowns that ring the cities, mounted dramatically after the 1970s, and now is a present danger throughout Central America, Brazil, and the drug-addled north of South America.

In the Northern Triangle countries—El Salvador, Guatemala, and Honduras—the gang that calls itself Mara Salvatrucha (MS-13) numbers seventy thousand angry young men, all dedicated to brutal acts of murder, rape, sex trafficking, kidnappings, extortion, drug violence. It is overwhelmingly responsible for the mass flight and displacement of families that has become so rampant in Central America. Curiously enough, MS-13 had its origins in the mean, crowded slums of Los Angeles during the 1980s and spread south like a virulent plague, overwhelming the countries in which MS-13 gang members had been born. The worst infusions of violence took place between 2000 and 2004, when the United States, fulfilling a get-tough immigration policy begun under President Bill Clinton, pulled twenty thousand gang members from jails around the country—all foreign-born refugees—and deported them to their old native *barrios* in the Northern Triangle. The convicts, who had little or no affiliation to their countries of birth, had difficulty integrating into the normal order of things. They resorted to what they knew best: gang life. They began recruiting a formidable army of disgruntled youths—boys accustomed to poverty and humiliation; the "born dead," as they call themselves—who were especially attracted to the status and power that MS-13 bestowed them. They inflicted a hecatomb of murders from the Sonora Desert to Panama City. The judicial systems of El Salvador, Guatemala, and Honduras were hardly equipped to deal with the bloodletting that followed: nations that had thought themselves budding exemplars of the democratic process were now forced to live under a de facto state of siege, ruled not by presidents and governments but by deadly gangs.

There are scarcely more violent societies than those of Central America, Brazil, and the vast territory of South America gripped by corruption and the drug trade. Most disturbing, perhaps, is the way gang violence seems to mimic the past: the severing of heads, so prevalent in Mesoamerica a thousand years ago, is ubiquitous today in El Salvador and Honduras. The gouged eyes and tongues, the ripping out of an enemy's heart—all these are eerily similar to ancient practices of pre-Columbian civilizations. The testimonials to this are legion. In 1983, for example, in the midst of the Shining Path terror in Peru, a mother named Angélica Mendoza de Ascarza went looking for her son. For twenty years, she peered into every mass grave, followed every possible clue. She searched for him in the reeking garbage dumps that line the roads on the periphery of Lima; she picked through bodies with no heads, heads with no eyes, broken jaws, dismembered fingers. In 2017 she died with no answers.

Thousands of miles away in Colinas de Santa Fe, a tiny suburb near Veracruz, the bustling port founded by Hernán Cortés, another mother, named María de Lourdes Rosales, went hunting for her child. Finding no trace of him, she marched with the mothers of the disappeared—protesting the two hundred thousand that had gone missing in Mexico in the murderous decade between 2005 and 2014. During the march, a mysterious man got out of a car to slip the women a hand-drawn, primitive map. It showed the location of an undiscovered mass grave. When María got to the site, the stench was overwhelming; the rotting, deracinated heads, unidentifiable. It was a grim, hallucinatory scene, one that might easily have been witnessed four hundred years before, during colonial times, in the pits of the dead, beside the mercury mines of Santa Barbara. Or just last year, in the killing fields of Mato Grosso, Brazil, where men lusting for land are still invading indigenous territories and cutting down every tree, man, and woman in their way. History has a way of slipping fitfully into the future.

There are other striking parallels between present and past. Today Mexican gang leaders are called *palabreros*, the men who carry the word, just as Montezuma and his ancestors called themselves *tlatoani*, the men who are allowed to speak. In the crime-riddled city of Juárez, just across the border from El Paso, Texas, it is not uncommon to find a flayed corpse or a body bristling with thirteen knives—ritual killings that hark back to bygone ceremonies. In the mountain villages of the Andes—in towns such as Juan Ochochoque's vertiginous gold mine in La Rinconada—miners will sacrifice one of their own in a calculated murder, and then deposit the body in a mine shaft to feed the god of the underworld, much as their ancestors did before them. In Miami, where Carlos Buergos eventually returned after his criminal peregrinations, and where life among drug hoods is all too cheap, men wear trophy ears dangling from gold necklaces, just as their forebears slung shrunken heads on their belts.

Ask any coroner in any murder capital of Latin America, and he or she will tell you: in this part of the world, anthropology is a teacher. The flint was displaced by the sword, and the sword was replaced by the gun. The old is made new again.

PART THREE

STONE

How is it, sir, that having persuaded me to trust our friendship, you then chose to destroy me, your friend and brother? You gave me the cross as a defense against my enemies, and then, with it, you tried to annihilate me.

—Casqui, a tribal headman, ca. 1520

CHAPTER 10

THE GODS BEFORE

---

*Is it possible that the great God who fills Heaven and Earth would
choose to be born in a stable among animals, then die on a cross
among thieves? Is there anything that inspires more horror and
admiration?*

—Fr. Luis de Granada, ca. 1554

It did not escape Xavier Albó, a tall, lanky, bright-eyed novice with the
Society of Jesus—the Catholic order of Jesuits—that he was arriving
in the Americas much as his priestly forebears had done five hundred
years before. Like them, he was young, ignorant of the world into which
he had come, but charged with an urgent mission: to win souls to the
Christian faith. His immediate impressions were four as he strode down
the plank of the ship *L'Auguste* and out onto hard land: the abandoned
port, the shuttered shops, the weeping women in the streets, and then the
surging mass of humanity as he entered the heart of Buenos Aires. It was
early August 1952, and Eva Duarte Perón, the much-loved first lady of
Argentina, had just died after a very public struggle with cancer. Three
million people had poured into the nation's capital to weep beside her
casket. The grief over "Santa Evita"—a towering, charismatic force in
the country—was acute, palpable. Xavier had never seen such a roiling
sea of souls, never witnessed such fervent worship for a mere mortal.
Except for the trip from the hills of Catalunya to his school in Barcelona,
he had traveled no more than a few miles from where he'd been born.
He had just turned seventeen.

He was a graduate of the Colegio San Ignacio, a sprawling, neo-
Gothic brick monolith that still straddles the heights of Barcelona. Trav-

eling to Bolivia with two other novices—friends since childhood—he was to form a novitiate in Cochabamba, spend two years in dedicated prayer, and then go on to ten more years of study, after which he would help bring Jesus to the rural poor. Xavier was a sunny, fresh-faced youth with a ready smile and close-cropped chestnut hair. In his trim, black cleric's shirt and starched white collar, he was the antithesis of a foot-loose boy on a world adventure, and, indeed, his arrival was a formal enterprise, the fulfillment of an obligation. The padre maestro who had seen him off had said in no uncertain terms: "Bid farewell to your families for good." It had been a sobering reminder. He had hardly begun to shave.

He was born in 1934 in La Garriga, a tiny resort surrounded by tall, leafy oaks in the heart of Catalan country. For years, this verdant little paradise had been a summer refuge for the wealthy of Barcelona. From the front door of his house on a clear day, he could see the magnificent church on Mount Tibidabo and imagine its perch over the city and its view to the shimmering sea. Life in that sleepy little exurb might have been an idyllic existence for a young boy with dreams. But it was not. From the moment Xavier saw his first light of day in that turbulent corner of Spain, his world had been choked by hostility, ready to burst with ill will. Days before his birth, the coal miners of Asturias had gone on strike, and the Spanish army had loosed a fierce military rout that left two thousand protesters dead, three thousand wounded, and thirty thousand more in prison. Street violence, political killings, and a viral anger had erupted throughout the countryside, and La Garriga, situated at the heart of Catalan and Basque resistance, braced itself for a restless future.

Two years later, in 1936, the populist fervor in Spain was such that a coalition of liberal, Socialist, and Communist parties—the Popular Front, known to conservatives as the "Reds"—swept to power in a surprising outcome in the national elections. The old, moneyed class of industrialists and landowners, as well as the Catholic Church, were outraged. In response, the head of the armed forces, General Francisco Franco, staged a violent coup to win back control. Ultimately, that military insurrection led to the Spanish Civil War, a bloody, harrowing conflagration between Republicans and Nationalists that ended up littering the country with corpses, spurring international fury, engaging Nazi and Soviet war machines, and serving as a rehearsal for the Second World War. Half a million lives would be lost in the process; half a million more spit out as refugees.

Xavier's father, who owned a small business in La Garriga, was one of the town's first casualties of war. As Xavier tells it, he was killed by Reds—landless, hungry, and desperate Spaniards—who marauded the landscape, killing conservatives, taking over their businesses, setting fire to churches, and trying to take back control of the government. Xavier, barely a few months old, was not old enough to remember his father's murder, but his sisters were: they watched as Communist rebels frog-marched him from their house, dragged him to a dark alley, and dispatched him with a bullet to the back of his head. His grandfather, a baker in La Garriga, was killed weeks later, leaving Xavier's mother both widow and orphan, forced to raise five children alone. In a nation paralyzed by rampant brutality, Señora Albó decided to keep her brood safely at home and commandeer their educations. Xavier became her pupil in all things, religious or secular. Three agonizing years later, in 1939, just as Hitler's armies overtook Poland and swarmed into France, just as Spain's Civil War sputtered to a close, ten Savoia-Marchetti warplanes from Franco's Nationalist forces roared overhead and, in a lesson lost on no one, rained bombs on Xavier's neighborhood and destroyed the heart of La Garriga.

By the time Xavier marked his fifth year of life, Generalísimo Franco had rid the country of Reds, clamped a steel vise on Spain, anointed himself "El Caudillo," the boss, and begun the business of executing or torturing four hundred thousand political prisoners in concentration camps around the country. Throughout that campaign, El Caudillo enjoyed the steadfast backing of the Catholic Church. For all his pugnacity, he was a devout believer (with a Jesuit confessor to boot). Pledging to keep Spain free from atheism, he promised the Church a central role in Spain's future. The Albós hung a large portrait of Franco in their living room alongside the portrait of Xavier's beloved father. Five years later, when Xavier turned ten and Spain was locked into a thirty-nine-year romance with the *mano dura*, Señora Albó packed up Xavier's things, hoped for the best, and sent him to Jesuit school in Barcelona.

It well may be that he had been destined for life in the New World. As a boy attending mass in La Garriga's main church, Xavier had prayed before an image of Saint Stephen that had hung there since 1492, the very year Columbus sailed to America. Having been born into the realities of a cruel and senseless war, he was determined to dedicate himself to peace, to the betterment of things, to social justice and human understanding. Toward those ends, Xavier was willing to go wherever the Jesuits decreed and pledge himself to a life of poverty, chastity, and obedience. Part devotion, part love of adventure, that tireless drive—a rare combination of curiosity and surrender—would light his way for the rest of his life.

Seeing the cult of Evita in its fullest expression, seeing that Spain was not alone in its petulant, pendulum swings, in its militarism and idolatry, Xavier felt he was entering a world that, for all its stark differences, resonated profoundly with his own. As he traveled north to Bolivia on a lumbering train, he viewed the majestic world unfolding before him—poor, backward, crippled, yet inexpressibly beautiful and infinitely kind—and his convictions deepened. He was entering a dynamic universe, witnessing a country that was on the verge of taking hold of its fate, changing the course of its future.

Bolivia had just emerged from a historic revolution. Four months before, in April 1952, Bolivian tin miners had risen up against a repressive oligarchy—much as the Spanish coal miners of Asturias had—but unlike them, the Bolivians had prevailed. Moreover, the populist Left of Bolivia had won in a democratic election, but, unlike its Spanish counterpart, it had gone on to retain that power. Bolivia was putting into place a number of radical reforms that gave peasants their rights, nationalized the mines, and won universal suffrage for women. And they were doing so seven years before Cuba would win greater fame for equivalent victories. Xavier was entering the country at a pivotal moment in its history. It was what the Indians called Pachacuti—a turning of the earth, a realignment of the stars—and the Church was being presented with a momentous choice. Would it protect the old, moneyed power base and the *mano dura*, as Spanish bishops had done during the Civil War? Or would it live by its precepts and side with the rights of the poor?

THE FOUNDATION OF HEAVEN

Who could conquer Tenochtitlán? Who could shake the foundation of heaven?

— "Cantares Mexicanos," Aztec songs, ca. 1560.

Xavier found very quickly that, despite the half millennium that had passed, the spirituality he was discovering in Bolivia was probably somewhat like the one his priestly forebears had encountered in the time of Pizarro. From what he could observe, the faithful of this "New World" were vastly more attuned to nature, their cosmic orientation tied keenly to the land beneath their feet, the sun overhead, the rains in between. When Spanish conquistadors and their priests had burst into these remote lands, they had come with lessons about sins and saints, abstract notions of redemption, and a ritual that demanded strict adherence to a written text. It had been a strange, asymmetrical junction. Deities in the New World were explanations, not questions—concrete correspondents to life on earth. The God of the conquistadors was something·else entirely—a proposition, a puzzle, recorded in incomprehensible code. Cortés himself had reported that the universe he had entered was "so wondrous as not to be believed." The sprawling metropolis of Tenochtitlán had been filled with such mind-boggling novelties that "we here who saw them with our own eyes could not understand them with our minds."

It is not surprising, then, how difficult it was for Xavier—as it had been for Cortés and continues to be for us—to fathom the contours of indigenous faith in its pure, aboriginal form. What stands as recorded history, after all, isn't history at all. Written after the conquest and heavily influenced by European prejudices, Spanish chronicles are filled with the firm conviction that the American Indian was, at best, ignorant and, at worst, diabolical. The writings of Columbus, Cortés, Pedro Pizarro, and others are filled with hyperbole and outright lies for obvious reasons: theirs was a mission to persuade, subjugate, and rule. Their accounts were addressed to the Crown as propaganda or justification, not as history. But even the most detailed journals by well-meaning, extraordinarily astute and observant priests are skewed by pronounced Christian doctrine. The view, every way we look—and absent any comprehensive documentation by the indigenous themselves—is warped by the eye of the beholder.

When it comes to matters of the spirit, the task of understanding the past is even more complicated. What little we have been able to deduce about the various tribal faiths, from Tierra del Fuego to the Rio Grande—from the Guaraní to the Aztecs—we have had to glean from artifacts that are frustratingly difficult to decode much less comprehend with any depth or certitude. Relics can tell us a great deal about burial practices or prevailing deities, or the heroics of war, or the state of scientific progress, or the geography of a people, or even the centrality of the natural world, but they don't reveal much about the essential soul. Nor do they tell us about the beliefs that inform the fears and hopes of an ancient and inscrutable people.

Here is what we do know: long before the Incas built their colossal temples in Cuzco, Sacsayhuaman, or Machu Picchu—long before the Mayans built Chichén Itzá, or Tikal, or Uxmal—the Waris and the Olmecs built sacred leviathans of stone, often perched on beds of rock. Sacred places in the indigenous Americas have been shown to hold a natural magnetism; a physical traction that suggests a deep understanding of the geology of stone. Indeed, the sanctity of stone seems to have united the spiritual life of the indigenous throughout the hemisphere. Creation myths, whether or not they have been embellished one way or another in the course of time, seem to share this commonality: they begin with a search for an ideal landform—a lake, a rock, a promontory— from which a strong faith might radiate. Often it is charged with telluric power. The heavens above, whether it was the North Star crossing the night sky, or the sun as it mounts the vaulting dome of day, might further inform the placement of a temple.

The Incas, who were the most impressive empire builders of their day, were all too aware of the concrete, physical nature of things. They had fashioned a muscular religion around it. Establishing the sun as their supreme god, they divided their empire into four quarters to reflect the four seasons, and split it in half (north, south) to represent the dry and wet halves of the year. The transition between seasons—when the Milky Way streamed from northeast to southwest—was precisely the moment when the skies rained life-giving water on the Earth Mother, Pachamama. A firm logic ruled their science even as it ruled their faith. The Aztecs, too, worshiped the sun above all, divided their universe into four, not only to mirror the seasons but also to correspond to the four successive suns, or periods, their civilization had experienced, and the four great catastrophes that had undone them. The cosmos was divided into four "directions"; the city of Tenochtitlán, into four *campans*.

Perhaps the most famous relic we have from the Aztecs is their stone calendar, a round disk depicting the great god Sun at the center, surrounded by the four iterations of civilization that went before. According to the calendar, the first Aztecs had been devoured by tigers; the second, overpowered by hurricanes; the third, obliterated by rains; the fourth, washed away in a great flood. The Aztecs whom Cortés would encounter were living under the Fifth Sun, and they understood that they would prevail only as long as they pleased the gods. This they could achieve only through human sacrifice. The period of the Fifth Sun, as legend went, had been born of sacrifice—indeed, humanity owed its very life's breath to it. According to the story, the forces that rule the cosmos had met at the dawn of creation and gathered around a blazing fire. They asked that one stand forth and show his loyalty by leaping bravely into the inferno. The most beautiful among them, handsome of face and encrusted with jewels, hesitated. The ugliest, a dwarfish creature pocked with ulcers, plunged in and was promptly reborn as the mighty sun. Mortified, the beautiful one leapt in and rose to the skies as the moon.

Clearly, if gods had sacrificed themselves to create the universe as we know it, the people of the Fifth Sun would need to pay down sacrifices in order to perdure. Human sacrifice was as obvious a necessity to the Aztecs as the sun above and the maize below. The logic was simple: the earth goddess, Coatlicue, needed to be fed in order to feed the rest of us. Human blood would need to water her loam. Beating hearts needed to be ripped from chests and held aloft, shown to her consort, the Sun. So it was that the Aztecs' faith mirrored the world around them. As seasons came and went, they were reminded of their fragility: How long would they last? How to prevail? How to fend off the dark forces that might swallow them again? Religion is a useful mirror on its followers' preoccupations. From it, we learn that the central preoccupation of the Mesoamerican Indians was that nature had to be loved and feared at once if they were to survive it. The ancients lived their beliefs, understood profoundly the connections. And because they were creatures of nature, dependent on its realities for both mortal and spiritual existence, they strove to adapt to the physical world, not alter it.

The worship of stones, and all that emerged from stone—gold, silver, copper, cinnabar, salt, gemstone—had a conspicuous role in the ancient Americas, as indeed it continues to have today. Mines in the time of the Incas were considered sacred, a gift from the earth, much as plants, crops, and all else that sprang from the land were considered hallowed and divine. These earthly things were constituents of a greater ambit, cogs in a larger wheelwork, in which humans played an integral part. Stones were where we were all headed—the realm of the hard, the calcified, the long dead—the great accumulation of animal and plant energy. Great piles of rock and towering mountains were our natural fathers, our spirit *apus*, who lived long before us and held ancient wisdom. The Sun was the great giver of being, the life force that sparked creation. Earth was his natural mate, his lover, the womb from which all the living sprang and the tomb to which we would all go. Water was the animating medium that flowed through nature and maintained it, even as veins flow through leaves and flesh. Most important in indigenous thinking—the indisputable germ at the heart of the logic—was the interconnectedness of life: the intrinsic interdependence, the breath, the air, the matrix we all share. This was as present and easily understood by ancient Americans as the global movement of money and commerce might be to us today: a grand, protean web that connected the world.

Confounding our ability to truly comprehend all this—given the paucity of indigenous accounts untainted by Spanish interpretation—there is the rudimentary problem of language. Western words simply cannot convey the significance that the natural world held for the Indian. It is an inadequacy that begins with the way we perceive the most fundamental aspects of our shared world. As Franz Boas, the father of American anthropology, once pointed out, although "the form is constant, the interpretation is variable," which is to say that if you put a tube in front of a contemporary European and an exact replica before an Alaskan Indian, the European may see it as a cylindrical object, a concrete object that happens to be hollow, whereas the Inuit whaler might focus on the emptiness within. Where words may be understood, on the other hand, the meaning may not: *The Florentine Codex*, the sixteenth-century record of Mesoamerican history, states that when emissaries of Montezuma rowed out with treasures to meet a wary Cortés, they "ate the earth" until he let them board his ship. What was meant was that they kowtowed and groveled. There is little doubt: language is a formidable wall against our understanding the ancient indigenous mind. Add to the myriad linguistic discordances our starkly differing mythologies, our attitudes about human relations, our uses of memory, the way we observe our physical surroundings—and you have a potential sea of misapprehension. If we perceive shapes as intrinsically different from the way an Andean might perceive them, how can we hope to understand the spiritual significance of stones?

And yet, from all evidence, stones were and continue to be essential to the culture. Pedro Sarmiento de Gamboa, a Spanish explorer who was commissioned to write a history of the Incas in 1572—when Spain had already destroyed the empire and the conquistadors held Tahuantinsuyu in their grip—described an origin myth that was striking in its difference from the prevailing legend put forward by the mestizo El Inca Garcilaso de la Vega a few decades later. In Inca Garcilaso's version— written in Spain in the 1600s, more than fifty years after he had left Peru—the Adam and Eve of the Incas, Manco Capac and Mama Ocllo, set out to find their land, holding a precious rod of gold. When that rod leapt from their hands and sank deep into the earth, they would know they had reached the umbilicus of their universe, the sacred Cuzco. It was a pretty tale, sure to interest Spaniards by virtue of that provocative, golden flourish. But the descendants of the Incas interviewed by Gamboa in the mountain aeries surrounding Cuzco had a very different story. In their version, four brothers—Ayar Uchu, Ayar Cachi, Ayar Mango, and Ayar Auca—set out from a cave at the very dawn of civilization and headed out to establish an empire. They wandered the land, sowing seeds in promising places, gathering harvests where they could. They were farmers at heart, and their trip was markedly ordinary, lasting for many years. They did, however, eliminate a pesky brother by trapping him in a cave; and they transformed a favored brother into a great rock—a sacred *huaca*—which they continued to consult. Eventually their grandmother, Mama Huaco, a fierce, feisty woman who had her fill of wandering, hurled two sticks toward the north. One fell in Colca-bamba and bounced, inhospitably, from the desiccated earth. The other sank comfortably into Cuzco. When the brothers stepped onto the exact location where the stick had disappeared, the earth had turned to stone.

Stone, to the ancient indigenous of the Americas, was transubstantial, mutable, as dynamic a concept as—in the Christian context—wine is to the blood of Christ. Its physicality was patent, but its significance was not. Petrification was but a brief suspension, a temporary immobiliza-tion from which life might spring anew. Just as mummies of the Lords Inca were meant to be preserved, fed, and consulted because they would live on in another dimension, stones, too, were living things—powerful, sentient, spiritually animate—whose specters could be summoned to teach us a thing or two. It is a starkly un-Western idea, one that sits more comfortably in an Oriental mind: the Ojibwe of North America, for instance, believed stones housed vital energies. So did the Cherokee, the Sioux, the Iroquois. In ancient China and Japan, rocks were valued for their telluric powers. The ancient druids of the Celtics who inhab-ited the British Isles were also worshipers of stone with strong notions about human sacrifice and distinct theories about the transmutability of souls, but—as would later befall the American indigenous—they were spurned as barbarians and eccentrics by their Roman conquerors, and rejected as pagans by the Christians who followed.

A thrall in stone was deeply embedded in the spiritual life of an-cient Mesoamericans, whose culture dominated the funnel of land that runs up the hemisphere from Panama to Colorado, and across from the Caribbean to the Pacific. The Mayans, so populous in that verdant, rain-rich terrain, made stone images of the dead and believed their souls inhabited them. The rock itself was possessed of a life force that tran-scended physicality and confounded time. So intrinsic to the Mayans was the connection between stone and everlasting life that their word for stone, *tun*, also means "time." The passing years—the raveling of history itself—were counted in *tun*. Like the Quechua word *pacha*, which in the Andes connotes the earth beneath our feet as well as the progress of time (a word impossible to translate accurately into English), these concepts suggest something beyond a physical presence: a promise; perhaps even a moral order. Through a constant communication with stone, humans could thwart mortality, talk to the dead, even manipulate events in the future. Stones had authority, agency—the ability to represent us to a higher power. Eventually, and for obvious reasons, human sacrifice came to be tied with stone worship. Blood was spilled on stone; human offerings were made on thick slabs of it so that rewards could be extracted from gods, and the living could coerce the spirits.

This romance with stone had many cultural ramifications. The Mayans would sculpt rock into great pyramids that marked the days of the year, the movement of the sun, and the time to plant, as well as the time to reap. The ancestors of the Guaraní, who lived two thousand years ago in the jungle that surrounds Paraguay's Amambay Hills, decorated massive rock ledges with abstract symbols of earth and sky. The Diquís, who inhabited Panama and Costa Rica eight hundred years before Columbus's arrival, carved great *bolas*, perfectly round fifteen-ton spheres of igneous rock that were scattered through jungle and field to mark the approach to a great man's house—perhaps a temple—although the true significance of *bolas* still remains a mystery. Another mystery resides in the cyclopean, fifty-ton stone heads left behind by the Olmecs, commemorating the strong, proud features of their race.

And then, of course, there are the magnificent edifices of the Incas, who were so aware of the spirituality of magnetic rock that they searched out natural outcroppings of it on which to build their temples. Where there were insufficient lodes, they forced armies of thousands to dig out and drag colossal, one-hundred-ton boulders from quarries more than twenty miles away. Stones were placed on the graves of great Inca leaders so that their spirits would live on in the stelae—their grave markers— and speak to us, the living. Like the cairns of Scotland, or the *mani* in Tibet, or the ovoo in Mongolia, piles of rock in the Andes were signals of good luck, and travelers would stack them, add to them—stone on stone—as they passed. Abandoned ruins were revered for their ability to connect to other worlds, other dimensions. These were the *huacas*, for which we also have no adequate word: they were not sacred in any abstract sense, not deities, not supernatural as we know it. They were powerful precisely because they reflected an earthly vitality. *"Huacas* are made of energized matter," just as everything else on this earth is, one scholar suggests, "and they act *within* nature, not over and outside it, as Western supernaturals do." They may look ordinary enough—craggy promontories, still lifes, silent bystanders—but they are as keenly aware of us as we are of them. This notion of the manifest sacredness all around us was, and still is, mirrored in the beliefs of rain forest Indians throughout the hemisphere. As one historian describes them, "Jungle dwellers live in a forest of eyes. A person moving through nature is never truly alone." Which is to say that the trees, the stones, the very earth—the whole material universe—is alive, catalytic, and flush with the clear potential to feed our souls.

That stones could be simultaneously holy and utilitarian was only logical to the ancients. Bartolomé de las Casas, a historian and Dominican friar who devoted himself to defending the rights of the indigenous against the depredations of the Spanish, told of Mesoamerican and Caribbean Indians who used precious stones to capture the breath of dying chieftains so that their spirits would live on and their wisdom continue to guide them. Like the little round Andean stone that sits at the head of Leonor Gonzáles's bed and houses the eternal soul of her husband, stones not only represented the dead, they became their vital personifications— they would see and speak for them—and they would accompany the living. Whole delegations of officials would form to guard these rock-hard avatars of the Lords Inca, guarantee sacrifices on their behalf, and promote their durability. Such rituals were available not only to the powerful. Even the most common among us might release her last breath to a stone—a simple, ordinary pebble plucked from the ground—and be immortalized forever.

As history wore on, many of these commemorative stone structures (whether they be monuments, statues, or stelae) were obliterated by Spanish missionaries intent on ridding the colonies of what they considered superstition, devilry, and the "black arts." But even as Spanish priests and conquistadors reduced evidence of *huaca* to rubble, they couldn't destroy it in the people. In the Andes—whether among Quechua, Huanca, or Aymara people—that reverence for spirited stone continues: in their awe at the beauty and power of jutting rock; or their sympathy for a random *piedra cansada*, a "tired stone," an abandoned hulk that never made it to the Herculean structure for which it was meant; or even their delight in small, perfectly shaped or unusually colored rocks they carve or choose to represent a loved one. In Central America, shamans treat sick children by taking a natural, unblemished stone that personifies a child's soul and burying it in a secret place by a spring or a river until the Earth Mother nurses the child back to health. Such are the ways the ancient lessons prevail.

The most commanding glories of the Mayans—the manses, the temples, the great pyramids of stone—were tucked away in jungles and, so, were eventually overtaken by boscage, lost to humanity for a thousand years. Many of them, discovered only in the last two centuries, were stumbled upon by hazard, as fearless explorers hacked through the tangle to be met with a multitude of elegant structures. Strangely enough, many of them shared a common trait: three mighty rocks at their foundation. The towering red sandstone monoliths at Quiriguá, found in the thickets of Guatemala's jungle, tell us why. According to their inscriptions, the three original stones that marked the beginning of time had been planted by the gods in 3114 BC—at approximately the same time as the birth of the Egyptian dynasty. Which is to say that the age-old practice of "sowing the stones"—installing three rocks as fundament and anchor—has been part of the culture for millennia. The monoliths at Quiriguá also tell us that each rock had its purpose and meaning: the first represents the throne of the jaguar, lord of the fertile earth; the second, the water throne, where sharks coexist with lilies; the third, the throne of the flying snake, emperor of the skies. Curiously enough, with slight variations, that trinity mirrors the beliefs of the Incas, who lived two thousand miles away and four millennia later. Like the Mayans, the Incas revered three spirit animals above all: the puma, the snake, and the condor—masters, respectively, of earth, water, and sky. It is a sensible enough worship: these are the only three habitats this planet offers its living beings.

Today the ritual planting of three hearth stones is still practiced by the people of Central America. Often without knowing quite why, descendants of the Mayans or Aztecs will insist on placing three solid rocks at the foot of their buildings or installing three mortar stones in their kitchens, with the simple explanation that if a stool needs three legs for stability, so does a human abode. In such ways does the centrality of stone persist in the lives of Latin American Indians, who continue to hold a profound reverence for nature and a firm conviction that they are custodians of a sacred life cycle. As one Aymara candidate of the indigenist party said to potential voters in Qhunqhu Liqiliqi, Bolivia, as he plucked a random rock from the ground and held it toward the sun, "We are this stone." Then, turning it in his hand, he parsed it more closely for his listeners, lest there be any doubt: "This stone is *us*." It was a declaration of affiliation, reciprocity, and responsibility to nature. But it was also a statement of faith.

The ancient indigenous cultures of Latin America may have been surrounded by oceans on all sides, isolated, hermetical, unknown to the rest of the world, but their highly developed religions and profound curiosity about the world—about the why of things—made for exuberant intellectual pursuits. The Mayans, for one, who still populate Central America, are heirs to almost three thousand years of cultivated history, all of it informed by an ancient faith. When Britain and Northern Europe were still being overrun by wild, primitive tribes, the Mayans had built great temples, invented hieroglyphic writing, devised an advanced numbering system sophisticated for its use of zero, and fashioned a calendar meant to advance the science of astronomy. Indeed, the formula to count days devised by Mayan priests in the sixth century was more accurate than European versions until Pope Gregory XIII installed the Gregorian calendar nearly a thousand years later. To cultures such as the Maya, Toltec, or Inca, science and religion were partners, working hand in hand to explain the mysteries of the world rather than stand contest for its souls.

Copán, in what is now Honduras, was the intellectual seat of the Mayans, a grand university city in which one of the most extensive displays of hieroglyphics can still be seen. Most of the codices are now gone, to be sure, destroyed in the blazing bonfires the Spanish conquerors held in their zeal to Christianize the hemisphere, but we see evidence of Mayan spirituality in books that have survived—the *Popol Vuh*, the *Chilám Balám*—which are replete with poetry, mythology, and a litany of beliefs that have not been extinguished completely in the Mayan people.

Indeed, the pyramids built throughout the great expanse of present-day Mexico—not just by Mayans but also by Olmecs, Toltecs, Zapotecs, Aztecs—stand as imposing testimony to an abiding faith. The six that adorn the ancient city of Tikal in Guatemala are triumphs of architecture, towering belvederes meant to survey a sweeping panorama of empire. The pyramid at Cholula—now a sprawl of stony ruin—was larger, grander than any that the Egyptian King Cheops built. The pyramid at Chichén-Itzá is remarkable for its star-gazing observatory and a vast, becolumned ball court, a tribute to the god of air, wind, and wisdom. The Pyramid of the Sun at Teotihuacán was the preeminent religious site in all pre-Columbian America and, in its time, one of the most teeming, populous cities of the ancient world.

Although historians can find no traceable communication between ancient Mexico and Peru, there are clear parallels in the religious iconography and spiritual lives of the people. Even as Olmecs and Mayans were raising temples to their gods, the nations that inhabited desert and mountain thousands of miles to the south—the Moche, Wari, and Tiwanaku—were building formidable monuments to strikingly similar deities: the omnipotent sun, the fecund earth, the fickle rains, the volatile sea. More striking still is how influences seemed to travel across inhospitable terrain: the Peruvian archaeologist Julio C. Tello discovered ruins on the Bolivian plateau that anticipate the architectural style of Peru's most ancient structure, the spectacular underground labyrinth of corridors called Chavín de Huántar, built a cordillera away and hundreds of years later. There are many such examples in which discrete cultures in the Andes echoed and mirrored one another, although they would not be joined politically until many centuries later when the Incas dominated a vast empire that stretched from Ecuador to Argentina. The same could be said of the various cultures conquered by the Mexicas, from the Gulf of Mexico to the Pacific. These interconnections seem logical: the distances are not overwhelming. Yet images of mystically charged creatures— fanged serpents, great cats, lizards, spiders, hummingbirds—appear in dramatically different topographies and in diverse mediums, from metal to stone, and from Mexico to Paraguay. The artifacts, like connective tissue, reveal the gods and precepts that were held in common: the sun, the moon, the earth; the essential sexuality of nature; the humanlike fallibility of the sacred world. Even more startling are the similarities in interpretation. Take, for instance, the adoration of a sorcerous, fiendish, but ultimately fertile female figure, whether she be the Lady of Cao, a tattooed, spider-bedecked, bloody-minded queen who ruled the coast of Peru more than fifteen centuries ago; or the mythical Earth Mother, Coatlicue—Aztec goddess of womb and tomb, creation and ruin, birther and destroyer of men—whose snake-skirted, ghoulish likeness is graven in stone thousands of miles away.

There are curious correlations, too, in myths of creation. According to one Andean legend, the god Viracocha forged man not once, but twice. On his first attempt, he fashioned a lumbering, brainless race, which he despised and quickly turned to stone. His second creation was shaped from smaller stones, perhaps even hardened clay, and the issue pleased him. Apart from conceiving all earthly life and all heavenly bodies, Viracocha, whose name means "foam of the sea," was a natural teacher, committed to wandering his newly wrought world to impart his wisdom. He was bearded—a curious feature for the god of a race virtually free of body hair—tall, inordinately wise, and, as some Spanish chronicles tell it for obvious reasons, fair skinned. When, in his peregrinations, he finally reached the coast, he sailed off into the Pacific, vowing to return someday, although he was never to be seen again. Viracocha's semblance is ubiquitous, rampant throughout the heartland of South America; clutching two thunderbolts, ringed by the sun's rays, preserved for all time in metal or stone. So beloved a figure was he that a later ruler, the Lord Inca Viracocha, eventually took his name.

Remarkable as it may seem, the creator god of the Aztecs, too, was reputed to be tall, bearded, and, according to some chroniclers, fair and blue eyed. He was "the plumed serpent" Quetzalcoatl, a protean figure who, it was said, would be reborn for each period of history, manifesting a different face every time. When the theologian Joseph Campbell set out to document the distinct manifestations of Quetzalcoatl, he quickly found that there were no fewer than a thousand of them, minted to appeal to specific peoples, specific regions. All the same, Quetzalcoatl, like his Andean counterpart Viracocha, represented heaven and earth: the radiant, orderly forces of a star-studded sky as well as the chaotic, generative powers of land and sea. For Incas as well as Aztecs, the worship of mysterious yet essential life forces was paramount. Just as believers today petition a Christian, Muslim, or Jewish god—along with a miscellany of saints and subalterns—to save their souls, the indigenous appealed to the Sun God and his attendant minions to allow them to harness nature. Toward that end, the conquering civilizations of South and Central America erected mighty temples, subjugated and converted alien tribes. The effort required a churning, uninterrupted mill of human lives—as slave labor, as sacrifices, as worshipers—a glorious, ever-expanding, continually evangelized mass of the faithful to ensure better rains, better sun, better harvests.

FOLLOW ME

Go and make disciples of all nations, baptizing them in the name of the Father and of the Son and of the Holy Spirit, and teaching them to obey.
—Matthew 28:19–20

Xavier Albó knew very well that his chief obligation to the Church would be to preach the Gospel and bring souls to Jesus, as it had been for every Jesuit friar entering the priesthood to emulate Saint Paul making his missionary journey to Cyprus. That commitment would change over the years and become something new—something deeper—but at the tender age of seventeen, with the weight of the Vatican's Department of Missions upon him, Xavier's goals were simple: he hoped to be educated, to grow, and to learn to communicate directly, meaningfully with those whose souls would be his responsibility. These were the thoughts uppermost in his mind as he wandered the Argentine capital, marveling at its mighty monuments, its evident political power, and the roiling humanity that surged through its rain-soaked, funereal streets, mourning the death of a beloved first lady. Even as Xavier booked his railway passage to Bolivia, another adolescent boy, Jorge Bergoglio, future Jesuit and pontiff, sat in a church on the other side of Buenos Aires, and glimpsed his destiny—a moment that presented itself to him with such physical force that he would describe it as being thrown from a horse, just as Saint Paul once had been. The paths of these two young Jesuits would not cross for another sixty-four years.

As Xavier's train lurched its way to Cochabamba, Bolivia, his window revealed a world he hadn't imagined in his most improbable dreams. Months before, sure that he would be assigned to the mission in Bombay, he had read everything on India his school could offer. But Pope Pius XII had urged the Church to send its young to Latin America, where Communism was taking root and threatened to unleash a wave of atheism among the poor. The younger and callower the novitiates, was the thinking, the more easily they would insert themselves into the population. Now, as the Argentine pampas scrolled by and the train heaved its way toward the airless heights of the Andes, Xavier realized how truly raw he was, how little he knew, how disadvantaged he was in his chosen profession. He had read little about these lands before his ship had skimmed to shore and dropped anchor in the port of Buenos Aires. The first he had heard of Eva Perón was on board, when the Argentine captain had called for fifteen minutes of silence, and a member of the crew read aloud an entire chapter from Evita's memoir, *La Razón de Mi Vida, The Reason of My Life.* Now, as his train puffed its way from the farmlands beyond the capital to the cactus plains of Tucumán, he could see Evita's likeness enshrined in every station. It was worship, pure and simple, and he was taken aback by its intensity. Evita, a former actress—and not a very good one—had made a career of establishing schools, orphanages, old-age homes, hospitals, charitable institutions, and encouraging woman's suffrage. She had done the kind of work missions strove to do.

By the time Xavier arrived in Cochabamba, he had learned a thing or two. Bolivia was nothing like Argentina. Whereas Buenos Aires was largely white, its population overwhelmingly European and purged of Indian blood, the country to which he would devote the rest of his life was markedly indigenous. Women, even the poorest among them, wore colorful, layered skirts (*polleras*), bowler hats, and long braids that signaled their marital status: loose if they were single, tied if they were married, sometimes plaited with black fringe if they were widows. Men were broad shouldered, deliberate, somber. He watched as they scurried vigorously down dusty trails or herded animals from field to field. One face after another glanced up from the rugged landscape to gaze at the boy in the lumbering iron behemoth, and, with each, he felt he had passed into a distinct—and timeless—universe. There were farmers with ruddy countenances, hewing tumescent stalks of quinoa; little girls tottering down hillsides with babies strapped to their backs; women squatting on brightly colored cloths, displaying cures for fertility, cataracts, leprosy; laughing boys running by, shouting up, offering him baby llamas; a lone fisherman in a canoe, slipping quietly past on a mud-brown river; laborers arguing in a cantina, drunk. These were his flock. It would be his job to love them.

Xavier had long sensed his calling was not to the priesthood as much as to missionary work. An adventurous, curious boy with a friendly and jovial streak, he was there to learn as much as to teach. He had not wanted to pursue a life of the cloth in a familiar place, in a Spanish town. Now, transplanted to a completely unfamiliar country, he looked around with a joy he had never felt before. There was plenty for him to learn here. The light-skinned Bolivians in Cochabamba who welcomed the novitiates and invited them to their sumptuous homes—those who had always held the power and the purse strings—seemed familiar enough, to be sure. They spoke Spanish, owned all there was to own, controlled 92 percent of the cultivable land, felt entitled to the nation's riches, and had enjoyed privileges for hundreds of years. But the people he had seen from the train window, the Quechua and Aymara—the humble, the poor, the laborers, the mountain folk—were the ones Xavier most wanted to know. As it happened, the country had just been convulsed by a violent wave of revolution that had swept through only months before his arrival. The Bolivians he had been watching were poised on the verge of change. Xavier could not possibly know it, but the people around him were lit with a sense that the world had turned, the god of revolution Pachacuti had sent it topsy-turvy, and the last would now be the first.

Xavier, shuttled by the Jesuits to his new quarters in Cochabamba and cloistered in a school where he would acquire a prodigious command of Quechua, would not learn about that revolution for some time. Studying the language of the land even as chickens and pigs wandered in and out of his classroom, he was blissfully unaware that the world outside was bubbling with a sense of newness; that it had made a cataclysmic transition. He had no idea that, for years, young intellectuals, frustrated with Bolivia's conservative rule—its rank oppression, its economic inefficiencies, its abject surrender to the demands of foreign bosses—had championed *indianismo*, a conviction that the country needed to return to ancient roots and a better organized, more broadly representative Socialist state akin to that of the Incas. The white elites and their puppet generals had brought nothing but misery. Only two decades before, they had presided over a humiliating war with Paraguay in which the country had sacrificed sixty-five thousand lives and a vast expanse of land—the oil-rich scrub of the Gran Chaco. For years, Chile, Peru, Argentina, and Brazil had hacked at Bolivia's borders, sensing a weak player. But it was Bolivia's own oligarchs—its tin mine owners, its rural landowners, its generals—and its old, repressive power structure, that had tyrannized the ordinary worker, sold out to foreign corporations, given away its riches, and brought rampant hunger to the people.

In 1946, in a fit of discontent, the people had thrown the government from power, abducted their president, Gualberto Villaroel, and hanged him from a lamppost outside the presidential palace. A turbulent five years followed. None of this was surprising: Bolivia had undergone 178 popular uprisings since its independence from Spain little more than a century before. These bouts of belligerence had paralyzed the economy, but they had been quashed easily by the powers that be. All the same, on April 9, 1952, even as Xavier Albó was sailing toward Buenos Aires en route to that country, Bolivia's National Revolutionary Movement declared itself a champion to beleaguered Bolivians, seized military arsenals in La Paz, and began distributing arms to citizens. Gunslinging miners from as far away as Potosí swarmed into the capital and blocked the army from seizing advantage. After three days of brutal fighting, and despite all efforts by the US government to thwart the rebels, the military surrendered, and a newly elected president, former economics professor Victor Paz Estenssoro, took the reins, sending a rare jolt of possibility into the rural hinterland. Almost immediately, Paz Estenssoro extended universal suffrage to all, including the most remote and illiterate. Just as immediately, he nationalized the country's mines—along with the world's legendary source of silver, the global economic catalyst Potosí—and instituted an agrarian reform that abolished forced labor and redistributed land to indigenous farmers. It was to this newly invented world that Xavier had come.

*   *   *

Xavier had been a victim of cultural imperialism all his life. As a speaker of Catalan, he belonged to a population that had suffered linguistic subjugation since the twelfth century, when Aragón had annexed the thriving, exuberantly independent people of Catalonia. Growing up under Generalísimo Franco's boot, he had been allowed to use the language of his ancestors only within the walls of his home, not in public places. He could empathize with the anguish of colonialism, the suppression and extermination of a native dialect for "the good" of the state. He knew what it must mean for the Quechua, speakers of an ancient tongue, to lose their children to an alien culture.

Getting to know the gentle, warmhearted Bolivians who welcomed him to that paradisiacal neighborhood where he was to train in the sacristy and learn their language—the jovial cook, the toothless caretaker, the friendly shopkeeper, the busy passersby—he began learning something more. Xavier began to hear about the difficult history through which they had passed. There was, of course, the revolution that had just rocked the country, sparked by miners who had borne the brunt of punishing demands for centuries. Before that, the dark, violent days of colonial rule. But even before all that, when conquering Incas had swept through these lands, annexing tribes, imposing their faith, and demanding their captives' labor, life had been harsh for these people. Sacrifices had been legion. No salve to the conquered masses, the ancient religions had made blood demands.

Indeed, from the northermost reaches of Mexica rule to the southernmost forests of the Guaraní, religion and tribal ritual had often demanded the ultimate sacrifice: offering up human lives to appease the gods. Faith had asked more than good acts and prayer from its followers. It had asked for life itself.

In the ancient Americas, human sacrifice was a test of religious conviction. Gods needed to be mollified. Bodies were required. Blood needed to be drawn. Rather than yielding their own to the sacrificial stone, the pre-Columbians, especially Mesoamericans, often provoked wars to gain victims. They went so far as to adapt rules of warfare to the task: warriors would only wound their enemies in battle so that they could take them prisoner and kill them—even eat them—in ritual sacrifice. Aztec codices describe these religious rites, performed in elaborate ceremonies atop great pyramid temples. High priests would choose the most virile among the captives; four lesser priests would wrestle the live victim to the ritual slab; and a fifth would cut open his thorax with a sharp obsidian knife, reach under his sternum, and rip out the still-beating heart. The victim's body would then be flung down the temple steps, spraying blood as it caromed down the barbed declivity, and then his heart would be burned, sending its smoke to a hungry god.

In Peru, during Inti Raymi celebrations for the winter solstice, human sacrifices were made with great pomp and ceremony, overseen by high priests of the Inca. But warriors and captives were not considered the highest blood tributes to a supreme god. The Incas sacrificed prepubescent children of both sexes, chosen for their innocence as well as their beauty, offered up in an effort to win the Sun's favor and ensure a bountiful harvest. They called it *capacocha*, and the sacrifice of a beautiful, virginal child would be called for whenever good fortune was needed: when an emperor was ill, or had celebrated the birth of a son, or had set out to war, or had died, or had just been succeeded. The diminutive victims were prepared in elaborate rituals, dressed, drugged, and then led up mountains to icy promontories where their skulls were crushed or throats strangled in solemn observances. Blood was never shed in these sacrifices: a victim who had been cut or bled would have been deemed imperfect, incomplete, unacceptable to the Lord Sun. In 1892 an excavation on Ecuador's Isla de la Plata produced the grisly remains of two such children, adorned with precious artifacts, killed without any evidence of blood, and buried in precisely the way that Inca emperors mandated such rituals to take place. One hundred years later, in 1995, the remains of a twelve-year-old mummified Inca girl were dug from the snows of Mount Ampato in southern Peru, along with a trove of gold and silver ornaments. "Juanita," she was subsequently called, the Ice Maiden, and she was wrapped in an exquisitely woven tapestry of bright colors and a shawl of the finest alpaca—with a silver clasp at her breast and a cap of red feathers on her brow. Her right eye socket bore a visible crack and, above it, a massive fracture: evidence that she had been dispatched by a brutal blow to the head. In the glacial heights of Chile and northwest Argentina, frozen for all time in the perpetual snows of Aconcagua, an assortment of mummified children was found—sometimes alone, sometimes in clusters, always exquisitely dressed, always bludgeoned or asphyxiated—anywhere from six to fifteen years old. In 2018, the skull of a boy—less than ten-years-old—was found in a sacrificial pit in the ruins of the Aztec Templo Mayor, under the very heart of Mexico City.

As gruesome as these child murders were, they were perceived as having great agency. In the way, perhaps, that we believe that sacrificing soldiers to war—ceding our youngest and strongest to the mayhem of battle—will bring us progress, the ancient Andeans believed that sacrificial ceremonies, meticulously planned and spiritedly offered, would go a long way to paying down sins and bringing good fortune. More important, they reckoned they had good evidence for their efficacy: when Arequipa's volcano Misti erupted in the early fifteenth century, and the surrounding area was razed by a tsunami of molten lava, the queen wife of Pachacutec Inca Yupanqui called for a flurry of sacrifices in Cuzco to mitigate the *apu*'s divine fury. But the volcano's fulminations did not cease until Pachacutec himself visited the mountain with his entourage of high priests and made the sacrificial offerings that eventually calmed its fiery depths. When the most sacred building in Cuzco, the Temple of the Sun, was constructed, a number of children were buried alive in the sanctuary's foundation, ensuring the requisite potency and energy that the holy space would have for all generations to come. So convinced were the Incas that there was a strong causality between the sacrifice of children and the benefits to empire, that fathers would offer up their daughters to the ritual of *capacocha*, believing that great favors would be won for the good of the people, and their "chosen" child would live on in eternal honor among the celestial deities.

In Paraguay and Uruguay, the Guaraní, an otherwise gentle and spiritual people who believed in one God as well as the Word—the knowledge that lived deep within and was passed on to unborn children—were also reputed to be cannibals. For all their poetry and sensibility, there was also this. We don't know whether they consumed the flesh of their enemies or, more likely—as some Amazon Indians still do—ate their dead in the clear conviction that it was abhorrent to leave their remains to the despoliations of the wild. Far better to take in a loved one's ashes, ingest his essence, incorporate him to an everlasting life than abandon his body to harsh fortune. Whatever their calculus, the Guaraní, whom Christian conquistadors may have accused falsely in order to vilify and vanquish them, became renowned the world over for the cruelties of their religion. In Álvar Núñez Cabeza de Vaca's *Comentarios*, published in 1542, the explorer told of the Guaraní custom to follow wars with sacred rituals. These occasions began innocently enough with singing and dancing, and they invited their prisoners to join them. They prepared the captives for weeks by fattening them, giving them all they desired, even allowing their wives and daughters to pleasure them. In the end, when the victims were sufficiently plump and content, shamans and children were sent to hack them to pieces. The butchered corpses would be cooked in large pots, the flesh devoured and savored, and the great Father thanked for this opportunity to settle scores.

Whether or not this was true about the Guaraní, there is good, concrete evidence that human sacrifice and cannibalism were practiced elsewhere in the New World. Historians recount the discovery of child sacrifices, live burials found under the walls of structures throughout the Andes—quite obviously a building-dedication rite. This is certainly nothing the pre-Columbians invented: decapitated infants used for the same purpose are on display in the Museum of the Pontifical Biblical Institute, in Jerusalem. According to that particular exhibit, they were found in towns near the Dead Sea, "invariably under house floors, and they were quite possibly foundation sacrifices, as encountered elsewhere in the Near East." The difference is that the Andean children sacrifices were common many thousands of years later, right up to the time of the conquest—and, some say, years after. At Ancón, along the Peruvian coast where I used to play as a little girl, a child was found interred beneath the corner of a stone house. In place of her eyes were brilliant little squares of mica; her stomach was replaced by a gourd; and where her heart should have been, there was a shimmering rock crystal. Sacred hearths needed to be fed with sacrifices such as these.

In such ways did violence and faith join hands in the pre-Columbian past, much as it had joined hands in Spain's fierce expulsion of its Jews, its autos-da-fé, and the Crusades it had mounted against Europe's conquering Muslim armies. Yet for all the bloodlust that had consumed Spain for centuries, the Spanish would claim indigenous "barbarism" and "profanity" as reason enough to enslave a hemisphere. To the Catholic Crown, ritual human sacrifice and cannibalism were untenable, diabolical heresies that needed to be purged unilaterally. So it was that the violence of Latin America's religious past became the perfect justification to impose a violent religious future. Seizing the opportunity that indigenous "blasphemies" offered, Spain moved quickly to grant the Church a firm toehold in its campaign of subjugation. Never had Scripture been so useful in the rout of a vast, unknown territory. Conquistadors, bishops, merchants, bankers all endorsed the calumniation, weighing in on the inherent savagery of all New World Indians, no matter how great the civilization, no matter how developed the religion. Now, as a perceptive, compassionate young Jesuit novitiate was beginning to see it, it was precisely to keep a firm dominion on the population five hundred years later that he had been sent to that far, mountain hinterland of America.

CHAPTER 11

STONE TRUMPS STONE

❖

The sword and the cross marched together in the conquest and plunder of Latin America, and captains and bishops, knights and evangelists, soldiers and monks joined forces to help themselves to its silver.

—Eduardo Galeano, *Open Veins of Latin America*

From the moment the Old World met the New, it wanted to evangelize it: plant a cross in all its public places, pile stone on its sacred stone. In Montezuma's first meeting with Cortés, the Spaniard warned the emperor about the supremacy of the Spanish God and the sacrilege of worshiping idols in His place. This was not surprising, neither for the man who said it nor for he who heard it. Cortés and Montezuma both inhabited worlds defined by faith. For Cortés, the cross was synonymous with patriotism, righteousness, manliness—intrinsic to his identity. The patron saint of Spain is Saint James—Santiago "Matamoros," the Moor Slayer—after all, and Santiago's name had been invoked for centuries in every show of swords, every charge against an enemy, every venture into the unknown.

For the Mexicas, too, and especially for the Aztecs who lorded over them, their gods, which numbered into the dozens, were as natural and present as the air they breathed, the blood that coursed through their veins. There were thirteen levels of heaven, nine layers of underworld in the Aztec pantheon, each stratum inhabited by its respective deities and celestial bodies. Gods were invoked for the growing of maize, the fermentation of liquor, the defeat of a foe, the birth of a child, the pleasures of sex. What *was* different, perhaps, was that the Aztecs did not impose their gods unilaterally. High priests understood that other cultures might have potent, useful faiths of their own. The Aztec god of fertility—Xipe Totec—had been adopted from the Yopi people. The god of the night sky or high wind—Tezcatlipoca, ruler of the underworld—central to the religion, had once been worshiped by Toltecs.

One of the first edicts Cortés proclaimed after conquering Tenochtitlán was that its temples were *not* to be torn down immediately—they might prove advantageous as fortresses—but the idols in them were to be ripped from their shrines and smashed to rubble. That, too, was not surprising in the long history of things. Since time immemorial, Christians had been vandalizing the temples of the vanquished. When Rome, perhaps the most militaristic of empires the world has ever known, decided to champion Christianity, its decrees about conquering "barbarians" became a ready manual for carnage. The primary targets—the first to be eliminated in any conquest—were the idols. When Christians took over Athens, a mob of looters tore down a statue of the goddess Athena, decapitated her, and hacked her to pieces; her head was installed, upside down, as a stepping-stone to a Christian home. When monks took over the Temple of Serapis in Alexandria, they ordered it to be leveled on the spot: thousands of books were destroyed, and the colossal statue of the deity was dismembered, paraded around the city, and burned in a mighty pyre. Gold-plated walls were carried away; silver and bronze ripped from the arches. When the looters were finished, only the stone of the temple floor remained; a church dedicated to Saint John the Baptist was built on it.

Later, during the Byzantine era, when the Parthenon—the apotheosis of Greek civilization—was seized and used as a church, two imperious bishops carved their names into its massive columns. It mattered not that they were defacing a sacred monument that predated them by a millennium. They were merely following suit: less than four hundred years after the birth of Christ, a law had gone into effect, declaring that those who rejected the cross would "pay with their life and blood." And pay with their lives they did. By the time Cortés set foot on the shores of Veracruz, that mind-set had been in place for more than a thousand years.

So it was that Cortés and his cohort felt no compunction about destroying a religion and inflicting their faith by force. The conquistadors had indicated from the very start that this would be the case. Within days of his arrival in Tenochtitlán, Cortés had asked to see one of Montezuma's great temples of worship. The emperor obliged, taking him on a personal tour to the sacred site of Huei Teocalli, showing him the soaring tower, the great hall, the blood-stained altars, the sacrificial knives, the enormous snakeskin drum, the dragon plinth, the cyclopean, bejeweled figures of Huitzilopochtli and Tezcatlipoca—gods of war and the underworld. Cortés was repelled: he turned to his host and expressed surprise at how so wise a man could worship such absurd and wicked idols. He proposed to erect a cross on top of it all and install an image of Virgin Mary in the very heart of the hall. Montezuma was stung, furious, and snapped back that he would not have admitted Cortés to his temple had he known he would insult his gods.

But religion wasn't the immediate order of business after the conquest: gold was. At first, when Cortés imprisoned Montezuma, shackled him, and declared Tenochtitlán for the Spanish Crown, he ordered his soldiers to ferret out all the precious loot they could find. In that frenzied aftermath, Montezuma's high priests were lulled into believing that, for all Cortés's initial talk about God, the son, the Virgin, and the Holy Spirit, his true gods were gold and silver. They believed they would be able to carry on their faith—reshape it at most, with an extra god here, a trifling ritual there, as they themselves had done with faiths of the conquered. They did not imagine the ferocity with which the Spanish would eventually inflict their worship. Aztec gods might have been demanding, ravenous, fastidious, but the priests never assumed they were the *only* gods. The empire had been built on diversity, with the presumption that religion among its ever-expanding subjects might actually be a matter of choice.

As time wore on, the Aztec priests understood that the Spaniards and their marauding cohort, the Tlaxcalans, would kill, maim, and destroy whatever stood between them and their supremacy. They also deduced that, as holy men, they stood a good chance of surviving. Given the conquerors' one-track minds about "the yellow metal and the white" and Spain's palpable disgust with human sacrifice, the priests were reasonably sure they weren't going to be butchered in rituals. Somehow, despite the mayhem that was occurring around them daily, they assumed that the faith itself would be safe. Especially since their own Supreme Creator—Ometeotl, Life Giver—did not appear to be all that different from the conquistadors' *Dios*. A cross here, a shrine there, did not necessarily mean that their fundamental beliefs, on which the very business of life rested, were in peril. They were soon disabused of that notion.

In 1524, after three years of decimating disease, rampant butchery, and wholesale pillage, twelve Franciscan monks arrived from Spain to do what Cortés in all his pugnacity had not: replace the Aztec priests and transform the pagan masses into Christian believers. By then, it was growing increasingly clear to the Mexicans that the Spaniards would not tolerate the old ways. On the contrary: they had stripped their temples, burned their idols, killed and enslaved thousands. They would now raze their culture to the ground, weed out the doubters, and erect crosses and virgins on their most holy of grounds.

The little band of Franciscans entrusted with the formidable task of evangelizing an entire civilization walked the full distance—two hundred miles of sand, silt, and volcanic rock—from Veracruz to Mexico City. History would remember them as "the Twelve" and, indeed, theirs was a deliberate number, meant to echo the Twelve Apostles who had carried Christ's Gospel to a wider world. Unshaven, exhausted after a month at sea, shuffling through the unfamiliar terrain in their battered sandals and tattered robes, the priests looked like a sorry lot, and the Indians who gathered to watch them pass whispered *"motolinia"*—the Nahuatl word for "beggars"—which one of the Spaniards overheard and eventually adopted as his name. From that day forward the Franciscan was simply known as Motolinía, the "poor one." When the shabby little delegation finally trooped into the capital, the Mexicans were stunned to see Cortés and his henchmen rush to greet them, fall to their knees, and kiss the hems of their mud-crusted habits. And yet, the Indians had witnessed so much that was strange and bewildering by now: their great metropolis was in the tumult of unimaginable change. The destruction of their physical world was evident everywhere. What they had not factored entirely was that, with the advent of twelve humble men, the last shred of their civilization would be taken from them. The spiritual conquest of Mexico had begun.

*   *   *

We would do well at this point in the crusade to recall the state of the Catholic enterprise at the time of "Discovery." Pope Alexander VI, as rapacious in his appetites as in his worldly ambitions, needed money; the entire Church was an institution in turmoil. Europe itself was in flux. It was certainly far less stable, far less unified as an economy or society than the ruling cultures of Mesoamerica or the Andes, where religion had served as a great integrating force. As one historian put it, Europe had become dangerously off kilter, contentious, a time bomb of animus. Its religion had not done the job of forging a sense of political purpose or fiscal unity, as the Aztec and Inca spiritual systems had done. Christianity hadn't been born to do those things. But what it had been born to do went seriously off track a millennium and a half into its history.

By the beginning of the sixteenth century, instead of dedicating itself to the salvation of souls, the Church was wallowing in a mire of corruption, using believers for rank financial gain. Pope Leo X, who presided over the Church at precisely the time when Cortés was cutting a bold path into the Yucatán, had been selling two thousand church offices every year for the round sum of 500,000 ducats ($100 million today), an astounding figure, given that the entire accumulated wealth of the richest nobleman in Europe was worth a fraction of that. With the annual income from those offices, the newly established officials paid their toadies a pittance to handle spiritual tasks while they raised money for Rome and helped themselves to the difference. Violations multiplied. The archbishop of Mainz, Germany, in grievous debt because he was funding a gaggle of mistresses, tried to buy a second archbishopric from Pope Leo in order to augment his income. To raise the money, he ordered a Dominican friar to hawk indulgences: certificates that assured a buyer that his sins—and their corresponding punishments—would be reduced in the afterlife. The friar, keen to please his archbishop, set out with a clever jingle: "As soon as the gold in the basin rings / Right then the soul to heaven springs." The faithful, eager to save their souls and buy free passage to heaven, were all too willing to pay the archbishop his fee.

The Catholic Church had become a bureaucracy, a sales operation, a vast financial network. Its goal, rather than shepherd the meek and poor, was its very own glorification. The pontiffs, each in turn, were obliged to generate the prodigious river of gold and silver it took to exalt the faith and maintain Catholicism's primacy. In 1506 they began erecting a monument that would lend full expression to their grandeur: Saint Peter's Basilica in Rome. A decade later, in 1517, a voice would rise up to decry the excesses. Enraged by the blatant venality on show, a young German monk from a small mining town compiled a document he called "Ninety-Five Theses" and nailed it to the chapel door of the University of Wittenberg. In it, he condemned the Church's practice of selling offices and indulgences to enrich itself.

Within two months, Martin Luther's accusations were circulating in capitals throughout Europe, aided by a burgeoning proliferation of printing presses. The schism could hardly have happened without Gutenberg's invention. To Rome's alarm, Luther's complaints were convincing princes and commoners alike to abandon Catholicism and join a new, Protestant church. By 1524, as twelve ragtag Franciscans wended their way from Veracruz to Mexico City, the rebellious spirit of the Reformation was producing a dramatic change of heart in Northern Europe, threatening Catholic preeminence. The Church—and its greatest champion, Spain—rallied to defend the faith. Both needed Cortés to score a victory that would buy Catholic ascendancy, ensure Spain's economic survival, and tighten the religion's grip on the Old World. Rather than stamp out the corruption that had contaminated the Church for decades, however, the Reformation had the opposite effect on the scrappy religious orders in the New World: greed grew even deeper roots. If evangelism was the key to conquest, it was also the key to territorial control. All the edicts and correctives Spain might put in place were now but distant rumblings to those forging a new frontier, marching to a different tune. The ring of gold was the only sound that mattered.

Ironically enough, to many of the religious who were swept into the enterprise, the New World represented a chance for the faith to remake itself, return to its roots—an opportunity to gather a tabula rasa of fresh souls and start the Christian process all over again. But if the evangelization of the Americas was ever meant to be a happy harvest of believers, history quickly overtook that plan. There was a fortune to be had, a purse on offer. Soon after the arrival of the Franciscan delegation, the conquistadors established a Christianizing routine—an armed spiritual conquest—that would be marshaled henceforward throughout the hemisphere.

It began with the *requerimiento*, the statement read out to villagers, declaring Spain's divinely ordained right to appropriate any territory of the New World, subjugate and enslave its inhabitants, and, if necessary, wage war and kill. In 1513, just as Michelangelo's magnificent fresco of the creation on the ceiling of the Sistine Chapel was shown for the first time—just as Bartolomé de las Casas was coming to the conclusion that three million Indians had already died in the conquest, and just as Vasco Núñez de Balboa expanded the scope of the invasion by reaching the Pacific coast—the Spanish Crown decided something needed to be done about the dying. It had assumed, and few argued against it, that lands inhabited by a lesser race belonged to no one. The New World had been there for the taking. Only a full twenty years into the conquest did the question about natives' rights arise.

To assuage the potential fallout, the Crown resolved that in all future sorties, conquistadors were to read out a pronunciamento allowing Indians to surrender peacefully to Christ and Spain, thereby absolving Spain of any crimes of violence. The *requerimiento* prefaced every attack, and it began with a seemingly innocuous disquisition on all the Catholic angels and holymen, including Saint James and Saint Peter, but it ended with an unmistakable threat: "If you do not comply—if you pit yourself against me—I swear that with God's help I shall engage all my powers against you, make war on you wherever and however I can, subject you to the yoke, force you to obey the Church and his Highness, and I will take you, your women, and your children and make you all slaves to sell or dispose of as his Highness sees fit, and I will take all that you own, and inflict every ill and possible harm."

Shouted from great distances—at times only mumbled—the declaration was little more than noise to the Indians who heard it, incomprehensible babble, hardly distinguishable from the barking of dogs. Some came to the cross peacefully; many resisted vehemently. In the end, in the face of guns, cannon, horses, and a raging disease, field after field fell to the soldiers of Jesus.

THE CONQUEST OF THE INDIAN SOUL

*I find only one fault, o most Christian of kings, with your Indies. And it
is that they are populated by vile people, stained and suspect.*
                                        —Gaspar Pérez de Villagra, 1610

The vanquished were assigned directly to *encomiendas*: land entrusted to
conquistadors, officials, or priests. Confused, disoriented, afraid—often
separated from their children and families—they were counted, herded,
given Spanish names, told through halting translations that they belonged
to a distant god, a distant king. Their owners, the *encomenderos*, were
now free to demand tributes, or taxes, from them: these could be paid
in labor or gold, and, in return, Indians were promised protection and a
Christian hereafter. In practice, however, little was given. The *encomiendas* were outright land grabs. Spaniards simply appropriated whole territories, enslaved any and all who lived on them, hunted down fugitives,
and forced their captives to work their mines in treacherous, often fatal
conditions, with no attention to spiritual matters. "In the nine years of
his government of this island," one friar said of the royal governor of the
West Indies, "he was no more interested in the indoctrination and salvation of the Indians than if they were sticks and stones, or cats and dogs."
And yet the governor had been dispatched precisely to correct the egregious injustices against Indians meted out under Columbus. Abuses were
so dire—death and disease so rampant—that the priests who accompanied the conquistadors began to send word back that, for all the high-
flown claims about curbing abuses and spreading the gospel of Christ, the
system of subjugation had grown more brutal, more inhumane.

Bartolomé de las Casas had not been raised to see the conquest from
an Indian point of view. On the contrary. His father, a merchant who
had joined Columbus's second voyage in hopes of bettering his lot, surprised his young son by returning with a slave as a souvenir. The Indian
Juanico, who was promptly put in the service of Bartolomé, had been
a gift from none other than Columbus. A few years later, in 1501, Bartolomé joined the priesthood as a sweet-faced novice of eighteen and
sailed to Hispaniola with his father. We know little about his first years

there, except that the Church had not quite taken root. There was no established path for a young cleric. Like everyone else, he was expected to help establish a colony, hunt slaves, and contribute to the budding economy.

A few years later, Bartolomé made a brief visit to Rome and was ordained as a Dominican friar before he returned, making him the first priest to preach his inaugural mass in the Americas. Granted his own *encomienda* and a wealth of slaves, he became a prosperous plantation owner, often finding himself party to slave raids against the Taíno to augment the ever-dwindling workforce. So entrenched was he in the slave economy that a flock of Dominican priests who arrived some years later, denied him—and all slaveowners, for that matter—the right to confession. One of the Dominicans, appalled by the heartlessness he was witnessing, the unbridled disease, scolded his fellow Spaniards in a fiery Christmas sermon: "Tell me by what right, what writ of justice, do you hold these Indians in such cruel and horrible servitude?" the priest shouted, red faced. "On what authority have you waged such despicable wars against these peaceful and meek people . . . to work them to death, kill them outright, in order to wrest and amass your daily gold?" In the presence of none other than Christopher Columbus's son Diego, the Dominican railed on and on, accusing all Spaniards in that little church of having lost every shred of conscience they'd ever had—that they were blind, steeped in sin, headed perilously for hellfire.

At first, Las Casas was taken aback by those accusations and defended the conquistadors. After all, the expeditions had been charged with bringing the Lord's Gospel to this wild frontier, and popes and kings had blessed the enterprise. But before long, the friar found himself contemplating the Dominican's fevered words. In 1513, just as the *requerimiento* was issued, he set out on the expedition to conquer Cuba along with Cortés, Diego Velázquez, Pánfilo de Narváez, and others who would eventually bring the island's Taíno population to virtual extinction. It was there as the expedition's chaplain, witnessing the wanton brutality, the serial burnings at the stake, the horrifying atrocities, the butchering of thousands—"without provocation or cause"—that Las Casas began to doubt Spain's civilizing mission. Rewarded for his part in the conquest with a gold mine in Cuba, even more slaves, and a picturesque *encomienda* overlooking the Arimao River, he settled into the quiet life of a hacienda owner, but he couldn't help weighing the contradictions between his religious vows and the inhumanities he had witnessed.

He had been present at the massacre of Caonao. He had seen the Indians come forward with baskets of bread and fish even as the conquistadors sharpened their swords on stone. That day, seven thousand were killed, most of them as sport—disemboweled, maimed, mauled—fleeing with their innards in their hands. He had watched a circle of his comrades send a dog against a helpless Indian and roar with merriment as he screamed for mercy, gutted before their eyes. He had looked on as slaves were forced to march 250 miles to mine gold. Whipped to work harder, they either died on their way home, or arrived—damaged and undernourished—unable to consummate their marriages. Babies were born stunted, if they were born at all. Men infected their villages with pox. The race wasted away, unable to meet the quotas.

Within a year, Las Casas was converted, radicalized, surprising his fellow haciendados by announcing that he would henceforward dedicate himself to the welfare of the conquered. The transformation was swift, startling: in blazing, indignant sermons and ferocious dispatches to the corridors of power in Valladolid, he excoriated his countrymen for the cruelties of the slave hunt and the rigors of the *encomienda*. He vowed to bring an end to their crimes. As for the claim that Spain was bringing the Christian religion to a profane and unruly world, Las Casas answered that if war were truly necessary to convert Indians, it would be more Christian to leave them alone.

If no one in the colonies was listening, at least the Church began to pay attention. For his forceful, unflagging advocacy, the Church eventually proclaimed Las Casas Protector of the Indians. For fifteen more years, he made a Herculean effort to travel to as many outposts as he could, preaching his message of leniency for the Mayans, the Nahua, the Inca, the Taíno—wherever conquistadors had raised crosses of conquest. He took his missionary work to the coast of Venezuela, where he attempted an experiment to convert natives by peaceful means. Those efforts failed, largely because Spaniards were so hostile to them; and because the new landowners—who had the most to lose—had begun to proclaim him mad, freakish, a demon in the flesh. All the same, he carried on, pledging himself to the Dominican order, which had inspired his change of heart in the first place. His travels took him to Mexico, Guatemala, Panama, Nicaragua, and then back to Mexico, where he narrowly escaped assassination. His work did not go unheeded: as a result of his petitions, a landmark papal bull was issued, proclaiming the Indian a man like any other, capable of Christianization. Not everyone was convinced.

If only by virtue of unflagging persistence, the friar eventually won his young king's ear. King Carlos I, Holy Roman emperor and impressionable young man of nineteen, found Las Casas's accounts of the atrocities compelling, horrifying. As the brash, quick-tempered priest with the piercing eyes recounted the barbarities, the adolescent king couldn't help but empathize. The slave trade that had flowed from Africa to Europe long before his reign had made house servants of its black captives—chambermaids, cooks, stable boys, valets—it had not necessarily reduced them to punishing, homicidal labor. This brutality, this carnage, was something new, altogether vile. Even as he grew older, amassing the riches and power that New World silver bestowed on him, King Carlos never stopped listening to the wiry, indefatigable priest.

There was good reason to listen. The atrocities had only multiplied since the deaths of King Carlos's grandparents Ferdinand and Isabella. With the colonization of Mexico and Peru, the genocide along the Río de la Plata, the bloodletting in the highlands of Bogotá—the growing consolidation of Spanish power across the hemisphere—Indians were dying off in alarming numbers. The decimation was evident everywhere: in the Caribbean, the isthmus, Mesoamerica, the Andes. The indigenous had fought back valiantly and given as much as they got; they had not succumbed as abjectly as some chroniclers have claimed. But there was no denying the calculus: population losses were so dire that another massive plunder, the Atlantic slave trade, was soon put into place to offset the shortage of laborers. Las Casas himself, in a moment of desperation, had suggested it. The shipping magnates of Europe's great nautical powers—Portugal, England, Holland—now leapt into that market with entrepreneurial gusto. Millions of black Africans were rounded up, shoved into the holds of ships, and sent off to die en route or labor in a cruel New World. Five million would be sent to Brazil; almost one and a half million to Spanish America. The mathematics couldn't have been clearer: Europe was growing rich on the backs of dead Indians, the commerce of black flesh, the pumped-up exploitation of the Indies, and an ever-expanding demand for silver and gold.

A priest called it all into question. Somehow Las Casas had managed to enter—physically, mentally, spiritually—the Indian experience, to see the onslaught as they did. As impossible as it was for a European to fully comprehend the indigenous world view, he had studied it as few others had, and his crisis of conscience went on to unleash a tempest of hostilities. In the New World, Las Casas was reviled by the *encomenderos*, the landed rich, the influential traders, the powerful conquistadors whose profits depended on a slave economy. Ironically, even Motolinía, one of the Twelve Apostles of Mexico—a ragtag Franciscan who had gone on to be named guardian of the Convent of San Francisco—became one of Las Casas's fiercest critics, demanding that his *Brief History of the Destruction of the Indies* be censored and the Dominican locked up in a monastery where he could do the ongoing conquest no further harm. They called Las Casas an Indian lover, an Indian puppet, a traitor to his race: "a grievous man, restless, importunate, turbulent, injurious, and prejudicial." In time, he become known as the author of the "Black Legend," the damning, exaggerated notion that Spain was more cruel and hateful than any other European nation marauding the Southern Hemisphere for mammon and slaves. The English, French, and Dutch, especially— including adherents of Lutheranism—latched on to the "Black Legend" and promoted it eagerly in a campaign to smear Spain, topple its vast global power, and malign Spaniards as a sadistic race and Catholicism as a corrupt religion.

By then, the debate on whether Indians were human or beasts of burden was raging in Europe, argued by philosophers, clerics, and lawmakers alike. Were the inhabitants of the New World even worth the arduous effort of Christianization? Could you physically force a lower race of man to join the higher realms of the spirit? In the midst of this furious war of words, King Carlos decided to suspend all future conquests until such questions were settled. Toward that end, he convened a conference in Valladolid's Colegio de San Gregorio, a glorious fifteenth-century triumph of stone, carved—absurdly enough—with statues of wild-eyed, hirsute beast-men cowering under fair-faced knights wielding swords and shields. It was there in those vaulted halls that Las Casas vied in long, spirited debates against Juan Ginés de Sepúlveda, the Crown's official historian, a widely respected scholar and proponent of Aristotle's theory of natural slavery. According to Aristotle's *Politics*, especially as most colonial powers chose to interpret it, some races by virtue of superior intellect were born to rule, while others, of crude, limited powers of reason, were fit only to serve them.

Sepúlveda had just produced a treatise in which he argued that war against the peoples of the New World was perfectly justified because they practiced abominable acts of cannibalism and human sacrifice. Following that logic, if Spain went to war against the defilers and won, it had every right—according to rules of combat—to enslave them. Sepúlveda went on to say that it was then incumbent on the Spanish Church, as an institution sworn to evangelization, to impose Christianity forcibly on those conquered pagans: to resort to the law of *compelle intrare*, a grotesquely distorted interpretation of Jesus's words, "compel people to come in that my house may be filled," by which Spain argued that it was perfectly justified in compelling heathen to "come in," accept the faith, and believe. Hadn't the fiendish Aztecs sacrificed twenty thousand souls a year, displaying their monstrous trophies on colossal racks? Hadn't the wicked Incas reveled in incest? Hadn't the diabolical Caribs roasted their enemies in big clay pots and feasted ghoulishly on their bones? And all that *before* the arrival of the Spaniards? At the core of Sepúlveda's conviction, naturally, was that a Spaniard was superior to an Indian—culturally, intellectually, corporally—and that though an Indian might not be a monkey, exactly, he was certainly a primate of an inferior order. As one contemporary historian comments: all this from a man who had never set eyes on the race.

But King Carlos listened to the priest, not the Aristotelean. In 1542 the monarch issued the New Laws of the Indies, forbidding all further enslavement in the New World and condemning the *encomienda* to extinction. The laws had a certain currency in Spain—priests and politicians commended them—and many a Spaniard congratulated the bright-eyed Dominican for the victory. But they had no adherents to speak of in the American colonies. There, every rung of the colonial hierarchy rose up to claim that the laws would undermine their livelihoods: the wealthy would be stripped of their riches; the poor, deprived of the opportunity to become rich. In Mexico, the emissary who was sent to put the king's laws into effect was eventually persuaded not to publish them at all. In Peru, when the viceroy attempted to enforce the laws, he was pursued, arrested, and beheaded by Francisco Pizarro's brother Gonzalo. When King Carlos made Las Casas the bishop of Chiapas, which included areas of Guatemala as well as southern Mexico, the municipal council of Guatemala—responsible for a colossal trade in indigo—wrote an urgent, terrified letter to the king, saying, "we are as disturbed as if the public executioner had been sent to cut off our heads." Even as King Carlos congratulated himself for his enlightened judgment, the priest had become a pariah, and the New Laws were having no effect on the very people they were meant to relieve. These were fleeting victories, worth only the paper on which they were printed. Conquistadors ignored them, landowners laughed them off—finding it easy to scoff at legislation that was signed and stamped thousands of miles away.

In the end, what was a king to do? The debate he had conjured in Valladolid had called into question the very legitimacy of Spain's rule in the Indies. King Carlos was not about to do what the full logic of his laws demanded: withdraw the abusive conquistadors, surrender his silver to Europe's circling vultures, and declare the conquest of the New World null and void. The only hope was to hasten the evangelization, make the Indians—and the new generations of mestizos that had been born in the intervening half century—more Catholic, more Spanish. But somehow for the king, the whole question trailed off in a slew of personal misfortunes. His wife had given birth to a stillborn son; two weeks later, she died, leaving him grief stricken, hardly able to function at all. Plagued by epileptic attacks, gout, and an aching jaw, he began to abdicate his empire piece by piece.

When King Carlos relinquished all power and his son, Philip II, took the throne in 1556, the rich conquistadors of Peru, including the silver barons of Potosí, lobbied furiously with the new king to keep their *encomiendas* into perpetuity so that their considerable wealth could pass down from son to son for the rest of time. They offered him an exorbitant bribe—nine million ducats, which would have paid off Spain's annual deficit for almost a decade—and Philip was sorely tempted. His father had left him a staggering debt and, traveling to London to wed Queen Mary I of England in hopes of revitalizing England's Catholic Church, Philip had wildly escalated his prodigal habits. He ordered the Council of the Indies to accept the conquistadors' offer right away. Las Casas, who had been battling to abolish the system of *encomiendas*, was outraged when he heard of it. The hyperindustrious priest set about persuading his allies as well as Peru's Indians to match the sum with a counteroffer, which they did, however empty the gesture might have seemed.

But eventually the Spanish colonial bureaucracy brought the whole business to a grinding halt. Peru's first conquistadors were ensured their riches into perpetuity, a few of the landowners were allowed to retain theirs during their lifetimes, and the rest had to revert all property to the Crown. The descendants of the Incas, who had struggled beneath the colonial boot for more than a generation now, were given little hope that their progeny would ever escape the cycle of exploitation. "We who were once brave and noble," one lamented, "are no more than pitiful servants now, *yanakunas*." So it was that the business of righting wrongs with the Indians was left entirely to a growing circle of mendicant priests, pledged to poverty, who knew all too well that the mission to evangelize had not fared well in Cortés's and Pizarro's hands. For all the bellowing of saints' names as the conquistadors had charged into villages—for all the planting of crosses atop the sacred *huacas*—the sword was never going to bring the Indians to Jesus.

A MISSIONARY'S WORK

With the faith, the scourge of God came into the country.

—*Jesuit Relations*, 1653

Bringing the Indians to Jesus was much on Xavier Albó's mind as he made his way through the two-year novitiate. It seemed to him that a missionary's work should be the other way around: Shouldn't a priest be bringing himself to the Indians? Wasn't a missionary's work to serve rather than to impose? He couldn't shake the thought that an entire mythology of inferiority had been inflicted on the race he had been sent to engage. The psychological offensive was still at work, fruit of a deep racial bigotry. Somewhere along the way, the assumption had been made that to truly conquer, a victor needed to disgrace and demoralize, make his subject believe in his own worthlessness. As one angry priest had shouted at his congregation five hundred years before: if the indigenous were a beleaguered, exhausted race, perhaps it was because their conquerors had not been practitioners of true Christian grace. "What care have you ever given to revealing God the creator in a way that they might understand the logic of baptism, of hearing mass, of consecrating holy days in His name?" the man had said. "Perhaps you think they are devoid of rational souls? Are you not obliged as Christians to love them as you love yourself?"

Xavier believed without a doubt that the Bolivian Indians he had come to know—the meek as well as the bold—often had higher spiritual capacities, sharper intelligences, and more natural abilities than their white masters recognized. But they'd had scant opportunities to flourish.

He became acutely aware that he was entering a cleft society, an apartheid nation. The whites and near-whites in the cities, all Spanish speakers, were thriving. The Indians and darker citizens in the countryside, the Quechua speakers, were desperately poor. The bilingual mestizos in the cities often hid their fluency in Quechua, ashamed to claim their indigenous roots. A sharp racial and linguistic divide separated the two Bolivias, and the composite wasn't working well. There was much a fledgling priest might do for the 62 percent pushed into the margins: the miners who needed justice, the campesinos who needed education, the mothers who needed relief, the children who needed doctors, the villages that needed water. Who was going to meet those needs if not the servants of God? Governments seemed to have abdicated all responsibility.

Arriving a few months after the agrarian revolution, Xavier could not have known about Bolivia's upheavals, its devastating losses to Paraguay in the Chaco War (1932–1935), or its new Socialist president, but he could sense an air of possibility in those who made the bread, swept the roads, tended the pigs. Cloistered from the world at large, without the benefit of any orientation or access to newspapers, he had to gather evidence from what he could see. Could it be that the country was poised on the brink of change? It was a daring thought, but Xavier imagined himself nudging that process along, winning the poor some measure of dignity, doing work that could truly be called Christian. To that end, he decided to commit himself body and soul to learning Quechua, the ancient language of the Andes. Even as he studied the fundamental lessons of priesthood, he pored over the caprices of Quechua grammar, its chip-chop phonology, its singular world view. By the time two years were done, the spiritual exercises of Jesuit founder Saint Ignatius learned, his vows of poverty, chastity, and obedience taken, and his novitiate over, he had a solid, working knowledge of the tongue.

Albó had a talent for languages, and his Jesuit teachers were keenly aware of it. Over the years, he had acquired a rudimentary command of Latin, French, Italian, English. At ease in the world—an outgoing boy with an impish streak, a frank tongue, and an adventurous heart— languages came easily to him. It was the liturgical curriculum, the rigors of history and philosophy, that required application. And yet for all the intensity of the classroom and imposed insularity of his group, he managed to have moments of collegial joy. His fellow novitiates were Catalan and Bolivian youths—the Catalans, from families of modest means; the Bolivians, from families with lavish haciendas. There was a spirited boy from Barcelona who had joined the Society of Jesus in order to travel the world; in time, he would leave the order to marry a Bolivian woman. There was the elegant Bolivian from an illustrious mining family, a descendant of the millionaire moguls of Potosí, whose Quechua was perfectly fluent because he had been raised by an Indian nanny. The teachers were no less fascinating—the old Jesuit astronomer, for instance, who stored his lenses in toilet paper tubes, fussed over celestial maps, and stared into the night sky, never quite trusting that scientists understood that radiant splendor. There were the taciturn *serranos*, mountain people who came and went, doubting the claims that Bolivia was entering a better world—they had heard it all too many times before. There were the señoras in wide skirts and bowler hats who sold *chicha*, chatted with Xavier amiably, and giggled when he made mistakes and unwittingly uttered salty language. His love for Bolivians came in such fleeting glimpses; it was electrifying, profound, immediate. He never lost the feeling that Bolivia was the land he had been destined to embrace; the Indians, his true people.

After two years, the Jesuit missions decided to send him to Ecuador for the next step in his formation. Understanding that surrender itself was part of a priest's curriculum, Xavier serenely gathered up his few worldly possessions—a scattering of clothes, a family prayerbook, a stack of notebooks with rows and rows of notations in a tidy hand—and boarded a puffing, squealing iron behemoth bound for Quito. He did not know it yet, but the pages tucked under his arm represented the rudiments of his first book, a Quechua primer.

Ecuador surprised him: a twentieth-century nation locked in a time warp, its collective head immersed in the colonial past. Seeing Indians in and around Quito confined to lives of servitude and hard labor, he began to understand the revolution that was taking place in Bolivia. Quechua was Ecuador's language, too, a lingua franca throughout these parts, given that the Inca Empire had exercised a long reach and an abiding grip. But the Inca pluck, that essential pride, that singular *pundonor*—to never lie, never steal, never be idle—had all but drained from the indigenous here. They didn't seem to know the inherent spirit they might reignite, the age-old power they had lost. All the same, Xavier continued his linguistic work, seeking out those who might teach him more, befriending the random passerby who might add to his mounting fluency. As he met more people—the rich along with the poor—he never lost the feeling that he was abroad in a land of the cowed: human casualties of five hundred years of domination. Traveling down the coast to Piura and Lima, he found the same doomed resignation in the indigenous and mixed-race *cholos* of Peru.

His observations couldn't have been more accurate. Ecuador, like Peru, was in the midst of a stern political backlash in the 1950s. The Communist wave that had swept the hemisphere had found a stunning corrective in both countries: in Ecuador, President José María Velasco had imposed a strict reactionary agenda; in Peru, General Manuel Odría was conducting an all-out military campaign against anyone who questioned the legitimacy of white rule. Indeed, throughout Latin America, a fierce campaign to stamp out Communism was afoot, supported by the United States and bolstered mightily by the ruling white Creole class. Xavier may have arrived at a transformative time for Bolivia, but the old-style oppression was all too evident in Bolivia's neighbors. From

1950 to 1966, fourteen governments were violently overthrown as dictatorial rule was forced on more than half of Latin America's population. Intrigued by the struggle between Right and Left—the haves and have-nots—Xavier began a systematic study of the philosophy of Latin American revolutionaries, particularly the founder of the Ecuadoran Communist Party, Manuel Agustín Aguirre. Unlike the priests who had marched with conquistadors, he found himself aligning with those who had no power at all. Nor was this unusual for a "soldier of God." The Jesuits had a long history of bucking power in Latin America.

As a neophyte, Xavier now entered the next stage of the fifteen years he would dedicate to preparing to serve the Society of Jesus. He would spend three years in Quito, studying philosophy, metaphysics, cosmology, anthropology, epistemology—all in Latin. A few of the subjects—physics, for example, or the history of philosophy—which required a deeper comprehension or a more ample canvas for argument, would be conducted in Spanish. If the education of a Jesuit was considered the most stringent in the Catholic clergy, there was a reason why. Its contours had been established four centuries earlier by the soldier Ignatius of Loyola—Basque founder of the "soldiers of God"—and little had changed since its inception.

Even as Columbus was scouring the Caribbean, hunting slaves, Ignatius had been at war in Europe, serving in Ferdinand and Isabella's army. Wounded when a cannonball shattered his legs, the nobleman was sent home to his estate in Loyola, where he experienced a vision that called him to religious life. That vision, embraced by the pope and seconded by the Spanish Crown, was to create an army of tough Christians, men prepared in the rigors of every academic discipline so that they might be sent anywhere in the world, ready to spread the word of Christ in the most Spartan of conditions. The training would be long and arduous, meant to test the loyalty, resilience, ingenuity, and endurance of any would-be warrior. Ignatius's idea couldn't have come at a more propitious time for Spain. There was a New World to Christianize, and militant Christians were needed to bring a hemisphere of Indians to heel.

But the Jesuits often found themselves warring on the side of the Indians. In the late sixteenth century, almost exactly four hundred years before Xavier pledged himself to the order, an eleven-year-old boy in the tiny Spanish town of Medina had taken the Jesuit pledge, eventually joining its forces in Peru and Mexico. He was José de Acosta, a liberal-minded priest who refused to accept that indigenous religions were little more than barbarian devil worship. Acosta argued that Indians inhabited another world of thought and knew God by the light of natural reason. He was vehemently opposed to the clean-slate strategy of Christianization, evangelism as practiced by conquistadors: the notion that you could win souls by smashing idols and razing temples, baptism by blood and fire. "To eradicate idolatry by force before Indians have spontaneously received the Gospel," he claimed, "has always seemed to me, as it has to other very wise and sober men, to close, lock and bar the door of the Gospel to those outside, rather than open it." Acosta wanted Jesuits to take a different tack: evangelize little by little, not by leaps and bounds but by small steps, gathering Indians together, learning from them, spreading the word of God by example. To that end, he established schools and universities for the native population throughout Peru, much to the consternation of the viceroy.

Throughout the 1500s and 1600s, Jesuits who hewed to Acosta's principles organized vast, economically successful *reducciones*—isolated settlements—of Indians in the Andes, Brazil, and the vast territory that reached from Argentina to Peru, known as Paraguay. The Crown approved heartily, on the assumption that these far-flung communities would hold Spain's frontiers against Portuguese expansion. The Jesuits, on the other hand, assumed these remote settlements would keep tribes safe and offer them full, productive lives, apart from the spoliations of colonial rule. The missions became sanctuaries from conquest, havens where priests operated as entrepreneurs, overseeing vast fields of corn or cotton, ranches of pigs and cattle; where the Guaraní or the Yaqui or the Amazon tribes learned to read books and play music; where they learned to worship the Christian God; where they could be safe from the marauding Portuguese paramilitaries—the *bandeirantes*—and their brutal slave raids. In the immense territory that surrounds the Río de la Plata, by the end of the seventeenth century, more than half the Indian population lived and worked on Jesuit lands.

But too much success proved to be the Jesuits' undoing. Over the course of 150 years, their missions became such thriving businesses that the Crown decided they were a competing economy—a state within a state—that needed to be stopped, ejected from the Americas entirely. On February 27, 1767, King Carlos III expelled the Jesuits from all Spanish territories. Priests were swiftly summoned to ports, herded on ships, sent home. Their buildings were confiscated, their settlements stripped of all possessions, their ranks interrogated for any property they still might hold. Eventually the pope declared the Society of Jesus "forever extinguished and silenced." Thousands of destitute priests—instantly transformed into pariahs—roamed Europe seeking refuge. The Indians who had inhabited their reductions in the wilds of South and Central America dispersed into jungle and mountain, dazed, disoriented, left to the caprices of circumstance. Many were prey to slavers and lubricious landlords who swept in to raid the missions and take advantage of the governing void. Whole populations were abducted and sold into the Brazilian slave markets. Corpses hung from trees in the missions. Many Indians simply slipped into the rain forests and disappeared. The violins, the flutes, the books, the libraries, the plows were all tossed into ovens, cooked down, and made into gunpowder cartridges. Those who persevered and remained, hoping for miraculous regeneration, grew ill, dying in far greater numbers than births could replace them.

Such was the grim history that Xavier absorbed, alongside knottier conundrums of philosophy and science. But the real lesson came later, when he learned about the brotherhood's resilience: almost fifty years after it was disbanded, the Jesuit order was restored to its former status in 1814. Like a dead plant that has left behind a strong seed, its new generation grew exuberantly, surpassing all former numbers and establishing prestigious universities throughout the Americas. By the time Xavier finished his studies in Ecuador in the late 1950s, it was a global enterprise. The black cassocks had proliferated, especially in the Southern Hemisphere, and the ranks of the Society of Jesus—the "pope's black guard," as they became known in Protestant Europe—peaked, reaching record numbers in missions around the world. In Latin America, where the political climate was growing increasingly volatile and the time bomb of oppression threatened to explode yet again, the missions took up the work for which they were renowned hundreds of years before: the welfare of the dispossessed. Xavier would become one of its leaders.

PREACHING THE GOSPEL AMONG BARBARIANS

Don't you understand that all that these friars say is lies? Our fathers,
our grandfathers—did they know these monks?
—Andrés Mixcoatl to the people of Metepec, 1537

It is generally accepted that Columbus had no priest with him on his first voyage—a surprising assumption, given his claims that he was embarking on a holy voyage and Queen Isabella's understanding that he was attempting exactly that for Spain. Early scholars argued the question, refusing to believe that a devout Christian, as Columbus certainly was, would have set sail without a chaplain, even putting forth names—Fray Juan Pérez, Fray Pedro de Arenas, and others—as possibilities who *must* have accompanied him. But Columbus's journal, which meticulously cites many of his companions on that inaugural expedition, makes no mention of a clergyman, and it is difficult to believe that he wouldn't have memorialized his priest's name in that singular, sprawling hand of his. To cast even more doubt on those early claims, the chronologies and logistics suffer stark inconsistencies. The more likely conclusion is that Columbus had no priest on that first expeditionary voyage. It may be because he didn't suspect that his journey would take longer than six months—an important point, since Catholic navigators measured voyages according to Catholic obligations and, in the fifteenth century, it was the rule rather than the exception that believers take Holy Communion every six months or, at least, once a year. We have it on good authority that the entire expeditionary party went to confession and received communion before their ships skimmed away from the port of Palos on that windless August night in 1492. Entirely ignorant about the boundless unknown into which they were headed, they may have assumed that a priest was unnecessary on a voyage of a few months.

The record is crystal clear, however, when it comes to Cortés's first contact with Montezuma, or Pizarro's confrontation with Atahualpa, or Gonzalo Jiménez de Quesada's brash rout of the Muíscas in Bogotá. In every one of those cases—the most significant conquests of the New World—a priest was present at the creation, playing a critical role in the unfolding drama. Curiously enough, all three conquistadors were distant cousins, and all three lived by the binding principle of their time, in which war and religion—the sword and the stone—were part and parcel of a national identity. It was an era in which warriors and priests marched together, one in which popes themselves led armies against any and all who defied them. More urgently, perhaps, all three understood that the damning accusations of malfeasance levied against Columbus had been made by men of the cloth. Having a priest at one's side to bless a victory was a convenient foil against any protests the Crown might make.

Two priests were pivotal in Cortés's legendary conquest. The first was Gerónimo de Aguilar, the hapless Franciscan who had been shipwrecked on the Yucatán coast, wandered the savannas of Quintana Roo, was captured by the Mayans and enslaved for eight years, and then was found, by sheer serendipity, as Cortés made his way to the Aztec capital. Aguilar, hardly recognizable as a Spaniard—skin burned brown, head shaven like a slave's, beggared and filthy—made himself known to Cortés by mumbling a few words in Spanish and pulling an old Book of Hours from beneath his rotting blanket. Saved from the sacrificial slab to which he was surely bound had he stayed among the Mayans, Aguilar was immediately useful to Cortés by virtue of his familiarity with the local tongue. Eventually, along with Cortés's winsome Nahua lover, La Malinche, Aguilar would play a crucial role in the conquistador's negotiations with Montezuma.

Another priest, Gonzalo Guerrero, had survived the shipwreck with Aguilar. But Guerrero eventually went native, pledging loyalty to his Mayan captors and fighting fearlessly alongside them. Elevated to the status of chief—his ears and lower lip ceremonially slashed in two—he married a Mayan woman and fathered numerous children. Whereas Aguilar had obeyed his vows of celibacy and paid for that loyalty with his freedom, Guerrero had been rewarded by the Indians for abandoning his religion, his culture, his entire past. But now that the tables had turned, and six hundred Spanish soldiers were marching to Tenochtitlán with cannons, guns, and legions of allies, Guerrero was loath to reveal himself as a fallen Franciscan. He took to the forest, hiding his shame, only to emerge again to fight the Spaniards as they swept through Mexico, cementing their conquest.

The other priest who stood with Cortés was Bartolomé de Olmedo, and it is to him that Cortés owes many of his early victories. Olmedo was at heart a temperate man, a deeply thoughtful theologian. Time and again, he curbed the conquistador's more brutal instincts, urging him toward compassion. Cortés, a man of grand ambition and carnal inclinations—a politician of few scruples—was well aware that he needed someone like Olmedo to temper his wilder nature and shape his image at home. And yet Olmedo was no enlightened hero, inclined to see Indians as fellow men. He had lived much, seen much. A seasoned priest when he had arrived in Hispaniola, he had a mandate to Christianize what was left of the Taíno. Swept by chance into Cortés's capricious and illicit campaign to conquer Mexico, he won the conquistador's trust and was delegated to diplomatic tasks apart from his priestly obligations. He converted and baptized the slave La Malinche, enabling Cortés to consort freely with her. He baptized the first Christian women of Mexico so that soldiers might indulge in sex without fear that they were consorting with pagans. He was dispatched to mollify the shiploads of angry troops sent to castigate Cortés for flagrantly countermanding his orders. Olmedo was also responsible for teaching Montezuma the basic tenets of Christianity before the emperor was murdered and dispatched to his gods.

Most important, when Cortés's impulse was to hack the Tlaxcalans' idols to rubble, Olmedo counseled a gentler approach, insisting that Christianizing by force would only reap the whirlwind. There were better ways to introduce innocents to the teachings of Jesus, he insisted. He proved right. At first, the Tlaxcalans balked at the Christian God; they had no use for another deity or prophet. But with Olmedo's quiet persistence, they finally submitted to the cross. The significance of this cannot be overestimated. Without the support and military muscle of the Tlaxcalans—inveterate enemies of the Aztecs—the history of Spanish America would have come to an abrupt halt a few miles outside of Veracruz. Without the hordes of Christianized Indians who marched with Cortés against the Aztec capital, Spanish would not be spoken in Mexico today. And then, once Tenochtitlán was taken: without the easy conversion of the Nahuas, who were accustomed to adopting foreign gods, the conquest of more recalcitrant Chichimecas or Mayans would have proved impossible. By the time twelve weary, cadaverous, and scruffy Franciscans wandered into the heart of Montezuma's empire to be greeted by kneeling Spaniards, the way was wide open for the spiritual conquest of Mexico.

We have much evidence that Cortés, by nature pugilistic about imposing his religion, was hardly Christian in meting out his ambitions. He was strategic, cunning, inclined to breathtaking violence, as every triumphant conquistador proved to be. For all the giddy claims that Cortés was a consummate hero, a devout Christian—"a man of unfeigned piety, of the stuff that martyrs are made of," as a judge crowed to the king—there is equal documentation that he was a heartless tyrant. How does a legend that begins with the promise of salvation turn to rank killing for no apparent reason or provocation? The cowardice of Montezuma, the genius of Cortés, the predestined arrival of the fairer race—these are fantasies that have been conjured by generations of Spanish storytellers. The fact remains that there are pieces to this puzzle that continue to elude us—five centuries of carefully devised political narrative we will probably never deconstruct—and yet, no matter how we choose to interpret history, two indisputable facts stand witness at beginning and end: Cortés entered Tenochtitlán freely, welcomed in with his priest and his legions; and two years later, after much death and destruction, an empire was won.

For all his illiteracy and lack of sophistication—for all the humiliations that an illegitimate son of a nobleman had to endure—Pizarro had done well for himself, even before he undertook the expedition that would win him the laurels of history. He was wealthy. He was respected. And, having been on expeditions to Cartagena, Panama, and the Pacific with Balboa, he had been well schooled in how the Church might be employed in the wild bonanza that was La Conquista. He understood the moral ballast that a few good priests would provide in a full-tilt offensive against the fabled land of "Pirú." Even in the earliest days of that grand idea, as he sat in Panama and dreamed of a bold exploration south, he allied with the rich clergyman Hernando de Luque, whose guidance would become essential in Pizarro's dealings with the Crown. When King Carlos finally approved the expedition, Pizarro decided on a priest from his own family ranks for the actual voyage. This was not unusual; a preference for family partners when engaging in potentially profitable ventures had become something of an instinct in the conquistadors. In the frenzied quest for riches and glory, only a brother or sworn comrade could be trusted—the temptations for mutiny or larceny were so great. Indeed, Pizarro would eventually fall out with his second associate, Diego de Almagro, over the jurisdiction of gold-rich Cuzco, and the Viejo Capitán (as Pizarro was called) would eventually order Almagro's execution. The passions and acrimonies provoked by this rash act led Almagro's followers to wreak revenge on Pizarro years later when they surprised the old governor in his palace and drove a sword through his throat.

Pizarro thought he was avoiding such a fate by populating his expedition with kin: three half brothers—Juan, Gonzalo, Hernando—two of whom, like him, were illegitimate sons of his father; and a number of cousins. One of these was Vicente de Valverde, a nobleman turned Dominican priest who was distantly related to Pizarro and marched with him to Cajamarca for the fateful meeting with Atahualpa. The rest of the story is well known: it was Valverde who shook a cross at the royal Inca and read aloud to him from his breviary, insisting that his Christian God was superior to the Indian's and that worshiping the sun was foolish. When Atahualpa took the priest's book in his hands, turned it over, and threw it to the ground, Valverde called on his cousin to avenge the blasphemy. Pizarro had always had it in mind to attack and capture the Inca emperor, but there was nothing so effective as having a priest order it. It was, as the Church would largely become throughout the Spanish colonies, a felicitous cooperation between religion and power.

That marriage of sword and stone had become part and parcel of a national character. Just as Castile's or Aragon's crusades against the infidels had forged a warrior race, trained and tested in crucibles of violence, the crusades had also implanted a blatantly militant religiosity. The Spaniards who undertook the feat of conquering the New World were endowed with keen capacities for courage, fatalism, stoicism, arrogance, and *pundonor*; they were also deeply convinced of their own Christian exceptionalism. They wielded the word of Jesus as a banner; as symbol and lodestar of Hispanicity. Conquest, colonization, missionary zeal— all three marched lockstep in the New World. Even as conquistadors cut bold paths of exploration, even as colonials surged in to make their fortunes, priests mobilized communities and civilized the conquered. As remarkable as it seems, Christian missions became the systematizing force, the vanguard of empire.

The religious who rushed in to remake these newly won lands wielded power they had nowhere else in the world. Catholic imperialism was a fact of life in the early Americas—an organizing principle—and it grew alongside the formidable bureaucracy Spain would build there. The bond between throne and altar was mutually reinforcing, unquestioned, and it resulted in a church whose rule would thrive, outlasting institutions long after conquistador and colonizer were gone. Catholicism would become a steadfast reality in that turbid world and the bedrock on which much would be built: the education of the Latin American elite, the permanence of white rule, the social safety net for the poor, the ordinary masses' ever ardent hope for progress. It was an orthodox church, conservative, but it was imbued nevertheless with a crusading spirit. In the thick of exploration's wildest improvisations, it proved more nimble and imaginative than the Crown. Ultimately, it would be far more resourceful than any frontiersman in the Americas. Priests went where the Crown's emissaries dared not go, and they pushed far beyond the boundaries that conquistadors had set for themselves. Much would be asked of the Church; much would be met. But at the heart of things was a struggle for control as fierce and enduring as the conquest itself.

The mendicant friars—the Dominicans, Franciscans, Augustinians—who made the first inroads into the New World were soon fighting to establish exclusive authority over their "pagan" charges. Convinced that they alone could transform the godless multitudes into a Christian ideal—a society that would embody the opposite of the corrupt, mercenary machine that the Church had become in Europe—they plunged into the business of moving populations into their *reducciones*, putting them to work, and indoctrinating them in the word of the Lord. Oblivious to the profound shock that this mass deracination and displacement created, they focused on what was uppermost in conquistadors' minds: the appropriation of large tracts of land, the soldiering that a large-scale reeducation would require. As the forced corralling of Indians continued, the sheer magnitude of the effort required more and more territory. An intense rivalry emerged between orders to ally with governors, gain larger footprints, and increase their ownership of the enterprise. Dominicans accused Franciscans of invading their territory and hijacking their operations; Augustinians complained that Dominicans preaching in Spanish instead of indigenous languages would render Catholicism an alien cult. Adding fuel to this intramural friction, the newly crowned king, Philip II, in his capacity as Vicar of Christ, decided to take the entire business of New World evangelization out of the hands of the monastic orders and place it under royal control. The Crown now assumed ultimate authority by handpicking bishops and assigning them to the colonies, dropping them into the troubled mix and expecting them to command discipline.

When the bishops arrived, they found a fully functioning ecclesiastical system that left little room for them. They were forced to insert themselves, impose, try to win the upper hand they had been promised. So it was that an abiding rift between bishops and religious orders—the secular church and the monks—entered the Americas and never left it. As one historian put it, a deep fissure ran down the very heart of the colonial church as bishop and monk tried to wrest control in a fervid struggle to win souls. The Church seldom spoke with one voice, leaving native populations to wonder how they might play off sides and profit from the divisions. On one hand, there was the secular institution, led by bishops, championed by governors, decreed by a king, and ready to ordain American-born priests in order to boost its power. On the other was a scattering of mendicant orders, pioneers in the hemisphere's evangelization yet rivals among themselves, squabbling over dominion, unwilling to pass the baton to anyone born in and of the New World.

In both camps, as was clearly evident, priests were Spanish or descendants of Spaniards, white, firmly tied to the hierarchy of power. But their antagonisms were striking, often spilling over into society itself, where everyone seemed to have a son or brother committed to religious life. Passions would grow so heated, brawls so common, that during one canonical election in Mexico, a meeting between two opposing factions prompted knives to be drawn and mutiny declared, until the viceroy himself was forced to intervene and sit with the holy men until tempers cooled.

Mendicants versus bishops, Creoles against Spanish-born, order against order, the contest for religious ascendancy shot like an electric charge through Spanish America. Yet for all the discord within the Church, its influence—in whatever guise—only grew stronger. The obligatory tithes, the tributes imposed on rich and poor, the demand that Indians labor to win God's blessing: all these conspired to make the Church an affluent enterprise. Peru and Mexico, leviathans of gold and silver, began to generate such unimagined wealth that viceroys rushed to build church after church to celebrate their dominion, each more magnificently gilded than the last. Religious orders became consumed by the appropriation of real estate, buying up urban plots in a frenzy to install convents, monasteries, schools, and universities. By 1620, a mere century after Cortés thrust a cross into the heart of Montezuma's temple, the glories of God were such a sight to behold in Latin America that the English priest Thomas Gage was moved to write:

> There are not above fifty churches and chapels, cloisters and nunneries, and parish churches in [Mexico] city, but those that are there are the fairest that ever my eyes beheld. The roofs and beams in many of them are all daubed with gold. Many altars have sundry marble pillars, and others are decorated with brazil-wood stays standing one above another with tabernacles for several saints richly wrought with golden colors, so that twenty thousand ducats is a common price of many of them. These cause admiration in the common sort of people, and admiration brings on daily adoration. . . . All the copes, canopies, hangings, altar cloths, candlesticks, jewels belonging to the saints, and crowns of gold and silver, and tabernacles of gold and crystal to carry about their sacrament in procession would mount to the worth of a reasonable mine of silver, and would be a rich prey for any nation that could make better use of wealth and riches. I will not speak much of the lives of the friars and nuns of that city, but only that there they enjoy more liberty than in parts of Europe and that surely the scandals committed by them do cry up to Heaven for vengeance, judgment, and destruction.

It is a lesson in how one man's sanctuary can be another's temple of the profane. Even when both worship the same god.

Indeed, the effort to build a cathedral that was mightier, more richly adorned than the Incas' Coricancha or the Aztecs' Huei Teocalli, inflicted far more demands on Spanish resources and Indian endurance than any project undertaken in the Anglo-American colonies. Tithing was compulsory, often punishing, put in place by Alexander VI's papal bull as early as 1501 precisely for the maintenance of the Church in the Indies. Anything grown on American soil as well as anything mined from it would henceforward be taxed, its proceeds assigned "for all time" to the "Church of the Catholic Kings." Supplemented by fees demanded for baptisms, communions, weddings, funerals, and special blessings, the coffers were always full, ensuring ever grander processions and richly embroidered chasubles. So wealthy, in fact, did the colonial clergy become, that by the nineteenth century, when revolutionaries stormed the palaces to seek independence from Spain, almost half of all property in Mexico City belonged to the Church. In Caracas, when Simón Bolívar inherited the wealth that would make him rich enough to fund the liberation of six republics, it was from an uncle priest, who had died and left a fortune in lay properties. In Lima, enterprising clergy had so much money to spare that the Peruvian Church became a muscular bank, the major supplier of credit to citizens of the viceroyalty.

Landowners as well as merchants—miners as well as farmers—relied on ecclesiastical institutions for loans, sometimes surrendering their properties as collateral. Donning the cassock became such a tried-and-true avenue to riches that Pope Gregory XIII issued a complaint, scolding Franciscans in silver-boom Mexico and Peru for doffing their robes and returning to Spain as fatcat aristocrats, having labored more to "enrich themselves than to mind the salvation of their flocks." But individual priests were not alone in material ambitions. Their organizations, too, were profiting mightily from the labors of evangelization. By the end of the eighteenth century, it became all too obvious to the Crown that the colonial Church had accumulated a massive amount of lucre. When the Jesuits were stripped of their missions, banished from the Americas and disbanded in disgrace, the Society of Jesus was the most affluent property owner in the colonies, owning more than four hundred successful haciendas throughout the continent and controlling great swaths of arable land.

In the course of three centuries of colonial rule, the Church had grown skilled at glorifying itself and lining its pockets, but it had also accomplished considerable good. Even as Las Casas was persuading the courts in Spain to classify Indians as *miserabiles*—a legal designation that demanded the Crown's protection—the Church established a General Indian Court meant to hear out any Indian who felt he had been wronged. At least its intention was just, whether or not its decisions were ever followed. The Church also constructed and oversaw hospitals, missions, and schools, essentially working alone to provide these services. As conquistadors focused on what they might extract, the Church looked about to see what it might leave behind. At first, it was the Franciscans, Dominicans, and Augustinians who undertook the education of the impoverished indigenous masses. Eventually the Jesuits—perhaps the greatest single educational force in the New World—established a network of schools and colleges that would serve white Creoles throughout Spanish America.

As splintered as the orders were, a set Catholic curriculum ensured a uniformity of thought—a programmed catechism, a coherent belief system—which the Crown and the Inquisition found convenient. For centuries, a Catholic education seemed the only thing the increasingly sprawling colonial system had in common. Eventually Bolívar would claim that a single faith and a single language, conditions of a grueling conquest, had turned out to be Latin America's best hope: two shared traits that suggested the potential for a solid and powerful union, an opportunity for South America to unite and create a mighty bulwark against the world. It was a brief salute to the good that Spain had wrought in the midst of all the bad. The solidarity he envisioned, however, would never come to pass. Although the Christianizing campaign, as messy and uneven as it was, had exerted its consolidating effects, it could not compete with the strict separation that Spain had demanded of its colonies. The mother country had proved masterful at keeping its territories isolated, ignorant, and suspicious of one another, although faith had made them one.

None of this is to say that the Church didn't commit egregious injustices—both by bishops and orders—against the very people they were pledged to "civilize." The Church had two faces, good and bad,

and too often the good had a habit of looking the other way when brutalities were committed in the name of evangelization. The Franciscans
imposed harsh corporal punishments on any Indian who was late to religion lessons, giving the transgressor five sharp blows on the back with
a spiked stick. Well into the eighteenth century, they maintained stocks
and jails for natives who didn't comply with their rules or practices. Presidios and missions employed armed soldiers as guards, an association
that would prove tricky as priests became identified with the strong arm
of conquest. But priests themselves were often to blame for these asso-
ciations. In their uncontrollable zeal to purge old faiths and install the
new, missionaries destroyed much of pre-Columbian culture, consigning
a large share of indigenous learning to the dustbin of history.

Often they were simply swept away by the violence of the times.
Frustrated by the fierce opposition of the Chichimecas in Mexico, some
friars joined the demand for a full-scale war of extermination—*guerra
a fuego y a sangre*—to purge the landscape of belligerent Indians and
facilitate a wholesale appropriation of Indian territories. In the late sixteenth century, the head of the Franciscan order in Yucatán, Diego de
Landa, outraged by evidence that the Mayans were still secretly worshiping their idols, unleashed a host of atrocities. Thousands of Indians
were subjected to *la estrapada* or *la garrucha*: hanged by their wrists with
irons strapped to their legs, one of the Inquisition's most dreaded tortures. Needless to say, hundreds died. Landa then called for five thousand Mayan statues and an abundance of precious books to be dragged
into the main plaza and pounded to rubble or burned to ash to teach
the Indians once and for all that their history was abhorrent; their only
salvation, the cross. One might argue that it is unfair for us to pass judgment on sixteenth-century barbarities from the vantage of present-day
sensibilities, except for one glaring fact: the Church, then as now, hewed
to the basic theological principle that faith had to be accepted freely. New
World friars had lost sight of that principle. That, along with the slave
raids, violent incursions, reductions, exploitations, diseases, wholesale
rapes—all the grievances associated with conquistadors—tended to turn
natives away from Christianity. As one humble Mexican put it: I don't
want to go to heaven if there are Spaniards there.

To be sure, there were churchmen who labored notably to preserve the Indian culture and its past—the Franciscans Bernardino de Sahagún and Motolinía, for instance, or the Dominican Las Casas—priests who held the firm conviction that in order to convert people, one must know and understand their ways. Anglo-America never produced a single defender of the American Indian comparable to those Spaniards. Likewise, the Las Casas–Sepúlveda debate in Valladolid, which strove to establish whether the indigenous were fully human, was remarkable for having happened at all—much less having been called for by a king. In the history of the world, there is nothing to equal that impassioned deliberation.

But Spain's mission frontier system, in which priests were the vanguard, was itself an invasion, meant to disrupt, transform, force natives from the godless fringes and into the orbit of Christianity. The intent may have been subtle persuasion, but the result was to turn the indigenous world upside down. The arrival of men in robes—unarmed trailblazers who ventured where others feared to tread—was a harbinger of the servitude that would follow, the loss of the old, a forced acceptance of the new. Unlike the British colonization of North America, in which pioneers pushed into territories, settled, and evicted the Indians by violent force, the Spanish did the reverse: they pushed in, settled, and *absorbed* the Indians. They reduced them, baptized them, reproduced with them. Mostly this worked. Sometimes it didn't. In what is now Chile, the Araucanian Indians were so defiant in their rejection of the colonists that the missionaries cautiously stepped aside while a bloody war lasting generations raged on, eventually producing a lucrative slave trade for Spain.

As religious orders pressed into the interior of the Americas, indoctrination became a calculated process. Along with evangelizing the masses, the Church struggled to do what a colonial government in all its greed and corruption could not: shape and advance the culture, tend to the welfare of the people. It was because of priests that Mexico had a printing press in 1539, and because of them that universities would crop up one after another to serve the children of whites—in Lima, Mexico City, La Plata, Santo Domingo, Bogotá—bastions of orthodoxy that strove to mirror the exuberant intellectual culture of the *madre patria*. In time, and although they differed wildly in approach, the mendicants succeeded in bringing more and more Indians into the fold precisely because they offered these services. Franciscans, seeped in millenarian and apocalyptic visions, hurried from village to village, baptizing hordes of Mexicans at a time, dispensing with the time-consuming business of teaching the rudiments of catechism. Dominicans, heritors of a great intellectual tradition, were the first evangelizers of Peru and the first to teach the natives Spanish, although they stopped short after a few basics and refused to teach them too much. The thinking was that a truly educated Indian would be at odds with the racial subjugation necessary to drive a burgeoning slave economy. Jesuits, on the other hand, taught natives all they knew, from Latin, to Bach, to astronomy. They founded prestigious schools in the urban centers, focusing on the children of the powerful; and then radiated into far corners of jungle to teach all the rest, building worlds unto themselves, proving themselves far better governors than their masters.

ACHIEVING UTOPIA

All monks have achieved is rank robbery and oppression, enriching themselves on the sweat and agony of Indians.
—Tupac Inca Yupanqui, 1783

At first, as priests proliferated through highlands and low, spreading Christ's word and warning the natives about the perils of worshiping false gods, the Indians suspected that they were demons. These were surely the *pishtacos* of Quechua lore, the *kharisiri* of Aymara legend: evil, white goblins that roamed the land, rendering the fat of their victims and using it for baptismal oil. The Indians had watched, horrified, as Spanish soldiers rummaged through fields of battle, searching for enemy dead and carving off chunks of body fat to apply to their own bleeding wounds. The practice was common enough in an age when priest-surgeons in the Old World used warm oil to speed healing, but from there, the rumors multiplied. This was a race of white foreigners, well equipped, charismatic, powerful—with silver tongues and fancy promises—but they needed the fat of Indians to make their church bells ring, their wheels spin, their cannons fire.

Much about the Spanish priests seemed foreign, otherworldly, downright peculiar. The high priests of the indigenous, for all their power and remove, had led normal lives with wives and children. Their worship of sun, rain, earth—abiding realities of life—seemed sensible, practical. But these strange, pale apparitions who pledged themselves to celibacy and worshiped a ruined prophet nailed to a wooden cross seemed bizarre, laughable. How could a celibate priest be a fully realized man if he had never attained personhood through the procreative power of sex, the most natural law there was? How could a tribe in long robes and shaved crowns aim to teach about matters of the spirit if its members were so naive about life itself?

Xavier Albó, joining the Jesuits centuries later, would encounter the same suspicions in rural Bolivia and Ecuador. Many was the time a giggling child would run up, boldly pull up his skirt, and shout, *"Dentro de este padrecito hay un hombre!"*—"There's a man inside this little priest!" A male in a robe seemed so alien; a gangly white male wandering the remote villages, more so. He made special efforts to ingratiate himself to the whispering señoras in the markets, the laborers shuffling home from the mines. He knew the history. He understood what it meant to be approached and preached to by a stranger from Spain. He would explain that, in truth, he was Catalan—an outsider like them, with a culture and language quite distinct from the Spanish. His listeners nodded and smiled politely. Eventually he began to call himself Bolivian. In time, he would shed his black cassock altogether.

The priest as party to conquest was very much on Xavier's mind as he finished his First Studies, the requisite years of Jesuit training before he committed himself fully to a specialization. An invader was not what he had ever intended to be. Growing up in the chaos of a rancorous civil war, in a world in which fathers and grandfathers were murdered for random passions, he had been given God's light; he simply wanted to pass it on. He was discovering now that he cared less about proselytizing than about the hand he might proffer, the work he might do to offset the stunning neglect that was all too evident around him. He had not imagined that the indigenous themselves—their language, their traditions, their fully formed spiritual dispositions—would captivate him as they had. The most humble, the stone poor—the *miserabiles*—had become his teachers. It was to them that he wanted to dedicate his work in these fields of the Lord. The cities might be full of rich, up-and-coming Latin

Americans, as he had learned in La Paz and now in Quito—the economically viable, the healthy, the educated 20 percent—but he was sure that it was the rural *indios* and their progeny, clinging to an ancestral past, keeping alive their daily rituals and beliefs, who held the fate of Latin America in their hands.

In these reflections, Xavier was little different from Jesuits who had created missions five hundred years before in what are now the borderlands between Paraguay and Brazil. As a newly minted order, trying to define its role in those wilds, the Jesuits had applied themselves to the welfare of those for whom Spaniards had little use: the Guaraní, who had fled slavery by penetrating deeper and deeper into the forests. Building an all-Guaraní army to defend their flock from Portuguese raiders and colonial bosses, the Jesuits began a long tradition of outmaneuvering governors and bishops, and doing things their own way. Jesuit reductions were largely humane enterprises, communities in which men of the cloth immersed themselves in tribal cultures, respectful of traditions they might not wholly understand. And they were profitable. Some observers in Europe went so far as to say that in the remote forests of an unfriendly continent, the Jesuits were achieving Utopia.

Xavier might as well have been living in the jungle of Madidi for all he heard about Cuba and the fateful revolution that promised to shape the Latin American future. Even as Castro and Guevara huddled in the pine-studded forests of Cuba's Sierra Cristal, awaiting the opportune moment to invade Havana, Xavier was doing fieldwork in Bolivia, learning all he could about the peculiarities of an ancient language. Quechua presented surprising subtleties, seemingly endless variations. Shaking the fleas from his blanket and moving from one village to another, he was determined to record a linguistic system that had never been documented adequately before. The most revolutionary thing on his mind was hardly the Marxist idea—the Spanish Civil War had cured him of that—but the pronunciations of *ka* and *kha*, a distinction that could make him a credible speaker or a ridiculous laughingstock. He listened to an older, more seasoned priest articulate the glottal and velar distinctions between those two consonants until his dentures fell out, prompting Xavier to quip that this was a pronunciation he couldn't possibly replicate.

He wandered into whorehouses unwittingly, seeing "señoras" gather on balconies, thinking it a convenient enough signal to chat. He went about meticulously recording the differences between northern and southern inflections. One day, in order to capture what sounded like an elegant accent, he interviewed a sweet, old woman, who turned out to be the mother of the interior minister, and so was arrested on suspicion of espionage. In short, he was documenting a culture as well as a language. He became a census taker so as to widen his contacts: knocking on doors, sitting on stones, conferring with mothers about children, fathers about aspirations, children about play. He scoured the countryside in a sputtering old motorcycle, his cassock fluttering in the wind. He was seeing Latin America as few outsiders did, and he was learning what it meant to be Andean, a mountain people, stubbornly marginal, living in a universe apart from the rich and powerful. He continued this work throughout his tenure as a novitiate, and he continued the fieldwork in Bolivia even as he was earning a doctorate in sociolinguistics at Cornell University in the United States.

When his newly won Bolivian friends asked him about his faith, Xavier simply told them about his own teacher: a man who began in a barn surrounded by animals and ended on a hillside surrounded by thieves. When his Jesuit brothers asked him about his work, he answered that he was trying to find how a country might heal its soul. He didn't specify what country he meant, exactly.

CHAPTER 12

HOUSE OF GOD

❖

Politics is in crisis, very much in crisis in Latin America. . . . It is more sick than well.

—Pope Francis I, 2018

By the time Jesuits were banished from Christian life at the end of the eighteenth century, it had become clear to many colonials—white, brown, black, and mestizo—that the Old European allegory about Latin America was false: the devil was not a godless Indian; the devil was a ruthless Spaniard. The view of colonialism as the personification of evil began to flourish among those born in the New World, product of the seed that Bartolomé de las Casas had planted centuries before, and it grew now with rebellious force, urged on by echoes of the "Black Legend" in Europe. Creole aristocrats—educated, wordly, savvy about the hemisphere they inhabited—chafed at their reduced status, stung by laws put in place by the Council of the Indies. They were white. They were sons of Spaniards. But because they had not been born in Spain, they wielded no clout. They were barred by law from holding office, or making laws, or taking positions of power. And though they ran thriving haciendas, businesses, and mines, they could not profit fully from their own successes. At the very top of any institution, whether it be mercantile, judicial, or social (and that included the Church), sat an overseer—an emissary, an import, a parvenu—from the *madre patria*. Very often, the mother country did not send its best and brightest, leaving sophisticated Creoles to stew that they had to answer to inept foreigners. Here, then, was the smoldering cinder that spurred the wars of independence. When it flared in the late 1700s and burst into full flame in 1810, revolution sped like a lit wick from the Río Plata to the Rio Grande, igniting the hemisphere and mowing down millions in war's hellfire. Throughout the carnage, the Church sided with Spain. This was no surprise, since priests had marched in with conquistadors, popes had allied with kings, and the evidence was there for all to see in every *plaza central:* the most colossal, most glorious church always sat next to the governor's mansion, and the bishop's house was just steps away.

When the Latin American revolutions were over and Spain was pushed back across the Atlantic, the destruction was cataclysmal. Entire cities had been wiped from the map. Civilian populations had been reduced by a third. Spain's expeditionary forces were virtually obliterated. In Venezuela alone, there were more human losses than in the United States Revolution and Civil War combined. The king's armies limped off to their battered ships, taking governors, archbishops, and bishops with them, creating a vacuum in Latin American leadership that would leave it in virtual chaos for generations to come. Whole missions were emptied out. Churches and convents that hadn't been destroyed in the fury fell into disrepair. There simply weren't enough Creole priests to maintain the vast webwork of Catholic enterprises that peppered the American landscape. In smaller towns, locals took over churches, unsure what to do with them. Indians in rural areas lost contact with the faith entirely. As whites swooped in to grab all the power and property the Spaniards had left behind, the darker races were left to get on as best they could.

No one paid much attention to how much control the Church had lost in those humbler communities. Generations passed without any record of their religion or their spiritual practices. The scattering of ordained Creole priests that remained tended to cling to the urban centers, the familiar settings, the whiter congregations, the bustling neighborhoods they knew. Complicating this, the governments of the new independent republics—as tumultuous and disordered as they were—were wary of engaging the Church in anything that smacked of a retreat to the old, colonial ways. In some areas of Central America, anticlerical governments moved to pare church influence to a minimum and curb the old tradition of acting as the Vatican's collection agency. Mexico, for instance, seized and nationalized all church property in the late 1800s, separated the Church and the state, and then had to live with the consequences: its clergy became radicalized, fighting the government at every turn, until Mexico's legislators—weary of the resistance—cast all foreign priests out of the country and decreed that only the Mexican born could be preachers. The Guatemalan response was even more austere: an edict rigorously restricted the number of Catholic priests to a maximum of one hundred for the entire country. It was meant as a temporary corrective, but it became the rule for more than seventy years.

Throughout this period, the upper class and upwardly mobile remained loyal to the Church. Ironically, with whiteness the most obvious ticket to power, flaunting one's high quotient of Hispanicity—and, by association, Catholicism—became an instrument of power in postrevolutionary Spanish America. To be dominant, it was essential to be white, wear a crucifix, sport one's religion on one's sleeve. But, in general and in sheer numbers, the Latin American Church was in grave crisis. Subjugated even more cruelly by postrevolutionary bosses than they ever had been by the Spanish, the campesinos who lived in dire poverty and were expected to do the lion's share of hard labor began to revisit their ancestors' indigenous rituals with a vengeance born of resentment. To be sure, their spiritual practices had always harbored vestiges of an ancient past, even under the harshest policies of colonial rule. But left to their own devices, rural churches allowed the worship of nature and idols, creating a highly syncretic religion—a fusion of Christian and tribal beliefs— unlike anything the Church had ever seen: a Virgin's image was likely in the shape of a mountain—a nod to the Earth Mother, Pachamama— with a sun crowning her head and a half moon cradling her feet. Or, in festivals commemorating Christian holidays, processions were led by men dressed as devils, with masks that bore the unmistakeable fangs of Coatlicue or Ai Apaec.

So it was that the revolutions that pulsed through the hemisphere had the unintended consequence of redefining Latin American Christianity for the masses. Eager to do away with the severities—the Christian obsession with sin, for instance, which had always been alien and imponderable— the darker races restored old legends more tolerant of human weakness, beliefs more aligned with the natural world around them. Caribbean blacks returned to the voodoo and trances of Santería, Yoruba, or Mandinga: to worshiping an abundance of *orisha* gods who corresponded to life as they knew it. The Indians reembraced their divinities—the earth, sun, and sea—and man's role as a creature of nature.

From the pampas of Argentina to the Yucatán jungle, the people left behind by the fleeing Christian missions began to retrofit faith to ancestral cosmogonies. In the isolated Mexican sierra of Nayarit, for example, the Coras, the last tribe of Mexicans to be evangelized by force, had not seen a priest since the Jesuit exodus of 1767. They remained cut off from Christianity for two centuries until a Franciscan wandered into the mesa in 1969 and resumed preaching the Gospel. What he found was that, in the course of two hundred years of solitude, the Coras had returned to worshiping the Sun. But, to his surprise, the Sun God was now Jesus Christ, complete with passion, crucifixion, and resurrection. Some Indians were even capable of reciting whole portions of the Mass in something that resembled Latin. Judas, an incomprehensible figure to the Coras—unlike any god they had ever had—no longer existed, but his tribe, the Jews, had become *los borrados*, "the erased ones," near-naked men smeared in ash and mud, and then brightly painted, sporting the snouts of beasts. In the spring ritual that still persists to this day, the Coras assume that guise, playing the part of Jesus's crucifiers, whom they believe to have been the Jews. To the loud, persistent beat of drums, men dressed as devils race through villages in pursuit of a boy representing the Christ Sun. Bringing the underworld to life in ways that Christian liturgy cannot, the Cora ritual is a lesson in forbearance: here are the black sheep of the world—a racing flock of human badness—that, for all their villainy, are fallible, human, just like us. Celebrating wickedness with a prodigal consumption of peyote, the *borrados* dance their way into night until the Easter sun rises, at which point they plunge into the river, wash off the ash and the evil, and, like Christ, are reborn.

Xavier Albó did not know it quite yet, but, as with the vanguard of priests that had penetrated those highlands four hundred years before, he was expected to start the Christian process all over again. Even as he contemplated his future, wondering how best to serve people with clearly observable, robust beliefs of their own, he was joined by a wave of foreign priests, who, like him, had been shunted to Latin America to spearhead a Catholic rebirth. Strolling through sleepy mountain towns in Bolivia and Ecuador, or corralled within mission walls, he was unaware he was in the thick of a worldwide initiative. He didn't realize it fully until he was at Cornell University seeking his doctorate in the late 1960s, when a worldwide peace movement was loosed at full throttle, and liberation theology was being born. The Church was reinventing itself in ways it had not anticipated.

Like sixteenth-century bishops thrust into a volatile hemisphere, twentieth-century friars were expected to intervene, stanch the ebb, fix things. But circumstances were very different now: the Church had considerably less political power. Latin Americans were hardly new to Christianity: they had absorbed it before, imagined its possibilities, tailored it to their uses. The work of priests this time around was not to impose faith so much as to rescue it—to reenter a world abandoned for more than a century and win it back with a gentler approach. It was either this or lose Latin America to Protestantism, evangelicals, atheism, agnosticism, apathy. With little more than a vague game plan to gain believers, Catholic missionaries from around the world, most of them survivors of a chastening World War, went about the work of immersing themselves in local cultures, insinuating themselves into the communities. It was evangelization of a different stripe.

In the cities, the elite were carrying on Christian traditions much as their Spanish forefathers had done before them. Children attended Catholic schools, parents baptized their infants, the dead were given Christian burials, those passing a church dutifully crossed themselves. But in the wider ambit of rural Latin America, campesinos had recast faith itself, making the life of the spirit more relevant than it ever had been under colonial powers. Religion was now community's full partner—a reason to gather together, share the work, assist the frail—even if that religion could no longer be called Catholicism. The ringleaders of this adapted Christianity were less priests than shamans; they celebrated solstices, the changing seasons, the harvests; they held indigenous fiestas, complete with native customs, even blood rituals. They returned to the abiding principle that worshiping nature was the binding glue of their civilization, a far more comprehensible belief system than anything the white men had taught them. If Jesus and Mary remained in that constellation of holies, it was not as redeemer and virgin but as the ever-present Sun and Earth.

As the Catholic orders of Europe undertook their reconquest of Latin America in the 1950s, seeking to restore and strengthen their hold, they were not alone. Maryknoll missionaries from the United States, having shifted their focus from China to Latin America, flooded into the region but found no ordained priests in the old Spanish churches that punctuated the rural landscape. What they found instead were spiritual chieftains who were startlingly resentful of the intrusion, openly skeptical. The North Americans were seen as usurpers, invaders, modern-day subjugators. Things got worse when those missionaries tried to take over the properties the prerevolutionary Church had left behind. The Indians refused to give them keys to the buildings, or grant access to abandoned schools, or even allow them to see prized images of patron saints the locals had been safeguarding for generations.

There was no doubt about it: the Catholic Church was in a deeply pitched battle to regain the hearts and minds of some fifty million indigenous souls. From the Vatican on down to the most modest mission, the Church's reentry was seen as a titanic struggle, as urgent as Pope Alexander VI's audacious campaign to convert all the godless heathen of the New World. More conscious of cultural sensibilities now—aware that the Church needed to shape itself to the people and not the other way around—Catholic missionaries poured into backwood and hinterland, prepared to salvage their losses. In Mexico, where church-state relations had been inflamed for more than a century, as well as in Uruguay, which had long broken diplomatic relations with the Vatican, missionaries swarmed in with the newfound conviction that they would do it right this time.

Integral to this new approach was the concept of "inculturation," a tacit understanding that in the process of evangelization, the priests themselves were being evangelized. If they were doing it right—learning the language and customs, deeply understanding the people—they were entering rather than altering cultures, winning through camaraderie rather than by force. To that end, priests expanded their evangelizing army by recruiting Indian and mixed-race "catechists," native laypeople who would act as avatars: teaching the faith, tending the sick, carrying out simple church duties. The Church would win locals with locals, create a human tsunami of Catholic conversion produced by the population itself. The strategy was not unfamiliar. It had been applied five centuries before when Franciscans had used the Nahuas to help convert the rebellious tribes. But it had never been done with the large-scale determination that the Church now marshaled.

There was much to set right. A stark system of discrimination had been afoot in the region's cities for centuries, and it seemed impossible to correct. Every day there was another affront to the darker, humbler races: a Quechua in native dress turned away from a Lima movie theater; a Yaqui arrested in Mexico City for wandering a white neighborhood; a Mayan prodigy refused admission at a prestigious Catholic school; an Aymara holy man denied a role in a church. "We affirm that both religions, Aymara and Christian, teach love and respect for life," a group of religious leaders announced at a conclave of priests in Bolivia. "These are not religions of hate. However, by its actions, the Christian religion is a contradiction. It divides. It puts no confidence in native leadership. We are its right arms, but not the head. A theological colonialism still reigns." And so it seemed. The wave of European and American evangelizers had brought a new sensibility to the task, but they continued to be as foreign as they had ever been, internationally funded, an invasion of sorts. Little appeared to have changed since the priest Pedro de Quiroga had gone home to Spain in 1563 with a Peruvian's bitter testimony in hand: "We cannot persuade ourselves to believe anything you preach or say, because in everything, you always have lied and deceived us."

As time progressed and very different civil wars, revolutions, and plagues of terrorism convulsed Latin America in the 1970s and 1980s, the missionaries, far more attuned now to the populations they were serving—far more inculturated than their predecessors—found themselves embracing the militant politics of the locals. Bartolomé de las Casas's outrage had rattled down the centuries to foment a twentieth-century insurgency. This was liberation theology in tooth and claw, and it exploded onto the Latin American stage with a force that surprised the Vatican and spurred a crisis of identity that still bedevils the Church.

WINDS OF A MOVEMENT

I come from a continent in which more than sixty percent of the population lives in a state of poverty, and eighty-two percent of those find themselves in extreme poverty. . . . How do you tell the poor that God loves them?

    —Father Gustavo Gutiérrez, *Theology of Liberation*, 1971

When Xavier Albó received his doctorate in anthropology from Cornell in 1969 and returned to Bolivia, determined to use his knowledge for the betterment of the American Indian, he was thirty-four years old. He had spent more than half his life in Bolivia, almost twenty years of it preparing to serve the Society of Jesus. He had watched liberation theology emerge among his cohort, a will-o-the-wisp notion, a fledgling concept that corresponded to his sympathies but had yet to spread its wings. That same year, Rubem Alves, a young priest from Minas Gerais, who had been driven out of Brazil by a violent clampdown on suspected Communists, completed his doctoral thesis at Princeton University. Titled "Toward a Theology of Liberation," it was among the first instances that phrase had been used in scholarly circles in the United States. But it was hardly a cogent expression of what had been aswirl in South America for some time—it was merely a wan declaration that Brazil's poor deserved better from the Church. Alves himself found his paper wanting; Princeton gave it the lowest possible grade.

    Coincidentally enough, at about the same time, Gustavo Gutiérrez, a Peruvian who had completed his ecclesiastical studies in Europe, organized a conference of priests in the bustling Peruvian fishing port of Chimbote, bringing together those who, for years, had been discussing a new approach for the region. He called it: *"Hacia una teología de la liberación,"* Toward a Theology of Liberation. Gutiérrez's definition of this new movement, bolstered by the surge of Socialist passions sweeping the hemisphere during that tumultuous year, was bold, clear, and had strong implications for a priest's role: "If faith is a commitment to God and fellow man, and if theology is the understanding of that faith, it's not the theory that matters. It's the commitment. It's action. A theology of liberation intends to forge an active relationship between man's earthly emancipation—social, political, economic—and the Kingdom of God."

In other words, if Latin America's most pressing wound was injustice—its gaping abyss between rich and poor, white and brown, privilege and neglect—it was incumbent on the Church as God's champion to address this flagrantly un-Christian state of affairs. Poverty was not a fatal disease, it was a treatable condition. Oppression was not a misfortune, it was a correctable injustice. As the rationale went: the persecution that had caused widespread indigence in Latin America had been artificially imposed by an unjust society, a twisted mentality, a conquering culture; and if that oppression was not innate but inflicted, it could be reversed. Aesop's wicked scorpion who spoke for all tyrants—"It's not my fault, it's just my nature"—was unacceptable. The Church needed to insert itself into the socioeconomic structures that were generating the suffering and dedicate itself to purging the underlying sin. What was the work of the Church, after all, if not Christian salvation? And what was salvation if not the liberation of man?

It was a revolutionary concept, calling for a priest's involvement far beyond his traditional role, and it meant to transform the social landscape as profoundly as the conquest had done five hundred years before. This time, however, the change would come from the bottom—from the grass roots, from the weakest among them—rather than from any ruling potentate. And this time, rather than assist conquistadors in cowing the indigenous masses, liberation priests would play a dynamic part in unwinding that scandalous history. If men of the cloth had to join rebellions in order to cure Latin America's poverty—if they had to arm themselves to win the poor some measure of justice—so be it.

The Vatican's reaction was swift and damning. The liberation sought by this new breed of Latin American priest was more allied with politics, in its view, than with Christianity. Human liberation, as far as the official church was concerned, was the process of freeing oneself from sin. Not rescuing oneself from oppression. It was the individual soul—not the one in a wider, political sphere—that was central to Vatican concerns. More crucial still, the Church wanted nothing to do with Marxism, which was on a disturbing ascendancy around the globe during the sixties and seventies and which, in its purest form, was anti-Christian—

antifaith as a whole—and built on an atheist creed. But Latin America's activist priests were testing the rules and protocols in ways that asked fundamental questions of faith itself. Where did the Church stand if it didn't stand for human rights? What was it prepared to do to correct endemic, historic abuse? Was Christianity a faith of words only, or one that lived by its commandments, by the lessons of its greatest teacher, Jesus Christ? At what point in human suffering would priests take action to defend the least among them?

In retrospect, looking back at the whirl of history, it is clear that liberation theology was a product of the Vatican itself. Many in Rome's hierarchy eventually understood that, and it made the sting of this new theology more potent still. It had begun in January 1959 when Pope John XXIII announced the Second Vatican Council and called for a total overhaul of the Church. (The First Vatican Council had been convoked in 1869 by Pope Pius IX to deal with the threat of—among other things—materialism.) Vatican II's freer interpretation of the missionary role had a profound impact on the Church and on young priests around the world. But in a fateful fluke of history that few in the Church would have predicted, at precisely the same time—January 1959—Fidel Castro swept into Havana, and the Cuban revolution erupted onto the world stage.

Cuba's revolution had an electrifying effect on Latin America in the 1960s. The gaping divide between rich and poor had long been a ticking bomb in the region, fueling furies, ready to detonate. The radical transformation of Cuba's wildly corrupt society—its topsy-turvy conversion to a Communist state—was as inspiring to Latin America's vast underclass as it was terrifying to the region's oligarchs and the institutions and powers that supported them. But it shook the foundations of the Latin American church. Cuba had taken it by complete surprise.

And yet it presented an opportunity for the new wave of priests charged with reevangelizing Latin America. Even as Xavier pursued his graduate studies at Cornell, Vatican II had thrown open the Church's windows, redefining Catholicism anew. Much as Cuba had dispensed with its flagrant dictator, Fulgencio Batista, and its old, corrupt system of rule, the Church had called for a clear-cut separation from hidebound strictures of the past. No longer would it be an institution that dictated from on high so much as a covenant with the faithful, "a pilgrim people of

God": a dynamic body of religious that spoke the language of the people, welcomed innovation, accepted ethnic versions of the faith, and took a sober look at the social and economic problems of its believers. Gone was the fusty old Latin Mass. Gone, for many priests and nuns, were the robes and cassocks. Gone was the notion that it was a sacrilege to infuse Catholicism with one's folk traditions. Most important, perhaps: gone was the meager consolation that the poor would find their reward in heaven. It was incumbent on the modern Church to abolish human suffering. Now.

No one could have suspected that the next vogue of Christian thought would come from Latin America. But the region's oppression, its violence, its institutional injustices, and its historic ties to the Catholic Church had created a perfect opportunity for rethinking the role of religion, for forging a new approach. It was not an easy birth. The unleashing of liberation theology brought with it much consternation for bishops in Rome. Who was this angry creed's adversary, exactly? And why was it dancing so close to Marxist thought? No one could doubt that Communism was posing a danger to organized religion. But so did a Church that had served power and perpetuated social inequities. In order to make good on Vatican II's promise of a more just world—in order to keep godless Communism from the door—the Church had decided to address poverty at its root, in the very fields and villages where young priests such as Xavier Albó had set their sights. Liberation theologists, too, had made the poor their target, but they were taking a more activist view. Poverty was the product of racism, a caste society, a systematic oppression, and they were betting that the leveling force of Marxism, for all its pronouncements that religion was the opiate of the people, might have a lesson or two for anyone who would remake Latin America.

It was a surly age. Priests in Rome continued to argue the fine, doctrinal points even as conflagrations around the world flared and consumed populations: the Vietnam War, the troubles in Laos, the Cuban Missile Crisis, the civil rights struggle in the United States, the fierce protests emerging in Europe, the Arab-Israeli conflict, the assassinations of more than a dozen world figures, the independence cry of thirty-two African nations. The time seemed ripe for making Vatican II into a true reversal of the old order. But the Church was willing to go only so far. Although the new pontiff, Pope Paul VI, had dedicated his life to fighting poverty, he declared liberation theology's declarations too political, too truculent, too harsh on the power elite that had kept the Church afloat for centuries.

It was not the first time the Church had censured priests for defending the underdogs of Latin America. Five hundred years before, Bartolomé de las Casas had decried the cruelties of conquest so stolidly that the Church ultimately tired of his complaints and consigned him to the margins of history. Priests were expected to follow Rome's orders, obey bishops, hew to the strict regulations of Spain's Council of the Indies, which was usually headed by a man of the cloth. Those who didn't— those who protested on behalf of the conquered—were frowned upon, sidelined, defrocked.

Three hundred years later, in 1810, falling in line with the Spanish Crown was still the default position. It was a rare priest who would wage a campaign against the imposing military-clerical complex that Spain's government represented. In precisely that year, when Father Miguel Hidalgo gave his desperate "Cry of Dolores" and rode out at the head of a peasant revolution—making him perhaps the first true liberation theologist in Latin America—all the weight of the institutional church fell upon him. Initially, his plea for justice was met with an outpouring of support from Mexico's priests and a vast army of the poor marched out under the banner of the Virgin of Guadalupe to protest the abuse that had racked Mexico for centuries. But the pope's rebuke, memorialized in a fiery encyclical, was adamantly on the other side. As far as the pope was concerned, Spain was a paragon of virtue, its king absolute, its children the sons of God. Rebel priests were the "evil ones." Revolution, "a plague from a sinister well." With that blistering encyclical in tow, the viceroy called on his archbishop to marshal the entire Mexican Church against the revolutionaries. The archbishop obliged. Warrior priests were sent out to defend Spain, shouting "Viva la Fe Católica!" and fighting under the banner of the Virgin of Remedios. As one historian commented wryly, it was one virgin battling another in the killing fields of Mexico— summoned by rebel and ruler alike—until Father Hidalgo was hunted down and beheaded, his head thrust on a hook and swung from a rooftop in Guanajuato.

*   *   *

Ironically, 150 years later, by virtue of another pope's hand, Church dissidents were once again emboldened. Vatican II had spurred a fresh generation of Latin American priests to aspire to make a difference. There was no doubt what their objective would be. In countries that held the largest indigenous and black populations—Mexico, Peru, Bolivia, Guatemala, Brazil, Venezuela among them—more than 80 percent of the people lived below the poverty line. Disease, hunger, misery, illiteracy, crime were endemic, and yet governments had proven incapable of addressing the racism that was so clearly at the root of these problems. Something had to be done. Three years after the declaration of Vatican II, a group of thirty theologians called for a conference in Medellín to discuss a new way to think about Catholicism. They called it "the preferential option for the poor." If the destitute were favored by God, as Scripture made very clear, then to place them at the center of the Church's work was to fulfill a biblical imperative. In the waning years of the twentieth century, in a hemisphere filled with staggeringly impoverished children of God, there seemed to be no end to the souls the Church might serve.

The world in which Xavier moved in the 1970s and 1980s was populated by those who would bring the philosophy of liberation to the favelas and *barriadas*, the *campo* and *pueblo*—the most desperate neighborhoods of Latin America. Among them was the Franciscan Leonardo Boff of Brazil, a resolute champion of this new thinking who openly supported Communists, excoriated the United States as a terrorist state, and accused the Vatican of being a rigid, fundamentalist dynasty. More than once, the guardians of Rome—especially Cardinal Joseph Ratzinger— censured Boff for his insolence. Ratzinger, who would go on to become Pope Benedict XVI, complained that liberation theology had produced nothing but "rebellion, division, dissent, offense, and anarchy." Its advocates were nothing less than architects of chaos.

In that supposedly ruinous company was Pedro Casaldáliga, a Brazilian bishop who had dedicated himself to defending field laborers and, for it, was targeted for assassination by hit men answering to the rich landowners of Mato Grosso. (His vicar, in a case of mistaken identity, was killed instead.) Casaldáliga, like Boff, was eventually dressed down by Pope John Paul II for sympathizing too strongly with the Left and for supporting Daniel Ortega's anti-American regime in Nicaragua. If Communism was the enemy, no aspect of it would be tolerated. The Hobbesian choice was to leave things as they were, which meant that poverty was the only thing on offer.

Passions ran so high in Brazil that the military soon mounted a campaign of violent oppression against anyone, including liberation theologists, who opposed or criticized the country's social policies. Eliminating freedoms one by one, army generals created a special arm of the secret police to monitor the Church's political activities—arresting, detaining, even murdering priests for their work in the poorest favelas of the land. And yet, one after another—in Brazil as well as elsewhere in the Americas—Xavier's young friends were drawn to the prospect of social revolutions.

In answer, the Church began a systematic purge of these unruly ranks. In addition to Boff, Casaldáliga, and numerous others who had come up through Xavier's ranks, Pope John Paul II defrocked two more: the Jesuit intellectuals Fernando and Ernesto Cardenal, brothers from a wealthy Managua family, who fought openly and unrepentantly against Nicaragua's grinding oppression. For decades, too, the Vatican treated Peru's liberation theologist Gustavo Gutiérrez with contempt, accusing him of undermining the Church's authority and twisting faith into an instrument of rebellion. In Colombia, the Marxist priest Camilo Torres, who joined the guerrilla fighters of the National Liberation Army and was killed in action, had been warned many times by the Church that he risked discharge. His only answer: "If Jesus were alive today, He would be a guerrilla." But one by one, liberation priests were disavowed, suspended *a divinis*, expelled.

Xavier might have joined his fellow priests' more militant efforts, but he never did. He participated in debates with liberation activists. He observed their growing radicalism, was witness to their mounting fury. For him, it was not a question of sympathies—all of which he shared—but of objectives. How best to achieve the social conscience that was sorely needed? Transient political ambitions seemed to pale in comparison to the one fundamental truth that could transform this battered corner of the world: racial bigotry was simply wrong, corrosive, abhorrent. You couldn't convince others of this through coercion or violence; it was possible only via concord and affiliation. He hoped for a true beacon of reason—akin to Gandhi's or Dr. Martin Luther King Jr.'s or Nelson Mandela's—that might change the fabric of Latin America by revealing the inhumanity of its age-old prejudices. In the end, it seemed simple: if each of us wants dignity and justice for ourselves, surely we will want these things for others. The calculus was obvious. It was Jesus's most potent lesson. Reasonable minds would prevail.

In a bellicose age, Xavier had chosen peace. As he saw it, the sword had held enough dominion in this part of the world. Judging from Potosí and the wreckage it had left behind, rapacity had been Latin America's ruin, too. More than anything, he hoped the Church was not a third curse. Like the Indians he had come to know, he would place one stone on another, keep his head down, work. He founded an organization devoted to the welfare of farmers. He worked to instill the Quechua and Aymara people with pride in their language, their history, their long cultural tradition. He installed, by sheer will and improvisation, schools for the young, conferences on ethnic pride, commissions on peace and human rights. He continued to assist the most humble communities, whose deep spirituality sustained him.

Into these quiet convictions, by sheer chance, stepped a priest who would become one of Xavier's closest friends and confidants. He was Luís Espinal—Lucho, as he was known to his colleagues—a fellow Catalan who had chosen a far more militant path. He had arrived in La Paz just as Xavier was organizing CIPCA (the Center for Research and Promotion of Farmers), and the two understood that they had much in common: as Catalans, as Jesuits, as men devoted to the betterment of the world around them. Lucho was a poet, journalist, filmmaker, and critic, a priest whose impulse to report events as he saw them led to an activism more in line with liberation theologists of his time. When Lucho spoke about the urgent need to be more aggressive, importunate, shrill, Xavier listened. When environmental disasters occurred, they sprang to address them together. When Xavier produced testimonials from child laborers in the cornfields, Lucho publicized them on his television program, *En Carne Viva*—In Living Flesh. When Che Guevara was hunted down and killed in Bolivia by special forces and their American military advisors in

1967, Lucho hiked into the cordillera to interview what was left of Che's guerrillas. When Salvador Allende was bombed and killed in his presidential palace, Lucho flew to Santiago, Chile, to walk among the corpses and pray. More and more radicalized by his work—especially with the region's silver miners—Lucho became a spokesman for the abuses. In his quest to improve conditions throughout the country, he cofounded the Permanent Assembly for Human Rights.

In 1977, already a prominent figure in workers' rights, Lucho joined a hunger strike staged by indigenous women whose husbands had been imprisoned for demanding better conditions in the mines. Out of sympathy for the Quechua and Aymara women, Xavier also joined the strike. Not long after—and presumably because of his activism—Lucho was kidnapped by paramilitaries of the ultra-right-wing government of President Hugo Banzer, tortured, and then killed, his naked corpse flung to one side of the road to Chacaltaya. It was later learned that Operation Condor, the wider campaign of state terror condoned by Henry Kissinger and funded by the United States, had purged him along with sixty thousand other Latin Americans suspected of being "dangerous subversives." Xavier was never quite the same after that. Most vivid in his mind as he looks back on the long days of that miners' strike—the racking hunger, the hard floor of the newspaper offices where he kept vigil with the prisoners' aggrieved wives—is the fleeting figure of a man who came to look on the two gaunt gringo priests amid the flock of starving Indians. His name was Evo Morales, a mere wisp of a youth with ink-black hair and the grim look of determination. Morales would go on to become the first Aymara president of Bolivia—the second indigenous American in five hundred years to be elected to rule his people.

If liberation theologists thought they had found the way to rescue the poor and win souls to their side, there were other parties intensely committed to that goal. In the decades between 1960 and 1990—in that volatile, bloody-minded era when liberals, dictators, and generals sparred to dominate the arena—no fewer than four spiritual initiatives vied for the soul of Latin America. The Roman Catholic Church declared it had seen the light: it would mend its ways and dedicate itself to addressing poverty through its new Vatican II reforms. Liberation theologists decided with a passion approaching belligerence that they would fight established powers—governments, mining corporations, exporters, banks, even the Church, if need be—to protect the powerless. Atheists, in terrorist insurgencies that tore through the hemisphere from Nicaragua to Peru, sought to win adherents by erasing religion altogether. And in the 1980s, as indigent communities longed for non-Spanish, non-Catholic, non-Communist, genuinely liberating places of worship, Pentecostalist and Evangelical Protestants began to pour into Latin America, eager to vie for the prize. The brown, black, the urban flotsam as well as the rural poor, began to crowd those houses of God, half of them yearning for ancient days when religion had been a tribe's binding glue, half in protest against a Church that was party to an old invasion. Most seductive about these new Protestant religions were precepts the brown populations could well understand: the faithful might speak in tongues, rituals could heal the sick, exorcisms would be necessary, prophets might walk among us. The Protestant evangelical experience, in other words, promised a life full of miracles, signs, and wonders; not a dour paying down of sins. More persuasive, perhaps, it argued that with faith and a strong commitment to the virtuous life, a poor man could move up the socioeconomic ladder. A pauper might become a prince.

BEHOLD, THE NEW HAS COME

It is now obvious that these facile millenarianisms are mistaken. I am convinced that it is here [in Latin America] that the future of the Catholic Church is being decided. This has always been evident to me.
—Pope Benedict XVI, on his flight to Brazil, 2007

When Pope Benedict XVI—formerly Cardinal Ratzinger, who had applied a virtual spiked stick to the backs of liberation theologists in the 1970s—flew to Brazil on his first papal visit in 2007, he was visiting a continent that was home to the vast majority of his flock. At the time, more than half of all practicing Catholics lived in Latin America, a remarkable figure for a religion that had been forcibly, even violently imposed five hundred years before. And yet, his was a visit of desperation.

The pope had carefully chosen Brazil for that inaugural voyage, and with good reason. Brazil boasted the largest Catholic population of any country on the planet. But there was a more pressing justification for that choice: for all its numbers, the Brazilian Church was losing adherents at alarming rates. In the span of a single generation, it had lost a full quarter of its flock to Protestant religions. Most had left in the course of a decade. The pace was startling; worse, there seemed to be no end to the hemorrhage. In the 515-year history of the Americas, the Church had always held a religious monopoly on these lands. Its only challenges had been atheism or the nettlesome recrudescence of some wicked Indian ritual. Things had changed, and they had done so with such velocity that the Church hadn't noticed until the bleeding had gone too far.

The tectonic shifts in Latin America's spiritual life have been so swift that it is difficult to report them with precision. The numbers change by the day. But the trend is clear. One out of five Brazilians today is a Protestant; the overwhelming majority of them Pentecostals. In Nicaragua, El Salvador, Honduras, and Guatemala—countries that have been racked by bloodshed—one out of three residents has abandoned Catholicism in favor of evangelical rebirth. Throughout the region, from Costa Rica to Argentina, believers are following suit in breathtaking numbers, prompting evangelical temples to sprout by the thousands even as Catholic churches sell off properties to survive. A Protestant conversion would have been unthinkable in most Latin American families just twenty-five years ago, but today it's a rare family that doesn't count an evangelical at the dinner table. Indeed, nearly 40 percent of all Pentecostals are estimated to live in Latin America. Nearly all began life as Catholics. Nearly all come from the humbler classes. The poor—victims of a lingering colonialism and toxic racism—are fleeing a church that has claimed them for more than five hundred years.

The phenomenon is, in many ways, part of a larger, seismic repositioning. In the course of the twentieth century, Christianity itself experienced a radical metamorphosis. It flipped hemispheres, fulfilling Pachacuti's prophecy that the world would eventually turn upside down. The "global north" (North America, Europe, Australia, and New Zealand), once home to four times as many Christians as the "global south" (the rest of the world), is no longer the most Christian place on earth. Whereas one hundred years ago a full 90 percent of all people in the global north called themselves Christians, only 69 percent do today. To put that in perspective, consider this: in the developed world, a married couple who are devout believers are more than likely to have grandchildren who will never worship in a church. Or this: in Europe, on the very soil where, four hundred years ago, Protestants and Catholics slaughtered each other in the bloodiest religious wars in recorded human history, religion is a dwindling enterprise. London's churches, emptied of worshipers, are re-emerging as restaurants. Of the thousand or so churches that were decommissioned and shuttered in the Netherlands in the 2000s, many are now extravagant houses. One is a skateboard park. In Germany, from Berlin to Mönchengladbach, deserted churches have been repurposed as mosques to accommodate a growing Islamic population. In Spain and Portugal, where conquistadors once fell to their knees at the sight of a cassock, monasteries have become resorts that market themselves as "foodie paradises." The United States is no stranger to this phenomenon: not far from the White House, houses of worship are being sold off as luxury apartments; venerable old churches reopen as breweries.

The opposite is happening in the global south. Over the same period, Christianity has blossomed in sub-Saharan Africa and Asia. So much so that the great majority of Christians now live in the Southern Hemisphere, making the developing world an exuberant field of expansion for Catholic missionaries. Even as the Church is struggling financially—even as it has forfeited Europeans to agnosticism, atheism, or sheer indifference—it has won a robust army of believers among the darker races. Much of that success is due to priests of Xavier's generation, who made it their goal in the 1950s and 1960s to spread the gospel in the Third World. If Catholicism is less white by the day, it is making spectacular gains among the brown.

All the same, as he stepped off his airplane in Rio de Janeiro, Pope Benedict was beset by two pressing questions: Why were Brazilians, Chileans, Argentines, Central Americans—a deeply spiritual people, the beating heart of Catholicism for so many centuries—renouncing the Church for an alien, fundamentalist faith? And how could his priests hold on to these Christian masses, who hadn't abandoned Jesus at all but were deserting the Church at the rate of ten thousand souls a day? As

Pope Benedict had come to realize, the future depended on Latin America. A full offensive was required. Nowhere was that sentiment more fervently held than in the papal conclave, which proceeded to install a sunny South American mender of fences, Cardinal Jorge Mario Bergoglio, on the papal throne when the crusty old German Benedict XVI surprised the world with his resignation in 2013. The weight of Catholicism's future now fell squarely on the shoulders of Pope Francis I, a Jesuit, a man expected to finish what his generation had been asked to accomplish fifty years before—a man who insisted he wanted a church of and for the poor.

The reasons for the public's estrangement from the Church had been many. Not least among them, as Pope Benedict pointed out, was the violence that had rattled through the latter half of the twentieth century as terrorists or drug traffickers swept through the Latin American countryside, and anyone who professed leftist views faced brutal retaliation. From Brazil to Nicaragua, dictators and generals had made it clear that pesky priests, liberals with Communist sympathies, warriors for Jesus— like any upstart revolutionaries—would be quashed wherever they were found. One after another, radicalized priests and nuns who dared take up populist causes were targeted, killed, exiled.

The Vatican was soon caught in the cross fire. It had flung wide its gates at the dawn of Vatican II, raising the clerics' hopes with a firm stand against poverty, only to slam it shut again when it thought they had gone too far. For all the heroics on behalf of the poor, for all the martyred priests and nuns who had made the ultimate sacrifice, the violence that ripped through Latin America in the latter half of the twentieth century—and the Church's implication in it—frightened away peasants and slum dwellers, who began to flock to Pentecostal temples, choosing a life of the spirit over the perils of the day. As one American pastor put it, "The Catholic Church opted for the poor, but the poor opted for the evangelicals." Pope Benedict, flying into Brazil to try to win back the fickle soul of a continent, perhaps failed to see the connection: by rejecting one activist priest after another—by siding with power, by protecting the Church's flanks from any criticism whatsoever, by failing to respond to the meek of the earth, by leaving renegade clerics to construct their own versions of liberation theology—the Vatican had reaped a whirlwind. The stone seemed to be passing into other hands.

* * *

Pope Benedict was not alone. His predecessor, Pope John Paul II, among the most beloved pontiffs in Latin America for his support of the "preferential option for the poor," had also neglected signs of the exodus. Touring South America in the 1980s, he was aware of the influx of evangelicals, but the reception in every country he visited had been nothing short of rapturous, as biblical crowds gathered to receive him and monuments were erected in his honor. It was easy to think it was just a passing romance. All the same, toward the end of his papacy, there were niggling indications that things were going awry: the increasing risks liberation theologists were taking, the mounting outrage over predatory sexual abuses among the clergy, the Church's patent unwillingness to address the sins of its own ranks, the various historical amends that needed to be made. Eventually John Paul II issued a resounding apology to the aboriginals of the Far Pacific: "The wrongs done to indigenous peoples need to be honestly acknowledged," he told Australians and Polynesians forthrightly. "The Church expresses deep regret and asks forgiveness where her children have been party to wrongs." But the Church had yet to acknowledge its part in the conquest and subjugation of the Americas, a fact not overlooked by the millions of indigent faithful who turned out to receive him year after year in country after country.

On those Latin American visits, the Polish pope had focused his attention on the ills of liberation theology, excoriating its Latin American practitioners and approaching its uniquely regional nature with an authoritarian, Eurocentric point of view. His all-consuming opposition to left-wing politics in general and Communism in particular prevented a more measured evaluation of the realities of Latin America's dysfunctions. When Bishop Óscar Romero of El Salvador pleaded with him to intercede on behalf of his countrymen and condemn a regime that was turning death squads on its own people, John Paul simply cautioned him to beware of politics and stick with the anti-Communist side. "But Holy Father," Romero protested with reason, "anti-Communism is what the Right [the proponent of violence] preaches!" Sticking with anti-Communism, the bishop insisted, would mean condoning the death squads. And indeed, the violent right-wing government in El Salvador had proven itself a mortal danger to its people. The National Guard had

made it very clear—had said so in a public forum—that it was prepared
to kill as many as three hundred thousand Salvadorans, if that's what it
took to squelch a leftist insurrection. At least forty thousand peasants
had already been slaughtered, a staggering percentage of the country's
population. The US equivalent would have been more than four million.
All the same, the Church did not listen to Romero's pleas. Months after
his visit to the pope to seek mercy for his fellow citizens, the bishop was
gunned down and killed in the full light of day while saying Mass in a
hospital chapel in El Salvador.

Even then, Pope John Paul II was unconvinced. In a visit to Nicaragua three years later, he publicly denounced priests who had taken
political stances, although the evidence of human misery was all around
him: two-thirds of the country lived in poverty, infant mortality was at
an all-time high, 93 percent of the population did not have safe, potable
water. As he addressed the half million Nicaraguans who had gathered
to hear him, many of them at patience's end, he was repeatedly drowned
out by hecklers who shouted, "We want peace!" "Power to the people!"
to which, visibly irritated, he barked back more than once, "Silence!"
When Ernesto Cardenal, a liberation priest, dropped to his knees afterward to kiss the pope's ring, John Paul snatched it away, shook a finger
in his face, and scolded him to "straighten out your position with the
Church!" Later, Cardenal had strong words in response: "Christ led me
to Marx!" he insisted. "I do not think the pope understands Marxism."
There had been reasons for the Vatican's blindness to spiraling Protestantism. It had been too busy waging war against its own priests.

When John Paul II finally did turn his attention to evangelical gains
in the region, he was curt, dismissive. In a 1992 address to Latin American bishops in the Dominican Republic, which was meant to celebrate
the five hundredth anniversary of Columbus's landing on those shores,
the pope warned of "rapacious wolves" among the evangelicals. He accused the intruders of being predators, promoters of "pseudospiritual
movements," sowers of nothing but division and discord. Their money
and designs, he warned ominously, were heavily funded from abroad.
That message was amplified by bishops throughout the region, who denounced the evangelical initiative as little more than a bald North American invasion, blessed by and paid for by the CIA. They had forgotten,

somehow, that the Catholic Church had been forced on the New World by an invasion of its own. The listening crowds, aware of the ironies of "celebrating" the quincentennial of a ruthless conquest, awaited some reference to the Church's complicity in the violence, but they never heard one. "From the very beginning, the Catholic Church has been a tireless defender of Indians," Pope John Paul told them instead, citing as heroes, with no irony whatsoever, the very friars the sixteenth-century Church had condemned for raising their voices against the savagery.

Five hundred years after the fact, the head of the Church was making the point Pope Alexander VI had made in 1493: that the Church would protect the First People if they believed in Christ, even though everyone knew better, and even though it was clear that the Indians of 1992 occupied virtually the same rung their ancestors had occupied in 1492—the very bottom. The pope then made a roundabout reference to present-day liberation priests, suggesting that their distractions might be the reason why Latin Americans were wary about Catholicism and looking around for other spiritual masters. "The great masses are without adequate religious attention," he fretted. "The faithful do not find in their pastoral ministers a strong sense of God."

Liberation priests had lost their grip on the people's pulse. That much was certainly true. Latin Americans had grown weary of so much violence; of the ceaseless rattling of swords that liberation theology had joined. In contrast, Pentecostals, Charismatics, Jehovah Witnesses, and other Protestant denominations were offering belief systems the struggling classes could understand: a more resolute connection to spiritual life and to their communities; a return to the virtues that had made their ancestors strong. In the ancient Inca way of thinking, a muscular code of ethics had been essential to society: *Ama suwa, ama llulla, ama qhella.* Do not steal, do not lie, do not be idle. What had the conquest given them in its stead? Enslavement. A culture of corruption. Wanton immorality. Rampant poverty. There was a hunger throughout the Americas for a more governed self, a more controlled society, a system that demanded principles and opened the door to a better life. The evangelicals were offering just that.

Pentecostal missionaries flowed into this flagging, angry terrain, proposing an apolitical alternative. Theirs was a brighter future, a way ahead. As one preacher put it, "We have all heard the old song—the song of hatred, sin, racism, intolerance, division, strife, brokenness. It's time to sing something new." Worshiping in their ranks, they claimed, offered a direct conversation with God, fewer intermediaries between man and his Creator. Even more attractive in those postcataclysmic years was the sense of order that Pentecostalism promised. Not only was its code of ethics as rigorous as the ancients', it was downright spartan: a convert was expected to attend religious services regularly, bond with neighbors, reject homosexuals, prohibit drinking, spurn sex before marriage, condemn abortion, decry racism, and place a man at the center of his family (although evangelical missionaries emphasized that it took a good woman to put him there). There was no need to travel a via crucis to reach salvation: conversion alone could win it. They called it spiritual rebirth, instant regeneration, the grace of being born again. Most important, according to missionaries, the Pentecostalist way was the road to upward mobility. Whereas the Catholic Church had told its believers that it was noble to be poor—that the wretched would find a special place in heaven—Pentecostalists were adamant that a believer could have it all right here on earth. They called it prosperity theology, and there was nothing wrong with wanting one's riches in the here and now.

Today Evangelical Christianity is having groundbreaking ramifications for ordinary Latin Americans. Women, who historically have borne the brunt of poverty and marginalization, now see themselves as agents of change. Although they are not necessarily better off politically as evangelicals, they stand to reform their households by luring men to the faith. A religion that brooks no drink, no extramarital sex, or domestic abuse can have a demonstrative impact on the family. And a family that is healthier, more educated, and more productive will move up the socioeconomic ladder. In countries throughout Latin America, the evangelical church is being credited with the creation of a new middle class. It is also being credited with the transformation of a number of conservative parties. In a funhouse distortion of all history that has gone before, evangelicals are joining right-wing political parties that historically have been oppressors of the poor, yet align with their socially conservative views on gay rights, abortion, and the role of women. Strangely enough, on the basis of these abiding shibboleths of culture, the Catholic Church cannot disagree.

These days, in Brazil, where a quarter of the population live in abject poverty and an evangelical preacher can fly from town to town in a private jet worth $45 million, stark economic differences only seem to inspire. Hundreds of thousands of aggravated, unemployed Brazilians stream to evangelical temples to learn how they can pray their way to financial paradise. Edir Macedo, a Brazilian preacher suspected by some of money laundering and charlatanism, nevertheless commands a major newspaper, a number of music companies, a television news station, and a personal fortune worth about $1 billion. A searing critic of the Vatican, he congratulates his ex-Catholic followers for leaving behind a crippling mentality. He assures them that they, too, can be as rich as he is, if only they follow the evangelical example. And they do. On one sunlit morning in Natal, Sandra Abdalla answered her doorbell to find two men applying for construction work in her house. Their pitch was direct: They were clean, they told her—God-fearing, upstanding members of Edir Macedo's Universal Church of the Kingdom of God. They didn't drink, steal, or raise hell. The senhora could count on them to be at her door every morning at seven, and—unlike the Catholic competition— she could trust them around her whisky, her silver, and, by all means, her daughter.

Other, less financially driven evangelicals have taken a more modest route. Willing to venture where Catholic priests will not go, they have penetrated deep into the Lacandón jungle, high into the snowcapped Andes. They don't simply pass through, greeting villagers on quick, proselytizing missions. They live with them, eat what they eat, work by their sides, collect water from the same rivers, bathe their children in the same gullies. They don't call Pentecostalism a religion but "a way." They don't occupy church grounds, but modest shacks. One icy dawn, as Leonor Gonzáles left her hut in the hyaline heights of La Rinconada to sift through the rock spill from the mines, she saw a makeshift sign nailed precariously on a nearby door. When she asked her daughter Senna what it said, she was told it was an invitation: "Come in, friend. We are Leaving Footprints. We are the Assemblies of God." The hut, like Leonor's, was built of stone.

BLOWS LIKE THE WRATH OF GOD

There are blows in life, so hard . . . I don't know! Blows like the wrath
of God, as if all at once the undertow of all that had ever been suffered
rushed in to swamp the soul . . . I don't know!

—César Vallejo, "The Black Heralds"

Xavier Albó was not immune to the passions of liberation priests, nor was
he unaware of the radical challenges they suggested. Like many of his fellow priests in Latin America—the overwhelming majority from Spain—
he had grown up among devout Catholics who, caught in the vicissitudes
of the Spanish Civil War, had followed the Church and saluted Generalísimo Franco. Their swing now to the Left seemed a natural enough
human response to the error of choosing a side that had exterminated
almost half a million. Not least, Xavier and his cohort had contemplated
history, studied the conquest, seen the ways that, for all the Church's efforts to appear apolitical, it had seldom been so. It had never been far
removed from the sword and throne. From the moment its priests had
set foot in Latin America, it had been the religion of domination, of faraway kings, of tyrants and despots and corridors of power. It had built
mighty institutions; it had been trusted, obeyed, respected. But it had not
attended to the miners, the peons, the bricklayers—the poor, persecuted,
and despised. How had the Church strayed so far from Christ's example?

He was more than fifty before he looked around and realized that
he had been living and working on a continent beset by violence since
the day he had arrived, a downy-cheeked, seventeen-year-old boy. His
dream had always been to immerse himself in this new land: to learn, to
understand the Guaraní, the Aymara, the Quechua, the Afro-Latins—
the great proliferation of cultures that were buried deep in the larger
American identity. This was not a sentimental or comfortable aspiration.
In the half century he had spent in South America, he had seen what
championing the poor could do to a man. He had lost fellow priests to
executions, skirmishes, revenge killings; he had prayed over their mutilated corpses, he had hazarded forays into the most remote jungles to
meet with liberation priests alongside their gun-toting comrades. He

had never been lured to aggression, but he could understand it. Perhaps it was because, as a student of anthropology, he had been trained to see the world through other eyes, to refrain from passing judgment. Certainly, he had never sought to protect himself from the harsher aspects of the Latin American reality. But for all his curiosity, for all his desire to plumb the heart of his adopted homeland, he had not been dealt the worst. He had been spared the sword.

Not Vicente Cañas, a Jesuit friend who had immersed himself so thoroughly in the indigenous cultures of Brazil and Paraguay that he had shed his robe, pierced his face, and joined the tribe of the Enawenê-Nawê. Working tirelessly to protect the tribal land from mining companies and land-razing ranchers, Cañas had been singled out as a target by Paraguay's cutthroat dictator, Alfredo Stroessner, who dismissed him as "that silly little priest"—an irritant, a pest, a mote in the churning universe of graft—who only got in the way. Cast out of Paraguay for his work with the Guaraní, Cañas then made his home in a cabin in Brazil six hours downriver by canoe from the Enawenê-Nawê, where he could conduct spiritual retreats and visit that tribe regularly, helping them plant, fend off aggressors, care for the sick. Cañas was found by his hut one fine morning, gutted and sprawled on the blood-soaked dirt, his skull crushed, his genitals cut off, his few worldly possessions destroyed. When Brazilian judges tried to get to the bottom of the crime, the police—paid off by rich, land-hungry *fazendeiros*—absconded with the priest's smashed cranium, the prima facie evidence, and no one was held accountable. His skull was eventually found in an abandoned box in a remote bus station in Minas Gerais.

Not spared, too, was João Bosco Burnier, his Jesuit colleague in a diamond mining town, who was pistol-whipped and shot point-blank in the neck with a *bala dundum*—an exploding bullet—when he tried to save two indigenous women from being torn apart by wild boars. A group of bored soldiers had tied down the women and were goading the animals to disembowel them alive, before the gory enterprise was interrupted by Brother João. The women were saved, but the Jesuit was not. It took more than twenty years for the military to admit that the women were a lure; the meddlesome priest had been their target all along.

And so it went throughout the hemisphere. One after another, activist missionary priests continued to be targets of the military, of foreign corporations, of rich owners of haciendas, of testosterone-driven caudillos. Their more conservative brothers gravitated to cities, to centers of privilege as they had done since time immemorial—safe and sound, working in prestigious schools and universities, attending to congregations of the rich and upwardly mobile. Once in a while, as priests were wont to do, they wandered onto dangerous ground.

WORD OF GOD

It is their natural right to be recognized as a culture distinct from the Western culture, a culture in which they live their own faith.
                                        —Bishop Samuel Ruíz, Chiapas

One of the more fearless was the Mexican bishop of Chiapas, Samuel Ruiz, whose work on behalf of the poor eventually blossomed into full-blown rebellion: the Zapatista uprising of 1994. It began when the Church sent catechists to serve a population boom in the Lacandón jungle. Before 1950, the Lacandón had relatively few inhabitants, but when the government began to urge landowners in to establish cattle ranches instead of farms, hundreds of thousands of peons laboring in Chiapas's agricultural fields were dismissed en masse. An escape to the forest seemed the only option, and the Indians—evicted, homeless, angry—flooded into the jungle, with catechists and revolutionaries in tow.

Bishop Ruiz, immediately sympathetic to their plight, took it upon himself to shepherd this newly displaced population. He determined to protect them from exploitation and, to that effort, installed a new category of spiritual worker: the *tuhuneles*, the lay deacons, eight thousand strong, who, unlike catechists, could preach as well as offer sacraments of baptism, communion, and marriage. This new breed corresponded to a centuries-old aspiration among the Indians: the ability to elect their own leaders, promote their own priests, grow their own religion. Ruíz and his fellow priests called this more muscular effort of proselytization "the Word of God." Eventually Ruiz found himself building an entire empire in Chiapas, attracting gun-toting militants—*brigadistas*—who

joined forces with deacons to organize honey farmers and coffee growers, raising political consciousnesses, demanding human rights. As time
went on and Ruiz's friend Bishop Óscar Romero was gunned down in El
Salvador, the villages of Chiapas began to fear the encroaching military
terror that sped uncontrolled through Nicaragua, Honduras, El Salvador, and Guatemala in the 1980s (as it did throughout Latin America in
those years). The Church's deacons, seeking stronger champions and defenders, eventually turned to an even more radical group: the Frente de
Liberación Nacional (FLN), which had tucked itself into the Lacandón
jungle in 1983, transformed itself into the Zapatista Army of National
Liberation (EZLN), and readied itself for all-out war against the Mexican state. So it was that Bishop Ruiz, who had become prophet, priest,
and king to the downtrodden people of Chiapas, came face-to-face with
Subcomandante Marcos.

It was a fractious confrontation. The declared terrorist and *guerrillero*
Subcomandante Marcos, a charismatic figure in his black ski mask and
pipe, commanded the Lacandón as whimsically and erratically as Robin
Hood had commanded Sherwood Forest. Outraged and radicalized by
the government's bloody 1968 Tlatelolco massacre of students in Mexico
City, which claimed 350 lives, Marcos had slipped into the jungle several
years later, joined forces with remnants of the FLN, and created an army
that would bedevil the Mexican authorities for twenty years. Trained by
Cuban guerrillas and a passionate apostle of Che Guevara, Marcos was
sharp tongued, fierce, unequivocal—the absolute opposite of the sweet-
faced *tatic* (father), the soft-spoken bishop with the gentle eyes.

And yet Marcos and Ruiz concurred on much: They were both sure
that their new peasant movement was a return to roots, a vindication of
the conquest's depredations, a resurgence of the most ancient of all pasts,
Indian Mexico. They understood that if oppression was their target, theirs
was inherently a political battle; and where there was political division,
violence was never far behind. They also concurred in the Marxist view:
that the underdevelopment of the Third World was a direct product of the
avaricious development of the First. Foreign ventures undertaken by rich
countries had promised much in the Americas and, indeed, had brought
fitful progress, but the overall effect had been subjugation, and those who
bore the brunt were always the lower classes, the darker races, the poor.

That much was agreed upon between the guerrilla and the priest. But whereas Bishop Ruiz was convinced that his "Word of God"—a Marxist interpretation of the gospel—and his *tuhuneles* and catechists were in themselves a redemptive force and liberating army, Subcomandante Marcos adamantly did not. Although the guerrilla's writings had an unmistakable biblical tone, damning the depravities Indians were too often prey to (prostitution, alcoholism, machismo, domestic violence), and although all the Zapatistas quickly adopted biblical names (Moisés, Josué, David, Daniel), Marcos was no believer in God. "God and his Word aren't worth a damn," he was often heard to say as he spurred his horse through the forest green, a semiautomatic strapped to his side, a pipe jutting from his trademark balaclava.

Eventually Marcos would draw a line with Bishop Ruiz: "Here there will be no Word of God," he announced to the denizens of the Lacandón jungle. "Here there will be no government of the republic, here there is only going to be the Zapatista Army of National Liberation." Little did he know that Bishop Ruiz had already crossed that line. To marshal God's word, Ruiz had created a radical organization known as Root (*slōp* in Tzeltal Mayan), a clandestine group whose charge was to prepare for a possible armed rebellion between the people of Chiapas and the shock troops of the republic. It had been meant as a back-up defense guard, but when Subcomandante Marcos swept into far corners of the Lacandón, recruiting terrorists for his Zapatista Army, there was already a core of armed peasants more than ready to sign up. They had been groomed for it by the *tatic*'s catechists. Bishop Ruiz shook his head and lamented, "These people [the Zapatistas] have arrived to mount a saddled horse." The Church had planted a seed, and the people of Mexico would now reap a bitter harvest. The Zapatista uprising erupted with full force on New Year's Day 1994, in a killing spree that left more than 150 dead. Three years later, even after peace talks had begun, the carnage would continue. Paramilitaries would invade churches and gun down whole congregations. Forty thousand government troops would descend on that forest paradise to suppress the rebels. Indians would sell their livestock to buy arms. "The truth is that for the indigenous," the *tatic* said sadly after weeks of rampant bloodshed, "there is no way out but that of the gun."

*   *   *

Ruiz was beset from all sides for his role in the bloody uprising: the Vatican tried to muzzle him; political enemies tried to assassinate him; the Mexican government waged a no-holds-barred campaign to discredit his name. Dubbed the "Red Bishop" by adversaries, Ruiz had become emblematic of the controversial role liberation theologists were playing in Latin America's ongoing crises. From the 1960s well into the twenty-first century—from the bizarre, self-inflicted genocide of Peru's Shining Path, to Brazil's scarring vendetta against its leftist rebels, to Guatemala's systematic purge of nearly a quarter million of its people—the Church was seen as siding with insurgents, goading the meek to think they might inherit the earth. The aftershocks continued to reverberate throughout the hemisphere for decades to come. Indeed, since 2006, Mexico has made the fury in Chiapas look trivial. Its drug wars have generated catastrophic human losses that dwarf the Zapatista uprising. In the last ten years, more than two hundred thousand Mexicans have died as a result of the illegal drug trade. There is a reason why Protestant missionaries are doing so well recruiting souls south of the Rio Grande: Mexico is the most dangerous country in Latin America for Catholic priests and nuns. Drug lords make a point to attend Catholic church services, carry and distribute Bibles, justify their violence as "divine justice" or orders from the Lord. Sometimes a priest just gets in the way.

As fate would have it, Xavier Albó was visiting Ruiz during the peace talks that took place in Chiapas in the late 1990s. Calling on him in the bright-yellow stucco cathedral that was the *tatic's* domain, he congratulated the bishop on his work with the indigenous but gently inserted his own thoughts about nonviolence. It was not the first they had met, and Ruíz remembered the Jesuit as the Bolivian who, like him, had dedicated his life to the disenfranchised of this increasingly fraying New World. Xavier glanced around to take in the scene of those historic mediations. It was jarring to see, but it was certainly nothing he didn't recognize—a norm for anyone who had cared to look in the past five hundred years: behind one cordon were the Indians, awaiting judgment. Behind another, dressed in white, members of the international peace groups that supported them. Behind the third, the military and police, with guns and grenades at the ready.

WHERE THE SPIRIT RESIDES

"Religion" suggests something structured, doctrinal, rigid. For us, it is more deep inside. Not a cult, not a building, not a bible.
                    —David Choquehuanca, chancellor of Bolivia, 2017

Why would an appraisal of the current state of Latin American faith include religions that are no longer practiced—religions that are mere vestiges of civilizations annihilated five hundred years ago? Perhaps because the fire has never quite been extinguished; because the rubble of conquest still holds abiding power over the land.

The native populations of the Americas—virtually stamped out in North America—have survived to different degrees in Latin America. Killed off or driven to near extinction in Argentina, Chile, Uruguay, and Brazil, the First People are still vibrantly present elsewhere, if not as pure indigenous stock then in the veins of the region's largely mixed-race population. Whereas the English and French rarely mixed with their colonial vassals in North America, Africa, and India, the Spanish and Portuguese conjugated freely with the colored races of Latin America, producing a vast racial fusion. With that diversity came a virulent, institutionalized racism, ruthlessly observed. As soon as Spain was able to impose some semblance of control over its colonies, it moved to enforce a strict separation of races. At the very top were the Spanish; immediately below, their American-born white offspring; below that, a torrent of admixtures: the mestizos, sambos, mulattos, quadroons, octoroons, moriscos, coyotes, chamisos, gíbaros, and so on, each shade of skin color recorded meticulously by the Church in official birth registries. For each hue in that broad spectrum of racial identity, there were concrete socioeconomic ramifications. If a newborn looked Indian and was duly recorded as such, he would grow up subject to the Spanish tribute; if he were unable to pay, he was forced to meet his debt through hard labor. Chained, herded in gangs, separated from families, stripped of all humanity, Indians were likely to be sent great distances to satisfy Spain's demands. Today those colonial hardships may be gone, but the racism endures.

From time to time, the deep racial prejudices rush back to haunt those who may be unaware of their own genealogical past. With the proliferation of genetics tests, Latin Americans who identify as "white" are gradually learning that they may be only partially so, the great majority descended from ancestors who represent every race of man. I myself am an example of this. Told throughout childhood that our family is *cien por ciento criolla*—100 percent Spanish blooded—although our history reaches back half a millennium in South America, I have learned since from genetic tests that I am only slightly more than half Caucasian: I am brown, I am yellow, I am black. I belong, as the Mexican philosopher José Vasconcelos put it, to the Cosmic Race. *La raza cósmica*. Most of us with deep roots in these Americas do.

Which brings us to a phenomenon particular to Latin America: that those who are visibly identifiable as descendants of Indians or Africans insist with a certitude bordering on defensiveness that they are not. For many, it is an insult to call out one's darker ancestry, "the stain"—*la mancha*—that the majority of us inherited from our colored races. But as Mexican writer Carlos Fuentes once wrote, "We are all men of La Mancha." We are people of the stain. Or, as the old joke goes, like bananas, we Latin Americans eventually show our black spots. Fuentes went on to spell this out more fully: "When we understand that none of us is pure, that we are all both real and ideal, heroic and absurd, made of desire and imagination as much as of blood and bone, and that each of us is part Christian, part Jew, part Moor, part Caucasian, part black, part Indian, without having to sacrifice any of the components— only then will we truly understand both the grandeur and vassalage of Spain."

This inherent and deeply ingrained racism has ways of emerging in strange ways. In the Andes, until the recent wave of *indigenismo*, an Indian seldom alluded to his or her race: Bolivia's Indians referred to themselves as *campesinos*, country people; Peruvians called themselves *serranos*, people of the mountain. Blacks of Venezuela call themselves *morenos*, which literally means Moorish but can also mean tanned or bronzed, as in *azucar morena*—the color of brown sugar. And then there are the nicknames (not always affectionate) for anyone with the slightest racial feature: slanted eyes (*chino*); indigenous features (*cholo*); dark skin (*sambo*); fair haired (*guero*). It is why, in Latin America, race is devilishly hard to catalog with any certitude in a census. An outward trait can belie the genome, and a person is likely to identify as an ethnicity he is not. Japanese are often mislabeled as *chinos* (as was the Peruvian president "El Chino" Alberto Fujimori); Arabs are called *turcos* (as is one of the richest men in the world, the Mexican billionaire "El Turco" Carlos Slim). Contradictions abound. Curiously enough, in Paraguay, where Guaraní is spoken by the overwhelming majority, were you to call a passerby a Guaraní, chances are he would be taken aback. The Guaraní represent a minuscule population—2 percent—in a country that was once entirely theirs. And yet 90 percent of all Paraguayans speak the Guaraní language.

What does this mean for matters of the spirit? For the 80 percent who count themselves Catholic, faith in this part of the world, like race, is an amalgamation. Even in urban, predominantly white areas, worship is more often syncretic than orthodox. Latin American Christianity, whether it be Catholic or evangelical, is infused with superstition, exorcism, sacrificial rites, curative rituals, dark powers, voodoo, nature worship, and the supernatural. Nowhere is this more richly documented than in the region's literature, in which devout Catholics—for all their prayers to the Holy Virgin—consult seers to communicate with the dead or shamans to purge evil from the living. A cobbled life of the spirit is as evident in the novels of Gabriel García Márquez as it is in the poetry of Octavio Paz. Since pre-Columbian days, religion in this turbulent sphere has had to tweak, mutate, make room for the incoming stranger. As the superior general of the Society of Jesus said when Xavier Albó took up his priestly work in South America, "You cannot be truly religious here if you are not interreligious; you cannot be a Catholic if you are not ecumenical." Faith in a nervous precinct, in other words, must be supple if it is to survive. The pre-Columbian Indians knew this. And although the impulse on Latin American ground since time immemorial—since long before Cortés or Pizarro or Columbus—is to believe in a higher power, to yearn for a currency beyond life on earth, the urge in this fickle landscape is also toward change.

*   *   *

Change is arguably very much on the mind of Francis I, the first Latin American pope, who was named pontiff at a point in history when his homeland represents Catholicism's best hope as well as its most precarious wound. On his 2018 papal trip to the region, Francis carefully avoided saying too much about the Church's raging sexual abuse scandal, but he spoke frankly about the corruption, greed, and violence that are taking a harsh toll on Latin Americans. "Politics is in crisis, very much in crisis in Latin America . . . more sick than well," he told those who had gathered to hear him in Lima. He deplored Brazil's Odebrecht scandal, the largest foreign bribery case in history, a scourge of corruption that involved billions of dollars and implicated presidents and politicians of more than a dozen countries from the Caribbean to the Southern Cone. "What is wrong with Peru," Francis scolded, "that when one finishes being president, one ends up behind bars?"

The pope was clearly determined to set things right in his part of the world. A few years earlier, and more remarkably, he did what his predecessors have never done in half a millennium of history: he apologized for the rank violation of Latin American Indians. In a landmark address in Bolivia, speaking to a hall of indigenous listeners, including President Evo Morales, he offered a stinging apology that did not mince words: "Many grave sins were committed against the native people of America in the name of God," he said plainly. The massive crowd of Aymara, Quechua, and Guaraní Bolivians leapt to its feet in euphoric recognition of the significance of that simple declaration. The pope, in his usual modesty, demurred. He added that he was not really saying anything new; he credited Pope John Paul II for apologizing for the Church's "infidelities to the Gospel . . . especially during the second millennium." But there was no question that Francis *was* saying something new. Xavier Albó, who was present, was struck by the intensity and candor of his admission. The pope didn't stop there, however; he continued his apology, not only on behalf of Rome but of Spain, Portugal, England, France—all the self-appointed conquerors of the Americas. "I humbly ask forgiveness," he said, "not only for the offense of the Church herself, but for crimes committed against the native peoples during the so-called conquest of America."

TO RIGHT THE UNRIGHTABLE WRONG

If someone asks me if I believe in kharisiri *[white ghouls who prey on
Indians], I will say, No, I do not, but I have the greatest respect for the
people who do.*

—Xavier Albó, 2017

Xavier has gone on to attain considerable stature in his beloved Bolivia.
Having inserted himself into the needs and aspirations of a never-ending
sea of underprivileged, the energetic eighty-five-year-old is known as
tata tapukillu or *el cura preguntón*: our father of endless questions,
friendly curiosity, gentle intrusions. With a traditional knit cap—an Andean *ch'ullo*—perched on his head and a worn alpaca sweater to guard
him against the chill, he putters through the streets of La Paz, stopping
to chat in Aymara with the fruit vendor, or in Quechua with a cluster
of schoolchildren. This is his daily ritual: the ongoing communion he
maintains with his people, a liturgy of the hours, a living rosary.

If he came to these shores to learn rather than to preach, he has accomplished his ambitions. He is, like celebrated priests before him—
Bartolomé de las Casas or Bernardino de Sahagún—well known as a
scholar of the First People. In 2017, for his abundant contributions, Bolivia's highest honor, Knight of the Order of the Condor of the Andes,
was conferred on him. He has advised presidents on native populations;
he has brokered peace among warring tribes; he has worked side by
side with evangelicals; he has raised foundations, libraries, and schools
to teach Indians about the larger world and the proud place they hold
within it. He has been both counselor and critic to the first indigenous
president of Bolivia, Evo Morales, a former bricklayer and coca farmer
whose election in 2005 Xavier celebrated with joy—and whose evolution
into a rock-ribbed, despotic caudillo he has vigorously censured.

A fount of good humor, he calls his fellow Jesuits "the most terrifying
tribe that ever descended on this mountain redoubt." He says it with a
mixture of pride for a brotherhood that has labored mightily to set history aright and regret for a church that too often has marched alongside
tyrants. He has represented Latin America in intense consultations with

eminences of the Holy See, and he has given testimony in Quechua at humble hearings in tumbledown hamlets. To him, it seems preposterous that a pastor would choose to communicate in Spanish—the language of the conquest—with those who have minded this land for thousands of years.

Albó represents a Latin American church in the crucible of transformation. To be sure, he is less concerned with doctrine than with the long-suffered spiritual afflictions of his flock. Comparing his ministry to the practice of medicine—an equally fragile discipline—one might say that he recognizes the patient's symptoms and is searching for cures. In the more than sixty years that he has devoted himself to Latin America, he has learned that his work is hard to explain to chance interlocutors. But eventually he puts it plainly: "I don't want to conquer souls. I don't want to be a master to anyone. I am here to keep company," he says. Nothing more.

In his lifetime, he has seen self-anointed redeemers come and go: Fidel Castro, Manuel Noriega, Evo Morales, Juan Perón, Alberto Fujimori, Hugo Chávez—leaders who promised much, delivered some, and clung to power far too long. He has watched democratically elected presidents become tinpot dictators, insatiable caesars like so many others in the region's history since Columbus was handed the pearls of Panama, or Cortés hijacked the riches of Montezuma, or Pizarro demanded roomfuls of gold and silver. For Xavier Albó, the real treasures, he tells me, are *las tres patas.* The three pillars of a sturdy society, nothing less than the three legs a good table requires: a balance among economic justice, social equality, and educational opportunity. Or, you might say: the do-not-steal, do-not-lie, do-not-be-idle foundational principles of civilizations that went before. "There is nothing religious about this," he says. And yet it is all about cardinal precepts, Christian commandments, a binding covenant on which human beings can agree. It is a question of the spirit.

"I am not one to pray," he tells me. "At least not in any ritualized, obligatory kind of way. I am not that kind of priest. It is more deep inside." And then he waits to see if I have caught the allusion to something David Choquehuanca, the Aymara chancellor of Bolivia, had once told him, something he had mentioned to me several days before. The chancellor had explained that the word *religion* did not appear in the Bolivian

constitution because faith was not something concrete or rigidly understood. "For us, it is more deep inside. Not a cult, not a building, not a
Bible."

It is no surprise that the Church's formalities have never appealed
to Xavier Albó. No surprise that he is staunchly apolitical. Having departed the Spanish Civil War to arrive at the Bolivian revolution, he is
wary of partisan allegiances. As I left him in his modest room after our
last interview in La Paz, he seemed smaller than I had found him, a little
spent by my endless questions, my curiosity, my intrusions. But his eyes
sparkled.

"There's an image I can't quite get out of my mind," he said as I
gathered my notebooks. "It's an old bit of history, but maybe it will tell
you something about the way I think." The image he had in mind was
of Julian de Lizardi, a young Basque priest who had left Spain in 1717
to join the Jesuit missions in Paraguay. Lizardi was sent deep into the
unexplored interior to evangelize the Chiriguanos, a hostile tribe of the
Guaraní that had fiercely resisted Christianization. Not long after he arrived, the Chiriguanos smeared their faces with war paint and mounted
an attack on the makeshift little church where he was holding mass.
They seized him, stripped him of his vestments, led him naked to an
immense rock, and bound him there while they sacked the altar, burned
the Church, and killed everyone in the vicinity. Weeks later, the Jesuit
was found strapped to that towering white stone, lanced, bludgeoned,
and pierced by a hundred arrows.

The question must have hung in my eyes.

"I'm telling you this, because you will understand why I couldn't very
well campaign for the man's canonization," he said. The prayer card
with Lizardi's likeness had stated: "Killed in a barbaric assassination by
savages."

"Savages! The Guaraní! The very people I was working with at the
time." Xavier waved his hand. "So you see. It's a fraught business. For
some, an intervention on behalf of God can be read as an act of war."

IT'S JUST OUR NATURE

—————————— ❖ ——————————

Stress is transgenerational [heritable], and a parent's exposure to it will risk PTSD in subsequent generations.
—*Biological Psychiatry*, September 1, 2015

Juan Gabriel Vásquez, one of Latin America's most distinguished novelists—an eloquent witness to the heartbreaking bloodbath that has plagued Colombia for generations—tells of the moment in the early 2000s when his twin daughters were born in Bogotá. It was in the heat of the killing, when tens of thousands were falling victim to a perfect storm of drugs, public truculence, and terror. Nestling the newborns into the young father's arms, the obstetrician suddenly recognized him as the novelist-journalist who was meticulously recording the ongoing trauma of Colombia's violence. The doctor insisted that Vásquez come to his home, saying he had something important to show him. Within hours, Vásquez was making his way through the vertiginous, winding streets of that Andean capital to see what the man so urgently wanted him to see. A knock on the door, and he was quickly led to a room where he was handed a small, sealed jar exuding a chemical stink and filled with a murky yellow liquid. Immediately, he understood that the ghoulish hunk suspended within were bones of a human spine.

Placing the jar into Vásquez's hands as tenderly as he had handed him his newborn infants, the physician explained that the bones had once belonged to Jorge Gaitán, the presidential candidate whose assassination in Bogotá almost sixty years before had erupted into a frenzy of killing known as La Violencia. Somehow, passed down from doctor to doctor, the specimen had ended up in a drawer in the obstetrician's house.

But the bones told only part of the story. For ten hours after Gaitán's murder on April 9, 1948, the people had rioted, stoning the presidential palace, torching the city's vehicles and houses, prompting a hellish government response that left Bogotá in ruins. Within hours, as news of the assassination spread throughout the country, the violence proliferated, provoking mayhem and carnage in Medellín, Bucaramanga, and Ibagué. For ten more years, the Colombian people would extract revenge for Gaitán's murder. That fury would spur a civil war, invite military crackdowns, spawn bands of angry guerrillas and paramilitary militias, and give rise to drug hoods whose cartels and operatives fanned through the countryside and held Colombia hostage into the twenty-first century. More than five million Colombians would be forced from their homes; forty-five thousand children would be killed.

Vásquez cradled the jar with Gaitán's spine in his hands—the very hands that, hours before, had held the tiny, flailing bodies of his daughters. Here, in his grasp, was a relic of the murder that had sparked rebellion and hatched a reign of terror. La Violencia had begun when his father was an infant in the 1940s, accelerated when Vásquez himself first saw light in 1973, and now was still ablaze three generations later, insinuating its way into the lives of his children. The question that occurred to Vásquez with sudden and urgent force was this: had violence—the impulse to it, the dread of it, the inevitability of it—been written into his country's genes? Was it a heritable trait? Had brutality been so deeply imprinted on his people that it had become the accepted norm, a way of life? Had it rattled down the generations to be engraved on the temporal lobes, ganglia, and hearts of two little girls who had entered this world only hours before?

The study of transgenerational epigenetic inheritance is a young science—much about it is tenuous and unproven, far from being accepted beyond a shadow of scientific doubt. Whereas we now know that a pregnant mother's trauma can chemically alter the cells of the fetus she is carrying, whether an entire generation's DNA can be marked by the horrors and abuses its parents and grandparents have endured is another question. And yet it doesn't have to be scientifically proven for Latin Americans to believe that this is so. In many of the region's cultures—

and certainly within the Catholic context—it is generally accepted that a curse can echo its way down the generations. As recently as my father's lifetime, it was believed that the sins of an ancestor might predispose you to be born with a tail. A woman who witnessed atrocities was bound to bear monstrously deformed children. Babies would be enslaved by the curse of their forefathers. Call it superstition, wrongheaded religious education, magical thinking—it is still alive and well in many precincts of Latin America. Whether or not science ever establishes conclusively that violence, fear, or cowardice can be genetically coded in the human helix, for centuries we have believed it to be so.

Perhaps that is why we are so predisposed to believe myths, extravagant political promises, outright lies. Perhaps it is why we have learned to witness history with a certain helplessness. For all the extraordinary advances Latin America has made in the past hundred years—for all the economic gains, the improved living conditions, the gradual eradication of poverty, the rise of a fledgling middle class—we look over our shoulders in fear that those fragile structures could easily tumble. Often they do. A sudden revolt, a foreign intervention, a pigheaded despot, a violent earthquake might bring down the house of cards. When Peru's poverty rose in 2018 for the first time in sixteen years and hundreds of thousands of Peruvians slipped back into desperate beggary, you could almost hear the collective sigh: Why did we ever think it could be otherwise? When rumors of impending coups cropped up after the impeachment of a president in one country and the rise of an ultra-right-wing president in another, these were more than rumors: they were fears steeped in history, anxieties deeply marked by the past.

How is it that Argentina, the fifth richest country in the world in the 1930s, with a per capita income equal to that of France and more automobiles than the United Kingdom, has been such a perpetual victim to corruption, stagnation, and disarray? How is it that Venezuela, with the largest proven oil reserves on the planet—potentially the wealthiest country in all of South America—is now patently unable to feed itself? When Venezuela's economy bottomed out under Nicolás Maduro, and all the pretty dreams woven by Hugo Chávez were sent into a spiral of desperation and hunger, millions of the disillusioned set out on an unprecedented exodus, abandoning their country, shaking their heads, wondering where it had all gone wrong. The wiser heads—haves along with have-nots—did not wonder at all. What had gone wrong was what always went wrong: the dictators, the rapine, the seemingly insurmountable indigence, corruption, inefficiency. It's just our nature.

The renowned Venezuelan intellectual Carlos Rangel once said that the ten thousand kilometers that separate Mexico from Argentina mark a geographic distance, not a spiritual one. There are sufficient commonalities of history and character in Spanish-speaking America to allow us to generalize about the whole. Rangel, who despised Castro's Communist dictatorship as much as the Fascist dictatorship of Pinochet, argued that to be a Latin American of the humbler class was to be trapped in a perpetual cycle of oppression and rebellion, either resigning oneself to the role of noble savage or taking up the revolutionary gauntlet. The champions of the poor place all blame for Latin America's ills on predatory foreigners: we are poor because wealthy nations exploit us; because they rob us of our riches, reduce us to vassals in service to a herculean First World. The rich's champions—guardians of the caste system and the status quo—are inclined to favor dictators, the iron fist, the military, the Church, even foreign interventions so that the haves can keep power in their favor, preserve things exactly as they are. To be a Latin American of the more comfortable class is to long for a firm hand. Whatever our class, Rangel contends, we fear we are congenitally doomed by the other. We assume we'll eventually fall prey to the ire of the opposing side—be it rich or poor—to bitter history, to the system's deficiencies, to our worst instincts. We believe failure is bred in the bone, handed down through generations. Why wouldn't we, if like Leonor Gonzáles—like too many Latin Americans—we are still pounding rock, still dragging water, still living much as our forebears did hundreds of years ago?

There is certainly plenty of evidence for the system's deficiencies. For all our love of family and tradition—for all our human warmth and natural ingenuity, for all our courage in the face of adversity—Latin America is rife with dysfunction. We are, if body counts are any measure, the most murderous place on earth. In a perpetual pendulum swing from street violence to government brutality, our acculturation to the sword is shocking. Nowhere has that terrible numbness been more evident during the last half century than the spate of Latin American countries where rebellion became terrorism, terrorism became "narconomics," and disorder swept the land to be met by genocidal military crackdowns. For decades, from the desert of Sonora to the altiplano of Peru, army ranks ballooned to form robust counterinsurgencies, and when those campaigns were done, legions of out-of-work warriors spilled into cities and villages: a ready-made fighting force for the drug trade. So it was that one generation's centurions became the next generation's criminals. Demobilized Colombian soldiers who once fought the FARC have been lured to the drug trade in forests outside Medellín, just as Peruvian troops that fought the Shining Path ended up toting guns for the cocaine lords of the Huallaga Valley. From paramilitary to coke thug is a familiar trajectory in these lands. Certainly that was the case for Carlos Buergos, a young Cuban warrior for Communism in Angola who found a profitable career as a drug hood in Washington, DC.

Illegal drugs, as one economist has suggested, are Latin America's new silver, extracted greedily from the very territories that historically have sent precious metals around the world: Colombia, Peru, Bolivia, Mexico, Brazil. Just as silver and gold have been dug from Latin America's bowels and shipped away for five hundred years, cocaine and heroin have been reaped, processed, and sent away for fifty. Though it is difficult to measure the exact volume of this clandestine market, we know that it involves veritable armies of narco-operatives and—in countries where drug production is massive—there are few citizens whose lives it doesn't touch. Once laundered, drug dollars flow through construction companies, service industries, tourism, banks, food businesses, political organizations, even churches, changing the very nature of the economy. Since the 1990s, illicit cocaine has commanded a vast web involving hundreds of thousands of employees, from farmers, to smugglers, to rehab counselors. With revenues in the hundreds of billions of dollars, it is among the most valuable single commodity chains in world history.

Although drug money typically finances a shady underworld of crime gangs, prostitution, and human trafficking, these days the prosperity one sees all about in certain Latin American cities—from Santiago to Mexico City—can be the result of drug-financed infusions. Indeed, whole countries can profit from black-market ebullience. Venezuela under President Nicolás Maduro has hitched its very survival to the commerce of illicit drugs: in a diabolical triangle of oil, cocaine money, and military muscle, Venezuela has succeeded in reinventing itself as a narco-mafia state. So it is that Latin American drug currency seems to be everywhere around us. Often we hold its ubiquitousness in our very hands: scientists report that 90 percent of all US dollar bills carry traces of cocaine.

As the daughter of a North American mother, I am outraged at the physical enslavement of twenty-three million human beings—nearly half of them citizens of the United States—to this veritable firehose of white "silver." As the daughter of a South American father, I am appalled at the insatiable hunger for illegal drugs in the United States and Europe and the ways it has shackled the Latin American economy to criminal gangs and a boundless, foreign addiction. There is plenty of blame to go around.

But trade in heroin, marijuana, and cocaine has given the region more than an exuberant underworld market. It has been a powerful generator of violence. More costly in human terms than terrorism, the drug wars have proven to be a grim reaper in these Americas. No other region formally at peace has equalled its levels of violence. Since 2006, more than a quarter million Mexicans have been killed in the US-backed government campaign to stamp out illegal drugs in Mexico. Those killings became so routine that it was hardly reported when thirteen thousand were mowed down in drug-related violence in the first nine months of 2011. Almost forty thousand Mexicans have gone missing. When five severed heads were flung onto a crowded dance floor in Michoacán in the name of "divine justice," the revelers cleared out in terror, but no one was particularly surprised.

The same can be said for Colombia. An equivalent number of Colombians—more than 220,000, to be exact—have been sacrificed in drug wars that have raged for generations. Almost 8 million souls have been displaced. Tens of thousands of children were kidnapped and recruited as combatants. The peace process in Colombia that began in 2016 reduced the murder rate dramatically, cutting it by a third. Even so, to date, Colombia has the highest number of internal refugees of any country in the world: higher than Syria, the Congo, Somalia, Yemen, or Iraq. Similarly, in Venezuela's increasingly violent and dysfunctional ambit, millions of refugees have fled, streaming across borders to seek safety elsewhere. And the litany goes on: according to the United Nations, Brazil's drug-related homicides in a single year rivaled the death toll of the Syrian civil war. Peru, which today is the largest source of coca leaf and a mighty force in the production of cocaine, has long suffered the rampant street violence that drug mafias generate. If forty-three of the fifty most violent cities of the world are in Latin America, illegal drugs are surely one of the big reasons why.

Just as silver brought enormous wealth to the Spanish elite but unspeakable cruelty to native Americans, the illegal drug culture has brought riches to a very few and conflagration to the overwhelming many. Here is an endlessly recurring history, nudged along by the region's gravest affliction: its dire inequality. Latin America is the most unequal region on earth precisely because it has never ceased to be colonized—by exploiters, conquerors, proselytizers—and, for the past two centuries, by its own tiny elite. As economists have long argued, extractive societies such as Latin America's are built on social injustice. They are designed and maintained by a ruling class whose primary goal is to enrich themselves and perpetuate their power. They thrive when absolute privilege reigns over absolute poverty. But extractive nations are also programmed to fail. The damage left behind in their endless raid on natural resources—by silver, if you will—is all too enduring. It is violence, resentment, poverty, environmental damage, crime. To paraphrase Bolívar: what you are left with is an ungovernable America, where revolutions only plow the sea.

If few places on this globe are as violent as Latin America, few are as corrupt. According to polls, the overwhelming majority of Latin Americans believe their governments are riddled with vice. That corruption is most pernicious precisely where probity is most needed: in the region's security forces. Too often in Latin America, the police and the army are co-opted by politicians, less likely to serve the letter of the law than whoever happens to be in power. Even as Latin American dictators go about rewriting constitutions and dismantling the checks on their power, police chiefs and generals are given free rein to brutalize the population. In El Salvador in 2015, the vice president—a former guerrilla chief himself—approved the police director's policy of killing gang members "without fear of suffering consequences." In Honduras, a drug czar investigating the government's collusion with cocaine cartels found that the National Police were reporting directly to drug lords and carrying out murders on their behalf. "We are rotten to the core," the drug czar said after he had been fired summarily for doing his job too well. "We are at the edge of an abyss. . . . You write a report, you give it to your boss, and then you realize that he was the very one committing the crimes you're documenting." Two weeks later, he was dead.

Playing no small part in the culture of corruption is colonialism's most faithful accomplice: the Church. When Pope Francis learned of the systemic and widespread graft being exposed in the Odebrecht bribery cases—a gargantuan Brazilian operation totaling billions of dollars of payoffs to politicians throughout the hemisphere, the largest foreign bribery case in history—his response was unequivocal outrage. Latin American politics was in crisis, he declared. Very much in crisis! It was more sick than well! Which was true. But as just about everyone in the region knew, this was no passing ailment. Corruption has been endemic since Columbus planted a cross in Hispaniola and, despite the good pontiff's lamentations, the Church was all too present in its foundation.

What do the colonized learn, after all, from a church that is willing to collaborate with the Crown to sell *cédulas de Gracias al Sacar*—certificates of "whiteness"—to those of the darker races so that they might be admitted to a schoolroom, or a government office, or even marry? What do the faithful learn from an institution that required their ancestors to pay tributes or, if they failed to do so, condemned them to hard labor? What do they learn from a religion whose cardinals and bishops side with strongmen—with Cortés, Pizarro, Perón, or Franco; who offer their services to tyrants, as Chilean Cardinal Raul Silva Henríquez once offered them to General Pinochet, in order to "put the right face" on a deadly coup? What do they learn from priests who boast that they have accepted donations from traffickers and filled their churches' coffers with ill-gained lucre? Or what do they learn when priests who refuse to capitulate to despots—as Bishop Óscar Romero did—are gunned down in the bright light of day? For all the mercies that the Church has extended to Latin America, and there have been many, the institution has been a tower of ambiguity. All too often, it wears two faces: one that champions the lowly, another that speaks for the lords. And when measured against the long train of history, it has failed in its most basic task: to impart the abiding virtues of a truly humane, law-abiding, egalitarian society. As the Jesuit Xavier Albó put it so aptly: those virtues were well in place long before Christianity arrived on American soil. They were written into the laws of civilizations it dismantled. To wit: *ama suwa, ama llulla, ama qhella.* Do not steal. Do not lie. Do not go idle.

Leonor Gonzáles has proven unable to live down-mountain from the reeking garbage heaps of La Rinconada. Although good fortune arrived in the form of an American documentary filmmaker who arranged to educate her children in exchange for filming her family, she was never quite able to adjust to life elsewhere. Leaving the raw violence and toxins of the illegal gold mines for the frenetic life of Juliaca—a Peruvian airport town thirty miles from Puno—she was considered little more than an illiterate rube in a wide skirt; an outsider with no skills to offer. Although her children enrolled in school and quickly adapted to their two-room cement shack in the slum behind the airport, Leonor was soon back in the gold mines, taking her chances on her hands and knees, scrabbling through rock spills again. Every Thursday she takes the diminutive stone that represents her husband, puts it in the pocket of her apron, and rides a rickety *combi* up-mountain for six hours, over bone-rattling dirt roads; and every Monday, she travels back to see that her children have eaten, studied, and have clean clothes for the next week. Her youngest daughter, Senna, has graduated from the Universidad Andina Nestor Cáceres. Her older daughter, Mari, is recovering from the suicide of a lover, a young miner in La Rinconada who drank too much, hanged himself in a mine shaft, and left her with an infant child. She is studying to be a pharmacist. The eldest, Jhon, still suffers multiple traumas—eye, brain, and lung damage—from the collapse of the mine that killed their father, but he manages to work fifty-four hours a week for a cable installation service. Leonor's youngest, Henrry, a high-spirited sixteen-year-old who might otherwise be laboring in the cyanide pits of Mount Ananea, receives the highest grades his ramshackle school can offer.

Carlos Buergos, thousands of miles north, somewhere between Florida and Louisiana—nobody really knows—is no less consigned to a life on the margins. Scrounging work wherever he can, he has drifted from city to suburb, making ends meet as a janitor, busboy, carwash, messenger boy, plying his wits on the streets. Now in his sixties and plagued by old injuries—the bullet to his head, the knife to his gut—he surely finds it hard to get up and out into the street at all. What deliverance he has found has been through the kindness of strangers. Most of them, older women looking to forget the past. Before marrying his round, spunky, no-nonsense Venezuelan wife, he had been living with Helen, a menopausal blonde he had met on the dance floor of a Washington, DC, bar. After serving a fifteen-year jail sentence for dealing cocaine—after his sickly six-year-old son died and his wife divorced him—he found himself using that strategy again. He sought out mature, unattached women in mambo bars, and offered to exchange a little tenderness for a place to stay. From time to time, he scored a few months of grace, especially with American women who found his impish good looks and thick Cuban accent charming. But age, weariness, and a long criminal record seem to have caught up with Carlos. He can no longer be found in his old haunts in Dade County or the jittery singles bars on the perimeter of New Orleans. Nor do court records that register his petty burglaries or his fleeting coke deals or his dustups with police suggest that he stays in one place very long. In those reports, under the rubric "Possible Employers," the record is clear: none found. The last coke kingpin he dealt with identifies himself only as "GOD."

Xavier Albó, a priest who has dedicated sixty-seven years of his life to the culture and welfare of Indians—who, being more inclined to spiritual than genealogical classifications, counts himself an *indio*, an Aymara, a Quechua—can claim with all certitude that he is no longer a Catalan. Nor even a Spaniard. He is Bolivian. He has seen Bolivia reborn, and he has seen it proceed through all hell's circles of transfiguration. Having worked to elect Evo Morales—the country's first indigenous president—with all the hope he could muster, Xavier has seen that hope run aground. Morales, who began as a poor coca leaf farmer, became what so many democratically elected Latin American presidents have become: rich, rabidly authoritarian, a hidebound dictator. Like Hugo Chávez, like Alberto Fujimori, like Juan Perón, like Daniel Ortega, he has used democracy to undermine democracy. Xavier is not shy to say so. He is forthright about the dreams, and he is forthright about the failures.

But like a father who loves his child no matter how errant, he is unwilling to abandon hope for what yet might be. Latin America's redemption is just around the corner. If only there were better courts, better schools, better leaders. He may be in his ninetieth decade, but Xavier still works tirelessly to champion what he has always believed in, the trinity that will redeem Latin America: justice, equality, education. It's as simple and as difficult as that.

Leonor, Carlos, and Xavier will never meet, but their stories are inextricably bound, just as the history of silver, sword, and stone have marched together in this hard and hopeful land. There are other narratives in Latin America, to be sure. Happier ones. But it is these, and the resolution of these, that define the hemisphere and its future. They have certainly defined its past.

Latin America's resources, its violence, and its religions were vital forces long before the conquest that birthed the land as we know it. Plunder, cruelty, and the imposition of faith were well known to the pre-Columbian people. But Columbus put the first brick in the lie of the Americas when he insisted he had found Asia, that he was in a land rich with gold, that its people were docile, easily enslaved, handily outfoxed. He had not; it was not; they were not. Although the natives were eventually reduced to servitude—men for their labor, women for their sex—their new masters never really learned who they were. The native Americans were never really appreciated, never understood as a people who might eventually claim their birthright. They were sent to the mines, herded into fields, their life force appropriated and their culture obliterated. Violence, meant to cow them, became the wound. Faith, meant to soothe them, became the unguent. Eventually they were subsumed. Mestizo-ized. Indoctrinated. Or, in the case of the countries of the Southern Cone—Chile, Argentina, Uruguay, Paraguay—obliterated entirely. And the lie continued. Orwell, in all his genius, could not have imagined a more surreal, mind-bending universe. Europe, Latin America's most prolific mythologizer—and its most prodigious profiteer—established the notion that the culture didn't matter, that Europe was superior, born to lord over them and bring them progress. In time, North America would expand the notion. And Latin Americans believed it all.

As James Baldwin once wrote, American history is longer, larger, more various, more beautiful, and more terrible than anything we have ever said about it. That much is certainly true about the Americas of the South. Chroniclers of old have accustomed us to see history from the eye of the invader, from the perspective of conquest. We imagine Latin America, as one eminent historian of pre-Columbian cultures has said, with a conquistador at its start. A Hispanic tale. The rest scatters into the haze, into the wings of history, into oblivion. We tend to think of the arc of these Americas as the story of Columbus *and* the Taíno. The story of Cortés . . . *and* the Aztecs. Pizarro . . . *and* the Incas. Cabeza de Vaca *and* the Guaraní. Spain *and* its colonies. The tinpot dictator *and* his unfortunate casualties. The Roman Catholic Church *and* the pagans. The vast world economy *and* the coveted veins that lie dormant in the earth. Even here, in this book, the juxtaposition of winners and losers seems to be the only way to frame the past.

But it is the *"ands,"* the second parties to each dyad, that reveal the underlying and often more enduring aspects of the story: it is the Taíno, the Aztec, the Inca, the Guaraní, the colonies, the pagans, the casualties, and the veins that lie dormant in the earth that tell the deeper tale. These are the constituent parts that, however trampled, remain deeply imprinted on the region's psyche. We cannot turn back time. We cannot unmake the world we have made. But until we understand the *"ands"* of history—the ghosts in the machinery, the victims of our collective amnesia—we cannot hope to understand the region as it is now. Nor will we ever understand the character of its people. To look at it squarely: a long litany of iniquities lies at the heart of the Latin American narrative. Until Latin America understands how its people have been shaped, sharpened, and stunted by those iniquities, the crucibles of silver, sword, and stone will continue to write its story.

ACKNOWLEDGMENTS

This book arose from a long conversation with the late María Isabel Arana Cisneros, my aunt and godmother, whose sparkling intellect and Brobdingnagian erudition never failed to make me look beyond my crimped horizons and think deeply about why things are the way they are. We had been sitting in her comfortable living room in Lima, talking about the differences between North American and South American revolutions, an exchange prompted by my book, *Bolivar: American Liberator*, when I began to list the characteristics that made Latin America's wars of independence (1804–1898) unique in history. My Tía Chaba peered over the rim of her glasses and said, "Well, that is all very well and good, Marisi, but here's a goal if you're really interested in explaining us: Get at what it is—*exactly*—that makes Latin Americans so different from the rest of the world, and you will be clarifying things."

Getting at things "exactly" is the rub. I am reminded of a sobering passage by the great Argentine novelist Ernesto Sabato, who once wrote that history is made of fallacy, specious argument, and forgetting. It all brings to mind Sir Walter Raleigh, an extravagant raconteur if ever there was one, who—sentenced to life imprisonment in the Tower of London—set about writing a sweeping history of England. Legend has it that as he was in the thick of the first chapters, there was a resounding uproar in the streets below—nothing less than a riot prompted by an assassination attempt on the king. The reports that reached him in his little aerie were so confusing and contradictory that he threw up his hands and gave up on the entire project, complaining that he could hardly write another word of history when he didn't even know what was happening outside his window.

So it is with me. Attempting a history of Latin America is a task filled with folly, given all the distortions that have gone before, not to mention the constant flux and reinventions to which our nations are prone. Change is constant. Volatility is the norm. A definitive history is impossible when so much is happening just outside the window. Clarifying things, as my aunt would have me do, is a job for Sisyphus. Trying to get at "what it is exactly" that makes Latin Americans the way we are has made me throw up my hands with every chapter. So let me be clear: This is not a book of history, although I have plowed through copious stacks of chronicles to tell it. Neither is it a work of journalism, although I have followed each of my subjects' lives with all the intensity of a hungry hound. This book is, like everything that comes out of Latin America, a mixed breed. A mutt. And it has many fathers.

I have had the extraordinary good fortune to know and collaborate with historians, journalists, and intellectuals, living and dead, whose works have guided me in myriad ways. None of them is in any way responsible for the errors in this book, and my shortcomings should not reflect on their excellence. I owe much, for instance, to the late, great Colombian historian Germán Arciniegas, whose highly original works I helped bring into English as a young editor in New York and whose good humor about the slippery Latin American past always made me laugh. I have learned much from friends: From Mario Vargas Llosa, my brilliant compatriot, whose penetrating insights via fiction as well as nonfiction have shed much light on the character of the region. From the Uruguayan Eduardo Galeano, with whom I shared many an evening's conversation about the long view, the millennium that precedes us. From the distinguished British historian John Hemming, whose profound knowledge about Latin American civilizations and unstinting generosity have been indispensable to my work. From the intrepid American explorer Loren MacIntyre, who called me on the phone in his last days on earth to demand that I get the facts of the terrain right. From the Mexican *sabios*—wise men—Carlos Fuentes and Enrique Krauze, whose unflinching gaze on Mexico's glorious and tumultuous history has taught me much.

But there are so many others who have been my teachers in this enterprise: Julia Álvarez, Cecilia Alvear, José Amor y Vázquez, Elizabeth Benson, Patricia Cepeda, Sandra Cisneros, Lawrence Clayton, Ariel Dorfman, Ronald Edward, Gustavo Gorriti, Alma Guillermoprieto,

John W. Hessler, Leonardo López Luján, Javier Lizarzaburu, Colin McEwan, Alberto Manguel, Senna Ochochoque, Mark J. Plotkin, Elena Poniatowska, Jorge Ramos, Laura Restrepo, Tina Rosenberg, María Rostworowski, Ilan Stavans, Richard Webb. I owe them an insurmountable debt of gratitude. There are also those, whom I may not know personally, but whose work, listed in my bibliography, has made deep impressions on these pages.

Then there are those who contributed concretely to this curious crossbreed of history and reportage. I am indebted to the late James H. Billington, Librarian of Congress and brilliant mentor, who welcomed me to the Library in 2013 and invited me to sit at his side and be a part of that great institution. I owe big thanks to Jane McAuliffe, former head of the Library's John W. Kluge Center, who invited me to leave that desk and spend a full year as the Chair of the Cultures of the Countries of the South, combing through the vast riches of the Latin American and Hispanic Collection. The Kluge Center has now been my benefactor for two books of history. I thank Erick Langer of Georgetown University, who suggested casually many years ago that I should look into the work of an elderly Jesuit priest in Bolivia whose life seemed a curious mirror on the past. That man was Xavier Albó, and his story lies at the very heart of this book. Similarly, I want to thank Richard Robbins and Kayce Freed Jennings of the Documentary Group and Girl Rising for sending me 18,000 feet into the Andean sky to write about a fourteen-year-old girl in the gold mines of La Rinconada. It was there that I met Leonor Gonzáles, whose life is not very different from her ancestors' who inhabited those mountains five hundred years ago. I am grateful, too, to my friend Clara, who gave me her blessing to take my *Washington Post* story about her Cuban husband, Carlos Buergos, and expand it to the fullness it finds here.

The bedrock on which this book stands is my dear friend and trusted literary agent, Amanda Urban. Binky, as all her literary brood knows, has no equal. She is a fierce warrior with a heart of gold, and I am fortunate to have her in my corner. My editor at Simon & Schuster, Bob Bender, was the soul of patience as two years stretched into five and a flimsy notion became a sprawling project. Bob is my ideal reader: firm, exacting, and thoroughly committed to his authors. I am grateful to him and his stalwart assistant Johanna Li, as I am to my thorough copy-editor, Phil Bashe; my talented designers, Carly Loman and Jackie Seow; and my tireless publicist, Julia Prosser. I am especially thankful for the encouragement and muscle of my publisher, the president of Simon & Schuster, Jonathan Karp.

None of this could have been accomplished without the help of countless friends and family: my children, Lalo Walsh and Adam Ward, who sat with me at their kitchen tables and allowed me to rattle on about the joys and indignities of a writing life; my stepson Jim Yardley, who noodled endlessly over the title with me as we lolled in the comforts of his London house; my other stepson Bill Yardley, who steered me from at least one perilous writer's precipice; my parents, Jorge and Marie, who live on although they are long gone, and who would have argued late into the night about the glories and blunders of this book; my brother and sister, George and Vicky Arana, faithful companions who traveled with me throughout the Americas as I tried to tie down loose ends; my neighbors Don and Betty Hawkins, who carried the final, copyedited manuscript lovingly from Lima to Washington, DC, and then posted it on to New York; and last, but not least, my late, irreplaceable Tía Chaba, who would have squinted at me over her glasses and asked if I really meant all that I've said.

The biggest thank you, however, is to my steadfast husband, Jonathan Yardley, who prompted me to leave my editorial desk twenty years ago and start writing books in the first place. It was Jon who patted me on the back, left me alone to stare at the wall, cooked the dinners, did the shopping, took out the dog, furminated the cat, paid the bills, told me to keep on doing whatever it was I was doing, and then greeted me with a smile and a cocktail at the close of each day. Now that is what I would call clarifying things.

NOTES

Chapter 1: Still Seeking El Dorado

1 Epigraph: *"Peru is a beggar sitting on a bench of gold"*: This phrase is often attributed to the nineteenth-century Italian scientist Antonio Raimondi, who lived and taught in Peru, but the attribution has never been confirmed. Nevertheless, it is an old and well-known adage throughout South America. The Institute of Mining Engineers of Peru (IIMP) has gone to great lengths to debunk the adage; indeed, its director proclaimed, "Peru is not a beggar on a bench of gold. In our country, mining is the principal motor of the economy; it represents more than 12% of the GNP and 60% of all exports." Which, of course, proves the point. Almost all its gold leaves the country, and one out of four Peruvians lives in poverty. IIMP, accessed January 29, 2019, www.iimp .org.pe/actualidad/el-peru-no-es-un-mendigo-sentado-en-un-banco-de-oro; Reuters, "Peru Poverty Rate Rises for First Time in 16 Years: Government," April 24, 2018. About the aphorism: A. Alcocer Martínez, "Conjetura y postura frente al dicho 'El Perú es un mendigo sentado en un banco de oro," *Boletín de la Academia Peruana de la Lengua* [Bulletin of the Peruvian Academy of Language] 41 (2006): 45–58.

1 *Leonor Gonzáles leaves her stone hut*: Information henceforward about Leonor Gonzáles is based on ongoing interviews with her in Peru as follows: La Rinconada, February 17–22, 2012; Putina, February 23, 2012; Juliaca, February 15–19, 2013; Juliaca and Puno, February 19–24, 2014; February 11–15, 2015; February 20–24, 2016; March 2–7, 2017; January 31–February 5, 2019. Since 2013, I have been in weekly, informal communication with the family, visiting them at least once a year in Juliaca.

3 *"choak'd up with Indian Blood and Gore"*: Fray Bartolomé de las Casas, *A Short History of the Destruction of the Indies*, penultimate paragraph, Project Gutenberg, www.gutenberg.org/files/23466-h.html.

3 *"His soul rests inside"*: Her actual words: *"Su alma ahí en el rumi."* The word *rumi* is Quechua for "stone."

5 *slate blades that Chimú warriors used*: Carmen Pérez-Maestro, "Armas de metal en el Perú prehispanico," Espacio, Tiempo y Forma, I, Prehistoria y Arquelogía, T-12, 1999, 321.

5 *The ten most dangerous cities in the world*: USA Today, July 17, 2018 (Belém,

Brazil; Ciudad Guayana, Venezuela; Ciudad Victoria, Mexico; Fortaleza,
Brazil; La Paz, Mexico; Tijuana, Mexico; Natal, Brazil; Acapulco, Mexico;
Caracas, Venezuela; Los Cabos, Mexico); World Atlas, October 5, 2018
(Caracas; Acapulco; San Pedro Sula, Honduras; Distrito Central, Honduras;
Victoria; Maturín, Venezuela; San Salvador, El Salvador; Ciudad Guayana;
Valencia, Venezuela; Natal, Brazil). See also David Luhnow, "Latin America
Is the Murder Capital of the World," *Wall Street Journal*, September 20, 2018.

5 *a flood of desperate immigrants*: US Department of Homeland Security, Office
of Immigration Statistics, *2013 Yearbook of Immigration Statistics*, August
2014, www.dhs.gov/sites/default/files/publications/ois_yb_2013_0.pdf. Miriam
Jordan, "More Migrants Are Crossing the Border This Year," *New York Times*
online, March 5, 2019.

5 *"turned the world"*: Pachacutec, or Pachacuti, literally means "he who turns
the world" or "earth shaker." Mark Cartwright, "Pachacuti Inqa Yupanqui,"
Ancient History Encyclopedia, last modified July 18, 2016, www.ancient.eu
/Pachacuti_Inca_Yupanqui.

5 *A full 40 percent of all the world's Catholics*: Pew Research Center online,
"The Global Catholic Population," last modified February 13, 2013, www
.pewforum.org/2013/02/13/the-global-catholic-population; US Central Intelligence Agency online, "Religions," in *The World Factbook*, accessed January 29,
2019, www.cia.gov/library/publications/the-world-factbook/fields/2122.html.

6 *most trusted institution in all of Latin America*: Edward L. Cleary, *How
Latin America Saved the Soul of the Catholic Church*, 3. See also Feline
Freier, "Maduro's Immorality and the Role of the Church in Venezuela,"
Georgetown University Berkley Center for Religion, Peace & World Affairs
online, last modified, June 15, 2018.

6 *"a continent made to undermine conventional truths"*: Eric Hobsbawm, *Viva la
Revolución*, ed. Leslie Bethell (New York: Little, Brown, 2016). Credit also to
Tony Wood's review of that book in the *Guardian* (UK edition), July 18, 2016.

7 *Spain's custom of sending sons into different walks of life*: This is referred
to as the abiding power triangle of *"los ricos, los militares, y los curas."* In
other words: a banker, a general, and a bishop. President Hugo Chávez of
Venezuela has been known to refer to this triad of power as a crippling force
in capitalism. See the distillation of his thinking in *Socialismo del Siglo XXI*
(Caracas, República Bolivariana de Venezuela: Ministerio del Poder Popular,
2007), 5.

Part i: Silver

9 Epigraph: *"Once upon a time, my little dove"*: Antonio Dominguez Hidalgo,
Mitos, Fabulas, y Leyendas del Antiguo México (México, DF: Editorial Umbral,
1987), 215.

CHAPTER 2: VEINS OF A MOUNTAIN GOD

11   Epigraph: *"Descend to the mineral depths"*: Pablo Neruda, "The Heights of
     Machu Picchu," from *Canto General*, trans. Jack Schmitt, in *The Poetry of Pablo
     Neruda*, ed. Ilan Stavans (New York: Farrar, Straus and Giroux, 2003), 207.

11   *a region of sparkling lakes*: Felipe Guaman Poma de Ayala, *El Primer nueva
     corónica y buen gobierno*, ed. John Murra, Rolena Adorno, and Jorge
     Urioste, vol. 1, figs. 49–78; El Inca Garcilaso, *Royal Commentaries of Peru*,
     1:330; *Monografía de Bolivia* (La Paz: Biblioteca del Sesquicentenario de la
     República, 1975), 3:27.

11   *a barrens that beggars the imagination*: For evidence of the environmental
     degradation in this area, see W. H. Strosnider, F. Llanos, and R. W. Nairn, "A
     Legacy of Nearly 500 Years of Mining in Potosí, Bolivia," a paper presented
     at the 2008 National Meeting of the American Society of Mining and
     Reclamation, Richmond, VA, www.asmr.us/Publications/Conference%20
     Proceedings/2008/1232-Strosnider-OK.pdf. See also Nicholas A. Robins,
     *Mercury, Mining, and Empire: The Human and Ecological Cost of Colonial Silver
     Mining in the Andes*, 184–86. The terrain is very similar to Mount Ananea,
     which I describe in my article "Dreaming of El Dorado," *Virginia Quarterly
     Review* online, last modified September 17, 2012, www.vqronline.org/essay
     /dreaming-el-dorado.

12   *as populous and vibrant as Paris or London*: Tertius Chandler, *Four Thousand
     Years of Urban Growth: An Historical Census* (Lewiston, NY: Edwin Mellen
     Press, 1987), 483, 529.

13   *a fragile grid on the verge of collapse*: William Neuman, "For Miners, Increasing
     Risk on a Mountain at the Heart of Bolivia's Identity," *New York Times* online,
     September 16, 2014.

13   *slaves scrabbled for silver with deer antlers*: Kendall Brown, *A History of Mining
     in Latin America: From the Colonial Era to the Present*, digital version, loc. 328,
     6%.

13   *they had only one use and only one consumer*: *Crónica franciscana de las provincias
     del Perú* (1651) (Washington, DC: American Academy of Franciscan History,
     1957), 1:16; Pedro de Cieza de León, *Crónica del Perú*, 39.

13   *Huayna Capac . . . loved gold and silver with an abandon*: Garcilaso, *Royal
     Commentaries*, 1:314.

13   *chambers' walls lined with silver*: Francisco de Xerez, quoted in Horatio H.
     Urteaga, *Biblioteca de Cultura Peruana: Los cronistas de la Conquista*, 55.

13   *This Lord Inca wanted to eat and drink from them*: José de Acosta, *Historia
     Natural y Moral de las Indias*, vol. 4, ch. 4.

14   *brought on a covetousness and oppression*: Garcilaso, *Royal Commentaries*, 1:314.

14   *Handsome, well built, a warrior king*: Guaman Poma, 1:93.

14   *Bigger than China's Ming dynasty*: Charles C. Mann, *1491: New Revelations of
     the Americas Before Columbus*, 74.

15 *Pointing to it, he opined*: Garcilaso, *Royal Commentaries*, 1:314.

15 *because the promontory was considered sacred*: Fray Diego de Ocaña, *Un viaje fascinante por la América Hispana del siglo 16*, 184; Teresa Gisbert, *Iconografía y mitos indígenas en el arte*, 19.

15 Epigraph: *"On the fourth day, the All Powerful"*: Bartolomé Arzáns de Orsúa y Vela, *Historia de la Villa Imperial de Potosí*, 3 vols. 1715. Repr., edited by Lewis Hanke and Gunnar Mendoza. Rhode Island: Brown University Press, 1965. This eighteenth-century manuscript purchased by the Church from a Parisian book dealer in 1905 is one of the most important items in any collection about the history of the conquest.

15 *letter to the celebrated explorer Alexander von Humboldt*: Alexander von Humboldt, Ueber die geographischen und geognostischen Arbeiten des Herrn Pentland im sudlichen Peru: Hertha, Zeitschr. f. Erd-Volker-und Staatenkunde Ano 5, 1–29, Stuttgart, Ger., 1829. See also Georg Petersen, *Mining and Metallurgy in Ancient Peru*, 44.

16 *after a grueling two-thousand-mile mule ride*: Joanne Pillsbury, ed., *Guide to Documentary Sources for Andean Studies*, vol. 2, *1530–1900*, 506.

16 *gold nuggets as large as a human skull*: Garcilaso, *Los mejores comentarios reales*, ed. Domingo Miliani (Ayacucho, Peru: Biblioteca Ayacucho, 1992), 202. Also Herbert Guillaume, *The Amazon Provinces of Peru as a Field for European Emigration* (Southampton, UK: self-pub., 1894), 300–1.

16 *El Inca Garcilaso de la Vega, Huayna Capac's great-nephew*: Garcilaso, *Los mejores comentarios reales*, 202; Guillaume, *Amazon Provinces of Peru*, 300–1.

16 *The Spanish, too, eventually abandoned their mines*: Guillaume, *Amazon Provinces of Peru*, 302.

16 *bored deeper into the glacial rock*: Joseph B. Pentland, *Report on Bolivia, 1827*, 73–74; Petersen, 26.

17 *Bolivian geologists revived Pentland's work*: Carlos Serrano Bravo, *Historia de la minería andina boliviana (Siglos 16–20)*. Paper published online, December 2004, www2.congreso.gob.pe/sicr/cendocbib/con4_uibd .nsf/6EF6AA797C1749E905257EFF005C493F/$FILE/Historia_de _Miner%C3%ADa_Andina_Boliviana.pdf.

17 *After his meager breakfast*: This account of Juan Sixto Ochochoque's mining routine is from interviews with Leonor Gonzáles and her family, cited earlier.

18 *strong constraints against forcing slaves*: Nicholas Tripcevich and Kevin J. Vaughn, eds., *Mining and Quarrying in the Ancient Andes: Sociopolitical Economic, and Symbolic Dimensions*, 217.

18 *mining in the time of the Incas*: Petersen, 44.

18 *plunging a three-hundred-meter hole into its flank*: This is an estimation, based on interviews with fellow miners in La Rinconada, who cited 250 to 300 meters from shaft entrance to end.

18 *would have represented a flagrant violation*: P. Gose, quoted in Tripcevich and Vaughn, 278.

18　*lion's share of gold that the indigenous extracted*: Bernabé Cobo, *Historia del Nuevo mundo* 1:300; Acosta, vol. 4, ch. 4.

18　*said to have been so laden with gold*: William H. Prescott, *History of the Conquest of Peru: With a Preliminary View of the Civilization of the Incas*, 56.

18　*for them, it consisted of different cycles*: María Rostworowski, *Historia del Tawantinsuyu*, 25, 28; Ronald Wright, *Stolen Continents: The Americas Through Indian Eyes*, 30–33.

18　*Aztec world view, too, was deeply binary*: Wright, 33.

18　*work was interchangeable, rotational*: Rostworowski, *Historia del Tawantinsuyu*, 227. What follows here on Inca culture is informed largely by Rostworowski.

20　*The walls of Coricancha, the "golden realm"*: Prescott, *Conquest of Peru*, 218–19.

20　*every utensil in his house*: Garcilaso, *Royal Commentaries*, 3:192.

20　*Gold was the "sweat of the sun"*: Cruz Martínez de la Torre, "El sudor del Sol y las lágrimas de la Luna: La metalurgia del oro y de la plata en el Antiguo Perú," Espacio, Tiempo y Forma, Serie VII, *Historia del Arte*, t.12, 1999, 11.

21　*to the Inca, gold was light's refuge*: Fundación ICO, *Oro y la plata de las Indias en la época de los Austrias*, 33.

21　*primogenitor, Christ, and king*: Wright, 72.

21　*His bowels were meticulously removed*: Ibid.

21　*chain of gold that reached from one end of Cuzco's marketplace*: El Inca Garcilaso put it at about seven hundred feet, which would be the length of two football fields. *Royal Commentaries*, 3:192.

21　*These metals were not forged in the same way*: Heather Lechtman, "Cloth and Metal: The Culture of Technology," in *Andean Art at Dumbarton Oaks*, vol. 1, ed. Elizabeth Hill Boone (Washington, DC: Dumbarton Oaks), 1996, 33–43; Charles C. Mann, 94.

22　*news of their love for them*: Miguel León Portilla. *De Teotihuacán a los aztecas: antología de fuentes e interpretaciones históricas*, (México, DF: UNAM, 1971), 21. Also, in many chronicles written by the conquistadors, it is clear that the indigenous of Mexico and Panama were aware that gold could be found in cultures to the south.

22　*began producing exquisite gold for its chieftains*: Jose Pérez de Barradas, *Orfebrería prehispánica de Colombia*, 93–98, 339–41.

22　*the legend of El Dorado took hold*: This was an exaggeration of other accounts in which the gold dust ritual was undertaken by a prince (*psihipqua*) upon the death of the ruling cacique (*zipa*) and before taking up the reins of power. Juan Rodríguez Freyle. *Conquista y Descubrimiento del Nuevo Reino de Granada* (Bogotá: Círculo de Lectores, 1985), 28–29.

23　Epigraph: *"There was no sin then"*: *"No había entonces pecado. No había entonces enfermedad. No había dolor de huesos. No había fiebre por el oro."* Chilám Balám de Chumayel, quoted in *Miguel León-Portilla, El Reverso de la Conquista: Relaciones aztecas, mayas e incas*, 22.

23　*brought metallurgy to Mesoamerica*: León-Portilla, *Reverso de la Conquista*, 23.

23 *as a mark of nobility; as a way to distinguish class*: Fray Diego Durán, *The Aztecs: The History of the Indies of New Spain*, trans. Doris Heyden and Fernando Horcasitas, 132.

23 *began fashioning copper spears*: León-Portilla, *Reverso de la Conquista*, 417.

24 *face-to-face with an original world, entirely distinct*: Rostworowski, *Historia del Tawantinsuyu*, 28.

24 *"great island, afloat in a primordial sea"*: Wright, 32.

24 *there were one hundred million of them*: William H. Denevan, *The Population of the Americas in 1492* (Milwaukee: University of Wisconsin, 1992), 1; Wright, 4. To be fair, this figure has fluctuated from as high as 112 million to as low as 10 million.

24 *home to a quarter million residents*: Wright, 11.

24 *quadruple the population of London*: The Aztec population was five million in 1500; London's was approximately fifty thousand; the United Kingdom's, four million. "Population of the British Isles," Tacitus.nu, accessed January 29, 2019, www.tacitus.nu/historical-atlas/population/british.htm; Boris Urlanis, *Rost naseleniya v Evrope* [Population growth in Europe] (Moscow: OGIZ-Gospolitizdam, 1941).

24 *Aztecs governed twenty-five million more*: Charles C. Mann, 107.

24 *The Inca capital, Cuzco, too, was a humming metropolis*: "Inca People," *Encyclopædia Britannica* online, www.britannica.com/topic/Inca.

24 *two hundred thousand citizens, with as many as thirty-seven million*: Gordon F. McEwan, in *After Collapse: The Regeneration of Complex Societies*, ed. Glenn Schwartz and John Nichols (Tucson: University of Arizona Press, 2010), 98.

25 *emeralds, amethysts, jade, turquoise*: George Folsom, intro., in Hernán Cortés, *The Despatches of Hernando Cortés* (New York: Wiley & Putnam, 1843), 35.

25 *"the excrement of the gods"*: The Aztec word for *gold* or *silver* is *teocuitlatl*, which literally means "excrement of the gods" (Classical Nahuatl-English Dictionary, Glosbe, https://en.glosbe.com/nci/en/teocuitlatl).

25 *"What can be grander than a barbarian lord"*: Hernán Cortés, "Segunda Carta," *Caretas de Relación*. See also *Hernán Cortés: Letters from Mexico*, trans. and ed. Anthony R. Pagden, 108.

26 *part of a vast family of languages*: Uto-Aztecan languages: Nahuatl, Cheme-huevi, Paiute, O'odham, Hopi, Tübatulabal, Comanche. See *Nahuatl: Nahuatl Dialects, Classical Nahuatl Grammar* (Memphis: General Books: 2010), 44; Germán Vázquez Chamorro, *Moctezuma*, 2006, 17.

26 *a territory the size of Britain*: The Aztec Empire was roughly 80,000 square miles; England is 50,346. World Atlas, accessed January 29, 2019, www.worldatlas.com.

26 *Montezuma II had been elected democratically*: Durán, 220.

26 *He was deliberate, serious*: Francisco Cervantes de Salazar, *Crónica de la Nueva España*, bk. 4, ch. 3, in cervantesvirtual.com. Also Durán, 220.

26 *sweeping the temple floors*: Vázquez, *Moctezuma*, 1987, 6–7.

26 *Charismatic, dignified, tall*: Details about Montezuma are from Cortés, *Cartas de Relación*, or Bernal Díaz del Castillo, *Historia verdadera de la conquista de la Nueva España*, ch. 91; Cervantes de Salazar, *Crónica*, bk. 4, ch. 3; Bernal Díaz del Castillo, in Enrique de Vedia, *Historiadores primitivos de Indias*, 2:86.

26 *special potions to boost his virility*: Cervantes de Salazar, *Crónica*, 8.

27 *strong, nimble, and an excellent archer*: Ibid., 3.

27 *Once the initiation rituals were done*: Vázquez, *Moctezuma*, 1987, 7; Durán, 178, 222.

27 *describe Montezuma II as a weak and anxious ruler*: The Florentine Codex: *General History of the Things of New Spain*, vol. 8, bk. 12, trans. Arthur J. O. Anderson and Charles E. Dibble, 13–26.

27 *as the Nahuatl name* Montezuma *actually means*: Vázquez, *Moctezuma*, 1987, 13.

27 *Tenochtitlán's military now commandeered every aspect*: Ibid., 14.

27 *serving as guard for a burgeoning class of powerful merchants*: Ibid.

27 *The central plaza of Tenochtitlán*: Cervantes de Salazar, *Crónica*, bk. 4, 18:356. The Mixtecs, during the time of Moctezuma I, also had extremely wealthy merchants and a lively marketplace of gold, silver, and precious stones. These practices may have been adopted from them.

28 *paid tributes to the state in bracelets*: Enrique Canudas Sandoval, *Venas de la plata en la historia de México* 1:182.

28 *A wealthy protobourgeoisie*: Vázquez, *Moctezuma*, 1987, 14.

28 *His government would clamp down*: Durán, 222–23.

28 *dressing down the plebeian soldiers*: Ibid., 223; Vázquez, *Moctezuma*, 2006, 104.

28 *a nobleman's bastard children*: Durán, 223; Vázquez, *Moctezuma*, 2006, 105.

28 *slay all the tutors and handmaids*: Durán, 227; Vázquez, *Moctezuma*, 2006, 106.

29 *reduce the power of the wealthy merchants*: Durán, 227–28; Vázquez, *Moctezuma*, 2006, 109–111.

29 *rule was eventually visited by all three*: Frances Berdan, *Aztec Archaeology and Ethnohistory* (New York: Cambridge University Press, 2014), 170.

29 *Evil omens began to be reported*: *Florentine Codex*, vol. 8, bk. 12, 1–3. It's worth mentioning here that the *Florentine Codex* reveals a distinct pro-Tlatelolco and anti-Tenochtitlán bent.

30 Epigraph: *"With the Pacific to the west and the Amazon to the east"*: John Hemming, *Conquest of the Incas*, 29.

30 *The marriage he finally consummated*: Gamboa, 177.

30 *paraded the seven-hundred-foot cable*: Agustin de Zárate, *Historia del descubrimiento y conquista del Perú*, vol. 1, ch. 14; Garcilaso, *Royal Commentaries*, vol. 1, bk. 9, ch. 1.

31 *Cruel, cowardly, and vain*: Rostworowski, *Historia del Tawantinsuyu*, 159.

31 *Tupac Inca Yupanqui, one of the most aggressive*: Guaman Poma, 1:91.

31 *metal making in full swing*: Tripcevich and Vaughn, 255.

31 *he was delighted to find*: Pedro Sarmiento de Gamboa, *History of the Incas* (2007), 160.

31 *booty of dark-skinned slaves, gold*: Ibid., 152.

31 *weighed down with gold, silver, emeralds*: Raúl Porras Barrenechea, ed., "Oro
    y leyenda del Perú," in *Indagaciones peruanos*, available at the National
    University of San Marcos Library System online, sisbib.unmsm.edu.pe
    /bibvirtual/libros/linguistica/legado_quechua/oro.htm.

32 *Near Tumbes and Quito, where rivers glittered with gold*: Petersen, 49.

32 *his governors had been found with their throats slit*: Rostworowski, *Historia del
    Tawantinsuyu*, 122.

32 *the magnificent Royal Road, the Capac Ñan*: El Inca Garcilaso tells us that this
    stretch of the road was built expressly for Huayna Capac's campaign to pacify
    Quito. *Royal Commentaries*, 8:370.

32 *Not least on Huayna Capac's mind . . . with a retinue*: Rostworowski, *Historia del
    Tawantinsuyu*, 123.

32 *Enamored of his father's glittering spoils*: Garcilaso, *Royal Commentaries*, 8:314.

32 *vast army of hundreds of thousands*: Juan de Santa Cruz Pachacuti Yamqui
    Salcamayhua says that there were more than a million of these soldiers.
    Clements R. Markham, *Narratives of the Rites and Laws of the Yncas*, 109.

32 *naked, wild men of the Quillacingas*: Garcilaso, *Royal Commentaries*, 8:315;
    Cobo, *Historia*, 1:157–59.

33 *ordered his armies to decapitate*: Cobo, *Historia*, 1:300; Antonio de Herrera y
    Tordesillas, *Historia de las Indias Occidentales*, 148.

33 *Yahuarcocha: "pool of blood"*: Cobo, *Historia*, 1:159.

33 *grisly process that took more than a decade*: Ibid. The struggle may have taken as
    long as seventeen years; see the current archeological evidence in Owen Jarus,
    "Ancient War Revealed in Discovery of Incan Fortresses," LiveScience, last
    modified May 31, 2011.

33 *hardly a Quiteño male left over the age of twelve*: José Echeverria Almeida,
    "Archeology of a Battle: The Lagoon of Yahuarcocha," Revista Arqueología
    Ecuatoriana, last modified June 12, 2007, http://revistas.arqueo-ecuatoriana.ec
    /es/apachita/apachita-9/88-arqueologia-de-una-batalla-la-laguna-de-yahuarcocha.

33 *"You are all children now"*: Frederick A. Kirkpatrick, 134.

33 *transferring his court from Cuzco*: Cobo, *Historia*, 1:161.

33 *creating a new capital in Quito, a rift*: Cieza de León, *Cronica del Perú*, 1:226.

34 *One Spanish friar recounted*: Fray Buenaventura de Salinas y Cordova,
    Memorial de las Historias del nuevo mundo: Pirú, 58–59.

34 *the Andean chronicler Felipe Guaman Poma de Ayala depicts*: Guaman Poma,
    2:343.

34 *A plague of epic proportions*: Juan B. Lastres, *La Salud Pública y la Prevención
    de la Viruela en el Perú*, intro; Noble David Cook, *Born to Die: Disease and
    New World Conquest, 1492–1650* (Cambridge: Cambridge University Press,
    1998), 13; Cook, *Demographic Collapse: Indian Peru, 1520–1620* (Cambridge,
    Cambridge University Press, 2004), 114, 116, 143–44, 252–54. Some historians
    have noted that the reports of the spread of smallpox do not conform with

what scientists know about the way the disease works. For example: "Almost every element of this received account is false, epidemiologically improbable, historiographically suspect, or logically dubious." Francis J. Brooks, "Revising the Conquest of Mexico: Smallpox, Sources, and Populations," *Journal of Interdisciplinary History* 24, no. 1 (Summer 1993), 1–29.

35 *aided by random vectors*: James B. Kiracofe and John S. Marr, "Marching to Disaster: The Catastrophic Convergence of Inca Imperial Policy, Sand Flies, and El Niño in the 1524 Andean Epidemic," paper, presented at the Inter-American Institute for Advanced Studies in Cultural History, Dumbarton Oaks Pre-Columbian Symposium, Washington, DC, February 14, 2003, published in *El Niño, Catastrophism, and Cultural Change in Ancient America*, ed. Daniel H. Sandweiss and Jeffrey Quilter (Cambridge, MA: Harvard University Press, 2009); Juan B. Lastres, *Las Neuro-bartonelosis*, 10–11.

35 *wiped out countless members of the royal family*: Sarmiento de Gamboa, *History of the Incas*, 164.

35 *Eventually Huayna Capac . . . infected with the disease*: There is some debate about the exact nature of Huayna Capac's disease. Nevertheless, many sixteenth-century chroniclers identify his sickness as smallpox. One of the most dependable is Juan de Betanzos, who was married to Huayna Capac's niece and describes the Inca's death as due to *"una sarna y lepra"* (a kind of scabies and leprosy). More recent historians and anthropologists have accepted that smallpox swept the hemisphere on numerous vectors after the conquistadors arrived in the late fifteenth century. For a good debate against this, see Robert McCaa, Aleta Nimlos, and Teodoro Hampe Martínez, "Why Blame Smallpox? The Death of the Inca Huayna Capac and the Demographic Destruction of Tawantinsuyu (Ancient Peru)" (paper, Minnesota Population Center, University of Minnesota, 2004), http://users.pop.umn.edu/~rmccaa /aha2004/why_blame_smallpox.pdf. Chroniclers who mention the plague in Peru and/or identify it as smallpox are numerous, but here is a short list: Cieza de León, *Crónica del Perú*, 1:199–200; Guaman Poma, 2:93; Marcos Jiménez de la Espada, ed., *Una Antigualla peruana*, 21; Lastres, *Historia de la Viruela*, 25; Pedro Pizarro, "Relación del descubrimiento y conquista de los reinos del Perú," in *Biblioteca de autores españoles desde la formación del lenguaje hasta nuestros días: Crónicas del Perú* [Narrative of the discovery and conquest of the kingdoms of Peru], vol. 5 (Madrid: Ediciones Atlas, 1965), 181.

35 *his throne should go to the eldest*: Sarmiento de Gamboa, *History of the Incas*, 165.

35 *The Lord Inca was hallucinating*: Cobo, *Historia*, 1:161; Lastres, *Historia de la viruela*, 21.

35 *Supay, who answered that*: Cobo, *Historia*, 1:161.

36 *possibly under psychotic delusions*: Lastres, *Historia de la viruela*, 21.

36 *Lord Inca's heart was gouged from his breast*: Cobo, *Historia*, 1:161.

36 *his embalmed body was carried to Cuzco*: Guaman Poma, 2:379.

36 *insisting he was still alive*: Rostworowski, *Historia del Tawantinsuyu*, 90.

36 *after many months of travel*: According to El Inca Garcilaso, it took four months to transport goods from Cuzco to Potosí and back, as it was all done on foot or on the backs of llamas. I have based this estimate on that fact. *Royal Commentaries*, 8:370.

36 *Four thousand family members, concubines, and servants*: R. J. Rummel, *Death by Government* (New Brunswick, NJ: Transaction, 1994), 63.

36 *Guaraquinga—a giant, solid gold*: Cobo, *Historia*, 1:162.

37 Epigraph: *"There it was. The face of the sun"*: Garcilaso, *Royal Commentaries*, 8:350.

37 *Almost five centuries later*: As mentioned earlier, all information on Juan Ochochoque was gathered from interviews with his wife, Leonor Gonzáles, and his children, Senna, Mariluz, Jhon, and Henrry, in La Rinconada, Putina, Juliaca, and Puno, as well as weekly or monthly contact since 2014.

37 *lives of his wife and seven children*: Ochochoque had two "compromisos," or commitments, as Andean Indians call them. These are not wives by marriage. His compromiso with Leonor Gonzáles produced four children. He had three older children by his first.

38 *masked by the tanning process*: Mark Cartwright, "Inca Mummies," Ancient History Encyclopedia, last modified June 16, 2014.

38 *his mummy was ferreted out of Cuzco*: W. H. Isbell, *Mummies and Mortuary Monuments* (Austin: University of Texas Press, 1997), 54–55.

CHAPTER 3: METAL HUNGER

39 Epigraph: *"Inca: 'Is this the gold you people eat?'"*: In Quechua—*Kay quritachu mikhunki?* Guaman Poma, 2:342.

41 *At the close of the fourteenth century, seven-eighths*: Antonio Miguel Bernal, *España, proyecto inacabado: Los Costes/beneficios del Imperio*, 274.

41 *By 1475, they had become keen participants*: Ibid.

42 *Isabella and Ferdinand called for a brutal and fanatical purge*: This was inspired by Alonso de Hojeda, a Dominican friar, who consulted with Isabella when she was visiting in Seville in 1478 and warned her that heresy was rampant. Henry Kamen, 35; Joseph Pérez, *The Spanish Inquisition* (New Haven, CT: Yale University Press, 2004), 19.

42 *filled the royal coffers*: Carlos Fuentes, *The Buried Mirror*, 82.

42 *a hundred thousand Moors were dead*: Kamen, 17.

42 *more than half the Jewish population of Castile*: Ibid., 37.

42 *an almost festive air*: Ibid., 255, 272.

42 *the ancestors of Saint Teresa of Ávila*: Anna Foa, "Teresa's 'Marrano' Grandfather," *L'Osservatore Romano* (Vatican), March 2, 2015. There is some debate about the converso roots of Cervantes, but many intellectuals, such as

Carlos Fuentes, consider them a certainty. Fuentes, 173–74; William Byron, *Cervantes: A Biography* (Garden City, NY: Doubleday, 1978), 24–32.

43 *That hunger hardened*: Cristóbal Colón (Christopher Columbus), *Relaciones y cartas de Cristóbal Colón*, prologue, 24.

43 *the production of this metal would not be enough*: Bernal, 269.

43 *written openly about his carnal appetites*: Pope Pius II, to his father, Silvio, 1443, in *Reject Aeneas, Accept Pius: Selected Letters of Aeneas Sylvius Piccolomini*, ed. and trans. Thomas M. Izbicki, Gerald Christianson, and Philip Krey (Washington, DC: Catholic University of America Press, 2006), 161.

43 *"The problem of money predominates"*: Pope Pius II to the council at Siena, 1436. Ibid., 95.

43 auri sacra fames: The saying *"Quid non mortal pectoral cogis, Auri sacra fames"* is a verse from Virgil's *The Aeneid*, bk. 3, v. 56–57. Its meaning translated loosely is "To what lengths will man's accursed greed for gold not lead him."

43 *as thirty-five of her caravels returned*: Malyn Newitt, *A History of Portuguese Overseas Expansion: 1400–1668* (New York: Routledge, 2005), 39–40.

43 *more than 1,500 pounds of gold*: It was 1,589, to be exact. Manuela Mendonça—*O Sonho da União Ibérica* (Lisbon: Quidnovi, 2007), 101–3—cites 106,676 *dobles* of gold; a *doble* at that time weighed 6.77 grams. That would add up to more than 700 kilos, or 1,589 pounds—about three-quarters of a ton.

44 *When the famous Portuguese explorer Bartolomeu Dias rounded*: Peter L. Bernstein, *The Power of Gold: The History of an Obsession*, 117.

44 *worrying his copy of* Imago Mundi: German Arciniegas, *America in Europe: A History of the New World in Reverse*, 27; Markham, 30.

44 *a letter and a map he had sent many years before*: Toscanelli sent a letter, dated 25 June 1474, and a map to Fernão Martins, a priest in Lisbon, detailing a westward course to the Spice Islands and Asia. Martins delivered that letter to King Afonso, whose advisors rejected its proposal. Columbus, 14; Markham, 31; Kirkpatrick, 6.

44 *The map placed the hulking island*: J. G. Bartholomew, *A Literary and Historical Atlas of America* (New York: E. P. Dutton, 1911), commons.wikimedia.org/wiki /File:Atlantic_Ocean,_Toscanelli,_1474.jpg.

44 *"This island is rich in gold, pearls, and gems"*: Kirkpatrick, 7.

45 Epigraph: *"Gold and slaves. The first corrupts all it touches"*: Simón Bolívar, Contestación de un americano meridional a un caballero de esta isla ("Letter from Jamaica"), Kingston, September 6, 1815, quoted in Marie Arana, *Simón Bolívar: American Liberator*, 310.

46 Epigraph: *"As centuries unfold"*: *"Venient annis saecula seris, quibus Oceanus vincula rerum laxet et ingens pateat tellus Tethysque novos detegat orbes nec sit terris ultima Thule."* Seneca, *Medea* (Oxford: Oxford University Press, 2014), 84.

47 *in a frayed coat*: James Reston Jr., *Dogs of God* (New York: Anchor, 2005), 238.

47 *prematurely white hair askew*: According to Columbus's son Fernando,

his father's "hair, which had been fair, snow-white at the age of thirty."
Kirkpatrick, 11; Markham, 136.

47 *little interested in personal riches*: Markham, 57.

47 *sailed out of Lisbon secretly*: Ibid., 9.

47 *prattling on to anyone willing to listen*: Reston, *Dogs*, 238.

47 *weary of dealing with intermediaries*: Eduardo Galeano, *Open Veins of Latin America: Five Centuries of the Pillage of a Continent*, 12.

47 *"Columbus's enterprise . . . will add many carats"*: Luis de Santálgel's letter to Ferdinand and Isabella, in Fray Bartolomé de las Casas, *Obras Completas*, 3:517.

47 *"Gold is a wonderful thing!"*: Columbus's letter to King Ferdinand and Queen Isabella, 1503, in Martin Fernandez de Navarrete, *Colección de los viajes y descubrimientos que hicieron por mar los españoles*, vol. 1 (Madrid: Imprenta Nacional, 1858), 456.

48 *"a handsome people: with hair not curly"*: Ibid., 175. Columbus, 24.

48 *naked, guileless, seemingly "poor in everything"*: Ibid. See also *Letter of Christopher Columbus to Rafael Sánchez, Facsimile of the First Publication Concerning America, Published at Barcelona, May 1493* (Chicago: W. H. Lowdermilk, 1893).

48 *drank from goblets of gold*: Fray Bartolomé de las Casas, *Vida de Cristóbal Colón*, 87.

48 *no fewer than one hundred allusions to gold and silver*: Columbus, 1–148; Bernstein, 120.

48 *The indigenous Americans, quick to see*: Las Casas, *Cristóbal Colón*, 90.

48 *"They have no experience with arms"*: Columbus, 1–148.

49 *gold his sailors raked from the riverbeds . . . "like chaff"*: Fernandez de Navarrete, 1:456.

49 *nearing the River Ganges*: Ibid., 367.

49 *"I have secured one thousand four hundred islands"*: Ibid. 348–49.

49 *"This island is Tarsus, Scythia, Ophir, Ophaz"*: He was implying that, in addition to Japan, he had found an equivalent source to that which had produced the riches of King Solomon, the most prosperous of biblical monarchs.

49 *sail triumphantly to the Spanish port of Palos*: Las Casas, *Obras*, 3:695.

49 *Columbus took his exotic caravan overland*: Markham, 135–36.

50 *It was a grand show—a* pars pro toto: Elvira Vilches, *New World Gold*, 65.

50 *Pope Alexander . . . was one of the first to receive a gift*: Las Casas, *Obras*, 4:834–38; Markham, 137. The Treaty of Tordesillas (1494), which set out the pope's line of demarcation, was confirmed by the pope's ambassadors in a meeting at Tordesillas. The line of demarcation was initially set by Alexander at 100 leagues west of the Cape Verde Islands. In 1506 it was shifted to 370 leagues west of those islands and sanctioned by Pope Julius II.

50 *given his own coat of arms*: Las Casas, *Obras*, 4:839.

50 *equipment to facilitate metal mining*: Ibid., 846–47.

50 *Sailors, swordsmen, gentlemen, miners*: Ibid.

51 *"Get gold! Humanly, if possible"*: Bernal, 279; Mario Arrubla, prologue in Ramiro Montoya, *Crónicas del oro y la plata americanos*, 11.

51 *In 1495, in desperation, he issued an infamous edict*: The edict is described in Brown, 11. The large containers, or "cascabeles grandes," were generally hawking bells, tied to the legs of hawks in falconry. The equivalent amount of gold would be sufficient to make dozens of rings. Of the chopping of hands, Las Casas writes, "[A]ll this did I behold with my bodily mortal eyes," Las Casas, *Historia*, 3:96.

51 *a commerce he knew well from his exploits in Africa*: Ramiro Montoya, 22.

51 *By the end of that trade, as many as five million souls*: Andrés Reséndez, *The Other Slavery: The Uncovered Story of Indian Enslavement in America*, 5.

51 *"Slaves are the primary source of income"*: Las Casas, quoted in F. P. Sullivan, *Indian Freedom* (Kansas City, MO: Sheed & Ward, 1995), 60.

51 *Blamed for appalling cruelties*: Bartolomé de las Casas, who had witnessed Columbus's magnificent parade as a young man, joined the gold rush, and become a Dominican friar, would later lament the captain general's excesses in his famously vivid *A Short History of the Destruction of the Indies*.

51 *Hadn't Columbus's dreams been a drain?*: Washington Irving, *A History of the Life and Voyages of Christopher Columbus*, vol. 1 (Paris: Galignani, 1828), 259.

51 *hadn't a great fraud been perpetrated?*: Ramiro Montoya, 25.

51 *teetotaling queen*: Luis Suárez Fernández, *Isabel I Reina*, 114.

52 *one-tenth of all royal profits*: Silvio Beding, *The Christopher Columbus Encyclopedia*, vol. 1 (New York: Simon & Schuster, 1992), 416.

52 *He had seen more parrots*: German Arciniegas, *Latin America: A Cultural History*, 27.

52 *He had lost his riches, his reputation, his eyesight*: Raúl Aguilar Rodas, *Cristobal Colón* (Medellín: Paniberica, 2006), 1.

53 Epigraph: *"Fateful omens in the sky. One like a spark of fire"*: Fray Bernardino de Sahagún, testimony from a Nahua witness, year of 12-House, 1517, in León-Portilla, *Visión de los vencidos: Crónicas indígenas*, 7; León-Portilla, *Reverso de la Conquista*, 29.

53 *crippled by gout, fending off mutineers*: Columbus, 303–23.

53 *Ten thousand pesos of gold had been harvested*: Ramiro Montoya, 24.

53 *It didn't take long for Cortés to grasp*: J. H. Elliott, in *Cortés: Letters*, xiv.

53 *Cortés was perhaps first to recognize*: Pagden, in *Cortés: Letters*, xli.

54 *sent by Queen Isabella with express instructions*: Pagden, in *Cortés: Letters*, xliii.

54 *But once declared free, the Taíno refused to mine*: Thomas Southey, *Chronological History of the West Indies*, vol. 1.

54 *"Forasmuch as my Lord"*: Queen Isabel I, *Decree on Indian Labor*, 1503, in John Parry, *New Iberian World: A Documentary History* (New York: Times Books, 1984), 1:262–63; see also Arana, *Bolívar*, 471.

54 *one Machiavellian scheme after another*: King Ferdinand was the model for Niccolò Machiavelli's *The Prince*. Niccolò Machiavelli, *The Letters of Machiavelli* (Chicago: University of Chicago, 1961), 52.

55 *romanced the island's women*: William H. Prescott, *History of the Conquest of*

Mexico, 109. This is admittedly something of a romantic view. He was either seducing the wives of his Spaniard cohort or taking rampant advantage of Indian females. Prescott describes them as "amorous propensities." See also Díaz, *Historia verdadera de la conquista de Nueva España*, ch. 203.

55 *a quarter million more pesos of gold*: 215,000, to be exact. Ramiro Montoya, 24.

55 *famine, disease, and suicide*: When the Taíno were forced to work the mines, they did not plant or harvest crops, as they had been accustomed to, and so a famine ensued. Smallpox, too, became rampant. Pietro Martire D'Anghiera, *De Orbe Novo, the Eight Decades of Peter Martyr D'Anghera*, 1625; New York: Knickerbocker (1912); digital version, BiblioBazaar (2009), 160, 376.

55 *reduced that robust community of a half million to a feeble sixty thousand*: The half-million figure comes from Karen Anderson Córdova, *Hispaniola and Puerto Rico: Indian Acculturation and Heterogeneity, 1492–1550* (Ann Arbor, MI: University Microfilms, 1990). Also: "sixty thousand"—"there were 60,000 people living on this island, including the Indians; so that from 1494 to 1508, over three million people had perished from war, slavery, and the mines." Las Casas, *A Short History of the Destruction of the Indies* (London: Penguin, 1974). The claim of "three million" is generally regarded as an exaggeration, whereas the sixty thousand were accounted for when Las Casas arrived in 1508.

55 *"I came to get gold!"*: Prescott, *Conquest of Mexico*, 109.

56 *slave hunters, returning to Cuba*: Cortés to Doña Juana and Carlos V, 10 July 1519, in *Cortés: Letters*, 4.

56 *"If you're so ravenous"*: *"Si tan ansiosos estáis de oro que abandonáis vuestra tierra para venir a inquietar la ajena, yo os mostraré una provincia donde podéis a manos llenas satisfacer ese deseo."* Jorge Guillermo Leguía, *Historia de América* (Lima: Rosay, 1934), 72.

57 *his father-in-law, Pedrarias*: Balboa to King Ferdinand, 16 October 1515, in *Archivo de Indias*, vol. 2 (Madrid: Imprenta Española, 1864). Balboa was betrothed to Pedrarias's oldest daughter—an arrangement suggested by the bishop, Fray Juan de Quevedo, to quell the jealousies between them.

57 *the "Wrath of God"*: David Marley, *Wars of the Americas: A Chronology* (Santa Barbara, CA: ABC-CLIO, 1998), 13.

57 *One of Balboa's men . . . Francisco Pizarro*: Jesús María Henao, *Historia de Colombia* (Bogotá: Librería Colombiana, 1920), 1:50–54.

57 *recruited five hundred of Velázquez's men*: To be exact, they numbered 508, not counting about 100 more shipmasters, pilots, and sailors. Bernal Díaz del Castillo, *The Discovery and Conquest of Mexico*, 42.

58 *Cortés rushed to set sail*: Gonzalo Fernández de Oviedo y Valdés, *Historia General y Natural de las Indias*, 1:539–41.

58 *"Fortune favors the daring!"*: Hernán Cortés, *Cartas del famoso conquistador Hernán Cortés al emperador Carlos Quinto*, 213.

58 *roaring with rage, charging his brash young captain*: Díaz, *Discovery and Conquest*, 39.

58 *he played on their greed for gold*: Ibid., 33–41.

58 *They were, after all, eager recruits*: Díaz, *Historia verdadera de la conquista*, 13–16.

58 *"God would see to it that the lands we found were teeming with gold"*: Ibid., 17.

59 Epigraph: *"There she is, the mountain"*: *"La montaña Bella Durmiente, ahí en mi pueblo de lágrimas."* From interviews with residents of La Rinconada, Mount Ananea, Peru, February 2013.

60 Epigraph: *"That's it?" said the captain*: Testimony of messengers in Nahuatl, 1519, in Miguel León-Portilla, *Visión de los vencidos*, 68.

60 *They had lost eight hundred men*: Ibid., 59.

61 *Cortés dashed all possible hope of desertion by scuttling his ships*: Ibid., 109.

61 *he had seen cities here that matched Granada*: *Cortés: Letters*, 67–68.

62 *From caciques, the tribal leaders who spoke candidly*: Díaz, *Historia verdadera de la conquista*, 3:156–57, 174–75.

62 *gigantic discs of gold and silver*: Ibid., 165–67, 171, 187–88.

62 *he and his troops crossed the towering Sierra Madre*: Díaz, *Historia verdadera de la conquista*, 3:168 map.

62 *on a blue lake, radiating such brilliance*: See ch. 2 epigraph—Dominguez Hidalgo, *Mitos, Fabulas, y Leyendas del Antiguo México*, 215.

62 *The Spaniards were as dazzled*: Díaz, *Historia verdadera de la conquista*, 3:190.

62 *"I do not know how to describe it"*: Ibid., 191.

63 *an additional three thousand pesos of gold*: *Cortés: Letters*, 69.

63 *annual tributes of these*: Ibid., 69, 79–81.

63 *he was being given a courtesy*: Ibid., 80.

63 *a diplomat would not*: Ibid.

63 *Some chroniclers—including Cortés himself—have claimed*: Anthony R. Pagden, commentary in *Cortés: Letters*, 42n, 467. The other chroniclers who promoted this notion are all Spaniards—Durán, chs. 53, 54, 394–408; Fray Bernardino de Sahagún, *Historia general de las cosas de Nueva España*, vol. 4, ch. 10. Also Don Antonio de Mendoza, the first viceroy of New Spain, quoted in J. H. Elliott, "The Mental World of Hernán Cortés," *Transactions of the Royal Historical Society* 17 (1967): 41–58, 53.

64 *But these are Western projections on the Amerindian mind*: The Quetzalcoatl myth was fabricated by Cortés in his second letter to King Carlos and then taken as fact by subsequent Spanish historians. There is no indigenous evidence for it. Bernal Díaz, the most reliable contemporary witness of the meeting between Montezuma and Cortés, never mentions Quetzalcoatl or any other god. He quotes Montezuma as saying, very simply, that his ancestors had predicted a foreign race of men would appear on his shores one day. Díaz, *Historia verdadera de la conquista*, 3:206; Jacques Lafaye, *Quetzalcóatl and Guadalupe: The Formation of Mexican National Consciousness* (Chicago: University of Chicago Press, 1976), 149. Henry Wagner mentions the Indian custom of dressing newly arrived visitors in native regalia. Indian chiefs

dressed Juan de Grijalva in Indian finery when he arrived at Rio Tabasco in 1518. It is said that Montezuma sent a reproduction of Quetzalcoatl's clothes in which to dress Grijalva, but the Spanish conquistador had already departed. A priest in Grijalva's expedition and subsequently in Cortés's expedition, Juan Díaz, describes this, and it may be the source of Cortés's inspired explanation to the king. Henry Wagner, *The Discovery of New Spain in 1518 by Juan de Grijalva* (Pasadena, CA: Cortés Society, 1942), 34–35.

64 *he arrived on a litter under a magnificent*: The entire account is in Díaz, *Discovery and Conquest*, 193. Also in *Cortés: Letters*, 85, with some differing flourishes.

64 *astonished by "the barbarian king's baubles"*: Cortés, *Despatches*, 35; *Cortés: Letters*, 108.

64 *To touch the great Aztec lord*: Díaz, *Discovery and Conquest*, 194; *Cortés: Letters*, 84.

64 *hygiene-conscious Aztecs*: Jacques Soustelle, *Daily Life of the Aztecs* (Mineola, NY: Dover Publications, 2002), 129–31. Aztecs often bathed twice a day with copalxocotl and washed their mouths with breath fresheners. (See also *Florentine Codex*, bk. 11, pt. 12.) The Spaniards, on the other hand, cleaned their teeth with urine. (See Ashenburg, below.)

64 *Sixteenth-century Europeans*: Katherine Ashenburg, *The Dirt on Clean* (Toronto: Knopf, 2007), 39–72. Ashenburg explains that in Spain, especially, there was a general disdain for bathing, heightened by Arab rituals of cleanliness. Moreover, water was feared as a carrier of the Black Death, and, for centuries, baths were perceived as opening the pores and admitting disease.

64 *they insisted on fumigating them with incense*: Díaz, *Discovery and Conquest*, 10, 90, 169.

64 *He lodged him splendidly*: Ibid., 196.

65 *"it would benefit" the king*: *Cortés: Letters*, 88.

65 *Cortés got word that two Spaniards had been killed*: Ibid., 89–91.

65 *He explained to his prisoner*: Ibid., 92.

65 *He insisted that he be shown the mines*: Ibid.

65 *He called for his servants to accompany*: Ibid., 92–93.

65 *Mexico's fields were bursting with maize*: Ibid., 94.

65 *Artists produced maps*: Ibid.

65 *defer to the Spaniards as they built fortresses*: Ibid., 96.

65 *silver sheets amounting to almost a million pesos*: Ibid., 100. Seven hundred thousand pesos, to be exact. Also Díaz, *Discovery and Conquest*, 256, 269.

66 *would have been worth more than $20 million*: Cortés wrote that what he sent King Carlos in his first shipment was worth more than 100,000 ducats. *Cortés: Letters*, 100. A ducat was 3.545 grams of 99.47 percent fine gold, which at market value today ($41.4 in 2016) is worth $20 million, www.goldgrambars .com, accessed April 20, 2019.

66 Epigraph: *"They come armed with lightning"*: Carlos Fuentes, *El espejo enterrado* (México, DF: House Grupo Editorial, 2016), 111.

66 *The small jade stones*, chalchihuites: H. W. Foshag, "Chalchihuitl, A Study in Jade," *American Minerologist* 40, nos. 11/12 (December 1, 1955): 1062–1070: "Among the Aztecs, chalchihuitl was the most precious of substances. As an indication of its value, one may quote Montezuma's words, as recorded by Bernal Díaz del Castillo (1632) upon the occasion of paying tribute to Cortés: 'I will also give you some very valuable stones, which you will send to him in my name; they are chalchihuites and are not to be given to anyone else but only to him, your great Prince. Each is worth two loads of gold.'"

66 *no one had more of it than the merchants of Venice*: Frederic C. Lane, *Venice: A Maritime Republic* (Baltimore: John Hopkins University Press, 1973), 323.

67 *"the total amount of gold in Europe in all forms"*: Bernstein, 109.

67 *the bullion reserves*: John Day, "The Great Bullion Famine of the Fifteenth Century," *Past and Present* 79 (May 1978): 3–54.

67 *"greater Kingdoms and Dominions"*: Cortés: *Letters*, 159.

67 *Rebellions flared*: Ibid., 97.

67 *another fleet of Spanish ships carrying nine hundred*: 880, to be exact—80 horsemen and 800 foot soldiers, Ibid., 113–27.

67 *Even as some of Cortés's men*: Díaz, *Historia verdadera de la conquista*, 256.

67 *secretly began sending gifts of gold and food*: Ibid., 257.

67 *more gold for their loyalty*: Ibid., 258.

67 *draped heavy gold chains—fanfarrones*: Ibid., 257.

68 *The retinue of Spaniards left behind*: Ibid., 300–9.

68 *butchering hundreds mercilessly*: Miguel León-Portilla, *The Broken Spears: The Aztec Account of the Conquest of Mexico*, 74–77; Francisco López de Gómara cites six hundred present and nearly all killed, *Historia General de las Indias: Conquista de México*, vol. 2 (Caracas: Fundación Biblioteca Ayacucho, 2007), 1996–98.

68 *Those last bitter blows at the hands of his own people*: This is taken from Prescott's fusion of eyewitness testimonies: Díaz, Oviedo, Torquemada, the noble Tlaxcalan Diego Muños Camargo, the celebrated chronicler Antonio de Herrera, and so on. Prescott, *Conquest of Mexico*, 350–51.

69 *newly conceived Council of the Indies*: King Carlos I made his first mention of this council in 1519, although it wasn't established until 1524.

69 *"Cortés ordered his . . . servants"*: Ibid., 313.

69 *seizing the jade along with the solid gold bars*: Díaz, *Historia verdadera de la conquista*, 313–14.

69 *Narvaéz troops, newly arrived*: Oviedo, 3:47.

70 *Looking back, a Spaniard caught a glimpse*: Díaz, *Historia verdadera de la conquista*, 314.

70 *With four thousand Tlaxcalans*: Prescott, *Conquest of Mexico*, 399; Díaz, *Historia verdadera de la conquista*, 332–33.

70 *"This order of Cortés's"*: Díaz, *Historia verdadera de la conquista*, 334.

71 *decided to change his coat of arms*: R. L. Kagan, *Clio and the Crown: The Politics*

of History in Medieval and Early Modern Spain (Baltimore: Johns Hopkins University Press, 2009), 61.

71 *This ambition, coupled with the superstition of the age*: William Dalton, *Cortés and Pizarro* (London: Griffin, Bohn, 1852), 8.

71 *"Under faith's banners"*: *"So color de religión/Van a buscar plata y oro."* Lope de Vega, *Obras de Lope de Vega*, vol. 11 (Madrid: Rivadeneyra, 1900), 110.

71 *"Santiago! Y cierra, España!"*: "Saint James! And charge, Spain!" The Spanish cry upon an attack on the battlefield. Saint James was also known in Iberia as Santiago Matamoros (Saint James the Moorslayer). The battle cry "Santiago! Y cierra!" is said to have been used at the Battle of Las Navas de Tolosa in 1212, when the Castilians, Aragonese, and Portuguese united against the Berber Almohad rulers of southern Iberia. "España" was added later, when Castile and Aragon became Spain.

71 *Only Napoleon I and Adolf Hitler at the heights of rule*: Bernstein, 130.

CHAPTER 4: TRAIL OF THE WHITE KING

73 Epigraph: *"Atahualpa had said there was a small mountain"*: Pedro Pizarro, *Relation of the Discovery*, 2 vols. (New York: Cortés Society, 1921), 234.

73 *some even related by blood*: Pizarro, Cortés, and Orellana were all distant cousins. Rómulo Cúneo-Vidal, *Vida del Conquistador del Perú, Don Francisco Pizarro y sus hermanos* (Barcelona: Maucci, 1925).

74 *"The men who went on these ventures"*: John Hemming, *The Search for El Dorado*, 50.

74 *Pizarro had studied Cortés's strategies of conquest meticulously*: H. T. Peck, *W. H. Prescott*, English Men of Letters (New York: Macmillan, 1905), 160–63.

75 *"discovered, conquered, and pacified Pirú."* José Antonio Busto Duthurburu, *Pizarro*, 1:120–22.

75 *The Pirú Andagoya had found*: Pirú was also reported variously as "Virú" in original chronicles. Cieza de León calls him Peruquete: Cieza, *The Discovery and Conquest of Peru: Chronicles of the New World Encounter*, 48–49.

75 *Pirú—the name now for all land south of Panama*: Busto, *Pizarro*, 1:139.

75 *the Guaraní Indians had told*: According to a conquistador's letter, even the king's vassals were wearing crowns of silver and plates of gold. From *Carta de Luis Ramírez a su padre*, San Salvador, 10 July 1528, *"vista la gran riqueza de la tierra, y como junto a la dicha sierra había un rey blanco que traía . . . vestidos como nosotros, se determinaron de ir allá, por ver lo que era, los cuales fueron y les embiaron cartas. Y que aún no habían llegado a las minas, más ya habían tenido plática con unos indios comarcanos a la sierra, y que traían en las cabezas unas coronas de plata y unas planchas de oro colgadas de los pescuezos y orejas, y ceñidas por cintos."* José Toribio Medina, *El veneciano Sebastian Cabot* (Santiago: Imprenta Universitaria, 1908), 442.

75 *the mutinous Sack of Rome*: In 1527, 34,000 soldiers of the armies of the Holy
Roman Empire, unpaid and furious, mutinied and marched against Rome,
pillaging the city. Pedro de Mendoza was among them.

75 *avid participant in the race for worldly riches*: Sarah de Laredo, intro., *From Panama
to Peru: The Conquest of Peru by the Pizarros* (London: Maggs Bros., 1925), v.

75 *Born the illegitimate son of a lesser nobleman*: Busto, *Pizarro*, 1:40–41.

76 *he was a loyal warrior, valiant in battle*: Oviedo, vol. 4, pt. 3, intro, 2.

76 *flush with grain and a thriving cattle business*: Rafael Varón Gabal, *Pizarro and
His Brothers* (Norman: University of Oklahoma, 1997), 17.

76 *Pizarro merged his plantation*: Busto, *Pizarro*, 1:124.

76 *They formalized their pact*: Francisco López de Gómara, *Historia General de las
Indias (1523–1548)*, vol. 1, pt. 1 ch. 108.

77 *a crew of more than one hundred men*: Zárate, bk. 1, ch. 1, 19; Francisco de
Xerez, *True Account of the Conquest of Peru (1522–48)*, ed. Iván R. Reyna;
Antononio de Herrera y Tordesillas, *The General History of the Vast Continent
and Islands of America*, 6 vols., trans. Captain John Stevens.

77 *Luque, manager of their funds*: According to the Sorbonne historian Bernard
Lavallé, Luque was serving as a front for someone else: *"Rafael Varón Gabai
insiste asimismo en el hecho de que el principal financista de la operación puede
muy bien haber sido en realidad el licenciado Espinosa, uno de los hombres más
conocidos y más ricos de Panamá en esa época, pero cuya posición en relación a
Pedrarias Dávila, de quien era alcalde mayor, lo ponía en una situación delicada.
No es pues imposible que Luque, quien de todos modos participaba en la empresa,
le haya servido de pantalla."* Bernard Lavallé, *Francisco Pizarro* (Madrid:
Espasa-Calpé, 2005), 58.

77 *the governor was not asked to contribute a penny*: There is some debate on this
and even the suggestion that he was paid to be a partner. For clarity on this
debate see Varón, *Pizarro*, 17–19.

77 *The first voyage was a rout*: This account is taken from various sources. See
Diego de Silva y Guzmán, *Conquista de la Nueva Castilla, "La Crónica rimada"*
(Lima: Biblioteca Peruana, 1968); Oviedo, vol. 4, pt. 3, intro., 2; Xerez, *True
Account*, vol. 3, 3–5; Cieza de León, *Discovery and Conquest of Peru*, 49–55;
Raúl Porras Barrenechea, *Cartas del Perú, Colección de documentos inéditos para
la historia del Perú (1524–1543)*, vol. 3, 13–18.

77 *no wind in their sails*: Silva y Guzman, *Conquista*, 1:21, cited in Busto, *Pizarro*,
1:138.

79 *"Ah, mister Governor!"*: "A señor gobernador/ miradlo bien por entero/allá va
el recogedor/y acá queda el carnicero." Cieza de León, in Vedia, *Historiadores
primitivos de Indias*, 2:436.

79 *under captain Bartolomé Ruiz*: Ruiz was a skilled former pilot who had sailed
with Columbus.

79 *Huayna Capac, who, at that moment*: Cieza de León claims he was still alive at
this point. Cieza de León, *The Discovery and Conquest of Peru, 113*.

79 *"They were carrying many pieces of silver"*: Raúl Porras Barrenechea, *Cronistas del Perú (1528–1650) y otros ensayos* (Lima: Banco de Crédito del Perú, 1986), 54–55. Quoted also in Hemming, *Conquest of the Incas* (1983), 25, and Wright, 64.

80 *they wept for joy to see*: Cieza de León, *Crónica del Perú*, vol. 16, fol. 17v.

80 *kept his emotions in check*: Ibid.

80 *"On that side . . . is Panama"*: José Antonio Busto Duthurburu, *La Conquista del Perú*, 26. The original Spanish has it "escoja el que fuere buen castellano lo que más bien le estuviere."

81 *dumped their allotment of maize on the sand*: Cieza de León, vol. 16, fol. 18v.

81 *Pizarro had six months to make his way back*: Lavallé, *Francisco Pizarro*, 66.

81 *a band of slaves*: As Alexandra Parma Cook and David Noble Cook noted in the 1998 edition of Cieza de León's book: "There were numerous Black slaves in Panama in the 1520s, and many participated in the Peruvian venture. A slave had saved the life of Almagro. As [James] Lockhart points out [in *Men of Cajamarca*], the records are remarkably silent regarding the sure partici-pation of Blacks in the conquest." Cieza de León, *Discovery and Conquest of Peru*, 111.

81 *enough supplies, but no weapons of war*: Hemming, *Conquest*, 27.

82 *"the product of centuries of development"*: Ibid., 27.

83 Epigraph: *"Castrate the sun!"*: From the *Chilám Balám de Chumayel*, quoted in León-Portilla, *Reverso de la Conquista*, 78.

83 *Cortés, with his natural charisma*: Cortés, *Cartas y relaciones de Hernán Cortés al emperador Carlos V* (Paris: Imprenta Central de los Ferro Carriles A. Chaix y ca., 1856) 539–58; Hemming, *Conquest*, 28.

83 *had not been having an easy time of it*: "Me ha sido más difícil luchar contra mis compatriotas que contra los aztecas." Julio Verne, *Viajeros extraordinarios* (1878) (Barcelona: Circulo Latino, 2006), 290.

83 *mingled easily and charmed the ladies*: José Luis Olaizola, *Francisco Pizarro* (Madrid: Planeta, 1998), available on BibliotecaOnline, 2012 digital edition, www.bibliotecaonline.net.

83 *a formidable river of silver*: The first Aztec mines Cortés's men tapped were the ancient sites at Taxco. Because of France's many covert attempts to seize the silver as it made its way across the Atlantic, Spain sent a fleet of ships to escort the shipments. Timothy R. Walton, *The Spanish Treasure Fleets* (Sarasota, FL: Pineapple Press, 1994), 44.

83 *They saw each other at least once*: Olaizola, *Francisco Pizarro*; Hemming, *Conquest*, 28.

84 *as Egypt is from Rome*: I owe these insights to Ronald Wright, in his masterful *Stolen Continents*.

85 *he had no real understanding of the people*: Ibid., 67.

85 *from the southernmost part of Colombia*: This was neither Colombia nor Chile at the time, of course, but I use these for ease of understanding by the contem-

porary reader. From here forward, I use these current geographic place markers for convenience's sake.

85 *"that there were about one hundred ninety"*: Edmundo Guillén Guillén, *La guerra de reconquista Inka* (Lima: Guillén Guillén, 1994), 44.

87 *"like a brilliantly star-studded sky"*: Cristóbal de Mena, in Miguel de Estete, *Noticia del Perú*, quoted in Hemming, *Conquest of the Incas*, 36.

87 *"I myself witnessed"*: Pedro Pizarro, 36.

88 *"Where are they?"*: Hemming, *Conquest*, 40.

88 *"Did you not see what just happened?"*: Cieza de León, *Crónica del Perú*, vol. 3, ch. 44, 255; Estete, 31; Porras Barrenechea, *Cartas del Perú*, 120.

89 *"Their efforts were of little avail"*: Cristóbal de Mena, *La conquista del Perú, llamada la Nueva Castilla*, 244.

89 *Pizarro was able to frog-march*: Pedro Pizarro, 230.

89 *"They pulled him from his litter by force"*: Tito Cusi Yupanqui, *A 16th-Century Account of the Conquest*, 136.

89 *In little more than two hours*: Xerez, 333; Mena, 244.

89 *He answered with a sad smile*: Mena, 246; Hemming, *Conquest*, 46.

90 *At least one historian has conjectured*: Hemming, *Conquest*, 46.

90 *"The Spaniards took all who were brave and noble"*: Guaman Poma, 2:357.

90 *an ongoing culture of rampant sexual abuse*: Sara Vicuña Guengerich, "Capac Women and the Politics of Marriage in Early Colonial Peru," *Colonial Latin American Review* 24, no. 2 (2015): 147–67, 147; Susan Socolow, *The Women of Colonial Latin America* (Cambridge: Cambridge University Press, 2000), 38.

90 *"eighty thousand pesos of gold"*: Hernando de Soto, in Porras Barrenechea, *Cartas del Perú*, 59.

91 *Spanish squadrons rode out into the countryside*: Guaman Poma, 2:369.

91 *one large room stacked to the ceiling with gold*: Xerez, 335. The room measured roughly twenty-five by eighteen feet, and eighteen feet high (an average taken from numerous chroniclers) (Hemming, *Conquest*, 535).

91 *Huascar was killed soon after*: Mena, 250; Estete, 35; Hemming, *Conquest*, 54.

92 *By 1534, the conquistadors had wrung an estimated ten metric tons*: Izumi Shimada and John Merkel, "Copper-Alloy Metallurgy in Ancient Peru," *Scientific American* 265, no. 1 (July 1991): 80.

92 *worth approximately a half billion dollars*: 24K gold in January 2019: 10 tons at $1,319.51 per ounce = $384,857,127; silver on same date: 70 tons at $16.06 per ounce = $32,789,170. Total: $417,646,297. Gold and silver prices, Gold Price, accessed January 30, 2019, http://goldprice.org/gold-price-usa.html.

92 *With the exception of a few objects*: Vilches, 135.

93 Epigraph: *"Stone upon stone on a bedrock of rags?"* (*"piedra en la piedra, y en la base, harapos?"*): Neruda, "Alturas de Machu Picchu," 207 (my translation).

93 *personal loans to the king*: Varón, *Pizarro*, 75.

93 *the most prosperous mogul in Mexico*: Buddy Levy, *Conquistador: Hernán Cortés, Montezuma, and the Last Stand of the Aztecs* (New York: Bantam Dell, 2008),

321. I use *Mexico* for ease of comprehension. Of course, it was not called
Mexico but New Spain.

93 *five times more blacks than whites*: Ramiro Montoya, 111.

95 *shoe their horses with the precious white substance*: Acosta, vol. 4, ch. 4.

95 *One conquistador whose jaw was blown off*: José Antonio Busto Duthurburu, *La
Platería en el Perú: dos mil años de arte e historia*, 68.

96 *palaces atop their places of government*: Indeed, Pizarro instructed his palace
in Lima to be built on top of the residence of Taulichusco, the *curaca* who
governed the region under the Incas. Churches were to be built atop temples.
In such ways did the Spaniards signify power over the conquered.

96 *Cortés's and Pizarro's conquests were soon producing*: Robins, *Mercury, Mining,
and Empire*, 4–6.

96 *An intense theological debate soon arose*: Rolena Adorno, *The Polemics of
Possession in Spanish American Narrative*, 82–86.

96 *"heretics, schismatics, accursed of God"*: K. W. Swart, *The Black Legend During
the Eighty Years War* (Amsterdam: Springer Netherlands, 1975), 36–57.

97 *As much as two million to three million pesos*: All the following information on
Sino-Spanish trade is from Frederick W. Mote and Denis Twitchett, eds., *The
Cambridge History of China*, vol. 8, *The Ming Dynasty, 1368–1644*, pt. 2 (New
York: Cambridge University Press, 1998), 389–96.

97 *Striking a productive vein in Potosí*: J. R. McNeill and William H. McNeill, *The
Human Web: A Bird's-Eye View of World History*, 203.

97 *Fleets that shipped silver to the Orient*: Mote and Twitchett, *Cambridge History:
Ming Dynasty*, 389–96.

97 *Potosí celebrated the coronation*: Luis Capoche, *Relación general de la villa
imperial de Potosí* (Madrid: Atlas, 1959), https://archive.org/stream
/RelacionGeneralDeLaVillaImperialDePotosiLUISCAPOCHE.

97 *"Vale un Potosí!"*: Miguel de Cervantes, *Don Quixote de la Mancha*, pt. 2, ch.
71, "*Si yo te hubiera de pagar, Sancho —respondió don Quijote,—conforme lo
que merece la grandeza y calidad deste remedio, el tesoro de Venecia, las minas
del Potosí fueran poco para pagarte; toma tú el tiento á lo que llevas mío, y pon el
precio á cada azote.*"

98 *All indigenous males between eighteen and fifty*: Acemoglu and Robinson, map
1, the mining *mita* catchment area. Also in Peter Bakewell, *Miners of the Red
Mountain: Indian Labor in Potosí, 1545–1650*, 181.

98 *but most hardly resisted*: Bakewell, 44–45.

98 *mining had never been so ruthless*: Rostworowski, *Historia del Tawantinsuyu*,
184.

98 *"Your excellence, I am the captain of these people"*: Alonso Enriquez de
Guzmán, *Libro de la vida y los costumbres de Don Alonso Enríquez de Guzmán*,
70–71; Sancho Rayon and de Zabalburu, *Coleccíon de documentos inéditos
para la historia de España*, 85:291 (my translation). "*Apo, yo soy capitán desta
gente, y hasta agora que eres venido á esta tierra á ponella en razón, yo he andado*

*alzado . . . por los muchos agravios de que después que entraron los cristianos en
esta tierra hemos recibido. . . . antes éramos señores y agora somos esclavos. No
solamente han querido los cristianos que los sirvamos, como nos servíamos, el
caballero como caballero y el oficial como oficial, y el villano como villano, sino
que á todos nos hacen unos, todos quieren que les trayamos las cargas á cuestas, que
seamos albañiles y les hagamos las casas, que seamos labradores y les hagamos las
sementeras. Mira si ha sido razón que se nos haga de mal."*

99   *As his corpse decomposed, puddles of mercury*: Brown, ch. 8.

99   *Legions of Indians disappeared into the mountains*: Pedro Pablo Arana, *Las minas
de azogue del Perú* (Lima: Imprenta El Lucero, 1901), 14. Pedro Pablo Arana,
governor of Cuzco, senator of Peru, and candidate for vice president of the
country in 1899, was my paternal great grandfather. He became owner of the
infamous mines of Santa Barbara (which were on his property in his hacienda
in Huancavelíca) long after they had been abandoned by the Spaniards.

99   *Mothers broke their children's bones*: Archivo de Indias, Audiencia de Lima,
legajo 442, Joseph Cornejo to Patiño, San Ildefonso, August 27, 1734.

99   *"living images of death, black shades of eternal hell"*: Salinas y Córdova,
Memorial de las historias, 297.

99   *that to be made to mine was a virtual death sentence*: John Miller, *Memoirs of
General Miller in the Service of the Republic of Peru* (New York: AMS, 1979),
207.

99   *a hell of a different kind*: Bartolomé Arzáns de Orsúa y Vela, *Relatos de la villa
imperial de Potosí* (1705) (La Paz: Plural, 2000), 180.

99   *By 1825, when Simón Bolívar's armies finally liberated those lands*: Pedro Pablo
Arana, *Azogue*, 14.

100   *"I am rich Potosí. Envy of all kings"*: *"Soy el Rico Potosí. Del mundo soy el tesoro.
Soy el rey de los montes. Envidia soy de los reyes."* Wilson Mendieta Pacheco,
Potosí, patrimonio de la humanidad (Potosí, Bol.: El Siglo, 1988), 9.

100   *"Out of its great wealth, the republic of Spain"*: Martín González de Cellorigo
(1600), quoted in J. H. Elliott, *Empires of the Atlantic World: Britain and Spain
in America*, 140.

100   *"easy money"*: Ibid.

101   Epigraph: *"One does not establish a dictatorship in order to safeguard a
revolution"*: George Orwell, *Nineteen Eighty-Four* (New York: Knopf, 1987),
276.

101   *"The Indies and Spain may be two powers under the same ruler"*: Charles de
Secondat baron de Montesquieu, *L'Esprit des lois* (1748), in *Oeuvres de Montesquieu* (Paris: Dalibon, 1822), 3:456. (My translation.)

102   *Never in the history of Spanish America*: Carlos Marichal, *Bankruptcy of Empire:
Mexican Silver and the Wars Between Spain, Britain and France, 1760–1810*, 20.
Also on p. 4: "As the richest tax colony of the 18th century, the viceroyalty
of New Spain served as a *fiscal sub-metropolis* that assured the capacity of the
imperial state to defend itself in a time of successive international conflicts."

102   *a dizzying 250 million silver pesos*: Ibid., 18.

102   *compensated with titles of nobility*: Ibid., 85.

102   *In the autumn of 1807, when Napoleon I invaded Spain*: Arana, *Bolívar*, 82–86.

103   *The prolific veins of the Veta Madre*: Margaret E. Rankine, "The Mexican Mining Industry in the Nineteenth Century," *Bulletin of Latin American Research* 11, no. 1 (1992): 29–48.

104   *"We slip in between!"*: George Canning, in H. W. V. Temperley, "The Later American Policy of George Canning," *American History Review* 11, no. 4 (July 1906): 781, quoted in Arana, *Bolívar*, 347.

104   *Thomas Jefferson's smug suggestion*: Jefferson to Archibald Stuart, 25 January 1786, Paris, in *The Works of Thomas Jefferson* 4:188, ed. Paul Ford, quoted in Arana, *Bolívar*, 74.

104   *One British company impounded black slaves to work the pits of Minas Gerais*: Courtney J. Campbell, "Making Abolition Brazilian: British Law and Brazilian Abolitionists in Nineteenth-Century Minas Gerais and Pernambuco," *Slavery & Abolition* 36, no 3 (2015): 521–43.

104   *American enterprises were investing hundreds of millions*: Mexican Mining Journal 8, no. 1 (January 1909): 14.

CHAPTER 5: BLIND AMBITION

105   Epigraph: *"In the long course of history"*: Ludwig Von Mises, *Nationalökonomie: Theorie des Handelns und Wirtschaftens* (Geneva: Editions Union, 1940), 441.

105   *Legend has it that Ai Apaec*: All descriptions of Ai Apaec here are taken from Ulla Holmquist, curator of the Larco Herrera Museum, the institution of record on the Moche culture, in Pueblo Libre, Lima, Peru. Also Juergen Golte, *Moche Cosmología y Sociedad* (Lima: Instituto de Estudios Peruanos), 2009, and Rafael Larco Hoyle, *Los Mochicas* (Lima: Museo Arqueológico Rafael Larco Herrera), 1942.

106   *There is a reason why Indians of Latin America are hesitant*: There is plenty of evidence for this in chronicles by the descendants of royal indigenous houses. As one example, Bartolomé Arzáns de Orsúa y Vela recorded this testimonial from a lowly Indian in his history of Potosí: *"decidles que al mal hombre Hualca, lo ha de castigar el gran Pachacamac, porque les ha descubierto el Potocsi, que a ninguno de nuestros Ingas se lo dio; y que si quieren paz y no guerra que se vayan de aquí y nos entreguen a Hualca para castigarlo en nombre de Pachacamac, y por haber faltado a la orden que nos dio a todos de que no sacásemos la plata del cerro."* Arzáns, *Historia de la villa imperial de Potosí* (1965), 1:39.

108   *priests have called him a demon—a devil who reigned over the mines*: Pascale Absi, "Los Hijos del diablo," in *Demonio, religión y sociedad entre España y América*, ed. Fermín del Pino Díaz, 271.

108 *Early chronicles tell us: "en lugar della usaban desta letra T, así, en lugar de decir Dios suelen pronunciar Tios."* Cobo, *Historia*, 1:155.

108 Epigraph: *"¡Oh, Perú de metal y de melancolía!"*: "Oh, Peru of metal and melancholy!" From the poem "A Carmela, la Peruana," Federico García Lorca, *Obras* 2:416 (Madrid: Akal, 1998).

108 *Peru is booming these days*: The material on La Rinconada is adapted and updated from Arana, "Dreaming of El Dorado."

109 *Minerals are the country's main export*: I owe this phrase to William Finnegan, "Tears of the Sun," *New Yorker*, April 20, 2015.

109 *In 2009 Peru extracted a total of 182 tons of gold*: "World Gold Production by Country," USAGold, accessed January 30, 2019, www.usagold.com/reference /globalgoldproduction.html.

109 *"In all history . . . only 161,000 tons of gold"*: Brook Larmer, *National Geographic*, January 2009.

109 *But multinational giants are not the only ones*: Suzanne Daley, "Peru Scrambles to Drive Out Illegal Gold Mining," *New York Times* online, July 26, 2016.

109 *Investigators report that more than a quarter of all gold*: *Organized Crime and Illegally Mined Gold in Latin America* (Geneva: Global Initiative Against Transnational Organized Crime, April 2016), https://arcominero.infoama zonia.org/GIATOC-OC_Illegally-Mined-Gold-in-Latin-America-3c3f978eef 80083bdd8780d7c5a21f1e.pdf.

109 *"Illegal mining is crowding out the legal"*: Guillermo Arbe Carbonel, an economist with Scotiabank, quoted in Daley, "Peru Scrambles."

109 *twice as profitable as trafficking cocaine*: "Muestra retrata el verdadero rostro de la minería ilegal," *La República* (Perú), May 24, 2017; Heather Walsh, "In Colombia, Gold Mining's Becoming More Dangerous Than Cocaine," *Financial Post* (Can.), October 12, 2011.

110 *Deforestation from mining in the Peruvian Amazon alone*: Dan Collyns, "Extent of Peruvian Amazon Lost to Illegal Goldmines Mapped for First Time," *Guardian* (UK edition), October 29, 2013; Jonathan Watts, "High Gold Prices Causing Increased Deforestation in South America, Study Finds," *Guardian* (UK edition), January 14, 2015, and "Brazilian Court Blocks Abolition of Vast Amazon Reserve," *Guardian* (UK edition), August 30, 2017. The exact figures went from 5,350 acres per year to 15,150 after 2008. They remained so for many years.

110 *equivalent to wiping out an area the size of Manhattan*: J. Watts, "Amazon Deforestation Picking Up Pace, Satellite Data Reveals." *Guardian* (UK edition), October 19, 2014. Metropolitan Denver is 153 square miles, Manhattan is 22.82 square miles; 402 square kilometers (155 square miles) were cleared in Brazil in September 2014. A. Fonseca, C. Souza Jr., and A. Veríssimo, *Deforestation Report for the Brazilian Amazon* (Belém, Br.: Institute of Man and Environment of the Amazon, January 2015), www.imazon.org.br.

110 *it cleans up our global emissions*: Trista Patterson and M. Sanjayan, "Amazon:

Lungs of the Planet," BBC Future online, video, November 18, 2014. 3:57, www.bbc.com/future/story/20130226-amazon-lungs-of-the-planet.

110   *up to $460 million on the open market*: A diachronic graph of gold prices at current (and constantly fluctuating) rates can be found on Gold Price, www.goldprice.org.

110   *Today there are seventy thousand souls*: "Puno," *Diario Correo* (Peru), March 4, 2015, https://diariocorreo.pe/edicion/puno/la-ciudad-mas-alta-del-mundo-y -sombrio-esta-ubicado-en-puno-video-696750/3.

112   *On average, a miner in La Rinconada earns $170*: Fritz Dubois, Peru 21, 31 mayo 2012. For size of family, see *Niños que trabajan: en minería artesanal de oro en el Perú*, Scribd, https://www.scribd.com/document/67842098/NINNOS -QUE-TRABAJAN-PIAZZA.

112   *thousands of hoodwinked, prepubescent girls*: A lawyer and social worker, Leon Quispe, who has dedicated himself to the welfare of the community, estimates that anywhere from five thousand to eight thousand girls, some as young as fourteen, move through La Rinconada's cantinas in any given year. They are held captive as sexual slaves. Leon Quispe, interview by author, Puno and La Rinconada, February 7–15, 2012. Follow-up interview with Quispe, Puno, February 20, 2016. See also "Trata de personas continúa impune en infierno de La Rinconada," *La República* (Perú), June 9, 2016.

112   *HIV and tuberculosis are common here*: "Mineros de La Rinconada portan tuberculosis y VIH-Sida," *Diario Correo* (Perú), March 25, 2015.

113   *an average miner—the highest paid in Latin America*: Heraclio Castillo, "Salarios en minería del estado," *Zacatecas en Imagen* (México), February 12, 2013, www .remam.org/2013/12/salarios-en-mineria-del-estado-mas-altos-en-el-pais/.

113   *In Cajamarca, which has poured nearly $1.5 billion*: Peru, the largest producer of gold in the world, produced 151 tons in 2017, equaling $5.5 billion. Of that total, Cajamarca produced 33 tons or $1.3 billion. Xinhua, February 7, 2018. One mine alone, Yanacocha, has produced 35 million ounces of gold in the last twenty-five years. Ben Hallman and Roxana Olivera, "Gold Rush," *Huffington Post*, last modified April 15, 2015, http://projects.huffingtonpost .com/worldbank-evicted-abandoned/how-worldbank-finances-environmental -destruction-peru.

113   *three in four residents live in numbing poverty*: It was approximately 76 percent in 2005, 51 percent in 2015. *Map of Provincial and District Poverty 2013* (Lima: Instituto Nacional de Estadística e Informática, 2015). El Fondo de Cooperación para el Desarrollo Social (FONCODES), 2005 and 2015.

113   Epigraph: *"To live perpetually at the mercy of two colossuses"*: Mario Vargas Llosa, "Socialism and the Tanks," in *Making Waves*, ed. and trans. John King (New York: Farrar, Straus and Giroux, 1996), 79.

114   *championed in the 1950s by US Secretary of State John Foster Dulles*: Dulles worked for the law offices that represented United Fruit, and he remained on its payroll for many years; Allen Dulles sat on its board of directors. Secretary

Dulles lobbied President Dwight Eisenhower to plot a military coup against President Jacobo Árbenz in Guatemala to protect United Fruit's interests. Rich Cohen, *The Fish That Ate the Whale* (New York: Farrar, Straus and Giroux, 2012), 186. See also: Cesar Ayala, *American Sugar Kingdom* (Chapel Hill: University of North Carolina Press, 1999), 48–74.

114 *they hired death squads*: Gary Giroux, *Business Scandals, Corruption, and Reform: An Encyclopedia* (Denver: Greenwood, 2013), 50.

115 *the US military invaded Latin America twenty-eight times*: Dan Koeppel, *Banana: The Fate of the Fruit That Changed the World* (New York: Penguin, 2008), 63.

115 *the most important agricultural product cultivated in South America*: Sidney W. Mintz, *Sweetness and Power: The Place of Sugar in Modern History* (New York: Penguin, 1985), 71–73.

115 *A German traveler in the sixteenth century*: Ibid., 134.

115 *"White gold" . . . "Mother of slavery"*: " 'The Slave Trade Developed Western Societies and Plunged Africa into Underdevelopment,'" interview with the writer and professor Didier Gondola, Rebelión, last modified April 24, 2009, www.rebelion.org/noticia.php?id=84242.

115 *By the nineteenth century, more than six million tons*: Mintz, *Sweetness and Power*, 73.

115 *Today almost two billion tons*: Groupes Sucres et Danrées, Sucden online, last modified January 30, 2019, www.sucden.com/en/products-and-services/sugar /global-trade-flows; see also "raw sugar trade," "world sugar trade" on the same website.

115 *"I do not know if sugar and coffee are essential to the happiness of Europe"*: J. H. Bernardin de Saint Pierre, *Voyage to Isle de France, Isle de Bourbon, The Cape of Good Hope* (1773), quoted in Mintz, *Sweetness and Power*, frontispiece.

116 *country with the largest hydrocarbon reserves*: Johannes Alvarez and James Fiorito, "Venezuelan Oil," ENG-297, *Ethics of Development in a Global Environment*, Stanford University, June 2, 2005.

116 *In the early 1900s, a number of London banks invested*: Robert Burroughs, *Travel Writing and Atrocities: Eyewitness Accounts of Colonialism* (New York: Routledge, 2011), 124. Julio César Arana's Anglo-Peruvian Rubber Company, which held a fierce monopoly on rubber extraction in the Putumayo region and was responsible for a hecatomb of cruelties perpetrated on the Amazon people, was controlled by a board of directors out of London and financed by London banks. See Ovidio Lagos, *Arana, Rey de Caucho* (Buenos Aires: Emecé, 2005). I have also written about Julio César Arana in my memoir *American Chica* (New York: Dial Press, 2001).

116 *earning the equivalent of $5 billion a year*: The Peruvian newsmagazine *Caretas* reported, in a history of the powerful Morey family of Iquitos—the family that ran all the barges in that neck of the Amazon River—that the Anglo-Peruvian Rubber Company (for whom the patriarch Luis Felipe Morey

worked) was exporting 3.8 million pounds of rubber a year, rubber being worth one pound sterling per pound at the time. "La Familia Morey y Otros Entronques Historicos," Raúl Morey Menacho, *Caretas*, no. 1351 (February 23, 1995); 3.8 million GBP (Great British Pounds, or pounds sterling) in 1900 is worth 4.2 billion GBP today, which translates to $5.5 billion ("relative output worth"), Measuring Worth, accessed January 30, 2019, www.measuringworth .com. I interviewed Humberto Morey extensively about the company for my memoir, *American Chica*.

117 *American middlemen muscled their way into the coffee business*: US Federal Trade Commission, as explained in Cid Silveira, *Café: Un drama na economia nacional* (Rio de Janeiro: Editôra Civilização Brasileira, 1962).

117 *"The day is not far distant when three Stars and Stripes"*: President William Taft in 1912, quoted in *Liberalization and Redemocratization in Latin America*, ed. George Lopez and Michael Stohl (New York: Greenwood, 1987), 258.

117 *marines were sent in "to protect the lives and interests of US citizens"*: Galeano, 107–8.

117 *"I know he is an SOB"*: Lopez and Stohl, *Liberalization and Redemocratization*, 258. This quote is variously attributed to Secretary of State Cordell Hull about Rafael Trujillo, or to Franklin D. Roosevelt about Anastasio Somoza. It is also claimed to have been said by FDR in reference to Generalísimo Francisco Franco of Spain. The conjecture by many historians and journalists is that it was probably a phrase used generally in the day about dictators and strongmen whom the United States supported. Kevin Drum, "But He's Our Son of a Bitch," *Washington Monthly*, May 16, 2006.

117 *"I spent thirty-three years and four months in active service"*: Excerpt from a speech delivered in 1933 by Major General Smedley Butler, USMC. Leo Huberman, *We the People* (New York: Monthly Review Press, 1970), 252; "Smedley Butler on Interventionism," Federation of American Scientists online, accessed January 30, 2019, https://fas.org/man/smedley.htm.

118 *As one historian explains: they didn't have to be*: Will Fowler, *Latin America Since 1780* (Abingdon, UK: Routledge, 2016), 67.

118 *"For the Americans of the north, the only Americans are themselves"*: *Epistolario de Diego Portales* (Santiago: Ediciones Universidad Diego Portales, 2007), 1:8.

119 *forced Indians to buy goods they didn't need*: Miller, *Memoirs*, 1:12.

119 *40 percent of all US exports*: Shlomo Ben-Ami, "Is the US Losing Latin America?" Project Syndicate, last modified June 5, 2013.

119 *It is a market that generates*: US Chamber of Commerce, "The Facts on Nafta," December 16, 2016, www.uschamber.com/sites/default/files/the_facts_on _nafta_-_2017.pdf.

119 *Chile's threat to nationalize Anaconda*: "CIA Activities in Chile," US Central Intelligence Agency online, last modified September 18, 2000.

119 *facing resistance by Colombian workers*: Dan Kovalik, "Colombia: The Empire Strikes Back," *The Blog, Huffington Post*, last modified May 8, 2012, www .huffingtonpost.com/dan-kovalik/colombia-the-empire-strik_b_1500062.html.

119 *"brigade commanders with hands-on counterinsurgency"*: "Obama Says 'Days of Meddling' in Latin America Are Past," BBC News online, last modified April 11, 2015,; Kovalik, "Colombia."

120 *"to do more to combat drug use on its own turf"*: Ben-Ami, "Is the US Losing?"

120 *"The days in which our agenda in this hemisphere"*: "Obama Says."

120 *even though China is the world's number one producer of iron*: www.worldatlas .com/articles/top-iron-ore-producing-countries-in-the-world.html.

120 *and even though Brazil loses money in the bargain*: Kenneth Rapoza, "Brazil's Vale Needs to Turn Its Iron Ore into Pixie Dust," *Forbes*, February 4, 2016.

120 *Peru may be one of the world's top ten producers of gold*: "Top 10 Gold-Producing Countries in the World," FinancesOnline, accessed March 15, 2019.

120 *They are owned, managed, and operated by*: *Peru's Mining & Metals Investment Guide, 2017/2018* (Lima: EY Peru, 2018), 31.

120 *Asia now consumes most of the gold*: More than 40 percent, to be precise. Heather Long, "China Is on a Massive Gold Buying Spree," CNN Money Investing Guide online, last modified February 10, 2016.

121 *for every $100 of gold it rips*: President Danilo Medina Sánchez, quoted in "Sickness and Wealth: Shiny New Mine, Rusty Pollution Problems," *Economist* online, last modified September 21, 2013.

121 *"That is simply unacceptable"*: Ibid.

121 *the fact that almost half of Colombia is managed*: PBI Colombia, no. 18, November 2011.

121 *Mexican mines are dominated by Canadians*: "Mexican Mining," *Engineering and Mining Journal* 212, no. 8 (October 2011): 52; *Mining Industry in Mexico* (Vancouver: Deloitte & Touche LLP, May 2012).

121 *For every simple gold ring that goes out into the world*: Arana, "Dreaming of El Dorado"; "The Real Price of Gold," *National Geographic*, January 2009. More than a pound of mercury, OIT/IPEC report, http://geco.mineroartesanal.com /tiki-download_wiki_attachment.php?attId=122, 5. Newmont moves thirty tons of rock for every ounce of gold. "By the time it is through, the company will have dug up billions of tons of earth." Jane Perlez and Lowell Bergman, "Tangled Strands in Fight over Peru Gold Mine," *New York Times* online, June 14, 2010.

121 Epigraph: *"Gold is chemically inert"*: Bernstein, 3.

122 *One ounce of gold, which sold on the global market for $271*: A graph of gold prices at past and current rates can be found on Gold Price, www.goldprice.org.

122 *The largest gold operation in all South America*: José Ramos, "La mineria peruana, la Newmont-Yanacocha y el Proyecto Conga," Globedia, last modified July 7, 2012, http://globedia.com/mineria-peruana-newmont-yana cocha-proyecto-conga; Francesc Relea, "Peru's Humala Shuffles Cabinet," *El País* (Madrid) online, last modified July 26, 2012, http://elpais.com/elpais /2012/07/26/inenglish/1343304801_310180.html.

123 *Their complaints were loud and clear*: Polya Lesova, "Peru Gold, Copper Mining Opposition Intensifies," MarketWatch, last modified July 25, 2012.

123 *Not long before, a German scientist had confirmed*: Reinhard Seifert, quoted in Alice Bernard and Diego Cupolo, "Scientist Calls Peru Conga Mining Project an 'Environmental Disaster': Interview with Reinhard Seifert," Upside Down World, last modified May 1, 2012, http://upsidedownworld.org/main/peru -archives-76/3608-scientist-calls-peru-conga-mining-project-an-environmental -disaster-interview-with-reinhard-seifert.

123 *the question of rank exploitation*: In 2010, a year in which the Yanacocha mines shipped $3.7 billion (3 million ounces at $1,290 an ounce) worth of gold from Cajamarca, more than half the residents of Cajamarca earned approximately $100 a month. Perlez and Bergman, "Tangled Strands"; Ben Hallman and Roxana Olivera, "Gold Rush," *Huffington Post*, last modified April 15, 2015; Apoyo Consultorio, *Study of the Yanacocha Mine's Economic Impacts: Final Report* (Lima: International Finance Corporation, September 2009), www.ifc .org/wps/wcm/connect/3853268048f9cc368651ee28c8cbc78b/Yanachocha-Peru .pdf?MOD=AJPERES.

123 *Peru stood to retain only 15 percent*: This is a generous reckoning. Some reports show gold sales in 2013 of $1.43 billion and a Peruvian tax of $137.8 million, which represents less than 10 percent retention by the state. Raúl Wiener and Juan Torres, *The Yanacocha Case* (Loreto, Peru: Impresión Arte, 2014), 47–58, https://justice-project.org/wp-content/uploads/2017/07/the-yanacocha-taxes -2015.pdf.

123 *troops in riot gear were called out to contain*: There has been no dearth of antimining protests in Peru or anywhere else in South America, with 215 recorded in 19 countries in 2014. "Mining in Latin America: From Conflict to Cooperation," *Economist* online, February 6, 2016.

123 *leader of the protest, a Catholic priest, was taken by force*: The priest was Marco Arana (no relation to this author), now a Peruvian congressman. "Agresión a Sacerdote Marco Arana 04 Julio 2012," uploaded to YouTube by Cajamar- caenvideo on July 4, 2012, 3:33, www.youtube.com/watch?v=w-amfIQn0OU).

124 *The diminutive Peruvian invited protesters onto her contested land*: For a testi- monial video by Acuña and live documentary evidence of the attacks on her and her family, see Roxana Olivera, "Life Yes, Gold No!" New Interna- tionalist, last modified November 21, 2012, https://newint.org/features/web -exclusive/2012/11/21/peru-gold-rush-threatens-indigenous-communities. See also "Máxima Acuña, la campesina peruana 'heredera' de la activista asesinada Berta Cáceres" [Máxima Acuña, the Peruvian peasant 'heir' of the murdered activist Berta Cáceres], BBC News Mundo, last modified April 18, 2016, www.bbc.com/mundo/noticias/2016/04/160418_peru_campesina_maxima _acuna_gana_premio_goldman_heredera_berta_caceres_lv.

124 *to walk away from the project*: Cecilia Jamasmie, "Community Opposition Forces Newmont to Abandon Conga Project in Peru," Mining.com, last modified April 18, 2016, www.mining.com.

124 *Máxima Acuña was given a prestigious international prize*: "Máxima Acuña,

2016 Goldman Environmental Prize Recipient, South and Central America," Goldman Environmental Prize online, accessed January 31, 2019, www .goldmanprize.org/recipient/maxima-acuna.

124 *a New York journalist dubbed her "the badass grandma"*: Anna Lekas Miller, "Meet the Badass Grandma Standing Up to Big Mining," Daily Beast, last modified April 18, 2016.

124 *promising sales of nearly $1 billion a year*: "Newmont Announces Full Year and Fourth Quarter 2016 Results," Business Wire, last modified February 21, 2017, www.businesswire.com/news/home/20170221006614/en/Newmont -Announces-Full-Year-Fourth-Quarter-2016.

124 *A few months later, a band of hit men*: Michael Brune, "Goldman Prize Winner Reportedly Attacked at Her Home by Mining Industry Hitmen," Eco Watch, last modified September 23, 2016.

124 Epigraph: *"We would not say Jesus, Mary, Joseph"*: A female miner, quoted in Michael Taussig, *The Devil and Commodity Fetishism in South America* (Chapel Hill: University of North Carolina Press, 1980), 148.

124 *Leonor Gonzáles could be Máxima Acuña's sister*: To remind: this section on the Ochochoque-Gonzáles family (as all material about them) is taken from a series of more than two dozen interviews and hundreds of Internet communications the author conducted with family members between January 2012 and April 2019 in La Rinconada, Putina, Juliaca, Puno, and Lima.

128 *most dynamic and productive branch*: Daley, "Peru Scrambles."

128 *some nations win, others lose*: Galeano, 1–2.

128 *the most unequal continent in the world*: Acemoglu and Robinson, 19.

129 *Latin American elites adopted policies and institutions*: Ibid., 67.

129 *by 1914, there were almost thirty thousand banks*: Ibid., 33–34.

129 *Latin American republics became extractive by nature*: Ibid., 81.

129 *Those who had served his revolution had ploughed the sea*: Simón Bolívar to Barranquilla Flores, 9 November 1830, in *Cartas del Libertador corregidas conforme a los originales* [Letters from the liberator conforming to the originals], ed. Vicente Lecuna, 10 vols. (Caracas, 1917), 9:370. See also Arana, *Bolívar*, 450.

129 *The strongest, as always in these Americas, did as they pleased*: Serge Gruzinski, *Man-Gods in the Mexican Highland* (Stanford, CA: Stanford University Press, 1989), 41.

130 *"Mining is the hole through which the vitality"*: Sergio Almaraz Paz, *Bolivia: Requiem para una República* (Montevideo, Bolivia: Biblioteca de Marcha, 1970), 83–84.

130 *"Of all those expensive and uncertain projects"*: Adam Smith, in Samuel D. Horton, *The Parity of Money as Regarded by Adam Smith, Ricardo, and Mill* (London: Macmillan, 1888), 79–80.

131 Epigraph: *"National wealth consists in the abundance"*: Ibid., 15.

131 *the vast majority of Latin Americans*: Jamele Rigolini and Renos Vakis,

"Four Facts About Poverty in Latin America You Probably Didn't Know," *Huffington Post, The Blog*, last modified December 6, 2017.

131 *Whereas open frontiers in the United States of America or trade routes in Europe*: Acemoglu and Robinson, 36.

132 *That extractive economy has been inimical to true prosperity*: Ibid., 37.

132 *Argentina, Ecuador, Brazil, Peru, and Colombia have seen*: George Gao, "Latin America's Middle Class Grows, but in Some Regions More Than Others," FactTank, Pew Research Center online, last modified July 20, 2015.

Part 2: Sword

133 Epigraph: *"The distant past never disappears completely"*: Octavio Paz, *El Laberinto de la soledad* (México, DF: Fondo de Cultura Económica, 1999), 13–14. In the original: *"Las épocas viejas nunca desaparecen completamente y todas las heridas, aún la más antiguas, manan sangre todavía."*

Chapter 6: Blood Lust

135 Epigraph: *"Question: When did Peru fuck up, exactly?"*: *"Cuando se jodió el Perú?,"* Mario Vargas Llosa, *Conversación en La Catedral.* Answered by Jeremías Gamboa: *"El Perú se jodió al momento mismo de nacer. Su concepción tuvo como base un hecho asimétrico y brutal que fundó una nación herida y enemistada con una de sus mitades, la indígena."* Gamboa, "En que momento se jodió el Perú? El dilema vargallosiano," *El Comercio* (Lima), March 29, 2017.

135 *He came barefoot to this country from Cuba*: Based on numerous interviews conducted from September 1995 through June 1996, and intermittent telephone communications thereafter with Carlos Buergos, inmate, Lorton Prison, VA.

135 *Seared into the memory of every Marielito*: Much of the following account about Marielitos and Carlos Buergos is taken from Marie Arana-Ward, "Three Marielitos, Three Manifest Destinies," *Washington Post*, July 9, 1996. The research continued in follow-up reporting on Carlos's family for two decades after that.

136 *the Mariel boat lift brought 125,000 Cubans to the United States*: Tomas Curi, Immigration and Naturalization Service, telephone interview by author, May 1996.

136 *"Give me your tired, your poor"*: Emma Lazarus, "The New Colossus," lines that are engraved on the Statue of Liberty, Poetry Foundation online, accessed February 1, 2019, www.poetryfoundation.org/poems/46550/the-new-colossus.

136 *"America . . . is the greatest of opportunities"*: George Santayana, an often-quoted line from *The Last Puritan: A Memoir in the Form of a Novel* (London: Constable, 1935).

137 *about 2,500—were convicts and mental cases*: Curi, interview.

138 Epigraph: *"Man wasn't born to live without purpose like a jungle animal"*: Editorial, *El Mercurio* (Chile), May 24, 1859, quoted in Leticia Reina, *La reindianización de América, Siglo XIX* [The re-Indianization of America, 19th century] (México, DF: XXI Century, 1997), 141.

139 *leaving three thousand men, women, and children to die*: Joyce Appleby, *Shores of Knowledge* (New York: Norton, 2013), 25.

139 *"I saw here cruelty on a scale no living being has ever seen"*: Las Casas, *A Short History*, 53–57.

139 *if Catholics were all going to heaven*: Appleby, *Shores*.

139 *whether they killed to eat or ate the already dead*: Neil L. Whitehead, "Carib Cannibalism: The Historical Evidence," *Journal de la Société des Américanistes* 70, no. 1 (1984): 69–87.

139 *Columbus's writings reveal that he was very aware*: Ibid., 70, 74; Carlos A. Jáuregui, *Canibalia: Canibalismo, calibanismo, antropofagia cultural y consumo en América Latina*, 62.

140 *The indigenous peoples of Mexico*: Whitehead, "Carib Cannibalism," 71.

140 *"showed all the ferocity and bestiality"*: Jáuregui, 62.

140 *"If such cannibals continue to resist and do not admit"*: Whitehead, "Carib Cannibalism," 70.

140 *conquistadors called for a broader definition of the criteria*: Ibid., 74.

140 *Sir Walter Raleigh . . . joked*: Richard Hakluyt, *Hakluyt's Voyages to the New World* (New York: Macmillan, 1972), 396.

141 *a sangre y fuego*: The Spanish literal meaning for this is "by blood and fire." The understanding is "unto extermination."

141 *"limpieza de sangre"*: Albert A. Sicroff, *Los Estatutos de Limpieza de Sangre* (Madrid: Taurus, 1985).

141 *"Spaniards would brag about their panoply of cruelties"*: Las Casas, *Historia*, vol. 3, bk. 2, sec. 6, ch. 17; *Obras*, 4:1363.

141 *"All this, and more, I saw, so foreign to human nature"*: Las Casas, *Historia*, Ibid.

141 *ten million Africans who were abducted*: "List of Voyages," Voyages Database, Emory University, accessed February 1, 2019, www.slavevoyages.org/voyage /search; Carson Claiborne, Stanford University, "Blacks in Latin America," Microsoft Encarta Online Encyclopedia 2000.

141 *the Muslims of Granada had slaughtered its Jews*: "Spain Viritual Jewish History Tour," Jewish Virtual Library, accessed January 31, 2019, www.jewishvirtual library.org/spain-virtual-jewish-history-tour: "In 1066 a Muslim mob stormed the royal palace in Granada, crucified Jewish vizier Joseph ibn Naghrela, and massacred most of the Jewish population of the city. Accounts of the Granada Massacre state that more than 1,500 Jewish families, numbering 4,000 persons, were murdered in just one day." The entire population of Granada was approximately 25,000.

141 *more than a hundred thousand Jews were massacred*: Edward Rothstein, "Was

the Islam of Old Spain Truly Tolerant?," *New York Times* online, September 27, 2003.

142   *Hadn't medieval lore held that the periphery*: This goes back to Pliny the Elder's first-century AD descriptions of extraordinary races that inhabited India and Ethiopia. See also Alixe Bovey, "Medieval Monsters," British Library online, last modified April 30, 2015.

142   *For all the contemporary revisionist scholarship that has portrayed*: One pair of scholars has gone so far as to say, "Before the whites came, our conflicts were brief and almost bloodless, resembling far more a professional football game than the lethal annihilations of the European conquest." Russell Means and Marvin Wolf, *Where White Men Fear to Tread* (New York: St. Martin's, 1995), 16. For a sobering corrective, see Richard J. Chacon and Rubén G. Mendoza's thorough and convincing *Latin American Indigenous Warfare and Ritual Violence*, which incorporates dozens of years of research in essays covering multidisciplinary studies. Much of what follows in this section is based on the scholarship therein.

142   *The skull towers at Tenochtitlán alone . . . as many as 136,000*: Michael Harner, "The Ecological Basis for Aztec Sacrifice," *American Ethnologist* 4, no. 1 (February 1977): 117–35, www.jstor.org/stable/643526. Others have calculated 60,000 skulls: Bernard R. Ortíz de Montellano, "Counting Skulls: Comment on the Aztec Cannibalism Theory of Harner-Harris," *American Anthropologist* 85, no. 2 (1983): 403–6.

143   *Montezuma II's predecessor, Ahuitzotl, conducted a mass execution*: Rubén G. Mendoza, "Aztec Militarism and Blood Sacrifice," in Chacon and Mendoza, 42.

143   *Xipe Totec, ruler of war as well as earthly abundance*: Eduardo Matos Moctezuma and Felipe Solis Olguín, *Aztecs* (London: Royal Academy of Arts, 2002), 423.

143   *ritual flaying among the Aztecs*: Ibid., 423–26.

143   *The Mayans, no strangers to these practices*: Chacon and Mendoza, 15–25.

143   *Before the start of a game*: Rubén G. Mendoza, "The Divine Gourd Tree," in *The Taking and Displaying of Human Body Parts as Trophies by Amerindians*, ed. Richard Chacon and David Dye (New York: Springer, 2007), 409.

143   *part and parcel of the ritual of worship*: There is plenty of evidence of this in the Mayan text of the *Popol Vuh*, or *Book of Counsel*.

144   *From the 700 men*: Jiménez de Quesada, "One After the Other They All Fell Under Your Majesty's Rule" (Excerpts from *Epitomé del Nuevo Reino de Granada*), *The Colombia Reader: History, Culture, Politics*, ed. Ann Farnsworth-Alvear, Marco Palacíos, and Ana María Gómez López (Durham, NC: Duke University Press, 2017), 22.

144   *Jiménez de Quesada issued the order to fight, slaughter*: Ibid.

145   *steal more than seven thousand emeralds*: Ibid.

145   Epigraph: *"It's not my fault. It's just my nature."*: A possible adaptation of Aesop's "The Farmer and the Viper." Certainly versions have appeared

among the Persians, the Central Asians, and other cultures. I have taken it
from the fable of the scorpion and the frog in Louis Pérez's lecture; see below.

145 *the ways that stress, social pressure, and hardship have affected certain races*:
C. W. Kuzawa and E. Sweet, "Epigenetics and the Embodiment of Race,"
American Journal of Human Biology 21, no. 1 (January/February 2009): 2–15.
See also the online index of Northwestern University Laboratory for Human
Biology Research/Christopher Kuzawa web files, www.groups.anthropology
.northwestern.edu/lhbr/kuzawa_web_files/pdfs.

145 *Others conclude that the effects of violence*: K. M. Radtke et al., "Transgenerational Impact of Intimate Partner Violence on Methylation in the Promoter of
the Glucocorticoid Receptor," *Translational Psychiatry* 1, no. 7 (July 2011): e21.

145 *Latin American historians*: One of them is Louis A. Pérez, the J. Carlyle Sitterson
Professor of History and director of the Institute for the Study of the Americas
at the University of North Carolina. On November 5, 2015, Pérez delivered
a stirring explanation of cultural differences in the Eqbal Ahmad Lecture at
Hampshire College, in which he explained transgenerational epigenetic inheritance and Cuba's historical disposition to the United States by telling Aesop's
story of the scorpion and the frog. Louis A. Pérez, "2015 Eqbal Ahmad Lecture,
Louis Pérez, Wayne Smith, Hampshire College," videotaped November 5,
2015, in Amherst, MA, 1:22.25, www.youtube.com/watch?v=IuBdKB8jX3I.

146 *a half million in one decade alone*: This was the decade between 1482 and 1492,
during Ferdinand's war against the Granada Emirate. A hundred thousand
Moors died or were enslaved; two hundred thousand Moors and two hundred
thousand Jews were forcibly expelled (Kamen, 37–38). See also Joseph
Telushkin, *Jewish Literacy*, New York: Morrow, 1991.

146 *contemporary historians depict the moment of first contact*: Means and Wolf,
White Men, 16.

146 *The evidence tells us this is not so*: The data presented in scholarly works and
symposia since 2003 ("Problems in Paradise," American Anthropological
Association Symposium on Amerindian Violence, 2003, Chicago) indicate that
indigenous warfare, ritual violence, and armed conflict were prevalent in every
major culture of Latin America before the conquest. Chacon and Mendoza, 4.

146 *miraculous "thundersticks"*: David J. Silverman, *Thundersticks: Firearms and
the Violent Transformation of Native America* (Cambridge, MA: Harvard
University Press, 2016).

147 *Cortés, Balboa, Pizarro—they had all bucked*: To this mutinous group many
could be added, but few so colorful as Lope de Aguirre, "El Loco," who
called himself Wrath of God, Prince of Freedom, King of Tierra Firme. He
countermanded Gonzalo Pizarro's orders in Peru and visited rampant cruelty
on the Indians. Charles Nicholl, *The Creature in the Map* (Chicago: University
of Chicago Press, 1997), 27.

147 *they had brought wild, rebellious impulses with them*: Arciniegas, *Latin America*,
137–38.

147   *In Paraguay, one of the conquistadors*: This was Domingo Martínez de Irala,
      a Basque conquistador who was part of Pedro de Mendoza's expedition to
      the southern regions of the continent in 1535. He helped found Buenos Aires
      and became captain general of Río de la Plata. Irala went against rank and
      accused Governor Cabeza de Vaca of being too sympathetic to the Indians and
      succeeded in having him shipped back to Spain as a traitor.

147   *When European intellectuals began to raise moral arguments*: Alonso Zorita,
      Leyes y ordenanzas reales de las Indias Del Mar Oceano (1574) (México, DF:
      Secretaria de Hacienda, 1983–1984), 355–56.

148   *Absolute rule became the hallmark*: From here to the end of this section on
      Spanish colonial rule, I have quoted liberally from my own work, *Bolívar:
      American Liberator*, 26–27. The sources for this information include:
      Leslie Bethell, *The Cambridge History of Latin America*, vol. 3 (Cambridge:
      Cambridge University Press, 1985); Carlos Eugenio Restrepo, *Historia de la
      Revolución*, vol. 1; Guillermo Antonio Sherwell, *Simón Bolívar (el Libertador):
      Patriot, Warrior, Statesman, Father of Five Nations* (Washington, DC: B. S.
      Adams, 1921).

149   *It was thought that the Inca ruler Pachacuti*: Betanzos, *Narrative of the Incas*
      (ca. 1576), trans. and ed., Roland Hamilton and Dana Buchanan (Austin:
      University of Texas Press, 1996); Burr Brundage, *Empire of the Inca* (Norman:
      University of Oklahoma Press, 1963), 112–24.

150   *Just as the Spaniards kept good records*: Bernabé Cobo, *Inca Religion and Customs*
      (1653), 135. See also Chacon and Mendoza, 120–21.

150   *"If a person dies, it is better for the fields"*: Graham Gori, Associated Press,
      "Ancient and Bloody Bolivian Ritual Draws a Crowd," *Los Angeles Times*,
      July 6, 2003.

150   *"It is like man and woman"*: Gori, "Ancient and Bloody."

150   *"Thank you, brother; we have tested each other"*: Gori, "Ancient and Bloody."

151   Epigraph: *"What concerns us most about the Inca civilization"*: Jose Carlos
      Mariátegui, quoted in Wright, 275.

151   *Scholars claim that a mere twenty-one years*: David Stannard, *American
      Holocaust: The Conquest of the New World* (New York: Oxford Press, 1993),
      prologue.

152   *An anthropologist claims that one lone slave*: Jared Diamond, *Guns, Germs, and
      Steel* (New York: Norton, 1997) e-book, ch. 12.

152   *by 1618, less than one hundred years later*: Ibid.; Ángel Rosenblat, *La Población
      Indígena de América: Desde 1492 Hasta la Actualidad* (Buenos Aires: Institución
      Cultural Española, 1945), http://pueblosoriginarios.com/textos/rosenblat/1492
      .html.

153   *"deafened the skies, making the heavens reecho"*: Martín de Murúa, *Historia
      general del Perú*, 2:270.

153   *"imbruted Spaniards"*: José García Hamilton, *El autoritarismo y la improduc-
      tividad en Hispanoamérica* (Buenos Aires: Ed. Sudamericana, 1998), ch. 1.

153 *silver economy that had more drastic consequences*: Galeano, 43.

153 *Ten years later, the vast majority of the hemisphere*: King Philip II of Spain ruled Portugal between 1581 and 1598, and so would have been the de facto ruler of Brazil, making this claim a resounding reality.

153 *infected blankets or tainted baubles*: Esther Wagner Stearn and Allen Edwin Stearn, *The Effect of Smallpox on the Destiny of the Amerindian* (Minneapolis: University of Minnesota, 1945), 13–20, 73–94, 97.

153 *by the time the Europeans got around to counting them*: "Selected Death Tolls for Wars, Massacres, and Atrocities Before the 20th Century," Necrometrics, last modified January 2012, http://necrometrics.com/pre1700a.htm#America.

153 *Scholars do tell us that when the Viceroyalty of Mexico celebrated*: Rosenblat, *La Población*, 185.

153 *the humming human population Cortés encountered*: Stannard, *American Holocaust*, 33.

154 *a veritable rainbow of crossbreeds*: These eventually garnered a colorful litany of names, depending on the shade of skin—*indios, cholos*, mestizos, negros, *pardos*, zambos, mulattos, *castizos, moriscos*, albinos, *torna-atrás, sambayos, cambujos, albarazados, barcinos, coyotes, chamizos, chinos, ahí te estás, tente en el aire, no te entiendo*. Ángel Rosenblat, *La población indígena y el mestizaje en América*, vol. 2 (Buenos Aires: Nova, 1954), 135.

155 *reclaim their identity after almost two centuries*: Nicholas A. Robins, *Native Insurgencies and the Genocidal Impulse in the Americas*, 3.

155 *The next large-scale uprising in the colonies*: Kenneth J. Andrien, "Economic Crisis, Taxes, and the Quito Insurrection of 1765," in *Past and Present*, no. 129 (November 1990): 104–131.

155 *bedeviled the Viceroyalty of Peru for decades*: Scarlett Godoy O'Phelan, *Un siglo de rebeliones anticoloniales* (Paris: Institut français d'études andines, 2015), 296–305.

156 *exterminating not only Spaniards*: "*Informe de los oidores Pedro Antonio Zernudas y Lorenzo Blanco Ciceron*," La Plata, March 14, 1781, Charcas, 596, Archivo General de las Indias (AGI). "Confesión de Asensio Pacheco," La Plata, April 18, 1781, AGI, ibid., 603, 20: Robins, *Native Insurgencies*, 39.

156 *The trouble began when a mestizo* curaca: Tupac Amaru II's name was José Gabriel Condorcanqui before he rose up against the Spanish. I have taken the lion's share of this account of Tupac Amaru II as well as the cameo of José Antonio Galán's insurgency directly from Arana, *Bolívar*, 29–30.

156 *"I have decided to shake off"*: Tupac Amaru II in José Félix Blanco and Ramón Azpurúa, *Documentos para la historia de la vida pública del Liberator de Colombia* (Caracas: La Opinión Nacional, 1875), 1:151.

156 *Tupac Amaru had said very clearly*: Ibid., 167.

156 *"to put an end to all Europeans"*: Jan Szeminski, "Why Kill the Spaniard?," in *Resistance, Rebellion, and Consciousness in the Andean Peasant World*, ed. Steve Stern (Madison: University of Wisconsin Press, 1987), 167.

157 *the victorious rebels danced, drunk, on the corpses of whites*: Robins, *Native Insurgencies*, 40–41, 54.

157 *they fed on white flesh*: Szeminski, "Why Kill?," 169–70.

157 *costing the Indians some hundred thousand lives*: Bethell, *History of Latin America*, 3:36.

157 *"I only know of two, and they are you and I"*: J. P. Viscardo y Guzmán, *Letter to the Spanish Americans* (1799) (Providence: John Carter Brown Library facsimile, 2002), from the introduction by David Brading, 20.

157 *cut out the Indian's tongue*: Antonio Núñez Jiménez, *Un mundo aparte* (Madrid: Ed. de la Torre, 1994), 216–17.

157 *"His hands and feet will be bound by strong cords"*: Ibid.

158 *signaled the end of Spanish dominion*: Justin Winsor, ed., *Narrative and Critical History of America* (Cambridge, MA: Houghton Mifflin, 1889), 317.

158 *when an army of twenty thousand*: Germán Arciniegas, *20,000 Comuneros hacia Santa Fe* (Bogotá: Pluma, 1981).

159 Epigraph: *"The men who knew how to use a machete"*: *"Los hombres que sabían usar un machete para cortar la caña, demostraron un día que sabían usar el machete también para combatir."* Fidel y Dolores Guerra Castro, *Fidel Castro y la historia como ciencia* (Havana: Centro de Estudios Martianos, 2007), 106.

159 monstrum horrendum: Fidel Castro, *Fidel Castro: Selección de documentos* (Havana: Editora Política, 2007), 11.

160 *handed over more than 60 percent of all sugar production*: Juan Triana Cordoví, "La Maldita Bendición de la Caña de Azucar," *On Cuba*, September 26, 2016.

160 *a few distinguished Americans had begun to grumble*: Among them, noted historian Arthur Schlesinger Jr., who by then had founded Americans for Democratic Action with former First Lady Eleanor Roosevelt, Minnesota senator Hubert Humphrey, economist John Kenneth Galbraith, and theologian Reinhold Niebuhr. Arthur Schlesinger Jr., *The Dynamics of World Power* (New York: McGraw-Hill, 1973), 512.

160 *"I believe the hour has come"*: Luis Báez, *Así es Fidel* (Havana: Casa Editora, 2010), 2:11.

160 *bedraggled, hungry, sea tossed*: Che Guevara, quoted in Douglas Kellner, *Ernesto "Che" Guevara* (World Leaders Past & Present) (Langhorne, PA: Chelsea House, 1989), 40.

161 *burgeoning sugar boom in Brazil*: "Appendix B: Supply-Demand Balances, 'Sugar,'" in *Commodity Markets Outlook* (Washington, DC: World Bank Group, October 2016), 58, http://pubdocs.worldbank.org/en/14308147680 4664222/CMO-October-2016-Full-Report.pdf.

162 *double the sugar output to ten million tons*: Kosmas Tsokhas, "The Political Economy of Cuban Dependence on the Soviet Union," *Theory and Society* 9 (March 1980): 319–62.

CHAPTER 7: REVOLUTIONS THAT SHAPED LATIN AMERICA'S PSYCHE

163 Epigraph: *"They say grand projects need to be built with calm!"*: Simón Bolívar, speech to the Patriotic Society, July 3–4, 1811, in Bolívar, *Doctrina del Libertador*, ed. Manuel Pérez Vila (Caracas: Fundación Biblioteca Ayacucho, 1992), 7.

163 *when an unexpected window of opportunity flung open*: Much of the following account of the wars for independence in Latin America is taken from my book *Bolívar: American Liberator*, which has an extensive account of these events.

166 *Anyone who dared express sympathy*: Pedro Fermín de Cevallos, *Resumen de la Historia de Ecuador*, vol. 3, ch. 2, Miguel de Cervantes Virtual Library Foundation, www.cervantesvirtual.com.

166 Epigraph: *"He rode, fighting all the way, more miles than Ulysses"*: Thomas Carlyle about Bolívar, in "Dr. Francia," *Foreign Quarterly Review*, no. 62 (1843).

168 *He had little patience for those who waved banners of liberty*: Arana, *Bolívar*, 80.

168 *"the sea that separates us from her"*: Bolívar, "Letter from Jamaica," Kingston, September 6, 1815, in *Reflexiones políticas* (Barcelona: www.lingkua.com, 2018), 63.

168 *That year, like dominos tumbling in a row*: Arana, *Bolívar*, 86.

170 *"The art of victory is learned in defeat"*: Simón Bolívar, in Felipe Larrazábal, *Vida y correspondencia general del Libertador Simón Bolívar*, vol. 1 (New York: Eduardo O. Jenkins, 1866), 580.

171 *massacred eighty thousand rebels*: Bolívar, to the editor of the *Royal Gazette*, Kingston, 15 August 1815, in *Cartas del Libertador*, ed. Lecuna, vol. 1, 29, 95.

172 *"almost without exception were shot"*: M. McKinley, *Pre-Revolutionary Caracas* (Cambridge: Cambridge University Press, 1985), 171. All the information about Bolívar's wars can be found in greater detail in my biography *Bolívar: American Liberator*.

172 *reduced civilian populations in Latin America by a third*: Christon Archer, *The Wars of Independence in Spanish America*, Jaguar Books on Latin America, no. 20 (Wilmington, DE: SR Books, 2000), 35–37, 283–92. Robert Scheina, *Latin America's Wars: The Age of the Caudillo, 1791–1899*, vol. 1 (Washington, DC: Potomac Books, 2003), 173, claims that in Ecuador, Venezuela, and Mexico, populations were reduced by a quarter.

172 *"There are no more provinces left"*: J. B. Trend, *Bolívar and the Independence of Spanish America* (New York, Macmillan, 1948), 109.

172 Epigraph: *"They are children of the devil, not of the Moon and Sun"*: El Inca Garcilaso, *La Florida*, bk. 3, ch. 26, 149.

172 *in unabated frenzy to sacrifice a million more*: Scheina, *Latin America's Wars*, 2:1845. Scheina, *Latin America's Wars: The Age of the Caudillo, 1791–1899*, vol. 1 (Dulles, VA: Brassey's, 2003), 84, specifies three hundred thousand combatants and seven hundred thousand civilians.

173 *almost half a million more Mexicans were lost*: More than six hundred thousand

is the claim in Juan González, *Harvest of Empire: A History of Latinos in America* (New York: Penguin, 2001).

173 *One-quarter of its population*: Scheina, *Latin America's Wars*, 2:1773. For a comparative number, see also Jan Lahmeyer, "Mexico: Historical Demographical Data of the Whole Country," Populstat, last modified February 4, 2002, www.populsat.info/Americas/mexicoc.htm, which claims 15 percent.

173 *Between 1910 and 1920, the Mexican population was reduced*: Sherburne F. Cook and Woodrow Borah show the native population imploding from 25.2 million in 1519, to 6.3 million by 1545, to 2.5 million in 1570, and bottoming out at 1.2 million in 1620. From some 5 million inhabitants in 1800, Mexico grew to 8 million by 1855 and to more than 15 million in 1910. So between 1519 and 1910, the population had dropped by 10 million people. Robert McCaa, "The Peopling of Mexico from Origins to Revolution" (preliminary draft), in *The Population History of North America*, ed. Richard Steckel and Michael Haines (Cambridge: Cambridge University Press, 1997), https://users .pop.umn.edu/~rmccaa/mxpoprev/cambridg3.htm. With the revolution, it dropped again by 1921 to a bit more than 14 million. Jan Lahmeyer: "Mexico: Historical Demographical Data of the Whole Country," Population Statistics, last modified February 2, 2004.

173 *landowners drove out or killed Chinese railroad laborers*: Enrique Krauze, "Mexico at War," *New York Review of Books*, September 27, 2012.

173 *a full half of the peasant class*: María Teresa Vázquez Castillo, *Land Privatization in Mexico: Urbanization, Formation of Regions, and Globalization in Ejidos* (New York: Routledge, 2004), 26.

173 *one of the ten most dangerous places in the world*: Amanda Macias and Pamela Engel, "The 50 Most Violent Cities in the World," Business Insider, last modified January 23, 2015; *Independent* (UK), April 2016.

174 *three of whose siblings were certifiably deranged*: George Frederick Masterman, *Seven Eventful Years in Paraguay: A Narrative of Personal Experience Amongst the Paraguayans* (London: Sampson Low, 1870), 46.

174 *windows in the houses of Asunción*: Julio Llanos, *El Dr. Francia* (Buenos Aires: Moen, 1907), 53.

174 *He had never forgotten that the parents*: Ibid., 45–46.

174 *he forbade the Spaniards of Paraguay*: Ibid., 36.

174 *"Here, under our own nose"*: Thomas Carlyle, "Dr. Francia," in *Critical and Miscellaneous Essays*, vol. 1, Carlyle's Complete Works (Boston: Standard, 1899), 17.

175 *"the only Latin American country that foreign capital could not warp"*: Galeano, 188.

175 *His remains were later exhumed, defiled, absconded with*: H. Leguizamón, letter to the editor of *La Nación*, June 23, 1906, in Llanos, *Dr. Francia*, 78–81.

177 *Meanwhile, a nation of 900,000*: W. D. Rubinstein, *Genocide: A History* (London: Pearson, 2004), 94.

177 *In centuries to come, dictators came in a multitude*: This and the following few lines ares taken directly from my own work: Arana, *Bolívar*, 463.

177 *a necessary corrective in the public mind, a mythic creature*: Gabriel García Márquez once said, "The only mythic creature that Latin America has ever produced is the dictator." *"Una naturaleza distinta en un mundo distinto al nuestro"* [A different nature in a world different from ours], *La Jornada* (Mexico City), October 28, 2010, 4.

177 *"The most stubborn conservatism"*: Ernesto Sabato, *"Inercia mental,"* in *Uno y el universo* (Buenos Aires: Editorial Seix Barral, 2003), 90.

177 *Peru, the jittery seat of a lapsed empire*: Arana, *Bolívar*, 456.

178 *In Bolivia, just after the revolution*: President Mariano Melgarejo, killed in exile in Lima, 1871. See also Lawrence A. Clayton, *The Bolivarian Nations of Latin America*, 22.

178 *In Ecuador, a roundly hated religous fundamentalist despot*: President Gabriel García Moreno, an intense Catholic. Ibid., 23.

178 *In Quito, a dictator who tried to seize power*: President José Eloy Álfaro, a Freemason, who attempted to dismantle the Church's power, Ibid., 36.

178 Epigraph: *"The people get the governments they deserve"*: José Martí, *Ideario cubano* (Havana: Municipio de la Habana, 1936), 144.

178 *losing half a million people—rebels and Spaniards*: Scheina, *Latin America's Wars*, vol. 1, quoted in "Statistics of Wars, Oppressions and Atrocities of the Nineteenth Century," Necrometrics, last modified March 2011, http://necrometrics.com/wars19c.htm#Max-Mex.

179 *By 1961, two thousand of them had been executed*: Hugh Thomas, *Cuba: The Pursuit of Freedom* (New York: Harper & Row, 1971), 1460.

179 *By 1970, five thousand had been shot*: Ibid.

179 *Twenty thousand more were rotting in dungeons*: "Impunity," ch. 11 in *Cuba's Repressive Machinery: Human Rights Forty Years After the Revolution* (report), Human Rights Watch online, last modified June 1999, www.hrw.org/reports/1999/cuba/Cuba996-11.htm; Thomas, *Cuba*, 1458–61.

179 *con un violín, una baraja y un gallo fino*: Rafael Fernández de Castro, *Para la historia de Cuba*, vol. 1 (Habana: La Propaganda Literaria, 1899), 315.

179 *"far more than tons of sugar"*: Norman Gall, "How Castro Failed," *Commentary*, November 1, 1971, 48.

180 *from every far corner of Cuba*: Ibid.

180 *Animals perished without fodder*: Fidel Castro himself admitted this. Castro, public speech, July 26, 1970, quoted in Gall, Ibid.

181 Epigraph: *"The chief says burn everything"*: UNITA General Arlindo Pena's nom de guerre in the Angolan wars was "General Ben Ben" after the Algerian revolutionary leader, Ahmed Ben Bella. After the 1992 Halloween Massacre in Luanda, General Ben Ben was shown on television shouting these words into his radio. Peter Polack, *The Last Hot Battle of the Cold War* (Philadelphia: Casemate, 2013), 84–85.

182 *Cuba would pour half a million men*: J. H. Williams, "Cuba: Havana's Military Machine," *Atlantic*, August 1988.

184 *A decade later, it would be more than seventy thousand*: Luis Cino Álvarez, "Valió la pena la muerte de miles de cubanos en Angola?," Blogs Cubanos, Radio Televisión Martí, November 2015.

184 *almost 350,000*: Jamie Miller, "Castro in Africa," *The Atlantic*, December 3, 2016.

184 *He found himself armed with an AK-47*: The following events were described to me in numerous interviews with Carlos Buergos, Lorton Prison, September 1995 through July 1996.

186 *"What have they done to us?"*: *"Qué han hecho de mi pueblo? Qué han hecho de nosotros?"* António Lobo Antunes, *En el culo del mundo* [The land at the end of the world] (Madrid: Debolsillo e-book, 2012), Ch. G. Antunes was drafted into the war in Angola as a Portuguese soldier in the early 1970s, before Portugal's revolution in 1974.

186 *Cubans were using flamethrowers*: "Absolute Hell over There," *Time*, January 17, 1977.

187 *fulfilling a doctrine*: The Monroe Doctrine, the US policy to oppose any foreign power trying to meddle in the hemisphere, began in 1823, just before Latin America achieved complete independence, although it was not called by this name until more than twenty-five years later. President James Monroe was its author.

188 *arrest, torture, disappear, and execute nearly fifty thousand*: Paul Lopes, *The Agrarian Crises in Modern Guatemala* (Madison: University of Wisconsin, 1985), 46; *Amnesty International Annual Report 1971–1972* (London: AI Publications, 1972), 45; *Amnesty International Annual Report 1972–1973* (London: AI Publications, 1973), 6. President Arana had been known to say, "If it is necessary to turn the country into a cemetery in order to pacify it, I will not hesitate to do so." James Dunkerley, *Power in the Isthmus* (London: Verso, 1988), 691.

188 "A Salvador Allende, de su compañero de armas": José Miguel Larraya, "Fidel Ante la Tumba de Allende," *El País* (Madrid), November 11, 1996; "Allende se suicidó con un fusil regalado por Fidel Castro," Libertad Digital SA, last modified July 20, 2011.

188 *Not long after, with the full blessings of the Central Intelligence Agency*: Peter Kornbluh, "Chile and the United States: Declassified Documents Relating to the Military Coup, September 11, 1973," *National Security Archive Electronic Briefing Book 8*, George Washington University National Security Archive (legacy online site), accessed February 1, 2019, https://nsarchive2.gwu.edu//NSAEBB/NSAEBB8/nsaebb8i.htm. Also: Kristian Gustafson, "CIA Machinations in Chile, 1970: Reexamining the Record," *Studies in Intelligence* 47, no. 3 (2003).

188 *"It is firm and continuing policy"*: Kornbluh, "Chile and the United States."

188 *"Make the economy scream!"*: Ibid.

189 *"Such things are not done here"*: Tina Rosenberg, *Children of Cain: Violence and the Violent in Latin America*, 338.

189 *force victims to lie on the ground*: Ibid., 334.

189 *The government response was merciless*: Juan Forero, "Details of Mexico's Dirty Wars from 1960s to 1980s Released," *Washington Post*, November 22, 2006.

189 *students and political sympathizers were executed on the spot*: Kevin Sullivan, "Memories of Massacre in Mexico," *Washington Post*, February 14, 2002.

189 *Almost a thousand were subsequently disappeared*: Forero, "Details of Mexico's Dirty Wars."

190 *a staggering count of two hundred thousand dead*: "Mass Atrocity Endings: Colombia—La Violencia," World Peace Foundation at the Fletcher School online, last modified December 14, 2016.

190 *"agreeable to the United States"*: John Adams to John Jay, London, 28 May 1786, in E. Taylor Parks, *Colombia and the United States: 1765–1934* (Durham, NC: Duke University Press, 1935), 36.

190 *"those People"*: Ibid.

191 *"What could I think of revolutions?"*: John Adams to politician James Lloyd, 30 March 1815, Quincy, MA, in *The Works of John Adams* (Boston: Little Brown, 1856), 150.

191 *"if the poison of unrest . . . infect"*: Richard Nixon, voice recording, Nixontapes .org, 735–001, June 15, 1972.

191 *"Latin America doesn't matter"*: Richard Nixon to US ambassador to NATO Donald Rumsfeld, quoted in James Mann, *Rise of the Vulcans: The History of Bush's War Cabinet* (New York: Viking, 2004), 16.

191 *"People don't give a shit about the place"*: Nixon phone call with H. R. Haldeman, October 20, 1971, George Washington University National Security Archive (legacy online site), accessed February 1, 2019, www.gwu.edu/~nsarchiv/NSAEBB /NSAEBB95/mex18.pdf, conversation 597-3, cassette 1293.

191 *"What happens in the south has no importance"*: Henry Kissinger, quoted in Seymour Hersh, "The Price of Power: Kissinger, Nixon, and Chile," *Atlantic*, December 1982.

191 *Infantilizing the region's people, dismissing them as irresponsible*: Kissinger: "I don't see why we need to stand by and watch a country go Communist due to the irresponsibility of its people. The issues are much too important for the Chilean voters to be left to decide for themselves." Meeting of the "40 Committee" on covert action in Chile (June 27, 1970), from Victor Marchetti and John D. Marks, *The CIA and the Cult of Intelligence* (New York: Knopf, 1974). See also Seymour Hersh, "Censored Matter in Book About CIA Said to Have Related Chile Activities; Damage Feared," *New York Times* online, September 11, 1974).

191 *"America's backyard"*: Walter Hixson, *American Foreign Relations: A New Diplomatic History* (New York: Routledge, 2016), 310.

CHAPTER 8: THE RISE OF THE STRONGMAN AND THE DRAGONS
ALONG THE WAY

192   Epigraph: *"Barbarians who resort to force"*: José Martí, *"Los bárbaros que todo lo confían a la fuerza y a la violencia nada construyen, porque sus simientes son de odio,"* cited in Eduardo Palomo y Trigueros, *Cita-logía* (Sevilla: Punto Rojo, 2013), 295. (My translation.)

192   *I fought for liberty with all my heart"*: José García Hamilton, *El autoritarismo y la improductividad en Hispanoamérica* (Buenos Aires: Ed. Sudamericana, 1998), digital .ersion.

192   *"We have tried everything under the sun, and nothing has worked"*: Simón Bolívar to Urdaneta, Buíjo, July 5, 1829, in Daniel Florencio O'Leary, *Memorias de General O'Leary* (Caracas: Imprenta Nacional, 1879–88), 23:416–18.

193   *"A democratic system, far from rescuing us"*: Bolívar, "Letter from Jamaica," addressed to "un caballero de esta isla," Kingston, September 6, 1815, in Vicente Lecuna, *Simón Bolívar, Obras* (Caracas: Ediciones de la CANTV, 1983), 1:161.

194   *reduced the Latin American populace by more than 25 percent*: Scheina, *Latin America's Wars*, vol. 1, 173.

194   Epigraph: *"My grandfather, as he drank his coffee"*: Octavio Paz, "Intermitencias del Oeste," from Canción Mexicana, *Collected Poems of Octavio Paz* (New York: New Directions, 1987), 222. (My translation.)

194   *each time burying and reburying*: Fuentes, 268–69.

194   *sold off or lost vast tracts of land to the United States*: Santa Anna lost North Texas to the United States as well as the whole northern area of Mexican territories, including Arizona, New Mexico, Colorado, Nevada, California, and parts of Utah. Most of this was part of the 1853 Gadsden Purchase, in order to facilitate the building of the railroads.

195   *Díaz was all too reliant on ruthless*: Stuart Easterling, *The Mexican Revolution: A Short History, 1910–1920* (Chicago: Haymarket, 2013), 34–40.

196   *Díaz had all the chieftains of the Yaquis and the Mayans*: Thirty thousand people were deported. Along the way, the men were forced to marry Chinese farmhands and forget all previous alliances. Fuentes, 286.

196   *One prominent Mexican historian reckons that no fewer than seven hundred thousand*: Enrique Krauze, "In Mexico, a War Every Century," *New York Times* Opinion online, September 14, 2010.

196   *the pro-Catholic Cristero rebellion of the 1920s*: Ibid.

196   Epigraph: *"The war will come, my darling"*: Lines from Gioconda Belli's "Canto de guerra," 1948, in Belli, *De la costilla de Eva* (Managua: Editorial Neuva Nicaragua, 1987). (My translation.)

197   *invaded by British forces in 1847*: Data on Nicaragua from "Timeline: Nicaragua," Stanford University online, last accessed, February 2, 2019, https://web.stanford.edu/group/arts/nicaragua/discovery_eng/timeline.

198 *"chronic wrongdoing"*: The Roosevelt Corollary (1904) to the Monroe Doctrine (1823) masked US strategic interests in the rhetoric of neighborly aid: "Chronic wrongdoing or an impotence which results in a general loosening of the ties of civilized society, may in America, as elsewhere, ultimately require intervention by some civilized nation, and in the Western Hemisphere the adherence of the United States to the Monroe Doctrine may force the United States, however reluctantly, in flagrant cases of such wrongdoing or impotence, to the exercise of an international police power." As quoted in Gaddis Smith, *The Last Years of the Monroe Doctrine* (New York: Hill and Wang, 1994), 25.

198 *as many as fifty thousand Nicaraguans had been murdered*: David Boddiger, *Tico Times* (Costa Rica), July 22, 2014.

198 Epigraph: *"The fukú ain't just ancient history"*: Junot Díaz, *The Brief Wondrous Life of Oscar Wao* (New York: Riverhead, 2007), 3.

200 *he ordered the massacre*: Robert Crassweller, *The Life and Times of a Caribbean Dictator* (New York: Macmillan, 1966), 156.

200 *he met his undoing via American pragmatism*: "I Shot the Cruellest Dictator in the Americas," BBC News online, last modified May 28, 2011, www.bbc.com /news/world-latin-america-13560512. The BBC confirms the CIA involvement and adds: "In a letter to his State Department superior in October 1960, Henry Dearborn, de facto CIA station chief in the Dominican Republic, wrote: 'If I were a Dominican, which thank heaven I am not, I would favour destroying Trujillo as being the first necessary step in the salvation of my country and I would regard this, in fact, as my Christian duty.'"

200 Epigraph: *"It's the sound of things falling"*: "Es el ruido de las cosas al caer desde la altura, un ruido interrumpido y por lo mismo eterno, un ruido que no termina nunca." Juan Gabriel Vásquez, *El ruido de las cosas al caer* (Madrid: Alfaguara, 20011), 87. (My translation.)

201 *As many as 130,000 Colombians died*: "La Guerra de los Mil Días," *Encyclopædia Britannica* online, January 5, 2018.

202 *Not until the Peruvian president*: This was Luis Sánchez Cerro, even as he reviewed troops being sent to the undeclared war.

202 *Gabriel García Márquez, who was witness to the deed*: Gabriel García Márquez, *Vivir para contarla* (Barcelona: Mondadori, 2002), 332–63.

203 *"They've murdered Gaitán!"*: *"Matarón a Gaitán!"* Georgie Anne Geyer, *Guerrilla Prince* (New York: Little, Brown, 1991), 77.

203 *strewn with more than three hundred thousand corpses*: The three-hundred-thousand figure comes from a number of sources gathered by Erna von der Walde and Carmen Burbano, "Violence in Colombia: A Timeline," North American Congress on Latin America online, last modified September 2007, https://nacla.org/article/violence-colombia-timeline. See also Rex A. Hudson, ed., *Colombia: A Country Study*, 5th ed. (Washington, DC: Library of Congress, 2010), 326. This study puts the figure at more than two hundred thousand.

203 *blamed variously on the CIA*: Hudson, *Colombia*, 43. Gloria Gaitán, the politician's daughter, who was eleven years old at the time, suggested that it was the CIA. A contemporary Colombian politician named Álvaro Leyva Durán has suggested that a jilted suitor of Gaitán's lover—a hostess at the nightclub El Gato Negro—might have been the killer. Otty Patiño, *Historia (privada) de la violencia* (Bogotá: Debate, 2017), 300.

203 *forcibly displaced three million souls*: Rosenberg, 142. Rosenberg refers to Chileans who fled from the countryside into the cities. A more conservative figure, two million, perhaps focusing on the ensuing Chilean diaspora, is given in "Mass Atrocity Endings: Colombia—LA Violencia," World Peace Foundation at the Fletcher School online, last modified December 14, 2016, https://sites.tufts.edu/atrocityendings/2016/12/14/colombia-la-violencia-2.

203 *"Trujillo was there!"*: This is from the account Castro gave when interviewed by Katiuska Blanco Castiñeira for *Fidel Castro Ruz: Guerrillero del tiempo* (Panamá: Ruth Casa Editorial, 2012), vol. 1, ch. 9.

204 *"Indian" in manner, "intelligent, clever, friendly"*: Ibid.

204 *Gaitán was polite*: Ibid.

204 *"When I arrived in Colombia"*: Ibid.

204 *Castro was on his way to Gaitán's office*: Ibid.

205 Epigraph: *"Castro was in Angola because Angola"*: Geyer, *Guerrilla Prince*, 339.

205 *stand against a sea of foes*: Indeed, Castro mustered the strongest per capita fighting force in Latin America: *Cuban Armed Forces and the Military Presence* (Special Report no. 103) (Washington, DC: US Department of State, August 1982), www.dtic.mil/dtic/tr/fulltext/u2/a497385.pdf.

205 *Buergos did not know he had been witness*: Again, these accounts, for a front-page feature in the *Washington Post*, July 9, 1996, are taken from my 1995–96 interviews with Buergos during his incarceration in Lorton Prison.

205 *forty-five thousand more Cubans like him*: John Darnton, "Castro Finds There Are Risks as the 'Policeman of Africa,'" *New York Times* online, November 12, 1978.

206 *Latin America's most lasting dictator*: Fidel Castro led Cuba for five decades and was the world's third-longest-serving head of state, after Britain's Queen Elizabeth and the King of Thailand. He temporarily ceded power to his brother Raul in July 2006 after undergoing intestinal surgery. The handover of power became official in 2008. Reuters, "Castro Among Longest-Serving Leaders, Known for Long Speeches," Voice of America online, November 26, 2016, www.voanews.com/a/fidel-castro-obituary-facts/3612417.html.

206 *the most efficient terrorist machine*: "Fidel Castro Proclaims Himself a Terrorist," Fidel Castro, speech at the fifteenth anniversary of MININT, the Republic of Cuba's Ministry of the Interior, June 1976.

206 *The country's cattle, copious in the 1950s*: Gary Marx, "Cubans Have Beef with Chronic Cattle Shortage," *Chicago Tribune*, March 18, 2004.

206 *Eventually the ban included horses*: "Por qué Cuba sanciona con tanta severidad el

sacrificio de ganado?" [Why does Cuba sanction cattle slaughter so severely?], BBC World online, last modified September 12, 2015.

207 *he would release three thousand "hard-core" criminals*: Reuters, "Castro Would Free 3,000," *New York Times* online, November 23, 1978.

208 Epigraph: *"Tierra del Fuego could prove suitable for cattle breeding"*: London *Daily News*, 1882, as quoted in Michael Taussig, *Mimesis and Alterity: A Particular History of the Senses* (London: Routledge, 1993), 86.

208 *"Eat or be eaten, there's no getting around it"*: *"O comes o te comen, no hay más remedio,"* Mario Vargas Llosa, *La Ciudad y los Perros* (Madrid: Alfaguara, 2005), 33.

209 *the region is overwhelmingly, numbingly homicidal*: Rosenberg, 8.

209 *"dangerous obstacles"*: Martín Gusinde, *Los indios de Tierra del Fuego* (Buenos Aires: Centro de Etnología Americana, 1982), 143. See also Jérémie Gilbert, *Nomadic Peoples and Human Rights* (New York: Routledge, 2014), 23–24.

210 *"These poor wretches were stunted in their growth"*: Charles Darwin, *The Voyage of the* Beagle (1845; London: Wordsworth Classics, 1997), 198–99.

210 *"There's so much . . . to eliminate the Fuegians"*: *London Daily News*, 1882, in Taussig, *Mimesis*, 86; Jérémie Gilbert, *Nomadic People and Human Rights*, 24.

210 *Several years later, Argentina admitted its largest European influx*: More than 1.6 million immigrants from Europe were welcomed in 1914. Hundreds of thousands had flowed in during the previous century. Fuentes, 282.

210 *"Quantity is not the whole issue. Violence in Latin America"*: Rosenberg, 8.

211 Epigraph: *"A single person killed is a tragedy"*: The phrase in Russian is translated variously as "one death is a tragedy, a million deaths a statistic" or "the death of one man is a tragedy, the death of millions is a statistic." See Elizabeth Knowles, *Oxford Dictionary of Quotations* (New York: Oxford University Press, 1999), 736.

211 *the word disappeared took on new currency*: Rosenberg, 79.

211 *a secret death squad called the Triple A*: Ignacio González Jansen, *La Triple A* (Buenos Aires: Contrapunto, 1986), 7–38.

212 *collecting some of the largest ransoms*: $14 million would be equivalent to $69 million today. This was Victor Samuelson, a refinery manager for a subsidiary of Exxon. Brian Berenty, "The Born Legacy: Kidnappings in 1970s Argentina," November 4, 2015. www.livinglifeinanopensuitcase.wordpress .com. The Born brothers ransom of $60 million would be equivalent to $293 million today. Gus Lubin and Shlomo Sprung, "The Largest Ransoms Ever Paid," Business Insider, last modified September 7, 2012.

212 *"The Trial"—eerily reminiscent*: This was El Proceso de Reorganizacíon Nacional (National Reorganization Process), which, when shortened became *El Processo*, or The Trial, the name given to General Videla's regime. Rosenberg, 82.

212 *Almost seven thousand more Argentines went missing*: Lubin and Sprung, "Largest Ransoms."

213 *"Who is a disappeared person?"*: "Pregunta a Videla sobre los desaparecidos," uploaded to YouTube by CADALTV on April 25, 2013, 5:24, www.youtube .com/watch?v=3A1UCjKOjuc. Videla's answer: *"Es un incognito. Es un desaparecido. No tiene identidad. No está ni muerto, ni vivo. Está desaparecido."*

213 *(supported by Peru, Colombia, and Venezuela)*: "Perú: Socio de Condor," John Dinges online, accessed February 2, 2019, http://johndinges.com/condor /documents/Peru%20and%20Condor.htm.

213 *under the auspices of General Videla*: At the time, Videla was the senior commander of the Argentine army. He rose to the presidency in March 1976.

213 *methods they might use against "subversives"*: "Lifting of Pinochet's Immunity Renews Focus on Operation Condor," George Washington University National Security Archive (legacy online site), last modified June 10, 2004, https://nsarchive2.gwu.edu/NSAEBB/NSAEBB125. Two excellent sources are John Dinges's *The Condor Years* (New York: Free Press, 2005) and Peter Kornbluh's *The Pinochet File* (New York: Free Press, 2003).

213 *The United States, a natural partner . . . was complicit*: A. J. Langguth, *Hidden Terrors: The Truth About U.S. Police Operatons in Latin America* (New York: Pantheon Books, 1978). The entire book is about US complicity. Langguth was a bureau chief for the *New York Times*, among several other media organizations.

213 *"however unpleasant"*: Kissinger transcript, staff meeting, US Department of State, October 1, 1973, available on George Washington University National Security Archive (legacy online site), accessed March 16, 2019, https://ns archive2.gwu.edu//NSAEBB/NSAEBB110/chile03.pdf, 26–27.

213 *"take no further action"*: Kissinger, in a September 20, 1976, memorandum, George Washington University National Security Archive (legacy online site), accessed February 2, 2019, https://nsarchive2.gwu.edu/NSAEBB/NSAE BB125/condor09.pdf.

214 *the military regime hosted the soccer World Cup*: Wright Thompson, "While the World Watched," *ESPN the Magazine*, June 9, 2014.

214 *dropped from biplanes and helicopters into the Atlantic or the Paraná River*: Vladimir Hernández, "Argentina: viaje al delta donde 'llovieron cuerpos'" [Argentina: Trip to the delta where "bodies rained"], BBC World online, last modified March 24, 2013.

214 *Videla swanned through festivities with Secretary Kissinger*: Thompson, "World Watched."

214 *Nineteen of the twenty-two players didn't join in the revelry*: Ibid.

214 *as many as thirty thousand Argentines*: "Obama Brings 'Declassified Diplomacy' to Argentina" (Security Advisor Susan Rice's public announcement in advance of President Obama's 2016 trip to that country), available on George Washington University National Security Archive (legacy online site), last modified March 18, 2016, https://nsarchive.gwu.edu/briefing-book/south ern-cone/2016-03-18/obama-brings-declassified-diplomacy-argentina;

accessed March 16, 2019. Reuters, Sarah Marsh and Maximiliano Rizzi, "Obama's Argentina Trip Raises Questions About Macri Rights Record," March 18, 2016. According to a secret Chilean intelligence report, at least twenty-two thousand Argentines were killed between 1975 and 1978. "On 30th Anniversary of Argentine Coup, New Declassified Details on Repression and US Support for Military Dictatorship," available on George Washington University National Security Archive (legacy online site), last modified March 23, 2006, https://nsarchive2.gwu.edu/NSAEBB/NSAEBB185/index.htm.

214   *In Chile, we know that a quarter million*: Edward Rhymes, "Operation Condor," TeleSUR online, last modified June 15, 2017.

214   *Paraguayan armed forces disposed of two thousand*: Nilson Mariano, *As Garras do Condor* (São Paulo: Vozes, 2003), 234.

214   *Because of the covert nature of Operation Condor*: Ibid.

214   *The human costs of Condor were higher*: American death tolls in select wars: Revolutionary War—8,000 combat deaths, 25,000 total US war dead, in Howard H. Peckham, ed., *The Toll of Independence* (Chicago: University of Chicago Press, 1974), 131. Vietnam War—47,424 combat deaths, 58,209 total US dead, in John Whiteclay Chambers II, ed., *The Oxford Companion to American Military History* (New York: Oxford University Press, 1999), 849. American engagements since then—7,788 total combat and war dead, Nese F. DeBruyne, "American War and Military Operations Casualties: Lists and Statistics," table 2-24, Congressional Research Service online, last modified September 14, 2018, https://fas.org/sgp/crs/natsec/RL32492.pdf. For comparative reference: combat losses in World War I reached 53,000 (116,000 overall, including disease); in the American Civil War, 618,000.

215   Epigraph: *"Let the history we lived"*: Personal testimony quoted in D. Rothenberg, ed., *Memory of Silence (Tz'inil na 'tab'al), The Guatemalan Truth Commission Report* (London: Palgrave Macmillan, 2012), 7, www.documentcloud.org /documents/357870-guatemala-memory-of-silence-the-commission-for.html.

216   *when poverty rates in El Salvador were at 90 percent*: Rosenberg, 243.

216   *With the help of $4.5 billion*: Ibid., 269.

216   *arms and guns that poured in from Ethiopia and Vietnam*: Jorge G. Castañeda, *Utopia Unarmed: The Latin American Left After the Cold War*, 98.

217   *Mutilated corpses littered the streets*: Mark Danner, "The Truth of El Mozote," *The New Yorker*, December 6, 1993.

217   *murdering nuns, declaring Jesuit priests enemies*: Ibid., 101.

217   *one million were displaced*: Mayra Gomez, *Human Rights in Cuba, El Salvador and Nicaragua* (New York: Routledge, 2003), 101.

217   *seventy-five thousand were murdered*: *Report of the UN Truth Commission on El Salvador* (New York: United Nations Security Council S25500, April 1, 1993), www.derechos.org/nizkor/salvador/informes/truth.html.

217   *controlled the railroads and the shipyards*: Walter LaFeber, *Inevitable Revolutions: The United States in Central America* (New York: Norton, 1993), 76–77.

218 *the Central Intelligence Agency . . . masterminded a coup*: Stephen Schlesinger and Stephen Kinzer, *Bitter Fruit: The Story of the American Coup in Guatemala* (Cambridge, MA: Harvard University Press, 1999), 100–1.

218 *the Guatemalan military . . . stepped in to make demands*: The numbers and information relating to the Guatemalan Civil War and genocide throughout these pages are largely from a report by the American Association for the Advancement of Science (AAAS) and the International Center for Human Rights Investigations. Patrick Ball, Paul Kobrak, and Herbert Spirer, *State Violence in Guatemala, 1960–1996* (Washington, DC: AAAS, 1999).

219 *in one month alone, August 1977, they murdered sixty-one*: Ibid., 21.

219 *the "internal enemy"*: Rothenberg, *Guatemala: Memory of Silence*, 20.

219 *Eighteen thousand Guatemalans fell victim*: Ibid., 12.

219 *Using techniques taught them by foreign advisors*: Ibid., 42. The aforementioned reports identify the advisors as Israeli and Argentine military personnel.

219 *"Methods of violence became ever more gruesome"*: Ibid., 40–41.

220 *President Ronald Reagan's administration portrayed the regime*: Ibid., 42; Greg Grandin, "Guatemalan Slaughter Was Part of Reagan's Hard Line," *New York Times* online, May 21, 2013; Elisabeth Malkin, "Former Leader of Guatemala Is Guilty of Genocide Against Mayan Group," *New York Times* online, May 10, 2013.

220 *He's "a man of great integrity"*: Grandin, "Guatemalan Slaughter," May 10, 2013.

220 *as many as two hundred thousand dead or disappeared*: Associated Press, April 29, 1999; Rothenberg, *Guatemala: Memory of Silence*, 13. The population in 1982 was about six million.

220 Epigraph: *"In 1980 the statue of the Virgin of Cuapa"*: Dirk Kruijt, "Revolución y contrarevolución: el gobierno sandinista y la guerra de la Contra en Nicaragua, 1980–1990," *Desafíos* 23, no. 2 (July–December 2011): 67.

220 *Most of Nicaragua's children under the age of five*: Rosenberg, 279.

220 *"I don't want educated people"*: Ibid.

220 *When an earthquake toppled Managua*: Ibid., 279–80.

221 *on August 22, 1978, the Sandinista vanguard,* la frente, *stormed*: "Así contó La Prensa el asalto al Palacio Nacional hace 39 años," *La Prensa* (Managua), August 22, 2017, www.laprensa.com.ni/2017/08/22/politica/2283511-el -asalto-al-palacio-nacional-1978.

221 *brother would fight brother, and fifty thousand Nicaraguans*: Rosenberg, 288; Gomez, *Human Rights*, 10.

222 *"You'd be surprised"*: Lou Cannon, "Latin Trip an Eye-Opener for Reagan," *Washington Post*, December 6, 1982.

222 Epigraph: *"I have lived inside that monster"*: José Martí to Manuel Mercado, 18 May 1895, Campo del Rios (English translation), HistoryofCuba.com, accessed March 16, 2016. In this letter, Martí was actually referring to the United States as the monster.

CHAPTER 9: SLOW BURN

223 Epigraph: *"Everybody in the Andes knows"*: Mario Vargas Llosa, *Death in the Andes* (New York: Farrar, Straus and Giroux, 1993), 127.

223 *Britain was roughed up by the Angry Brigade*: The Angry Brigade was a leftwing revolutionary group that led a number of terrorist bombings between 1970 and 1972 in England.

223 *a formidable body count alongside its profits*: Business boomed during Colombia's La Violencia. Between 1948 and 1953, when the violence was at its peak, the country's growth rate was 6.2 percent. Rosenberg, 41.

223 *Colombia . . . continued to be the largest exporter of gold*: *Colombia: The Colombian Economy* (World Bank report, International Bank for Reconstruction and Development, Eastern Latin American Division, March 25, 1948), http://documents.worldbank.org/curated/en/582941468247471820/pdf /L31000Colombia000The0Colombian0economy.pdf.

224 *more than twenty thousand armed commandos*: Hudson, *Colombia*, 327.

224 *a formidable infantry of twenty-three thousand*: twenty thousand FARC at its height; three thousand ELN. Juan Guillermo Mercado, "Desmovilización, principal arma contra las guerrillas," *El Tiempo* (Colombia) online, last modified September 22, 2013. Also, *Contribución al entendimiento del conflicto armado en Colombia* [Contribution to the understanding of the armed conflict in Colombia] (Havana: Comisión Histórica del Conflicto y sus Víctimas [Historical commission of the conflict and its victims], February 2015), 50–65.

224 *more than ten million avid American users*: "The Global Cocaine Market," in *World Drug Report 2010* (Geneva: United Nations Office on Drugs and Crime, June 2010), 30, www.unodc.org/documents/wdr/WDR_2010/1.3_The_globa _cocaine_market.pdf.

224 *a record $165 billion*: Ibid., 69. The agricultural and mining businesses in the United States in 1995 totaled about $200 billion in profits. US Department of Commerce, *Survey of Current Business 79*, table B-3, https://fraser.stlouisfed .org/files/docs/publications/SCB/1990–99/SCB_071999.pdf.

224 *Billions of drug dollars flowed into Colombia*: Hudson, *Colombia*, 329.

225 *a fiercer, more random level of violence*: *Contribución al entendimiento*, 56–64.

225 *as many as three mass killings a month*: Hudson, *Colombia*, 34–38.

225 Epigraph: *"Everything but the power is an illusion"*: Abimael Guzmán, also known as "Gonzalo," the leader of Sendero Luminoso (Shining Path) in Peru. Fernando Salazar Paredes, "Salvo el poder todo es ilusión," La Opinion, *Pagina Siete* (La Paz), May 4, 2016.

226 *a sudden efflorescence of educational opportunity*: I owe these insights and much of what follows on Huamanga University and the Sendero Luminoso to Jorge G. Castañeda's superb *Utopia Unarmed*, 98–125.

226 *Ayacucho's Huamanga University*: This is more formally known as the National University of San Cristóbal de Huamanga.

226 *one of the strongest—as well as the most violent*: Castañeda, *Utopia Unarmed*, 120.

226 *Guzmán, the illegitimate son of a reasonably well-off merchant*: These details of his childhood are from Juan Carlos Soto and Giuliana Retamozo, "La Madre Chilena de Abimael Guzmán," *La República* (Arequipa, Peru), March 22, 2008.

228 *He ruled with all the absolutism of an iron-fisted dictator*: His plan, as laid out in Shining Path documents, intended to be (1) violent: power would be seized through violent means and would be held by a dictatorship; (2) thorough: it would obliterate the imperialists as well as the feudal-minded underdogs; (3) long: the engagement would consist of a prolonged, massive, total war; and (4) new: it would engage masses—not armies as previously conceived—and it would transform the Path into a new, never-before-seen populist force. Guzmán's philosophy is clearly laid out in a paper by the Peruvian historian Nelson Manrique, "*Pensamiento, acción y base político del movimiento Sendero Luminoso*," available on Historicizing the Living Past in Latin America, www.historizarelpasadovivo.cl.

228 *cross national borders and spark world revolution*: El Diario (La Paz) interview, quoted in C. Kistler, "PCM: To Defend the Life of Chairman Gonzalo is to Defend Maoism!" Redspark (an international Communist Party publication), last modified October 25, 2107, http://www.redspark.nu/en/imperialist-states/to -defend-the-life-of-chairman-gonzalo-is-to-defend-maoism.

228 *taken every opportunity to penetrate that system*: Gustavo Gorriti, *Shining Path: A History of the Millenarian War in Peru*, 84; Dora Tramontana Cubas, "*La Violencia Terrorista en el Perú, Sendero Luminoso*," *Revista Persona*, nos. 25, 26, Argentina, 2004.

229 *Lima awoke to find dead dogs hanging from lampposts*: Lucero Yrigoyen MQ, "Sendero Luminoso y los perros," *Semanario Siete* (Peru), September 10, 2012.

229 *At first, the youths who populated the Path*: Gorriti, 86.

229 *It was the first armed insurrection in Latin America*: Castañeda, *Utopia Unarmed*, 127. The Path's financial arrangement with the drug trade may well have been a precursor to and model for the FARC's collaboration with Colombian drug lords. See also Manrique, "The War for the Central Sierra," in *Shining and Other Paths: War and Society in Peru, 1980–1995*, ed. Steve J. Stern, 215.

230 *If a female guerrilla flirted with a policeman*: Rosenberg, 146.

230 *stuff dismembered penises into mouths*: Anne Lambright, *Andean Truths*, Liverpool, UK: Liverpool University Press, 2015, 158–59.

230 *"a river of blood!"*: Carlos Iván Degregori, "Harvesting Storms: Peasant *Rondas* and the Defeat of Sendero Luminoso in Ayacucho," in Stern, *Shining and Other Paths*, 128.

230 *hammer the countryside*: Ibid.; PCP-SL (Communist Party of Peru document), December 1982, quoted in Gorriti, 283.

230   *"the local mayor; the health post's nurse"*: Rosenberg, 146.

230   *surpassed the death toll for the American Revolution*: Charles F. Walker, *The Tupac Amaru Rebellion* (Cambridge, MA: Belknap Press, 2016), 277.

231   "La cuota," *Guzmán called it*: Gorriti, 282.

231   *the most radical expression of a desperate revolutionary body*: Rodrigo Montoya, "*Izquierda unida y Sendero, potencialidad y limite,*" *Sociedad y política*, August 13, 1983.

231   *It cut through the shantytowns, killing the civic leaders*: Jo-Marie Burt, "The Case of Villa El Salvador," in Stern, *Shining and Other Paths*, 270–71.

232   *had cost Peru 70,000 souls*: "Abimael Guzmán," *Encyclopædia Britannica* online, www.britannica.com/biography/Abimael-Guzman.

232   *The displaced rural population*: Castañeda, *Utopia Unarmed*, 125.

232   *one out of every two Lima residents lived in a slum*: Ibid.

232   *sickened 322,000*: Marcus Cueto, *El regreso de las epidemias: salud y sociedad en el Perú del siglo XX* (Lima: Instituto de Estudios Peruanos, 2000), 175. Cueto's figure is 322,562.

232   *cut down a thousand more*: James Brooke, "Cholera Kills 1,100 in Peru and Marches On," *New York Times* online, April 19, 1991.

232   *Twenty-five students and teachers were abducted*: Also, "*Confirman que restos de víctimas de La Cantuta fueron quemados*" [It is confirmed that the remains of the La Cantuta victims were burned], *El Mercurio* (Santiago), August 18, 2008, www.emol.mundo.

232   *Not one was a member of the Shining Path*: "Victims of the Barrios Altos and La Cantuta Massacres Were Not Terrorists," *El Comercio* (Lima), April 7, 2009, http://archivo.elcomercio.pe/politica/gobierno/victimas-masacres-barrios-al tos-cantuta-no-eran-terroristas-noticia-270253.

232   *supported by $36 million*: This money was provided by the United States Agency for International Development (USAID), an independent agency that provides civilian foreign aid and development assistance, https://newrepublic .com/article/151599/dont-talk-perus-forced-sterilizations. Support for the Peruvian armed forces also came from the American military in the form of counterinsurgency training at Fort Gulick in Panama (Manrique, "War for Central Sierra," 193). The figures are from Françoise Berthélémy, "*Stérilisa-tions forcés des Indiennes du Pérou,*" *Le Monde diplomatique*, May 2004.

232   Epigraph: "*America is the greatest of opportunities and the worst of influences*": *The Works of George Santayana*, vol. 5, bk. 6, ed. Herman J. Saatkamp Jr. and William G. Holzberger (Cambridge, MA: MIT Press, 2004), 423.

233   *Castro called "human refuse" and "scum"*: David Piñeiro, "The Exodus of Mariel," Una Breve Historia, accessed March 16, 2019, www.unabrevehistoria .com/exodo-desde-mariel.html.

233   *"To the Cuban refugees: This great nation"*: Mariel boat lift flyer, "The Cuban Experience in Florida," image number, PR30565, Florida Memory: State Library & Archives of Florida.

234 *he was whisked through a processing center in Key West*: Arana-Ward, "Three Marielitos."

234 *fifty-five had criminal records*: "Cuban Refugee Crisis," *The [Online] Encyclopedia of Arkansas History and Culture*, last modified March 12, 2015.

234 *All the same, the people who inhabited the small town*: "Cuban Refugee Crisis."

234 *At the Immigration and Naturalization Service*: Arana-Ward, "Three Marielitos."

235 *The city's leaders didn't seem to care*: Robert Pierre Pierre, "DC Anti-Gang Efforts Marked by Frustration," *Washington Post* online, March 9, 1997.

236 *"I was with a group of Cubans both times"*: Arana-Ward, "Three Marielitos."

237 *"I was getting right"*: Ibid.

238 *He drifted from one town to another*: These more recent details were gathered in the author's follow-up reporting on Buergos's whereabouts in 2017–18.

238 Epigraph: *"The conquest has not yet ended"*: Juan Adolfo Vásquez, 1982, quoted in Wright, 52.

238 *The Spanish . . . had been reliant on* hermandades: Kamen, *Spain*, 21–22.

239 *he sent unwanted, hardened criminals*: John Hemming, *Red Gold: The Conquest of the Brazilian Indians. 1500–1700*, 40.

239 *"la época del perrero"*: Moreno Parra, Héctor Alonso, and Rodriguez Sanchez, *Etnicidad, resistencias y políticas públicas* (Cali, Co.: University del Valle, 2014), 102.

239 *"a primitiveness, a ferocity"*: Mario Vargas Llosa, *El Pez en agua* (Madrid: Alfaguara, 2006), 520.

239 *could easily be reduced to vileness*: "*Vargas Llosa dice que descubrió la literatura latinoamericana en París*," *La Vanguardia* (Barcelona), May 1, 2014. These are not Vargas Llosa's words, but the reviewer's.

239 *"The conquest of America was cruel, violent"*: Mario Vargas Llosa, Nobel lecture, December 7, 2010, Stockholm.

240 *For a hundred years*, limpieza de sangre *was law*: María Elena Martínez, *Genealogical Fictions: Limpieza de Sangre, Religion, and Gender in Colonial Mexico* (Stanford, CA: Stanford University Press, 2008), 10–12.

240 cédulas de Gracias al Sacar: Bethell, *History of Latin America*, 3:30.

241 *Of the fifty most violent cities in the world*: Macias and Engel, "50 Most Violent Cities."

241 *easy as going to Facebook or a digital marketplace called "Qué Barato!"*: "*Sicarios trujillanos se promocionan en página web de anuncios*," *Trujillo Informa* (Trujillo, Peru), January 20, 2014; "*Sicarios de Trujillo que se promocionan por Facebook*," *El Comercio* (Lima), May 11, 2013.

241 *no country at peace has registered Colombia's extreme levels*: Hudson, *Colombia*, 337.

241 *In Buenos Aires, Argentina*: Gabriel DiNicolaand Germán de los Santos, "*Sicarios: mandar a matar en la Argentina puede costar $10,000*," *La Nación* (Buenos Aires), January 29, 2017.

241 *As one journalist has said*, sicarios: Rosenberg, 34.

241 *the product of a numbing spiral of righteous violence*: Eric Johnson, Ricardo Salvatore, and Pieter Spierenburg, eds., *Murder and Violence in Latin America* (Malden, MA: Wiley-Blackwell, 2013), 269.

241 *more than a dozen Salvadorans were cut down in gang warfare*: "Shining Light on Latin America's Homicide Epidemic," *Economist*, April 5, 2018.

241 *108 homicides per 100,000 people*: *Homicide Counts and Rates*, United Nations Office on Drugs and Crime (UNODC) online, 2000–2013, www.unodc.org /documents/gsh/data/GSH2013_Homicide_count_and_rate.xlsx; https://www .unodc.org/documents/gsh/pdfs/2014_GLOBAL_HOMICIDE_BOOK_web .pdf. General data and statistics on global crime, 2013–17, www.unodc.org/unodc /en/data-and-analysis/statistics.html.

241 *a region that accounts for a mere 8 percent*: "Shining Light Latin America's Homicide Epidemic."

242 *Venezuelan government stopped reporting homicides in 2005*: Miriam Wells, "Venezuela Government Admits Keeping Crime Figures Secret," InSight Crime online, last modified July 15, 2013.

243 *buying off dozens of presidents and government officials*: Among them, Brazil, Venezuela, the Dominican Republic, Panama, Argentina, Ecuador, Peru, Guatemala, Colombia, Mexico, El Salvador, Chile. See also "Odebrecht Case: Politicians Worldwide Suspected in Bribery Scandal," BBC News online, last modified December 15, 2017, www.bbc.com/news/world-latin-america -41109132; Anthony Faiola, "The Corruptions Scandal That Started in Brazil," *Washington Post*, January 23, 2018.

243 *kickbacks totaling $800 million*: Michael Smith, Sabrina Valle, and Blake Schmidt, "No One Has Ever Made a Corruption Machine Like This One," *Bloomberg Businessweek*, June 8, 2017.

243 *According to the anticorruption activist organization Transparency International*: Karen McVeigh, "Bribes for Public Services Rife in Latin America," *Guardian* (UK edition), October 10, 2017.

243 *If history holds, the people's fury will be followed by rebellion*: For this and the commentary and specifics that follow, I owe a large debt to the excellent anthology of scholarship in Johnson, Salvatore, and Spierenburg, *Murder and Violence*, 269.

243 *The people may even long for it*: Anthony Faiola and Marina Lopes, "Stop and Search? This Poor Community in Rio Says Yes, Please," *Washington Post*, March 25, 2018.

243 *the plague that has held Latin America fast since*: Corruption, which has deep roots in Spain and Portugal, spiraled on an intense and virulent scale during the reign of Philip III, who ruled in Lisbon as well as in Madrid (1598–1621). Government posts were for sale, the courts could be bought, and bribery was rampant. Latin America did not invent its corruption. Fuentes, 166–67.

244 *the most hardheaded conservatism*: Ernesto Sabato, "Inercia mental," in *Uno y el universo*, 90.

245 *No other country in the region*: Enrique Krauze, "In the Shadow of the Patriarch," *New Republic*, October 23, 2009.

245 *A population that was approximately twenty million*: Tim Merrill and Ramón Miró, eds., *Mexico: A Country Study* (Washington, DC: Library of Congress, 1996), 91.

245 *Some call it genocide*: Johnson, Salvatore, and Spierenburg, *Murder and Violence*, 244.

245 *sending more than two hundred thousand to their graves*: Nina Lakhani and Erubiel Tirado, "Mexico's War on Drugs," *Guardian* (UK edition), December 8, 2016. "Since 2007, almost 200,000 people have been murdered and more than 28,000 reported as disappeared. . . . The US donated at least $1.5bn" to this initiative by 2016. To put things in perspective, the United States has spent more than $2.5 trillion on the war on drugs between 1973 and 2016.

246 *the slums have exhibited an exponential growth in violent crime*: Salvatore, in Johnson, Salvatore, and Spierenburg, *Murder and Violence*, 236.

246 *began to flock to the urban hearts*: "Shining Light."

246 *Mara Salvatrucha (MS-13) numbers seventy thousand*: Steven Dudley et al., "The MS13," InSight Crime and Center for Latin American and Latino Studies at American University online, last modified February 2018.

246 *pulled twenty thousand gang members from jails*: Ibid.

246 *hardly equipped to deal with the bloodletting that followed*: Jose Miguel Cruz, "The Root Causes of the Central American Crisis," *Current History* 114, no. 769 (February 2015): 43–48.

247 *a mother named Angélica Mendoza de Ascarza went looking*: Phil Davison, "Activist Protested Peruvian Government to Get Answers About Missing People," *Washington Post*, September 10, 2017.

247 *another mother named Maria de Lourdes Rosales*: Ioan Grillo, "The Paradox of Mexico's Mass Graves," *New York Times* online, July 19, 2017.

247 *Or just last year, in the killing fields of Mato Grosso*: Chris Arsenault, "Politics of Death: Land Conflict and Murder Go 'Hand in Hand' in Brazil," Reuters, June 26, 2017.

247 *gang leaders are called* palabreros, *the men who carry the word*: Dudley et al., "MS13."

PART 3: STONE

249 Epigraph: *"How is it, sir, that having persuaded me to trust our friendship"*: *"¿Cómo, señor, es posible que habiéndome dado la fe de amistad."* Gonzalo Fernández de Oviedo y Valdés reports this testimonial from Casqui, an evangelized Tainan cacique who traveled to Barcelona on Columbus's return trip from the Caribbean. Oviedo, 2:118, 179–80.

Chapter 10: The Gods Before

251   Epigraph: *"Is it possible that the great God"*: Fray Luis de Granada, *Obras del VP Maestro Fr. Luis de Granada* [Collected works of the venerable father priest Luis de Granada] (Madrid: Antonio Gonçalez de Reyes, 1711), vol. 21, pt. 5, tratado 4, para. 20.

251   *It did not escape Xavier Albó*: All the information on and descriptions of Xavier Albó's life, career, and opinions are taken from a series of interviews I did with him in the Jesuit House in La Paz, Bolivia, from February 20 to February 27, 2016, including correspondence before and after, as well as his very thorough autobiography, *Un curioso incorregible*, published in Bolivia in 2017.

251   *Society of Jesus*: The Jesuits (Societas Iesu, SJ), established in Loyola in 1534. It is known in Spanish as Compañía de Jesús, the original name given to the order by Ignatius of Loyola and his first six companions. They also called themselves Amigos en El Señor. "Society" derives from the Latin translation.

252   *the coal miners of Asturias had gone on strike*: *"La Revolución de Asturias, octubre de 1934: La Revolución minera,"* Association for the Recovery of Historical Memory online, last modified October 5, 2017, www.radiorecuperandomemoria.com

253   *Half a million lives would be lost*: Adam Hochschild, *Spain in Our Hearts* (New York: Houghton Mifflin, 2016), 343. Historians estimate that, outside combat, the Nationalists killed 150,000 opponents between 1936 and 1939, and Franco's regime executed an additional 20,000 more after coming to power. Many more were arrested and tortured, or maimed for life. But the Republicans committed their share of atrocities, killing about 49,000. The rest were civilian deaths (James McAuley and Pamela Rolfe, "Spain Plans to Exhume Franco," *Washington Post*, October 20, 2018).

253   *ten Savoia-Marchetti warplanes from Franco's Nationalist forces roared overhead*: Josep María y Joan Villarroya Solé i Sabaté, *España en llamas: La guerra civil desde el aire* (Madrid: Temas de Hoy, 2003), 239.

255   Epigraph: *"Who could conquer Tenochtitlán?"*: *"Cantares Mexicanos,"* quoted in David Carrasco, *Quetzalcoatl and the Irony of Empire* (Chicago: University of Chicago Press, 1982), 150.

255   *Cortés himself had reported*: Cortés, *Cartas de Relación* (1993), 232–48. Quoted in Restall, *When Montezuma Met Cortés*, 4.

255   *What stands as recorded history, after all, isn't history at all*: This concept is lucidly and amply explored in the erudite and well-argued book *When Montezuma Met Cortés: The True Story of the Meeting That Changed History*, by Pennsylvania State University historian Matthew Restall.

256   *Often it is charged with telluric power*: James Mann, *Rise of the Vulcans*, 82.

256   *the most impressive empire builders of their day*: Felipe Fernandez-Armesto, *Civilization* (New York: Touchstone, 2001), 390–402.

256   *The transition between seasons—when the Milky Way streamed*: James Mann,
      Rise of the Vulcans 83.

258   *Mines in the time of the Incas were considered sacred*: Tripcevich and Vaughn,
      3–10.

258   *the indisputable germ at the heart*: Catherine J. Allen, "When Pebbles
      Move Mountains," in *Creating Context in Andean Cultures*, ed. Rosaleen
      Howard-Malverde (New York: Oxford University Press, 1997), 73–83.

258   *"the form is constant, the interpretation is variable"*: Franz Boas, *Primitive Art*
      (1927) (New York: Dover Publications, 1955), 128. Cited in Krista Ulujuk
      Zawadski, "Lines of Discovery on Inuit Needle Cases, *Kakpiit*, in Museum
      Collections," *Museum Anthropology* 41, no. 1 (Spring 2018): 61–75, https://
      anthrosource.onlinelibrary.wiley.com/toc/15481379/2018/41/1.

259   The Florentine Codex . . . *emissaries of Montezuma*: Sahagún, 12:13.

259   *But the descendants of the Incas interviewed by Gamboa*: Rostworowski, *Historia
      del Tawantinsuyu*, 46–47.

260   *Stone, to the ancient indigenous of the Americas, was transubstantial*: Carolyn
      Dean, *A Culture of Stone: Inka Perspectives on Rock*, 5.

260   *A thrall in stone was deeply embedded*: Lars Frühsorge, "Sowing the Stone,"
      Estudios de Cultura: Maya, vol. 45 (México, DF: Universidad Nacional
      Autónoma de Mexico [UNAM], 2015): 72–189.

260   *their word for stone*, tun, *also means "time"*: Ibid.

260   *Like the Quechua word* pacha: Tamara L. Bray, ed., *The Archaeology of Wak'as:
      Explorations of the Sacred in the Pre-Columbian Andes* 25–27.

261   *the living could coerce the spirits*: David Stuart, "Kings of Stone," *RES: Anthro-
      pology and Aesthetics* 29/30 (Spring/Autumn 1996): 148–71.

262   *"Huacas are made of energized matter"*: Frank Salomon, *The Huarochirí
      Manuscript* (Austin: University of Texas, 1991), 19. The italics are mine.

262   *"Jungle dwellers live in a forest of eyes"*: Richard K. Nelson, "The Watchful
      World," in *Readings in Indigenous Religions*, ed. Graham Harvey (London:
      Continuum, 2002), 345.

262   *Bartolomé de las Casas . . . told of Mesoamerican*: Las Casas, in *Apologética Historia
      Sumaria*, ed. Juan Pérez de Tudela (Madrid: Editorial Atlas, 1958), 527.

263   *a random* piedra cansada: Dean, 50. A tired stone. These were originally
      reported by Guaman Poma in *El primer nueva corónica y buen gobierno* [The
      first new chronicle and good government], in which he describes six thousand
      workers hauling huge boulders to the site of Sacsayhuamán using "great
      cables of hemp and rope," and—sometimes unable to haul them all—leaving
      some randomly on the landscape.

263   *shamans treat sick children*: Frühsorge, "Sowing," 72–189.

263   *the three original stones that marked the beginning of time*: David Freidel, Linda
      Schele, and Joy Parker, *Maya Cosos: Three Thousand Years on the Shaman's Path*
      (New York: Morrow, 1993), 67; Matthew G. Looper, *To Be Like Gods: Dance
      in Ancient Maya Civilization* (Austin: University of Texas Press, 2009), 116.

263 *the age-old practice of "sowing the stones"*: Frühsorge, "Sowing," 72–189.

263 *descendants of the Mayans or Aztecs will insist*: Matthew G. Looper, *The Three Stones of Maya Creation Mythology*, Wired Humanities Projects, University of Oregon Mesoamerican Archives, quoted in Dr. Frances Karttunen, "Why Always *Three* Hearth Stones?," Aztecs at Mexicolore, accessed February 3, 2019, www.mexicolore.co.uk/aztecs/ask-experts/why-always-three-hearth -stones.

264 *"We are this stone"*: John Janusek, "Of Monoliths and Men," in Bray, 335–36. The italics are mine.

265 *The pyramid at Cholula . . . grander than any that the Egyptian king Cheops built*: The Cholula structure, which is known as Tlachihualtepetl ("man-made mountain") and built about 300 BC, has a base four times larger than Giza's and nearly twice the volume. Josh Hrala, "The World's Largest Pyramid Is Hidden Under a Mountain in Mexico," Science Alert, last modified August 25, 2016, https://www.sciencealert.com/the-world-s-largest-pyramid-is-hidden -under-a-mountain-in-mexico.

265 *the Peruvian archaeologist Julio C. Tello discovered ruins*: preface, *Anthropological Papers of the American Museum of Natural History* (New York: AMNC, Board of Trustees, 1944–45), 39:5.

266 *According to one Andean legend*: This was recorded by one of Pizarro's cohort, Juan de Betanzos, a Spaniard married to Atahualpa's cousin (who was also a former concubine of Pizarro's). *Narrative of the Incas*, 7–10.

267 Epigraph: *"Go and make disciples of all nations"*: Matthew 28:19–20.

267 *presented itself to him with such physical force*: "Pope Francis and Saint Matthew," *Today's Catholic*, September 15, 2015.

269 *controlled 92 percent of the cultivable land*: Maria Luise Wagner, "The Sexenio (1946–52)," in *Bolivia: A Country Study*, ed. Rex A. Hudson and Dennis M. Hanratty (Washington, DC: Library of Congress, 1989).

270 *the country had sacrificed sixty-five thousand lives*: Matthew Hughes, "Logistics and the Chaco War: Bolivia Versus Paraguay," *Journal of Military History* 69, no. 2 (April 2005): 412.

270 *178 popular uprisings*: Guillermo Yeatts, *The Roots of Poverty in Latin America* (Jefferson, NC: McFarland, 2005), 53.

271 *even eat them—in ritual sacrifice*: Rubén Mendoza, "Aztec Militarism and Blood Sacrifice," in Chacon and Mendoza, 47–48.

271 *Aztec codices describe these religious rites*: See *Codex Magliabechiano*, fol. 70, Biblioteca Nazionale Centrale, Florence, Italy, www.art.com/products/p11 726751-sa-i1352276/a-human-sacrifice-from-the-codex-magliabechiano.htm.

272 *In Peru, during Inti Raymi celebrations*: Guaman Poma, 2:38.

272 *They called it* capacocha: *Qhapaq hucha*, in Quechua, "royal sins." The rite is well explained in Valerie Andrushko et al., "Investigating a Child Sacrifice Event from the Inca Heartland," *Journal of Archaeological Science* 38, no. 2 (February 2011): 323–33. See also Maria Constanza Ceruti, "Frozen Mummies

from Andean Mountaintop Shrines: Bioarchaeology and Ethnohistory of Inca Human Sacrifice," *BioMed Research International* 2015, article ID 439428 (2015): 12 pages, http://www.dx.doi.org/10.1155/2015/439428.

272   *Blood was never shed in these sacrifices*: Martín de Murúa, *Historia del orígen y genealogía real de los reyes incas del Perú* (1590), 2:263–64.

272   *In 1892 an excavation on Ecuador's Isla de la Plata*: Richard J. Chacon, Yamilette Chacon, and Angel Guandinango, "The Inti Raymi Festival Among the Cotacachi and Otavalo of Highland Ecuador: Blood for the Earth," in Chacon and Mendoza, 123.

272   *in 1995, the remains of a twelve-year-old mummified Inca girl*: Johan Reinhard: "Peru's Ice Maidens," *National Geographic*, June 1996, 62–81.

273   *In 2018, the skull of a boy*: Natasha Frost, "Grisly Child Sacrifice Found at Foot of Ancient Aztec Temple," www.history.com, July 30, 2018. The discoveries in the archaeological dig led by Leonardo López Luján and taking place now in Templo Mayor, under the heart of Mexico City, have been astounding, including the unearthing of skull racks and skull towers numbering hundreds of victims.

273   *when Arequipa's volcano Misti erupted*: Murúa, *Historia General del Perú*, 16:48.

273   *a number of children were buried alive*: Colin McEwan and M. Van de Guchte, "Ancestral Time and Sacred Space in Inca State Ritual," in *The Ancient Americas: Art from Sacred Landscapes*, ed. R. Townsend (Chicago: Art Institute of Chicago, 1992), 359–71; Gordon McEwan, *The Incas: New Perspectives* (New York: Norton, 2006), 150.

274   *They prepared the captives for weeks by fattening them*: Alvar Nuñez Cabeza de Vaca, "Comentarios," *Relación y comentarios*, ch. 16, 558.

274   *Historians recount the discovery of child sacrifices*: Elizabeth Benson and Anita Cook, 2–3.

274   *up to the time of the conquest—and, some say, years after*: Chacon, Chacon, and Guandinango, "Inti Raymi Festival," 120–25.

CHAPTER 11: STONE TRUMPS STONE

276   Epigraph: *"The sword and the cross marched together"*: Galeano, 20.

277   *The god of the night sky or high wind*: Guilhem Olivier, *Mockeries and Metamorphoses of an Aztec God: Tezcatlipoca, "Lord of the Smoking Mirror"* (Boulder: University Press of Colorado, 2003), 14–15.

277   *One of the first edicts Cortés proclaimed*: Acosta, vol. 4, ch. 4.

277   *When Christians took over Athens*: Linda Jones Roccos, "Athena from a House on the Areopagus," *Hesperia: The Journal of the American School of Classical Studies at Athens* 60, no. 3 (1991): 397–410.

277   *a church dedicated to Saint John the Baptist*: Alan Rowe and B. R. Rees, "A Contribution to the Archaeology of the Western Desert IV: The Great

Serapeum of Alexandria," Bulletin of the John Rylands Library, Manchester 39: (1957), 485–520, https://www.escholar.manchester.ac.uk /api/datastream?publicationPid=uk-ac-man-scw:1m1914&datastream Id=POST-PEER-REVIEW-PUBLISHERS-DOCUMENT.PDF.

277 *Later, during the Byzantine era, when the Parthenon*: John Pollini, "Christian Destruction and Mutilation of the Parthenon," in *Athenische Mitteilungen*, 122 (2007), 207–28. When Athens subsequently fell to the Ottomans, the conquering Muslims used the Parthenon's sacred halls as a gunpowder arsenal.

277 *those who rejected the cross would "pay with their life and blood"*: In AD 380 the Roman emperor Theodosius I issued the Edict of Thessalonica. This established Christianity as the official state religion; all other sects were declared heretical. Five years later capital punishment for nonadherents began. Ibid. Also: Sidney Zdeneck Ehler and J. B. Morrall, *Church and State Through the Centuries* (Cheshire, CT: Biblo-Moser, 1988), 6–7.

278 *The emperor obliged, taking him on a personal tour*: Díaz, *Historia verdadera de la conquista*, 145–47.

278 *Montezuma's high priests were lulled into believing*: Wright, 145.

278 *Aztec gods might have been demanding, ravenous*: Ibid.

278 *"the yellow metal and the white"*: *Cozticteocuítlatl*, "yellow metal" in Nahuatl; *iztacteocuítlatl*, "white metal." León Portilla, *Visión de los vencidos*, 149.

279 *Supreme Creator—Ometeotl, Life Giver*: Miguel Léon-Portilla, "*Ometeotl, el supremo dios dual, y Tezcatlipoca 'Dios Principal,'*" *Estudios de Cultura Náhuatl* (México, DF: UNAM, 1999), 30.

279 *The little band of Franciscans*: Fray Gerónimo de Mendieta, *Historia eclesiástica indiana* (New York: Edwin Mellen Press, 1997), 60–62.

279 *The spiritual conquest of Mexico*: See Robert Ricard, *The Spiritual Conquest of Mexico*. Also Stafford Poole, "Expansion and Evangelism: Central and North America, 1492–1600," in Charles H. Lippy, Robert Choquette, and Stafford Poole, *Christianity Comes to the Americas, 1492–1776*, 32.

280 *as rapacious in his appetites*: The passions of Pope Alexander VI (1492–1503) "were for gold, women, and the careers of his [illegitimate] children." Norman Davies, *A History of Europe* (New York: Harper, 1996), 484.

280 *far less stable, far less unified as an economy*: Steven J. Keillor, *This Rebellious House: American History and the Truth of Christianity* (Downers Grove, IL: InterVarsity Press, 1996), 21.

280 *As one historian put it, Europe had become dangerously off kilter*: Ibid., 20.

280 *the richest nobleman in Europe*: Giovanni de Medici, who was worth about two hundred thousand ducats (or the equivalent of $36 million) at the time. Carrie Hojnicki, "Famiglia De Medici," Business Insider, last modified July 5, 2012.

280 *officials paid their toadies a pittance*: Keillor, *This Rebellious House*, 22.

280 *To raise the money, he ordered a Dominican friar*: Ibid. This was Johann Tetzel, whose indulgences and financial transactions provoked the ire of Martin Luther and the start of the Reformation.

280 *"As soon as the gold in the basin rings"*: Ibid.

281 *nailed it to the chapel door of the University of Wittenberg*: Reformation historian Andrew Pettegree of the University of St. Andrews doubts the ancient legend about the nailing and claims that, since the chapel door was the common notice board of the university, it was probably pasted or affixed in another way. Billy Perrigo, "Martin Luther's 95 Theses," *Time*, October 31, 2017.

281 *Within two months, Martin Luther's accusations were circulating*: Richard J. Evans, "The Monk Who Shook the World," *Wall Street Journal*, March 31, 2017.

282 *Soon after the arrival of the Franciscan delegation*: Lippy, Choquette, and Poole, 32.

282 *just as Bartolomé de las Casas was coming to the conclusion*: Las Casas, *History of the Indies* (New York: Harper and Row, 1979), 35. Las Casas arrived in 1508. His reckoning covers 1492–1508. The figure of three million dead is hotly argued by historians, who posit that Las Casas couldn't possibly have known either the numbers for the general population or the numbers who fell victim to the Conquest. See David Henige, *Numbers from Nowhere: The American Indian Contact Debate* (Norman: Oklahoma University Press, 1998), 133–35.

282 *something needed to be done about the dying*: In 1510 a delegation of Dominican friars arrived in Hispaniola and immediately expressed outrage against the treatment of the Indians. The Dominicans then led a formidable campaign against what they considered a genocide of the population of the Indies. H. R. Wagner and H. R. Parish, *The Life and Writings of Bartolomé de Las Casas* (Albuquerque: University of New Mexico Press, 1967), 11.

282 *"If you do not comply"*: El Requerimiento. Ficción jurídica: Texto completo. Monarquía Española, 1513, redactado por Juan López de Palacios, Scribd, accessed March 16, 2019, www.scribd.com/document/125487670.

283 Epigraph: *"I find only one fault, o most Christian of kings"*: Gaspar Pérez de Villagrá, *Historia de la Nueva México*, epic tale written in 1610 (México, DF: Museo Nacional, 1900), quoted in Jorge Cañizares-Esguerra, *Puritan Conquistadors: Iberianizing the Atlantic, 1550–1700*, 243.

283 *with no attention to spiritual matters*: Poole, in Lippy, Choquette, and Poole, 82.

283 *"In the nine years of his government of this island"*: Las Casas, in reference to Governor Ovando of Hispaniola, in *Obras*, 4:1355; also quoted in Lawrence A. Clayton, *Bartolomé de las Casas and the Conquest of the Americas*, ed. Jürgen Buchenau, 30.

283 *The Indian Juanico, who was promptly put in the service*: When Columbus was being investigated for his alleged crimes, Queen Isabella angrily insisted that Juanico, and all the others, be sent back to Hispaniola. "What right does the Admiral have to give my vassals to anyone?" she exclaimed. Las Casas, *Obras* 4:1243. Also in Clayton, *Bolivian Nations*, 17.

284 *So entrenched was he in the slave economy*: Lippy, Choquette, and Poole, 82.

284 *"Tell me by what right, what writ of justice?"*: This was Fray Antonio de Montesinos. Luis Alfredo Fajardo Sánchez, "Fray Antón de Montesinos: His Narrative

and the Rights of Indigenous Peoples in the Constitutions of Our America,"
SciELO Colombia, accessed February 2, 2019, www.scielo.org.co/pdf/hall
/v10n20/v10n20a14.pdf; also George Sanderlin, ed., *Witness: Writing of Bartolomé de las Casas* (Maryknoll, NY: Orbis, 1993), 66–67.

284 *In the presence of none other than Christopher Columbus's son Diego*: Clayton, *Bolivian Nations*, 41.

284 *the butchering of thousands—"without provocation or cause"*: Fray Bartolomé de las Casas, *Brevísima relación* (Medellín, Colombia: Universdad de Antioquia, 2011), 39.

285 *He had been present at the massacre of Caonao*: Las Casas, *Historia*, 3:1243, in *Obras completas* 4:1363ff.

285 *He had looked on as slaves were forced to march*: Ibid., vol. 2, ch. 7, 1318–19.

285 *if war were truly necessary to convert Indians*: Lewis Hanke, "A Modest Proposal for a Moratorium on Grand Generalizations: Some Thoughts on the Black Legend," *Hispanic American Historical Review* 51, no. 1 (February 1971): 124.

286 *where he narrowly escaped assassination*: M. Giménez Fernández, "Fray Bartolomé de las Casas," in *Bartolomé de las Casas in History*, ed. Friede and Keen (DeKalb: Northern Illinois University, 1971), 67–126.

286 *King Carlos I, Holy Roman emperor*: He was also known as King Charles V or Carlos V, ruler of the Duchy of Burgundy from 1506, Spain from 1516, and the Holy Roman Empire from 1519.

286 *Las Casas himself . . . had suggested it*: Clayton, *Bolivian Nations*, 135–36.

286 *Five million would be sent to Brazil*: Trans-Atlantic Slave Trade Database, www.slavevoyages.org. These figures reflect the slave trade between 1500 and 1875. No other country would receive as many slaves as Brazil.

287 *Somehow Las Casas had managed to enter*: Clayton, *Bolivian Nations*, 36.

287 *Ironically, even Motolinía, one of the Twelve Apostles of Mexico*: This was the priest who named himself Motolinía—Nahuatl for "beggar"—whose original name was Toribio de Benavente and who supported the notion that Indians were savages and needed to be Christianized in order to be protected. Ibid., 146.

287 *"a grievous man, restless, importunate"*: "Motolinía," in James Lockhart and Enrique Otte, eds., *Letters and People of the Spanish Indies, Sixteenth Century* (Cambridge: Cambridge University Press, 1976), 226.

287 *the "Black Legend," the damning, exaggerated notion*: Eventually this legend (*la leyenda negra*) produced a counterargument, when twentieth-century Spanish historians proposed a "White Legend," arguing that Spaniards were no worse than other Europeans and that the accusations of Las Casas and others were unjust and overblown. See also Hanke, "A Modest Proposal," 112–27.

288 *long, spirited debates against Juan Ginés de Sepúlveda*: The description of the debate with Sepúlveda is adapted from Lippy, Choquette, and Poole, 86–87. Aristotle's theory of natural slavery is in the fifth book of his *Politics*.

288 *Sepúlveda had just produced a treatise*: This was *The Second Democrates,*

or Reasons That Justify War Against the Indians, circulated in 1546–47 and produced at the request of Cardinal Juan García Loaysa, president of the Council of the Indies and a staunch critic of Las Casas.

288 *claim that the laws would undermine their livelihoods*: Clayton, *Bolivian Nations*, 119.

289 *In Mexico, the emissary who was sent*: Ibid., 119–24. The emissary in Mexico was Francisco de Tello Sandoval. The viceroy in Peru was Viceroy Blasco Núñez de Vela.

289 *"we are as disturbed as if the public executioner"*: Benno Biermann, "Bartolomé de las Casas," in *Bartolomé de las Casas in History*, 468. Quoted in Clayton, *Bolivian Nations*, 116.

289 *the New Laws were having no effect*: Benjamin Keen, "The Black Legend Revisited: Assumptions and Realities," *Hispanic American Historical Review* 49, no. 4 (November 1969): 704.

289 *When King Carlos relinquished all power and his son, Philip II, took the throne*: I owe much of this information to the context provided in Lawrence A. Clayton's excellent biography of Las Casas, *Bartolomé de las Casas and the Conquest of the Americas*, 145–50.

290 *"We who were once brave and noble"*: Guaman Poma, 2:357.

290 Epigraph: *"With the faith, the scourge of God came"*: The quote continues—"and, in proportion as the one increased, the other smote them more severely." Francesco G. Bressani, *Jesuit Relations* (1653), vol. 39, no. 141 (New York: Pageant, 1959). *Jesuit Relations* was the collection of documents and chronicles compiled by missionaries in the field in New France and printed between 1632 and 1673.

290 *Bringing the Indians to Jesus*: All the information about Xavier and his opinions is either from my interviews with him in La Paz in 2016, email correspondence from 2015 to 2018, or from his own memoir, Xavier Albó Corrons and Carmen Beatríz Ruiz, *Un curioso incorregible*.

291 *"What care have you ever given"*: Fray Antonio de Montesinos, Ibid.

293 *the rudiments of his first book, a Quechua primer*: Xavier Albó, *Un Metodo para aprender el quechua* (La Paz: Instituto Jesuita, 1964).

295 *José de Acosta, a liberal-minded priest who*: Manuel M. Marzal et al., *The Indian Face of God in Latin America*, 2.

295 *"To eradicate idolatry by force before Indians"*: José de Acosta, quoted in Marzal et al., 3.

295 *The Crown approved heartily, on the assumption*: Massimo Livi Bacci, *Estragos de la Conquista* (Madrid: Grupo Planeta, 2006), 235.

295 *more than half the Indian population*: Ibid., 237.

296 *"forever extinguished and silenced"*: Pope Clement XIV, in his papal brief *Dominus ac Redemptor Noster*, issued on July 21, 1773.

296 *Many were prey to slavers and lubricious landlords*: Jorge A. Ramos, *Historia de la nación latinoamericana* (Buenos Aires: Continente, 2011), 97–101.

296 *dying in far greater numbers than births*: Bacci, *Estragos*, 265.

296 *the "pope's black guard"*: Jorge A. Ramos, *Historia*, 97–101. Quoted also in Galeano, 190–91.

297 Title: *Preaching the Gospel Among Barbarians*: This is an echo of the Jesuit José de Acosta's treatise *De promulgatione Evangelii apud Barbaros* [On promulgating the gospel among barbarians], written in 1575 and published in Salamanca in 1589 by Apud Guillelmum Foquel.

297 Epigraph: *"Don't you understand that all that these friars say is lies?"*: Andrés Mixcoatl to the people of Metepec, Zacatepec, and Atliztaca, in Gruzinski, *Man-Gods*, 54.

298 *The first was Gerónimo de Aguilar, the hapless*: Díaz, *Historia verdadera de la conquista*, ch. 36–37.

299 *Bartolomé de Olmedo, and it is to him that Cortés owes*: Ibid., ch. 38–40; Ricard, 82–84.

299 *Cortés, a man of grand ambition and carnal inclinations*: Ricard, 79.

299 *without the easy conversion of the Nahuas*: Lippy, Choquete, and Poole, 38.

300 *For all the giddy claims that Cortés was a consummate hero*: I owe these insights to a remarkably original book, *When Montezuma Met Cortés*, by the historian Matthew Restall. In this case, see especially 301–54.

300 *"a man of unfeigned piety"*: The *oidor* Alonso de Zorita to King Philip, letter, 1 April 1562, *General de Indias*, Patronato, 182, ramo 2; partially transcribed in Ignacio Romero Vargas y Iturbide, *Montezuma el Magnífico y la Invasion de Anáhuac* (México, DF: Editorial Romero Vargas, 1963). Quoted in Restall, *When Montzeuma Met Cortés*, 334–35.

301 *Viejo Capitán*: Among the indigenous, Pizarro was variously known as "Apu" (earthly god) or "Machu Capitán" (old captain). Among the Spaniards, he was referred to as "Marqués" (marquis) for the honor bestowed on him by the Crown, Marqués de los Atavillos. R. Cunéo-Vidal, *Los hijos americanos de los Pizarro* (Alicante, Sp.: Miguel de Cervantes Virtual Library Foundation, 2006), www.cervantesvirtual.com/obra-visor/los-hijos-americanos-de-los -pizarros-de-la-conquista-0/html/00a6b998-82b2-11df-acc7-002185ce6064_2 .html.

301 *it was Valverde who shook a cross at the royal Inca*: Guaman Poma, 353–57.

301 *keen capacities for courage, fatalism, stoicism*: Lippy, Choquette, and Poole, 4.

302 *missions became . . . the vanguard of empire*: Ibid., 3.

302 *In the thick of exploration's wildest improvisations*: Arciniegas, *Latin America*, 139.

302 *The mendicant friars . . . who made the first inroads*: I owe much of these insights to J. H. Elliott's superb synthesis *Empires of the Atlantic World*, especially his chapter "America as Sacred Space."

302 *Oblivious to the profound shock that this mass deracination*: Lippy, Choquette, and Poole, 40.

302 *An intense rivalry emerged*: Elliott, *Empires of the Atlantic World*, 201.

303 *invading their territory and hijacking their operations*: Lippy, Choquette, and Poole, 90.

303 *Augustinians complained that Dominicans preaching in Spanish*: J. L. González and O. González, *Christianity in Latin America* (New York: Cambridge University Press, 2008), 51.

303 *they found a fully functioning ecclesiastical system*: Stafford Poole, *Pedro Moya de Contreras: Catholic Reform and Royal Power in New Spain, 1571–1591* (Norman: University of Oklahoma Press, 2011), 80.

303 *As one historian put it, a deep fissure ran down the very heart*: Elliott, *Empires of the Atlantic World*, 198.

303 *Passions would grow so heated, brawls so common*: Thomas Gage, *The English-American His Travails by Sea and Land* (1648), 71–72, quoted in H. McKennie Goodpasture, *Cross and Sword: An Eyewitness History of Christianity in Latin America* (Eugene, OR: Wipf & Stock, 1989), 56.

303 *Mendicants versus bishops, Creoles against Spanish-born*: Elliott, *Empires of the Atlantic World*, 201.

304 *"There are not above fifty churches and chapels"*: Gage, in *Cross and Sword*, 71–72.

304 *"so that twenty thousand ducats"*: Within the Gage quotation above, the worth of the brazilwood stays "wrought with golden colors." The amount quoted is equivalent to $2.7 million today. "Current Gold Gram Bar Values," GoldGramBars.com, last modified January 25, 2019, www.goldgrambars.com.

305 *"enrich themselves than to mind the salvation"*: Roberto Levillier, *Organización de la iglesia y ordenes religiosas en el virreinato del Perú en el siglo 16* (Madrid: Rivadeneyra, 1919), 148. Cited also in Ricard, 424.

306 *persuading the courts in Spain to classify Indians as* miserabiles: Woodrow Borah, *Justice by Insurance: The General Indian Court of Colonial Mexico* (Los Angeles: University of California Press, 1983), 81.

306 *the Church established a General Indian Court*: Hanke, "A Modest Proposal," 118.

306 *perhaps the greatest single educational force in the New World*: Lippy, Choquette, and Poole, 42.

306 *which the Crown and the Inquisition found convenient*: The Spanish Inquisition was far more aggressive in Spain than it would ever be in the Americas. The Black Legend, perpetrated by England and France, exaggerated its reach and terror. English efforts against witchcraft—both in the British Isles and its colonies—executed thirty to fifty times more people than the Inquistion did. Arciniegas, *Latin America*, 139.

306 *Eventually Bolívar would claim that a single faith*: Arana, *Bolívar*, 353.

307 *The Franciscans imposed harsh corporal punishments*: Poole, in Lippy, Choquette, and Poole, 57, 124.

307 *Presidios and missions employed armed soldiers*: Ibid., 38.

307 *missionaries destroyed much of pre-Columbian culture*: Ibid., 41.

307   *a full-scale war of extermination*: Ibid., 38.

307   *the head of the Franciscan order in Yucatán, Diego de Landa*: Felipe Fernandez-
      Armesto, *The Americas: A Hemispheric History*, 68; "Diego de Landa,"
      Encyclopædia Britannica online, www.britannica.com.

307   *One might argue that it is unfair for us to pass judgment*: Poole, in Lippy,
      Choquette, and Poole, 124–25.

307   *That, along with the slave raids, violent incursions, reductions*: Ibid., 123.

307   *As one humble Mexican put it*: Ibid.

308   *Anglo-America never produced a single defender of the American Indian*: Ibid., 126.

308   *nothing to equal that impassioned deliberation*: Ibid.

308   *But Spain's mission frontier system*: This paragraph in general owes much to
      Elliott, *Empires of the Atlantic World*, 268–69.

308   *It was because of priests that Mexico had a printing press*: Ibid., 205.

309   *Dominicans, heritors of a great intellectual tradition*: The Dominican schools
      did not found a single secondary school, and they refused to teach Indians or
      mestizos Latin (Lippy, Choquette, and Poole, 42).

309   Epigraph: *"All monks have achieved"*: Tupac Inca Yupanqui, "Reos de la
      sublevación de la provincia de Huarochiri" (1783), fs. 277–78, Audencia de
      Lima 1047, Archivo General de Indias.

309   *the Indians suspected that they were demons*: Marzal et al., 222.

309   *These were surely the* pishtacos *of Quechua lore*: Ibid; C. Wofenzon, "El
      'Pishtaco' y el conflicto entre la costa y la sierra," *Latin American Literary
      Review* 38, no. 75 (January–June 2019): 24–45.

309   *The practice was common enough in an age*: R. D. Forrest, "Development of
      Wound Therapy from the Dark Ages to the Present," *Journal of the Royal
      Society of Medicine* 75, no. 4 (April 1982): 268–69.

310   *How could a celibate priest be a fully realized man*: Marzal et al., 222.

310   "Dentro de este padrecito hay un hombre!": Albó and Ruiz, 54.

311   *the healthy, the educated 20 percent*: Latin American income-inequality levels
      were among the highest in the world in the 1950s, and they still are today.
      E. Frankema, "The Historical Evolution of Inequality in Latin America:
      A Comparative Analysis, 1870–2000" (thesis, Groningen University, 2008);
      United Nations University-World Institute for Development Economics
      Research, UNU/WIDER (2005) World Income Inequality Database (WIID),
      version 2.0a, www.wider.unu.edu/project/wiid-world-income-inequality
      -database?query=Latin+America.

311   *Some observers in Europe went so far as to say*: Girolamo Imbruglia, *The Jesuit
      Missions of Paraguay and a Cultural History of Utopia*, Studies in Christian
      Mission, vol. 51 (Boston: Brill, 2017), 22–23, 144.

312   *how a country might heal its soul*: He may have been referring to one of his
      indigenous informants, who had told him in all candor, *"el país me hace
      sufrir"*—the country makes me suffer. Albó, Television interview, La Paz,
      "No Mentiras PAT," April 9, 2016.

Chapter 12: House of God

313   Epigraph: " *"Politics is in crisis"*: Pope Francis I, quoted in Caroline Stauffer and Philip Pullella, "Pope Ends Latin American Trip with Warning About Political Corruption," Reuters, January 21, 2018.

313   *the Old European allegory about Latin America was false*: Cañizares-Esguerra, 71.

314   *When the Latin American revolutions were over*: Arana, *Bolívar*, 458.

314   *Civilian populations had been reduced by a third*: Christon Archer, ed. *The Wars of Independence in Spanish America*, Jaguar Books on Latin America, no. 20 (Wilmington, DE: SR Books, 2000), 35–37, 283–92.

314   *Churches and convents that hadn't been destroyed*: Hanke, "A Modest Proposal," 126.

314   *No one paid much attention to how much control the Church had lost*: Cleary, *How Latin America*, 115.

314   *curb the old tradition of acting as the Vatican's collection agency*: John Frederick Schwaller, *The History of the Catholic Church in Latin America: From Conquest to Revolution and Beyond*, 132.

314   *Mexico, for instance, seized and nationalized all church property*: Arturo Elias, consul general of Mexico, in the *New York Times*, February 21, 1926. It's worth adding here that Mexico is closer to a fuller separation of church and state than the United States is. In Mexico, the church is forbidden from certain rights and activities. Anthony T. C. Cowden, "The Role of Religion in the Mexican Drug War" (paper, Naval War College, Newport, RI, October 2011), www.researchgate.net/publication/277760802.

315   *the Latin American Church was in grave crisis*: Ibid., 114.

315   *Caribbean blacks returned to the voodoo and trances*: T. L. Smith, "Three Specimens of Religious Syncretism in Latin America," *International Review of Modern Sociology* 4, no. 1 (Spring 1974): 1–18.

316   *In the isolated Mexican sierra of Nayarit*: Aldana Guillermo, "Mesa del Nayar's Strange Holy Week," *National Geographic*, June 1971, 780–95.

318   *Maryknoll missionaries from the United States, having shifted*: Cleary, *How Latin America*, 116.

318   *the Catholic Church was in a deeply pitched battle*: Ibid.

318   *the concept of "inculturation"*: Xavier Albó, in interviews with me, volunteered repeatedly that he had been evangelized in the course of his sixty-five years among the indigenous.

318   *by recruiting Indian and mixed-race "catechists"*: Cleary, *How Latin America*, 183.

319   *"We affirm that both religions, Aymara and Christian, teach love"*: Xavier Albó, "The Aymara Religious Experience," in Marzal et al., 165.

319   *"We cannot persuade ourselves to believe anything you preach"*: Pedro de Quiroga, testimonial taken from a Peruvian Indian, "Coloquio de la verdad,"

in *El indio dividido: fractures de conciencia en el Perú colonial*, ed. Ana Vian Herrero (Madrid: Iberoamericana, 2009), 505.

320 Epigraph: *"I come from a continent in which more than sixty percent"*: Gustavo Gutiérrez Merino, *Teología de la liberación* (Salamanca, Sp.: Ediciones Sígueme, 1971), 15. See also Gutiérrez, "Teología de la liberación y contexto literario" [Theology of liberation and literary context], www.ensayistas.org /critica/liberacion/TL/documentos/gutierrez.htm.

320 *"If faith is a commitment to God and fellow man"*: Gutiérrez, *Teología*, 15.

321 *Poverty was not a fatal disease, it was a treatable condition*: Gustavo Gutiérrez Merino, in *Páginas*, vols. 191–96 (Lima: Centro de estudios y publicaciones, 2005). See also the Jesuit website Pastoralsj, https://pastoralsj.org/creer/1298 -gustavo-gutierrez.

321 *The Vatican's reaction was swift and damning*: For a variety of perspectives on this, see Juan Luis Segundo, *Theology and the Church: A Response to Cardinal Ratzinger and a Warning to the Whole Church* (San Francisco: Harper & Row, 1987) and Christian Smith, *The Emergence of Liberation Theology: Radical Religion and Social Movement Theory* (Chicago: University of Chicago, 1991).

322 *Pope John XXIII announced the Second Vatican Council*: See "Second Vatican Council," *Encyclopædia Britannica* online, www.britannica.com/event/Second -Vatican-Council.

322 *"a pilgrim people of God"*: *Lumen Gentium*, no. 48, Pope Paul VI, November 21, 1964, Vatican Council; Father Joshua Brommer, "The Church: A Pilgrim People of God," Diocese of Harrisburg online, accessed February 2, 2019, www.hbgdiocese.org/wp-content/uploads/2013/05/042613-Vatican-II-article -the-Church.pdf.

323 *assassinations of more than a dozen world figures*: Among them, Humberto Delgado (Portugal), Ngo Dinh Diem (Vietnam), Medgar Evers (US), Che Guevara (Bolivia), John F. Kennedy (US), Robert F. Kennedy (US), Martin Luther King Jr. (US), Grigoris Lambrakis (Greece), Patrice Lumumba (Congo), Malcolm X (US), Sylvanus Olympio (Togo), Jason Sendwe (Congo), Rafael Trujillo (Dominican Republic), Hendrik Verwoerd (South Africa).

324 *a vast army of the poor marched out under the banner*: Diego Barros Arana, "La Acción del clero en la revolución de la independencia americana," in Miguel Amunátegui and Barros Arana, *La Iglesia frente a la emancipación americana*, 111–21.

324 *"evil ones" . . . "a plague from a sinister well"*: Amunátegui and Barros Arana, *La Iglesia*, 18.

324 *With that blistering encyclical in tow*: Ibid.

325 *"the preferential option for the poor"*: Cleary, *How Latin America*, 53.

325 *accused the Vatican of being a rigid, fundamentalist dynasty*: "Nao existe guerra justa," Comunità Italiana, last modified November 2001, www.comunitaitaliana .com.br/Entrevistas/boff.htm.

325 *"rebellion, division, dissent, offense, and anarchy"*: Pope Benedict XVI, in a

December 7, 2009, address to Brazilian bishops, as quoted in Stephanie Kirchgaessner and Jonathan Watts, "Catholic Church Warms to Liberation," *Guardian* (UK edition), May 11, 2015, www.theguardian.com/world/2015/may /11/vatican-new-chapter-liberation-theology-founder-gustavo-gutierrez.

325 *targeted for assassination by hit men*: Juan Arias, "Casaldáliga reta a Roma," *El País* (Madrid), January 16, 2005.

326 *in Brazil that the military soon mounted a campaign*: Schwaller, *Catholic Church in Latin America*, 234–35.

326 *Pope John Paul II defrocked two more*: "Father Fernando Cardenal's Decision," *Envío*, Información sobre Nicaragua y Centroamérica, no. 43, January 1985, www.envio.org.ni/articulo/3387.

326 *"If Jesus were alive today, He would be a guerrilla"*: Manlio Graziano, *Holy Wars and Holy Alliances* (New York: Columbia University Press, 2017), 249.

326 *disavowed, suspended* a divinis: Ibid.

327 *He was Luís Espinal—Lucho, as he was known*: Espinal is well known to the Bolivian public, not only as a priest but also as a poet, playwright, journalist, and activist. His best-known published work is probably *Oraciones a quemarropa*, Prayers at point-blank range. Among his films are *Chuquiago* and *El embrujo de mi tierra*.

328 *his naked corpse flung to one side of the road to Chacaltaya*: "El cuerpo de Espinal tenía 17 orificios de bala," *El Deber* (Bol.), January 1, 2017.

328 *state of terror condoned by Henry Kissinger and funded*: "Operation Condor: National Security Archive Presents Trove of Declassified Documentation in Historic Trial in Argentina," George Washington University National Security Archive (legacy online site), last modified May 6, 2015, https://nsarchive2.gwu .edu/NSAEBB/NSAEBB514; Ben Norton, "Documents Detail US Complicity in Operation Condor Terror Campaign," Truthout online, last modified May 23, 2015, https://truthout.org/articles/documents-detail-us-complicity -in-operation-condor-terror-campaign; John Dinges, *Condor Years*.

328 *suspected of being "dangerous subversives"*: "El Papa rezará en silencio por el jesuita Luís Espinal," *Periodista Digital*, May 15, 2015.

328 *the first Aymara president of Bolivia*: The first South American president of full-blooded indigenous descent was Alejandro Toledo of Peru, who was elected in 2001. Morales was elected in 2005.

329 Epigraph: *"It is now obvious that these facile millenarianisms"*: "Interview of His Holiness Benedict XVI During the Flight to Brazil, Wednesday, 9 May 2007," accessed on March 16, 2009, https://w2.vatican.va/content/benedict-xvi/en /speeches/2007/may/documents/hf_ben-xvi_spe_20070509_interview-brazil.html.

329 *When Pope Benedict XVI . . . flew to Brazil*: Cleary, *How Latin America*, 1.

329 *more than half of all practicing Catholics lived in Latin America*: All statistics in this segment on Catholics and Pentecostalists are taken from the following reports by the Pew Research Center online, Washington, DC: "Religion in Latin America," last modified November 13, 2014; "The Global Catholic

Population," last modified February 13, 2013; "Global Christianity—A Report on the Size and Distribution of the World's Christian Population," last modified December 19, 2011; "Spirit and Power—A 10-Country Survey of Pentecostals," last modified October 5, 2006; "Overview: Pentecostalism in Latin America," last modified October 5, 2006.

330 *"global north"*: Technically, this also includes Japan, although, for the purposes of this point, Japan is excluded, since it is not a Christian country.

331 *Whereas one hundred years ago a full 90 percent*: "Global Christianity," Pew Research Center online.

331 *the bloodiest religious wars in recorded human history*: Europe's Thirty Years War at the verge of the Reformation (1618–48), which took eight million lives and triggered a famine as well as a flurry of diseases.

331 *London's churches, emptied of worshipers, are reemerging*: Lindsey Olander, "13 Grandiose Churches Reincarnated as Restaurants," *Travel + Leisure*, May 12, 2015.

331 *decommissioned and shuttered in the Netherlands*: Naftali Bendavid, "Europe's Empty Churches," *Wall Street Journal*, January 2, 2015; "Netherlands: Abandoned Church Converted into Skatepark," video uploaded January 31, 2015, by RT, 1:18, www.youtube.com/watch?v=fV3k5UntyL4.

331 *In Germany, from Berlin to Mönchengladbach*: Soeren Kern, "German Church Becomes Mosque: The New Normal," Gatestone Institute online, last modified February 13, 2013, www.gatestoneinstitute.org/3585/german -church-becomes-mosque.

331 *In Spain and Portugal*: Alice Newell-Hanson, "19 Hotels That Used to Be Churches," *Condé Nast Traveler*, March 29, 2018.

331 *not far from the White House, houses of worship*: Helen Wieffering, "DC's Old School and Church Buildings Are Getting New Life," *Greater Greater Washington*, February 1, 2018.

331 *venerable old churches reopen as breweries*: Dake Kang, Associated Press, "Holy Spirits: Closed Churches Find Second Life as Breweries," October 6, 2017.

331 *So much so that the great majority of Christians*: 61 percent, according to "Global Christianity," Pew Research Center online; Joey Marshall, "The World's Most Committed Christians," FactTank, Pew Research Center online, last modified August 22, 2018.

331 *Even as the Church is struggling financially*: In my own neighborhood in Lima, Peru, the well-known Iglesia de la Virgen Fátima is currently contemplating selling its adjoining monastery to a five-star hotel chain. The neighborhood was told it was because all the Church's money had been rerouted from Latin America to Asia or Africa, and the management needed desperately to raise funds. According to *Fortune*, February 17, 2013: "For all its splendor, the Vatican is nearly broke. . . . With investments of some $500 million, the Vatican commands fewer financial resources than many U.S. universities. . . . Curiously, the Vatican finds itself in financial straits when the Church is

showing new vitality around the world. . . . Energetic missionary work and the Pope's frequent, triumphal visits have swelled the ranks of Catholics in Africa and Asia, particularly in Nigeria and India."

331 *at the rate of ten thousand souls a day?*: Brian Smith, *Religious Politics in Latin America: Pentecostal Vs. Catholic*, 2.

332 *a man who insisted he wanted a church of and for the poor*: "Pope Francis Reveals Why He Chose His Name," *Catholic Herald*, March 16, 2013.

332 *as Pope Benedict pointed out*: "Interview of His Holiness Benedict XVI."

332 *the violence that had rattled through the latter half*: Brian Smith, 6–7.

332 *"The Catholic Church opted for the poor"*: John Berryman, quoted in Kenneth Serbin, "The Catholic Church, Religious Pluralism" (working paper 3263, Kellogg Institute for International Studies, Notre Dame, IN, February 1999).

333 *most beloved pontiffs . . . the "preferential option for the poor"*: Cleary, *How Latin America*, 90.

333 *"The wrongs done to indigenous peoples need to be"*: Pope John Paul II, "Ecclesia in Oceania," given in Rome, Saint Peter's, November 22, 2001, Apostolic Exhortation, Catholic News Agency online, www.catholicnewsagency.com /document/ecclesia-in-oceania-675.

333 *When Bishop Óscar Romero of El Salvador pleaded with him*: Gina Pianigiani, "Pope Paves Way for Sainthood for Archbishop Óscar Romero," *New York Times*, March 7, 2018.

333 *John Paul simply cautioned him*: Holly Sklar, *Washington's War on Nicaragua* (Cambridge, MA: *South End Press*, 1988), 51.

333 *"But Holy Father," Romero protested*: Ibid.

334 *it was prepared to kill as many as three hundred thousand*: The head of the National Guard, Carlos Eugenio Vides Casanova, is quoted as saying, "Today the armed forces are prepared to kill two hundred thousand to three hundred thousand, if that's what it takes to stop a Communist takeover." Ibid., 50.

334 *"We want peace!" "Power to the people!"*: Christopher Dickey, "Pope Heckled During Mass in Nicaragua," *Washington Post*, March 5, 1983.

334 *"straighten out your position with the Church!"*: Pope John Paul II, quoted in Alan Riding, "Pope Says Taking Sides in Nicaragua Is Peril to Church," *New York Times*, March 5, 1983.

334 *"Christ led me to Marx!"*: Michael Novak, "The Case Against Liberation Theology," *New York Times* online, October 21, 1984.

334 *"rapacious wolves . . . pseudospiritual movements"*: Brian Smith, 4; Edward L. Cleary, "John Paul Cries 'Wolf': Misreading the Pentecostals," *Commonweal*, November 20, 1992.

334 *blessed by and paid for by the CIA*: Brian Smith, 4.

335 *"From the very beginning, the Catholic Church"*: John Paul II, in a speech in Mexico in 1993. *"Discurso del Santo Padre Juan Pablo II,"* Viaje Apostólico a Jamaica, México y Denver, Santuario de Nuestra Señora de Izamal, August 11, 1993, Libreria Editrice Vaticana.

335 *"The great masses are without adequate"*: John Paul II, discourse in Santo Domingo, 1992, quoted in Brian Smith, 7.

336 *"We have all heard the old song"*: Samuel Rodríguez, "America: It's Time for a New Song," sermon, 2016, National Hispanic Christian Leadership Conference (the largest Evangelical/Pentecostal organization in the world).

336 *a convert was expected to attend religious services regularly*: All expectations and promises here are taken from the Pew Research report "Religion in Latin America."

336 *evangelical church is being credited with the creation of a new middle class*: Anderson Antunes, "The Richest Pastors of Brazil," *Forbes*, January 17, 2013.

336 *credited with the transformation of a number of conservative parties*: Javier Corrales, "A Perfect Marriage: Evangelicals and Conservatives in Latin America," *New York Times*, January 17, 2018.

337 *in Brazil, where a quarter of the population live in abject poverty*: Jay Forte, "More Than 50 Million Brazilians Living Below Poverty Line," *Rio Times*, December 16, 2017.

337 *a private jet worth $45 million*: This is Edir Macedo of the Universal Church of the Kingdom of God, in Rio de Janeiro. Anderson Antunes, "Richest Pastors."

337 *On one sunlit morning in Natal*: Marie Arana, "Preparing for the Pope," *New York Times*, June 19, 2013.

338 Epigraph: *"There are blows in life, so hard"*: César Vallejo, "Los heraldos negros," *Cesar Vallejo: Antología Poética* (Madrid: EDAF, 1999), 67. (My translation.)

338 *exterminated almost half a million*: J. Rodrigo, *Cautivos: Campos de concentración en la España franquista, 1936–1947* (Madrid: Editorial Crítica, 2005).

339 *Vicente Cañas, a Jesuit friend who had immersed himself so thoroughly in the indigenous*: Tamara Fariñas, "El Jesuita español que se volvió indio," *El Confidencial*, November 8, 2017.

339 *"that silly little priest"*: Ibid.

339 *pistol-whipped and shot point-blank in the neck*: C. Machado, "Secretaria de Direitos Humanos reconhece que religioso morreu vítima do regime militar," Agência Brasil, April 19, 2010. Also "João Bosco Penio Burnier, S.J.," 1976, Ignatian Solidarity Nework online, https://ignatiansolidarity.net/blog/portfolio -item/joao-bosco-penido-burnier-1976-brazil.

340 Epigraph: *"It is their natural right to be recognized"*: "Bishop Samuel Ruíz Garcia," Emily Fund online, accessed February 3, 2019, www.doonething.org/heroes /pages-r/ruiz-quotes.htm.

340 *It began when the Church sent catechists*: Enrique Krauze, *Redeemers*, 414–16.

340 *the lay deacons, eight thousand strong*: Ginger Thompson, "Vatican Curbing Deacons in Mexico," *New York Times*, March 12, 2002.

340 *a centuries-old aspiration among the Indians*: Krauze, *Redeemers*, 419.

341 *Ruíz, who had become prophet, priest, and king*: Ibid., 420.

341 *radicalized by the government's bloody 1968 Tlatelolco massacre*: James

McKinley, "Bodies Found in Mexico City May Be Victims of 1968 Massacre," *New York Times*, July 11, 2007.

341 *Trained by Cuban guerrillas*: Krauze, *Redeemers*, 437–38.

341 *a return to roots*: This is a direct quote from Octavio Paz, *In Search of the Present: Nobel Lecture 1990* (San Diego: Harcourt Brace & Company, 1990), 22.

341 *resurgence of the most ancient of all pasts, Indian Mexico*: Quote from Krauze, *Redeemers*, 433.

342 *damning the depravities Indians were too often prey to*: Ibid., 446.

342 *Zapatistas quickly adopted biblical names*: Ibid., 424.

342 *"God and his Word aren't worth a damn"*: Ibid.

342 *"Here there will be no Word of God"*: Ibid., 425.

342 *Root (slōp in Tzeltal Mayan), a clandestine group*: John Womack Jr. et al., in *Rebellion in Chiapas: An Historical Reader*, ed. Womack (New York: New Press, 1999). Also quoted in Enrique Krauze, "Chiapas: The Indians' Prophet," *New York Review of Books* 45, December 16, 1999.

342 *"These people [the Zapatistas] have arrived to mount a saddled horse"*: Krauze, *Redeemers*, 425.

342 *Three years later . . . the carnage would continue*: On December 22, 1997, in the tiny village of Acteal, forty-five people (twenty-one women, fifteen children, and nine men) were murdered in a local shrine. Krauze, "Chiapas."

342 *Forty thousand government troops would descend*: Ibid.

342 *"The truth is that for the indigenous"*: Womack, *Rebellion in Chiapas*.

343 *the Vatican tried to muzzle him*: Molly Moore, "Embattled Chiapas Mediator Steps Aside," *Washington Post*, August 3, 1998.

343 *Dubbed the "Red Bishop"*: Ibid.

343 *Guatemala's systematic purge of nearly a quarter million*: "Press Briefing: Guatemala Historical Clarification Commission, United Nations, March 1, 1999"; Mireya Navarro, "Guatemalan Army Waged 'Genocide,' New Report Finds," *New York Times*, February 26, 1999.

343 *Its drug wars have generated catastrophic human losses*: "Mexico Drug War Fast Facts," CNN online, last modified July 26, 2018, https://edition.cnn .com/2013/09/02/world/americas/mexico-drug-war-fast-facts/index.html.

343 *Mexico is the most dangerous country*: "Mexico Is One of the Most Dangerous Countries for Priests," Aid to the Church in Need (CAN) online, last modified March 8, 2018, www.churchinneed.org/mexico-one-dangerous-countries-priests.

343 *Drug lords make a point to attend Catholic Church services*: La Familia Michoacana, which does this, "became widely known in 2006 when its members stormed a disco and threw the severed heads of five men on the dance floor along with a sign that read 'La Familia doesn't kill for money, doesn't kill women doesn't kill innocents. Those who die deserve to die. Let everyone know, this is divine justice.'" Dudley Althaus, "Mexico Catches Reputed Leader of La Familia Cartel," *Houston Chronicle*, June 21, 2011; also George

Grayson, *La Familia Drug Cartel: Implications for U.S. Mexican Security* (Carlisle, PA: Strategic Studies Institute, 2010), 5, 35–37, 46, 101.

343 *Xavier Albó was visiting with Ruíz during the peace talks*: Albó and Ruiz, 465–66.

344 Epigraph: *"'Religion' suggests something structured"*: David Choquehuanca, chancellor of Bolivia, in conversation with Xavier Albó. Ibid., 357.

344 *The native populations . . . have survived to different degrees*: Useful statistics can be found in the CIA's World Factbook (www.cia.gov/library/publications /the-world-factbook), which is constantly updated. According to it, Brazil, for instance, is 47.7 percent white, 43.1 percent mulatto, and only .4 percent indigenous; Argentina is 97.2 percent European descent and 2.4 percent Amerindian; Ecuador is 71.9 percent mestizo; Bolivia is 68 percent mestizo and 20 percent indigenous; Colombia is 84.2 percent mestizo/white and 10.4 percent mulatto.

344 *As soon as Spain was able to impose some semblance of control*: Arana, *Bolívar*, 11–12; John Miller, *Memoirs of General Miller* (London: Longman, Rees, Orme, Brown & Green, 1828), 1:5.

345 *the Cosmic Race. La raza cósmica*: José Vasconcelos, *La raza cósmica* (México, DF: Espasa Calpe, 1948), 47–51.

345 *"We are all men of La Mancha"*: Fuentes, 192.

345 *"When we understand that none of us is pure"*: Ibid, 193.

345 *Bolivia's Indians referred to themselves instead as* campesinos: Albó and Ruiz, 385–68.

346 *race is devilishly hard to catalog*: Peter Wade, *Race and Ethnicity in Latin America* (London: Pluto, 2010), 155–61.

346 *("El Chino" Alberto Fujimori)*: Gille Fromka, "Why Did Peruvians Call President Alberto Fujimori 'El Chino' When He Was of Japanese Heritage?," Quora, April 7, 2017.

346 *the Mexican billionaire "El Turco" Carlos Slim*: "A True Eastern Star: Carlos Selim El Turco," World Turkish Coalition, March 12, 2010. Slim is actually of Lebanese origin.

346 *Guaraní is spoken by the overwhelming majority*: Simon Romero, "An Indigenous Language with Staying Power," *New York Times*, March 12, 2012.

346 *a minuscule population—2 percent*: Ibid.

346 *90 percent of all Paraguayans*: Oishimaya Sen Nag, "What Languages Are Spoken in Paraguay?," World Atlas, last modified August 1, 2017, www .worldatlas.com/articles/what-languages-are-spoken-in-paraguay.

346 *For the 80 percent who count themselves Catholic*: A full 80 percent, although only 25 percent attend church regularly. Ronnie Kahn, "Religion in Latin America," *Newsletter of the Outreach Services of the African, Asian, Latin American, and Russian Studies Centers University of Illinois at Urbana-Champaign*, no. 86 (Spring 2002).

346 *Latin American Christianity . . . is infused with superstition*: Aldo Rubén Ameigeiras, "Ortodoxia doctrinaria y viejas ritualidades," in *Cruces, intersecciones, conflictos: Relaciones Político-Religiosas en Latinoamérica*, 212–26.

346 *"You cannot be truly religious here if you are not interreligious"*: Albó does not name the superior general who said this, but it was probably Pedro Arrupe, a Basque, who was the superior general of the Jesuits from 1965–1983. Albó and Ruiz, 307.

346 *the urge in this fickle landscape is also toward change*: Nine percent of Brazilians now say they follow no religion. Forty percent of Uruguayans claim no religious affiliation whatsoever. Philip Jenkins, "A Secular Latin America?" *Christian Century*, March 12, 2013. Other harbingers of change: Journalist Paulina Trujillo has established an atheist news organization in Quito, "Gracias a Dios soy Ateo, Thank God I'm an Atheist," https://www.atheism andhumor.com. Juan Gabriel Vásquez, an established novelist-journalist in Bogotá and a self-professed atheist, insists on a secular education for his children. Such bold, public rejections of the church would have been unthinkable a generation ago.

347 *Francis carefully avoided . . . sexual abuse scandal*: "Iglesia y abusos," editorial, *El País* (Madrid), September 15, 2018.

347 *"Politics is in crisis"*: Pope Francis I, in Stauffer and Pullella, "Pope Ends Latin American Trip."

347 *Odebrecht scandal, the largest foreign bribery case*: Linda Pressly, BBC World Service online, last modified April 22, 2018, www.bbc.com/news/business -43825294.

347 *"What is wrong with Peru"*: Stauffer and Pullella, "Pope Ends Latin American Trip."

347 *"Many grave sins were committed"*: Pope Francis I, quoted in Jim Yardley, "In Bolivia, Pope Francis Apologizes for Church's 'Grave Sins,'" *New York Times* online, July 9, 2015. Also "Pope Francis Asks for Forgiveness for Crimes Committed During the Conquest of America," uploaded to YouTube by Rome Reports on July 9, 2015, 1:42, www.youtube.com/watch?v=xi-KjE HBFjg.

347 *"infidelities to the Gospel . . . especially during the second millennium"*: Pope John Paul II, "Homily of the Holy Father, 'Day of Pardon,' Sunday, 12 March 2000," https://w2.vatican.va/content/john-paul-ii/en/homilies/2000/documents /hf_jp-ii_hom_20000312_pardon.html.

347 *"I humbly ask forgiveness"*: Pope Francis I, quoted in Yardley, "Pope Francis Apologizes."

348 Epigraph: *"If someone asks me if I believe in kharisiri"*: *"Si me pregunta si creo en los kharisiri, diré que no, pero respeto profundamente a quienes creen en eso."* *Kharisiri* is the Aymara equivalent of *pishtaco* (Quechua), evil phantom goblins that come from foreign lands to exploit the Indians. Albó and Ruiz, 301.

348 tata tapukillu: *our father of endless questions*: Ibid., 288.

348 *"the most terrifying tribe"*: Albó, interview by author, February 20, 2016. He is paraphrasing the Catalan sociologist Carmen Salcedo, who said this to him about the Jesuits in Bolivia.

349 *"I don't want to conquer souls"*: Ibid., February 21, 2016.

349 las tres patas: Ibid., February 22, 2016.

349 *"There is nothing religious about this"*: Ibid.

349 *"I am not one to pray"*: Ibid., February 20, 2016.

350 *"For us, it is more deep inside"*: Albó and Ruiz, 301.

350 *"There's an image I can't quite get out of my mind"*: Ibid., February 22, 2016. Albó later told the gist of this story in his memoir, *Un curioso incorregible*, 218, 313.

350 *"I'm telling you this"*: Ibid., February 23, 2016.

350 *The prayer card with Lizardi's likeness*: Albó and Ruiz, 218.

350 *"So you see. It's a fraught business"*: Albó, interview by author, February 22, 2016. He essentially repeats this thought in *Un curioso incorregible*, 313.

EPILOGUE: IT'S JUST OUR NATURE

351 Epigraph: *"Stress is transgenerational"*: Ali B. Rodgers and Tracy L. Bale, "Germ Cell Origins of Posttraumatic Stress Disorder Risk—The Transgenerational Impact of Parental Stress Experience," *Biological Psychiatry* 78, no. 5 (September 1, 2015): 307–14. This is paraphrased for clarity. The full quote is: "Critically, the consequences of *stress experiences are transgenerational, with parental stress exposure impacting stress reactivity and PTSD risk in subsequent generations.* Potential molecular mechanisms underlying this transmission have been explored in rodent models that specifically examine the paternal lineage, identifying epigenetic signatures in male germ cells as possible substrates of transgenerational programming." (The italics are mine to indicate what is quoted.)

351 *Juan Gabriel Vásquez . . . tells of the moment*: Juan Gabriel Vásquez in conversation with Jonathan Yardley at Politics and Prose bookstore, Washington, DC, October 5, 2018. A photograph of the jar with the segment of Gaitán's vertebrae also appears in his novel *The Shape of the Ruins* (New York: Riverhead, 2018), 66.

353 *Perhaps that is why we are so predisposed*: Carlos Rangel, *Del buen salvage al buen revolucionario* (Madrid: Editorial FAES, 2007), loc. 258–319.

353 *When Peru's poverty rose in 2018*: Reuters, "Peru Poverty Rate Rises for the First Time in 16 Years," April 24, 2018.

353 *When rumors of impending coups cropped up*: Natalia Sobrevilla, "El espectro del golpe de Estado," *El Comercio* (Lima), November, 7, 2018.

353 *How is it that Argentina, the fifth richest country in the world*: Rosenberg, 118.

353 *How is it that Venezuela, with the largest proven oil reserves*: Jessica Dillinger, "The World's Largest Oil Reserves by Country," World Atlas, last modified January 8, 2019, www.worldatlas.com/articles/the-world-s-largest-oil-re serves-by-country.html. The top three are Venezuela, 300,878 billion barrels; Saudi Arabia, 266,455 billion barrels; and Canada, 169,709 barrels.

354 *Carlos Rangel once said that the ten thousand kilometers that separate*: Rangel, *Del buen salvage*, loc. 258–319.

354 *Rangel, who despised Castro's Communist dictatorship*: Enrique de Diego, "Retratos: Carlos Rangel," Club de Libertad Digital, no. 2, www.clublibertad digital.com/ilustracion-liberal/2/carlos-rangel-enrique-de-diego.html.

354 *the spate of Latin American countries*: Specifically, Brazil, Colombia, Peru, Mexico, and Central America's Northern Triangle (Guatemala, Honduras, El Salvador).

355 *terrorism became "narconomics"*: This is Tom Wainwright's term, coined when he was the Mexico correspondent for the *Economist* and explained in his book *Narconomics: How to Run a Drug Cartel* (New York: PublicAffairs, 2016).

355 *a ready-made fighting force for the drug trade*: Bello, "Peace, at Last, in Colombia," *Economist*, June 25, 2016. See also "Growth of *Bandas Crimi-nales*," US Department of State Bureau for International Narcotics and Law Enforcement Affairs, *International Narcotics Control Strategy Report*, vol. 1, *Drug and Chemical Control* (Washington, DC: March 2012), 170–71.

355 *Illegal drugs, as one economist has suggested, are Latin America's new silver*: Steven Topik, Carlos Marichal, and Zephyr Frank, eds., *From Silver to Cocaine: Latin America Commodity Chains and the Building of the World Economy, 1500–2000*, esp. ch. 12, Paul Gootenberg, "Cocaine in Chains: The Rise and Demise of Global Commodity, 1860–1950" (Durham, NC: Duke University Press, 2006), 321–51.

355 *it involves veritable armies of narco-operatives*: Jeremy Haken, "Transnational Crime in the Developing World," Global Financial Integrity online, last modified February 8, 2011.

355 *few citizens whose lives it doesn't touch*: Saalar Aghili, "The Rise of Cocaine in Peru," *Berkeley Political Review*, May 16, 2016.

355 *With revenues in the hundreds of billions of dollars*: Haken, "Transnational Crime," 4.

355 *among the most valuable single commodity chains in world history*: Gootenberg, "Cocaine in Chains," 345–46.

355 *from Santiago to Mexico City*: The Andean drug trade flows through Chile, much as the Colombian and Caribbean trade flows north through Mexico. According to the nonprofit investigative organization InSight Crime: "Chile serves as a transshipment point for cocaine leaving the coca-producing countries of Bolivia and Peru. . . . With an estimated 71 percent of the cocaine from Bolivia passing through Arica, the Chilean port appears to be one of the major transshipment points in the country, along with the other coastal cities of Iquique, Antofagasta, and Mejillones." Tristan Clavel, "Report Finds Drug Trafficking Through Chile Is on the Rise," InSight Crime, last modified December 19, 2016. See also Jason Lange, "From Spas to Banks, Mexico Economy Rides on Drugs," Reuters, January 22, 2010.

356 *Venezuela has succeeded in reinventing itself as a narco-mafia state*: The

Venezuelan oil powerhouse PDVSA (Petróleos de Venezuela) worked independently for decades, but under Chávez and Maduro, it financed government projects. In 1979–81 Venezuela was responsible for laundering narco-dollars from one metric ton of illegal drugs; thirty-seven years later, it was laundering the equivalent of fifty to sixty metric tons. Profits from the sale of drugs empowers it to control the politics of the nation. Panel discussion between Ambassador William Brownfield and Juan Zarate, moderated by Moisés Rendon, Center for Strategic and International Studies, October 12, 2018, www.csis.org.

356 *90 percent of all US dollar bills*: Yuegang Zuo, professor of biochemistry, University of Massachusetts, Dartmouth. Bills turned up positive for cocaine in these percentages in certain cities: 100 percent: Detroit, Boston, Orlando, Miami, Los Angeles; 88 percent: Toronto; 77 percent: Salt Lake City. Madison Park, CNN online, last modified August 17, 2009.

356 *the physical enslavement of twenty-three million human beings*: To be exact, it is 22.85 million; 6 million in the United States; 10 million in all the Americas; 5 million in Europe. "Number of Cocaine Users Worldwide from 2010 to 2016, by Region (in Millions)," Statista, accessed February 3, 2019, www.statista .com.

356 *Since 2006, more than a quarter million Mexicans*: "Drug War Statistics," Drug Policy Alliance online, accessed February 3, 2019, www.drugpolicy.org/issues /drug-war-statistics; see also José de Córdoba and Juan Montes, "It's a Crisis of Civilization in Mexico," *Wall Street Journal*, November 14, 2018.

356 *thirteen thousand were mowed down in drug-related violence*: "Mexico Drug War Fast Facts," CNN online, last modified July 16, 2018.

356 *Almost forty thousand Mexicans*: Córdoba and Montes, "Crisis of Civilization."

356 *five severed heads were flung onto a crowded dance floor*: "Human Heads Dumped in Mexico Bar," BBC News online, modified September 7, 2006.

356 *An equivalent number of Colombians—more than 220,000 to be exact*: Nick Miroff, "The Staggering Toll of Colombia's War with FARC Rebels, Explained in Numbers," *Washington Post* online, August 24, 2016.

356 *Almost 8 million souls have been displaced*: "The Countries with Most Internal Displacement," in *Global Trends: Forced Displacement in 2017* (Geneva: United Nations Refugee Agency, 2018), https://www.unhcr.org/5b27be547.pdf.

356 *Tens of thousands of children were kidnapped*: Hudson, *Colombia*, 335.

356 *peace process in Colombia . . . reduced the murder rate*: "Murder South of the Border," Editorial, *Washington Post* online, September 30, 2018.

356 *millions of refugees have fled*: Brownfield and Zarate, discussion.

357 *Brazil's drug-related homicides in a single year*: The year is 2017. Chris Feliciano Arnold, "Brazil Has Become a Gangland," *Foreign Policy*, June 6, 2017, https:// foreignpolicy.com/2017/06/06/brazil-has-become-a-gangland-prison-riot.

357 *forty-three of the fifty most violent cities of the world are in Latin America*: Macias and Engel, "50 Most Violent Cities."

357 *extractive societies . . . are built on social injustice*: Acemoglu and Robinson,
399. The cost of Latin America's reliance on mining and farming were in
full evidence by the end of the nineteenth century when life expectancy in
certain areas was below twenty-seven years, literacy was as low as 2 percent,
and considerably more than half the total population lived in utter poverty.
Fuentes, 281–82.

357 *According to polls, the overwhelming majority believe*: Four in five believe
their governments are corrupt, while three out of four have no confidence
in government institutions. That level has fallen since 2010. A quarter of the
population live in poverty; 40 percent of all Latin Americans belong to the
"vulnerable" middle class, and this year, in some countries, a portion of those
have slipped back into poverty. The CAF report *Economic Outlook for Latin
America 2018* is described in "Confidence in Government Institutions, the Key
to Growth in Latin America," CAF Development Bank of Latin America
online, last modified April 9, 2018.

357 *the police and the army are co-opted*: Rachel Kleinfeld, "The Violence Driving
Migration Isn't Just Gangs," *Wall Street Journal*, November 10, 2018. Klein-
feld's essay is from her book *A Savage Order: How the World's Deadliest
Countries Can Forge a Path to Security* (New York: Pantheon, 2018).

357 *In El Salvador in 2015, the vice president*: This is Óscar Ortíz Ascencio.
Kleinfeld, "Violence Driving Migration."

357 *"without fear of suffering consequences"*: Ibid.

358 *"We are rotten to the core," the drug czar said*: This is Gustavo Alberto
Landaverde, former deputy drug czar of Honduras, who was fired from
his job, sued for libel, and, two weeks after this interview, killed by hit men
on motorbikes. Frances Robles, "Honduras Becomes Murder Capital of the
World," *Miami Herald*, January 23, 2012.

358 *a gargantuan Brazilian operation totaling billions of dollars*: $4.5 billion is the
total dollar amount of penalties levied on Odebrecht so far for its bribes and
payoffs. US Department of Justice, Office of Public Affairs, "Odebrecht and
Braskem Plead Guilty," December 21, 2016. Also Extra Fieser, "Colombia
Reveals Odebrecht Bribes Were Three Times Larger Than Previously
Known," Bloomberg, August 15, 2018.

358 *Latin American politics was in crisis*: Stauffer and Pullella, "Pope Ends Latin
American Trip."

358 cédulas de Gracias al Sacar: Bethell, *History of Latin America*, 3:30.

358 *as Chilean Cardinal Raul Silva Henríquez once offered them to General Pinochet*:
Rosenberg, 344. To be fair, Silva was probably hoping to put a foot in the
palace door. He became a stubborn opponent of Pinochet once the dictator
took absolute power into his hands.

358 *priests who boast that they have accepted donations*: This was documented in
Colombia in the 1980s and 1990s. Rosenberg, 62.

359 *As the Jesuit Xavier Albó put it so aptly*: Albó, interview by author, February 21,

2016. The three commandments of Inca society—*ama suwa, ama llulla, ama qhella*—actually correspond to the "*tres patas*," the three legs of the stool Albó claimed was necessary for a healthy polity. Do not steal (economic); do not lie (political); do not go idle (educational).

359 *American documentary filmmaker who arranged to educate her children*: This is the Oscar-nominated director Richard E. Robbins, whose film *Girl Rising* (New York: the Documentary Group, 2013) centered on the lives of ten young girls from underprivileged pockets around the world. Senna, Leonor's youngest daughter, was one of those girls. The film's associated campaign (also called "Girl Rising") assisted the family in educating Senna and her little brother, Henrry. I was one of the scriptwriters for the film.

360 *Nor do court records that register his petty burglaries*: County court records, Dade County, Florida, and Metairie, Louisiana, 2004 to 2017.

360 *he has used democracy to undermine democracy*: I have taken this phrase from Enrique Krauze's brilliant essay on Hugo Chávez, "The Shah of Venezuela," *New Republic*, April 1, 2009.

361 *Columbus put the first brick in the lie*: Rangel, *Del buen salvage*, loc. 258–319.

361 *American history is longer, larger, more various*: James Baldwin, "A Talk to Teachers," *The Price of the Ticket* (New York: St. Martin's Press, 1985), 332.

362 *one eminent historian of pre-Columbian cultures*: I owe this insight about the "ands" of Latin American history to my colleague John W. Hessler, distinguished curator of the Jay I. Kislak Collection, fellow of the Royal Geographical Society, author of numerous books, and specialist in geographic information science in the Geography and Map Division of the Library of Congress. John spoke of the "ands" at a tribute to the late Jay I. Kislak at a meeting of the library's Madison Council on October 18, 2019. I echo his remarks in these last paragraphs.

BIBLIOGRAPHY

Primary Sources

Acosta, Padre Ioseph (José) de. *Historia Natural y Moral de las Indias.* 4 vols. Sevilla: Juan de León, 1590.

Arzáns de Orsúa y Vela, Bartolomé, *Historia de la villa imperial de Potosí* (1736). La Paz: Plural, 2000.

———. *Historia de la villa imperial de Potosí.* 3 vols. Edited by Lewis Hanke and Gunnar Mendoza. Providence: Brown University Press, 1965.

Betanzos, Juan de. *Suma y narración de los Yngas* (1576). 3 vols. Cochabamba, Bo.: Fondo Rotatorio, 1993.

Cervantes de Salazar, Francisco. *Life in the Imperial and Loyal City of Mexico in New Spain* (1554). Facsimile of original. Translated by Minnie Lee Barrett Shepard. Austin: University of Texas Press, 1953. Digital version available at Miguel de Cervantes Virtual Library Foundation, www.cervantesvirtual.com.

Chimalpahin Quauhtlehuanitzin, Domingo Francisco de San Antón Muñon. *Historia Mexicana (1606–31).* Lincoln Center, MA: Conemex Associates, 1978.

Cieza de León, Pedro de. *Crónica del Perú* (Sevilla, 1533). 3 vols. Lima: Pontificia Universidad Católica del Perú, 1984.

———. *The Discovery and Conquest of Peru: Chronicles of the New World Encounter.* Durham, NC: Duke University Press, 1998.

Cobo, Bernabé. *Historia del Nuevo mundo* (1653). 4 vols. Sevilla: Impresa E. Rasco, 1890–95.

———. *History of the Inca Empire: An Account of the Indians' Customs and Their Origin.* Translated and edited by Roland Hamilton. Austin: University of Texas Press, 1979.

———. *Inca Religion and Customs* (1653). Translated and edited by Roland Hamilton. Austin: University of Texas Press, 1990.

Collapiña, Supno y otros Quipucamayos. "Relación de los Quipucamayos." In *Relación de la descendencia, gobierno y conquista de los Incas*, edited by Juan José Vega. Lima: Biblioteca Universitaria, 1974.

Colón, Cristóbal (Christopher Columbus). *Relaciones y cartas de Cristóbal Colón.* Madrid: Librería de la Viuda de Hernández, 1892.

Colón, Fernando. *Vida del almirante don Cristóbal Colón.* Edited by Ramón Iglesia. Madrid: Librería de la Viuda de Hernández, 1892.

Cortés, Hernán. *Cartas del famoso conquistador Hernán Cortés al emperador Carlos Quinto*. México, DF: Imprenta de I. Escalante, 1870.

———. *Cartas de Relación*, 12 vols. Seville: Jacobo Cromberger, 1522 (John Carter Brown Library).

———. *Cartas de Relación*. Edited by Angel Delgado Gómez. Madrid: Clásicos Castalia, 1993.

———. *Cartas y relaciones de Hernán Cortés al emperador Carlos V.* Paris: Imprenta Central de los Ferro-Carriles A. Chaix y, ca. 1856.

———. *Hernán Cortés: Letters from Mexico.* Translated and edited by Anthony R. Pagden, New York: Grossman, 1971.

Díaz del Castillo, Bernal. *The Discovery and Conquest of Mexico.* New York: Da Capo Press, 1996.

———. *Historia verdadera de la conquista de la Nueva España* (1632). Madrid: Biblioteca Americana, 1992.

Durán, Fray Diego. *The Aztecs: The History of the Indies of New Spain (1586–88).* Translated by Doris Heyden and Fernando Horcasitas. New York: Orion, 1964.

Enríquez de Guzmán, Alonso. *Libro de la vida y los costumbres de Don Alonso Enríquez de Guzmán.* Madrid: Ediciones Atlas, 1960. Also Barcelona: www.linkgua-digital.com, 2016.

———. *Vida y aventuras de un caballero noble desbaratado: Crónica de la Conquista del Perú: 1535–1539.* Cantuta, Perú: Ediciones Universidad Nacional de Educación, 1970.

Estete, Miguel de. *Noticia del Perú* (1540). Quito: Boletín de la Sociedad Ecuatoriana de Estudios Históricos, 1919.

Florentine Codex: General History of the Things of New Spain. Translated by Arthur J. O. Anderson and Charles E. Dibble. Pts. 1–13. Provo: School of American Research, University of Utah, 1970–82.

García Icazbalceta, Joaquín. *Nueva colección de documentos para la historia de México.* 3 vols. México, DF: Salvador Chavez Hayhoe, 1941.

Garcilaso, El Inca. *La Florida* (Lisbon, 1605). Madrid: Rodriguez Franco, 1723.

———. *Royal Commentaries of Peru.* 4 vols. Translated by Sir Paul Ricaut. London: Flesher, 1688.

Grijalva, Juan de. *The Discovery of New Spain in 1518.* Translated and edited by Henry R. Wagner. Pasadena, CA: Cortés Society, 1942.

Guaman Poma de Ayala, Felipe [Waman Puma]. *El primer nueva corónica y buen gobierno* (Madrid, 1615). 3 vols. Edited by John V. Mirra and Rolena Adorno. México, DF: Siglo Veintiuno, 1980.

Herrera y Tordesillas, Antonio de. *The General History of the Vast Continent and Islands of America.* 6 vols. Translated by Captain John Stevens. Reprint from 1740 edition. New York: AMS Press, 1973.

Las Casas, Fray Bartolomé de. *Historia de las Indias (1523–1548).* 3 vols. Madrid: Biblioteca Nacional, 1947.

———. *Obras completas*, 15 vols. Madrid: Alianza, 1988–98.

————. *A Short History of the Destruction of the Indies* (1542). London: Penguin, 1974.

————. *Vida de Cristóbal Colón*. Barcelona: Red ediciones, www.linkgua-digital.com, 2018.

López de Gómara, Francisco. *Historia General de las Indias* (1552). 2 vols. Madrid: Espasa-Calpe, 1932.

Mena, Cristóbal de [attributed to]. *La conquista del Perú, llamada la Nueva Castilla* (Seville, 1534). New York: New York Public Library Edition, 1929.

Murúa, Martín de. *Historia del origen y genealogía de los reyes incas del Perú* (Madrid, 1590). Madrid: Instituto Santo Toribio de Mogrovejo, 1946.

————. *Historia general del Perú*. Edited by Manuel Ballesteros. Madrid: Ediciones Historia, 1986.

Nuñez Cabeza de Vaca, Álvar. *La relación y comentarios del gobernador Alvar nuñez cabeça de vaca, de lo acaescido en las dos jornadas que hizo a las Indias* (Valladolid, Sp.: Los señores del consejo, 1555). In Enrique de Vedias: *Historiadores Primitivos de Indias*. Vol. 1 (Madrid: Rivadeneyra, 1852).

————. and Ulrich Schmidt. *The Conquest of the River Plate (1535–1555)*. Vol. 1, *Voyage of Ulrich Schmidt* (1567). Vol. 2, *The Commentaries of Alvar Nuñez Cabeza de Vaca* (1555). Edited by Luis L. Domínguez. New York: Burt Franklin, 1890. Also available on Project Gutenberg, www.gutenberg.org/ebooks/48058.

Ocaña, Fray Diego de. *Un viaje fascinante por la América Hispana del siglo 16*. Madrid: Studium, 1969.

Oviedo y Valdés, Gonzalo Fernandez de. *Historia General y Natural de las Indias* (1547). 4 vols. Madrid: Imprenta de la Real Academia de la Historia, 1851.

Pané, Fray Ramón. *An Account of the Antiquities of the Indians* (1571). Durham, NC: Duke University Press, 1999.

Pentland, Joseph B. *Informe sobre Bolivia, 1827*. Potosí, Bol.: Editorial Potosí, 1975.

————. *Report on Bolivia, 1827*. Condensed in English. Edited by J. Valerie Fifer. Royal Historical Society. London: *Camden Miscellany*, no. 35, 1974.

Pizarro, Pedro. *Relación del Descubrimiento y Conquista de los Reinos del Perú* (1571). Buenos Aires: Editorial Futuro, 1944.

————. *Relation of the Discovery*. 2 vols. Translated by Philip Ainsworth Means. New York: Cortés Society, 1921.

Porras Barrenechea, Raúl, ed. *Cartas del Perú, Colección de documentos inéditos para la historia del Perú*. Vol. 3. Lima: Edición de la Sociedad de Bibliófilos Peruanos, 1959.

————. *Relaciones primitivas de la conquista del Perú*. Lima: Universidad de San Marcos, 1967.

Quintana, Manuel José. *Vidas de Españoles Célebres* (1805). Barcelona: R. Plana, 1941.

Ruiz de Montoya, Antonio. *Conquista espiritual hecha por los religiosos de la Compañía de Jesús en las provincias de Paraguay, Paraná, Uruguay y Tape* (ca. 1650). Translated by Arthur Rabuske. Porto Alegre, Brazil: Martins Livreiro, 1985.

Sahagún, Fray Bernardino de. *Historia general de las cosas de Nueva España* (1547–80). 3 vols. México, DF: Imprenta Alejandro Valdés, 1829–30.

Salinas y Cordova, Fray Buenaventura de. *Memorial de las historias del nuevo mundo: Pirú* (1630). Lima: Universidad de San Marcos, 1957.

Sancho de Hoz, Pedro. *Relación de la conquista del Perú* (1539). Rioja, Spain: Amigos de la Historia de Calahorra, 2004.

Sancho Rayon, José and Francisco de Zabalburu. *Colección de documentos inéditos para la historia de España*. Vol. 85. Madrid: Imprenta de Miguel Ginesta, 1886.

Santa Cruz Pachacuti Yamqui Salcamayhua, Juan de. *Relación de antigüedades de este reino del Perú* (1613). Edited by Carlos Araníbar. Lima: Fondo de Cultura Económica, 1995.

Sarmiento de Gamboa, Pedro. *Historia de los Incas* (1572). Buenos Aires: Colección Hórreo, Emecé Editores, 1942.

———. *History of the Incas*. Translated by Brian Bauer and Vania Smith. Austin: University of Texas Press, 2007.

———. *History of the Incas*. Translated by Clements Markham. Project Gutenberg, www.gutenberg.org/ebooks/20218.

Tito Cusi Yupanqui. *A 16th-Century Account of the Conquest*. Originally published as *Instrucción del Inga Don Diego de Castro Titu Cusi Yumangui para el muy ilustre Señor el Licenciado Lope García de Castro* (1570). Cambridge, MA: Harvard University Press, 2005.

Torquemada, Fray Juan de. *Los veinte i un libros rituales y Monarquía Indiana* (Madrid, 1615), 6 vols. México, DF: Universidad Nacional Autónomo de México, 1975.

Xerez, Francisco de. *True Account of the Conquest of Peru (1522–48)*. Edited by Iván R. Reyna. New York: Peter Lang, 2013.

Zárate, Agustin de. *Historia del descubrimiento y conquista del Peru* (1548). 4 vols. Baltimore: Penguin, 1968.

CONTEMPORARY SOURCES

Acemoglu, Daron, and James A. Robinson. *Why Nations Fail: The Origins of Power, Prosperity, and Poverty*. New York: Crown, 2012.

Adorno, Rolena. *Guaman Poma: Writing and Resistance in Colonial Peru*. Austin: University of Texas Press, 1986.

———. *The Polemics of Possession in Spanish American Narrative*. New Haven, CT: Yale University Press, 2007.

Albó Corrons, Xavier. *Cabalgando entre dos mundos*. Eds. Albó, Tomás Greaves, Godofredo Sandoval. La Paz: Centro de Investigación y Promoción del Campesinado (CIPCA), 1983.

———. *La comunidad hoy*. La Paz: CIPCA, 1990.

———. *Obras selectas*, 4 vols. La Paz: Fundación Xavier Albó y CIPCA, 2016.

Albó Corrons, Xavier, and Matías Preiswerk. *Los Señores del Gran Poder*. La Paz: Centro de Teología Popular, 1986.

Albó Corrons, Xavier, and Carmen Beatriz Ruiz. *Un curioso incorregible*. La Paz: Fundación Xavier Albó, 2017.

Ameigeiras, Aldo Rubén, ed. *Cruces, intersecciones, conflictos: Relaciones Político-Religiosas en Latinoamérica*. Buenos Aires: CLACSO, 2012.

Amunátegui, Miguel Luis, y Diego Barros Arana. *La iglesia frente a la emancipación americana*. Santiago: Empresa Editora Austral, 1960.

Anderson, Charles L. G. *Old Panama and Castilla del Oro*. Boston: Page, 1911.

Andrien, Kenneth J. *The Human Tradition in Colonial Latin America*. Wilmington, DE: SR Books, 2002.

Andrien, Kenneth, and Rolena Adorno. *Transatlantic Encounters: Europeans and Andeans in the Sixteenth Century*. Berkeley: University of California Press, 1991.

Arana, Marie. *Simón Bolívar: American Liberator*. New York: Simon & Schuster, 2013.

Arana, Pedro Pablo. *Las minas de azogue del Perú*. Lima: El Luvero, 1901.

Arciniegas, Germán. *America in Europe: A History of the New World in Reverse*. Translated by R. Victoria Arana. San Diego: Harcourt Brace Jovanovich, 1986.

———. *Con América nace la nueva historia*. Bogotá: Tercer Mundo, 1990.

———. *Latin America: A Cultural History*. New York: Knopf, 1967.

Bakewell, Peter. *Miners of the Red Mountain: Indian Labor in Potosí, 1545–1650*. Albuquerque: University of New Mexico, 1984.

Barradas, Jose Pérez de. *Orfebrería prehispánica de Colombia*. Madrid: Jura, 1958.

Bassett, Molly H. *The Fate of Earthly Things: Aztec Gods and God-Bodies*. Austin: University of Texas, 2015.

Benson, Elizabeth P., and Anita G. Cook. *Ritual Sacrifice in Ancient Peru*. Austin: University of Texas, 2001.

Betances, Emelio. *The Catholic Church and Power Politics in Latin America: The Dominican Case in Comparative Perspective*. Lanham, MD: Rowman & Littlefield, 2007.

Bernal, Antonio Miguel. *España, proyecto inacabado: Los Costes/beneficios del Imperio*. Madrid: Fundación Carolina, 2005.

Bernstein, Peter L. *The Power of Gold: The History of an Obsession*. Hoboken, NJ: Wiley & Sons, 2000.

Brading, David. *El Ocaso Novohispano: Testimonios Documentales*. México: Instituto Nacional de Antropología e Historia, 1996.

Bray, Tamara L., ed. *The Archaeology of Wak'as: Explorations of the Sacred in the Pre-Columbian Andes*. Boulder: University Press of Colorado, 2015.

Brown, Kendall. *A History of Mining in Latin America: From the Colonial Era to the Present*. Albuquerque: University of New Mexico, 2012.

Busto Duthurburu, José Antonio. *La Conquista del Perú*. Lima: Librería Studium Editores, 1981.

———. *Pizarro*. 2 vols. Lima: Ediciones COPÉ, 2001.

———. *La Platería en el Perú: dos mil años de arte e historia*. Lima: Banco del Sur del Perú, 1996.

Canudas Sandoval, Enrique. *Las Venas de plata en la historia de México.* 3 vols. Tabasco, Mexico: Universidad Juárez, 2005.

Cañizares Esguerra, Jorge. *Puritan Conquistadors: Iberianizing the Atlantic, 1550–1700.* Stanford, CA: Stanford University Press, 2006.

Casaús Arzú, Marta Elena. *Genocidio: ¿La máxima expresión del racismo en Guatemala?* Ciudad de Guatemala: F&G Editores, 2008.

———. *Guatemala: Linaje y racismo.* Ciudad de Guatemala: FLACSO, 2007.

Castañeda, Jorge G. *Utopia Unarmed: The Latin American Left After the Cold War.* New York: Knopf, 1993.

Chacon, Richard J., and Rubén G. Mendoza. *Latin American Indigenous Warfare and Ritual Violence.* Tucson: University of Arizona, 2007.

Cisneros Velarde, Leonor, and Luis Guillermo Lumbreras. *Historia General del Ejercito Peruano.* 5 vols. Lima: Imprenta del Ministerio de Guerra, 1980.

Clayton, Lawrence A. *Bartolomé de las Casas and the Conquest of the Americas.* Viewpoints/Puntos de Vista. Edited by Jürgen Buchenau. West Sussex, UK: John Wiley & Sons, 2011.

———. *The Bolivarian Nations of Latin America.* Arlington, IL: Forum, 1984.

Cleary, Edward L. *How Latin America Saved the Soul of the Catholic Church.* Mahwah, NJ: Paulist Press, 2009.

Cleary, Edward L., and Hannah W. Stewart-Gambino. *Power, Politics, and Pentecostals in Latin America.* Boulder, CO: Westview Press, 1997.

Dean, Carolyn. *A Culture of Stone: Inka Perspectives on Rock.* Durham, NC: Duke University Press, 2010.

Doral, Paul J. *Power in Transition: The Rise of Guatemala's Industrial Oligarchy, 1871–1994.* Westport, CT: Prayer, 1995.

Elliott, J. H. *Empires of the Atlantic World: Britain and Spain in America.* New Haven, CT: Yale University Press, 2006.

Fernandez de Navarrete, Martín, *Colección de los viajes y descubrimientos que hicieron por mar los españoles.* Vol. 1. Madrid: Imprenta Nacional, 1858.

Fernández-Armesto, Felipe. *Pathfinders: A Global History of Exploration.* New York: Norton, 2006.

———. *The Americas: A Hemispheric History.* New York: Modern Library, 2003.

Fuentes, Carlos. *The Buried Mirror.* New York: Houghton Mifflin, 1992.

Galeano, Eduardo. *Open Veins of Latin America: Five Centuries of the Pillage of a Continent.* Translated by Cedric Belfrage. New York: Monthly Review, 1973.

Gibson, Charles. *The Aztecs Under Spanish Rule: A History of the Indians of the Valley of Mexico, 1519–1810.* Stanford, CA: Stanford University Press, 1964.

Gisbert, Teresa. *Iconografía y mitos indígenas en el arte.* La Paz: Gisbert, 1980.

Gorriti, Gustavo. *Shining Path: A History of the Millenarian War in Peru.* Chapel Hill: University of North Carolina Press, 1999.

Gruzinski, Serge. *The Mestizo Mind: The Intellectual Dynamics of Colonization and Globalization.* Translated by Deke Dusinberre. New York: Routledge, 2002.

Gutiérrez Merino, Gustavo. *Cristianismo y Tercer Mundo.* Bilbao, Sp.: Zero, 1973.

———. *Dios o el oro en las Indias.* San Salvador: UCA, 1991.

Hanke, Lewis. "A Modest Proposal for a Moratorium on Generalizations: Some Thoughts on the Black Legend." *Hispanic American Historical Review* 51, no. 1 (February, 1971): 112–27.

Hemming, John. *The Conquest of the Incas.* London: Macmillan, 1970. Also: New York, Penguin, 1983.

———. *Red Gold: The Conquest of the Brazilian Indians, 1500–1700.* Cambridge, MA: Harvard University Press, 1978.

———. *The Search for El Dorado.* New York: E. P. Dutton, 1978.

Hewitt, Edgar L. *Fray Bernardino De Sahagún and the Great Florentine Codex.* Santa Fe, NM: Archaeological Institute of America, 1944.

Historia de la Compañía de Jesús en la provincia del Paraguay. Vol. 1 (6 vols.). Madrid: V. Suárez, 1912–49.

Hoffman, Philip T., and Kathryn Norberg. *Fiscal Crises, Liberty, and Representative Government, 1450–1789.* Stanford, CA: Stanford University Press, 1994.

Hoyos, Juan José. *El Oro y la sangre.* Bogotá: Planeta, 1994.

Jáuregui, Carlos A. *Canibalia: Canibalismo, calibanismo, antropofagia cultural y consumo en América Latina.* Madrid: Iberoamericana, 2008.

Jiménez de la Espada, Marcos, ed. *Una Antigualla peruana.* Madrid: Manuel Gines Hernández, 1892.

Kamen, Henry. *The Spanish Inquisition: A Historical Revision.* New Haven, CT: Yale University Press, 2014.

Kirkpatrick, Frederick A. *The Spanish Conquistadores.* London: Adam and Charles Black, 1946.

Krauze, Enrique. *Redeemers: Ideas and Power in Latin America.* New York: Harper-Collins, 2011.

Langenscheidt, Adolphus. *Historia Minima de la Minería en la Sierra Gorda.* Ontario: Rolston-Bain, 1988.

Lastres, Juan B. *Las Neuro-bartonelosis.* Lima: Editora Medica Peruana, 1945.

———. *Historia de la viruela en el Perú.* Lima: Ministerio de Salud Pública y Asistencia Social, 1954.

———. *La Salud Pública y la Prevención de la Viruela en el Perú.* Lima: Ministerio de Hacienda y Comercio, 1957.

León-Portilla, Miguel, ed. *The Broken Spears: The Aztec Account of the Conquest of Mexico.* Beacon Press, Boston, 1962.

———. *El Reverso de la Conquista: Relaciones aztecas, mayas e incas.* México, DF: Editorial Mortiz, 1964.

———. *Visión de los vencidos: Crónicas indigenas.* Madrid: Historia 16, 1985.

———, ed. *Visión de los vencidos: Relaciones indigenas de la Conquista.* México, DF: Universidad Nacional Autónoma de México, 1961.

Lippy, Charles H., Robert Choquette, and Stafford Poole. *Christianity Comes to the Americas, 1492–1776.* New York: Paragon, 1992.

Livi Bacci, Massimo. *Los estragos de la conquista: Quebranto y declive de los indios de América*. Barcelona: Crítica, 2006.

McCaa, Robert, Aleta Nimlos, and Teodoro Hampe Martínez. "Why Blame Smallpox? The Death of the Inca Huayna Capac and the Demographic Destruction of Tawantinsuyu (Ancient Peru)." Paper, Minnesota Population Center, University of Minnesota, 2004. http://users.pop.umn.edu/~rmccaa/aha2004/why_blame_small pox.pdf.

McEwan, Colin, and Leonardo López Luján, eds. *Moctezuma: Aztec Ruler*. London: British Museum Press, 2009.

McNeill, J. R., and William H. McNeill. *The Human Web: A Bird's-Eye View of World History*. New York: Norton, 2003.

Mann, Charles C. *1491: New Revelations of the Americas Before Columbus*. New York: Random House, 2005.

Marichal, Carlos. *Bankruptcy of Empire: Mexican Silver and the Wars Between Spain, Britain and France, 1760–1810*. New York: Cambridge University Press, 2007.

Marzal, Manuel M., Eugenio Maurer, Xavier Albó, and Bartomeu Melia. *The Indian Face of God in Latin America*. New York: Orbis, 1996.

Markham, Clements R. *Narratives of the Rites and Laws of the Yncas*. New York: Burt Franklin, 1970.

Montoya, Ramiro. *Crónicas del oro y la plata americanos*. Madrid: Visión Libros, 2015.

———. Sangre del sol: crónicas del oro y plata que España sacó de América. Madrid: Visión Libros, 2013.

Moreyra Loredo, Manuel, et al. *El cristiano ante el Perú de 1985: crisis económica, violencia . . .* Lima: Centro de Proyección Cristiana, 1984.

Oro y la plata de las Indias en la época de los Austrias. Madrid: Fundación ICO, 1999.

Petersen, Georg. *Mining and Metallurgy in Ancient Peru*. Translated by William E. Brooks. Boulder, CO: Geological Society of America, 2010.

Pino Díaz, Fermín del, ed. *Demonio, Religión y Sociedad entre España y América*. Madrid: Consejo Superior de Investigaciones Científicas, Departamento de Antropología, 2002.

Pillsbury, Joanne, ed. *Guide to Documentary Sources for Andean Studies, 1530–1900*. 3 vols. Norman: University of Oklahoma Press, 2008.

Prescott, William H. *History of the Conquest of Mexico*. Edited by John F. Kirk. London: Routledge, 1893.

———. *History of the Conquest of Peru: With a Preliminary View of the Civilization of the Incas*. Edited by John F. Kirk. London: Routledge, 1893.

Quintana, Manuel José. *Vidas de españoles celebres*. Paris: Baudry, 1845.

Quiroz, Alfonso W. *Historia de la corrupción en el Perú*. Lima: Instituto de Estudios Peruanos, 2013.

Raimondi, Antonio. *El Perú*. 3 vols. Lima: Imprenta del Estado, 1874.

Reséndez, Andrés. *The Other Slavery: The Uncovered Story of Indian Enslavement in America*. New York: Houghton Mifflin Harcourt, 2016.

Restall, Matthew. *Seven Myths of the Spanish Conquest.* New York: Oxford University Press, 2003.

———. *When Montezuma Met Cortés: The True Story of the Meeting That Changed History.* New York: Ecco, 2018.

Ricard, Robert. *The Spiritual Conquest of Mexico.* Translated by Lesley Byrd Simpson. Berkeley: University of California Press, 1966.

Robins, Nicholas A. *Mercury, Mining, and Empire: The Human and Ecological Cost of Colonial Silver Mining in the Andes.* Bloomington: Indiana University Press, 2011.

———. *Native Insurgencies and the Genocidal Impulse in the Americas.* Bloomington: Indiana University Press, 2005.

Rosenberg, Tina. *Children of Cain: Violence and the Violent in Latin America.* New York: Morrow, 1991.

Rostworowski de Diez Canseco, María. *Conflicts over Coca Fields in Sixteenth-Century Perú.* Ann Arbor: University of Michigan, 1988.

———. *Costa peruana prehispánica.* Lima: Instituto de Estudios Peruanos Ediciones, 1977.

———. *Doña Francisca Pizarro.* Lima: IEP Ediciones, 1989.

———. *Historia del Tawantinsuyu.* Lima: IEP Ediciones, 1988.

———. *History of the Inca Realm.* Translated by Harry Iceland. Cambridge: Cambridge University Press, 1999.

———. *Pachacamac y el señor de los milagros.* Lima: IEP Ediciones, 1992.

———. *Pachacutec y la leyenda de los chancas.* Lima: IEP Ediciones, 1997.

Schwaller, John Frederick. *The History of the Catholic Church in Latin America: From Conquest to Revolution and Beyond.* New York: New York University Press, 2011.

Smith, Brian. *Religious Politics in Latin America: Pentecostal Vs. Catholic.* Notre Dame, IN: University of Notre Dame Press, 1998.

Solís, Felipe, and Martha Carmona. *El Oro precolombino de México: Colecciones Mixteca y Azteca.* Milan: Américo Artes Editores, 1995.

Southey, Thomas. *Chronological History of the West Indies.* 3 vols. London: Longman, Rees, 1827.

Stein, Stanley J., and Barbara H. Stein. *Silver, Trade, and War: Spain and America in the Making of Early Modern Europe.* Baltimore: Johns Hopkins University Press, 2000.

Stern, Steve J., ed. *Shining and Other Paths: War and Society in Peru, 1980–1995.* Durham, NC: Duke University Press, 1998.

Suárez Fernández, Luis. *Isabel I Reina.* Barcelona: Planeta, 2012.

TePaske, John J. *A New World of Gold and Silver.* Leiden, Netherlands: Brill, 2010.

Thompson, I. A. A. *Crown and Cortés: Government, Institutions and Representation in Early-Modern Castile.* Hampshire, UK: Variorum, 1993.

Tripcevich, Nicholas, and Kevin J. Vaughn, eds. *Mining and Quarrying in the Ancient Andes: Sociopolitical, Economic, and Symbolic Dimensions.* New York: Springer, 2013.

Urteaga, Horacio H. *Biblioteca de Cultura Peruana: Los cronistas de la Conquista*. Paris: Desclée de Brouwer, 1938.

Vargas Llosa, Mario. *Conversation in the Cathedral*. Translated by Gregory Rabassa. New York: Rayo, 2005.

——————. *A Fish in the Water*. Translated by Helen Lane. New York: Farrar Straus Giroux, 1994.

Vázquez Chamorro, Germán. *Moctezuma*. Madrid: Cambio 16, 1987.

———. *Moctezuma*. Madrid: Algaba, 2006.

Vedia, Enrique de. *Historiadores primitivos de Indias*. 2 vols. Madrid: Rivadeneyra, 1852.

Vilches, Elvira. *New World Gold*. Chicago: University of Chicago Press, 2010.

Whitaker, Arthur Preston. *The Huancavelica Mercury Mine*. Cambridge, MA: Harvard University Press, 1941.

Wright, Ronald. *Stolen Continents: The Americas Through Indian Eyes*. Boston: Houghton Mifflin, 1992.

INDEX

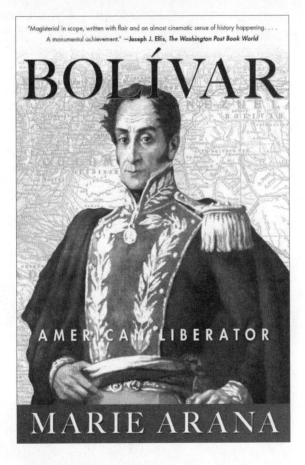